PURITANISM
and
DEMOCRACY

RALPH BARTON PERRY

PROFESSOR OF PHILOSOPHY, HARVARD UNIVERSITY

Author of "The Thought and Character of William James," "Shall Not Perish From the Earth," etc.

New York · The Vanguard Press

Seventh Printing

Designed by Stefan Salter
Manufactured in the United States of America
by H. Wolff, New York, N. Y.

THIS BOOK IS GRATEFULLY

DEDICATED TO

The Vanguard Press

REBELLION TO TYRANTS

IS OBEDIENCE TO GOD

Thomas Jefferson

CONTENTS

Part One

REVIEW OF THE PAST

CHAPTER ONE

DOUBT AND DISILLUSIONMENT

CHAPTER TWO

THE POWER OF IDEALS

CHAPTER THREE

THE APPRAISAL OF A HISTORIC CREED

CHAPTER FOUR

WHO WERE THE PURITANS?

CHAPTER FIVE

WHAT DID THE PURITANS BELIEVE?

CHAPTER SIX

THE DECLARATION OF INDEPENDENCE

CHAPTER SEVEN

THE ENLIGHTENED PHILOSOPHY OF THE DECLARATION

CHAPTER EIGHT

THE MAKING OF THE AMERICAN MIND

Part Two

APPRAISAL OF PURITANISM

CHAPTER NINE

THE IMPORTANCE OF SALVATION

CHAPTER TEN

THE MORAL ATHLETE

CHAPTER ELEVEN

THE ULTIMATE INDIVIDUAL

CHAPTER TWELVE

THE ECONOMIC VIRTUES

CHAPTER THIRTEEN

THE COMMUNITY OF RIGHTEOUSNESS

CHAPTER FOURTEEN

THE SOVEREIGNTY OF GOD

Part Three
APPRAISAL OF DEMOCRACY

CHAPTER FIFTEEN
THE SUPREMACY OF REASON AND CONSCIENCE

CHAPTER SIXTEEN
THE INDIVIDUAL AS THE SEAT OF VALUE

CHAPTER SEVENTEEN

POPULAR GOVERNMENT

CHAPTER EIGHTEEN

LIBERTY AND THE LIMITS OF GOVERNMENT

CHAPTER NINETEEN

EQUALITY AND FRATERNITY

CHAPTER TWENTY

THE UNIVERSAL HUMANITY

CONCLUSION

PREFACE

THE PRESENT BOOK grew out of a course, given some years ago at Harvard, which I at first called 'American Ideals.' This broader subject was gradually narrowed, and became a study of two ideals—puritanism and democracy—which in their persistence, their wide pervasiveness, and their mutual antithesis and reinforcement seemed to me to embrace what was most central to my theme, and to provide unity without oversimplification. This opinion was confirmed by the authority of V. L. Parrington, who said that "the two most characteristic qualities of the American temper are Puritanism and optimism."[1] For since American democracy, as I conceived it, expressed the hopeful view of man which prevailed in the Age of the Enlightenment, together with the sense of limitless possibility felt by vigorous settlers in a new land, it could be taken as the equivalent of Parrington's 'optimism.'

Among the unpublished papers of William James there is a note which reads: "Philosophic history is an attempt to connect together our hopes of the future with our misconceptions of the past." Assuming that the term "misconceptions" expresses a lively sense of fallibility, rather than willful deception or intellectual indolence, I accept this description of my task: namely, to conceive the thought of the past as truly as possible, and to connect it with the future through a present analysis and appraisal.

Over the years I have accumulated a sum of indebtedness which it is now quite impossible either to repay or to allocate. I have profited by the resources of Harvard University—its rich library, courteously and generously administered, grants from its Milton Fund, and, above all, the fraternal intercourse of its scholars. I have had near at hand such friends as Perry Miller, Arthur M. Schlesinger, and others, ready, as well as able, to answer such questions as I knew enough to ask. And I have had 'secretaries,' in the most honorific sense of that term. Constance R. McClellan, Louise S. Korns, and Jean S. Aiken by their skill and loyal interest have made it possible that the manuscript should be prepared for the press despite the Author's wartime preoccupations. Rosamond Hart Chapman has had a large part in the making of this book from its earliest beginnings; for her wise judgment, her scholarship, and her genius for accuracy I am abidingly grateful.

Cambridge, May 15, 1944 RALPH BARTON PERRY

Part One

REVIEW OF THE PAST

CHAPTER ONE

DOUBT AND DISILLUSIONMENT

1

IN THE COURSE of the present century Americans have devoted a great deal of attention to the appraisal of their national legacy, and with widely varying results. "What does it mean to be an American?" has become a question of prime importance not only for Americans themselves but for an apprehensive world.

Before the First World War America had already assumed a major role in world politics and felt the need of self-justification. At the same time the rapid flow of immigration had raised doubts as to the capacity of the 'melting pot' to preserve the American standard of living. The restriction of immigration was conceived as necessary in order that the salt wherewith new increments of population were seasoned might not lose its savor. Aliens whose single-minded loyalty was doubted were 'hyphenated Americans,' and the suspicion that many felt some prior allegiance elsewhere gave currency to the slogan 'America First.'

The opening of the First World War disclosed the extent to which Americans were divided among themselves by conflicting European sympathies, and when in 1917 America itself entered the war, it became necessary to formulate a creed on which all Americans might agree as Americans. In proportion as war has become a comprehensive effort, mobilizing all members of the group and all social agencies, economic and cultural as well as political and military, it has become an increasingly important function of government to formulate the national creed. The state papers of President Wilson abounded in statements designed to touch the hearts and fortify the wills of all Americans through invoking their common sentiments and habits of thought. The national creed was not only formulated by the President but methodically propagated by official agencies, civil and military, devoted to 'morale,' 'public information,' and 'war aims.' During and after the war these agencies assumed a broadly educational form. All Americans attended a school of Americanism. The deliberate effort to teach Americanism necessarily involved a scrutiny of the subject-matter to be taught. It no longer sufficed to be unconsciously or instinctively American, but the substance of the matter must be defined, and lines be drawn in order to distinguish orthodoxy from opposing heresies.

As yet America may be said to have enjoyed a 'good conscience.' It was necessary, no doubt, to remind Americans of their underlying convictions, but concerning the convictions themselves there was no widely pervasive doubt. The first phase of disillusionment that followed the war did not shake these convictions but narrowed their application. The repudiation of the League of Nations did not imply any disloyalty to the traditional creed but only a loss of the crusading spirit. America was to return to its ancient role of illuminating the world by precept and example rather than by active participation in affairs abroad. The revival of the old suspicions of Europe only accentuated the confidence of Americans in their own moral and material destiny. Withdrawing to their own continent, Americans rededicated themselves to their ancient idols and awaited the future with confidence. The Republican party, entrenched in power for twelve years, was the self-appointed instrument of this ingrowing piety. Its essential spirit was conveyed in 1920 by Will H. Hays, chairman of the Republican National Committee:

> The big issue . . . is "Americanism and patriotism." No political party, of course, can claim a monopoly of patriotism. But patriotism can be easily weakened by centrifugal forces. The Republican party stands for that type of centripetal patriotism that strives to make and keep conditions right in America and *in America first*.[1] *

2

So far, then, the chief concern of Americans was for the reaffirmation and preservation of their ideals. To slow down the flow of immigration to the rate of assimilation, to consolidate American opinion and senti-

* References for numbered notes for each chapter will be found at the end of the text.

ment, to distill their essence for purposes of indoctrination, to make the world 'safe' for democracy, or to retreat from the world in order to preserve the purity of democracy at home—all of these purposes presupposed that the value of Americanism itself was unquestioned. Meanwhile, however, many Americans were already reaching a very different conclusion, and proclaiming the poverty, if not the bankruptcy, of America's spiritual estate.

In the adolescent era of national piety following the American Revolution the famous Parson Weems delivered himself as follows:

> Who can reflect on that gracious guardian power of America, which brought us safely through our alarming war against Great Britain, which not only enabled us to repel Lord North's attempts on our liberties, but, far beyond our first and most sanguine expectations, to establish ourselves Free and Independent States; and then, without the least struggle or blood-shed among ourselves, kindly spread over our favoured heads, the heavenly canopy of an excellent government, pouring down on us all the blessings of just and equitable society; securing to every honest man and his family, the sweet and precious safeties of his liberty, his life, his health, his character, his property, his religion, and in fine, of every blessing connected with his highest happiness in this world, and with his preparation for eternal happiness in the next—who, I say, can think of this profusion of riches, mercies conferred on our country, above all other countries in the world, without feeling his soul oppressed and almost overwhelmed with a sense of the Divine munificence . . . ? *

Fulsome patriotism reached its height in America toward the middle of the last century, before the impending tragedy of disunion had yet cast too palpable a shadow:

> Poetry! Why, America is *all* poetry! The pages of our Constitution,—the deeds of our patriot sires,—the deliberations of our sages and statesmen,—the civilization and progress of our people,—the wisdom of our laws,—the greatness of our name,—are all covered over with the living fire of poetry; and *such* poetry, too, as no single brain could conceive, or pen delineate. What

---

* Mason L. Weems, *A History of the Life and Death, Virtues and Exploits of General George Washington,* 3d ed., Philadelphia, 1801? p. 71. This book was a best-seller in its day and has passed through over seventy editions, the hatchet and the cherry tree making their appearance in the fifth edition in 1806. It was only one of many edifying works produced by this strange combination of Anglican clergyman and commercial traveler.

are the machinery of rhymes and metre and strophes and apostrophes, compared with the living and breathing soul of the ideal made practical, which dwells within every American bosom, and sheds a halo of immortal glory over this free soil! [2]

The following passage, taken from the annual report in 1853 of the directors of the New York Mercantile Library Association, illustrates the American manner of eulogizing national heroes:

> Among the early engagements entered into on your behalf, was one for the delivery of a Lecture by the late Hon. Daniel Webster. But the gloom of death rolled over the intellect of the Lecturer; the eye of the Statesman no longer peers into futurity, anticipating the movements of [the] nation; the tongue of the eloquent orator speaks to us now only in the gigantic words which he has left behind him—monuments of imperishable grandeur, which will remain so long as the language in which they were spoken, and the constitution which they defended, shall be remembered amongst men. It may not be improper in this connection, gentlemen, to remark that, since our last annual gathering, another of those great and brilliant lights which adorned the intellectual heavens of the 19th century has passed away forever. He, the eloquent defender of liberty and independence, to whose firmness and foresight we are indebted for the acquisition of the waters of the Mississippi and the blessings of honorable peace, Henry Clay, has bequeathed to his countrymen
>
> *"His lofty name,*
> *A light, a landmark on the cliffs of fame."* [3]

3

The derision excited by such passages is largely due, no doubt, to their flamboyant rhetoric. But their rhetoric was the fitting vehicle of their sentiment. If they had ceased to carry conviction seventy-five years later, it was not owing to a mere change of literary style, but because the minds of Americans were no longer attuned to their simple-minded and fervid patriotism. Such sentiment could no longer be uttered or heard without a sense of insincerity, begotten by fundamental doubts and by the yawning gap between profession and practice.

The literature of disillusionment was in full swing by 1920. In the last quarter of the nineteenth century American fiction, under the lead of Howells, had turned definitively in the direction of realism, and in Frank Norris and Stephen Crane realism passed over into that profounder disillusionment known as 'naturalism.' This last development belonged to the broad stream of scientific pessimism represented most notably in Europe by Flaubert and Zola: man was no longer conceived as either the creation of God or the creator of his own destiny, but as a biological survival and a victim of circumstance.

Naturalism was not, however, merely a local manifestation of a literary fashion. Nor was it merely an application to literature of the rising prestige of science and of the world-wide vogue, after the middle of the nineteenth century, of the cult of materialism and positivism. It signified a growing queasiness of the American stomach: the essential flavor of American life had become unsavory and unpalatable. The close of the century witnessed the apotheosis of the captain of industry; but although he symbolized the self-made man, the march of technological progress, and the social benefits of competitive ambition, he began to wear the aspect of a monster rather than of a demigod. His sordid motives, his unscrupulous crushing of competition, his unholy alliance with the political boss, and his exploitation of labor belied his profession of public service. The triumph of the captain of industry was discordantly attended by the counter-demonstrations of the 'muckraker,' carried on chiefly in the pages of *McClure's Magazine* and the *American Magazine* during the years between 1903 and 1914.

Hjalmar Hjorth Boyesen's *Mammon of Unrighteousness* (1891) was among the first and most penetrating literary exposures of the seamy side of American plutocracy. He was followed by Winston Churchill and Robert Herrick. At the same time the frontier was being divested of its romance by Hamlin Garland. An increasing tone of bitterness and despair appeared in the naturalism of Theodore Dreiser, whose *Sister Carrie* appeared in 1900 and was followed by other works culminating in his *An American Tragedy* in 1925. Sinclair Lewis began with *Main Street* in 1920 to devote himself systematically to the task of making Americans appear not hateful but contemptible. The most characteristic manifestations of Americanism—the small rural town, the well-meaning and optimistic businessman—became symbols of derision not only to Europeans, but to Americans themselves. Sherwood Anderson, William Faulkner, Erskine Caldwell, John Dos Passos, and other novelists, together with poets such as Edwin Markham, Edgar Lee Masters, and Carl Sandburg and attended by a similar school of playwrights and painters, forced a half-reluctant public to focus attention upon the unpleasant aspects of the American scene. Veils were drawn aside, idols shattered, and sentiments 'debunked.'

In short, American literature during the early decades of the present century expressed the growth of a profound iconoclastic impulse. Speaking for his fellow poets, Conrad Aiken said that they had "little enough in common—nothing, perhaps, save the fact that they were all a good deal actuated at the outset by a disgust with the dead level of sentimentality and prettiness and moralism to which poetry had fallen between 1890 and 1910." [4] The key word here is "disgust"—disgust with evasion and unreality, together with the strong conviction that for the hygiene of the American soul a bath, even a mud bath, was better than rosewater.

4

Criticism followed a similar course. E. L. Godkin, founder of *The Nation* and its editor during the years 1865–81, had been the exponent of American orthodoxy in its pristine purity. Civil-service reform, anti-imperialism, the attack on monopoly in business and corruption in politics, implied no dissent from the American creed, but rather its more faithful observance. There was no change of heart. But in 1922 "Thirty Americans" expressed their assorted doubts concerning *Civilization in the United States,* agreeing only that Americans were chiefly governed by the fear of "being found out," and that America suffered from "emotional and aesthetic starvation." "We must change our hearts," they said.[5]

This heartsickness had, in 1900, driven Henry Adams to seek salvation in the writing of *Mont Saint-Michel and Chartres.* In H. L. Mencken and the "Americana" of the *American Mercury* it took the form of avowed intellectual snobbery. It turned Ludwig Lewisohn toward the richer culture of Europe:

> Americanization means . . . assimilation. But that is an empty concept, a mere cry of rage or tyranny, until the question is answered which would never be asked were the answer ripe: Assimilation to what? To what homogeneous culture, to what folkways of festival and song, to what common instincts concerning love and beauty, to what imaginative passions, to what roads of thought? We have none such that can unite us. Two things are nation wide and engage the passions of the Anglo-American stock: baseball and the prohibition of wine, love, speculation and art.[6]

Among the profounder critics conviction of sin took the form of a repudiation of American economic life—not its abuses, merely, but its fundamental motives and preoccupations. The struggle for wealth having become more bitter, it was suddenly revealed to a more sensitive conscience that one man's success implied another's failure, and that the terms of the competition predetermined the qualities of the survivors. The popular esteem for wealth gave its sanction and its blessing not only to industry and thrift but to cunning and hardness of heart. As early as 1895 Brooks Adams had published his *Law of Civilization and Decay,* which was both anti-capitalistic and pessimistic. Of this writer V. L. Parrington said:

> His lot had been cast, unfortunately, in an age of capitalism, when the acquisitive mind was triumphing over the imaginative, the banker over the priest and craftsman and mystic; but he could see no reason in heaven or earth . . . to apply the term progress to the spread of greed that was crowning the usurer as master of men.[7]

Critics such as Parrington and Charles A. Beard, while professing liberals, were convinced of the bankruptcy of the older individualist economy, with its associated polity and ethos. Speaking of Sinclair Lewis's *Babbitt,* the former said:

> Historically he marks the final passing in America of the civilization that came from the fruitful loins of the eighteenth century. For a hundred and fifty years western civilization had sustained its hopes on the rich nourishment provided by the great age of the Enlightenment. Faith in the excellence of man, in the law of progress, in the ultimate reign of justice, in the conquest of nature, in the finality and sufficiency of democracy, faith, in short, in the

excellence of life, was the great driving force in those earlier, simpler days. It was a noble dream—that dream of the Enlightenment—but it was slowly dissipated by an encompassing materialism that came likewise out of the eighteenth century. Faith in machinery came to supersede faith in man; the Industrial Revolution submerged the hopes of the French Revolution. And now we have fallen so low that our faith in justice, progress, the potentialities of human nature, the excellence of democracy, is stricken with pernicious anemia, and even faith in the machine is dying. Only science remains to take the place of the old romantic creed, and science with its psychology and physics is fast reducing man to a complex bundle of glands, at the mercy of a mechanistic universe.[8]

5

Although muckraking had lost its journalistic appeal through a growing distaste for muck, and owing to the counter-attractions of superficial prosperity, the deeper cause of its decline lay in the disillusionment of the rakers themselves. Critics of American life came to the conclusion that 'tainted money,' 'frenzied finance,' and Tammany bosses were not superficial excrescences which could be cured by the plastic surgeon, but symptoms of a grave central disorder. The cure for this disorder lay in some form of economic collectivism. Lincoln Steffens, the disillusioned muckraker, came to see in the subordination of politics to business, and in the subordination of ownership to management, the gradual development of a centrally directed and efficiently organized community of consumer-producers. The passing of the old America, which he as a liberal had once hoped to reform, was a metamorphosis rather than a death—the attainment by evolution of what it had cost a bloody revolution to secure in Russia.[9]

Socialism was an old story in America. Before the Civil War the influence of Owen and Fourier was widely disseminated, and socialist communities such as Brook Farm sprang up in various parts of the country. This movement was, however, not so much a protest as an extravagance of zeal. It was a premature enjoyment of utopia made possible by the very bounty of circumstance. Its communities were enclaves, supported and indulged by the existing capitalistic system. They represented no departure from the ideals of traditional Americanism, but were rather momentary embodiments of that state of nature which was the norm and premise of the Declaration of Independence.

After the Civil War the rapid industrialization of the North, with the development of a class-conscious proletariat, stimulated the organization of labor, and created conditions favorable to the reception of Marxian ideas. The single-tax movement, reaching its climax in the candidacy of Henry George in 1886 for the mayoralty of New York, had at least its common ground with socialism. As early as 1888 Edward Bellamy's *Looking Backward* had depicted a socialist utopia and attacked the impotence of the state to control the forces of competitive capitalism. The immense popular success of this book was due, no doubt, to astonishment rather than to conviction, but it was a sign of things to come.

Revolutionary socialism did not as yet make serious headway against the influence of 'prosperity.' But despite factional rivalries and the conservatism of the mass of American labor, the Socialist party in 1910 polled a vote of 600,000 and elected a member of Congress. Although organized labor has thrown its collective weight into the balance against socialism, it has also assisted in the diffusion of that doctrine, not only through the doctrine of its more radical wing, but through its development of class-consciousness, its insistent emphasis on the injustices of the existing system, and the education of its members in social thinking.

The Russian Revolution of 1917 exerted upon the contemporary world an effect scarcely less electrifying than that of the French Revolution of 1789. Its very excesses and cataclysmic character appeared to demonstrate the limitless possibilities of social reconstruction. To Americans it was not a manifestation of historical determinism but a demonstration of the power of the moral will. At the same time it promised a remedy for every grievance. Its effects were powerfully reinforced by the great economic depression of 1929.

The swift and dramatic transition from unparalleled 'prosperity' to impoverishment and wholesale unemployment—from pride to humiliation—dealt a staggering blow to American prestige. Within a few months America passed from the role of exemplar to that of a pathological case foreshadowing the doom of western civilization. It was impossible that American institutions, which had been in full and effective operation from 1920 to 1929, should not be held responsible for the disastrous sequel. American youth of the more generous type, eager for some fundamental cure of the world's ills, began to look with hopeful interest in the direction of the great experiment which was being conducted in Moscow. Sensing a more decisive Armageddon than Americans had hitherto dreamt of, the privileged classes in America began to speak with a bitterness inspired by fear—a deeper and more desperate fear than any hitherto harbored in the American breast.

To economic doubts as to the soundness of that laissez-faire capitalism on which America's material greatness had been founded, there were added even deeper misgivings as to the framework of government itself. Abroad, dictatorships superseded democracies and constitutional monarchies. A new age of despots began, and while Lenin, Stalin, Mussolini, Hitler, and their lesser imitators were officially condemned as un-American, they exercised an unmistakable fascination upon the American mind. American travelers were converted to a new political gospel. As Americans have always yielded to the spell of kings, so they succumbed to the public pomp or private blandishments of these new rulers. By a curious inverse effect of provincialism, traveling Americans were eager to show themselves to be cosmopolitan, and became, in each country which they visited, *plus royaliste que le roi.* Exhibiting the characteristic weakness of the liberal mind, Americans made allowances and found excuses for practices which they should have detested from the bottom of their American hearts. And no doubt the American businessman felt a secret sympathy for these dictators who had risen from the ranks, and who exhibited in politics that ruthlessness, opportunism, and technological skill which distinguished the captain of industry at home.

Economic and political doubts reinforced one another. There crept into the American consciousness the surmise that if the capitalistic system was in jeopardy, the only remedy lay in a profound political change. Whether the old system was to be preserved intact, reconstructed to suit new economic exigencies, or superseded altogether—in any case it was widely believed that the abandonment of the traditional political creed was inevitable. This political change might take the form of direct action masked by existing legal procedures, or a constitutional shift toward centralized control, or open revolution. All three alternatives, whether of 'Fascism,' 'New Deal,' or 'Communism,' threatened a radical departure from traditional American principles, arousing a sense of alarm in 'liberal' breasts and precipitating a new issue of 'constitutionalism.'

6

Movements in letters, criticism, economics, and politics found a parallel in the American rewriting of American history. Apropos of the realists in American literature, Percy H. Boynton said: "Their forebears had started an ambitious experiment from a theory, and the later generations had done their best to develop a legend to fit it; yet the facts were out of harmony with both." [10] Historians now began to find in the past the same gulf between profession and practice which writers of fiction, poetry, and criticism were finding in the present. Thus Sydney George Fisher, whose *True History of the American Revolution* was published in 1902, prepared his readers to be shocked:

> The Revolution was a much more ugly and unpleasant affair than most of us imagine. I know of many people who talk a great deal about their ancestors, but who I am quite sure would not now take the side their ancestors chose. Nor was it a great, spontaneous, unanimous uprising, all righteousness, perfection, and infallibility, a marvel of success at every step, and incapable of failure, as many of us very naturally believe from what we have read.[11]

In 1896 Paul Leicester Ford had published *The True George Washington.*[12] Fisher's history of the American Revolution had been preceded by his *True William Penn* and *True Benjamin Franklin.* The term 'true' in these and other titles implied that the history of the Revolution and of the great founders of the nation had up to that time *not* been true, had perhaps not *meant* to be true, and had, in any case, been too *good* to be true.

It is a remarkable fact that until the close of the nineteenth century the history of the Revolution had been based directly or indirectly on a prejudiced source, namely, on the summaries written for the *Annual Register* by Edmund Burke.[13] These summaries represented the Whig view that the American Revolution was the result of the stupidity and wickedness of the King and the Tory ministry—a view not only flattering to American pride, since it represented the colonists as the reasonable and long-suffering victims of oppression, but based on the same fundamental philosophy as the Declaration of Independence itself. This version of the Revolution was stereotyped and perpetuated by a long series of later historians, and was implanted in the mind of the American public by the edifying rhetoric of popular writers such as Parson Weems. *

Up to the close of the nineteenth century this period of ancestral heroism and primitive piety had been set apart as sacrosanct. But now it was violated by the profane historians, armed with evidence derived from original sources hitherto unused. The effect was to humanize the demigods, to recognize that the colonists were in some measure governed by ignoble passions, to excite sympathy with the 'Tories,' and to ascribe the Revolution itself to non-moral causes, rather than to the 'reasons' professed in the Declaration and reaffirmed on its subsequent anniversaries.[14] This 'new' and 'true' history of America, having begun through its introduction into school textbooks and popular literature to affect the public mind, provoked a vigorous reaction on the part of those who believed the national piety to be jeopardized.[15] But the spell was broken. Options and doubts superseded uncritical piety.

An increasing emphasis on the economic rather than the political aspects of history served to diminish the significance of the original democratic creed, and invited attention to the unreality of that creed under changed social conditions. As early as 1893 attention had been called to the disappearance of the frontier. The limitless opportunity, the free and hardy life, the direct challenge of nature—the experience and outlook that made the great West at once the source and the symbol

* For example: "And in 1774, when Lord North had resolved, Uzzah-like, to lay his unhallowed hand upon the sacred ark of our liberties, then it was that the patriotism of Washington broke forth in a blaze of glory to himself, and of honor to human nature." *Op. cit.*, p. 39.

of so much that is characteristically American—were all but gone. In 1921 Frederick Jackson Turner in his memorable book *The Frontier in American History* epitomized this American West and the peculiar tang which it has given to our national character:

She gave to the world such types as the farmer Thomas Jefferson, with his Declaration of Independence, his statute for religious toleration, and his purchase of Louisiana. She gave us Andrew Jackson, that fierce Tennessee spirit who broke down the traditions of conservative rule, swept away the privacies and privileges of officialdom, and, like a Gothic leader, opened the temple of the nation to the populace. She gave us Abraham Lincoln, whose gaunt frontier form and gnarled, massive hand told of the conflict with the forest, whose grasp of the ax-handle of the pioneer was no firmer than his grasp of the helm of the ship of state as it breasted the seas of civil war. . . . Best of all, the West gave, not only to the American, but to the unhappy and oppressed of all lands, a vision of hope, and assurance that the world held a place where were to be found high faith in man and the will and power to furnish him the opportunity to grow to the full measure of his own capacity. . . . The paths of the pioneer have widened into broad highways. The forest clearing has expanded into affluent commonwealths. Let us see to it that the ideals of the pioneer in his log cabin shall enlarge into the spiritual life of a democracy where civic power shall dominate and utilize individual achievement for the common good.[16]

"Let us see to it!" These very words implied a doubt as well as a resolve. Americanism was distilled out of the common experience of hardship; could it keep its flavor in times of privileged affluence? It arose in times of rural simplicity; could it survive amidst the urban congestion and social complexity of the modern industrial age? It was originally founded on the fact or fiction of opportunity; would it persist in an age of intensified economic pressure, in which a man could no longer find room in the outer fringe of settlement but must somehow make shift in the place where he was born?

The rewriting of American history in economic rather than in moral or political terms coincided with the increasing vogue of the Marxian conceptions of class struggle and dialectical materialism. Charles A. Beard, whose *Economic Interpretation of the Constitution of the United States* appeared in 1913, was preceded and attended by a cloud of lesser witnesses, of varying degrees of Marxian orthodoxy. By historians of this school the key to the understanding of American institutions was found, not in the doctrine of the Declaration of Independence, but rather in the institution of capitalism. Doubts concerning the validity of capitalism became doubts concerning the validity of Americanism. The way was thus prepared for the Marxian dialectic. If capitalism had run its course and was about to be supplanted by socialism, and if America was essentially capitalistic, then America was moribund; or if it was to live on it must be born again, through a 'social revolution,' with a new Marxian soul.

7

"And all the harsh conclusions of this sort," to borrow the words of a contemporary critic, "were given devastating significance through the growing suspicion that the Book of Genesis was no less a legend than Weems's *Life of Washington.*" [17] To secular doubt was added the waning influence of protestant Christianity. Although Catholicism grew less rapidly than protestantism, the absolute number of its adherents steadily increased, and Catholic opinion exercised a more conscious political influence. At the same time an increasing number of Americans were without religious adherence of any kind.

This religious change was to be measured not so much in terms of the numbers of church members as in a wavering and thinning of faith among professing protestants. A contemporary historian has described the last quarter of the nineteenth century as "A Critical Period in American Religion." [18] The theory of evolution seemed to assimilate man, soul and body, to nature. The development of Biblical criticism struck a blow at the authority which protestantism had substituted for the church. New cults, such as Ethical Culture and Christian Science, won adherents from the recognized protestant sects. The World's Parliament of Religions held in Chicago in 1893 disseminated the idea that non-Christian religions possessed claims equal, or even superior, to those of Christianity. In the protestant sects themselves latitudinarian and modernist tendencies dulled the edge of orthodoxy and tended to obliterate the line between the religious and the moral sanctions.

Traditionally the American moral code had been associated, if not always with strict orthodoxy, at least with a belief in the divine creation and government of the world. The high destiny of man and the authority of conscience had been based on the premise of their agreement with the constitution of the universe. Could the American mores survive the decline of the puritan and evangelical religious consciousness? Or was the Christian moral code as obsolete as was, to many Americans, the system of Christian dogma?

8

There is no cardinal principle of American life, no article of our central faith, that has not during the early decades of the present century been challenged and, by some critic or dissenting group, rejected. Today we are engaged in a Second World War which threatens to be of long duration and of unparalleled destructiveness. In 1914 there was only one question: Shall America, or shall America not, resort to arms in defense of Americanism? Twenty-five years later, in 1939, there were two questions: First, shall America intervene, and if so, in what way and at what time? Where does its frontier lie? On the Rhine or on the China Sea? On what shore of the Atlantic or the Pacific Ocean? On the Canadian or the Mexican border or at the northern or southern extremities of the hemisphere? Shall America intervene today or tomorrow, or postpone intervention to a last hour of extremity, in the hope that that hour will never come? Shall America intervene, if at all, by force of arms, by "aid short of war," by economic pressure, or only by moral suasion? But to these questions of defensive strategy, dictated by events beyond our control, there was now added a second question: For what should America intervene? What was that Americanism, other than bodily lives and possessions, which was worth defending? Even if America were to withdraw within its narrowest territorial frontiers, to what end should it devote itself in its own house? Was its purpose of national life consistent with locked gates and closed shutters, or would isolation itself be an admission of moral defeat? On this second major question the minds of Americans were confused and divided.

The first of these questions has been answered, and there remains only the issue of victory or defeat on the field of battle. To the second question the answer is not yet clear. The answer which America gives will not only govern its policy in the postwar epoch, but its motivation and its faith during the struggle itself. The degree of conviction and unanimity with which the answer is accepted may determine the outcome of that struggle. It is the hope of throwing some light on this second question, and of identifying the American cause with the American tradition, that inspires the writing of this book.

CHAPTER TWO

THE POWER OF IDEALS

1

THE TERM 'IDEAL' signifies a fusion of two components. 'Ideas,' as distinguished from 'ideals,' are objects of contemplation or intellectual affirmation. The letter 'l' added to 'idea' signifies the idea's appeal to emotion and will. Ideals are ideas or beliefs when these are objects not only of contemplation or affirmation but also of hope, desire, endeavor, admiration, and resolve. Or, if this definition appears too wide and too promiscuous, then one may limit the term to the case in which ideas, by evoking a community of emotion and will, play a social and not merely an individual role in human affairs.

When to 'ideal' one adds the adjective 'American,' this limiting condition of unanimity is expressly stipulated. The inhabitants of a certain area of the earth's surface during a certain period of time share the same loves and likings, or detestations and aversions, adopt a common standard of criticism, set themselves a common goal, and recognize their joint participation in a common task.

There are two slurs upon ideals that have acquired a wide vogue, and have derived some of their credibility from the hint of scandal which they convey, and from an almost morbid fear of being thought naïve or pious. It is held, in the first place, that ideals are causally impotent, or at least negligible. They glisten on the surface, and lend color to life; but it is their function to express, rather than to govern, events. It is held, in the second place, that ideals are fictitious or nonverifiable. They are not, as they purport to be, judgments that can be checked objectively by experience or logic, but are myths, or verbal elaborations of attitudes.

These two slurs upon ideals may or may not be combined. Those who, like despairing liberals, acknowledge the impotence of their ideal may yet hold that it is true; and those who, like candid Fascists, hold their ideology to be a myth, may at the same time employ it as an indispensable political force. Whether accepted independently or in combination, these slurs do at any rate have the effect of reinforcing one another to the discredit of ideals. Both alike, in the view of 'emancipated' minds, discredit the attitude of the sectarian adherent, who both *believes* his ideals as true and believes *in* them as efficacious.

2

The present chapter is devoted to an examination of the charge that ideas are impotent. The only ultimate scientific or philosophical support for this view is 'epiphenomenalism,' a by-product of the attempt to force nature into the strait jacket of a materialistic system. Consciousness is construed as a sort of excrescence of the physical world, designed for no purpose, apparently, but to annoy materialists. It appears to be forgotten that excrescences, be they blemishes or beauty spots, ordinarily interact with the organism on whose surface they appear.

Such supporting argument as there is for the epiphenomenalistic view rests on the false supposition that because causes are analyzable they are therefore inoperative. Let us assume that chemical and biological causes are 'reducible' to the laws of physics. The chemist or the biologist does not on that account abandon his own specific categories, or deny their causal validity. He supposes that they are consistent with physical concepts, but takes the ground that the physicist is under the same obligation of consistency as himself. A physics which explained chemical and biological events would not be 'mere' physics in a sense excluding chemistry and biology, but should properly be called 'bio-chemico-physics.' Similarly, when psychological causes are 'reduced' to biological, chemical, and physical terms, they are not eliminated, but systematically related. Fear and hunger can be construed as biochemical complexes only, provided biology and chemistry are themselves so extended as to embrace them within a science of psycho-bio-chemistry.

To limit the dynamics of human behavior to causes of the strictly physico-chemical type would be considered an excess of scientific zeal. Such a method, though it has been professed in principle, has never been employed in practice. But there is another epiphenomenalism which enjoys high repute, even though it is open to precisely the same objections. According to this halfway doctrine, low-grade mentality is causal, while high-grade mentality is epiphenomenal. Human affairs, so it is contended, are governed by passion, by blind 'drives,' by fears or needs; while rational purposes, moral codes, and philosophies are a mere façade behind which these more primitive and less reputable impulsions do their work. But if there is any ground for imputing causal efficacy to low-grade mentality, there is the same ground for acknowledging the power of high-grade mentality. Appetitive acts are caused by appetite; but if this is so, then personal acts are caused by personal choices, ambitions, scruples, or aspirations.

In human behavior, furthermore, the primitive impulsions such as appetites, instincts, and reflexes are inextricably mingled with so-called 'higher' processes. When hunger is humanly effective, it is so through judgments or assumptions that particular objects are edible. If men are moved by fear, their action is conditioned by the belief that an object is fearful. If men are moved both by hunger and by fear, then action requires some qualification of the one by the other, as when, for example, hunger is appeased within limits prescribed by fear. Whether the object of fear be a dark place, or a hereditary enemy, or an angry God, or an outraged public opinion, the essential mechanism is the same; namely, impulsions of escape *mediated* by judgments of danger. There are at the present moment millions of human beings who execrate 'Hitler.' Very few of these millions enjoy his personal acquaintance. Strictly speaking, they do not hate the man, but a stereotyped representation. They hate what they judge Hitler to be, and if certain judgments of his appearance, personal traits, and actions were not widely current in the world, this hate would have no object whatever —and, having no object, would cease to exist.

What is true of hunger, fear, and hate is true of love, or any other form of motivation. Whether the situation be novel or familiar, and the response extempore or habitual, the primitive impulsion is effective through being built into complex emotional and ideational systems.

If primitive impulses are potent, then those mediations and integrations of impulses which constitute acts of conscious volition are no less potent. If mind makes a difference, then the *making-up* of a mind makes a difference, including all of the expectations, comparisons, and inferences by which decisions are reached.

3

What is true of individual behavior is true of social behavior. As individual behavior depends on decisions embracing purposes and judgments, so social behavior depends on common purposes and common judgments. Men act when they decide; they act together when they agree. Having gone so far, there is no just ground for denying the potency, the unique social potency, of those interrelations, reciprocities, and identities of emotion and expectation which constitute collective ideals.

A signal instance of the social effectiveness of ideas is afforded by current explanations of belligerent aggrandizement. It used to be said that nations were impelled to conquest by the pressure of population and by hunger. But since it has become apparent that there is no pressure of population that is not effectively corrected by a decline of the birth rate, or by a more intensive cultivation of the land, or by peaceful emigration, and no need for food or raw materials that cannot be supplied by peaceful trade—then the ground of the explanation has been shifted. We are now told that a state engages in conquest because the possession of colonies is regarded as a symbol of national vitality, or because territorial expansion is identified in the public mind with the nation's historical destiny. And those whose business it is to supply the necessary motivation for the exertions and sacrifices of war assume that some such 'fictions' must be implanted in the collective mind, no matter how contrary to the economic facts, and no matter how contrary to the felt needs of unindoctrinated minds.

In short, those practical leaders whose business it is to engineer the making of history pay to the causal efficacy of ideals the highest possible tribute. Since experience teaches them that ideologies must be created where they do not exist, they testify to the power of ideologies where these are already implanted by tradition. And since they testify to the power of fictitious ideals, created ad hoc, they cannot very well deny the power of true ideals, if such there be, and if happily men discover them.

Acts of choice and agreement are not in themselves *sufficient* causes. They do not operate in vacuo, but in conjunction with some set of necessary conditions. The adoption of an ideal is said to be *the* cause of an event in situations in which it is the culminating condition. The other necessary conditions being present, the ideal may pull the trigger, ignite the spark, or tip the scale—being fateful in the sense that the event hangs in the balance until the weight of the ideal is added. Such situations are characteristic of human conduct, sets of conditions being present which with a slight supplemental force will precipitate far-reaching and widely divergent trains of events. If a factor such as an ideal makes *any* difference, then there may be situations in which it makes all the difference.

4

The term 'tradition' has misleading associations: it suggests the past, whereas the essential role of tradition is to define the present. A society lives in "the foremost files of time" by virtue of its accumulated legacy.

Tradition is inescapable whether one reaffirms or repudiates it. Even those who depart from the established creed do well to reflect upon that creed, since it is at least their point of departure. Said Joseph Glanvill:

> *Opinions* have their *Climes* and *National* diversities: And as some Regions have their proper Vices, not so generally found in others; so have they their mental depravities, which are drawn in with the common air of the Countrey. And I take this for one of the most considerable causes of the diversity of *Laws, Customes, Religions, natural* and *moral* doctrines, which is to be found in the divided Regions of the inhabited Earth. . . . So that what some

Astrologers say of our *Fortunes* and the passages of our lives; may by the allowance of a *Metaphor* be said of our *Opinions:* That they are written in our *stars,* being to the most as fatal as those involuntary occurrences, and as little in their Power as the *placits* of *destiny.*[1]

Despite the fatality with which the individual is assimilated to ancestral ways of thought and feeling, he starts life without them. According to the present consensus of experts, ideas are acquired and not inherited; because it is both biologically impossible to understand how they could be inherited, and psychologically possible to understand how they could be acquired.

To understand how ideas are acquired, and to account for the continuity of tradition, it is important to recognize that a 'generation' is a fiction. The procession of mankind is not a succession of companies marching in line, but a stream of individuals. The curtain does not go down upon a contemporary scene, but new actors enter and take their 'cues' before the old retire. Those who are nearing the end of their lap run side by side with new runners, and hand on the torch before their course is finished. Whatever the individual's age, to the last month or week or day he lives in the same world with younger and with older men.

During the first years of life inborn and general capacities are translated into specific habits which reflect the usage of the elders. Thus the child is born with a capacity to talk, and learns not only the native language but the local dialect and accent. Similarly, he learns how to eat and rest, how to work and play, how to clothe and protect himself, how to use tools, how to take care of his body and his possessions; and he learns how to feel and think and act in relation to his physical and social environment. In each case the 'how' denotes that specific manner of exercising these functions which is in vogue in his time and place. So insidious and unconscious is this process that when the developing individual first finds himself at all, he is already a product of his age.

Man is distinguished among animals by the extent to which he learns. His hereditary endowment is relatively flexible, his capacities of thought, memory, and imagination are relatively high, and his period of docility is relatively protracted. He learns in two ways. By word and example he learns from those who already have a mind of their own, without suffering the pains which it has cost them. Then, having thriftily taken over the achievement of those who have gone before, he adds to his possessions by his own experience and invention. If men learned only by experience, or only by example, their lives would be, at best, repetitive. Human life is progressive by virtue of the fact that the individual, having taken over the old ready-made, can learn for himself something which is new not only to him but to the race.

The full force of these considerations is evident when we realize that a newborn babe of the year 1944 is in no significant sense representative of that year. He is new, but not modern; he is born *into* his age, but is not *of* his age. He possesses the general traits of man, certain more specific racial traits, and certain still more specific idiosyncrasies. But he is as innocent of the fruits of civilization and culture as though he had been born in the stone age. And were he to be isolated from all social contacts save with his fellow babes, he would be compelled to begin again at the beginning and repeat the first faltering steps of human development. Though he be the most recent fruit of biological history, the babe is older than the man. His inborn mentality, which is all the mentality he has, is primitive. He comes down to date only when he has had time to assimilate the past; and he moves with the times only in his ripe manhood, when he is on the crest of the advancing wave of innovation. From then he is left behind and grows old again—though never so old as he was at the beginning.

An individual becomes a man of his time and place only when he has been dipped in the bath of tradition and stained with its latest hues. This stain is the basic coloring by which the individual's divergence and innovations are measured. The past as embodied in contemporary adults is both the bed of reactionaries and the springboard of innovators. It provides a man's working capital, whether he squanders it, lives on the interest, or invests it in new enterprises. The extent of his education is the extent to which he enters into effective possession of this patrimony, to which all members of the group have the same hereditary title.

5

The dependence of human life on ideas, and of co-operative social life on a community of ideas, has been vividly illustrated by the late Graham Wallas:

> If the earth were struck by one of Mr. Wells's comets, and if, in consequence, every human being now alive were to lose all the knowledge and habits which he had acquired from preceding generations (though retaining unchanged all his own powers of invention, and memory, and habituation), nine tenths of the inhabitants of London or New York would be dead within a month, and 99 per cent of the remaining tenth would be dead in six months. They would have no language to express their thoughts, and no thoughts but vague reverie. They could not read notices, or drive motors or horses. They would wander about, led by the inarticulate cries of a few naturally dominant individuals, drowning themselves, as thirst came on, in hundreds at the riverside landing places, looting those shops where the smell of decaying food attracted them, and perhaps at the end stumbling on the expedient of cannibalism. Even in the country districts, men could not invent, in time to preserve their lives, methods of growing food, or taming animals, or making fire, or so clothing themselves as to endure a northern winter. . . . The white races would probably become extinct everywhere. A few primitive races might live on fruit and small animals in those fertile tropical regions where the human species was originally evolved, until they had slowly accumulated a new social heritage.[2]

It is important that relics of the past should be saved from destruction, and that by communication and travel they should be rendered generally accessible. The significance of Wallas's illustration, however, lies in its proving that the whole effectiveness of relics consists in the *ideas* that are transmitted with them.

Organic matter is relatively unstable, and by a curious paradox dead things outlast the life that creates them, as the crustacean is outlasted by its shell. The house of man survives its tenant, and the tool the hand that fashions or uses it. Paper disintegrates and ink fades less quickly than the poet. The poem is happily more durable than either.

The value of physical relics lies in what they record. They are useful as aids to the racial memory, enabling that memory to retain a greater volume and complexity than would be possible through oral tradition alone; just as written memoranda enable a man to possess a greater learning than he can carry in his head. But there is no value in memoranda that cannot be read and understood. If their meaning is lost, relics do little to restore it, whereas if the meaning is preserved, it is comparatively easy to record it again. The poetry of Homer, the philosophy of Plato, and the science of Newton are not dependent upon the preservation of their first editions. To a certain extent they are even independent of the very language in which they were originally expressed. They are essentially systems of ideas, and, provided these are preserved, they can be retold in different symbols, just as a musical composition may be preserved in different notations and reproduced by different musicians with different instruments.

In order that the technology of the twentieth century may be transmitted to the next it is not necessary that any machine should be preserved from dissolution, but it is necessary that its essential formulas and aptitudes should be remembered, in order to be re-embodied in new machines. And even ideas and skills do not suffice unless they are linked with the purposes for which they are used, or the feelings which give them value. It is necessary, furthermore, that these purposes and feelings should be shared, in order that they may afford a basis of reciprocal action. When thus socialized and charged with emotion, durable ideas constitute the essence of culture and of civilization.

6

What is an institution? One might infer from certain contemporary practices that it is a building. The visitor who is 'shown' a public institution is encouraged to believe that it consists in the particular architectural monstrosity that occupies the adjacent hill. But even a hospital or a university does not consist in its plant. The government is neither the capitol, nor the capital; nor, a certain famous monarch to the contrary notwithstanding, is the state the ruler. Nor is the state the written constitution, or the other official papers deposited in its archives. The state is a system of ideal offices, services, and authorities, successively embodied in different men and instrumentalities; or, more fundamentally, it is a system of political habits, of ways of thinking, feeling, and acting, which are shared and reciprocally adjusted. So long as this system remains intact the state remains the same, and in proportion as this changes, the state changes. There must be a high degree of stability in order that there shall be a state at all, and the term 'habit,' literally construed, does not adequately describe this condition. There must be not only concrete habits (which perish with their organic mechanisms) but generalized uniformities which are repeated in their specific embodiments and transmitted to different individuals.

Legal institutions are embodied in records. But written statutes and judicial decisions do not constitute law except insofar as they have meaning. Destroy the continuity of thought by which they are interpreted, and legal records are no more than marks on paper. The law is no law without a community of understanding, shared by those who enforce it and those who submit. Furthermore, while the law does, it is true, invoke the sanction of force, it does so as a last resort and in exceptional cases. The efficacy of law depends on a pervasive and continuing law-abidingness, which consists of a common understanding and general acceptance, perpetually renewed. A 'reign of law' is a condition of society in which certain adjustments of man to man are rooted in the sentiment of the community and presupposed as the basis of reciprocal intercourse.

Economic institutions afford a not less convincing example. Their ideational and emotional character has been obscured because their objects are physical, whether commodities or services. But such objects are not *economic* objects unless related to human needs, desires, and judgments. Their 'value' in the economic sense is not a function of their physical properties or quantity, or of the physical force by which they are created, but of the demands which they satisfy and by which their production is induced. There is no physical entity whatsoever that would not be completely divested of its economic meaning if the human interests which it is supposed to serve should be withdrawn. If, as is conceivable, mankind should be converted to a gospel of complete apathy toward physical survival, then the entire economic system would be annihilated at a stroke. Although this fact is evident and implied in every type of economic doctrine, the term 'economic' retains a confused association with the material as opposed to the mental domain of existence.

The confusion has been confounded by the loose conception of 'natural' economic forces associated with the history of laissez-faire capitalism. Because this particular mode of economic procedure is relatively individualistic, and relatively unregulated by the state, it is considered as occurring after the manner of the tides or the rotation of the earth. But it requires no great penetration to see that laissez-faire capitalism rests on laws of property and contract, and on the general conviction that its encouragement of thrift and its stimulation of competitive invention and effort tend to lowered costs, technological progress, and the material well-being of society at large. On these legal guarantees, and on this general social philosophy, rests a vast network of controls, of correlative expectations, of long-range purposes and enterprises, which in their continuity and relative stability constitute what is meant by an economic institution. Were these unanimities of interest and belief to be destroyed, existing economic institutions would be destroyed, even though the sum of physico-chemical entities should be in no wise altered.

7

Ideas having a certain spread and permanence constitute the essential factor in what is called 'nationality.' We shall be able to avoid the pitfalls that beset this subject if instead of dividing human groups into nations and non-nations, we regard nationality as a form of life which social groups possess in greater or less degree; as a standard, in other words, rather than as a principle of classification. We can then understand its relation to the more definite bonds by which men are united, such as race, language, religion, economy, art, territory, and state. These will all prove to be conditions favorable to nationality, some of them indispensable, but none of them constitutive. That none of them is constitutive is proved by the fact that, taking each in turn, it is possible to deny nationality in its presence and affirm nationality in its absence.

Racial homogeneity does not prevent English and Americans of the same Anglo-Saxon stock from belonging to different nations; while American nationality testifies eloquently to the fact that a common nationality is consistent with a wide range of ethnic differences. The 'Unknown Soldier' is a recognized symbol of the fact that the degree of a man's Americanism does not depend on the color of his skin or the roots of his family tree.

The national difference between English-speaking Americans and English-speaking Englishmen proves that a common language is not a sufficient condition of nationality; while Switzerland proves the possibility of reconciling national sameness with linguistic diversity. Religious differences have long since ceased to coincide with national differences—otherwise it would be meaningless to speak of Christian nations in the plural, or to profess religious tolerance. Art has been notoriously vagrant and unpatriotic. Italian art has domesticated itself readily in all parts of Europe. America has lived most of its national life without a national art.

National boundaries do not coincide with economic boundaries, although some modern nationalists have blindly assumed that they do, or have striven desperately to make them do so. The valley of the Rhine has usually belonged to one economy and to several nations; the people of the southern half of the North American continent form one nation, though their economic interests are varied and conflicting. The very existence of trade across national frontiers is a standing demonstration that economic processes do not respect national differences, but are forever ignoring or resisting them, and tending to bring all nations to the same market.

Territorial propinquity is not essential to nationality, if it means anything to speak of the Jews as a dispersed nation. Nor does territorial propinquity always unite men nationally—on the contrary, national differences are most intense and violent at the border. National frontiers do not coincide with 'natural' frontiers any more than they do with economic frontiers. As to statehood, the history of nationality turns on the two facts that there have been states which were not nations, and nations which have lost or acquired statehood.

We shall understand the meaning of nationality if, instead of identifying it with any of these more definite social bonds, we inquire why these bonds are favorable to it, and why the presence of *some* of these bonds is necessary for its existence. Racial homogeneity is favorable to nationality, and racial diversity, if it goes beyond a certain point, may be fatal to it. Why? Because people of one race are relatively receptive to the same ideas; and because members of the same race have a common history, and a fund of common memories. The idea of common blood is itself a common idea of high emotional value; hence nations seek to conceal the variety of their ethnic origins, and even create mythologies for the purpose.

Why does a common language facilitate nationality? Because it is through a common language that men can have a common literature which commemorates their common heroes and gives articulate and stable expression to their common ideas. Why does diversity of religion diminish nationality? Because in proportion as men differ in their sanctions of good and evil they may be disqualified for that community of resolve which is implied in nationality.

Economic conflicts of interest not only work against mutual dependence and co-operation but tend to divergent social philosophies. There may be doubts as to the possibility of nationality without territorial propinquity. It may be argued that the Jews do not constitute a nation, or that they would not constitute a nation had they not formerly occupied the same territory. But if so, why? Because without propinquity men cannot have the contact that creates like-mindedness; or because attachment to a common soil constitutes a strong nucleus of common feeling.

Finally, what shall we say of the dependence of nationality on the state? If we accept the existence of non-national states, such as ancient Egypt or Persia, it is because we believe that the people of these states were unaware of any community of mind. If we doubt the possibility of non-national states, it is because we find it difficult to believe that people who participate in the great collective enterprises of war and religion could lack all consciousness of a common purpose. When, on the other hand, we assume that a nation may legitimately aspire to a statehood which it lacks, it is because we believe it unjust that a group should be forced under alien political institutions to belie its own creed.

An examination of the conditions favorable to nationality thus reveals its meaning. A social group constitutes a nation insofar as its members are of one mind, and insofar as this common system of ideas penetrates and relates its several institutions, regulates the lives of its members, and sets them, thus unified, apart from other social groups. It was in such terms that Washington affirmed and invoked American nationality:

> The name of AMERICAN, which belongs to you, in your national capacity, must always exalt the just pride of Patriotism, more than any appellation derived from local discriminations.—With slight shades of difference, you have the same Religion, Manners, Habits, and political Principles.—You have in a common cause fought and triumphed together. The Independence and Liberty you possess are the work of joint councils, and joint efforts—of common dangers, sufferings and successes.[3]

A complete nationalization is fortunately impossible. A modern German statesman has said:

> As far as I was concerned there was neither a Protestant nor a Catholic, neither a Conservative nor a Liberal Germany: before my eyes there was always the one and indivisible Nation, indivisible materially and spiritually.[4]

Prince von Bülow deceived himself. The impossibility of a complete nationalization lies in the fact that men are necessarily united in other ways that counteract and weaken the bond of nationality. Fanatical nationalists recognize these limitations and seek vainly to overcome them. The cosmopolitanism of contemporary culture, the bonds of commerce and of universal religions, the conscience of mankind, the common interests of special economic or professional classes, the dissenting or unassimilated idiosyncrasies of individuals—these are the forces which extreme nationalists seek to destroy, as hostile to that mentality by which they would have the group unified and set apart.

8

Tradition, culture, institutions, nationality, are constituted of common or interrelated interests and beliefs. They cannot be adequately described, or their changes adequately explained, save in these terms. Once this is admitted, it follows that a fundamental description and explanation of human history will embrace—not in a temper of reluctant concession but with positive emphasis—those deeper convictions and resolves whose causal potency it is now fashionable to disparage.

To acknowledge the dynamic importance of ideals does not imply the denial or the neglect of other causes. Linguistic usage has given rise to what might be called 'the fallacy of the definite article.' It is customary to refer to *any* reason or cause by which an event can be explained or controlled as *the* reason or cause. But in all historical situations there are many reasons and many causes; and if one of these is singled out for attention, it should be referred to as *a* reason or *a* cause. It is no part of the present argument to reject climatological, ethnic, demographic, economic, or psychological causes, or motives of the baser sort. The truth to be acknowledged is the limited truth that the creed which men profess is one cause among others—a cause which operates in a specific way as a condition of concerted action, and which may in any given historical context be a necessary cause of the occurrence of momentous events.

These broad considerations have a clear application to the subject-matter of the present work. Among the ideals embraced within the social heritage of Americans a peculiar importance attaches to puritanism and democracy. These are not ideas in any merely intellectual sense, like, for example, that of the quantum theory. They are charged with emotional appeal and provide incentives to action. Both are so complex that it would be more accurate to refer to them as *systems* of related ideals. They have been peculiarly pervasive, reaching not only through the whole length of American history, but breadthwise from center to extremities, touching American experience and behavior at every point. religious, moral, social, cultural, and political. Puritan ideals were acquired before and during the colonial period, and democratic ideals before and during the revolutionary period, so that both may be said to have molded the American mind from the beginning. They originated in the prenatal phase of American life and have predetermined the whole of its later development.

I am not unaware of the presence of other ideals, such, for example, as those introduced in colonial days by Anglicans and Catholics, and by the Spanish and Mexican settlers of the Southwest. I am not unaware of the great waves of immigration from central, southern, and eastern Europe during the nineteenth century. Nor am I forgetful of the ideals acquired as a result of the perpetual economic and cultural development of America, or as a result of the internal interaction between American, European, and even Oriental thought. I do not minimize the importance of economic institutions such as capitalism. These will appear in the discussion as implicated in the meanings of puritanism and democracy—but I do not attempt to do them justice.

In short, I have no desire to simplify the story, and it is not to be inferred that I deny what I do not mention. I claim only that a large part of the distinctively American tradition, culture, institutions, and nationality consists in these two systems of ideals: the puritanism implanted in the seventeenth century, and the democratic creed disseminated in the eighteenth century. And I hope that the method employed in the study of these two ideals may be extended to such other ideals as may deserve a place in any complete account of American development.

The history of puritanism and democracy testifies abundantly to the power of ideals. The puritan creed has repeatedly served as the basis of concerted action. It provided a reason for the reforming and separatist movements in the Anglican church, for the English Revolution and Commonwealth, for the English migrations to New England at the opening of the seventeenth century, and for the transformation of these settlements into a theocratic state. Blending with other ideologies, and modified by experience and environment, the puritan philosophy has formed an important part of that fundamental agreement of mind and purpose by which the United States has played its peculiar role in the modern world. The democratic creed of the Declaration of Independence formed a platform on which the insurrectionary colonies took their common stand. Interwoven as it was with economic and psychological motives which should not be either denied or disparaged, it has throughout American history been invoked whenever in times of crisis, such as the Civil War and the two World Wars, it has been necessary for Americans to mobilize their spiritual resources and find a common path amidst diverse and conflicting interests.

THE APPRAISAL OF A HISTORIC CREED

1

To QUOTE AGAIN from Joseph Glanvill:

> We came into the world like the unformed *Cub;* 'tis *education* is our *Plastick:* we are baptized into our opinions by our Juvenile nurture, and our growing years confirm those unexamined Principles. For our first task is to learn the *Creed* of our Countrey; and our next to maintain it.[1]

Goethe says in effect the same thing: "*Was du ererbt von deinen Vätern hast, erwirb es, um es zu besitzen.*" * Many Americans have become doubtful of the traditional creed which is the basis of their culture, the presupposition of their institutions, and the essence of their nationalism. Shall that creed be not only rediscovered but also reaffirmed?

Once a creed is doubted, it can be reaffirmed, if at all, only by conscious choice. The critical faculties which expelled the creed stand guard at the door, and must either withdraw or be satisfied before the creed can be readmitted. The choice between these two ways turns upon the second of the slurs which the modern sophisticated mind casts upon ideals. The first of these slurs—that ideals are impotent—has been abundantly disproved. But, granting their dynamic role in human life, there remains the charge that they are mere manifestations of subjective bias, incapable of proof or rational justification.

Those who accept this charge and at the same time recognize the indispensable part which ideals play in collective action must consciously suspend their critical faculties and connive at the formation of irrational beliefs. The critical faculties must be persuaded to abdicate, the last act of reason being to resign its post to unreason. As a theoretically un-

* "You must win your ancestral inheritance for yourself if you are really to possess it."

tenable dogmatism was corrected by methodical doubt, so a practically untenable doubt would then be corrected by a methodical dogmatism. The other alternative is that the critical faculties themselves should appraise a creed, or reappraise an old creed, by seeing the reasons for its adoption. This alternative implies that there *are* reasons or grounds for the preference of one creed to another, and that when a creed is defended by these reasons, it possesses a claim upon the acceptance of all rational men.

As regards the appraisal of a historic creed, there is no doubt whatsoever of the existence of subjective bias or relativity. Emancipated minds understate, rather than overstate, its range. The fact is that all judgments whatsoever are relative; and the task here, as elsewhere, is not to escape relativity, but to discount it, correct it, and turn it to profit.

The appraisal of a historic creed involves one or both of two forms of relativity—a relativity to the *time* of the historian's appraisal, and a relativity to its *standard.* The past is viewed *from* the present, and judged *in terms of* the present.

2

The past viewed from the present is retrospect—a prolongation to yesterday, or last year, or a century ago, of the line which leads in immediate experience from now to an instant ago. There is an effect of remoteness, direction, perspective, and intermediate passage, analogous to the spacial perception of the physical object as over-there-from-here. It is naïve to suppose that the object of perception possesses its spacial perspectives *where it is.* Similarly, the object of retrospection has characteristics of obsoleteness, venerable antiquity, patina, irrevocability, and familiarity—relatively to the changing present and to the impending novelty of the future. But it is naïve to suppose that the past bore in its own time these traces of time's subsequent passage.

Such naïveté is corrected as soon as the concealed frame of temporal reference is brought into the picture. There is no error in imputing to the past the characteristics of pastness, provided one introduces the relationship in full, and specifies 'pastness from this present.' All tenses —'is,' 'was,' and 'will be'—express characters of a temporal event or epoch. That which is *in* time is shared, through memory, expectation, or immediate action, by all times. It is some time's present, some time's future, and some time's past. A thrifty critic will not summarily dismiss these temporal characteristics because of the vulgar error of relativity, but will acknowledge the full truth in its amended form.

As regards any given epoch, there is a certain understanding which is reserved for posterity. It belongs to the nature of historic ideals that they should point toward the future, and that their meaning should be progressively revealed. There is an insight which is reserved for those who look back over the path already traversed, and which will escape the most prophetic imagination of earlier times as well as the experience of contemporaries. At the same time there is a merit in oblivion. Seen from the remote present, the past loses the greater part of its detail. But this omission has its positive as well as its negative effect—while it limits and excludes, it also accentuates. There is such a thing as the 'light of perspective.' Through its condensation of minutiae it throws into high relief the contour and proportionateness of the whole. Intensive historical research, with its anatomical dissection and rummaging among household effects, may distort as well as amplify. As regards the moral unities of an epoch—its scale of values and hierarchy of motives—the telescope of thought or the naked eye of memory may be a better instrument than microscopic analysis.

3

With the characteristics of pastness are associated certain emotional attitudes, or values, which it is naïve to impute to the past *as it was.* There is the aesthetic preference for the primitive or the archaic. To tired old age, to timid or cautious temperaments, to the mood of complacent success, or to a state of diminished vitality, any past is attractive. Its venerability, its entrenched solidity, and its agreement with habit alike commend it. Owing to these same characteristics, the past is repugnant to youth, or to ardent and adventurous temperaments, or to the mood of recklessness induced by failure, or to the state of superabounding vigor.

Strange indeed are the paradoxes to which this sort of naïveté gives rise. There is, for example, the phenomenon of the conservative who loves the revolutions of the past better than the mildest reforms of the present. Ideals generate reforms, and reformers are the radicals of their day, suspected or hated by the safe and sane. This is true of Christianity, of protestantism, of Americanism, and of the Republican party. Nevertheless Christian, protestant, American Republicanism—which is a coral reef deposited by radicals—is today the creed of arch-conservatism. To the conservative the only good radical is a dead radical. The conservative by age or temperament may be quite indifferent to the material or the architecture of his ideas, provided they are overgrown with ivy. The radical, on the other hand, likes ideas when they are fresh from the factory and have hardly yet been put to use. He does not object to the smell of varnish, and likes garish colors. The conservative, with a taste for antiquities, regards the radical as a philistine, a parvenu, and an adventurer—as indeed he is, and boasts of being.

The past has been a long time dead, and is therefore old. But by inverting the order of time, it is the present that is old and the past that is young. The past is both the aged and also the newborn. The scene of the past is the 'cradle of the race,' and is endeared by the association of infancy with innocence and infinite promise. "Bliss was it in that dawn to be alive." Or, as John Buchan wrote:

> The memories of a happy past are in themselves a solid possession:—
>
> *"Is it so small a thing*
> *To have enjoy'd the sun,*
> *To have lived light in the spring?"*
>
> The possession is the more valuable if such memories are readily evoked, so that past and present dwell in friendly proximity. This gift has always been mine. I cannot recover the vigour of youth for my limbs, but through memory I can recapture something of its ardour for my mind. The smell of wood smoke and heather, for instance, or a whiff of salt will recall shining morning-lands of the spirit.[2]

There is an even simpler illusion begotten by the *remoteness* of past time. "Distance," we say, "lends enchantment." Insofar as the present is weary or painful, as it often is, the past will take on a complementary hue of tranquillity or delightfulness. The non-present negates the evil of the present, together with its presence. But distance does not always lend enchantment. If the lover's heart is with his mistress, then his enchantment is here and now, if she is here and now; and in that case the past or any other distant region is an aching void.

These nostalgic feelings, due to contrasts of now and long ago, of old and new, of absence and presence, tend, then, to qualify our judgments of the past; or to lend it values, positive and negative, which it possesses only in relation to the judge's temporal subjectivity. The error lies in imputing such values intrinsically, rather than in seeing them in their conditioning relation.

4

The ideas of the remote past are not, except in a figurative sense, remembered; they must be reconstructed and conceived. The power of conceptual thought to transcend the limits of time and link together the past and the present is presupposed in all historical knowledge. Even physical science is called upon to explain events that are past in time as well as distant in space. It transcends the relativity of memory in the one case as it transcends the relativity of perception in the other. The 'scientific object,' such as the atom, or the orbit of a planet, is so conceived as to provide systematically for an infinitude of experiences at different times and places. This is ordinarily expressed by saying that the conceptual world of science yields by deduction the appearances by which it is verified. It is the distinguishing feature of conceptual thought that it can thus embrace and surmount the station and personal biography of the individual thinker. It creates objects and at the same time gives them freedom. Without loss of identity they can be embodied in diverse natural and historical events, approached from different 'points of view,' and thought by diverse individual thinkers.

But while conceptual thought provides an escape from perceptual relativity, it introduces a relativity of its own. The perceptual relativities of the solid are corrected by geometry—by the Euclidian conception of its internal relations and the projective conception of its external relations. But the geometrical conception of the solid is relative to the postulates and other theorems of geometry.

Similarly, a conception of the past event or epoch is not a memory, and is to that extent freed from the specific memorial remoteness and intermediate regions of retrospection. But, like the scientific object of physics, it must be conceived in terms of some conceptual frame of reference. The historian of past ideas, whatever his own place in history, must be able to rethink the identical thoughts of the past epoch. They must 'make sense' to him, and be logically related to his other ideas. He cannot even understand the logic of the past as another logic, or as 'non-logical,' except in terms of his own logic.

This type of relativity raises no radically new problem. It means that the logic of the past must be embraced within the logic of the present. The thinker of the past may, for example, think in terms of Euclidian geometry. The mathematician of the present, thinking in terms of non-Euclidian geometry, will transcend the limits of the past; but he will embrace Euclidian geometry within his more comprehensive system, and his thought will be identical with the past within the common area. He will see wider relationships, but will leave the narrower relationships intact. Similarly, the modern astronomer can understand the geocentric astronomy of earlier times, or the modern logician the Aristotelian logic of the syllogism, or the more highly developed linguist the speech of the child or of primitive society. In all of these cases it is necessary to suppose that a more limited system of meanings can be contained identically within a more elaborate system of meanings. At the same time the mind of the later historian cannot recover the limitations of the past, since to recognize limits is to transcend them; nor can the mind of the past be supposed to have grasped those fuller implications of its thought which are reserved for posterity.

There is no inherent impossibility in rethinking the thoughts of the past. There remains the problem of determining whether, in any given case, this identity does or does not occur. The problem is essentially the same as that of sharing the ideas of other contemporary minds. There are two checks on identity of meaning—the logical and the empirical. If I frame a definition or think an idea, I commit myself to its logical nexus with other ideas. When I meet another mind which gives these back to me, explicating what is implicit in my own idea and finding in my discourse a similar confirmation of his own, I possess evidence that his concept and mine are the same. The empirical check is found in the reference of the idea to external observable facts, and to action. If the other man's idea points to the same physical objects within my field of perception, or leads to the same action, I identify his idea with my own. If I have any doubts, they will be cleared up by questions which lead to a more and more explicit empirical reference, until, if necessary, he and I touch hands in the same concrete object while uttering the same word.

In the case of the past, such reciprocity is impossible. Dead writers, as Plato regretfully pointed out, can answer no questions. But there is a substitute for reciprocity in the fact of continuity of tradition. Identical meanings have been preserved through being communicated by each generation to the next during the period of their overlapping. As to the logical test, in proportion as a thinker of the past has elaborated the implications of his idea, I can compare them with the pattern of mine. An empirical test is provided by the sameness of the physical environment. Sun, moon, and stars, food and drink, the human body, the familial relationships, are presumed to be a part of the experience and action of the past, as they are of the present. The Greeks will have had 'a name for it,' if it falls within this area. These parts of the physical environment have their further physical relations, and whatever meanings fit this pattern may also safely be assumed.

In understanding an idea of the past, I must first conceive it clearly. Vagueness does not contribute to understanding here any more than elsewhere. I must then, in accordance with the above tests, impute the idea to the thought of the past. I must not impute to the past the images, memories, associations, or other contextual irradiations which are peculiar to my own biography. I must move in the direction of an objective meaning. In short, when I read the record of the thought of the past I must do so with a view to understanding it, getting its 'point,' or grasping its cogency. This effort, instead of leading us away from the past, may arrive at an identity between the present and the past.

The identity of conceptual objects paves the way for judgments of truth and error. It is impossible to appraise the ideals of the past unless one is allowed to define them. One must be able to say, "This ideal, *by which I mean precisely thus and so*, is open to the following objections, as is proved by the following evidence."

The purpose of the present book is to determine how far the ideals of puritanism and democracy are acceptable. To this end it will be necessary that these ideals should be so conceived as to mean something now, mean something definite, refer directly or indirectly to the present field of experience, and satisfy present logical standards. If the objection were raised that no puritan of the seventeenth century or democrat of the eighteenth actually conceived his ideals precisely as I conceive them, I could not disprove the objection, for the tests of conceptual identity are not absolutely conclusive. But for the purposes of this study it is more important that an idea should be an idea, and that it should be true or false, than that anybody should ever have believed it. I shall hope, in other words, that even though the historical difficulties be grave, I shall in any case have exhibited certain meanings and thrown some light on their validity.

5

The way has now been cleared for the central problem with which we are concerned in the present chapter. It is assumed that the meaning of a creed of the past can be grasped by a historian of the present; and that it can be largely divested of those temporal values which attach to it by virtue of its pastness. There remains the problem of its appraisal.

The problem of relativity again arises. As the understanding of a past creed requires that it shall be intelligible to the mind of the present, so its appraisal requires that it shall be measured by the critic's present standard. Some writers, as, for example, Professor Carl L. Becker, seem to think that it is sufficient simply to call attention to

> the truth that all historical writing, even the most honest, is unconsciously subjective, since every age is bound, in spite of itself, to make the dead perform whatever tricks it finds necessary for its own peace of mind.[3]

But why need historical writing be "unconsciously subjective"? Here again the solution of the problem lies in the fact that a relativity is transcended when it is brought to light. Relativity of appraisal is fallacious only when the critic's standard is omitted from the appraising judgment. Its omission arises from the union of two common linguistic practices—the practice of supplying meaning from the context, and the practice of using sentences for expressive rather than declaratory purposes.

It is a mistake to suppose that all verbal statements are true or false *as they stand*, divorced from the occasion on which they are uttered. When statements are made, there is a speaker, an audience, a time, and a place, and these commonly enter into the meaning of the statement. It is evident that words such as 'I,' 'you,' 'now,' 'then,' 'here,' and 'there' depend for their meaning on him who uses them, on him to whom they are addressed, on when and where they are uttered. Thus the statement 'Chicago is remote' means to say more than is included in the statement, and is true or false only when account is taken of the location of the speaker. If one Bostonian makes the statement to another Bostonian, it means "Chicago is remote from Boston." Among Bostonians it is unnecessary to say this explicitly, since the Bostonian's provincialism or taciturnity will usually prevail over his pedantry.

Sentences are used not only as elliptical statements of fact, but also as expressions of attitudes. Thus the sentence "Chicago is awful" can be used merely to express the speaker's distaste for that city, or his intention to disparage it in the esteem of him to whom the remark is addressed; the term 'awful' being 'emotive' and not descriptive. In that case the reply "No, Chicago does not inspire one with awe" would be inappropriate; as would any other reply that appealed to the evidence of fact. A reply in kind would be "It's a great place." Such expressions of attitude are not in themselves true or false, but true or false statements can be made about them, to the effect that Bostonians are against, and Middle Westerners for, Chicago.

These two linguistic practices are combined when the term which is elided is the speaker's own emotional attitude. The reception of news provides a case in point. When a group of anti-Axis partisans learn of the adherence of Bulgaria to the Axis, and one says to the other "That's bad," the fuller statement would be "To me, as one who desires the victory of Britain and Greece over the Axis, the adherence of Bulgaria to the Axis is unwelcome." The speaker is not merely expressing his present regret; he is also judging the effect of the reported event upon the defeat of the Axis. This part of the meaning of his statement is supplied by the hearers. The evidence of this tacit assumption might appear in the admitted relevance of such a remark as "But don't you think that Germany may be weakened by fighting the war on another front?" This question being raised, a military expert might be called on, and the matter debated in a spirit of disinterested inquiry. All of which would prove that the original remark "That's bad," taken in the context in which it was made, had a double meaning: it expressed the speaker's present attitude to the reported event, and at the same time asserted a relation (either in agreement with fact, or contrary to fact) between that event and what the speaker desired.

Appraisals, estimates, and approbations commonly take this elliptical and expressive form. They represent a present attitude of favor or disfavor based on an assumed standard. As they stand they are neither true nor false; but they *are not* merely as they stand—they mean more than they say. In effect and by intent they judge something *by* something, and become true or false when that by which they judge is made explicit.

This elliptical and expressive use of language may give rise to misunderstanding, both among the naïve and among the sophisticated. The naïve may make the mistake of supposing that the statement—such a statement as "That's bad"—is true or false as it stands. The sophisticated, discovering that this is not the case, may leap to the conclusion that statements of this type are not true or false at all. The fact is that the statement is true or false when the context is supplied. It is best that the maker of the statement should make this context explicit. Dutiable or non-dutiable goods may be brought across the frontier if they are 'declared' and the import tax, if there be any, paid; it is a mistake to conceal them in one's baggage and have them accusingly and triumphantly discovered by the inspector.

Let us see how this applies to the appraisal of a historic creed. Suppose a certain creed of the past to be understood—the Mormon creed, for example, concerning plural marriages; and suppose that a later critic condemns it, applying some term of disapproval, such as 'evil' or 'wrong.' Such an utterance as "The Mormon creed of plural marriages was wrong" *may* express no more than the speaker's or writer's personal dislike of plural marriages, or his intent to excite a similar dislike in those who hear or read his words. Having in mind instances of this sort, certain critics then take the view that *all* utterances employing such a predicate as 'wrong' have a merely 'emotive meaning.'

But to say "Plural marriages are wrong" may also mean that the Mormon creed is contrary to the creed of the writer or speaker, or of his reader or hearer, this creed being supplied by the context. The full meaning of the utterance is then "To us *as Christians* plural marriage is a sin"; and when so supplemented, the utterance becomes a statement of fact whose truth or falsity can be ascertained by citations from Scripture or other authoritative Christian sources. Similarly, if I say, "The puritan moral discipline was good," "The puritan theocracy was wrong," "The New England colonies ought not to have persecuted the Quakers," "The American colonists were right in seceding from the British Empire," the statements may be taken as relative to a norm which is tacitly assumed. When this norm is made explicit, and the judgment embraces the clause "according to the American creed," it is then true or false.

Norms are not only goals sought, perfections admired, or scruples which forbid, but standards by which to appraise actions or other norms. So to appraise means to compare; that is, to discover some degree, positive or negative, of correspondence. It is not necessary that the norm which is employed in judgments of appraisal should be the personal or social norm of the judge, or of those to whom the judgment is addressed. The conduct, precepts, or ideals of the past may be judged by a present norm, or by the norm of their own time, or by the norm of a third party, or by a norm abstracted from any specific historical setting.

Thus historical puritanism and democracy may be judged by the norm of twentieth-century America; and twentieth-century America may be judged by the norm imputed to puritan Englishmen of the seventeenth century, or to the American revolutionary party of the eighteenth century. A peculiar weight attaches to those appraisals of the past in which the norm is common to the past and the present. Only such judgments constitute a national self-criticism in the proper sense. They not only estimate the past in its own terms, but at the same time derive 'lessons' from the past which are applicable to current and impending action.

6

It is clear, then, that a judgment of appraisal, if by this is meant a judgment in which conduct, personal character, maxims, and policies are judged by an explicit standard, is objective and verifiable. If by describing such judgments as 'relative' it is meant that they employ a standard of comparison, then they are relative; but then they are at the same time absolute—absolute judgments of comparison.

There remains the question of the plurality of standards. That there are many standards is a plain matter of historical fact. In the very act of making one's own standard explicit one achieves objective detachment, and sees that standard to be one among others. These standards cannot be *reduced* to one, either by showing that there is one which is implied in all the others, or by showing that there is only one which can be adhered to with consistency, or by showing that the only difference between one standard and another is a difference of enlightenment. All these reductions have been attempted by moralists, but without success. Admitting the plurality of standards, of which of them shall we say that it is *the* standard by which the others can be judged 'morally,' in a sense that is universally acceptable? What standard, if any, is qualified to be considered as the standard of standards?

Standards may be distinguished by their agreement with reality. It has been claimed of the Christian standard, for example, that it is the design of Creation and the purpose of Divine Providence. Similarly it has been claimed that the nationalistic standard of Germany, or the economic standard of Communism, coincides with the forces of history; and that a certain code is destined to prevail over other codes in the struggle for existence.

There are two objections to adopting the actual constitution of things, whether defined in terms of religion, philosophy of history, or natural evolution, as the criterion of the moral standard. In the first place, all of these theories are at best of dubious validity. But in the second place, in proportion as a standard is conceived as coinciding with the actual constitution of things it ceases to be a standard. For a standard is essentially a goal to be reached, or a state of affairs to be realized through the will of him who adopts it. When the standard is conceived as actual rather than ideal, it ceases to be an object of endeavor and becomes an object of contemplation, endorsement, and gratification. Desire and will remain outside and project ideals of their own.

This contradiction between acceptance and action has given rise in the history of human thought to the insistence on freedom of the will as a postulate of the moral consciousness. In spite of all the subterfuges, confusions, and intellectual lapses that have obscured it, the contradiction still remains. The moral question is: What shall I do? What is that which ought to be done, and which but for me will not be done? To say that there is nothing to be done, since what ought to be done is already done, does not provide an answer but rejects the question. Meanwhile men have continued to ask the question, even nominal adherents of philosophies which reject it.

We address ourselves, then, to the moral question, Which of the several standards is fitted to be the ultimate standard of action, the highest ideal to be realized, the final goal of endeavor? There is, I think, an answer. There is a certain standard which plays a unique role in relation to the human will, and which may appropriately be called the 'moral' standard, the standard of standards, the standard by which all others shall be judged. It may be described in several ways, each of which presents it in a certain aspect.

Described as 'disinterestedness' or 'total benevolence,' this standard represents the claims of all interests, without bias in favor of any interest, such as self-interest, class interest, or national interest. Described as 'harmonious happiness,' this standard recognizes that the satisfaction of each interest must be so adjusted and restricted as to be compatible with the satisfaction of other interests. Described as 'reflective agreement,' this standard recognizes that the method of harmonizing all interests is an extension of the method by which a single person, taking account of all of his interests, seeks his own good on the whole. Reflective agreement requires that each person shall through sympathy adopt the interests of others, and that several persons, being reciprocally sympathetic, shall through discussion create a purpose of common good out of their total interests. Described as 'inclusiveness,' this standard forbids the disregard of any interest, or the exclusion of any interest except the interest which refuses to be included.

This standard is capable of being adopted and is capable of being applied. What title has it to speak the last word in moral matters?

First, it is a comparatively clear statement of the standard which, in various guises and verbal formulations, has been most widely in vogue in Western Europe, pagan or Christian, and whether in the social conscience of the average man or in the doctrines of moral philosophers. It is the standard most likely to be assumed as the standard of final appraisal among those who inherit the European tradition. It best states what is meant by 'humanitarianism,' 'general welfare,' and 'the public interest.' It reveals the principle common to Plato's conception of justice, the Christian commandment of love, Kant's 'categorical imperative,' and the utilitarian's 'greatest happiness of the greatest number.' To accept this standard as the 'moral' standard best agrees with the use of the word 'moral.'

Second, this standard plays a unique role in the development of the social arts and institutions. Economy, law, and polity arise out of the conflict of human interests, and serve the purpose of rendering interests compatible and mutually supporting; and they express themselves in the form of enduring institutions because this purpose is a continuing task, which concerns the total community. Reflective agreement, harmonious happiness, inclusive provision for all interests of all individuals, is the standard by which the function of these institutions is distinguished from their personal agents, and by which their failure and success as institutions are judged. And when, as at present, men look for a 'moral' solution of the problem of war, they hope to bring about a similar organization through which all nations can agree upon a common plan which takes account of the aggregate interests of mankind.

The third and strongest claim of this standard to be considered the moral standard par excellence lies in the fact that it is commonly presupposed in moral discussion as the principle by which differences of moral opinion can be resolved. Moral discussion takes place on two levels. There are questions of fact which arise between two individuals who presuppose the same end—questions concerning the nature of things, and questions of cause and effect. But when the dispute is carried further and concerns itself with conflicting ends, the agreement which is contemplated as the outcome of discussion is an agreement of wills, in which the several parties to the discussion shall have pooled their interests and adopted a common purpose which satisfies, or attempts to satisfy, them all.

William James has defended this view by saying that this standard is the "philosophical" standard, that is, the standard of the impartial and enlightened judge. The right of a claim or an interest to be satisfied is the root meaning of 'right,' and the obligation to take account of a claim or an interest is the root meaning of 'ought.' The only right or obligation to deny a claim or an interest must therefore spring from a counter-claim or an opposing interest. It follows that the philosopher, pledged to take the rounded and detached view of life, must take as his 'guiding principle' the satisfaction of as many demands as possible:

> That act must be the best act, accordingly, which makes for the best whole, in the sense of awakening the least sum of dissatisfactions. . . . The course of history is nothing but the story of men's struggles from generation to generation to find the more and more inclusive order.[4]

7

With the moral norm is associated a specific bias. The desire to find a common will creates a form of wishful thinking which exercises a profound influence on the nation's image of its own past. It behooves the critic to be aware of this bias, and at the same time to recognize that it springs from no trifling prejudice, but from the profoundest depths of the moral consciousness.

The individual in his biographical retrospect views his earlier life as *his* youth—as an earlier phase of the same life cycle. Similarly, the moral consciousness of today—its fundamental bond of agreement—tends, by selection, oblivion, and fiction, to find common ground with the past, and to impute to the past such attitudes and beliefs as will bring the past and the present together into a single, continuous, and enduring national life. This moral motive in itself affords no evidence that such attitudes were actually held in the past. The evidence appropriate to such a historical judgment is evidence disclosed by the *records* of yesterday. He whose judgment concerning the past is wholly dictated by the moral bias of the present is guilty of dogmatism.

Dogmatic judgments of the past arising from the moral bias assume various forms. There is the judgment which affirms the present to be the purpose of the past. When one looks back from a present eminence, the continuous path which has been traversed appears to *lead to* that eminence even when the path is errant and newly broken. Its beginnings seem to have been aware of their destination and to have been motivated by it. Thus a retrospective nationalism will impute to its own past a germ of destiny. This 'pathetic fallacy' leads men not only to impute the present creed to the past, but to exaggerate its role *in* the past. A nation now imbued with the puritan and democratic creeds tends to neglect the past diversity of opinions and motives, and to ignore other motives—such, for example, as economic interests—which prompted both the settlement of New England and the separation from the mother country.

Having detected this bias, the over-emancipated critic thereupon proceeds in a spirit of reprisal to belittle the earlier vogue and importance of the puritan and democratic creeds. A more discriminating and genial critic, on the other hand, will refuse to be prejudiced against a historical judgment by the fact that it is dogmatically affirmed. Granting that the judgment has hitherto lacked its appropriate evidence, he will be none the less receptive to that evidence. Nay, he will *hope* to find it, since, if he is successful, his conclusion will be doubly attested, as historically true and as suiting the moral exigencies of the present.

The adherents of a present national creed tend, then, for moral reasons, both to ascribe that creed to the nation's past, and to invest it with a dominant role. They tend also to eulogize the past, or credit it with the *realization* of a creed which is in the present only a standard and an aspiration. There is a powerful impulsion to view the national past in a rosy light, and to mix history with edification.

This tendency expresses, no doubt, that same instinctive avoidance of the painful which leads the individual to remember the good and forget the evil in his own past. A second motive is the laudatory fulsomeness of love. In the love of country, as in the love of a mistress, the whole vocabulary of praise is indiscriminately poured upon its object. Thus the Honorable Ole Hanson, Mayor of Seattle, published in 1920 a book entitled *Americanism versus Bolshevism*, in which he identified Americanism with liberty, equality, progress, law, hope, family life, prosperity, strength, morality, God and good, truth, justice, education, ideals, and several dozen other items of excellence. Bolshevism, of course, was identified with their opposites. If in his description of America the author omitted any laudatory terms, it was only because he did not think of them. When in his perorational eloquence he stated that "our countryside rings with happy song and laughter," while Russia "knows neither happiness nor song," we know that the support for this statement is to be found in the author's heart rather than in the data of sociology.

The fundamental explanation, however, lies in the fact that it is impossible to believe in ideals without a craving for their concrete embodiment. To be devoted to a creed implies a conviction that it is realizable, and the line between the realizable and the realized is naturally and easily crossed. Passionate devotees look for exemplars of perfection. When such exemplars are the objects of a collective idolatry, they serve the double purpose of confirmation and union. The only earthly realm of actuality in which such exemplars can dwell uncontradicted by too palpable disproof is the past. Faith swings round the circle, and places its vision of perfection at the beginning rather than at the end. The nation's history becomes a pantheon of collective hero-worship.

Parson Weems was an influential disseminator of idolatrous Americanism. It is to him more than to any other single writer that Americans owe their immaculate George Washington. He offered his *History of the Life and Death, Virtues and Exploits of General George Washington* to those "who wish to see human nature in its most finished form"; and in the Dedication to Martha Washington he said:

> One of my reasons for writing this sketch of your husband's life, and virtues, is derived from those virtues themselves, which are such *true brilliants* as to *assure* me, that even in my simple style, like diamonds on the earth, they will so play their part at *sparkling,* that many an honest youth shall long to place them in the casket of his own bosom.[5]

Recent historians, employing stricter methods of research, and being less ardent moralists, have discovered that George Washington was not without blemish. Indeed, it appears doubtful whether, despite the "excellent lady" to whom Weems attributes the story, Washington and his father ever had the edifying conversation about the hatchet and the cherry tree. Similarly, historians have now for some years been discovering that colonials of the seventeenth century were not so puritan, or colonials of the eighteenth century so democratic, as reverent democratic-puritans have liked to suppose.

So far so good. But the 'rigorous' historian is not without his failings. There is in history, as in literature, an instinctive avoidance of the obvious and banal, even when it is true; more joy in the kingdom of knowledge over one novelty than over ninety and nine familiar facts, with great credit to the missionary who triumphantly brings it in. And facts, like sinners, gain something from an unsavory reputation. There is a morbid curiosity among the readers, and sometimes even among the writers, of history, which puts a premium on scandal and disillusionment.

These are forms of bias which will also bear watching. There is no greater presumption of truth in a disparagement that springs from pruriency or boredom than in a eulogy that springs from piety. An anti-moral bias has no title to precedence over a moral bias. The attitude of disillusionment has at times so warped the historical mind as to make it necessary to insist that because a certain attribute is a virtue, it does not follow that George Washington or Abraham Lincoln may not have possessed it. And it may be necessary for future historians to discover that puritan New England was after all puritan, and that the signers of the Declaration of Independence and a considerable body of their contemporaries were democratic in practice as well as in profession.

Genuinely unbiased history does not, as a matter of fact, make the past less venerable. Excessive edification arouses ridicule or distaste. Or perhaps one should say that there are fashions in edification, and that to be effective in the twentieth century edification must not be too flagrant. The moral hook has to be baited. Parson Weems is a case in point. Over and above his confusion of history and edification, Parson Weems is ineffectively edifying. There is a verse (presumably his own) which is inscribed on the title page of an embellished edition of his life of Washington:

A life how useful to his country led!
How loved! While living!—how revered! now dead!
Lisp! lisp! his name, ye children yet unborn!
And with like deeds your own great names adorn.[6]

This verse does not produce on the children (now that they are born) precisely the effect intended. It disposes them to laughter rather than to reverent lisping. Nowadays we want our virtues embodied in the flesh and compounded with their opposites. Indeed, it is felt to be rather indecent to refer to them in public at all. The art of refined discourse now requires a dyslogistic vocabulary with which to make veiled allusions to virtue, as euphemisms were once required to avoid indelicate allusions to vice. So it happens that the historians' determination to include vice in the picture, or even to assign it the larger place, seems only to make the residuum of virtue more palatable.

Sacrosanct ideals tend to become stereotyped, verbal, unreal, and their pure embodiments do not make them less so. Only the unbiased historian can guide us to the age in which the ideal was born, and introduce us into the presence of its living embodiments. He puts life into the abstraction by dipping it in the bath of reality. Provided the essential meaning of the ideal is not obscured, historical realism enhances its power. The vulgarities of Lincoln or the frailties of Washington do not sully the perfections which these heroes symbolize, but humanize them and bring them within the range of mortal attainment. The same is true of the imperfect puritanism of New England, or the faltering democracy of the founding fathers. The worshiper needs intimacy with his heroes as well as with his gods, and veracious history gives to the cult of nationalism that tissue of circumstance through which the ideal is domesticated. For veracious history is always unique, and mortality and finitude are human. Because our forerunners, being like ourselves, were no better than they should be, and waged a doubtful struggle on particular and memorable battlefields, we may feel that we are peculiarly their successors and inherit their unfinished task.

8

In the chapters that follow, puritanism and democracy will be not only expounded but appraised. They will be appraised in terms of the moral standard explicitly defined, so that the conclusions may be verified by any reader for himself. Deviations from the standard will be condemned, and will be referred to as moral errors; agreements will be considered exemplary and admirable, and will be referred to as moral truths. Insofar as the standard is accepted by the reader, this study will be not only historical but also edifying. Insofar as its judgments of appraisal employ a standard shared by contemporary Americans, they will constitute 'our' appraisal and not merely mine. In proportion as the thought, sentiment, and organized life of the past employed the same standard as ours, we shall be appraising the puritan and democratic past 'in its own terms'; so that were it not for the accident of physical absence, that past might confirm or dispute our verdict. So far as this is the case our appraisal will be 'ours' not only in the contemporary, but also in the historical, sense, and will constitute, in short, a national self-appraisal.

Appraisal of the past discloses defects of commission and of omission, merits of antithesis, and merits and defects of exaggeration. Defects of commission, flat incongruence with the selected standard, require no special comment. The omissions of a past cult follow from its very pastness. It is judged by a posterity which commands a wider sweep—both before and after. The puritanism of the seventeenth century and the democracy of the eighteenth, thus roundly surveyed, will be seen to lie within limits; and to have missed or lost, as well as found.

Defects both of commission and of omission derive a certain extenuation from antithesis to their opposites. Moral cults arise as a recoil from the evil of their day, and are rightly loved for the enemies they make. A judge of puritanism and democracy should, before concluding his verdict, ask himself whether he would prefer the licentiousness and tyranny which these cults condemned.

Omission creates an effect of exaggeration which is both a merit and a defect—a merit in what it affirms, a defect in the degree of its emphasis—and it may be considered under either aspect. It may serve the purpose of driving home a partial truth. It sometimes happens that partial truth is obliged to raise its voice in order to get a hearing, and then its very exaggeration serves the purpose of completeness. On the other hand, exaggeration may exhibit the grotesqueness of partiality; and when seen in this monstrous aspect it may have the effect of discrediting the modicum of truth which it contains.

9

Granting that a cult of the past such as puritanism or democracy represents limited moral truths, there is an option as to whether as a whole it shall be taken as a symbol of its truths or as a caricature of its limitations. Whether the past shall be put on a pedestal or in the stocks is no affair of the descriptive historian, who provides the materials for both; but the existence of this option makes it possible to revere the past, and to treasure "that large utterance of the early Gods," [7] without a repudiation of the critical faculties. It is possible, to quote one of my colleagues, that there should be "disillusion without disenchantment." [8]

There is an instinct of moral self-preservation which prompts mankind to select and revere whatever of the past is most akin to the aspiration of the present. Said Barrett Wendell:

> The only thing that can make humanity godlike is unviolated tradition. . . . "It is the sin and the tumult and the passion of human life that die. Enshrined in art the beauty of the old days lives, and it will live forever."

And even though science nowadays teaches us the suggestive truth that the old days which we have reverenced were, after all, when the sun still shone on them, days of turbulence and wickedness, disheartening as any that surges about us now, that same science, one often thinks, is prone to forget the deep law of human nature which makes each generation, in the end, remember instinctively of those that are gone before only or chiefly those traits and deeds which shall add to the wisdom and the power of humanity.[9]

Caricature and satire are purges—occasionally beneficent, but without nutritive value. Laughter is a moral opiate, or an illusion of innocence, but it provides no positive moral incentive or illumination. It can be used to obtain temporary relief from the pressure of any ideal. Thus Nietzsche, for example, has made of Franciscan Christianity, with its exaggerated insistence on humility, obedience, simplicity, and nonresistance, a symbol of slavish weakness and mediocrity; while his own superman, conceived by him as the image of nobility and perfection, has become among rival wits an impersonation of bombast and arrogance. Treat all ideals in the same way and the result is to leave nothing but the sum of all partial errors. The most that can be said for this result is that it comforts the man of *no* purpose and *no* standards, who would like to be allowed to go to the devil as he likes.

The excessive use of satire robs life of symbolic reinforcement. History is stripped of heroes, saints, and martyrs, and peopled only with monsters. Those to whom puritanism or democracy means not what the puritan or the democrat has done, but only what he has overdone or left undone, are guilty of a double folly: they shut out a ray of light, and deprive the will of a powerful tonic. They hear no martial chant of the faithful, but only chuckles of derision. It is doubly wise to regard these traditional cults as the exaggerated and limited, but often for that very reason the heroic and dramatic, embodiments of moral truth.

He who undertakes a discriminating and provident criticism cannot fail to think wistfully of the partisan rewards which he renounces. The easiest laughter to excite is at the expense of seriousness. It is a part of my purpose to rebuke the cynics and satirists, but in so doing I cannot hope to be equally entertaining. They have a double advantage. In the first place, they collide with moral prejudices and produce a pleasurable shock. In the second place, the force of moral inertia works with them—

they offer a release from the yoke of duty, so that their audience is glad to believe them.

"It is the fault of our rhetoric," said Emerson, "that we cannot strongly state one fact without seeming to belie some other." [10] Since I am unwilling to belie or seem to belie any moral truth, however partial, I suffer the rhetorical penalty. The elder Henry James once said of the writings of Swedenborg that they were "insipid with veracity." [11] I am willing to be as insipid as necessary, in order to be as veracious as possible.

10

In this spirit of dull sobriety I submit that puritanism and democracy, being a complex set of complex ideas, are in some respects morally true and in other respects false. They are true and they are false both in what they accept and in what they reject. They are true and they are false as regards the amount and the proportion of their ingredients. Since their truth and their falsity are thus mixed, one must pronounce mixed verdicts upon them.

Thus puritanism contains ingredients which an ethics of reflective agreement must accept: the adoption of an order of values, culminating in a supreme good; a belief in the paramount importance of right conduct; the recognition of evil and of failure, above all in oneself; the adoption of a standard, and of a consistent distinction between right and wrong in terms of that standard; a scrupulous adherence to the right and avoidance of the wrong, as one sees them.

Puritanism proclaims the moral necessity of subordinating all partial good to total good. One may, it is true, postpone the best and last things to a future that is illusory or too remote. Some joy in the present is consistent with a greater joy in the future, and if joy were not sometimes present it would never occur at all. Nevertheless there remains the lucid truth, intelligible even to the simple intelligence of Bunyan's Christian, that the greatest goods are cut off from those passionate children of this world who seize too avidly upon the pleasures spread before them.

Unquestionably the way to be entertaining about a puritan is to caricature him. Secretly everyone would rather have an idealist *shown* up than *held* up—it relieves moral tension, and justifies that state of comparative failure which is the common lot. If Christian could have sat down at home in the City of Destruction with some of the leading wags of the place, and enjoyed a hearty laugh at the expense of Evangelist, his burden would have rolled off at once, and he would have been saved that hard journey to the foot of the Cross. But he would have sacrificed the greater to the lesser good.

Or, consider the original democratic creed of equality and natural rights as this is embodied in the Declaration of Independence and was professed by the founders of the Republic. Shall we ridicule it as a stupid error, and wittily expose the actual inequalities of human society? Shall we condemn it as abstract and doctrinaire, since it largely ignores the organic unity of society and the constructive possibilities of social legislation? Or shall we pursue the more thrifty course and use it as a symbol of its essential, though partial, truths?

Here are some of its essential truths. Men may justly challenge existing authority if it ignores their interests. The human individual is the proper judge of civil institutions, and it is to their fruitfulness in terms of human happiness and well-being that these institutions owe their justification. Submission to government should be an act of free consent based on a sense of benefits received. All great human achievement, and most of all in a democracy, must rest upon a faith in human nature. If one is to make the most of a man, one must give him the benefit of that doubt which always attaches to the limits of human capacity.

These are the truths of 1776, and I see nothing in them that is obsolete in the year 1944. He who takes these truths to heart is in no sense compelled to shut his eyes to the dangers of democracy: to the tyrannies and vulgarities of the majority; to the need in every democracy of an express insistence on quality and distinction; or to the incompleteness of a democracy that has not as yet entered into industry as well as politics. But by imputing essential truths to our fathers we can acknowledge them with filial piety, nourish ourselves upon them, and at the same time resolve to transmit to our own children a wider and fuller inheritance.

In 1916 the young Van Wyck Brooks deplored the absence in America of a rich intellectual and social experience:

> The hour of the epos had struck. It had struck, bequeathing to us only one human tradition. . . . Primitive competition, the competition of the jungle itself, the only mode of life our fathers knew, had left us cold and dumb in spirit, incoherent and uncohesive as between man and man, given to many devices, without community in aim or purpose. . . . One looks out to-day over the immense vista of our society, stretching westward in a succession of dreary steppes, a universe of talent and thwarted personality evaporating in stale culture, and one sees the inevitable result of possessing no tradition to fill in the interstices of energy and maintain a steady current of life over and above the ebb and flow of individual impulses, of individual destinies.[12]

There is a tragic irony in the fact that American critics have helped to create the very impoverishment which they so bitterly lament. The political and religious traditions, even the economic tradition, of America are as rich as any human society has ever enjoyed. America does not lack tradition, but fidelity.

The effect of the present challenge to our national piety is to arouse in the exponents of tradition an exaggerated fear of change and desperate attachment to the past which serve only to justify the charges of their opponents. We thus tend to a condition of blind struggle between two false gospels, the gospel of reaction and the gospel of revolution, or the gospel of the mere past and the gospel of the mere future. But the party of blind fidelity and the party of radical disillusionment must both be mistaken. Either of these errors may rise to heights of sincerity and courage that give it a sort of dignity. Nevertheless I do not hesitate to call both of these gospels false, because we cannot live in either the past or the future, but only in the present, which is both. We live out of the past and into the future. Our ideals, therefore, must be both old and new—both *memories* and *plans.* They must enable us to preserve our national identity, and draw inspiration from heroic days; but they must also find new content in the facts of life about us, reveal our faults, and help us with courage and invention to find new solutions of new problems.

It is only when an ideal is thus capable of bearing new fruit in each successive season because it is deeply and tenaciously rooted that it can serve its purpose of giving to a nation both integrity and nobility. Integrity comes of being true to the past, and nobility comes of being true to the future. The ideal serves a double role, as something to live *by*, and something to live *for*. As something to live by, the ideal gives to a nation its stability, its monumental greatness, its place in history; while to the individual it gives a sense of membership and participation, a pride and code of honor—and ancestry, in something better than a strictly genealogical sense. As something to live for, the ideal lifts our associated life above the plane of barter, or economic partnership, or a mere truce among self-seeking individuals, to the plane of a common cause.

CHAPTER FOUR

WHO WERE THE PURITANS?

1

Puritanism and democracy are historic creeds: the first, the creed of certain Englishmen of the sixteenth and seventeenth centuries, some of whom migrated to America, where they lived their creed, and sought to maintain it against the transforming influences of environment and internal change; the second, the creed of certain colonial Americans who waged a war of liberation, and created a new political constitution, at the close of the eighteenth century. Both are systems of ideas; and both are historical, that is, referred to a certain place and a certain period in past time. The nature of their historical anchorage is, however, different. Puritanism is a sect, identified by the group of its adherents. Democracy, in the specific American sense here intended, is the self-justification of a nation, finding authentic expression in public documents, and identified with the birth and development of a state.

In identifying a historical creed such as puritanism it is not possible to subordinate either the doctrine or its adherents. Shall we say that 'puritanism' is what the puritans believed, or that the 'puritans' were those who believed in puritanism? If we are wise we shall refuse to accept either horn of this dilemma. A school (sect, cult, or party) exists when a group of historical persons, independently identifiable in time and place, are associated through adherence to a common belief independently identifiable in the realm of ideas. This equal independence of doctrine and adherents being understood, it does not greatly matter with which the exposition begins. The historical fact is the union of the two: the fact that certain historical persons held a common and characteristic body of doctrine.

Every historical creed will have stricter meanings, together with a limitless range of approximations. The adherents are identified by the name which they adopt, or by which they are 'known' to their contemporaries and immediate posterity. But the doctrine may be abstracted from this historical setting, discovered in other times and places, and then named by analogy, as when one discovers 'Christians' before Christ.

Extended meanings are further multiplied by the complexity of the creed itself. Puritanism is a system of beliefs; and the name may be confined to the integral system, or extended to any of its parts, great or small. All beliefs have degrees of particularity and generality, and these also afford options of definition. All beliefs have degrees of purity and impurity. They develop in a subjective setting and an objective environment, both of which enter into and adulterate them. Again, doctrines and systems of doctrines have degrees of centrality. It will not do, perhaps, to identify a sectarian doctrine with all of the beliefs of all of its adherents. Puritanism, one is tempted to say, does not include what the so-called puritans believed about the cure for gout. Yet this statement is no sooner made than doubted, when one reflects upon the therapeutic implications of sin and prayer. In short, puritanism is not only a multiple system of ideas, but has a more or less concentric structure, with degrees of remoteness spreading from an essential core to an indefinitely remote periphery.

This complexity of meaning is further aggravated by the fact that every cult passes through the phases of development which are common to all cults, and which must not, therefore, be confused with the ideas which are peculiar to a particular cult. Thus every historic cult passes from a phase of innovation in which it challenges established things, to a phase of consolidation in which it seeks to establish and defend itself against later innovations. During their heroic days, when their conviction is most ardent, its adherents are filled with a crusading spirit, and with a combative resentfulness of tradition and authority. Innovators differ in the tempo of their reforming zeal: some are cautious, hoping to avoid an open breach; others are impatient and reckless. But at their height these same cults become jealous of their own authority, and fearful of attack from within or without.

Another recognizable change of phase is that from exuberant vitality to sclerosis. This process of desiccation, though perhaps characteristic of all cultural change, is peculiarly characteristic of moral ideas; which may retain their negations, automatisms, or external forms, when the last spark of hopeful faith has expired. Since all moral ideas imply some restraint upon the natural man, there will also be oscillations of strictness and laxity—harsh discipline alternating with concessions to appetite and inclination.

The presence of these elements of phase greatly complicates the problem of definition. It is clear that radicalism and conservatism, youth and age, or restriction and expansion, are not defining characteristics of puritanism and democracy. A 'last puritanism' will be a blend of puritanism and lastness—of the doctrinal peculiarities of puritanism with the mentality characteristic of any cult in its phase of decadence. Thus Santayana's famous book is an account not of the living puritan creed, but of its death; and its death resembles the death of any creed when its subordinations have become negations, its convictions rigidities, and its surviving zealots monstrosities. Just as the biographer must find some way of distinguishing the unique way in which his individual subject traverses the cycle of the seven ages from the infant in the nurse's arms to second childishness and mere oblivion, so the historian of ideas must seek to show how a juvenile or senile puritanism will differ from the juvenility or senility of any other cult.

It is characteristic of America that its inhabitants are of migrating stock. They or their ancestors came to America in order to escape some form of frustration, and they may be assumed, therefore, to have possessed certain migratory characteristics such as independence, ambition, or lawlessness. Being in America, they never wholly cease to be a people with two homes—the home of their adoption, and the home of their origin endeared to them by early attachment and the glamour of remoteness. But since puritans came to America to escape cavaliers and cavaliers to escape puritans, it would evidently be a mistake to define the meaning of either cult in terms of the psychology of escape, adventure, or nostalgia.

Every historical creed is thus an overlapping of continua, a region of thought defined by many intersecting series: anticipations and memories; waxing and waning; degrees of generalization; centrality or place in the system; relations to other ideas outside the system; relations to environment and to subjective conditions. Such a congeries should not and cannot be sharply bounded. How broadly or narrowly, how loosely or strictly—to what remote relation, to what mixtures or dilutions, to what foreshadowings or echoes—one shall apply the name, is arbitrary. A historical creed is like the sun, appearing as a clear-cut and uniform disk when low on the distant horizon, but revealing itself on closer inspection as a vast caldron of molten matter, emanating gases, and with corona and streamers projecting indefinitely into surrounding space.

The theological and moral distinctions that are central in puritanism are uncongenial to the present age. There is, therefore, a peculiar obligation to give them significance as well as clarity. The subtleties of puritanism are no more fantastic than those fine points which now divide radicals, liberals, capitalists, Communists, and Fascists; but they seem less important. In the one case, as in the other, there can be no understanding until the issues seem grave, and the rival doctrines convincing. Puritanism must therefore be presented in relation to the experience, the presuppositions, and the reasoning, which to its most enlightened and honest exponents gave it the weight of truth. It should be possible to capture something of the feeling which moved Thomas Goodwin to say: "I also read *Calvin's* Institutions, and O how sweet was the reading of some Parts of that Book to me! How Pleasing was the Delivery of Truths in a solid manner then to me!" [1]

2

The term 'puritan' must be defined in terms both of the human individuals whom it denotes and of the doctrines which it connotes. The present chapter is devoted to the first part of the definition. To whom is the name of 'puritan' properly applicable?

The puritans were protestants *à outrance,* and the name is sometimes extended to embrace those Christian sects or schools which manifested the protestant spirit even before the Protestant Reformation. Puritanism in this generic sense, as 'strictness of living and simplicity of worship'—Christianity in its pristine purity, and opposed to fleshly and worldly compromise, as well as to ecclesiasticism, ritualism, the multiplication of sacramental mysteries, and the elaboration of dogma—is a recurrent phenomenon in Christian history. The Paulicians, who were in evidence in Armenia and elsewhere as early as the fifth century, and whose Greek name, *Cathari* ('pure,' 'spotless,' 'clean'), suggests a verbal analogy to puritanism, afford an early instance. The Albigenses of the twelfth and thirteenth centuries defended a similar creed. The most important of the precursors of the Protestant Reformation was, however, John Wycliffe (c. 1320-1384), who translated the Bible, made a popular appeal through itinerant preachers, attacked the papacy and sacerdotalism, and advocated justification by faith, the right of private judgment, and the priesthood of believers. His followers, the Lollards, and those of his younger contemporary, John Huss, renewed themselves from generation to generation, and at the opening of the sixteenth century constituted a considerable body of Christendom already protestant in thought and feeling and predisposed to accept the teachings of Luther and Calvin.

But it is not necessary to look for this generic puritanism in such flagrantly reforming sects. Considered as the effort to purge the extreme Christian teaching of every admixture of compromise, it appears, for example, in the teachings of the great schoolman William of Occam:

> The Occamists, at least in spirit, were not dissidents, but were eager to maintain against the ever-menacing naturalism, against the eternal paganism, the fundamental Christian doctrine—the gratuitousness, the transcendence, the necessity, of the divine gift which makes us children of God—drawing from these essential truths certain unwelcome consequences, conceiving in the most relentless fashion the rights of God, the principles of morality, the wretchedness of fallen man. . . . Luther and Calvin undoubtedly pressed this inhuman doctrine to even further extremes, but they were not the first to support it.[2]

In a stricter historical sense, excluding both precursors and successors, the name of 'puritan' is applicable to the following groups:

1. The reformers in the Anglican church, 1559-1662
2. The New England settlers of 1620 and 1630

3. The makers and victors of the Puritan Revolution in England, 1642-60
4. The New England theocracy, 1650-90
5. Jonathan Edwards and the Great Awakening, 1730-50

3

1. The puritans in the strictest sense were the left-wing protestants *within* the Anglican church during the century from the liberal policy of Elizabeth to the repressive policy of Charles II, or from Thomas Cartwright, the reformer, to Richard Baxter, the outlaw. The puritan movement so defined was an effect of the peculiar history of the Reformation in England. A considerable portion of the English protestants were governed by political rather than by religious motives. They felt a nationalistic resentment of the pretensions of the papacy, and an anti-clericalism that ranged from a high-principled distrust of priestly privileges to a frankly sordid coveting of ecclesiastical property. To such protestants Catholic doctrine and worship were objectionable only insofar as they tended to support the papal or priestly claims; otherwise they commended themselves, on grounds of tradition, habit, and a spirit of moderation.

During more than a century it was a question as to whether the English church should be stabilized at this point. The leaders of the moderate party were monarchists, who were wholly out of sympathy with the stubborn individualism, sectarian factiousness, and theocratic republicanism which were the natural fruits of reformed protestantism. To the reformers of the Continent, protestantism of the moderate Anglican type was an arrested development.

The spirit of full-blown protestantism had already developed widely among the humbler classes in England as a result of the influence of Wycliffe in the fourteenth century, and it was inevitable that it should continue to assert itself, gathering strength from its own internal development and reinforced by contacts with the Continent.

During the reign of Edward VI (1547-53), and under his liberal bishops, Cranmer, Ridley, Hooper, and Latimer, the English Reformation developed rapidly in the direction of the Calvinistic movement of the Continent. The persecution and exile of these reformers during the reign of Mary only served to intensify their zeal, and led to the formation in Geneva in 1556 of an exile congregation under John Knox. When Elizabeth succeeded to the throne in 1558, and attempted in the following year to establish a moderate policy in the spirit of her father, the struggle was renewed. The extreme reforming party now sought in effect to model the national church of England on the church of Geneva.

Elizabeth's problem as a statesman was to reconcile the policy of a state church with the divided and rapidly changing sentiment of the people. It is evident that the forces at play were as much political as religious. The crown was at one and the same time supreme in matters temporal and in matters spiritual and ecclesiastical, so that whenever the royal prerogatives were asserted, religious dissent became indistinguishable from civil sedition. There must be 'uniformity,' otherwise there would be no common church and no state control; but this uniformity must not be too rigid lest it violate not only conscience and religious conviction but the Englishman's constitutional liberties.

The Acts of Supremacy and Uniformity promulgated by Elizabeth in 1559 were strict in tone, but leniently enforced. They affirmed the royal authority over the episcopal hierarchy; they prescribed uniformity of worship; and they imposed penalties upon any minister who failed to conform. But "heresies, errors, schisms, abuses, offences, contempts and enormities" [3] continued, and were overlooked even within the Anglican ministry. The substitution of tables for altars, the wearing of copes and surplices, "making the cross in the child's forehead" in the sacrament of baptism [4]—these and like matters were to the reformers questions of conscience and Scripture, on which they did not hesitate to challenge the authorities of church and state.

According to a church historian of the seventeenth century, those who refused "to subscribe to the *Liturgie, Ceremonies* and *Discipline* of the *Church*" were for the first time in 1564 "branded with the odious name of *Puritanes*." [5] The "invidious" name of "puritan" was current in 1568, being applied to those (especially ministers) who agreed only in attacking, by resistance, petition, or admonition, what they regarded as "popish abuses yet remaining in the English Church"; who represented "contentions, sects and disquietness . . . and, for one godly and uniform order, diversity of rites and ceremonies, disputations and contentions, schism and divisions already risen, and more like to ensue." These puritans, the Queen complained, were "over-bold with God Almighty, making too many subtle scannings of His blessed will, as lawyers do with human testaments." It was "dangerous to a kingly rule" to have private men citing Scripture against the government.[6]

The same resentment of the puritans' unruly temper appears in the speech of James I at the opening of Parliament in 1604:

> At my first coming, although I found but one religion, and that which by myself is professed, publicly allowed and by the law maintained, yet found I another sort of religion, besides a private sect, lurking within the bowels of this nation. The first is the true religion, which by me is professed and by the law is established: the second is the falsely called Catholics, but truly Papists: the third, which I call a sect rather than a religion, is the Puritans and Novelists, who do not so far differ from us in points of religion as in their confused form of policy and parity; being ever discontented with the present government and impatient to suffer any superiority, which maketh their sect unable to be suffered in any well-governed commonwealth.[7]

With Charles I the political motive was reinforced by his personal religious feelings and convictions; and, advised by Archbishop Laud and the Earl of Strafford, he launched upon an uncompromising policy of suppression. Parliament became the protector and the rallying point of the puritan party, and the religious conflict thus became at the same time a civil struggle between monarchy and republicanism.

After the Restoration Charles II resumed the Stuart policy, now supported by a cavalier Parliament which was more resentfully anti-puritan than the King. In 1662 a new and stricter Act of Uniformity, later supplemented by the Corporation Act of 1665, drove from the Anglican church two thousand ministers who refused to abjure the "solemn league and covenant,"[8] and give their "unfeigned assent and consent" to all things "contained and prescribed" in the Book of Common Prayer, to the "rites and ceremonies of the church, according to the use of the Church of England," and to "the form or manner of making, ordaining, and consecrating of bishops, priests, and deacons." [9] Severe penalties and disabilities were imposed upon those who conducted worship in any manner other than that prescribed for the Church of England; all teachers were compelled solemnly to declare their allegiance to both king and church.

The King and his advisers, laying it down that "nothing conduced more to the settling of the peace of this nation . . . than an universal agreement in the public worship of almighty God," [10] discovered that nothing conduced less to the peace of the nation than the attempt to enforce such agreement. Puritanism was driven from the state church and outlawed altogether; but it lost little of its vigor and none of its recalcitrancy. The puritans became nonconformists and dissenters, and were prosecuted and penalized for twenty-five years—until the Revolution of 1688, when religious toleration became an established policy of the realm.[11]

During this long and bitter struggle puritanism was both a force and a product. It is evident that it touched every aspect of English life. Considered as a purely religious phenomenon, puritanism was an attempt to purge the Anglican compromise of its 'dregs of Romanism.' It was not, however, and could not be, a purely religious phenomenon. It involved a struggle for power—the power to exist, or the power to control. Puritanism found itself in the position of defying authority, and was thus identified with the party of revolution. Like all revolutionary parties, it was internally divided according to the temper of its partisans. It had its right, its left, and its center, according to the degree of impatience and boldness. The struggle, once inaugurated, developed all the complex mentality of civil dissension. Suppression aggravated resistance, persecution created grievances and begot reprisals. The cavalier party tended to represent the landholding aristocracy, and the puritan party the rising class of tradesmen and merchants. But both parties were divided as well as united by their economic or cultural bias. Regardless of religious differences, men of property shrank from extreme measures which jeopardized their security, while men of taste instinctively dissociated themselves from excesses of sectarian zeal or of emotional piety.

4

2. The New England immigrants of 1620 fled from the England of James I to escape the officers of the law. The greater migration of 1630, a year after the dissolution of Parliament by Charles I, expressed the widespread conviction that it was no longer possible to hope for a reform of the Anglican church *in England.* Taking advantage of a charter issued in 1629 to the Company of Massachusetts Bay, these immigrants, selected for their piety and character, sought to promote their reform more effectively in a new world.

The 'Pilgrim Fathers' of Plymouth who disembarked from the *Mayflower* in 1620 were 'Separatists,' that is, they had already seceded from the Church of England and created independent churches of their own, on the congregational model. They were therefore not puritans in the strict sense of reforming Anglicans. They sprang from a Separatist church which was founded in 1607 at Scrooby, and which drew its members from the plain farmers of the surrounding countryside: "For they were of sundrie townes and vilages, some in Notingamshire, some of Lincollinshire, and some of Yorkshire, wher they border nearest togeather." [12] It was this church, seeking to escape persecution, and held together by the piety and courage of John Robinson, a clergyman, and William Brewster, the Scrooby postmaster, which found its way first to Holland and then by the accidents of weather and ignorance to the obscure harbor of Plymouth.

The settlement of Massachusetts Bay in 1630, on the other hand, was a large-scale movement, led by men who had never forfeited their legal standing. As described by a recent historian, their migration reflected the widespread belief that in Europe even the general cause of protestantism was hopeless:

> Gloomy indeed was the outlook for the Puritans in the 1630's. A wave of triumphant Catholicism seemed to be rolling over Europe. The Thirty Years' War was favoring the Catholic cause; the French Huguenots suffered a sorrowful defeat in 1628; the English queen, Henrietta Maria of France, was a devoted Catholic; the impecunious government of Charles I refused to aid

the Protestants on the Continent; and the policies of Archbishop Laud seemed to the Puritans to proclaim a forthcoming reunion between England and Rome.[13]

This gloom was unfounded. In ten years, as Governor Winthrop said, it was the puritans who expected "a new world" [14] at home, while their enemies were seeking refuge in Virginia and Maryland.

Although these settlers of 1630 accepted the congregational form of church polity, they had firmly rejected, and continued to reject, the principle of Separatism. They adhered to the principle of uniformity in the hope that they might eventually realize a uniformity of their own—a *reformed uniformity.*[15] They included men of wealth, education, and position, such as John Winthrop, their first governor, and John Cotton, their leading minister and doctrinal advocate. While the Pilgrims, being victims of persecution, and wanting to be let alone, were pervaded by a gentle spirit of communal life, the Massachusetts Bay colonists were militant and expansive.

By the migration to America, however, these differences were diminished and eventually obliterated. Reforming Anglicans, being separated from England by three thousand miles of sea and seven weeks or more of hazardous travel, and being thus almost wholly delivered from the royal and ecclesiastical control to which they professed allegiance, were from the standpoint of English authority scarcely distinguishable from Separatists. The Plymouth Separatists, on the other hand, their separation having been achieved, and being now free to create a homogeneous community of their own, were in New England scarcely distinguishable from the exponents of uniformity who were their neighbors to the north. Differences of social condition and of wealth lost much of their importance under pioneer conditions. The common environment, the common needs and hazards, the common Bible, and above all the common Calvinistic creed, filled a much greater place in their lives than the abstract issue of Separatism or the circumstances of their migration. The theocratic ideal, and the moral qualities which enabled both groups to survive and to realize that ideal, were essentially the same.

Making every allowance for the admixture of economic and political motives which influenced the settlers of Plymouth and Massachusetts

Bay, there remains the indisputable fact that this body of people were to an exceptional degree bound together by the consciousness of their common faith. This appears strikingly in the difference between New England on the one hand, and Virginia on the other. Virginia was pervaded by Anglican sentiment, and the distinguished families whose representatives played the leading part in the revolutionary and post-revolutionary periods of American history—families such as those of Washington, Madison, Monroe, Randolph, Lee, and Jefferson—sprang from cavalier ancestry. But taken as a whole, the form of Virginia society was due to the cult of tobacco rather than to a cult of piety.* Being more moderate in temper, more liberal in its conception of church membership, and more vulnerable to latitudinarian influences, Anglicanism provided no such theocratic impulse as moved the covenanted elect of New England.

5

3. The revolution which culminated in the Protectorate of Oliver Cromwell is commonly called the Puritan Revolution, and it would be as pedantic to question this use of the name as to deny its application to the Pilgrims of Plymouth. American puritanism claims the leaders of the English puritan party as its spiritual ancestors. "Hampden and Pym and Eliot and Baxter and Milton and Cromwell," says an American essayist, "have left a deeper impress upon America than all the Mathers." [16]

The differences which divided the parliamentary party served only to accentuate the body of ideas by which they were united. This party embraced liberal Anglicans, presbyterians, Separatists or Independents, and divers lesser sects, but they fought and triumphed for a common

---

* For the geographic, economic, and social influences which weakened the Anglican church in Virginia, *cf.* Thomas Jefferson Wertenbaker, *The First Americans, 1607-1690*, Macmillan, 1927, Chap. V, "A Transplanted Church," p. 138. "The influence of the Anglican church [in the colonies] continued to decline until during the American Revolution it reached its lowest ebb. Its history throughout the entire colonial period is one long recital of disappointment, of wasted opportunities, and gradually diminishing strength."

cause. There was bitter opposition between Independents and presbyterians. Presbyterianism was relatively authoritarian and hierarchical, and was therefore uncongenial to the temper of revolt and individualism that was rife in England during the Revolution. When the Revolution triumphed, and its leaders were confronted with the task of establishing religious uniformity under parliamentary control, they inevitably looked with favor upon the presbyterian system of church government. But Cromwell himself was an Independent, and his desire to hold his fighting forces together and to establish a stable peace inclined him to prevent any sect from claiming autocratic control. It is one of the minor ironies of history that the triumph of Cromwell in 1649, and the inauguration of a decade of religious toleration in England, should have synchronized with the consummation in New England of an intolerant theocracy.

6

4. There are certain characteristics of the American puritan which are associated with the theocratic state created and maintained in New England during the years from 1650 to 1690. During the forty years dating roughly from the adoption of the Cambridge Platform in New England in 1648 to the English Revolution of 1688, the puritan colonists of Massachusetts developed the social and political implications of their creed on a scale that has never been equaled before or since. Constituting the influential part of the population, having all the agencies of control in their hands, separated by a great distance from alien influences, and called upon to create a new society, they enjoyed a unique opportunity for creating an institutional embodiment of their characteristic doctrines. The New England theocracy was puritanism in being, puritanism true to its own genius, its seeds developing unhampered upon favorable soil.

That New England puritanism should have taken a theocratic form was implicit not only in its uniformitarian doctrine, but in the nature of the migration itself. The settlers were rigidly selected for their morality and piety. The Plymouth colonists were a church, a joint-stock company, and a state, all in one. For the larger Massachusetts group, who carried their charter in their pockets, the economic and political functions were means by which to sustain and regulate a community imbued with a religious purpose. As the population grew, this puritan nucleus became a minority and a party, exercising a control through representative institutions, but with a franchise limited to church members in good standing. The suppression of heresy by the magistrates was a function wholly appropriate to a society in which public order and religious conformity were identified.

But the period of the theocracy was both a period of culmination and a period of dissension and persecution. Puritanism inculcated the spirit of resistance in its own members, and sent many of its own reformers into a second exile. In New England, as in England, religious toleration eventually became the necessary condition of public order and stability.

7

5. Of all the exponents of American puritanism, Jonathan Edwards has acquired the greatest notoriety. His sensational emphasis on certain of the sinister aspects of Calvinistic theology has eclipsed the memory of his greater gifts. Instead of being taken as the distinguished philosopher and man of letters that he was—great mind and great spirit—he has become a topic of jest and ribaldry, whom any vulgarian feels authorized to deride as one who preached of *Sinners in the Hands of an Angry God.*

While Edwards is a familiar symbol of puritanism to its detractors, he is by no means the most characteristic of its representatives. His personal thought and experience lie on too exalted a plane. In his theology he represented a purity of Calvinistic doctrine, and a logical adherence to its major premise of divine sovereignty, exceeding anything known in New England in the preceding century. But he was not a mere dogmatic theologian: he was a speculative genius nourished on the philosophy of the past, and quickened by the influence of the Enlightenment. Like Augustine and Thomas Aquinas, he placed the orthodox tenets of Christianity within a framework of systematic metaphysics, and verified them from his own spiritual life.

While Edwards revived and rationalized Calvinistic doctrine, he at the same time revived piety. He lived in an age in which puritanism had lost much of its earnestness and inner conviction. In spite of their remoteness from Europe, the New England colonists felt the epochal change in the direction of the wind, now blowing from the quarter of reason rather than from that of faith. During the century which had elapsed between the original settlement of Massachusetts and Edwards's coming of age the colonial society had multiplied its secular preoccupations. The problem of salvation had retreated farther into the background. Belief, worship, and churchgoing had become externalized. Even the clergy did not consider it necessary to experience conversion. It was the mission of Edwards to reawaken the sense of sin, and to turn men's hearts again toward God. It was the sense of this mission which goaded him, despite misgivings, to emotional preaching, and which identified him broadly with the evangelical revival represented contemporaneously by the preaching of Wesley and Whitefield, and commonly known as the Great Awakening.

Evangelism springs from an eager interest in the saving of souls, and tends, therefore, to be humanitarian and popular. It emphasizes the religious emotions because of their effectiveness as a means of propagating belief, and because of their evident power to transform the individual. So it came about that Edwards as an evangelist—as an *alarmist* —acquired something of that character of intemperate 'enthusiasm' which was repugnant not only to his own gentleness and intellectuality, and to the temper of the eighteenth century, but to that emphasis on uniformity and civil order which had characterized the New England theocracy at its height.

The earlier persecutions of Anne Hutchinson, Roger Williams, and the Quakers had not turned on the abstract principle of tolerance. These radical dissenters stood for individualistic, anarchical, and subjectivistic tendencies which were believed to be fatal to social cohesion. They claimed a private inspiration by which they knew that they were 'justified'—even though their justification should bear no clearly defined relation to works, morals, doctrinal adherence, or any other generally accepted test. Thus the individual escaped all regulation, theological, moral, even political, because his private sanction was placed above every public sanction. His attitude was dangerous and troublesome to any civil order, and inconsistent with a civil order based upon a common moral and religious creed.[17]

Edwards felt that his evangelical methods, and the emotional outbursts to which they gave rise, were in need of some defense, and he published *Thoughts* on the subject.[18] Charles Chauncy replied with other *Thoughts—Seasonable Thoughts on the State of Religion in New England*, published in 1743. He believed that he spoke for the genuine puritan tradition when he condemned "the Prevalence of *Enthusiasm*, *Superstition*, and *Intemperate Zeal*, in all the *Wildness* and *Extravagance* that can be conceived of." Calvinists, he said, "now are, and always have been from the Beginning the *principal* and most *inveterate* Enemies to our growing *Confusions*."

'Tis readily own'd, it ought not to be expected of Persons under the *saving Operations* of the SPIRIT, that they should appear like *Angels;* but yet, it may, with all Reason, be expected, they should appear like *Men who have been renewed after the Image of* GOD, *in Knowledge, and Righteousness, and true Holiness.* 'Tis not enough that they have *Heat* in their *Affections,* but they must have *Light* in their *Minds;* 'tis not enough that they talk speciously, and *profess highly,* but they must be really possest of a truly *Christian Temper:* And this they must discover by *putting away from them all Bitterness, and Wrath, and Anger, and Clamour, and evil-speaking, with all Malice;* and not only so, but by living in the habitual Practice of that *Piety* towards GOD, and *Righteousness* and *Charity* towards *Men,* in all the genuine Expressions of them, which are required in the Gospel.[19]

In other words, puritanism was a form of social and intellectual orthodoxy, and was opposed to sectarian anarchy on grounds of public order and intellectual sobriety. Hence the evangelical revival, although revivifying the protestant religious consciousness, found itself under attack from two quarters, on the one hand from the exponents of enlightenment, and on the other hand from the representatives of the crystallized and established puritan tradition.

8

In estimating the volume of the puritan influence in America, or the number of Americans to whom the name of 'puritan' may with varying degrees of exactness be applied, it is necessary to take account, first, of the fecundity and expansion of the New England puritan. The descendants of the original puritan settlers spread to adjacent parts of New England, to New York, and to the Ohio Valley; and while they carried little baggage, they took their creed, and held to it all the more tenaciously as being their chief link with the past.

Other waves of immigration embraced Calvinists from Great Britain and from the continent of Europe. As early as 1651 the Scottish prisoners of war taken at the battle of Worcester were shipped to the colonies. The great Scotch-Irish influx brought over 150,000 presbyterians during the eighteenth century.[20] They were descendants of the presbyterian Scots who in the reign of James I had been settled in Ulster on the confiscated estates of rebellious nobles. Economic discrimination, religious persecution, and land evictions drove them from their new homes in a stream which between 1772 and 1774 amounted to 30,000. Entering for the most part at Middle Atlantic ports, this stream flowed south along the Great Valley, parallel to the seacoast, between the Blue Ridge and the Allegheny plateau. Turning west over the Alleghenies, it traversed the present states of Kentucky and Tennessee, and finally followed the course of the Ohio Valley. This stream was confluent during most of its course with a stream of German immigrants who had, as a rule, arrived earlier and possessed themselves of the best land. These Germans were mainly from the Palatinate and from Switzerland, and belonged in large part to the 'reformed' or Calvinistic branch of protestantism. Their migration, beginning in 1709 and culminating in the middle of the century, was an effect of the civil war, invasion, persecution, and economic distress that had continued almost uninterruptedly since the outbreak of the Thirty Years' War.

To these two major groups are to be added the French Huguenots, who came to America after the Revocation of the Edict of Nantes in

1685, and the Dutch, who settled in New York in 1608 and constituted an independent colony until 1664. The former settled in considerable numbers in South Carolina. The latter were in the main of the Dutch Reformed Church and, like the Huguenots, good Calvinists, as was a fraction of the immigrants (mainly Lutheran) who in the first half of the seventeenth century came from the Scandinavian countries.

Other colonists were drawn into the large and powerful evangelical sects. Of these the Baptists, except for the 'Free Will Baptists' of Rhode Island, were Calvinistic in profession, and their emphasis on emotional appeal and on the simpler teachings of the gospel suited the less-educated classes in Pennsylvania and the tidewater regions of the South. The Wesleyan teaching was tinged with Arminianism, extending to every man a hope of salvation based on the universality of redemption. This more compassionate and optimistic note, as well as its emotional methods of appeal, commended the Methodist Church to a wide following, and reinforced the broadly protestant, though not strictly Calvinistic, features of puritanism.

The multiplication of lesser sects has been a characteristic form of religious revival. An ardent reviver will be impatient and will find it quicker to form a new church than reform an old. Hence, as the vitality of older churches declined, something of the earlier zeal was renewed in the Mormons, Millerites, Seventh Day Adventists, Campbellites, Churches of Christ, Nazarenes, Church of God, Jehovah's Witnesses, Shakers, and Dunkers.[21] Of many of these sects might have been said what was said of Mormonism, that it was "an after-clap of puritanism." [22]

Before the Revolution the Catholics of Maryland were an intermittently persecuted group. Although their total number (of whom more than half lived in Maryland, the remainder in Pennsylvania, New York, and Virginia) was small, in John Carroll and Thomas Fitzsimmons they provided distinguished leaders of the revolutionary cause. Anglicanism was especially strong in the tidewater regions of the South, where colonial churches were 'established' in the seventeenth century.[23] But it is evident that an established English church in America contradicted the Revolution. The role of the great Virginia leaders of the

American Revolution is to be attributed to their religious moderation rather than to their religious zeal. Their ready acceptance of the philosophy of the Enlightenment had its roots in the religious struggles of England, in which the Anglican party was broadly identified with 'Arminianism' as opposed to the uncompromising temper of the Calvinistic puritans. The rule of Anglicanism, moreover, was mild, and tended to be perfunctory. Its practice and teachings left the greater part of the lives of its adherents untouched, and exposed to the liberalizing influences of the day. Neither Catholics nor Anglicans were likely to stamp their distinctive religious creed or social philosophy on the American nation in the heroic days of its emancipation.

The religious statistics of the colonial and revolutionary periods are notoriously unreliable, but even after making a liberal allowance for error, the figures are striking. According to the best available evidence the population of the Thirteen Colonies in 1776 was approximately 2,500,000.[24] The estimated number of those who were in the broad sense[25] adherents of Calvinistic or closely allied sects is as follows:[26]

Congregationalists (mainly New England puritans)	575,000
Presbyterians (mainly Scotch-Irish)	410,000
Dutch Reformed	75,000
German Reformed	50,000
Baptists	25,000
Total	1,135,000

It is to be assumed that the balance of the population in 1776 was mainly Anglican. It also embraced Methodists, Lutherans, and others of non-Calvinistic dissenting groups, but their number was at this time small. The great Methodist expansion was just beginning.[27] The number of Catholics was approximately 25,000, and that of Jews 2,000. An indeterminate number of the population were of no religious creed.[28]

Deducting these lesser groups, the number of Anglicans must have been well in excess of 1,000,000. This figure includes, however, the bulk of the Negro population, which in 1776 was 533,500, of whom 476,500 lived in Southern states, where their adherence to the creed of their masters was largely nominal. And on the whole Anglicans were less zealous than other sects, and their piety was less central to their thinking and practice.

It is safe to assume, then, that the influence of puritanism, in the broad Calvinistic sense, was a major force in the late colonial period, and that it contributed uniquely and profoundly to the making of the American mind when the American mind was in the making.

CHAPTER FIVE

WHAT DID THE PURITANS BELIEVE?

1

FOR THE PURPOSE of summarizing its essential doctrine puritanism may be described as theocratic, congregational-presbyterian, Calvinistic, protestant, medieval Christianity. Each of these five factors comprises a set of ideas, and they compose an orderly succession in which each in turn qualifies its predecessor. Thus protestantism is a form of medieval Christianity, Calvinism a form of protestantism, presbyterianism and congregationalism are forms of Calvinism, and puritan theocracy a form of presbyterianism and congregationalism.

The merit of this formula lies in its calling attention to the comparative magnitude of different areas of doctrine. In each case the adjective is less than the substantive which it qualifies. Puritanism, in short, is predominantly Christian, in the medieval sense of that term; and it is further qualified by the successively more restricted characteristics of protestantism, Calvinism, presbyterianism or congregationalism, and theocracy.

The tendency to conceive a sectarian doctrine in terms of its *special,* to the exclusion of its *generic,* characteristics is important enough to deserve a name—'the fallacy of difference.' In the present case it has led to a reduction of puritanism to what is *merely* puritan, as, for example, theocracy. Such a reduction is not only narrow, but false; because the differences lose their meaning when divorced from the genus. Puritan theocracy means nothing except as a species of presbyterianism or congregationalism; and these, in turn, borrow their substance from successively more generic characteristics until we reach the broadest generic characteristics of Christianity.

The avoidance of this fallacy is necessary, not only for understanding, but for appraisal. The fallacy of difference leads to the complete rejection of a doctrine by those who may in fact object only to its peculiar idiosyncrasy. In the case of puritanism this has led to its complete rejection by liberals, who, being obsessed by its theocracy, have forgotten that it was protestant; or by Catholics, who, in their polemic against its protestantism, have forgotten that it was Christian. And those who have doubts even on the score of its Christianity should not be permitted to forget that, in an even broader generic sense, puritanism was ethical and religious.

2

The main body of puritan doctrine, then, is medieval Christianity. In America, it was the chief link of continuity with the medieval past, being a traditional rather than an innovating doctrine. Thus in academic circles of puritan thought, such as the Harvard College of the seventeenth century, the Schoolmen were held in high respect. Puritanism was an offshoot from the main stem of Christian belief, and puritans, equally with Catholics, claimed descent from St. Paul and Augustine. They claimed, in fact, to be the legitimate heirs, and the only legitimate heirs, of the Christian succession. Like other varieties of protestantism, puritanism was a 'reformation' and not a revolution. A denizen of the modern world who would recover the essential spirit of Christian medievalism would do well to saturate himself with the orthodox protestantism of the seventeenth century. He will find more of its authentic presence there than in the contemporary cult of neo-medievalism, with its fancy for Gothic architecture or Thomistic philosophy. *

What was this medieval Christianity that formed the substance of puritanism? It comprised that anthropomorphic and anthropocentric view of the world which Santayana has called "The Christian Epic":

---

* What James Harvey Robinson in his *The Mind in the Making*, Harper, 1921, Chap. V, p. 123, calls "Our Medieval Intellectual Inheritance" was in all its essentials transplanted to America by the puritans of the seventeenth century and conserved in successive generations of protestant believers. For the traditional elements of Christian belief retained by Luther, *cf.* A. C. McGiffert, *Protestant Thought before Kant*, Scribner, 1919, pp. 46-60.

The opening and close of this drama were marked by two magnificent tableaux. In the first, in obedience to the word of God, sun, moon, and stars, and earth with all her plants and animals, assumed their appropriate places, and nature sprang into being with all her laws. The first man was made out of clay, by a special act of God, and the first woman was fashioned from one of his ribs, extracted while he lay in a deep sleep. . . . He suffered them to range at will and eat of all the fruits he had planted save that of one tree only. But they, incited by a devil, transgressed this single prohibition, and were banished from that paradise with a curse upon their head, the man to live by the sweat of his brow and the woman to bear children in labour. These children possessed from the moment of conception the inordinate natures which their parents had acquired. They were born to sin and to find disorder and death everywhere within and without them.

At the same time God, lest the work of his hands should wholly perish, promised to redeem in his good season some of Adam's children and restore them to a natural life. . . . Henceforth there were two spirits, two parties, or, as Saint Augustine called them, two cities in the world. The City of Satan, whatever its artifices in art, war, or philosophy, was essentially corrupt and impious. . . . Lost, as it seemed, within this Babylon, or visible only in its obscure and forgotten purlieus, lived on at the same time the City of God, the society of all the souls God predestined to salvation. . . . For salvation had indeed come with the fulness of time . . . through the incarnation of the Son of God in the Virgin Mary, his death upon a cross, his descent into hell, and his resurrection at the third day according to the Scriptures. . . .

All history was henceforth essentially nothing but the conflict between these two cities; two moralities, one natural, the other supernatural; two philosophies, one rational, the other revealed; two beauties, one corporeal, the other spiritual; two glories, one temporal, the other eternal; two institutions, one the world, the other the Church. . . . Their conflict was to fill the ages until, when wheat and tares had long flourished together . . . the harvest should come. . . . Whereupon the blessed would enter eternal bliss with God their master and the wicked everlasting torments with the devil whom they served.[1]

The Creator's benevolent plan having been dislocated by the sinful ingratitude of his creatures, the history of man's spiritual fortunes had assumed an aspect of tragedy. The natural man was afflicted with a hereditary taint so central and pervasive as to contaminate every natural impulse, every human faculty, and every social or creative achievement. Christianity absorbed and translated into its own terms the two great articles of that pessimism which represented the last, if not the profoundest, word of the ancient wisdom: a distrust of appetite, as the irreconcilable enemy of the moral will; and a conviction of the vanity of wealth, power, and social station.

But whereas pagan pessimism found a curb of appetite and a retreat from the world in the cult of the intellect, Christian pessimism was more radical. The seeming self-sufficiency of the sage was deemed the last stronghold of pride, which must be surrendered to faith before man can attain that complete humility which is the condition of his reconciliation with God. There is yet a hope of salvation, but that salvation can come only through God's indulgence. Acknowledging his undeservingness, and placing no reliance on his own natural powers, a man may qualify himself to be a vehicle of that mercy with which God softens the rigors of strict justice.

The theological ideal of medieval Christianity formed the complement of this doctrine of human salvation. The infinity of man's sin can be atoned only by God's own self-sacrifice, through Christ, who is God incarnate. The helplessness of the natural man places the whole burden of his regeneration on the efficacy of divine grace. Man's destiny is transposed from this world to the next, where he forever suffers the deserved penalty for his sin, or in his regenerate condition forever enjoys the restored favor of God. These highest truths are accessible, not through reason, but through faith and revelation: like salvation, they are a gift of God to such men as are, through the cult of humility, fit for their reception.

Religion is essentially a counsel of perfection, and can never correspond precisely with the conditions of human life or the level of human attainment. During the course of his natural life man inhabits a body, and, however much he may repudiate the flesh, he must obey its appetites. He also lives in the world, and however much he condemns it as vain, he must accept the conditions which it imposes. He cannot escape his relations to the state, to the prevailing economic system, and to other social institutions. In some measure he will not only adapt himself to these bodily and secular environments, but will be moved by their needs, their pleasures, and their ambitions. And however much the

Christian may condemn the natural intellect, he cannot live by faith alone. He needs his intellectual powers, not only to adapt himself to his natural and secular environment, but to elucidate and interpret faith itself.

The compromise of spirituality with the flesh, of the kingdom of God with the kingdoms of this world, and of faith with reason, was not recognized merely as a fatality but as an element in the ideal Christian life. Monasticism represents the attempt to escape this compromise, but, while it was permitted by Christian authority, and served as a symbol of Christian aspiration, it was expressly rejected as the universal rule of life. [2] Christ was God made man. He was born and died, sanctioned marriage by his presence, ate and drank like other men, grew weary and slept, and rendered unto Caesar as well as unto God. The saints were symbols of humanity as well as of spiritual purity; the church was a palpable and historical institution. The cult of piety was at the same time a cult of the intellect and of the creative imagination. Science and technology maintained their separate places, ministering to human needs, and doing no violence to religion. The sum of medieval Christian wisdom contained the truths of philosophy; and worship was embellished by the arts. The Christian life was, in short, a human life, saturated with its natural and temporal surroundings, and ennobled by human faculties.

Medieval Christianity affirmed, however, the *supremacy* of religion. Philosophy was the handmaid and auxiliary of faith; and the arts were dedicated to the uses of piety. The renunciation of the world and the flesh, the humble disavowal of the natural faculties, and the sense of the total dependence of man on his Creator, defined an order of values. They gave the Christian his uneasy conscience and his seasons of repentance. They furnished the content of his meditation, and the object of his devotion on all the solemn occasions of life—above all, when facing the prospect of death. And the ultimate generalizations in terms of which men represented the world in which they lived were moral and spiritual—the will of the Creator, his providence and moral government, the sin and the immortal destiny of man, the miracles of saints. The idea that certain palpable entities such as the church and the Bible might rightfully speak in the name of God combined with the feudal economic and political order to induce a widespread acceptance of authority, and a readiness to obey what came, or seemed to come, from above.

3

But puritanism is protestant Christianity. What, then, was protestantism? Above all, it was Christianity; indeed, its aim was to be more Christian than the Christians. At the opening of his *History of Plymouth Plantation*, Governor Bradford referred to Satan "as being loath his kingdom should goe downe, the trueth prevaile; and the churches of God reverte to their anciente puritie; and recover their primitive order, libertie, and bewtie . . . the right worship of God, and discipline of christ . . . according to the simplisitie of the Gospell; without the mixture of mens inventions." [3] The New England puritan here expressed the sense of his solidarity with all protestantism, meaning by protestantism not an innovation but a reform in which Christianity was to be restored to its original perfection.

Any cult such as Christianity tends to change. Because its practical teaching is against nature, there are inevitable relaxations and concessions. There is a perpetual accretion of new thought and usage—a cumulative effect of slight innovations of doctrine and ritual. These tendencies united to create a body of Christian practices and beliefs which, whatever their intrinsic value, were in any case posthumous. On the theory of a continuous historical revelation such developments may assume a place of equal rank with the first beginnings. On another and simpler view, however, they are incrustations, surrounding and hiding the essence under superimposed layers of foreign matter; or departures to increasing distances from the essential teachings and events set forth in the Bible. Hence the attempt, both intelligible and inevitable, to recover the Christian truth and life as they were in their pristine purity, when God and his chosen people enjoyed familiar and almost familial relations, and when Christ lived among men. In such times a man needed no intermediaries between himself and deity. He witnessed God's miraculous interventions, heard the warnings of inspired prophets, or saw Christ with his own eyes, and thus himself possessed the ultimate evidence for faith. The truth of the gospel was then plain to the humblest man. Heaven and hell, like God, were near at hand; events obeyed the decisions of the moral will and the retributions of the moral law; and the gospel could be accepted quite literally and unqualifiedly.

Here, then, is a perpetual protestantism always latent in Christian teaching, finding some degree of expression in every epoch of its history, and giving birth periodically to outbursts of 'reform,' of which the so-called Protestant Reformation of the sixteenth century was only the most cataclysmic instance. In its universality protestantism means the sweeping away or abridgment of those intermediaries—historical, theological, dogmatic, metaphysical, ecclesiastical, or liturgical—which tend perpetually to arise between man and God.

Let us consider the simplest possible example. Christianity begins by the interpolation of Christ, who mediates God to man and man to God. But interpolations multiply. The Virgin Mary mediates between man and Christ, the saint between man and the Virgin, and finally the priest between man and the saint. In this particular and limited application, then, generic protestantism is theism rather than Christolatry, Christolatry rather than Mariolatry, Mariolatry rather than hagiolatry, and hagiolatry rather than sacerdotalism. It is the tendency to refuse the services of any deputy, and go directly to headquarters. It restores in vivid directness man's sense of dependence on his Creator. Face to face as he is with his ultimate origin and destiny, he overlooks the foreground of life; his mind leaps at once to the momentous alternative of divine wrath or mercy.

Protestantism charges its Catholic opponents with neglecting the bolder and grimmer lessons of the gospel through preoccupation with its channels and agencies; to which the counter-charge is oversimplification, rigidity, and a disregard of the nuances. Catholicism is symbolized by the cathedral, protestantism by the nonconformist's chapel. It is significant that it should have been Catholicism and not protestantism which was more receptive to the humanistic movement of the Renaissance.

4

The general character of protestantism affords the clue to those specific elements of Christian doctrine which protestantism singled out for emphasis. Thus the doctrine of 'justification by faith' means that the human condition of salvation lies not in the merit of 'works' but in a "steady and certain knowledge of the Divine benevolence towards us."[4] This doctrine has two important implications.

In the first place, a man's salvation is not achieved externally, or through human agencies outside himself; he himself consciously participates. He understands God's offer of salvation, and accepts it in his own individual behalf. "No one," said Luther, "can understand God or God's word, unless he has it directly from the Holy Spirit, and no one has it unless he experiences and is conscious of it."[5] Other human agencies, such as the church, may make the offer known to him and awaken him to its momentous import, but he must himself grasp its meaning and credit its truth. In the last analysis, whether he is saved or not lies between himself and God. The religious experience of the individual thus assumes the first place, not in rare moments of mystical exaltation reserved for the elite, but in the everyday religion of the common man.

Justification by faith means, in the second place, that the believer must not only understand and accept God's offer of salvation but have confidence in its application to himself. He must not only believe it, but believe *in* it. Herein lies an important difference between the protestant and the Catholic attitudes. The Catholic has no initial assurance of salvation, but must wait until his faith has been put to the test of perseverance, and has been followed by regeneration. For the protestant, on the other hand, the state of faith itself is a guarantee of salvation, of which perseverance and the regenerative work of grace are the necessary sequel. Hence the protestant enjoys, so long as his faith is secure, a peculiar sense of certainty and finality. His strength lies in this, as does also his tendency to cocksureness and self-righteousness. But as the Catholic has doubts as to his regeneration, the protestant may also have his doubts; for the state of faith is itself an uncertain and wavering achievement.

In protestantism the Bible is made directly accessible to the believer himself. He may read, quote, and interpret it for himself. This 'right of private judgment' found ample warrant in authentic sources. According to St. John, "ye have an unction from the Holy One, and ye know all things . . . the anointing which ye have received of him abideth in you, and ye need not that any man teach you." [6] The effect of the vulgarization of Scripture is to encourage its literal acceptance, and to substitute a bibliolatry for those other forms of mediation which protestantism swept away. The acceptance of documentary in place of institutional authority tends to inflexibility, and to the multiplication of sectarian fanaticisms, at the same time that it elevates the dignity of the individual as having himself direct access to the very word of God.

The same broad principles—the elimination of intermediaries between man and God, the heightened sense of human dependence, the focusing of attention upon the individual religious consciousness—govern the protestant attitude in other matters of worship and doctrine. The rejection of the Roman doctrine of the mass, in which at the moment of its elevation the host becomes the actual body and blood of Christ, expresses an unwillingness to impute miraculous virtue to any agency, whether sacerdotal or ritual, which operates externally to the religious experience itself. The doctrine of 'Christian liberty' means that salvation, in the specifically religious sense, supersedes the coercive rule of law. Judged strictly by standards of legality, human works must, even at their best, remain deserving of punishment. Through God's indulgence the Christian is relieved from this oppressive sense of hopeless guilt, and may live in the 'cheerful' sense of paternal forgiveness.[7]

According to the doctrine of predestination and election, salvation is the free gift of God. Adopting a strict Augustinianism, and refusing every compromise,[8] the protestant claims no power to save himself, or even to contribute to his own salvation, and throws himself wholly upon the divine mercy. But this rigorous determinism, while it deprives the human individual of any freedom to achieve or to lose salvation by his own will, gives him a fanatical self-confidence of the type common to all fatalistic creeds. Finally, in the doctrine of 'the priesthood of believers,' protestantism elevates the Christian laity to a new dignity. Men of the true faith, whosoever they be, are competent to transact their spiritual affairs for themselves, without the offices of any sacerdotal caste.

5

As protestantism is not the rejection of traditional Christianity, but rather the attempt to purify and conserve it, so Calvinism represents the attempt to save protestantism, both from its enemies and from itself. The Calvinists were the shock troops of protestantism—organized, disciplined, and militant. Their modern analogy is to be found in the 'party,' whether Fascist, Nazi, communist, or nationalist, whose members are distinguished within the larger movement by their more uncompromising doctrinal allegiance, their high morale, and their cohesiveness.* Protestant individualism and sectarianism tended to anarchy, and its innovations to fantastic exaggeration. From without it was threatened by a vigorous Catholic counter-reformation; and at the same time, like all religious sects, it was perpetually subject to encroachment from the world, to corruption by the flesh, and to a loss of identity through compromise. To define protestantism, to keep it intact, to consolidate its gains, to spread its empire—this became the task of Calvin and his followers.

Calvin's *Institutes of the Christian Religion* (1536) and the Five Points of Calvinism adopted by the Synod of Dort in 1619 achieved that doctrinal systematization which is necessary for any durable sect. Calvinism was here distinguished by its comparatively rigorous adherence to Scripture. The effect was to narrow its content and to exclude elements derived from tradition or from philosophy. The emphasis was on logical coherence rather than on richness of thought and experience.

Calvinism not only defined and systematized the doctrinal content

---

* Illustrated, for example, by the greater success of the Calvinistic Baptists, as compared with the Arminian Baptists, in maintaining their identity during the period of the Puritan Revolution.[9]

of protestantism but accentuated that which was most characteristic of protestant doctrine; namely, its theocentrism. The Five Points of Calvinism went beyond Calvin himself in exalting the role of God in the drama of creation and salvation. 'Unconditional predestination,' which denies any factor of unpredictability contingent on the human will; 'limited atonement,' which restricts the efficacy of Christ's sacrifice to the elect; 'human inability,' which removes from man any shred of power to save himself; the 'irresistibility of grace,' and 'the perseverance of the saints,' meaning that once men are elected nothing can prevent their salvation—these are so many ways of affirming and reaffirming beyond any possibility of misunderstanding the doctrine that the entire spiritual history of man, including the role of Christ, is embraced within the antemundane decree of God. Time is the mere enactment of eternity.

The doctrinal rigidity of Calvinism was paralleled by the rigor of its ethics. It fixed moral responsibility on the individual and demanded the strictest rectitude. Calvin was not a philosophical moralist any more than he was a metaphysician. He took the Christian code as he found it in the Bible. The Ten Commandments provided the framework of this code, and the Bible was searched for texts which limited every natural weakness or worldly indulgence, from the recognized crimes of thievery and violence to gambling, avarice, dancing, theatergoing, drunkenness, unchastity, immodesty, pride, and vanity.[10] Assuming the form of rules imposed by the will of God, Calvinistic ethics was legalistic and authoritarian.

Calvinistic piety embraced within itself the whole civil and economic life of the community. It made such concessions to the world as would enable the man of God to take his place in the world. Calvin, like Luther, sanctioned the marriage of the clergy, and himself set an example. To beget offspring and to perpetuate the institution of the family was a social function of man which, like every other function, must be exercised and perfected in the Christian manner. Piety proves itself not by withdrawal into a sphere of its own, but by excelling in every province of secular life. The man of God should be a braver warrior, a more enlightened ruler, a more skillful and industrious artisan, and a more successful tradesman because of the divine favor and appointment.

6

Strict Calvinism was a hard doctrine, which did violence to human nature. It confronted man with the alternatives of salvation and damnation, and filled him with the utmost anxiety for the fate of his soul, while at the same time giving him no control of the forces by which that fate was governed. Now among strong-willed men anxiety and passivity do not sit well together, and if this incompatibility was not always manifest, it was because the will of the early reformers was largely absorbed by the struggle to prevail against their enemies within and without the church. In the degree to which this victory was assured, the Calvinist's will was released for the inner struggle to save his own soul, and protestant apologists of the late sixteenth and early seventeenth centuries sought to interpret Calvinism in a manner that would give meaning to this struggle.

The form of Calvinism which prevailed in New England was the so-called covenant or federal theology, of which the leading English exponent was William Ames and whose most distinguished representative in New England was John Cotton. These men, and their associates and followers, "are clearly the most quoted, most respected, and most influential of contemporary authors in the writings and sermons of early Massachusetts." *

In the covenant theology there is a filling-in of the framework of Calvinism with the content of reason and conscience. Calvinism is not rejected: its compelling implications create the problem, and there is no thought of rejecting them. The covenant theology is an attempt to

---

* Perry Miller, "The Marrow of Puritan Divinity," *Publications of the Colonial Society of Massachusetts,* Vol. XXXII, p. 257. It is only recently, and owing largely to the work of Professor Miller, that the importance of this movement has been recognized. (*Cf.* his *Orthodoxy in Massachusetts,* and *The New England Mind,* Macmillan, 1939.) It originated in Zurich in the sixteenth century and was developed in the seventeenth century in Holland, where it was known as Cocceianism, after the Dutch theologian Cocceius (1603-69). Its most important English representatives, in addition to Ames and Cotton, were William Perkins, John Preston, and Richard Sibbes in England; Thomas Shepard, Thomas Hooker, and Peter Bulkeley in New England. It strongly influenced the Westminster Confession of Faith.

preserve, in form at least, the Five Points of Calvinism, while at the same time, to quote Professor Perry Miller, providing for "the validity of reason in man, the regularity of secondary causes in nature, the harmony of knowledge and faith, the coincidence of the arbitrary with inherent goodness, the intimate connection between grace and the incitements that generate grace, the necessity for moral responsibility and activity." [11] In other words, God, though supreme, is a constitutional and not a capricious ruler. Salvation is an orderly progression in which those intellectual and moral attainments which fit a man to be saved are adopted by God as the antecedents of salvation.

This doctrine has the profoundest practical consequences. Man sets the salvation of his soul above all other goods, and believes that this good depends on the favor of God. Being deeply concerned, he is impelled to do what he can about it. And he can now, on the premises of the covenant theology, do precisely what he would do if he were seeking to effect his own salvation, save that he will ascribe the whole spiritual cycle to God and will enjoy the sense of God's support. He will exert himself to achieve spiritual perfection, even if it be only to prove that he is the recipient of God's favor. If he be likewise prompted to this effort by reason and conscience themselves, or by the social impulses of his time, he will find these natural and secular motives to be in harmony with his faith.

In this development of Calvinism piety is reconciled with human self-reliance, not only by concessions to the natural capacities, but by emphasis on the doctrine of 'the covenant of grace.' According to Peter Bulkeley, God has laid down the conditions of salvation and engaged himself to those who fulfill them:

> The promise of life is made onely to beleevers, who are described by other graces accompanying their faith, and therefore termed sometimes such as love God, sometimes mercifull, poor in heart, upright, and such other, all these flowing from faith, faith shewing it selfe by them. Now then, faith being the condition of the Covenant, (as we shall shew afterwards) and being knowne by these other graces accompanying it, here is the way for us to try our selves before God, whether the promise of salvation doe belong unto us, even by looking to the condition of faith, and such other graces, as doe accompany it in them that do believe.[12]

Those who have fulfilled the conditions laid down in the covenant are not themselves the authors of their salvation. God has bound himself freely, and has himself given to the elect the power to fulfill the terms of that bond:

> We acknowledge no such condition as by which we might receive life from the hand of Justice, as putting a price into our hand to be a meritorious cause of life; such a condition could not indeed stand with grace; but the condition wee put, is both received by grace, is by grace wrought in us, and doth also receive all from grace, and therefore doth nothing derogate from the grace of the Covenant. . . . The grace of the Covenant is free notwithstanding the condition, because we doe not put any condition as antecedent to the Covenant on God's part, whereby to induce and move the Lord to enter into covenant with us, as if there were any thing supposed in us, which might invite and draw him to take us into covenant with himselfe; but onely we suppose a condition antecedent to the promise of life, which condition we are to observe and walke in.[13]

But those who have fulfilled the terms do nonetheless have a claim upon God. They have not merited salvation by anything which they have done for themselves, but being by grace 'sanctified,' they may confidently count upon the sequel of 'justification.' They enjoy the dignity of beings who can stand up and assert their rights even before God, who granted them!

If a man believes that God's grace is governed by no principle, or that its principle is wholly inscrutable, he can seek to please God only by the degree of his humility. He will be suspicious of secular virtue and wisdom as evidences of pride, and will renounce and despise them; or, believing that they are irrelevant to salvation, he will neglect them. If he moves far enough in this direction he will deny, with Anne Hutchinson, that there is any necessary relation between 'sanctification' and 'justification.' He will, in short, dissociate salvation entirely from human capacity and attainment, and cultivate those distinctively religious emotions which he takes to be evidence of God's direct intervention.

It is evident that the 'antinomian' cult of helplessness, of unmoral religiosity, of civic irresponsibility, and of obscurantism is contrary to human nature and to the organized life of society. It is evident that it would ill accord with the dawning life of the modern world, and with the self-reliant spirit of the New England colonists, devoted as they were, with increasing hopefulness and success, to the construction of a new society. Through the covenant theology the New England puritans were possessed of the more congenial creed that God helps those who help themselves.

7

The task of interpreting Calvinism was beset by two kinds of dangers, the dangers to be escaped and the dangers which arose from the escape itself. How to cure the disease without being corrupted by the remedy—how to escape excessive religiosity without falling into secularism, how to escape superstition without falling into naturalism—this question generated the opposite heresies which bounded the area of puritan orthodoxy. Antinomianism, Anabaptism, and Quakerism represented the dangers of fanaticism—the dangers to be escaped; while the dangers inherent in the rationalistic escape itself were represented by Socinianism and Arminianism, as well as by the older heresies of gnosticism, Arianism, and Pelagianism.

Antinomianism, originating with Agricola (1492-1566), sprang from excessive emphasis on the doctrine of Christian liberty, or a divorce of the distinctively religious experiences from the standard moral and civic virtues. It suggests a too ready acceptance of divine forgiveness, or too great a reliance on the divine indulgence. It expresses the fact that any cult which exalts its members *above* the law will find itself in conflict with the law.

Terms denoting heresies have an emotional meaning, and are often applied as mere epithets of abuse. In the seventeenth century this was especially true of the term 'Anabaptist.' Spreading from South Germany and Switzerland to the Low Countries early in the sixteenth century, Anabaptism was so named for its rejection of infant baptism or its insistence that believers should be rebaptized at the time of conversion. Its radicalism and fanaticism, its conflicts with authority, and its tendency to communism, pacifism, and millennialism arose primarily from its endeavor to segregate the Christian community of saints under their own rule of life. It found its scriptural sanction in passages in the Old and New Testaments in which true believers are commanded to live apart lest their purity be contaminated:

> And what agreement hath the temple of God with idols? for ye are the temple of the living God; as God hath said, I will dwell in them, and walk in them; and I will be their God, and they shall be my people.
>
> Wherefore come out from among them, and be ye separate, saith the Lord, and touch not the unclean thing; and I will receive you.[14]

The importance of the Anabaptists thus lay in their thoroughgoing 'Separatism.' Isolated in the midst of society by a sense of their peculiar vocation, they resisted every authority, whether secular or ecclesiastical, which sought to impose uniformity. Their resistance to authority and their fanatical excesses made them the objects of cruel persecution—by the state as well as by the church, and by the more sober protestants as well as by Catholics. Their persecution and martyrdom in turn intensified their fanaticism and culminated in their seizure of the Westphalian city of Münster, where for three years (1532-35), under the leadership of Johann Matthiesen of Haarlem and Johann Bockholdt of Leyden, their unruly and licentious behavior justified the worst charges of their enemies. In spite of the sober piety of the Mennonites,* who were an outgrowth of the same movement in its later phases, the name 'Anabaptism' became synonymous with almost every breach of morals, good taste, enlightenment, and civil order attributable to protestant zeal.

The fact remains, however, that the Anabaptists sowed the seeds of religious freedom, and fought stoutly for toleration and the separation of church and state. Their doctrine of adult baptism rested on the principle that the church was a voluntary covenant among believers, set apart by their conviction and not by any accident of infancy or other external circumstance. Believing this, they could not, and did not, accept any external human authority, civil or ecclesiastical. Religion being an affair between each soul and God, and residing in the heart rather than in outer action or profession, any attempt at compulsion was regarded as wicked and fruitless. The civil authorities must remain within their own bounds and leave whatever concerns the salvation of the soul to its own proper spiritual agencies.

---

* So named from Menno Simons of Friesland (1492-1559).

These liberating ideas—anticipating by nearly a hundred years the utterances of the accredited leaders of religious toleration—were taught by men such as Hans Denck of South Germany and Switzerland, by Caspar Schwenckfeld, a Silesian noble, and by the Flemings, Pieters and Terwoort, who were martyred under Elizabeth in 1575.[15] Their basic ideas were carried over into the Baptist movement which later developed in England. Anabaptists driven from Holland by the repressive rule of Charles V fled after 1550 to England,* where their Separatist teachings blended with those of the forerunners of congregationalism.

After 1581, when the tolerant policy of William the Silent provided an asylum from the growing persecution in England, the current of religious refugees was reversed, and Holland again became the seed ground of the more radical sects. In 1600, John Smyth, Thomas Helwys, and other English exiles of a Separatist persuasion formed a church in Amsterdam; and late in 1611 (or early in 1612) this group, returning under the leadership of Helwys, founded the first Baptist church on English soil. Their creed, anticipated by the Dutch Anabaptists, and influenced by the congregational teachings of Robert Browne,† embraced the memorable declaration that "no Church ought to challenge any prerogative over any other," and that "the magistrate is not by virtue of his office to meddle with religion, or matters of conscience, to force and compel men to this or that form of religion or doctrine."[17]

Quakerism, founded by George Fox (1624-1690), and introduced and spread in the American colonies by William Penn (1644-1718), agreed with the Anabaptists and Baptists in its Separatism. But the peculiar root of its offending was its complete rejection of the distinction between clergy and laity, and its acceptance of 'inner light' as an authoritative source of inspiration and guidance. "We utter Words," said John Woolman, "from an inward Knowledge that they arise from the heavenly Spring."[18]

---

* How their advent was hailed by orthodox Englishmen is thus described by the ecclesiastical historian and biographer, John Strype: "With these [the Dutch] came our Anabaptists also and sectaries holding heretical and ill opinions . . . and doctrines sprung from some of these foreigners; begin now, if not before, to be dispersed in the nation, dangerous to the established and orthodox religion and civil government."[16]

† See below, p. 108.

Quakerism tended to reduce priest to believer rather than, as with the Anabaptists, to exalt believer to priest, but it had the same tendency to render its adherents recalcitrant to any mode of organized control, whether through civil or through ecclesiastical institutions. The quietism of this sect and its later reputation for sobriety and liberality must not be allowed to obscure the fact that in the seventeenth century it was associated with factiousness, intolerance, and obscurantism.[19] Passive resistance is nonetheless resistance, and because the Quaker's passivity made it difficult to convict him of overt crimes, it did not make him less obnoxious to authority.

While antinomianism, Quakerism, and Anabaptism were forms of excessive religious zeal, Socinianism and Arminianism, like their forerunners gnosticism, Arianism, and Pelagianism, represented the encroachments of secularism.

Socinianism, named for Laelius (1525-1562) and Faustus Socinus (1539-1604), rejected the central doctrines of Augustinian orthodoxy, both its strict trinitarianism and its doctrine of predestination. As a persistent influence, however, this heresy stands for the influence on protestantism of the humanistic and rationalizing tendencies of the Renaissance. It diminishes the emphasis on dogma, and construes Christianity as the true way of life, revealed to man through his enlightenment, and realized through his freedom of choice and natural capacity for virtue.

Arminianism, although its doctrines were of earlier origin and widely diffused, took its name from the Dutch theologian Jacobus Arminius (1560-1609), the exponent of that softer version of Augustinianism which the Five Points of Calvinism rejected point for point at the Synod of Dort in 1619. As set forth in the Remonstrance presented to the states of Holland in 1610, Arminianism affirmed conditional predestination, universal atonement, and the resistibility of grace.

What Arminianism meant to a good Calvinist is thus set forth by Dr. Thomas Goodwin, writing of his youthful impressions in Norwich and Christ's College, Cambridge:

As I grew up, the Noise of the *Arminian* Controversy in *Holland* . . . began to be every Man's Talk and Enquiry, and possessed my Ears. . . . I perceiv'd by their Doctrine, which I understood being inquisitive, that they acknowledged a Work of the Spirit of God to begin with Men, by moving and stirring the Soul; but Freewill then from its Freedom carried it, tho assisted by those Aids and Helps. And this Work of the Spirit they called Grace, sufficient in the first beginnings of it, exciting, moving and helping the Will of Man, to turn to God, and giving him Power to turn, when being thus helped he would set himself to do it: but withal they affirm'd, that tho Men are thus converted, yet by the Freedom of the same Will they may, and do, often in time fall away totally; and then upon another fit through the liberty of the Will, again assisted with the like former Helps, they return to Repentance.*

Wherever Arminianism reserved for the human will some part, however subordinate, in determining the issue of salvation, Calvinism denied that part. Whatever Arminians took from God and gave to man orthodox Calvinism restored to God. Where Arminianism made concessions, however small, Calvinism made none. The controversy represented the immense psychological and moral difference between the absolute and the approximate; the all and the almost all. The Arminian was reasonable and moderate, the Calvinist strict. To the Calvinist the Arminian moderation was loose; to the Arminian the Calvinistic strictness was harsh. So in England in the seventeenth century the term 'Arminian' became a label for the relatively latitudinarian position of the Anglican party in its struggles with puritanism.[20]

8

The theology of Jonathan Edwards, like that of the Calvinism of Dort, was directed primarily against Arminianism, from which he recoiled as from the verge of the Pelagian abyss. It is granted by all parties to the dispute that God saves a portion of mankind from the just penalty of sin through Christ's atonement. There arises, then, the problem of the roles which are played in this transaction, on the one hand, by God,

* "The Life of Dr. Thomas Goodwin," *The Works of Thomas Goodwin*, Vol. V, pp. x, vi. The elder Goodwin was born in Norwich in 1600 and educated at Cambridge University. Both places were at this time (1613-16, 1619-20) important centers of religious ferment. *Cf.* below, pages 108-109.

and, on the other hand, by those who are saved. There are two conditions which must be satisfied by any solution—the omnipotence of God's will, and the identification of the elect by some ascertainable mark; and beyond a certain point the satisfaction of one of these conditions tends to negate the other. An extreme emphasis upon God's part will make salvation irrelevant to human conduct and experience, the saved being distinguished only by their destiny. When the emphasis is shifted to the other extreme, and is placed on the attributes of the elect, men will cultivate these attributes and will seem to save themselves. Between these two extremes of a fatalistic supernaturalism and a naturalistic self-sufficiency there lies an almost infinitely divisible range of doctrinal difference.

Strict Calvinistic orthodoxy stands near the first of these extremes, in that it identifies the moment of a man's salvation with God's act of choosing him. Being so chosen, the fortunate but undeserving sinner experiences faith, a release from anxiety, and a vocation of righteousness. To the left of this position stands the covenant theology, with its insistence that a man is not saved until he has demonstrated a worthiness to be saved. As yet nothing happens independently of God. Although salvation is conditional, man's power to satisfy the condition comes from the same divine power that fulfills the condition. Next toward the left stands the Arminian doctrine, which recognizes the freedom of the human will, but so limits its efficacy as to safeguard the divine control. Salvation requires an increment of grace which God gives or withholds in accordance with his foreknown and predestined plan. Freedom having thus secured a foothold, the next step is to give it a decisive role. In the semi-Pelagianism of the evangelical sects, although salvation is still impossible without divine grace, that grace is open to all who will avail themselves of it by the sacraments, by penance, and by right conduct. From here it is but a short step to the full Pelagian view that, as the sinner sins through his freedom, so he can by that same freedom achieve salvation, with grace as a useful but not indispensable adjunct.

It is customary to say that Jonathan Edwards was a pure Calvinist, but this is true only in a limited sense. Calvin was a literal-minded Biblical theologian and political leader, who distrusted philosophy as an exercise of man's natural faculty of reason. Edwards, on the other hand, was a gifted speculative thinker whose mind was nourished by the great thinkers of the past, and freshened by the 'new' currents flowing from the Cambridge Platonists, from Locke, and from Berkeley. With strict Calvinism Edwards shared an uncompromising emphasis upon God. But he gave this theocentric doctrine a philosophical, and not merely a dogmatic and authoritarian, meaning. The human will, he argued, is governed by motives, and since these are linked by causation with the will of God, which in turn is the expression of the nature of God, the human will together with all of creation is an emanation of the divine being.[21] Creation itself is not directed to any end beyond the Creator, but is a manifestation of God's self-love. The virtue of man, though it may divide itself into many forms, is in essence the love of God, that is to say, the turning of the emanation toward its source—the love of partial being for the fullness of being. As to God himself, while his perfection is exalted above understanding, his nature is most nearly approximated in the sense of harmony, which is at one and the same time the quality of beauty and the spirit of love.[22]

Throughout his discussions of all of the specific Calvinistic dogmas there is in Edwards the same resort to reason and experience. Thus he explained the fall of all men through Adam, not by supposing that Adam's sin was 'imputed' to his posterity because he was their legal representative, but by defending the metaphysical solidarity of all mankind. He accepted the dogma of total depravity, not for reasons of orthodoxy, but on the evidence of the facts, which disclose man's universal tendency to every sort of sin.[23] Even the wrath of God found a philosophical interpretation in the idea of justice, and was thus a necessary part of the divine perfection.

The essence of Jonathan Edwards can best be understood when he is compared with the covenant theologians, to whom he stood so close. According to the covenant theologians salvation is, in a carefully guarded sense, conditional. It is a condition of a man's salvation that he should be fit to be saved. It is true that both the condition and the consequence come from God—whom God would save he first makes fit; but nevertheless the consequence is justified by the condition—the salvation by the fitness. It is of the essence of Edwards's piety, on the other hand, that all the parts of creation should be justified by the whole: not the fitness by the salvation or the salvation by the fitness, but both the salvation and the fitness by their harmony as expressions of the same divine will:

> When he [God] decrees diligence and industry, he decrees riches and prosperity; when he decrees prudence, he often decrees success; when he decrees striving, then he often decrees the obtaining the kingdom of heaven; when he decrees the preaching of the gospel, then he decrees the bringing home of souls to Christ; when he decrees good natural faculties, diligence, and good advantages, then he decrees learning; when he decrees summer then he decrees the growing of plants; when he decrees conformity to his Son, then he decrees calling; when he decrees calling, then he decrees justification; and when he decrees justification, then he decrees everlasting glory. Thus, all the decrees of God are harmonious; and this is all that can be said for or against absolute or conditional decrees. But this I say, it is as improper to make one decree a condition of another, as to make the other a condition of that: but there is a harmony between both.[24]

Similarly, fatalism is to be escaped, not by diminishing, but by increasing, the role of God. God does not decree the consequence in advance of the antecedent, but decrees both together as parts of a total plan. It is then meaningless to complain that the consequences will occur *no matter what* the antecedent:

> They say, to what purpose are praying, and striving, and attending on means, if all was irreversibly determined by God before? But, to say that all was determined before these prayers and strivings, is a very wrong way of speaking, and begets those ideas in the mind, which correspond with no realities with respect to God. The decrees of our everlasting state were not before our prayers and strivings; for these are as much present with God from all eternity, as they are the moment they are present with us.[25]

Evil, too, is explained, not by placing it outside of God in the errant will of man, but by giving it a place within the fullness of God's moral and spiritual perfection. Man's fault lies in his divorcing evil from the higher good, and cleaving to it for its own sake. Of this fault God is not guilty.

> God, though he hates a thing as it is simply, may incline to it with reference to the universality of things. Though he hates sin in itself, yet he may will to permit it, for the greater promotion of holiness in this universality, including all things, and at all times. . . . God inclines to excellency, which is

harmony, but yet he may incline to suffer that which is unharmonious in itself, for the promotion of universal harmony. . . . He wills what is contrary to excellency in some particulars, for the sake of a more general excellency and order. . . . Thus it is necessary, that God's awful majesty, his authority and dreadful greatness, justice, and holiness, should be manifested. But this could not be, unless sin and punishment had been decreed; so that the shining forth of God's glory would be very imperfect, both because these parts of divine glory would not shine forth as the others do, and also the glory of his goodness, love, and holiness would be faint without them.[26]

To love God is to love God as he is, and judge him only on his own terms. Such a love of God makes no claims upon him. He should be loved for his justice even by those who suffer its penalties.* He should be loved by all his creatures, as their author, for the sheer fullness of his being.

God is the universal cause, and is also a voluntary cause. He is therefore responsible as well as omnipotent—responsible for that which is commonly called evil, but which when conceived as the will of God becomes good. Edwards differs from other orthodox Christians, not in a failure to relieve God of responsibility, but in his rejection of the attempt. Semi-Pelagians, Arminians, and even the covenant theologians do not succeed in exculpating God; their attempt to do so only betrays their unwillingness to love God as he is. It signifies a conditional love of God, a judgment of God by standards other than himself. For Edwards God needs no justification. To emphasize secondary causes, and especially the will of man, while paying a lip service to the divine first cause, is not only illogical but is the essence of impiety.

9

In proportion as protestantism endeavored to establish itself permanently in the world, the problem of organization assumed increasing importance. This problem is divisible into the problem of church polity

* Hence the famous challenge of Samuel Hopkins: "Are you willing to be damned for the glory of God?" This idea is traceable to the medieval Christian mystics, to St. Paul, and even to Moses.[27]

and the problem of the relation of church and state. But while these two problems are abstractly distinguishable, historically they are closely related, both to one another and to the underlying body of theological belief.

It is customary to distinguish three forms of Christian polity—the episcopal, the presbyterian, and the congregational. Episcopacy is the government of the church by prelates, that is, by clergy of a higher order: ecclesiastical authority descending from above through a priestly hierarchy, and from the past through apostolic succession. Of this type of polity the papal Church of Rome is the most perfect expression.

With presbyterianism and congregationalism, on the other hand, all ecclesiastical authority springs from the body of believers. The 'visible' church is an aggregation of believers who make an open avowal of their faith, and organize voluntarily for the purpose of instruction, edification, and worship. It is organized in obedience to God's will as communicated through the Bible, and since each believer is the direct recipient of this command, he is qualified to participate in its execution.

In principle, the difference between the presbyterian and congregational polities is very simple. In congregationalism, two or more believers unite to form a church; and choose certain of their more gifted members [28] as ministers to preach the gospel and administer the sacraments, or as elders to impose discipline, or as deacons to dispense charity to the sick and poor. The individual church, thus organized, remains the ultimate ecclesiastical unit. In presbyterianism, on the other hand, two or more churches unite to form a presbytery; while beyond the presbytery lies the provincial synod, and the national synod or general assembly. The individual congregation is thus governed by a higher authority in which it is directly or indirectly represented.

Episcopacy, presbyterianism, and congregationalism permit of endless intermediate gradations. An episcopal, even a papal, church may be liberal, that is, responsive to the opinion and sentiment of the Christian people under its jurisdiction. A presbyterian church, on the other hand, may readily assume the form of an oligarchy, especially when the presbytery or synod reserves the function of ordination, and is thus enabled to perpetuate its own power. In a congregational church the minister and elders may acquire a high degree of authority through their administrative functions and through the prestige of their acknowledged expertness in matters of religion. Or congregational churches in the same area, professing the same doctrines, and fearing the same enemies, may form a confederation, with varying degrees of cohesion.

Presbyterianism and congregationalism stand together, however, in their denial of any gradation of priestly rank, in their practice of lay representation in all governing ecclesiastical bodies, and in their more or less strict adherence to the principle that all such authorities shall, directly or indirectly, be chosen by, and be responsible to, a body of believers who are equal before God. And Calvinism, both historically and logically, stands with them.

The presbyterian and congregational ecclesiastical polities were argued from Scripture and defended as a return to the purer practices of the primitive church, but their deeper ground lay in their agreement with the broad trend of reformed protestantism—the elimination or reduction of intermediaries between man and God, the alleged priesthood of all believers, the exaltation of the elect, the emphasis on the self-validating force of the religious experience, the substitution of Biblical for institutional authority, and the acknowledgment of the right of private judgment.

10

As between presbyterianism and congregationalism, the choice of puritanism was to some extent dictated by circumstance. Where, as in Geneva and Scotland, it was possible for a time to organize puritanism on a scale coextensive with the secular state, the polity was presbyterian. Wherever such a state-wide organization was impossible, owing to the division of sects, or to the remoteness of pioneer settlement, puritanism tended to organize itself in independent congregations. Such a form of organization was better fitted to troubled or changing conditions. It could be instituted locally on a small scale, and could be divided without being destroyed.

The drift of puritanism toward congregationalism found its deeper cause, however, in the same principle which impelled it to reject episcopacy; namely, the equal rights of all true believers, owing to their knowledge of God's Word and their privileged status as the vehicles of God's grace. Being directly under God, they acknowledged no allegiance to any hierarchy. Such human government as they required they were competent to institute themselves. In the Bible they found warrant for the belief that a voluntary association of the faithful would enjoy the direct presence of Christ: "For where two or three are gathered together in my name, there am I in the midst of them." In the Bible they could also find warrant for the belief that such an association should embrace *only* the faithful. For did not St. Paul exhort his church at Corinth to "purge out therefore the old leaven, that ye may be a new lump, as ye are unleavened"; and did he not forbid his brethren to "keep the feast" or even "keep company" with evildoers and idolaters? [29]

To the idea that the church may be small in size, self-constituted, and independent, and the idea that its membership must be pure, there was added the revolutionary impulse to complete the protestant reform without delay. Theoretically, there are three ways in which the purity of a church can be attained: by purifying the impure, by the expulsion of the impure, or by the withdrawal of the pure. To purify the impure takes time, and meanwhile it is necessary to keep company or even keep the feast with them. To expel the impure requires that the pure shall control the church; and if the pure be a minority, this also takes time, or may be unattainable. The third or 'Separatist' alternative can be put into practice at once. Separatist congregations would naturally be sporadic, obscure, and subject to persecution. They would be impromptu and highly mobile. They would appear from year to year in whatever locality they could find refuge, usually in England or in Holland, whichever at any given time was the safer of the two.

The Dutch Anabaptists, and the later English Baptists who followed Smyth and Helwys, were Separatists, and insofar as congregationalism is a species of Separatism its early beginnings are indistinguishable from the history of that movement. Congregationalism as a distinct movement began with certain Separatist leaders to whom polity was a matter of primary doctrinal importance rather than a corollary of other doctrines or a mere effect of circumstance; and whose doctrines of baptism and election were in the orthodox Calvinistic line. Robert Browne, Henry Barrow, John Greenwood, Henry Ainsworth, Francis Johnson, and John Robinson were among their early martyrs or refugees, and in their writings the congregational theory of ecclesiastical polity was crystallized and defended. Of these Browne and Robinson have achieved the greatest fame.

In 1580 or 1581 Browne founded a congregational church at Norwich, and in 1582, having fled to Middelburg in Zeeland, he published his famous *Treatise of Reformation without tarying for anie.* Afterward, in justifying Separatism, he took the ground that "the Kingdom off God Was not to be begun by whole parishes, but rather off the worthiest, Were they never so fewe." [30] Like the Anabaptists, he insisted that the church is a voluntary association:

> The church planted or gathered is a companie or number of Christians or beleeuers, which by a willing couenant made with their God, are vnder the gouernment of God and Christ, and kepe his lawes in one holie communion.[31]

John Robinson, like Browne, was a graduate of Cambridge University and an exile. Having for several years labored in the Separatist and Brownist circle at Norwich, he joined in 1604 the "verie forward" reformers of Gainsborough and Scrooby,[32] whence in 1607 or 1608 he and his congregation migrated to Amsterdam, and thence to Leyden in 1609. His congregational doctrine, on which the Plymouth church was founded, was set forth in his *Justification of Separation from the Church of England,* published in 1610:

> This we hold and affirm, that a company, consisting though but of two or three, separated from the world . . . and gathered into the name of Christ by a covenant made to walk in all the ways of God known unto them, is a church, and so hath the whole power of Christ. . . . A company of faithful people thus covenanting together are a church, though they be without any officers among them, contrary to your Popish opinion. . . . This company being a church hath interest in all the holy things of Christ, within and amongst themselves, immediately under him the head, without any foreign aid, and assistance.[33]

It made a great deal of difference at this time what kind of congregationalist one was. To be a congregationalist at all was to incur the suspicion of the authorities,* and it meant much if one could dissociate oneself from the *radical* Separatists of the day, such as the Anabaptists. Thus Robinson made much of the difference between a theory which placed the rule of the church directly in the body of the congregation, and a theory which accepted the rule of elders chosen and controlled by the congregation.[34] And he hedged on the issue of Separatism itself. Even in his *Justification of Separation* he insisted that those who had separated from the true church were not he and his kind, but the members of the Church of England—"all the profane rowt in the Kingdom vnder the Prelates tyranny . . . it is not we which refuse them, but they vs." [35] The true church, that is, the congregational church, was in principle one and indivisible: "There is but one body, the church, and but one Lord, or head of that body, Christ: and whosoever separates from the body, the church, separates from the head, Christ." [36] Thus Robinson found himself in the strange predicament of having to condemn that promiscuous hospitality of the Dutch by which he himself had benefited.[37]

The puritans who migrated to Massachusetts Bay in 1630 explicitly rejected the principle of Separatism altogether, despite the Separatist origins of that very congregational polity which they defended. They took the position that if congregationalism was the true form of Christian polity, it should prevail throughout Christendom. With William Ames, they rejected the schism as "a Cutting, a Separation, a dis-junction, or dissolution of that Vnion, which among Christians ought to be kept. . . . It is against the honour of Christ . . . it destroyeth the Vnitie of Christs Mysticall body." [38]

The non-separating congregationalists hoped to reconcile the unity

---

* In 1608, Joseph Hall, formerly Robinson's senior at Cambridge and later Bishop of Exeter (1627) and of Norwich (1641), published a *Letter to M. Smyth, and M. Robinson, Ringleaders of the late Separation at Amsterdam*, containing the following warning:". . . your souls shall find too late that it had been a thousand times better to swallow a ceremony, than to rend a chvrch; yea, that euen whoredoms and mvrders shall abide an easier answer than Separation." Quoted by H. M. Dexter, *Congregationalism . . . as Seen in Its Literature*, p. 382.

of the church with their congregational principles, and to transform an Anglican uniformity into a congregational uniformity. Their policy of peaceful penetration, of maintaining a position of technical regularity while harboring revolutionary designs, could not, however, be pursued indefinitely. To the Anglican authorities, who judged them by their designs, they were little better than Separatists. At the critical moment the organization of the Massachusetts Bay Company created an unlooked-for alternative. By migrating to New England, charter in hand, the non-Separatist congregationalists could maintain a nominal adherence to the Anglican church and continue to profess their regularity, while accomplishing their reforms without further delay.[39] In a land of their own they could now realize, unhampered by hostile authority, their dream of an all-congregational Christian society.

Their difficulties henceforth were internal rather than external. Conceiving the church as essentially a voluntary compact among the believers, and assuming, therefore, that "the predestined elect could be distinguished in the flesh from the predestined reprobate," [40] they were embarrassed by the difficulty of finding reliable criteria, and by the fact that the children of the saints, enjoying through infant baptism a sort of hereditary claim to membership in the church, frequently presented no evidence whatever of regeneration. In order to create and maintain a uniformity of faith and worship they found it necessary to exalt the power of ministers and elders and to develop through 'consociation' a centralized system of control that bore a striking resemblance to presbyterianism. They invoked the power of the magistrates to suppress heresy and enforce external observances. These measures encountered a growing resistance which was motivated not only by the spirit of secularism, and by an insistence on political rights, but by the deepest impulses of congregationalism itself. There was, in short, an inherent conflict between the idea of the single church as an autonomous group of believers, and the idea that there was one authentic polity and doctrine which was prescribed for all churches.

11

The question of Separatism and congregationalism is bound up with that of church and state. The church from which the English Separatists separated was a state church, so that their Separatism involved a challenge to the civil as well as to the ecclesiastical authorities.

There is, as has often been pointed out, a parallelism between civil and ecclesiastical polity, and this may be a cause of harmony or conflict. The constitution of the church will reflect the habits and convictions which govern its members in the civil polity in which they also participate. In the sixteenth and seventeenth centuries absolute monarchists tended to episcopacy, republicans and limited monarchists to presbyterianism,* and democrats to congregationalism. Presbyterianism and congregationalism reflected degrees of political liberalism, presbyterianism expressing fear of the masses, and congregationalism the extreme suspicion of authority.

Both presbyterianism and congregationalism were more congenial than episcopacy to the parliamentary party. In 1571 a committee of the British Parliament prepared a confession of faith which omitted the consecration of bishops and kindred matters. Archbishop Parker demanded an explanation of these omissions:

> Peter Wentworth replied they had done so because they had not yet made up their minds as to whether they were agreeable to the Word of God or not. "But surely," said the archbishop, "in these things you will refer yourselves wholly to us, the bishops." With some warmth Wentworth replied that "they meant to pass nothing they did not understand; for that would be to make the bishops into popes." [42]

This defiant reply suggests not so much the rejection of *what* the bishops prescribed, or the rejection of the episcopal office, as the rejection of any authority which would presume to prescribe what did not commend itself to those who were called upon to obey. In this recalcitrance to human authority puritanism was animated by the same claim

---

* The Independents occupied an intermediate position—more democratic than the presbyterians but disappointing the hopes of their more radical allies to the left.[41]

of autonomy that found simultaneous expression in civil matters. There was thus not only a parallelism between ecclesiastical and civil polities, but a perpetual interaction between the two, owing to the temper of the men who composed them.

It is possible, however, to exaggerate the importance of this analogy. Even the congregational form of polity did not offset the strain of authoritarianism in traditional Christianity. God was accustomed to address his people in the imperative mood; and whatever might be said of popes and bishops, Christ was the head and king of the church. The Scriptures were searched in order to discover the revealed authority, and its discovery implied a readiness to obey. The reformers were much more concerned with the rival power of the civil authority than with its constitutional form. The essential question as between church and state was the question of control. In Scandinavian countries, in the German principalities, and in Switzerland, where the secular authorities were friendly to the Reformation, the civil polity was not challenged. Even bishops of the established hierarchy were willingly accepted whenever they showed themselves complaisant. Had the Anglican hierarchy led or supported the reform, it is quite possible that presbyterianism and congregationalism would never have arisen in England. Calvin's emphasis upon a representative ecclesiastical polity was due in large measure to the fact that he was compelled to meet and overcome the hostility of the civil authorities as well as of the bishops.[43]

The fundamental issue concerning the relation of church and state is, then, independent of the question of the form of polity which prevails in either. Nor is the issue clearly conveyed by the term 'establishment.' If by an established church is meant a state church, whose head is the civil ruler, or which is supported by general taxation, or whose officers are in whole or in part appointed by the public authorities, then an established church may be subordinate to the state; and be merely an agency by which the habit of political obedience to authority is inculcated, or by which its purpose of civil order and its political ideology are promoted, as was advocated by Hobbes.[44] Or, the established church may administer a single religious doctrine and discipline to be enforced exclusively upon all by civil penalties. Or, finally, it may enjoy a favored position in the sphere of religion, and yet be only one of many forms of faith and worship recognized by the law. It is with the second and third of these alternatives that we are here concerned, and they are not distinguished either from one another or from the first alternative by the mere fact of establishment.

The second or uniformitarian alternative, according to which one religious doctrine and discipline is enforced by the public authorities, was the prevailing theory and practice throughout Christendom in the sixteenth and seventeenth centuries. It assumed either the Erastian or the ecclesiastical form. Erastianism represented the idea that the definition as well as the enforcement of religious orthodoxy should be entrusted to the civil authorities.[45] The state being itself a divine institution, it was assumed that its officers were competent in spiritual as well as in temporal matters. Lutheranism, as well as Anglicanism, tended to this view. The ecclesiastical form, on the other hand, represented the well-grounded suspicion that the state, once given control over matters of faith and conscience, would substitute its own political ideology for that of religion. It expressed a jealousy of the prerogative of the church as alone authorized to interpret the belief and practice which are to be imposed upon all members of the community; and was exemplified by the Catholic tradition,* by the Calvinistic republic of Geneva, by the Scotch presbyterianism of John Knox, by English puritanism before Cromwell, and by the puritanism of New England. This rivalry between state and church as the agencies of uniformitarian control signifies the fact that the power which enforces tends in the long run to determine the content of what is enforced.

The third alternative, according to which several churches are protected by the state, and no man is persecuted because of his religion, found its earliest advocates among Anabaptists, Quakers, and other extreme Separatists, and its first effective political expressions under William of Orange in 1581 [46] and in the Independency of Oliver Cromwell.

Whether uniformitarianism, or the enforcement of a single religious doctrine and discipline, does or does not deserve the name 'theocracy' is a question that can receive no absolute answer. The general principle

---

* Especially as represented by the Jesuits.

permits of varying degrees in the strictness and thoroughness of its application.

The principle itself involves, in the first place, a monopolistic orthodoxy: it becomes a function of the state to suppress heretical churches or sects. But the policy of repression may vary widely in severity. Since it is not possible to enforce the inner attitude of faith, in proportion as this inner attitude is emphasized, there is a tendency to oppose the intervention of the state, as useless, or as conducive to hypocrisy. But when the religious creed is so expanded and elaborated as to embrace overt conduct and social practices, it falls to an increasing extent within the scope of effective law. Even worship itself, so far as this consists of church attendance, public profession of faith, or other external observances, can be made uniform by the power of the civil authorities reinforced by public opinion. There will then be two forms of orthodoxy: the inner faith of the regenerate and the outward conformity of the unregenerate. No greater uniformity than this can be expected on the assumption that many are called but few are chosen.

The principle of legalized orthodoxy involves the priority of the religious to the political sanction. Even in Erastianism the credentials of political authority derive in the last analysis from the will of God, as revealed in his Word or in the experience and conviction of religiously-minded men; while an ecclesiasticism will allow comparatively little latitude to the civil authorities. Finally, the practice of monopolistic orthodoxy involves a subjective sense of certainty. The will to impose a uniform faith and worship reflects an absence of doubt, and an assumption by believers that dissent is a symptom of blindness or obstinacy. This is also a matter of degree.

Thus in proportion as protestantism was *severe* in its repression of heresy, *pervasive* in its cult, *arrogant* in its claims of revelation, and *confident* in its belief, it tended to theocracy.

12

Puritanism tended to theocracy. It was intolerant of other creeds—in this resembling its God, who might be merciful, but was not tolerant. It was disposed to make its own creed all-pervasive, and to perfect, after the scriptural model, all the aspects and social relationships of life. To achieve this end it did not scruple to employ the full force of the civil authorities, to limit citizenship to members of the church, and to identify its religious ideal with public policy. It enjoyed an invincible sense of truth and felt no compunction in saving unwilling men from the effects of their own blindness. The master motive was the desire to be pure, thorough, strict, and sound—cost what it might. This utopian dream was thus set forth in 1659 in Richard Baxter's *Holy Commonwealth*:

> It is this Theocratical Policy or Divine Commonwealth, which is the unquestionable reign of Christ on earth, which all Christians are agreed may be justly sought; and that temporal dignity of Saints, which undoubtedly would much bless the world.[47]

In New England in the seventeenth century it seemed that such a dream might be realized. The opportunity seemed providential. The true belief had been transplanted to a new world, where it was the animating creed of the dominant and most articulate element of the population—a region of space and time free from the deposit of the past, and from the contaminations and hindrances of an alien social environment.

But in England before the end of the Puritan Revolution, and in New England before the close of the century, it became clear that Baxter's "Theocratical Policy or Divine Commonwealth" did violence both to the genius of protestantism in particular, and to human nature in general. It might persecute this sect and that, and drive them underground or into exile; but it had itself begotten the spirit of sectarianism and nourished that spirit in its own bosom. It had taught, and continued to teach, that religious truth lay within the reach of every man who could read the Bible and experience the grace of God; and that a man's first duty was to the truth that he thus found and experienced for himself. At the same time, man's original faculties were ineradicable and must perpetually bear their own appropriate fruits, of usage, of attachments, and of ideas. Piety was a condition of strain requiring effort and exhortation; while secularism was a line of least resistance requiring only a relaxation of zeal. The theocratical state must, then, be perpetually engaged in crushing sectarian rivals and in negating the natural ways of man. Such a state could not in the long run do the state's business.

Calvin had taught that the objects of the state were:

> to cherish and support the external worship of God, to preserve the pure doctrine of religion, to defend the constitution of the Church, to regulate our lives in a manner requisite for the society of men, to form our manners to civil justice, to promote our concord with each other, and to establish general peace and tranquillity. . . . Its objects . . . are, that idolatry, sacrileges against the name of God, blasphemies against his truth, and other offences against religion, may not openly appear and be disseminated among the people.[48]

To this teaching was inevitably opposed the idea of the secular state, the object of which should be "to form our manners to civil justice, to promote our concord with each other, and to establish general peace and tranquillity"; but which would leave Calvin's other objects to conscience and to religion, and recognize that a diversity of faith and worship, however regrettable it might be from the standpoint of this or that particular creed, was consistent with the limited purpose of civil society.

This is the idea which was already in the sixteenth century advocated by those small and desperate sects who saw no hope of dominating the entire community and wanted only to be left in peace. It was the way of Roger Williams, who converted the defensive creed of a persecuted minority into a broad principle of polity, incorporated in the royal charter granted to Rhode Island by Charles II in 1663: no person should be "any wise molested, punished, disquieted, or called in question, for any differences in opinione in matters of religion," provided he "doe not actually disturb the civill peace." [49]

The name of this idea is religious toleration, and if it cannot be said to have been characteristic of puritanism in the strict sense, or in the original American sense, it nevertheless emerged from puritanism, both as the escape from its difficulties and as the natural expression of certain of its central motives. Whether as a defeat or as a culmination, it constituted the final chapter in the history of puritan polity.

CHAPTER SIX

THE DECLARATION OF INDEPENDENCE

1

THE WORD 'DEMOCRACY' * in its political application means popular government. Thus the Oxford Dictionary cites the following usage, dating from the sixteenth century: "The Democratian commen wealth . . . is the gouernment of the people; where all their counsell and aduise is had together in one." [1] The idea of popular government is variable in two respects: as regards what kind of people 'the people' are; and as regards how the people govern.

The term 'people' has a disparaging and a eulogistic meaning. To the critics of democracy, it usually means the relatively unprivileged, untutored, undisciplined, and impecunious masses. A democratic revolution is then an inversion of the social pyramid, in which the dregs are raised to the top, and government is by the most numerous class of the relatively unfit. In the eighteenth century, on the other hand, the people came to be thought of in terms of the virtues of the 'common man'; or in terms of the higher faculties which are possessed, at least potentially, by every man.

The people, however defined, may govern directly; or indirectly through elected representatives; or both directly and indirectly. In this respect democracy is capable of degrees. When the representative system is emphasized or highly developed, a democracy is sometimes called a 'republic'; as, for example, by James Madison, when he emphasized the fact that "the republican or representative form of government" can be extended over a "greater sphere of country." †

---

* After the French *démocratie,* originally the Greek *δημοκράτια.*

† "The Numerous Advantages of the Union," *The Federalist,* Paper X, Colonial Press, 1901, p. 48. There is no standardized usage of the term 'republic,' since it means literally no more than 'commonwealth' or 'polity.' It is often used to distinguish a government in which the supreme executive is elected, so that Great

These two variants are interdependent. A confidence in the intellectual and moral capacity of the people tends to direct democracy; while a less flattering view of the generality of mankind tends to an indirect democracy in which the masses are protected against their own weaknesses by the delegation of power to their more eminent representatives.

Over and above its strictly political meaning, democracy has also a broader social meaning. It then refers, not to government itself, but to the equal rights and privileges of those who live under government, and to the spirit of equality that prevails among them.

In order to understand the historical reference of the present study it is necessary to speak of 'American democracy of the eighteenth century.' In his *Modern Democracies,* which, although published in 1924, was written before the First World War, James Bryce pointed out that the American and French revolutionary thinkers went back across two thousand years for their "models." But although, especially in its literary manifestations, this democracy shared something of the neoclassicism of its times, it was by no means an imitation of antiquity. It sprang from new economic conditions, from the English legal tradition, from Christian humanitarianism, and from a radically individualistic philosophy, no one of which was anticipated in Greece or Rome. And it created forms of representation suitable to the magnitude and social complexity of the modern nation-state.

The democracy with which we are here concerned is, furthermore, specifically American, rather than broadly Occidental, or European. It reflected the particular manifestations of the American society of the eighteenth century—its protestant-puritan religious inheritance, its colonial status, and its peculiar physical environment. It was, it is true, of English parentage, but the American branch of descent advanced more rapidly than the mother stem. The yeoman class which had prospered in the England of the seventeenth century, which had comprised one-sixth of the population, which had fought the victorious battles of Cromwell and Fairfax, and which had provided the stock of the colonial migrations, was, in the eighteenth century, greatly diminished. The control

---

Britain, for example, would then be a democracy but not a republic. It cannot properly be opposed to democracy, but only to direct or 'absolute' democracy.

of society was in the hands of the great landowners, and public opinion and sentiment, even in Whig circles, was strongly resistant to revolutionary change. The seeds of English democracy matured at home more tardily than in the American soil to which they were transplanted.

The democracies of the South American continent were inspired by American democracy, and the democracies of the British Dominions were similarly influenced, or were parallel manifestations deriving broadly from the same sources. The French Revolution came after the American Revolution, and was fully conscious of the American precedent. The Swiss democracy, in turn, was extended and developed as a result of the French Revolution. Hence it may be said that the American democracy, decreed in 1776, and established in 1789, was the original and prototype of that modern democracy of which James Bryce said that prior to the First World War it was widely accepted as "the normal and natural form of government." [2]

2

For the purposes of the present study, then, 'democracy' means 'American democracy,' and 'American democracy' means that political and social creed which was the professed ground of the American Revolution of the eighteenth century. The Declaration of Independence was both a formulation of doctrine and an act of political revolution, the first being offered in justification of the second. We shall be concerned in the present chapter with precisely this relationship of doctrine to act, or with the role of the Declaration of Independence in that historical event known as the American Revolution.

A revolution, like any major historical event, is the effect of a confluence of many causes—economic, political, racial, geographical, and ideological. Some of these causes are necessary; some portion of them would, perhaps, be sufficient; though of this there can be no certainty, since historical events do not lend themselves to experiment. Applying this method of broad inclusiveness to the explanation of the American Revolution, we have first to note a set of causes that created its immediate background. It was to these causes that John Adams referred when, on August 24, 1815, he wrote to Jefferson:

> As to the history of the revolution, my ideas may be peculiar, perhaps singular. What do we mean by the revolution? The war? That was no part of the revolution; it was only an effect and consequence of it. The revolution was in the minds of the people, and this was effected from 1760 to 1775, in the course of fifteen years, before a drop of blood was shed at Lexington.[3]

The Peace of Paris was signed in 1763, just after the 'Great Awakening,' and approximately one hundred years after the puritan theocracy of New England had reached its height. This peace terminated the world-wide conflict variously known as the Seven Years' War, the Third Silesian War, and, on the American continent, the French and Indian War. In this far-flung struggle Prussia under Frederick the Great, together with Hannover, was allied with England under George II and George III, against Austria under Maria Theresa, Russia under the Empress Elizabeth, France under Louis XV, Saxony, and Sweden, and, for a part of the time, Spain. Since England, France, and Spain were great colonial empires, the war extended to India and the American continent as well as to Europe. The outcome of the war was to drive France from the American mainland, leaving England in possession of the disputed area between the Appalachians and the Mississippi, and of Florida and Canada, as well as of the Thirteen Colonies; Spain receiving possession of Louisiana, which at that time implied an area of indefinite extent west of the Mississippi.

This outcome created a problem and a policy for England, and at the same time a new state of mind in the Thirteen Colonies. England's policy was dictated by the need of reorganizing and consolidating a vast empire, while at the same time paying the costs of the war. The problem of colonial administration and taxation was assigned to Lord Grenville, who sympathized with the effort of George III to increase the royal prerogatives. On the side of England, then, there was a tendency to the assertion of a centralized authority. On the side of the Thirteen Colonies, the war had created a disposition to resist precisely such a policy. The colonists had fought their part in the war, and shared the sense of victory and merit. They had acquired a feeling of solidarity and a capacity for concerted action. Their population had reached 2,000,000, and was rapidly growing in wealth as well as in numbers. They had produced leaders of high repute. Washington had already earned a military reputation; Franklin, a scientist of international repute, had predicted "that the *foundations of the future grandeur and stability of the British Empire lie in America.*"[4] In other words, destiny was already 'manifest.' The American Revolution was precipitated by the resentments stirred in the new American mind, thus indisposed to submission, by the execution of the new imperial policy.

3

The mercantile-financial class and the rural-debtor class, though divided in interest, were both disposed to resistance. The former was sensitive to any restriction of trade; it resented the suppression of smuggling, the imposition of customs duties, and the writs of assistance and search warrants that grew out of the enforcement of the trade regulations imposed in 1763. The planters and landed proprietors of the South, on the other hand, were in debt to the London houses through which they marketed their produce, and were favorably inclined to repudiation. At the same time, the backwoodsmen and frontiersmen were interested in westward expansion, and resented the proclamation of 1763 prohibiting the extension of territorial boundaries beyond the Allegheny Mountains. The attempts to raise revenues in the colonies incurred the unpopularity usual with all tax measures, aggravated by the fact that the taxes were imposed and expended by a distant authority. Other causes conspired with economic causes. The tradition of religious dissent identified the intrusive imperial authority with the threat of episcopacy and monarchy. The settler was by habit self-reliant, intractable, and emotionally inflammable. Geographical remoteness and the inevitable laxity of imperial control at its outer boundaries had begotten habits of defiance.

Organized resistance began with the Stamp Act Congress of 1765. From this point, though specific measures might be repealed or moderated, the situation entered upon a mounting spiral: measures of coercion heated the blood, and induced a violence which, in turn, necessitated more vigorous measures of coercion. Thus the 'Boston Massacre' of 1770 was the result of sending two regiments of British regulars to overcome the resistance to the Townshend Duty Act of 1767. When, in the early '70's, the differences with England gave every sign of composing themselves, radical agitators such as Samuel Adams fanned the flames, deploring

> the Effect of a *mistaken* Prudence, which springs from Indolence or Cowardice or Hypocricy. . . . Too many are affraid to appear for the publick Liberty, and would fain flatter themselves that their Pusilanimity is true Prudence. For the sake of their own Ease or their own Safety, they preach the People into Paltry Ideas of Moderation.[5]

By the time of the 'Boston Tea Party' of 1773 the issue had ceased to concern the merits of any particular measure, and had become a head-on collision between the will to impose authority and the stubborn unwillingness to obey. The colonies were not united. As in every revolution, there were loyalists, who were 'liquidated,' and whose story forms no part of the heroic legend. But the men of action, who knew what they wanted and were prepared to stake their fortunes, held a growing ascendancy. These men had defied authority and rendered themselves liable to punishment; they must either render that authority powerless, or suffer at its hands; they must be either heroes or victims. Theirs was the positive and energetic course which enlisted sympathy, appealed to every natural instinct, and aroused every contagious emotion.

Event followed event in obedience to the psychology and the logic of revolution. The coercive or 'Intolerable' Acts of 1774, closing the port of Boston and altering the constitution of Massachusetts, brought the other colonies to its support. Support implied concert of action, and for that purpose there must be organization. The First Continental Congress met in 1774. War 'broke out' in 1775, in the battles of Lexington, Concord, and Bunker Hill, and in the siege of Boston. The colonies, now united in action, found their commander-in-chief in Washington. When independence was 'declared' in 1776, the determination to achieve it was already formed and in process of execution.

4

The American Revolution was a successful rebellion against the constituted authority. It was not a crusade undertaken in behalf of a creed formulated in advance, but a summary effect of interests and of mental dispositions, compounded among themselves and facilitated by the circumstances of time and place. Nevertheless, since the revolution assumed the form of a deliberate enterprise, calling for unanimity, prolonged effort, and sacrifice, it was necessary to invoke 'reasons.' There was need of an approving conscience, an assenting judgment, and a confirmation by the disinterested opinion of mankind. There was need for these because they are elements of strength and bonds of effective union. The rebellious colonists, then, took certain 'grounds': first, a legal ground; and then, in the last resort, a philosophical ground.

The first attempt of the colonists to justify their resistance to authority looked to the existing body of law. [6] This attempt proceeded from more specific to more general grounds. It was first argued that the imperial authority was justified in imposing external taxes and trade regulations, but not direct internal taxes, such as the stamp tax. This distinction broke down, partly because it was difficult to draw the line, and partly because if it were drawn, it became increasingly clear that the colonists did not propose to submit to *any* kind of taxation. The famous slogan "No taxation without representation" took the broader ground that Parliament's prerogative of taxation was based on its representative character: the colonists sent no member to Parliament, and their interests, being remote, had no effective spokesman in that body. But even this ground was too narrow, since it was limited to the power of taxation. Hence the next step was to insist that as constituents of the British Empire the colonists owed allegiance not to Parliament, but only to the King. This claim has been supported by recent authorities, on the precedent of Ireland; [7] and was in line with the subsequent development of the British Empire. But it afforded no justification of the defiance of the King, and when it became evident that the colonists did not propose to obey British authority at all, this, like the other and narrower legal arguments, lost its force.

There was, finally, the appeal from the British imperial constitution to 'natural law,' or 'the fundamental rights of Englishmen.' This would have been a legal justification had it been submitted to duly constituted judicial authorities. But the colonists did not propose to submit to British judges any more than to Parliament or the King. They proposed to make up their minds for themselves as to the 'justice' of their cause. The issue was to be submitted to the arbitrament of reason, and that authority spoke within their own breasts. At this point their justification became extra-legal—a justification of illegality in terms of the philosophical principles on which law itself is based. A political philosophy, says Leslie Stephen, is usually "the offspring of a recent, or the symptom of an approaching, revolution." [8] It arises when the habit of obedience is broken: when men have, in effect, suspended their allegiance until their interests and intellectual faculties shall have been satisfied.

5

On July 2, 1776, the Continental Congress, on the motion of Richard Henry Lee, adopted the following resolution: "That these United Colonies are, and of right ought to be, free and independent States, that they are absolved from all allegiance to the British Crown, and that all political connection between them and the State of Great Britain is, and ought to be, totally dissolved." [9] The resolve and the act were unmistakably and uncompromisingly illegal. The Declaration of Independence, which was adopted two days later, was a philosophical creed designed to justify the action of men who had taken the law into their own hands. It was at one and the same time a justification of rebellion and a statement of those common principles on which was to be founded a new state. It is as though men should say: "This is what government and law are for. Judged by this standard, the existing authority has forfeited its claim to obedience. This is at the same time the ground on which to erect a new authority which shall in the future be obeyed as commending itself to our reason and conscience." History affords few parallel instances of a state thus abruptly created, and consciously dedicated to a body of ideas whose acceptance constitutes its underlying bond of agreement.

This American democratic creed, designed to justify the past and chart the future, began as follows:

> When in the Course of human events, it becomes necessary for one people to dissolve the political bands, which have connected them with another, and to assume among the powers of the earth, the separate and equal station to which the Laws of Nature and of Nature's God entitle them, a decent respect to the opinions of mankind requires that they should declare the causes which impel them to the separation.—We hold these truths to be self-evident, that all men are created equal, that they are endowed by their Creator with certain unalienable Rights, that among these are Life, Liberty and the pursuit of Happiness.—That to secure these rights, Governments are instituted among Men, deriving their just powers from the consent of the governed,—That whenever any Form of Government becomes destructive of these ends, it is the Right of the People to alter or to abolish it, and to institute new Government, laying its foundation on such principles and organizing its powers in such form, as to them shall seem most likely to effect their Safety and Happiness.[10]

Not the least extraordinary feature of this remarkable document is the compactness and simplicity of statement with which a complete system of philosophy is embraced within a few brief paragraphs. It contains a political philosophy, setting forth the reasons that justify the authority of the state and define the fundamental rights which underlie the positive law; an ethics, which sets up the aggregate happiness of individuals as the supreme end; and a theistic and creationist doctrine of the origins of nature and man.

The Declaration of Independence was composed by Thomas Jefferson. It owes much to his intellect as well as to his pen, for he was no phrasemaker, ghost-writer, or unconscious plagiarist. But in this document he was giving the imprint of his genius to the current wisdom of the age. To quote Jefferson himself:

> With respect to our rights, and the acts of the British government contravening those rights, there was but one opinion on this side of the water. All American whigs thought alike on these subjects. When forced, therefore, to resort to arms for redress, an appeal to the tribunal of the world was deemed proper for our justification. This was the object of the Declaration of Inde-

pendence. Not to find out new principles, or new arguments, never before thought of, not merely to say things which had never been said before; but to place before mankind the common sense of the subject, in terms so plain and firm as to command their assent, and to justify ourselves in the independent stand we are compelled to take. Neither aiming at originality of principle or sentiment, nor yet copied from any particular and previous writing, it was intended to be an expression of the American mind, and to give to that expression the proper tone and spirit called for by the occasion. All its authority rests then on the harmonizing sentiments of the day, whether expressed in conversation, in letters, printed essays, or in the elementary books of public right, as Aristotle, Cicero, Locke, Sidney, &c.[11]

The question of Jefferson's sources is one on which authorities disagree. The earlier view that he was inspired by Rousseau has long since been abandoned. Rousseau's *Social Contract* was not published until 1762, and the essential ingredients of the thought of the Declaration were current in America before that time. There is no clear evidence, furthermore, that Jefferson had read Rousseau. A recent authority attaches importance to the fact that Jefferson had read and summarized the tracts of Lord Kames, the Scottish jurist, and traces Jefferson's political thinking to Anglo-Saxon history and jurisprudence: the Jeffersonian democracy "was born under the sign of Hengist and Horsa, not of the Goddess of Reason."[12] But to attribute the Declaration of Independence to any single source, whether French or English, is to miss its historical significance altogether. If special importance be attributed to the influence of Locke, this is not because of the fact that Jefferson is known to have been familiar with Locke's writings, or because of close parallels between the text of the Declaration and that of Locke's *Second Treatise of Civil Government;* but because Locke was the greatest and most representative exponent of the thought of the Enlightenment—which, arising in England in the seventeenth century, gave a distinctive character to the mind of Europe and America in the century that followed.

The political ideas of the Declaration, while explained in the language and the temper of the Enlightenment, were in full accord with the principles embodied in the earliest colonial charters. For one hundred and fifty years the American mind had been prepared for their reception. The charter of Maryland (1632) provided that Lord Baltimore and his heirs should make laws "consonant to Reason" and "Agreeable to the Laws, Statutes, Customs and Rights of . . . England." [13] Similar provisions were contained in the Fundamental Orders of Connecticut (1639), in the Massachusetts Body of Liberties (1641), and in William Penn's Frame of Government of Pennsylvania (1682). In the First Continental Congress John Adams was insistent that the colonies should "recur to the law of nature, as well as to the British constitution, and our American charters and grants," because he foresaw a necessity of avoiding any implied acceptance of existing authority.[14] But whether they were termed "natural," as became usual after 1760; or were referred to as "fundamental" or "ancient," or "customary," as "the laws of God," or as "the rights of Englishmen," [15] in any case there were recognized basic principles which might be invoked against the powers of any human government, and which found their sanction in reason, conscience, and piety.

6

The Declaration of Independence was an ex post facto justification of the American Revolution, as Locke's *Treatises of Civil Government* were an ex post facto justification of the English Revolution of 1688. Both wordings were avowedly apologetic. The Declaration of Independence was animated by "a decent respect to the opinions of mankind." Locke's *Treatises* were written

> to establish the throne of our great restorer, our present king William; to make good his title, in the consent of the people . . . and to justify to the world the people of England, whose love of their just and natural rights, with their resolution to preserve them, saved the nation when it was on the very brink of slavery and ruin.[16]

Jefferson, like Locke, gathered and reaffirmed the reasons. This does not imply that these reasons were first in the mind of the revolutionary party, in advance of any other condition or interest; and that they were then executed by purposeful action. They were the reasons by which the revolution was justified to its proponents, to its opponents, and to neutral observers. They constituted the defense of the revolution against the scruples of its own agents; they were designed to enlist the support of adherents in the enemy's camp; and to win the approval of the world and of posterity. Through this rationalization it was hoped that the revolution might be put on higher ground than sordid or partisan interest. But because it was a rationalization, the Declaration of Independence was not insulated from the stream of historical events. It expressed, and in turn affected, the minds of men. It was, in short, a *cause*—not the initial cause, not the only cause, not the sufficient cause, but, for all one can know to the contrary, a *necessary* cause. It occurred in response to a felt need, as the condition of a full and enduring concert of action.

That the Declaration of Independence should have been a social cause, reinforcing the effects of interest, habit, and passion, does not imply that its doctrines were not true. Whether they were or were not true in the sense in which political, moral, or religious doctrines can be true, is for philosophers to determine. In any case, they were intended as true, and taken as true. They expressed and were designed to invoke the 'enlightenment' of their age; and by the same token they lend themselves either to reaffirmation, or to correction, in terms of the more advanced enlightenment of later times.

The author of the best book on the Declaration of Independence, a book distinguished by its wit as well as by its penetration, delivers himself of the following judgment on the subject: "To ask whether the natural rights philosophy of the Declaration of Independence is true or false is essentially a meaningless question." As though in defense of his pronouncement, Professor Becker proceeds to show that the philosophy of the Declaration, like similar philosophies professed under similar conditions, is appealed to "in justification of actions which the community condemns as immoral or criminal." Revolutionists formulate the sort of philosophy which brings their action, despite its conflict with established law and custom, "into harmony with a rightly ordered universe, and enables them to think of themselves as having chosen the nobler part." They invoke a "higher law," which may be a law of God, or of conscience, or of nature. Such a law, says the author, when it provides "emotional inspiration," is 'true' to them whom it so fortifies; but, we are allowed to infer, not *really* true (or false) at all.[17]

This argument employs the method unhappily characteristic of the newer school of critical historians. It rests upon an unformulated philosophy of truth, which is itself assumed to be true. If the terms 'laws of nature,' 'God,' 'self-evident,' 'rights,' 'equality,' 'just,' and 'happiness,' meant anything to the Americans of 1776, then the propositions containing these terms were of necessity either true or false; and if we can recover the meanings, we can detect the truth or falsehood. That they *did* mean something can be proved only by setting forth their meanings—which I shall hope to do, ably assisted by the critical historians themselves.

The belittlement of the doctrines of the Declaration of Independence takes other forms. Thus Alvin Johnson has recently written:

> American democracy has proved itself an irrepressible force for the reason that it is not a matter of philosophical definition or legal status but a complex of impulses more or less trained and of experience more or less substantial deep in the heart of the individual democrat. Three centuries of life almost wholly civil in character, within an environment rich enough to offer opportunity for independence to most men, represent the chief conditioning circumstances for the development of this peculiar and tenacious plant, the American democratic spirit.[18]

This judgment is true in what it affirms, and false in what it denies. It is false to deny that American democracy is "a matter of philosophical definition or legal status"—peculiarly false. No polity in human history has owed so much to philosophy and jurisprudence. To hold to this indisputable historical fact is quite consistent with an ample recognition of the debt which American democracy owes to its environment and experience.

It was inevitable that historians of today should rewrite the history of the American Revolution in terms of 'propaganda' and the 'ruling class':

> The work of the propagandists has spoken for itself; by their fruits we have known them. Without their work independence would not have been declared in 1776 nor recognized in 1783. . . . The provincial ruling class, threatened in its position, used legal agencies of government and already

> established social institutions to undermine and ultimately to overthrow the British control. Through propaganda they spread the alarm to all classes. The propagandists identified the interests of the provincial ruling class with national interests and created a war psychosis. It was the propagandists who made inchoate feelings articulate opinion and provided the compulsive ideals which led to concrete action. . . . Nationalism was not the cause of the revolution, nor was it democratic in its origin, but the work of the revolutionary propagandists aided in developing the feeling of nationalism and in stimulating the ideals of a new democracy. [19]

This account adds nothing and subtracts nothing. Leaders, statesmen, philosophers, men of influence, and founding fathers remain the same when they are called "the provincial ruling class"; and persuasion, argument, or emotional appeal is not changed in character when it is called "propaganda." It remains as necessary as ever to acknowledge, define, interpret, and explain "the feeling of nationalism" and "the ideals of a new democracy."

7

The Declaration of Independence contains the essential ideas of American democracy, and has remained its creed and standard throughout the years of its subsequent development. "For the first time in the history of the world," says Professor Corwin, "the principles of revolution are made the basis of settled political institutions." [20] These principles have been challenged by individual thinkers, and even, as in the epoch of the Civil War, by sections or classes; but they have invariably been invoked in times of crisis or of patriotic fervor as constituting the moral bond of American nationality. The later history of the ideas of the Declaration concerns us only so far as may be necessary to establish their permanence and pervasiveness. They were promptly embodied, if they had not been anticipated, in the constitutions of the several states. Their public reading on successive anniversaries has solemnized the national memory and aspiration. They have proved broad enough to embrace partisan differences and cycles of political change.

When the Federal Constitution was under discussion in the year

1787-88 the problem of the colonists had shifted from revolution to reconstruction. It was a time of recoil and suspended activity. Even the conquest of the continent had lost much of its momentum. Men felt the pains and costs of change rather than its impetus. In 1803 the Reverend Jedediah Morse was minded to say, "Let us guard against the insidious encroachments of *innovation,* that evil and beguiling spirit which is now stalking to and fro through the earth, seeking whom he may destroy."[21] The "political bands which [had] connected them with another" had been dissolved, and it was now imperative for Americans "to form a more perfect union" among themselves.

The sentiment and emphasis which are effective for purposes of revolution are the precise opposites of those required "to institute new Government." Revolution is associated with the defiance of authority and the resort to violence; it is the task of political reconstruction to persuade men once again to obey. Revolution begets the feeling that a man can have what he wants; reconstruction compels him again to submit his particular interest to law and to the general good. The problem of reconstruction is to escape from that state of nature to which, in the act of revolution, society has reverted. In 1783 factionalism and personal jealousies were rife. The defects of human nature and the evils of anarchy were everywhere apparent. It was natural that in such a mood, and in response to the exigencies of such a crisis, there should be a swing toward political conservatism.

The Federal Constitution, then, expressed a fear of the excesses of revolutionary democracy, and of the mind of the masses. These fears inspired John Adams, Alexander Hamilton, and other leaders of the Federalist party; they represented the mood of reconstruction, as had Samuel Adams that of revolution. The motive of these leaders was to set such limits to popular government as should save it from self-destruction. Neither they nor Burke and the Whig party in England had any intention of denying popular government, but they desired that government should express the sober second thought of the people rather than their haste or passion. To this end they retarded the popular will and multiplied its intermediaries.[22] They sought to accomplish their purpose not by strengthening the executive, but by a division of powers, and by the six-year term of senators. *The Federalist* defended this last provision as follows:

> To a people as little blinded by prejudice or corrupted by flattery as those whom I address, I shall not scruple to add that such an institution may be sometimes necessary as a defence to the people against their own temporary errors and delusions. As the cool and deliberate sense of the community ought, in all governments, and actually will, in all free governments, ultimately prevail over the views of its rulers; so there are particular moments in public affairs when the people, stimulated by some irregular passion, or some illicit advantage, or misled by the artful misrepresentations of interested men, may call for measures which they themselves will afterwards be most ready to lament and condemn. In these critical moments, how salutary will be the interference of some temperate and respectable body of citizens in order to check the misguided career, and to suspend the blow meditated by the people against themselves, until reason, justice, and truth can regain their authority over the public mind? [23]

While the Federal Constitution represented a different mood and emphasis, it did not reject the doctrine of the Declaration of Independence. It rested upon the principle that men erect governments by agreement, and for their good as they consciously envisage it. In the last analysis, the sovereignty lay in the will of the people—if possible their thoughtful will, but nonetheless their will. The state rested upon sound moral premises, and was devoted to a moral end. Its purpose was to keep the peace among men in order that as individuals they might enjoy their fundamental rights and attain a maximum of personal development and happiness. Whenever the controversy over the Constitution turned on the fundamentals of political philosophy it was to the doctrine of natural law and natural rights that all parties appealed. As has been abundantly proved and documented by a recent political writer, "it seems safe to say that no member of the convention . . . ever questioned the validity of this concept." They took it for granted as the common ground of their differences.*

---

* B. F. Wright, Jr., *American Interpretations of Natural Law*, pp. 125, 248-51, 342-43, and Chap. VI, *passim*. Carl Becker, on the other hand, has contended that the "natural rights doctrine of the eighteenth century" was reaffirmed "in few if any of the constitutions now in force"; and that English democracy turned from this doctrine to Bentham, who rejected "the eighteenth century doctrine of natural rights alto-

It should be added that the Federalists represented not only a conservative emphasis on strong government and a delay of the popular will, but also the economic interest of the financial and mercantile classes of the eastern seaboard. These motives tend to agree, since creditors are more dependent than debtors upon public order and stability. At the moment when a debt is to be paid it is the debtor who suffers, and the creditor who profits, by a strict compliance with the law. The debtor is more disposed to welcome, if he does not actually foment, a state of disorder which permits of repudiation. He can 'afford' to be more reckless.

During its later history American democracy has had, under various names, its constitutional and its revolutionary parties. The constitutional party has emphasized the system of government in its integrity and has insisted on legality of procedure. It has attracted those whose advantage lay in economic stability, and in the status quo. The revolutionary party, on the other hand, has emphasized the popular will as directly expressed in the vote of the majority, and has attracted those whose advantage lay in change. The second of these parties represents the forward impulses of American democracy; the first, its sober thought. The second has been retarded by the first, but never stopped or reversed. The history of American democracy is a gradual realization, too slow for some and too rapid for others, of the implications of the Declaration of Independence.[25]

---

gether." (*Op. cit.*, pp. 234, 236.) Bentham rejected natural law only as an a priori truth of reason. He also rejected the contract theory in its literal acceptance as reducing political obligation to the sheer keeping of a promise. He insisted on carrying every question of right back to the principle of utility. But fundamentally Bentham is on the side of the natural-rights theory. The political authority is justified by the fact that "the benefit" outweighs "the mischief"—for the individual members of society. It is only insofar as individuals see this that their acceptance of "political society" in place of a merely "natural society" is rational.[24]

Bentham, according to Professor Becker, held that "the object of society is to achieve the greatest good of all its members; do not ask what rights men have in society, but what benefits they derive from it." (*Op. cit.*, p. 236.) It is only in the most superficial sense, however, that rights (for the eighteenth century) can be divorced from benefits. Bentham himself was shallow in controversy, and rarely understood the philosophy which he rejected.

8

Jeffersonian democracy was distinguished by this great leader's adherence to the revolutionary temper, as well as the philosophical doctrines, of the Declaration of Independence. He had been abroad during the years 1784-89, when the political reaction was at its height; and preserved an unshakable confidence in the natural man, stripped of station, office, and wealth. He would, it is true, have him educated, but he believed him to be educable. For leadership he looked to talent rather than hereditary aristocracy.

Whoe'er amidst the Sons
Of Reason, Valour, Liberty, and Virtue,
Displays distinguish'd Merit, is a Noble
Of Nature's own creating.[26]

Trusting human nature in the universal rather than the privileged sense, Jefferson had no fear of popular rule. He wrote to Du Pont de Nemours:

> We both consider the people as our children, and love them with parental affection. But you love them as infants whom you are afraid to trust without nurses; and I as adults whom I freely leave to self-government.

Not only did Jefferson remain loyal to the revolutionary spirit of 1776, but he believed that this spirit should be perpetuated:

> God forbid we should ever be 20 years without . . . a rebellion. The people cannot be all, & always, well informed. The part which is wrong will be discontented in proportion to the importance of the facts which they misconceive. If they remain quiet under such misconceptions it is a lethargy, the forerunner of death to the public liberty. . . . What country can preserve it's liberties if their rulers are not warned from time to time that their people preserve the spirit of resistance? Let them take arms. The remedy is to set them right as to facts, pardon & pacify them. . . . The tree of liberty must be refreshed from time to time with the blood of patriots & tyrants. It is it's natural manure.[27]

By two notable political acts, Jefferson brought American democracy into closer alignment with the underlying philosophy of the Declaration: by his advocacy of the first ten amendments to the Constitution, adopted in 1791; and by his opposition, in 1798, to the Alien and Sedition Laws.

The first ten amendments incorporated into the framework of American government the so-called Bill of Rights,[28] including the civil liberties of thought, speech, and assembly. The Bill of Rights was designed to prevent encroachments of government on life, liberty, and the pursuit of happiness. Since it was the very purpose of government to protect and foster these fundamental goods, it could not *rightly* destroy or negate them, where 'rightly' means not 'legally,' but 'morally.' Hence the authors of the Constitution were correct in referring to the Bill of Rights as "aphorisms . . . which would sound much better in a treatise of ethics, than in a constitution of government." [29]

The first ten amendments of the Constitution, like the 'due process' clause of the fifth and the reserved liberties of the fourteenth amendment, refer beyond government to a fundamental social philosophy. This is the "inarticulate major premise" referred to in Justice Holmes's famous dissenting opinion of 1905. They appeal to "fundamental principles as they have been understood by the traditions of our people and our law." To quote a well-known authority:

> Here is the whole story behind the failure of all formulae connected with 'due process' and all the meaningless and circular statements as to what acts are and what are not 'due process.' . . . Acts depriving any person of liberty or property are arbitrary and void if they have no substantial and rational or reasonable relation to the health, safety, morals, or welfare of the public or a part of the public. Whether the act has such 'substantial and rational' or 'reasonable' relation to the objects enumerated is determined by balancing all the interests and determining whether the predominant effect of the act is such that any generalization resulting from sustaining it will open a way for attack by the majority upon a fundamental condition of the existence of the social order.[30]

This statement, however, is not sufficiently explicit. For the major premise is not social order in general or the existing social order, but the particular ideal of social order—humane, individualistic, and equalitarian—which is "understood by the traditions of our people."

Shortly after these "fundamental principles" serving as the higher sanction of government were explicitly or implicitly incorporated in the Constitution, Chief Justice Marshall asserted the right of the Supreme Court to declare acts of Congress unconstitutional; and the Federal judiciary thus became the custodian of these principles. If the Court has failed to serve this purpose, it is because its members have been unwilling to exercise the role of philosophers, and have in the *name* of strict legality been the exponents of habit and usage; or because, hesitating to be consciously or articulately philosophical, they have become the spokesmen of their unconscious philosophies—that is to say, of their prejudices.

The Alien and Sedition Laws, passed during the administration of John Adams, were held to be unconstitutional by the Virginia and the Kentucky Resolutions, written in 1798 by Madison and Jefferson respectively. These Resolutions served a double purpose. In the first place, their enactment was in itself a declaration of the right of a state to declare unconstitutional an act of the Federal Government. They thus embodied the germ of the idea of secession, and placed their authors on the side of states' rights. But in the second place, they pledged the Republican party to the jealous guardianship of toleration, and thereby again reaffirmed the fundamental doctrine of the Declaration. They represented the view that if government derives its power from its acceptability to the reason of those who live under it, then reason must be free to speak freely in the light of evidence and discussion.[31]

Jefferson reaffirmed the principles of the Declaration; and in his seeing the application of these principles to constitutional questions, to individual rights, to slavery, to education, to primogeniture and entail, and to the separation of church and state, Jefferson was the most representative democrat of his age. But like all doctrinaire exponents of democracy, he was too ready to identify men with MAN, forgetting that human limitations are as human as are human prerogatives and potentialities. He tended to identify the universal man, definable in terms of reason and conscience, with the common man, forgetting that the commonness of the common man connotes vulgarity—the average, rather than the eminent, quality—and that men in the mass are brought even lower than their average by the effect of emotional contagion, and by their envy of superiors.

Jefferson's judgment of mankind was further limited by his own social station and experience. He belonged to an old frontier, already highly civilized; and he and his planter associates of Virginia were gentlemen in the social, and not merely in the natural, sense. They constituted, furthermore, during the successive presidencies of Jefferson, Madison, and Monroe, a veritable dynasty accustomed to the self-perpetuating leadership of their own elite. Jefferson's parochialism found expression in his famous apotheosis of his own rural society:

> Generally speaking, the proportion which the aggregate of the other classes of citizens bears in any State to that of its husbandmen is the proportion of its unsound to its healthy parts, and is a good enough barometer whereby to measure its degree of corruption. . . . Those who labor in the earth are the chosen people of God if ever he had a chosen people, whose breasts he has made his peculiar deposit for substantial and genuine virtue.[32]

Jefferson was out of touch with the ruder frontiersmen of the West, as well as with the working classes of the East. The translation of the democratic creed into the realities of popular rule was reserved for the era and the leadership of Andrew Jackson.

9

Jackson was elected to the presidency in 1828, when the reaction against the French Revolution had spent itself and was succeeded by a world-wide current of liberalism. In America, the Jacksonian era represents the reaffirmation of democratic principles in terms of the relatively untutored and unprivileged masses. This realistic expression of the new democratic spirit is symbolized by the famous scene at the White House on the occasion of Jackson's inauguration, and by the scandal which it created. "It was a glorious day . . . for the *sovereigns*," says one of the guests. According to a recent historian:

> The rabble fell on the refreshments, jostling the waiters as they appeared at the doors, breaking the china and glassware, standing in muddy boots on damask covered chairs, spoiling the carpets, and creating such a press that it was no longer possible for those on the inside to escape by the doors. The windows were used for exits for the suffocating masses. . . . Several thousand dollars' worth of broken china and cut glass and many bleeding noses attested the fierceness of the struggle.[33]

These ill-mannered guests, making themselves so insolently at home in the seat of power, symbolized the new and broader base of American democracy. Against the resistance of the old leaders, Federalists and Republicans alike—against the advice of John Adams, Daniel Webster, Joseph Story, Chancellor Kent, Madison, Monroe, Marshall, and Randolph, who held that only property-holders could have a responsible interest in government—shortly after the middle of the century suffrage was extended to all white male citizens above the age of twenty-one. Religious qualifications were likewise abolished, and all vestiges of union between church and state removed. Thus there came into actual realization the idea, implied in the doctrine of the Declaration, that political power ascends from those who live under it.

At the same time that the suffrage was extended, its role was magnified by substitution of popular election for executive or legislative appointment, the shortening of terms of office, and the continuing development of political parties. The introduction of the so-called spoils system signified not so much a desire for plunder as the assertion that the average rather than the eminent man was qualified for office. As Jackson expressed it, the prime requisite for office is not "talent" but "moral" quality:

> It shall be my care to fill the various offices at the disposal of the Executive with individuals uniting as far as possible the qualifications of the head and heart, always recollecting that in a free government the demand for moral qualities should be made superior to that of talents. In other forms of government where the people are not regarded as composing the sovereign power, it is easy to perceive that the safeguard of the empire consists chiefly in the skill by which the monarch can wield the bigoted acquiescence of his Subjects. But it is different with us. Here the will of the people, prescribed in a constitution of their own choice, controuls the service of the public functionaries, and is interested more deeply in the preservation of those qualities which ensures [*sic*] fidelity and honest devotion to their interests.[34]

Although Jacksonian democracy expressed a suspicion of officials, it tended to support the executive: as the leader and friend of the people, against vested interests; or as the man of action, against the more complicated and dilatory procedures of the legislature or the judiciary.

A significant omen of the future of American democracy was the growing self-consciousness of labor and the beginning of labor organization. The growth of industrial centers created a mass of hired workers, dependent, compelled to labor for twelve hours a day six days of the week, and with living conditions that were often squalid and unwholesome. The 'people' began to mean, not the inspired voice of free men, asserting and enjoying their natural rights, but the protest of oppressed and resentful classes—both the industrial workers of the East, and the small farmers of the West.[35] These were Jackson's supporters. He understood them, catered to them, and won their confidence.

Jackson is to be credited with a stubborn and truculent championship of individual rights, and with a sympathetic understanding of the underprivileged masses. But while Jacksonian democracy thus represented an advance from piety toward reality, it at the same time revealed the inherent and besetting evils of democracy: the envy of superiority, and the compensatory pride of inferiority; the loss of standards of excellence; the transfer of political authority from the higher faculties of man to his baser passions; the arts of the demagogue by which ambitious men acquire power through flattery.

10

The romantic humanitarianism which began in the Jacksonian era is a part of the history of American democracy, and not merely of American letters. It profoundly affected social thinking, gave new meaning to American institutions, and through stimulating the movement for the abolition of slavery was one of the contributing causes of the Civil War. As Jacksonian democracy represented the harsh-self-assertion of the individual, the new humanitarian movement represented democracy's benevolent and universalistic aspect; as Jacksonian democracy was practical and realistic, the humanitarian movement represented the aspiration to perfection. It incited the individual to reform himself, and it was a part of his self-reform that he should devote himself to the corrections of social evils and to the making of a better society.

The efflorescence of humanitarian sentiment, especially in New England and in other parts of the settled eastern seaboard, where contacts with intellectual tradition and with Europe were most intimate, has often been described. The following account, written by James Russell Lowell in 1865, referred to the decade of the 1840's:

> Every possible form of intellectual and physical dyspepsia brought forth its gospel. . . . Everybody had a mission (with a capital M) to attend to everybody-else's business. No brain but had its private maggot, which must have found pitiably short commons sometimes. Not a few impecunious zealots abjured the use of money (unless earned by other people), professing to live on the internal revenues of the spirit. Some had an assurance of instant millennium so soon as hooks and eyes should be substituted for buttons. Communities were established where everything was to be common but common-sense. Men renounced their old gods, and hesitated only whether to bestow their furloughed allegiance on Thor or Budh. Conventions were held for every hitherto inconceivable purpose. . . . Many foreign revolutionists out of work added to the general misunderstanding their contribution of broken English in every most ingenious form of fracture.[36]

Lowell's account of the humanitarian movement was written with an eye to its absurdities. But this movement achieved enduring results. It gave a new social impulse to religion—to unitarianism, universalism, and congregationalism in New England, and to evangelical revivalism in other regions. It stimulated temperance reform; the application of democratic principles to the status of women; the creation of hospitals and other institutions for the care of dependents and defectives; prison reform; and above all, under the leadership of such men as Henry Barnard and Horace Mann, the expansion of popular education and the foundation of colleges.*

Philanthropy was an original ingredient of the democracy of the Declaration. The individual's concern for his fellow men, for the amelioration of the condition of the relatively unfortunate, and for the development of a community of good is a deeper motive in democracy than the ambition or the discontent which the individual feels in his own behalf. The 'right' which the individual has to assert himself is a right only in a sense in which it is also the other's right; it is either reciprocal

* Sixty-seven colleges and universities were founded between 1830 and 1840.[37]

and universal, or it is, in the moral sense, no right at all. Apart, then, from the merit of its concrete achievements, the humanitarian revival was a manifestation of that charity to all without which Jacksonian democracy was no more than a sordid manifestation of greed and covetousness.

This revival had its humanistic as well as its humanitarian aspect. It demanded that individuals should merit their liberty, and utilize it for the development of the higher potentialities of human nature. It supplemented the concern for men's bodies, appetites, and needs with a concern for their personal development. The great intellectual, artistic, and moral "flowering" of this era, has recently been described by Van Wyck Brooks.[38] Emerson, Webster, Everett, Choate, Wendell Phillips, Theodore Parker, Charles Sumner, Ticknor, Sparks, Prescott, Bancroft, Motley, Parkman, Whittier, Longfellow, Hawthorne, Lowell, Holmes, Thoreau within New England, Irving, Cooper, and Poe in New York—these and dozens of men of lesser caliber constituted not a fortuitous combination of accidents, but the cultural ripening of a whole society living under free political institutions. This not only brought the assurance that creative faculty and high aspiration were consistent with democracy, but was to an originally colonial and frontier society, preoccupied with economic necessities and the pursuit of wealth, the pledge of a more exalted ambition. Patriotism no longer meant the pride of political independence and material gain, but the vision of a society whose individual members should participate in the best life and profit by the gifts of genius.

The romantic movement, finding its way to America, reaffirmed and enriched the cult of individual self-reliance. Emerson taught men to be themselves, with confidence in their inner sense of worth:

> Every spirit builds itself a house, and beyond its house a world, and beyond its world a heaven. Know then that the world exists for you. For you is the phenomenon perfect. . . . Build therefore your own world. As fast as you conform your life to the pure idea in your mind, that will unfold its great proportions. . . . In like manner, let a man fall into the divine circuits, and he is enlarged. Obedience to his genius is the only liberating influence. We wish to escape from subjection and a sense of inferiority, and we make self-denying ordinances, we drink water, we eat grass, we refuse

the laws, we go to jail: it is all in vain; only by obedience to his genius, only by the freest activity in the way constitutional to him, does an angel seem to arise before a man and lead him by the hand out of all the wards of the prison.[39]

Self-reliance in this sense was not the bare self-assertion of the ego, but the valid claim of personality. The self which was deemed worthy of reliance was not the enemy or rival of other selves, but a self which through the immanence of some spiritual principle, or through the attunement of its will to the objective deliverances of reason, or through its devotion to that good which is every man's good, was predisposed to social and cosmic harmony.

11

The connecting link between the romantic humanitarian movement and the issues of the Civil War is to be found in the creed of the radical abolitionists, for the most part of New England extraction. The antislavery sentiment was both humanitarian and humanistic, humanitarian in its reference to human suffering, humanistic in its reference to human dignity. The older reform which had led to the abolition of slavery in the northern states was superseded in 1830, when Garrison founded *The Liberator*, by a new and more radical movement. The 'come-outers,' as opposed to the 'gradualists,' were so revolutionary in temper that they were prepared to turn against church and state because these moved too slowly.[40] There gradually emerged the idea of a free nation—freed from the disgrace of slavery, and rededicated to the fundamental rights of man. The war for the Union was thus a war to preserve at all costs the purity, as well as the stability, of democratic institutions.

That the radical antislavery movement was based on the creed of the Declaration of Independence is confirmed by the fact that the apologists for slavery found themselves obliged to reject that creed. Equality and natural rights were disproved; real liberty was held to be a privilege created by society, natural liberty an evil; the best society was conceived in terms of an aristocracy, in which the perfection of the few was conditioned by the compulsory or hired labor of the many; and even the humanitarian impulse itself was disparaged as false sentimentality.[41]

Since the Civil War, in its moral aspect, thus represents a struggle for the essential ideas of American democracy, it is fitting that Lincoln, the leader of the Unionist cause, should have epitomized these ideas in his personal life, in his policy, and in his gift of public utterance. In his address of February twenty-second, 1861, made in that same Independence Hall in which the American democratic creed was formally adopted, he said:

> You have kindly suggested to me that in my hands is the task of restoring peace to our distracted country. I can say in return, sir, that all the political sentiments I entertain have been drawn, so far as I have been able to draw them, from the sentiments which originated in and were given to the world from this hall. I have never had a feeling, politically, that did not spring from the sentiments embodied in the Declaration of Independence.[42]

Lincoln was not a reckless agitator, but a constructive statesman, painfully conscious of his public responsibilities. He was not by nature doctrinaire, but shrewdly aware of circumstances and of the necessity of compromise. To Lincoln, therefore, the Declaration of Independence was not a mere affirmation of formulas quoted from the philosophers, or a rationalization of expediency, or a false account of the origins of human society; but an ideal of the good life, to be approximated by social development, to be earned by education and self-discipline, and to be employed as the norm of political measures:

> I think the authors of that notable instrument intended to include *all* men, but they did not intend to declare all men equal *in all respects.* They did not mean to say that all were equal in color, size, intellect, moral developments, or social capacity. They defined with tolerable distinctness in what respects they did consider all men created equal,—equal with "certain inalienable rights, among which are life, liberty, and the pursuit of happiness." This they said, and this they meant. They did not mean to assert the obvious untruth that all were then actually enjoying that equality, nor yet that they were about to confer it immediately upon them. In fact, they had no power to confer such a boon. They meant simply to declare the right, so that the enforcement of it might follow as fast as circumstances should permit.
>
> They meant to set up a standard maxim for free society, which should be familiar to all, and revered by all; constantly looked to, constantly labored

for, and even though never perfectly attained, constantly approximated, and thereby constantly spreading and deepening its influence and augmenting the happiness and value of life to all people of all colors everywhere. The assertion that "all men are created equal" was of no practical use in effecting our separation from Great Britain; and it was placed in the Declaration not for that, but for future use. Its authors meant it to be—as, thank God, it is now proving itself—a stumbling block to all those who in after times might seek to turn a free people back into the hateful paths of despotism.[43]

With Lincoln, furthermore, the privileges of democracy were conceived under the aspect of giving rather than of demanding. "This is a world of compensation," he said, "and he who would be no slave, must consent to have no slave. They who deny freedom to others, deserve it not for themselves, and under a just God cannot long retain it." [44] Lincoln's democracy was instinct with his profound humanity. He did not use the arts of the demagogue, but owing to his origin and his natural fellow feeling he spoke for others. As Lowell said, "He forgets himself so entirely in his object as to give his *I* the sympathetic and persuasive effect of *We* with the great body of his countrymen." [45]

12

The victory of the North in the Civil War signified the triumph of the democratic creed. At the same time it established national unity against the doctrine of secession. This second issue concerns us only so far as it led to the discussion of political philosophy, and to the explicit rejection of the organic theory of the state, imported from Germanic sources and profoundly opposed to the political premises of the Declaration.

There were two grounds on which secession was defended (and refuted) in keeping with traditional modes of political thinking. In the first place, it was argued that certain powers were 'reserved' to the states under the provisions of the Constitution. But their very reservation by the Constitution was an assertion of its authority to give or to withhold. Not only did the Federal Constitution divide the power among the several branches of the government, but the Federal Supreme Court was a court of last appeal in any dispute among them. And behind the Constitution lay the amending power lodged in Congress and in the several legislatures, and ultimately in the people by whom they were elected. In short, the Federal Constitution was "the supreme law of the land." [46]

In the second place, the case for secession was argued on the ground of compact. But if the compact was among the states—if they had in fact created a new sovereignty—then the seceding state was in the position of rejecting the legally constituted authority; in other words, of committing an act of revolution. If, on the other hand, the Constitution was a contract among the individuals of the United States, as is suggested by the expression, "We, the people . . .", then the state as such did not enjoy even the right of revolution.[47] Hence the more logical secessionists were driven to deny the compact theory altogether, and to consider the Federal Union as a mere 'treaty,' among states whose sovereignty was inalienable, being rooted in their history as organic entities.

The leading proponent of this view, which involved a radical repudiation of the first principles of the traditional American philosophy, was John C. Calhoun. To this statesman, who felt himself to be politically a South Carolinian, united with other South Carolinians by a common bond of interest and will, and to whom any other sovereignty had an alien and tyrannical aspect, it seemed clear that the original thirteen states were the only authentic political entities on the American continent. The Federal Constitution was a mere arrangement of convenience, terminable at pleasure.

But this manner of thinking was doubly dangerous for a secessionist. On the one hand, it implied a similar right of nullification for any minority within the state, whenever such minority should achieve a similar sense of historical solidarity; and on the other hand, it implied that the Federal Union might itself claim the right of sovereignty whenever its own political unity should have become sufficiently mature.

The doctrine of Calhoun was not a mere rationalization of secessionism. It expressed the historical and nationalistic reaction of the nineteenth century against the doctrinaire individualism of the eighteenth century. But it has retained what Professor Merriam has called its "Teutonic flavor," [48] and has never been domesticated on American soil, flourishing, as a rule, in academic circles rather than in the minds of American statesmen or in popular habits of political thought. It has, together with other similar influences of the nineteenth century, served as a corrective of abstract individualism. Nationalism as a force, subtly compounded of tradition, community of interest, and all the solidarities of habit, language, environment, imitation, and continuity, has to be assimilated to any modern theory of the state, and requires a vast amplification of the simple logic of the Declaration.

But Americans have never ceased to think of their political society as erected and maintained by themselves for the sake of benefits individually enjoyed—as an organization which they have made, rather than as organism of which they are members. Nor have Americans ever lost their original determination to be their own masters. An absolute authority which claims to speak for a higher corporate will does not to them differ from any other autocracy. It stands in irreconcilable opposition to the American democratic tradition which construes government as a trusteeship responsible to the felt interests and political judgments of the several individuals whose obedience it claims.

13

The principles which survived the crisis of the Civil War have remained, as Lincoln would have them, the standard of American public policy. The growth of nationalism and of industrialism during the second half of the nineteenth century, the international alignments of the First World War, and the problems of the post-war period of disillusionment, brought no fundamental change in the *professed* creed of American democracy. The evidence of this, abundant and eloquent, is to be found in the state papers of public officials, in congressional debates and political campaigns, and in the form of popular appeal employed whenever it was necessary to evoke the full force of American opinion and sentiment. Each forward impulse, such as the 'progressive' movement of the first Roosevelt and the 'new freedom' of Woodrow Wilson, was an attempt to apply, extend, and realize the maxims of the Declaration of Independence.

CHAPTER SEVEN

THE ENLIGHTENED PHILOSOPHY OF THE DECLARATION

1

IN A LETTER of June 8, 1783, to the governors of the states, General Washington said:

> The foundation of our empire was not laid in the gloomy age of ignorance and superstition; but at an epocha when the rights of mankind were better understood and more clearly defined, than at any former period. The researches of the human mind after social happiness have been carried to a great extent; the treasures of knowledge, acquired by the labors of philosophers, sages, and legislators, through a long succession of years, are laid open for our use, and their collected wisdom may be happily applied in the establishment of our forms of government.[1]

Washington did not ignore the fact that Providence had provided a spacious and bountiful continent for the new "empire," but he emphasized "the treasures of knowledge"—the unique opportunity afforded and enjoyed by Americans of combining the resources of nature and the resources of mind. Similarly, to admiring contemporaries abroad the new American nation afforded the unusual spectacle of an *actual* utopia—"agricultural, philosophical, tolerant, pious, rational and happy."[2]

The date of Washington's significant utterance was approximately one hundred years after the publication by Locke of those works which constitute the classic embodiment and most important philosophical source of the so-called Enlightenment.* During the intervening century two general attitudes—a trust in human faculties when freed from prejudice, tyranny, and superstition, and the confident belief that the

* Locke's *Second Treatise of Civil Government* and his *Essay Concerning Human Understanding* were both published in 1690. The first *Letter Concerning Toleration* had first appeared in English in the previous year.

world disclosed to these faculties was harmonious and beneficent—were so widely diffused as to create a characteristic epochal physiognomy. These attitudes of the Enlightenment constituted the spiritual environment of American democracy in the period of its gestation, birth, and childhood.

It might well be argued that the Enlightenment was no more than the belated blossoming of the Renaissance, which had been retarded by the medievalist revivals of the Reformation and the Counter-Reformation. But in the Enlightenment the spirit of the Renaissance was no longer reserved to the elite or to the theoretic life; it was in the air men breathed, and had penetrated into the strongholds of religion, morals, and politics. The new spirit, in contrast to the old, has been described in broad terms by Arthur McGiffert:

> The humility, the self-distrust, the dependence upon supernatural powers, the submission to external authority, the subordination of time to eternity and of fact to symbol, the conviction of the insignificance and meanness of the present life, the somber sense of the sin of man and the evil of the world, the static interpretation of reality, the passive acceptance of existing conditions and the belief that amelioration can come only in another world beyond the grave, the dualism between God and man, heaven and earth, spirit and flesh, the ascetic renunciation of the world and its pleasures—all of which characterized the Middle Ages—were widely overcome, and men faced life with a new confidence in themselves, with a new recognition of human power and achievement, with a new appreciation of present values, and with a new conviction of the onward progress of the race in past and future.[3]

The Declaration of Independence not only expressed the spirit of the Enlightenment, but also set forth its philosophy, and affirmed this philosophy as the major premise of American democracy. It epitomized the common ideas which underlay the united act of revolution, and which corresponded in their depth to the gravity of the decision. These ideas were in some degree intelligible and credible to the people at large; to thoughtful and educated men they meant volumes of natural, religious, moral, and political philosophy. Though they flowered in the present, their roots were deep in the past.

2

The confidence in human faculties which pervaded the eighteenth century was well justified. It has been said of Galileo, Descartes, Huygens, and Newton that "the issue of the combined labours of these four men has some right to be considered as the greatest single intellectual success which mankind has achieved." [4] Employing the work of his predecessors, Newton constructed the imposing edifice of universal mechanics, which until the close of the nineteenth century maintained its architecture unchanged, despite the building of new wings and the redecoration of the interior. The "incomparable Mr. Newton," as Locke called him,[5] shared with Locke himself the role of supreme exemplar of the power of the human mind. When the poet Gray referred to Locke as "Angliacae . . . lux altera gentis," [6] the twin luminary was Newton. The vogue of his *Principia,* published in 1687, was the scientific parallel of the vogue of Locke's *Essay,* published in 1690.

For the ultimate explanation of the force of gravitation, Newton appealed to the sustaining and all-pervading power of God. Thus his discovery of the mechanical order of nature was not felt to be hostile to religion: on the contrary, it gave confirmation to, as it derived support from, the traditional faith in a divine order. It testified to the glory of the Creation, and proved its intelligent and beneficent authorship.[7] The specific as well as the general teachings of Newton seemed to confirm this theistic belief. Action at a distance and the instantaneous transmission of light suggested the omnipresence of the divine causality. The fact that Newton spoke as a scientist free from religious bias, and from subjection to the Aristotelian tradition, gave added force to his testimony.

The broad scope of the Newtonian influence, as understood in the eighteenth century, was summarized as follows by one of his commentators:

> To describe the *phenomena* of nature, to explain their causes, to trace the relations and dependencies of those causes, and to inquire into the whole constitution of the universe, is the business of natural philosophy. . . . But

natural philosophy is subservient to purposes of a higher kind, and is chiefly to be valued as it lays a sure foundation for natural religion and moral philosophy; by leading us, in a satisfactory manner, to the knowledge of the Author and Governor of the universe. . . . Our views of Nature, however imperfect, serve to represent to us in the most sensible manner, that mighty power which prevails throughout, acting with a force and efficacy that appears to suffer no diminution from the greatest distances of space or intervals of time; and that wisdom which we see equally displayed in the exquisite structure and just motions of the greatest and subtilest parts. These, with perfect *goodness*, by which they are evidently directed, constitute the supreme object of the speculations of a philosopher; who, while he contemplates and admires so excellent a system, cannot but be himself excited and animated to correspond with the general harmony of nature.[8]

Newton's achievement was at one and the same time a discovery of nature and an exaltation of man, testifying both to the intelligible order of the one and to the intellectual powers of the other. He had made nature translucent, dispelling both doubt and mystery, and created an intoxicating sense of mental ease and mastery—"and clear ideas," said Erasmus Darwin, "charm the thinking mind."[9] Newton's works were republished in many editions, and widely popularized. They flattered the pride of the layman who, though he might not be able to 'understand mathematics,' saw in Newton a vicarious achievement of his own faculty of reason. It is not surprising that in their enthusiasm men ignored the difficulties and uncertainties that dog the footsteps of science, as it ascends its tortuous course; or that they should have celebrated a single victorious battle as though it were the final conquest. It is not surprising that men neglected the difference between a scientific law, mathematically formulated and scrupulously verified, and those laws of God and nature which seemed to be self-evidently true only because they were familiar and habitually accepted.

Though Newton was ten years the younger, he and Locke were close friends. Locke admired Newton's scientific achievement, but he conversed with him on theology. Locke said of his friend: "Mr. Newton is really a very valuable man, not only for his wonderful skill in mathematics, but in divinity too, and his great knowledge in the scriptures, wherein I know few his equals." And Locke's biographer said of both:

Such men as Locke and Newton and Boyle were the great upholders of Christianity in England. But it was Christian religion, not Christian theology, that they cared for; and, in the case of Locke especially, it was a very broad Christianity indeed.[10]

3

The Declaration of Independence invoked the sanction of "Nature's God," "the Creator," and "the Supreme Judge of the World," and thus inserted a clause of piety in the general democratic creed. This piety received characteristic expression in Washington's First Inaugural Address, delivered on April 30, 1789, when he first presented himself to Congress:

> It would be peculiarly improper to omit, in this first official act, my fervent supplications to that Almighty Being, who rules over the universe. . . . No people can be bound to acknowledge and adore the invisible hand, which conducts the affairs of men, more than the people of the United States. Every step, by which they have advanced to the character of an independent nation, seems to have been distinguished by some token of providential agency.[11]

American official piety goes back to 'the election sermon' of colonial times.[12] George Whitfield was urged to participate as chaplain in the siege of Louisburg in 1745, and though he declined, he selected for the banners of the expedition the motto, "Nothing is to be despaired of, with Christ for our leader." At the Constitutional Convention in 1787 Benjamin Franklin complained that "we have not hitherto once thought of humbly applying to the Father of lights to illuminate our understandings." But the Convention, "except three or four persons, thought Prayers unnecessary"! [13]

The position of American democracy toward religion in general might be described as that of friendly neutrality. As to religious differences, it has not only tolerated them, but protected them. What this signified in the early decades of our history was set down in 1857 by Lorenzo Dow Johnson:

> Negatively considered, we are a Christian nation, that is, we are not a Jewish, nor a Mahomedan, nor a heathen nation. . . . Believing that all men

are responsible, in matters of conscience, to God only, our laws do not define religion as in the union of Church and State; they only defend it. Yet in our national capacity we do recognize the moral obligations of Christianity, and therefore, positively considered, we are a Christian nation. Our national and municipal laws commit us to the acknowledgment of one Almighty God, the Creator and Ruler of the universe, and to one Lord Jesus Christ, as furnishing for all men, in his model life and teachings, our only rule of conduct. This may be seen in the oath of allegiance, required of all foreigners . . . and also in our oaths of office and trust, which are alike administered to the Chief Magistrate of the nation, and to the humblest witness in a court of justice. . . . This national acknowledgment of our faith, may also be seen in the provision made by the General Government for the support of religious teachers, to accompany those sent far away by the public service. . . . And lastly, but not least, we see it in the usage of government, in having both Houses of Congress opened with prayer by a Christian minister; to implore the guidance and blessing of Almighty God on their deliberations.[14] *

The public piety of American democracy embraced that portion of Christianity which was founded on reason, leaving the field of revelation to the private faith of divers churches and sects. This rational nucleus of Christianity, embodied in the Declaration of Independence, was derived from the doctrines of 'natural religion' and 'deism.'

The idea of natural religion suited the peculiar temper of the Enlightenment. It signified religion divested of mystery and of dogmatism, as well as of sectarian bigotry. Man's religious needs and problems, like every other exigency of life, were to be met by the exercise of his natural faculties. Religion is not unreasonable, nor is reason irreligious. Religion is 'natural' because it is the reasonable response of man to that cosmic environment which is plain to his emancipated

* In revolutionary and early days there were occasional instances of Catholic priests serving with the Catholic members of the American army, although not regularly commissioned as chaplains. From the time of the Mexican War Catholic chaplains have been officially attached to our armed services. The only Roman Catholic ever attached to Congress officiated as chaplain in the Senate from 1832 to 1883. There has never been either a Catholic or a Jewish chaplain in the House of Representatives. The first appointment of a Jewish chaplain for the armed services was to a hospital during the Civil War. In the early days Presbyterian chaplains predominated in the House, and Episcopalian in the Senate and armed services, especially in the Army. This information was made available through the courtesy of Miss Anne L. Baden, acting chief bibliographer of the Library of Congress.

intellect. The secondary causes of physical nature require a First Cause; it is evident from the harmonies and marvels of nature that the First Cause is not only all-powerful, but wise and benevolent; under such circumstances man should obey and rejoice in God. Conscience or 'natural light' adds its testimony, communicating to man those rules of life which God has ordained for the happiness of his creatures, and by which they may be brought into accord with the whole of his creation.

The current of British liberal religious thought divided (though never sharply) into two streams. Moderate deists such as John Tillotson, Samuel Clarke, and Locke remained within the bounds of tradition. They accepted natural religion as the achievement of reason; but added positive religion because the natural intellect, being obscured by superstition and other human limitations, needs to be supplemented by revelation. It is characteristic of Locke that his chief apologetic work should have been entitled *The Reasonableness of Christianity,* and that he should have described revelation as "*natural reason enlarged.*"[15]

The more radical deism proposed to *reduce* positive religion to natural religion.* Its exponents, such as John Toland, Anthony Collins, Matthew Tindal, Thomas Chubb, and Thomas Paine, were moved by a negative and revolutionary temper of mind. They were *anti*-clerical, *anti*-ecclesiastical, *anti*-scriptural, and *anti*-authoritarian. They found an adequate revelation of God in the constitution of nature:

> It can't be imputed to any Defect in the Light of Nature, that the Pagan World ran into Idolatry; but to their being intirely govern'd by Priests, who pretended Communication with their Gods; and to have thence their Revelations, which they impos'd on the Credulous as divine Oracles: Whereas the Business of the Christian Dispensation was to destroy all those traditional Revelations; and restore, free from all Idolatry, the true primitive, and natural Religion, implanted in Mankind from the Creation.[16]

Between Locke and Tindal there was room for many intermediate degrees. Men could be either church members or freethinkers and yet find common ground in a distrust of mysticism, a recalcitrancy to ec-

* The term 'deism' is sometimes used to refer to the whole movement from Herbert of Cherbury and embracing Locke, and is sometimes limited to this more radical group.

clesiastical authority, and a shift of emphasis from specific dogmas to the broad theistic truths of a divine Creator, Providence, and Ruler. At the same time there was an undoubted decline in the fervor of piety. Theism as a branch of knowledge tended to supplant religion as an emotional experience. In the words of Mark Pattison:

> With some trifling exceptions, the whole of religious literature was drawn into the endeavour to "prove the truth" of Christianity. The essay and the sermon, the learned treatise and the philosophical disquisition, Addison the polite writer, and Bentley the classical philologian, the astronomer Newton, no less than the theologians by profession, were all engaged upon the same task. . . . Every one who had anything to say on sacred subjects drilled it into an array of argument against a supposed objector. Christianity appeared made for nothing else but to be "proved"; what use to make of it when it was proved was not much thought about. . . . The only quality in Scripture which was dwelt upon was its "credibility." [17]

4

In the Declaration of Independence, "the Representatives of the United States of America, in General Congress assembled," appealed to the Supreme Judge of the World for the "Rectitude" of their "Intentions." What did the term "rectitude" signify—to Jefferson, or to the 'enlightened' men of his times?

What rectitude did *not* signify is clear enough. It did not signify mere self-interest, for it was designed to win the approval both of God and of mankind. It did not signify obedience to political authority, for it was designed to justify revolution. The moral philosophy of the Enlightenment on its negative side consisted in the rejection of precisely these two principles—selfishness and political authoritarianism—both of which were associated with the ill repute of the notorious Hobbes. "This account of things," said Adam Smith, "was attacked from all quarters, and by all sorts of weapons, by sober reason as well as by furious declamation." [18]

The first step in the repudiation of Hobbes was the insistence by

Ralph Cudworth and Samuel Clarke on the independent and "immutable" validity of moral principles; morality, like mathematics, being founded upon the "eternal and necessary differences of things." Even God could not make right right by the sheer force of his will.[19] But moral principles were not a mere collection of axioms. With Richard Cumberland and later with Locke, Shaftesbury, Hutcheson, Hume, and the deists, the emphasis shifted from the independent validity of moral principles to their general beneficence—their conduciveness to harmonious well-being and happiness.

The exaltation of moral principles above calculations of selfish prudence suggested a higher faculty for their apprehension. This faculty might be identified, as it was by Thomas Wollaston, with the same intellectual faculty that apprehends the truths of mathematics. Or it might be considered, as it was by Shaftesbury, as the faculty of taste, by which certain actions are deemed "fair," "harmonious," "shapely," "proportion'd," and "becoming."[20] Or it might be held, as it was by Hutcheson and Butler, to be a special faculty of "conscience" attuned exclusively to moral truths, as the eye to color.

These three ideas—the independence of moral principles, their general beneficence, and the direct apprehension of them by a human faculty—constituted evidence of God; while God, in turn, provided the guarantee of the moral constitution of the universe at large. Thus rectitude, benevolence, conscience, and piety became one.

So great has been the emphasis of philosophers on Locke's empirical theory of ideas, as distinguishing him from the earlier rationalism of Descartes and Spinoza and the later rationalism of Kant, that his role as the major exponent of the Age of Reason has been obscured. However posterity may have interpreted his mission, Locke himself was primarily interested in philosophy on account of its moral and religious implications.[21] "We have the knowledge of *our own* existence by intuition," he said; "of the existence of *God* by demonstration"; and of "*other things*—by sensation." Of this last sort of knowledge, which embraced among "other things" the physical world, even Locke felt somewhat doubtful: ". . . it is an assurance that deserves the name of *knowledge*," but it is "not altogether so certain as our intuitive knowledge, or the deductions of our reason."[22]

Later philosophers shared Locke's doubts without accepting his "assurance"; and, ignoring the more "certain" parts of his knowledge, considered him as the progenitor of Hume's skepticism. Being so considered, he was then credited with an unnatural audacity for having said that "morality is capable of demonstration," consisting of "necessary consequences, as incontestible as those in mathematics." [23] * Precisely the opposite is true. Locke's acceptance of the intuitive certainty of self-existence, and the demonstrable certainty of God's existence, laid the grounds for the moral certainty which was simply a deduction from the two: "the idea of a Supreme Being, infinite in power, goodness, and wisdom, whose workmanship we are, and on whom we depend; and the idea of ourselves, as understanding, rational creatures." [24] This interpretation of Locke, which is no more than an acceptance of his own explicit statements, assimilates him to the rationalistic optimism of the Enlightenment, and bridges the gap between his theory of knowledge and his social and political philosophy.

Turning over the pages of Locke's *Essay*, we read, first, that:

> Nature . . . has put into man a desire of happiness and an aversion to misery: these indeed are innate practical principles which . . . *do* continue constantly to operate and influence all our actions without ceasing: these may be observed in all persons and all ages, steady and universal.[25]

Secondly, we read that "things . . . are good or evil, only in reference to pleasure or pain." We call "*good*" that which "is apt to cause or increase pleasure, or diminish pain in us."

Finally, "*moral good and evil* . . . is only *the conformity or disagreement of our voluntary actions to some law, whereby good or evil is drawn on us, from the will and power of the lawmaker.*" These laws, which are not innate, but must be learned by the exercise of our faculties, are of three types: "the *divine* law," "the *civil* law," and "the law of *opinion* or *reputation.*" "Actions in their own nature right and wrong" are actions "coincident with the divine law." The divine law becomes the "law of nature" of the *Second Treatise of Civil Government.*[26]

Locke's ethics is thus explicitly 'theological.' An act is good relatively

* Moral knowledge would even have an advantage over mathematics in that its essences are real and not merely nominal.

to any given human agent when he deems it conducive to his own happiness; it is morally right when this happiness flows from the act's conformity to the commands of God. Why does obedience to God's commands bring happiness? Because, as we learn from revelation, God rewards obedience and penalizes disobedience. But there is a deeper reason. God's commands are not arbitrary, since he is good as well as powerful. The deeper reason lies in the inherent beneficence of the law itself—that "unshaken rule of morality and foundation of all social virtue, 'That one should do as he would be done unto.' " [27] This rule is widely approved even by those who are ignorant of God:

> God having, by an inseparable connexion, joined virtue and public happiness together, and made the practice thereof necessary to the preservation of society . . . it is no wonder that every one should not only allow, but recommend and magnify those rules to others, from whose observance of them he is sure to reap advantage to himself.[28]

Men require revelation because they are 'in the dark.' "Our Saviour found mankind under a corruption of manners and principles, which ages after ages had prevailed, and must be confessed, was not in a way or tendency to be mended." But even so, "those just measures of right and wrong, which necessity had anywhere introduced, the civil laws prescribed, or philosophy recommended, stood on their true foundations. They were looked on as bonds of society, and conveniences of human life, and laudable practices." The moral, like the theological, teachings of Christianity are inherently reasonable; [29] and the commands of God are promulgated to men by "the light of nature," as well as by "the voice of revelation." [30] Were his enlightenment perfect, man would see that the greatest good lay in an obedience to God's commands, without being either bribed or intimidated. For these commands coincide with the design of creation by which the greatest happiness of each is brought into accord with the greatest happiness of all.

5

Adam Smith's *Theory of Moral Sentiments* appeared in 1759, and his more famous *Wealth of Nations* in the memorable year 1776. He cannot be said to have contributed significantly to the thought embodied in the Declaration of Independence—here he was a parallel manifestation rather than a source. His significance lies in the fact that being himself a product of the Enlightenment, he applied its ideas in the field of economics. He provided for Jefferson * and others in the eighteenth century, and to an increasing degree during the nineteenth century, that form of economic thought which most closely paralleled democratic political thought—individualism, rationalism, freedom of commerce, freedom of contract, freedom from oppressive government. Above all, he provided the standard form of reconciliation between the professed benevolence of the democratic man and the acknowledged selfishness of the economic man. To those who see democracy under its economic rather than its political aspect, Smith rather than Locke is its prophet.

That which distinguished Adam Smith's ethics was his emphasis on the principle of sympathy. Through sympathy the individual transcends his private subjectivity and attains the attitude of a 'disinterested spectator.' Like his predecessors, Smith rejected the Hobbesian reduction of the moral consciousness to calculating self-interest. Acts are morally approved for their sheer "propriety," regardless of their consequences. That which is approved is not the useful, but the fit, the convenient, the beautiful, the "happy contrivance." Moral rules or laws are inductions from these immediate judgments of propriety. But though we do not approve acts *for* their usefulness, "Nature . . . seems to have so happily adjusted our sentiments of approbation and disapprobation, to the conveniency both of the individual and of the society, that after the strictest examination it will be found" that all of the approved ac-

* "In political economy I think Smith's wealth of nations the best book extant, in the science of government Montesquieu's spirit of laws is generally recommended . . . Locke's little book is perfect as far as it goes." [31]

tions and rules of action are, in fact, useful. This is the happiest contrivance of all.[32]

There appears, on the surface, to be a contradiction between the sympathetic principle of Smith's *Theory of Moral Sentiments* and the selfish principle of his *Wealth of Nations*.[33] There was, no doubt, a shift of emphasis and of preoccupation during the years between 1759 and 1776, but the apparent inconsistency is illuminating rather than baffling. Smith's "moral" philosophy was the larger outlook within which his economic science found its place. His economic science was, it is true, based on man's selfish desire to "possess more means of happiness," and on his "ingenious and artful adjustment of those means to the ends for which they were intended":

> It is not from the benevolence of the butcher, the brewer, or the baker that we expect our dinner, but from their regard to their own interest. We address ourselves, not to their humanity but to their self-love.[34]

But the disinterested spectator admires artful self-interest, along with the frugality and industry which are the conditions of wealth and happiness.[35] Each man not only *is* prudent, but *approves* of prudence; he acts from self-interest—with a good conscience. Similarly, he approves of justice, which defines and gives legal sanction to those rules of fair play by which competitive prudence serves a social end. Finally, the disinterested spectator approves of the humanity, the generosity, and the public spirit which distinguish human life on its highest plane.[36]

The deeper doctrine of Adam Smith, as of Locke and the Age of Enlightenment generally, was the principle of harmony—or the "invisible hand" of God.[37] Men are so constituted by nature, under God's beneficent reign, that each man in obeying the dictates of enlightened self-love is at the same time the perfect instrument of universal benevolence. Loving oneself is *in effect* the same as loving one's neighbor. The laissez-faire doctrine in economics did not merely preach this edifying doctrine, but verified it from that side of human life which is deemed least edifying. The rules under which competitive self-interest and the division of labor promote man's material well-being are the laws of nature. Their beneficent operation, implemented, but not created, by positive law, is the "wisdom of nature." [38] The economic order, motivated by self-interest and regulated by justice, takes its place within the divine order, which it both executes and exemplifies.

6

In the opening paragraph of the Declaration, Jefferson claimed for the American people that to which "the Laws of Nature and of Nature's God" entitled them. In the following paragraph these "Laws," at once natural and divine, were identified with certain "self-evident Truths": to wit, that men are "created equal" and endowed by their Creator with certain "unalienable rights," such as "Life, Liberty and the Pursuit of Happiness," to ensure which "Governments are instituted among men."

The doctrine of natural law is complex and has had a long history—coextensive, in fact, with the whole stream of European thought. Greek metaphysics, Roman jurisprudence, Christian theology, medieval scholasticism, the Protestant Reformation, the philosophy and political thought of the Renaissance and of the early seventeenth century, have all contributed to its meaning. To understand the form which this doctrine assumed in Locke it is, however, not necessary to look beyond two of his precursors: the "judicious" Richard Hooker, whom Locke so frequently cited in his support; and Thomas Hobbes, who served Locke, as he served so many of his successors, as both stimulant and irritant.*

Although Richard Hooker wrote at the close of the sixteenth century, his moderate temper was that of a later age. In the famous *Of the*

---

* I do not mean to belittle Locke's other sources, such as Grotius, of whom a recent writer says: "The immense prestige of the natural law doctrine in the seventeenth and eighteenth centuries was due particularly to the work of two men, Grotius and Newton. . . . Yet even more important [than his emphasis on the law of nations] was Grotius' revival of the Ciceronian idea of natural law. . . . Once again natural law is defined as right reason; and is described as at once a law of, and a law to, God. God himself, Grotius asserted, could not make twice two other than four; nor would his rational nature fail to guide man even though there were no God, or though God lacked interest in human affairs." [39]

Laws of Ecclesiastical Polity, published in 1594, and written in defense of Anglicanism against both puritanism and Catholicism, Hooker offered the following statement of the general nature of law:

> All things that are, have some operation not violent or casual. Neither doth any thing ever begin to exercise the same, without some fore-conceived end for which it worketh. And the end which it worketh for is not obtained, unless the work be also fit to obtain it by. For unto every end every operation will not serve. That which doth assign unto each thing the kind, that which doth moderate the force and power, that which doth appoint the form and measure, of working, the same we term a Law.[40]

God chooses his own end, and imposes upon himself the appropriate "manner of working." This self-regulation of God constitutes the "first law eternal." Considered as imposed or enjoined by God on his creatures, this same regulation constitutes the "second law eternal": there is a "manner of working which God hath set for each created thing to keep." This "second law eternal" assumes different forms suited to the creature on which it is imposed. There are "nature's laws," that is, the laws adapted to "natural agents"—"the heavens and elements of the world . . . which keep the law of their kind unwittingly." There are also laws for the angels, who are moved by "delectable love arising from the visible apprehension of the purity, glory, and beauty of God." [41] Finally, there are the laws applied to man. These are the "laws of reason," commonly called "laws of nature," or "natural laws," as distinguished from "nature's laws." Their control is exerted in a manner appropriate to human subjects: "God which moveth mere natural agents as an efficient only, doth otherwise move intellectual creatures"—namely, by knowledge and choice of the good:

> Laws of Reason have these marks to be known by. Such as keep them resemble most lively in their voluntary actions that very manner of working which Nature herself doth necessarily observe in the course of the whole world. The works of Nature are all behoveful, beautiful, without superfluity or defect; even so theirs, if they be framed according to that which the Law of Reason teacheth. Secondly, those Laws are investigable by Reason, without the help of Revelation supernatural and divine. Finally, in such sort they are investigable, that the knowledge of them is general, the world hath always been acquainted with them.[42]

In short, rational or natural law is neither a mere description of matters of fact, nor a mere definition of the ideal. It is both: it is the law of what ought to be in a world in which things are, normally, what they ought to be. The term 'natural,' as used here, is honorific as opposed to that more modern sense of the term, in which it connotes what is base and rudimentary. Natural law is primitive [43] only in the sense of being prior to civil and religious institutions. It is metaphysical, as affirming the essence of man; moral, as defining the right and the good; rational, in the double sense of being apprehended by reason and applied to rational beings.

But though men possess the capacity to discern these laws of reason or nature and to be guided by them, this capacity is weak and corrupted, so that immediate or private good is preferred to the true good. Therein lies the necessity of positive commands which are supported by rewards and punishments: rewards "which may more allure unto good than any hardness deterreth from it, and punishments, which may more deter from evil than any sweetness thereto allureth."

First in order come the divine commands supported by the rewards of heaven and hell. Next are the commands of the human ruler, or the positive law of government. Left to their own selfish depravity men fall into violent disputes:

> To take away all such mutual grievances, injuries, and wrongs, there was no way but only by growing unto composition and agreement amongst themselves, by ordaining some kind of government public, and by yielding themselves subject thereunto; that unto whom they granted authority to rule and govern, by them the peace, tranquility, and happy estate of the rest might be procured.[44]

The "second law eternal" is summarized by Hooker as follows:

> That part of it which ordereth natural agents we call usually Nature's law; that which Angels do clearly behold and without any swerving observe is a law Celestial and heavenly; the law of Reason, that which bindeth creatures reasonable in this world, and with which by reason they may most plainly perceive themselves bound; that which bindeth them, and is not known but by special revelation from God, Divine law; Human law, that which out of the law either of reason or of God men probably gathering to be expedient, they make it a law.[45]

7

The significance of Richard Hooker lies in his linking of medieval Christian thought with the Age of the Enlightenment. The divine law confirms, supplements, extends, and reinforces the light of nature; it "rectifies nature's obliquity" and "helps our imbecility."[46] Such being the condition of man—endowed with *natural faculties* which direct him to his sovereign good, but dependent on *revelation* to eke them out—he may place his reliance in different degrees on the one or the other. In the Age of the Enlightenment, as compared with the twilight of the Age of Faith in which Hooker lived, the emphasis was shifted from revelation to reason. Man was less disposed to recognize "nature's obliquity" or to admit his own "imbecility."

The human law, like the divine law, is an adjunct of natural law, required "now that man and his offspring are grown . . . corrupt and sinful." But there are important differences. In the first place, while the divine law is infallible and unquestionable, the human law reflects the limitations of mortal men: "that which probably gathering to be expedient, they make it a law." In the second place, human law has a special province. It deals with "civil perfection," with what serves men "living in public society," and "toucheth them as they are sociable parts united into one body." And to the universal natural law it adds laws that are of merely local and temporary convenience.[47]

In the third place, divine law is prior to human law, and in this respect resembles natural law. The law of nature and the law of God thus tended to be named together, as defining the underlying ground and proving the derivative authority of the political power. But in proportion as the spirit of the Enlightenment prevailed, men tended to turn from the authority of rulers, whether human or divine, and to seek a body of rules which were directly conducive to "civil perfection," and which men could ascertain independently by the light of their natural reason. The divine law tended to consist in little more than a pious verbalism, or the dogma that social harmony under natural law is a reproduction of the universal harmony.

Parallel to this tendency to divorce natural law from religious presuppositions ran a tendency to conceive natural law itself, not as absolute but as the means to a human end. Just as the positive law of God or man professes to execute the natural law, and may properly be judged by this, so natural law, professing to achieve a certain condition of "civil perfection," may be examined in the light of that achievement. Reason, instead of discovering a body of self-evident principles assumed to have a social end, derives the principles *from* the end.

The social end or "civil perfection" which the natural law is designed to achieve is the harmonious happiness of equal persons. Speaking of the second of the 'two great' Biblical commandments, which prescribes that it is a man's duty to love others as himself, Hooker said:

> From which relation of equality between ourselves and them that are as ourselves, what several rules and canons natural Reason hath drawn for direction of life no man is ignorant; as namely, "That because we would take no harm, we must therefore do none"; "That sith we would not be in any thing extremely dealt with, we must ourselves avoid all extremity in our dealings"; "that from all violence and wrong we are utterly to abstain"; with such like.[48]

The natural law not only takes cognizance of the equality of personal claims, but recognizes human desires and the material conditions of their satisfaction:

> All men desire to lead in this world a happy life. That life is led most happily, wherein all virtue is exercised without impediment or let. The Apostle, in exhorting men to contentment although they have in this world no more than very bare food and raiment, giveth us thereby to understand that those are even the lowest of things necessary; that if we should be stripped of all those things without which we might possibly be, yet these must be left; that destitution in these is such an impediment, as till it be removed suffereth not the mind of man to admit any other care. . . . Inasmuch as righteous life presupposeth life; inasmuch as to live virtuously it is impossible except we live; therefore the first impediment, which naturally we endeavour to remove, is penury and want of things without which we cannot live. Unto life many implements are necessary; more, if we seek (as all men naturally do) such a life as hath in it joy, comfort, delight, and pleasure.[49]

Thus natural law, as a set of categorical maxims, tended to be superseded by a body of rules judged to yield a certain result—namely, a justly ordered society. Natural law tended to be superseded by individual rights, and intuitive principles by the methodical pursuit of human happiness. The peculiar character of the doctrine of natural law, with its overtones and emotional meanings, depended on the gradual character of these transitions. Terms began to take on a new meaning before they had lost the old, and enjoyed the sanctions of tradition at the same time that they commended themselves to the spirit of free inquiry.

8

Nearly a century had elapsed between Hooker's *Ecclesiastical Polity* and Locke's *Second Treatise of Civil Government*—the century of the Puritan Revolution, the Restoration, and the settlement of 1688. Hooker had written before the Puritan Revolution as an orthodox Anglican partisan; Locke, a disillusioned puritan, and a moderate, though professing, Anglican, represented a "reasonable" Christianity in which the sects might find common ground. He died "in perfect charity with all men, and in sincere communion with the whole church of Christ, by whatever names Christ's followers call themselves." [50] Theism was still a common assumption in all practical philosophy. But moral, social, and political ideas were becoming secularized in terms of human faculties, human experience, and human needs.

Locke's *First Treatise of Civil Government* was devoted to a refutation of Sir Robert Filmer's *Patriarcha,* in which that author had defended the Stuart claim to an absolute sovereignty by divine choice. Locke's own theory, as presented in the *Second Treatise,* was designed to justify King William, who had been chosen by Parliament. God does not drop out of the picture, but retires into the background, where instead of creating human institutions, he lays down the guiding principles by which men create their own. In his ethics as set forth in the *Essay* Locke had emphasized the theological sanction, and in the *Second Treatise* the law of nature was still referred to as the command of God. But this remote theological reference now lost its primary importance, and the content of the law of nature assumed a specifically political meaning. Its priority to the positive law was affirmed in the doctrine of a 'state of nature,' when the law of nature (or of God) reigned without the sanction of civil government. The political beneficence of the law of nature was set forth in terms of 'natural rights,' which were the basic goods of individuals so limited as to be mutually compatible. The autonomy which the individual derives from his direct knowledge of the law of nature was reconciled with the authority of government by the theory of 'compact,' and his control of government was secured by the representative legislature and the right of revolution.

In summarizing these conceptions it will be instructive to compare the views of Locke with those of Hobbes. Both men were emphatically individualistic; they employed a similar vocabulary, and their reasoning was often parallel; but they reached politically opposite results.

For Hobbes, the individual man was governed by appetites, and by a desire of power wherewith to obtain 'felicity'; that is, the satisfaction of his appetites as they arise. Each man pursues power blindly and ruthlessly, and the result is war. Only the occasional man (like Hobbes himself!) is reasonable enough to see that the condition of enjoying felicity at all is peace, purchased by self-restraint and moderation. The average man has to be induced to do the reasonable thing by fear of punishment. Hobbes, in short, was both egoistic and pessimistic—egoistic in regarding individual self-interest as the only motive governing human behavior, pessimistic in his distrust of the degree to which even this motive is enlightened.

Locke, on the other hand, took a more flattering view of man, crediting him with a social nature and a high capacity for enlightenment. His will is not merely his strongest appetite, but his thoughtful preference for a good which embraces others as well as himself; and as a forerunner of the Age of Reason, Locke believed that such an enlightened will could fairly be expected of the general run of men.[51]

As regards natural law, the application is evident. With Hobbes, as with Locke, natural law coincided with the principles—such as the Golden Rule—by which the interests of individuals are brought into peaceful accord. With Hobbes these principles, in order to justify themselves to any given individual, have first to be translated into terms of self-interest, as the means of augmenting his own power and felicity. He must see that he himself gains more from peace than from war. But his enlightenment will tell him that he can enjoy the advantages of peace only provided others keep it, and his distrust will tell him that others cannot be counted on to keep the peace unless they are made to do so. Hobbes expressed this by saying that while the laws of nature prescribe the ways of peace as the "immutable and eternal" conditions of the preservation of the individual's life and the augmenting of his power, until the creation of the civil polity they oblige him only "in foro interno," that is, they regulate his aspirations. They oblige "in foro externo," that is, as rules of conduct, only within an authoritarian state.[52]

With Locke, on the other hand, the law of nature is binding on the individual because it appeals to his reason, whether or not he can justify it to himself in terms of his private gain; and this direct rational appeal is strong enough both to govern his own action and to be counted upon in others. There is, Locke quotes Hooker as saying, a "natural inducement," which "hath brought men to know that it is no less their duty to love others than themselves"; and, added Locke, "reason . . . teaches all mankind who will but consult it, that being all equal and independent, no one ought to harm another in his life, health, liberty, or possessions," but "ought . . . as much as he can to preserve the rest of mankind."[53] When this natural inducement is not strong enough, then men will still obey the law of nature out of wholesome respect for the will of God. The civil enforcement is only a last resort, useful, but not absolutely indispensable.

Even after the political sanction has been introduced, it does not supersede the divine and natural law which is "unwritten, and so nowhere to be found but in the minds of men":

> The obligations of the law of Nature cease not in society, but only in many cases are drawn closer, and have, by human laws, known penalties annexed to them to enforce their observation. Thus the law of Nature stands as an eternal rule to all men, legislators as well as others. The rules that they make for other men's actions must . . . be conformable to the law of Nature, *i.e.*, to the will of God, of which that is a declaration, and the fundamental law of Nature being the preservation of mankind, no human sanction can be good or valid against it.[54]

9

The difference between Hobbes and Locke is clearly reflected in their views of the so-called state of nature. For both men, the state of nature represents that condition of man, hypothetical or historical, in which he is free from the control of the civil authority. All men are then equal in respect of authority—that is, no man has any rightful authority over any other man. For Hobbes, this is a condition of private war, in which life is "solitary, poore, nasty, brutish, and short." [55]

With Locke, on the other hand, the state of nature represents the reign of the law of nature through the spontaneous operation of human faculties. To an age which was sensitive to the evils of political (as well as of ecclesiastical) tyranny, it represented a deliverance from oppression. Even in the state of nature there must, it is true, be rule, but it is the self-rule of rational and pious men. To Locke, this condition of mankind seemed practically as well as theoretically possible:

> Let me ask you, whether it be not possible that men, to whom the rivers and woods afforded the spontaneous provisions of life, and so with no private possessions of land had no enlarged desires after riches or power; should live together in society, make one people of one language under one chieftain, who shall have no other power but to command them in time of common war against their common enemies, without any municipal laws, judges, or any person with superiority established amongst them, but ended all their private differences, if any arose, by the extemporary determination of their neighbours, or of arbitrators chosen by the parties.[56]

It is true that this condition of man would be 'inconvenient,' for reasons which Locke plainly set forth. But it is clear that Locke, despite his moderation, was not out of accord with those retrospective utopians by whom the state of nature was not only idealized but regretted as an actual epoch in human history antedating the existence of political institutions. There is a difference between Locke and Pope, but it is largely a difference between the prosaic and the poetic mind:

> *Nor think in Nature's state they blindly trod;*
> *The state of Nature was the reign of God:*
> *Self-love and Social at her birth began,*
> *Union the bond of all things, and of Man.*[57]

Or, had Locke been a poet, he might have exclaimed with Shelley: "Perhaps ere Man had lost reason, and lived an happy, happy race: no Tyranny, No Priestcraft, No War.—Adieu to the dazzling picture!" [58]

"The outstanding feature of Locke's treatment of natural law," says a recent writer, "is the almost complete dissolution which this concept undergoes through his handling into the natural rights of the individual." [59] A right is a justifiable claim; a natural right is a claim justifiable in the absence of government and positive law.* Their treatment of this conception again reveals the basic difference between Hobbes and Locke.

In both philosophers there was the same ultimate individualism. In Hobbes the only right which was recognized as natural was the individual's unlimited private claim to self-preservation:

> The Right of Nature, which Writers commonly call *Jus Naturale,* is the Liberty each man hath, to use his own power, as he will himselfe, for the preservation of his own Nature; that is to say, of his own Life; and consequently, of doing any thing, which in his own Judgement, and Reason, hee shall conceive to be the aptest means thereunto.[60]

Locke recognized the same primitive right *in a state of war,* that is, where the individual is faced with implacable enmity:

> For by the fundamental law of Nature, man being to be preserved as much as possible, when all cannot be preserved, the safety of the innocent is to be preferred, and one may destroy a man who makes war upon him . . . for the same reason that he may kill a wolf or a lion, because they are not under the ties of the common law of reason, have no other rule but that of force and violence, and so may be treated as a beast of prey.

But, said Locke, with an unmistakable reference to Hobbes, there is a "plain difference between the state of Nature and the state of war, which however some men have confounded, are as far distant as a state of peace, goodwill, mutual assistance, and preservation; and a state of enmity, malice, violence, and mutual destruction are one from another." The "estate all men are naturally in" is "a state of perfect freedom to

---

* The French word *'droit'* and the German word *'Recht'* are not equivalent to the English word 'right,' but refer to law as a body of basic principles underlying the positive law, and constituting a branch of moral science.

order their actions, and dispose of their possessions and persons as they think fit, within the bounds of the law of Nature." [61]

In other words, in Locke's state of nature the rights of the individual were rights to be respected in others, as well as asserted for oneself. Their "bounds" were moral bounds and their observance was a moral obligation sanctioned by reason and conscience. While rights in this universal and reciprocal sense existed for Hobbes only in the form of legal rights guaranteed by the force of the sovereign, for Locke they were prior to the positive law and served as a norm by which the positive law was to be limited and guided.*

As regards the natural rights which Locke enumerated—life, person, health, limb, liberty, possessions, estate, property—they are all essentially the same. Thus Locke said that men unite in society "for the mutual preservation of their lives, liberties and estates, which I call by the general name—property." [63] This does not mean that Locke was an arch-capitalist who believed that the fundamental purpose of the state was to protect the individual's material possessions, or his control of the means of production. It means that with Locke "property" in this limited and debatable sense was absorbed into the fundamental idea of individualism. If the individual is to exist and flourish, he must be able to call something his *own* and be given exclusive right to its use, within the limits imposed by the similar rights of others. If a communist society allows a man to call his soul his own, or his breath, or his body, or his clothes, or his portion of food, then that society recognizes the right of property—in Locke's basic sense of the term. The "possession of outward things," † or property in external goods, is a special case of property in this basic sense. A man is dependent on the appropriation of physical resources beyond his own body—they do him "good for the support of his life." [65]

---

* They were "implied in the basic arrangements of society at all times and in all places." [62]

† In his first and most famous "Letter Concerning Toleration" he uses the expression "civil interest" to embrace "life, liberty, health, and indolency of body; and the possession of outward things, such as money, lands, houses, furniture, and the like." [64]

It is because he thought of property in this fundamental moral sense as the condition of an individualized human life that he could speak of it as a natural right having a meaning prior to its elaboration and its safeguarding by government. Property as a moral institution, independent of any laws of property, appears in Locke's notion of an ideal condition of things which existed "a long time in the world"—a condition of natural plenty, in which a man could use the resources of nature and multiply the fruits of his labor without fear of depriving others:

> And thus, I think, it is very easy to conceive, without any difficulty, how labour could at first begin a title of property in the common things of Nature, and how the spending it upon our uses bounded it; so that there could then be no reason of quarrelling about title, nor any doubt about the largeness of possession it gave. Right and conveniency went together. For as a man had a right to all he could employ his labour upon, so he had no temptation to labour for more than he could make use of. This left no room for controversy about the title, nor for encroachment on the right of others. What portion a man carved to himself was easily seen; and it was useless, as well as dishonest, to carve himself too much, or take more than he needed.[66]

10

Among the self-evident truths of the Declaration is the truth that to secure the rights of life, liberty, and the pursuit of happiness, "governments are instituted among men, deriving their just powers from the consent of the governed." The institution of government is related to natural law and natural rights through the idea of 'compact.'

Here again the difference between Locke and Hobbes is instructive. In both cases the political authority is "instituted"—is, in other words, a secondary form of society which supersedes a condition in which authority is equal; that is, in which no man has authority over any other man. In both cases political obedience is a contractual obligation which rests upon the keeping of promises, or the payment of what one 'owes'; and which rests, more fundamentally, upon the profitableness of a bargain to both parties, and their voluntary agreement upon it for the sake of the profit.* In both Hobbes and Locke the conditions of the origin of the state, both psychological and logical, must be assumed to exist prior to the state in the natural faculties of man. In both Hobbes and Locke the contracting parties are and remain individuals.†

Hobbes was confronted with the difficulty of imputing such an act of concerted reason to men in the state of nature. The creation of the civil polity implies not only a widely distributed enlightenment, but also an attitude of disinterestedness, since even an enlightened egoist might think that he had more to gain for himself in a state of nature, in which his force and cunning were unrestrained, than under a government which compelled him to make large concessions to others. With Hobbes, in other words, there should have been a sovereign already possessing the power to impose penalties, and thus enabled to provide the unscrupulous and the ignorant with incentives to create sovereignty!

With Locke the difficulty was the reverse of that of Hobbes. How is it that men whose conscience and reason already prompt them to seek the end of government, namely, "the good of mankind," [69] should feel the necessity of instituting government? Men's very competence to create government seems to render it supererogatory. This is Locke's question, and the following is his answer:

> If a man in the state of Nature be so free as has been said, if he be absolute lord of his own person and possessions, equal to the greatest and subject to nobody, why will he part with his freedom, this empire, and subject himself to the dominion and control of any other power? To which it is obvious to answer, that though in the state of Nature he hath such a right, yet the enjoyment of it is very uncertain and constantly exposed to the invasion of others; for all being kings as much as he, every man his equal, and the greater part

---

* Whether one thinks of promises, contracts, covenants, etc., as absolute—"so great and so strong . . . that Omnipotency itself can be tied by them," or as justified by their benefits to the parties concerned, depends on how far one's ethical thinking has advanced from intuitionism towards utilitarianism.[67]

† That Rousseau exerted comparatively little influence on American political thought was not due to the fact that Americans did not read French. From the standpoint of the eighteenth century Rousseau was either a backslider or a prophet ahead of his times. In thinking of a collective will as absorbing and superseding individuals, and as being in its solidarity the ultimate source of sovereignty, he was thinking the thoughts of a Spinoza, or of a Hegel, rather than those of the Enlightenment.[68]

no strict observers of equity and justice, the enjoyment of the property he has in this state is very unsafe, very insecure.[70]

In other words, government was for Locke a reinforcement of reason and conscience whereby their reign was made more firm and reliable. It also saved the unofficial man from the trouble of being his neighbor's keeper. For in the state of nature the "execution of the law of Nature is . . . put into every man's hands," which exposes men to "inconveniences." [71]

The same difference occurs in connection with the right of revolution—the "right of a people to alter or abolish" their government whenever it "becomes destructive of the ends for which it is created." It is now a question not of the right of a private individual to assert himself against his private enemy, but of the right of the private individual to disobey the public authority. For this there could, in Hobbes, be neither incentive nor justification: no incentive, because the only alternative was an intolerable state of war, which was worse than the worst of governments; no justification, because once the political sovereignty is created the individual has already authorized it to speak in his name.[72]

With Locke, on the other hand, the moral right, which was prior to legal right, always remained as a reserved right. It is true that Hobbes also recognized such a reserved right, but he limited it to the right of self-preservation. The only limit to sovereignty once it is established is the individual's right to defend himself against violence. With Locke, reason and conscience not only afforded a basis for the creation of the state, but remained a standing court of appeal for its rectification; or, if needs be, for its overthrow. The compact was revocable. The public power was to be obeyed "unless there be reason showed which may necessarily enforce that the law of reason or of God doth enjoin the contrary." [73] It was neither reasonable nor right that men should accept the authority of government when it has ceased to serve the purpose for which its exactions were originally accepted: "Rebellion to Tyrants is Obedience to God." *

In other words, for Hobbes there was only one contract: that, namely,

* The motto on the engraved seal used by Jefferson in his private correspondence.[74]

among the private individuals creating the state. For Locke, on the other hand, there was a contract between the people and the government. The English Revolution of 1688, like the American Revolution, was justified on this ground.*

11

The general character of the Enlightenment, together with its religious, moral, and political ideas, culminated in its notorious optimism. Whether this optimism was or was not 'shallow,' as the present age is disposed to think, is a question for further examination. In any case it was not a mere gush of sentimentality, but rested upon a systematic philosophy. Its fundamental concept was that of the constitutional harmony of the universe, so plainly set forth by the 'judicious Hooker':

> For we see the whole world and each part thereof so compacted, that as long as each thing performeth only that work which is natural unto it, it thereby preserveth both other things and also itself. . . . All things (God only excepted), besides the nature which they have in themselves, receive externally some perfection from other things, as hath been shewed. Insomuch as there is in the whole world no one thing great or small, but either in respect of knowledge or of use it may unto our perfection add somewhat.[76]

There was a harmony of nature and man, since both were conceived and executed by the same beneficent Creator. There was a harmony of human faculties with their objects of knowledge: the rational order of the cosmos was attuned to the reason implanted in man, and the eternal principles of rectitude were revealed to conscience. Corresponding to the nature of things there was a 'light of nature' which illuminated the mind. There was a harmony between self-love and benevolence, since each man was so constituted as to find his personal happiness in

---

* Thus "the Convention Parliament of 1689 justified the Revolution on the Calvinistic grounds: 'that King James having endeavored to subvert the constitution of the kingdom by breaking the original contract between King and people . . . having violated the Fundamental law and having withdrawn himself hath abdicated, and that the throne is vacant.' "[75]

that course of action which was at the same time conducive to the good of mankind at large. Obedience to God and to the political authority coincided with the dictates of reason and utility. The ideal social order consisted in a harmony of individuals amply guaranteed: it was supported by the testimony of man's higher faculties, concurrent with his private interests, commanded by God, and enforced by the state. Evil there was, no doubt, but it was accidental, and not intrinsic to the world; being a temporary lapse resulting from ignorance and tyranny, and remediable by the new enlightenment and the new liberty. Were these to fail, as seemed to the men of the eighteenth century highly improbable, it was always possible to fall back on the promises of God and the rectifications of the Divine Government.

CHAPTER EIGHT

THE MAKING OF THE AMERICAN MIND

1

So WELL did the Declaration of Independence accomplish its purpose of formulating "the common-sense of the subject" that its doctrines might have been gathered from the air. No American could have lived in the second half of the eighteenth century without imbibing them. To argue one source against another is misleading; but to emphasize the diversity of sources may serve to demonstrate how far "the American mind" [1] reflected the mind of the age. Jefferson's contemporaries and fellow leaders breathed the same intellectual atmosphere and were nourished on the same tradition as his own. Samuel Adams, James Otis, Patrick Henry, John Adams, James Madison, George Washington, even Alexander Hamilton, spoke, each with an individual accent, the same fundamental language.

A few scattered colonists across three thousand miles of water gave back to Europe a company of representative men saturated with its ripest tradition and motivated by its latest hopes. In the perspective of history there are no more typical embodiments of the Enlightenment than Tom Paine, Benjamin Franklin, and Thomas Jefferson. Poles asunder as they were in temperament, vocation, habits of mind, there is nevertheless a common physiognomy that makes it unimaginable that they should have lived in any other age.

Of these Paine represented the Enlightenment in its more radical and polemical aspects. To his contemporaries and to posterity he filled the double role of revolutionary hero and stench in the nostrils of conservative piety.* An Englishman by birth, he came to America on the invitation of Franklin in 1774, and at once adopted its cause as his own. His *Common Sense* (1776), in which he set forth the theory of compact

* Even Theodore Roosevelt spoke of him as a "filthy little atheist." [2]

and the state of nature in bold and simplified form, and *The American Crisis* (1776-1783), containing the famous "These are the times that try men's souls," played an important part in creating the popular demand for complete independence. Later he allied himself with the cause of the French Revolution and thus became a link between French and American radicalism. His *Rights of Man* (1791) and *Age of Reason* (1794) were brilliant popularizations of the general philosophy of the Enlightenment, both political and religious. In the latter field he carried deism to the length of denying positive religion altogether, and defended a piety that should be based wholly on reason and nature: "Do we want to know what God is? Search not the book called the scripture, which any human hand might make, but the scripture called the Creation." [3]

Although Benjamin Franklin was an experimental scientist, statesman, diplomat, moralizer, and journalist, rather than speculative philosopher, his mind was in complete harmony with the fundamental thinking of his age. In his shrewdness and simplicity he was to contemporaries the perfect embodiment of the new America, while his many years of residence in England and France between 1757 and 1785 brought him into close touch with the reigning tendencies of European thought, and thus enabled him to be, no less than Paine, an embodiment of the cosmopolitan spirit of the Enlightenment. Illustrations might be taken from his zeal for "natural philosophy," or from his simplified, deistic form of Christian piety; but nothing could more perfectly express the optimism of the Enlightenment than his affirmation of the harmony between prudence and benevolence:

> . . . for self-denial is never a duty or a reasonable action but as it is a natural means of procuring more pleasure than you can taste without it; so that this grave, saint-like guide to happiness, as rough and dreadful as she has been made to appear, is in truth the kindest and most beautiful mistress in the world. . . . It is doing all the good we can to others, by acts of humanity, friendship, generosity, and benevolence; this is that constant and durable good which will afford contentment and satisfaction always alike, without variation or diminution . . . their happiness or chief good consists in acting up to their chief faculty, or that faculty which distinguishes them from all creatures of a different species. The chief faculty in man is his reason, and consequently his chief good, or that which may be justly called his good, con-

sists not merely in action, but in reasonable action. By reasonable actions we understand those actions which are preservative of the human kind and naturally tend to produce real and unmixed happiness.[4]

Thomas Jefferson remains the most complete American exponent of the Enlightenment—both in its general tone and in its diverse doctrines. He was not only a man of affairs, but a sage—recognized as such in Europe as well as in America. He was the exponent of a mild and tolerant deism, of a Christian-humanitarian ethics, of the Newtonian science, and of the political doctrines of natural law and natural rights. He was optimistic, as well as unqualifiedly individualistic, in his view of human nature and of human institutions. In his statesmanship and in his extensive philosophical writings, as well as in his classic formulation of the doctrines of the Declaration, he was the epitome of the American mind, as that mind, together with the creed of American democracy, emerged from the reigning tradition and atmospheric conditions of the eighteenth century.

2

The American mind which produced at the close of the eighteenth century so remarkable a galaxy of leaders, and which fixed the framework of American democratic institutions, reflected the economic evolution, the legal and political habits, and the racial traits of the Englishman.

I am not unaware of the mixed character of the colonial population—of the Spanish elements of the Floridas and the Southwest, the wide diffusion of French pioneers in the Mississippi Valley, and the powerful concentration of Dutch in New York. The last of these groups was imbued with a traditional spirit of liberty, and familiar, in the Union of Utrecht (1579), with political practices which strikingly anticipated the procedures of American democracy.[5] Still less am I disposed to ignore or belittle the streams of immigration which after the middle of the eighteenth century brought to these shores not only Germans and Scotch-Irish, but numerous recruits from eastern and southern Europe. But this wider ethnic synthesis, creating the new American of the nineteenth century, did not take place until after American society was sufficiently crystallized to assimilate new material without a sudden or radical alteration of type.

It will be granted that on the Atlantic seaboard and in the adolescent period of institutional development the Englishman and the English way prevailed. The predominance of this influence was favored by the paucity and weakness of the indigenous population, which permitted a purity both of racial stock and of cultural tradition. Here lies the major explanation of the impressive difference between the political and social developments of the North American continent and those of the sister continent to the south, where the conquerors were of Latin origin, and where the Indian survived as a racial and cultural component.

The English settlers came in large part from the yeomanry and rising bourgeoisie which constituted the major force of the Puritan Revolution. They brought with them specific forms of 'open-field' farming, and of artisanship. Transplanted to American soil, this economic group suffered neither frustration nor the necessity of a resort to violence. Mounting rapidly in wealth and power, they proceeded to achieve the social reconstruction which was the logical sequel to their economic evolution.

The Englishman brought with him not only his economic self-reliance and ambition but those customary legal practices which safeguarded his traditional rights. Magna Carta was a part of his inheritance, and the Revolution of 1688 was a part of his destiny. The English common law acknowledged a set of principles more fundamental than executive authority or legislative enactment. It afforded a man protection against discrimination, arbitrariness, and tyrannical exploitation. It assumed that he was, for better or for worse, responsible for his own acts, entitled to their fruits, and deserving of punishment if their consequences were injurious to others. The common law was, in short, profoundly individualistic, and imbued with the idea that there are moral claims which both the law and the state are bound to respect.

With the Englishman came also his political habits. He was accustomed to living in a village or town having a certain autonomous and communal character—hence the incorporated New England township, with its 'town meeting' having authority over local affairs. He was a confirmed and practiced adherent of parliamentary government. Hence when Englishmen found it necessary or expedient to erect a state government they turned as a matter of course to the representative assembly or 'General Court.' In their struggles with their governors appointed from above, they were re-enacting the age-long controversy between Parliament and Crown. Constitutions were adopted before the middle of the seventeenth century which were, as regards popular sovereignty and the protection of individual liberties, anticipations of political democracy.

The effectiveness of institutions depends on the temper of the people who possess them—which brings us to the Englishman himself. Although disposed to accept the rule of law and disinclined to sudden and disorderly change, he was stubbornly insistent on his 'rights,' especially when he was animated by the spirit of frontier protestantism. He did not propose to be either exploited or patronized. He claimed what he considered his own, and was prepared to take what action might be necessary to secure it. Thus the essential Englishman, together with the social institutions to which he was habituated and tenaciously addicted, helped to prepare the way for American democracy.

This fact is quite consistent with the complementary fact that the temper of the English colonial society was on the whole conservative. An eminent historian has contended that because the American colonists were primarily insistent on the rights of Englishmen, they "contributed little or nothing to the cause of progressive liberalism or to the advancement of those democratic ideals that are a characteristic of the United States of America at the present time":

> Just what were the rights, immunities, and franchises of Englishmen at this time it would be difficult to state exactly. One thing, however, is quite clear: they were neither theoretical nor metaphysical but specific and concrete—rights that men were actually enjoying in England at the time. They were not the "liberty" but the "liberties"—quite a different matter—that Englishmen had won in the long years of their history and that concerned their position before the law, the titles to their lands, their freedom from arbitrary exactions, and the right of their representatives in parliament to certain privileges. . . . But whatever these rights were, they had nothing to do with democracy and represented nothing that was in advance of the age in which the colonists

lived. In our search for the conservative factors in our early colonial history we shall find nowhere any manifestations of democracy or even the suspicions of democracy in any form, any aspirations that anticipated future political ideals. any beginnings anywhere of an American mind.[6]

This judgment ignores the fact that the struggle for general rights is commonly motivated by their translation into particular rights. It fails to take account of the fact that the same temper of mind which prompted Englishmen to insist upon their specific legal rights qualified them to become the exponents of a liberalistic philosophy. Above all, it neglects the fact that the common law itself was impregnated with the 'theoretical' and the 'metaphysical.'

3

In preparing "the American mind" for the reception of the doctrines of the Declaration the law was a highly effective instrument. "What," said Alexander Hamilton, "is . . . the great body of the common law? Natural law and natural reason applied to the purposes of society." [7] John Adams said of James Otis, the famous Massachusetts lawyer and patriot:

> Otis . . . was . . . a great master of the laws of nature and nations. He had read Pufendorf, Grotius, Barbeyrac, Burlamaqui, Vattel, Heineccius. . . . It was a maxim which he inculcated on his pupils . . . *"that a lawyer ought never to be without a volume of natural or public law, or moral philosophy, on his table or in his pocket."* [8]

How the philosophy of the Enlightenment entered into the American conception of law, and how it there received confirmation and reflected the individualistic emphasis of puritanism and pioneer experience, is set forth by Roscoe Pound:

> Puritanism put individual judgment and individual conscience in the first place where the traditional modes of thought had put authority and the reason and judgment of the prince. This mode of thinking on religious and political questions entered into legal thinking during the contests between the courts and the crown in seventeenth century England. When the colonists

came to insist on the immemorial common law rights of Englishmen, as against the crown and Parliament, those rights were identified with the natural rights of man. Thus a continental philosophical theory got a concrete content of English law. The resulting tradition of legal thought was congenial to pioneer America. The pioneer was jealous of government and administration and had a rooted dislike of supervision. The conception of the common law as standing between the subject and the crown became in his mind one of the common law as standing between the individual and society.[9]

In his *Commentaries on the Laws of England* (1765-69), familiar to colonial students of law, Blackstone said:

> Man, considered as a creature, must necessarily be subject to the laws of his Creator. . . . This will of his Maker is called the law of nature. . . . This law of nature . . . is binding over all the globe . . . at all times: no human laws are of any validity, if contrary to this; and such of them as are valid derive all their force, and all their authority, mediately or immediately, from this original. . . . If any human law should allow or enjoin us to commit it [murder], we are bound to transgress that human law, or else we must offend both the natural and the divine.[10]

Both Otis and Blackstone relied on Locke; Otis also argued his case from Coke.[11]

Sir Edward Coke, who has been called "the greatest common lawyer of all time," [12] was the most redoubtable legal champion of Parliament against the pretensions of the Stuarts. In the name of the common law he fought the church, the admiralty, the Star Chamber, and even the royal prerogative—all with success. Referring to the pre-Revolutionary period, Jefferson wrote:

> Coke Littleton was the universal elementary book of law students, and a sounder whig never wrote, nor of profounder learning in the orthodox doctrines of the British constitution, or in what were called English liberties.[13]

The Petition of Right (passed by Parliament in 1628) was a chief source of the American 'Bill of Rights,' and this in turn was based on Coke's "Bill of Liberties." [14] To Coke the common law was based on natural, moral, and divine law. Here are his own words:

> And it appears in our books, that in many cases, the common law will controul acts of parliament, and sometimes adjudge them to be utterly void: for when an act of parliament is against common right and reason, or repugnant, or impossible to be performed, the common law will controul it and

adjudge such act to be void. . . . The law of nature is that which God at the time of creation of the nature of man infused into his heart, for his preservation and direction; and this is *Lex aeterna,* the moral law, called also the law of nature. And by this law, written with the finger of God in the heart of man, were the people of God a long time governed before the law was written by Moses who was the first reporter or writer of law in the world.[15]

Professor Edward S. Corwin has said:

The influence of higher law doctrine associated with the names of Coke and Locke was at its height in England during the period when the American colonies were being most actively settled, which means that Coke had, to begin with, the advantage since he was first on the ground. The presence of Coke's doctrines in the colonies during the latter two-thirds of the seventeenth century is widely evidenced by the repeated efforts of colonial legislatures to secure for their constituencies the benefits of *Magna Carta* and particularly of the twenty-ninth chapter thereof.[16]

It was Coke who was largely responsible for the revival of Magna Carta at the opening of the seventeenth century. In 1721 Benjamin Franklin's brother published in Boston a fifth edition of a little volume compiled by Henry Care, entitled *English Liberties, or The Free-Born Subject's Inheritance,* and containing Magna Carta with notes taken from "that Oracle of our Law, the Sage and Learned *Coke.*" Magna Carta, taken out of its original historical context, came to be regarded as a general charter of "English liberties," with emphasis on its famous twenty-ninth chapter:

No Freeman shall be taken or imprisoned, or disseised of his Freehold, or Liberties, or free Customs, or be outlawed, or exiled, or any otherwise destroyed, nor will we pass upon him, nor condemn him, but by lawful Judgment of his Peers, or by the Law of the Land. We will sell to no Man, we will not deny or defer to any Man, either Justice or Right.[17]

The American colonists were accustomed to the idea that the law of nature or of God should be 'engrafted' in their political constitutions, beginning with Magna Carta and the principles of the English constitution,[18] and extending to the charters and frames of government of the colonies. The 'rights of Englishmen,' although they had assumed the form of law, were felt to have in reason or in religion a sanction higher than the civil authority, and to be entitled to set limits to that authority. The Massachusetts Body of Liberties, adopted in 1641, affords a classic instance. The Preamble of that document contains the following paragraphs:

> The free fruition of such liberties Immunities and priveledges as humanitie, Civilitie, and Christianitie call for as due to every man in his place and proportion; without impeachment and Infringement hath ever bene and ever will be the tranquillitie and Stabilitie of Churches and Commonwealths. And the deniall or deprivall thereof, the disturbance if not the ruine of both.
>
> We hould it therefore our dutie and safetie whilst we are about the further establishing of this Government to collect and expresse all such freedomes as for present we foresee may concerne us, and our posteritie after us, And to ratify them with our sollemne consent.
>
> Wee doe therefore this day religiously and unanimously decree and confirme these following Rites, liberties, and priveledges concerneing our Churches, and Civill State to be respectively impartiallie and inviolably enjoyed and observed throughout our Jurisdiction for ever.[19]

Thus by the influence of lawyers, judges, and lawmakers the American mind was thoroughly impregnated with the idea of human rights which are prior to the commands of government, which are identified with the rule of God, which are revealed in reason and conscience, and which give to the human individual through his possession of those faculties a ground on which to impeach even a legislature of his own choosing. The 'higher law' was a meeting-place of legalism, of rationalism, of moralism, and of piety. Having prepared the mind of America for the Revolution, this idea was then embodied, not only in its professed creed, but in its constitutional theory and practice.

4

In political philosophy Americans had direct access not only to Locke but to Locke's antecedents, contemporaries, and followers near and remote. Acting under the neoclassical impulse of the eighteenth century, they read the Stoic doctrines in Cicero and in Seneca. The ancient orators and statesmen were quoted, Greek democracy and Roman republicanism were invoked as models. Through Richard Hooker they drew, as did Locke, upon the medieval doctrines of law eternal, divine, natural, and human. From two famous works of the sixteenth century, the *De Jure Regni* (1579) of George Buchanan, and the *Vindiciae contra Tyrannos* (1579),[20] they learned that men may rightly resist tyrants, that is, rulers who exceeded their limited constitutional powers. They were familiar with the Cambridge Platonists and the early deists.

Of seventeenth- or eighteenth-century writers, their libraries contained the works of John Milton, including his *Tenure of Kings and Magistrates* (1649), and his other prose writings. From James Harrington's *Commonwealth of Oceana* (1656) they borrowed many specific democratic ideas—the secret ballot, rotation in office, and compulsory education under state control. Montesquieu's great *L'Esprit des lois* (1743) was a guidebook for American framers of constitutions, and exercised a profound influence on Jefferson and other leading minds. The Swiss Emrich de Vattel's *Le Droit des gens* (1758) was a well-known popularization of the philosophy of natural law. More influential and widely read was Algernon Sidney, whose life and martyrdom made him a potent symbol. The following is from his *Discourses Concerning Government* (1698):

> *That which is not just, is not law; and that which is not law, ought not to be obeyed. . . .* [We] shall find that to be the law, which is founded upon the eternal principles of reason and truth, and not on the depraved will of man, which fluctuating according to the different interests, humours, and passions that reign in different nations, one day abrogates what had been enacted the other. The sanction therefore that deserves the name of a law, "which derives not its excellency from antiquity, or from the dignity of the legislators, but from intrinsick equity and justice," ought to be made in pursuance of that universal reason to which all nations at all times owe an equal veneration and obedience.[21]

It has been argued[22] that the Swiss publicist Jean Jacques Burlamaqui was responsible for the expression "pursuit of happiness" used by Jefferson in the Declaration of Independence, and that Jefferson was here opposed to Locke, who had spoken of "property." It is true that Burlamaqui was explicit in his insistence on the individual's claim to benefit from social institutions, and was peculiarly inclined to use the word 'happiness' to express the end of natural law. In his *Principles of Natural Law,* first published in 1747, he said:

My design is to inquire into those rules which nature alone prescribes to man, in order to conduct him safely to the end, which every one has, and indeed ought to have, in view, namely, true and solid happiness. By *happiness* we are to understand the internal satisfaction of the soul, arising from the possession of good; and by good, whatever is suitable or agreeable to man for his preservation, perfection, conveniency, or pleasure. The idea of good determines that of evil, which in its most general signification, implies whatever is opposite to the preservation, perfection, conveniency, or pleasure of man. . . . Right . . . is nothing else but whatever reason certainly acknowledges as a sure and concise means of attaining happiness, and approves as such.[23]

But Burlamaqui was not enunciating a new principle. If he had been an innovator he would scarcely have suited Jefferson's purpose of placing before mankind "the common sense of the subject," and of expressing "the American mind." That Burlamaqui was read and quoted by persons of importance, and that he may have influenced the framers of the Constitution in matters of detail, cannot be denied. But to say that in the "underlying philosophy of the Declaration of Independence Jefferson and Locke are at two opposite poles" [24] is to follow words rather than ideas.

Jefferson no doubt hesitated to include 'property' in the list of natural rights, because he thought of it as a civil right, protected by law.[25] Whatever may have been Jefferson's reasons for omitting 'property,' Locke's reasons for omitting 'pursuit of happiness' cannot be doubted. It is presupposed in his entire theory. It is implied in the beneficence of natural law, and in the meaning of beneficence. The individual's rights are his claims to happiness, or to the conditions of its pursuit and achievement. If Locke did not emphasize this in the *Second Treatise,* it was because he had said it so abundantly elsewhere.[26]

James Wilson of Pennsylvania, distinguished political leader and philosopher, wrote in 1774:

All men are, by nature, equal and free: no one has a right to any authority over another without his consent: all lawful government is founded on the consent of those who are subject to it: such consent was given with a view to ensure and to increase the happiness of the governed, above what they could enjoy in an independent and unconnected state of nature. The consequence is, that the happiness of the society is the *first* law of every government.[27]

To this passage Wilson appended a reference to Burlamaqui. In quoting the passage Professor Carl Becker remarks that this "sounds as if Wilson were making a summary of Locke"! [28] George Mason, author of the Virginia Bill of Rights (1776), found it natural to embrace both property and happiness in one list of rights:

All men are created equally free and independent, and have certain inherent natural rights, of which they cannot, by any compact, deprive or divest their posterity; among which are the enjoyment of life and liberty, with the means of acquiring and possessing property, and pursuing and obtaining happiness and safety.[29]

This was good Locke, good Jefferson, and good Burlamaqui, because it was the common doctrine of the times.

5

The minds of Americans, like the minds of Europeans, were prepared for the philosophy of the Enlightenment by their religious tradition. The clergy played an important role in spreading the revolutionary temper of mind and in popularizing the broad premises of American democracy. They could play this role not only because of the great influence of the pulpit as an agency of education and publicity, and because its occupants shared the patriotic fervor of the times, but because the Christian faith itself contained elements of agreement with the doctrines of the Declaration of Independence. An American who knew his Bible was familiar with the teachings of St. Paul:

For when the Gentiles, which have not the law, do by nature the things contained in the law, these, having not the law, are a law unto themselves: Which shew the work of the law written in their hearts, their conscience also bearing witness, and their thoughts the mean while accusing or else excusing one another.[30]

Catholics could and did rightly claim an affinity of doctrine with the Age of the Enlightenment. The conception of natural law was a recognized part of the scholastic teaching. Catholicism consistently refused to accept the supremacy of the state in matters of morals and conscience, so that there was an appeal from the civil authority,[31] which might, at least in principle, be invoked as a sanction of political revolution. Catholicism's conception of man was closer to the optimistic attitude of the Enlightenment than was protestantism's emphasis on human depravity. And Catholics, as a minority, were glad to avail themselves of the guarantees of religious liberty. On these and similar grounds leaders of Catholic thought in America repeatedly affirmed their accord both with the Declaration of Independence and with the Constitution.

On the other hand, although the state derived its authority from God, the Catholic God usually conferred authority on the established regime, and the Catholic Church was rarely a rallying-point for civil disaffection. Furthermore the Church was authoritarian in its own structure, and the tendency of ecclesiastical and civil polities to agree in their pattern here worked against democracy, rather than, as in the case of congregationalism, in its favor. More important than any or all of these points of doctrine was the fact that in the eighteenth century the struggles of the Reformation were still fresh in men's minds. Revolutionary agitators, such as Samuel Adams, who wished to inflame men against authority found it easy to revive the old hatred of the 'tyrannies' and 'superstitions' of the 'Romish' church, and patriotic protestant preachers found it natural and effective to identify the new political revolt against the King with the old ecclesiastical revolt against the Pope.

More than half of the signers of the Declaration of Independence were Anglicans, as were the members of the great Virginia dynasty. But this is to be explained not so much by the positive influence of Anglicanism, as by its mildness of discipline and liberality of doctrine. American Anglicans were so free from religious control as to be relatively susceptible to the secular and rationalistic influences of their day. Furthermore, the body of the revolutionary movement in the South was provided not by the Anglican planters but by the humbler folk of the dissenting sects. Anglicanism with its 'dregs of Romanism' suffered, like Romanism itself, from the prejudices excited by the religious wars. Anglican bishops were associated in tradition and in theory with Anglican kings, and the agitation for an American episcopate was resented as a step toward the extension to the colonies of a centralized ecclesiastical control.[32]

These suspicions were confirmed by experience. Many of the Anglican clergy "not only espoused the adverse side, but abandoned their flocks and their country." It is stated that when the British evacuated Philadelphia every clergyman of the Anglican church save one departed with them.[33] Even more palpable was the church affiliation of the class which represented and executed the hated tyranny from abroad. An American historian says:

> We must remember that all governors, lieutenant-governors, secretaries, councillors, attorneys general, chief justices, customs-officers—all colonial officers, in fact, who were appointed by the British government—were 'ruffle-shirted Episcopalians,' and attended the Anglican church.[34]

The popular emotional appeal of the evangelical sects tended to dignify the common man. The clergy were distinguished by their eloquence as preachers, rather than by their personal eminence. Authorities of every sort, intellectual, political, and ecclesiastical, were disparaged, and the rank and file of sinners or of souls-to-be-saved were exalted. The Methodists were avowedly Arminian, and held that God's offer of salvation was democratically open to all men. Baptists were for the most part professed Calvinists, and both the Baptist and the Methodist clergy turned for a justification of their revolutionary teachings to the theory of compact. But the revolutionary sympathies of the evangelical sects were due to social rather than to doctrinal causes. They belonged for the most part to the unprivileged classes, and they looked to their clergy for evangelical fervor rather than for intellectual guidance. Says Professor Corwin:

> Whitfield's doctrine was distinctly and disturbingly equalitarian. A spirit of criticism of superiors by inferiors, of elders by juniors ensued from it; while, at the same time the intellectual superiority of the clergy was menaced by the sudden appearance of a great crop of popular exhorters.[35]

But when account is taken of the Scotch-Irish presbyterians,[36] the Germans of the middle and southern colonies, and the New England congregationalists, it is safe to say that the bulk of the revolutionary armies came from dissenters of the reformed or Calvinistic sects.* From the clergy of these sects came also the religious leadership. If, therefore, we are to understand the religious impulse of the Revolution, we must examine the relation between puritanism, in the broad sense, and the democratic philosophy of the Enlightenment—both their opposition and their deeper bonds of agreement.

6

The transition from American puritanism to American democracy was at one and the same time a revolution and an evolution. As a revolution it represented the triumph of the Enlightenment over the Awakening of which the resurgent puritanism of Jonathan Edwards was an embodiment. Whereas puritanism taught men to rely on faith, revelation, and authority, and especially on the authority of the Bible as an authentic revelation of the will of God, the Enlightenment proclaimed the accessibility of truth, even basic truths of religion, to the faculty of reason.

Puritanism prolonged in America the medieval Christian view of the world and of human destiny. It taught men to distrust their natural inclinations as well as their natural faculties, and to find both their origin and their salvation in a supernatural order. It proclaimed a spiritual rebirth, and disparaged biological birth as a nexus of corruption. It was a cult of misanthropy, holding men to be irremedially tainted with sin unless healed by the miraculous and unmerited intervention of divine grace. This same harsh spirit was reflected, together with the principle of authority, in the puritan ethics—in its rigorism and legalism, and in its insistence on duty rather than on desire and love of the good.

* It is to be noted that over one-half of the "regulars enlisted for the Continental service from the beginning to the close of the struggle" were recruited, "equipped and maintained" by the New England states.[37]

The Enlightenment, on the other hand, was humane, optimistic, and eudaemonistic. The fact that Benjamin Franklin formulated maxims for conduct only served to accentuate the difference in the ultimate ground of moral appeal. The puritan maxims consisted largely in prohibitions, and were imposed by the will of God; the maxims of the new philosophy were recipes for success, discovered by common sense, and motivated by the end of happiness.[38]

There was a similar antithesis in the realm of political ideas. Emphasis on the sovereignty of God disposed puritans to the acceptance of a theocratic state which derived its sanction from above. The idea of election, according to which only a favored few, chosen for reasons known only to God, could hope for salvation, accustomed a puritan community to the idea of privilege, and hardened the hearts of the elite to the plight of the unfortunate. Richard Baxter, though with some slight qualms, had made this point clear a century before in his *Saints' Everlasting Rest:*

> The persons for whom this rest is designed, whom the text calls "the people of God," are "*chosen of God before the foundation of the world,* that they should be holy and without blame before him in love." That they are but a part of mankind, is apparent in Scripture and experience. They are the little flock, to whom "it is their Father's good pleasure to give the kingdom." [39]

A society of puritan believers was essentially intolerant. Ideas derived from authority were untroubled by doubt and imposed without qualms. Both for their own good, and for the well-being of the integral community, dissenters were, if not punished or exiled, at least saved from evil ways by emotional appeal and the pressure of public opinion.

Deism and latitudinarianism began before the close of the seventeenth century to pervade the colonies and to soften the temper of puritan piety, as well as the letter of puritan doctrine. Supernaturalism was attacked by science, dogma by rationalism, pessimism by optimism and humanitarianism, and the theocratic oligarchy by the rising forces of democracy. When, under the leadership of Jonathan Edwards, historical puritanism fought its last battle against the spirit of the new age, the difference between these two orientations of the human spirit was thrown into sharp relief. But the battle was already lost. Puritanism could not resist an opposition with which it had so deep a kinship. A leaven working within itself conspired with external forces to bring about a gradual transition rather than an abrupt reversal.

7

The deepest bond between puritanism and democracy was their common respect for the human individual irrespective of his place in any ecclesiastical, political, social, economic, or other institution. This individualism, with its far-reaching implications, modified every difference of method and doctrine.

While puritanism was authoritarian in its conception of God, the fact that the Bible was taken as the revelation of the divine will, and at the same time placed in the hands of every believer to read and interpret for himself, encouraged the individual to exercise his own wits. So long as he quoted Scripture he took high and unimpeachable grounds. He could always appeal directly to God against any human authority, whether church or state. This Biblical literalism did, no doubt, promote credulity and sanction the undisciplined vagaries of ignorance; but it taught the common man to conduct his own private search for truth, and to regulate his belief by the evidence presented to his own mind. This implied a corresponding intellectual capacity in human nature: truth was vulgarized, but, at the same time, human faculties were exalted.

This intellectual self-reliance favored the coalescence of puritan awakening and democratic enlightenment. In both cults there was a body of higher truths to which the individual might aspire through his own efforts. In both cults there was a popular ideology, the higher truths being the *plain* truths. And both cults stimulated popular education, because common men were assumed to have minds and encouraged to use them. Among the puritans religion itself was education. The minister, who must be a learned man, was a teacher; and the congregation was intellectually responsive, if only in matters of theology and Biblical exegesis.[40] The founding of Harvard College and of high schools by the New England puritans, and the gospel of public education proclaimed by Jefferson, were thus manifestations of a common impulse. Whether a man's business was the saving of his soul or the conduct of his temporal affairs, he must possess the requisite information and judgment. The puritan mind would have been favorably disposed to the general "objects of *primary* education," as set forth by Jefferson:

1. To give to every citizen the information he needs for the transaction of his own business.
2. To enable him to calculate for himself, and to express and preserve his ideas, his contracts and accounts in writing.
3. To improve, by reading, his morals and faculties.
4. To understand his duties to his neighbors and country, and to discharge with competence the functions confided to him by either.
5. To know his rights; to exercise with order and justice those he retains; to choose with discretion the fiduciary of those he delegates; and to notice their conduct with diligence, with candor and judgment.
6. And, in general, to observe with intelligence and faithfulness all the social relations under which he shall be placed.[41]

Although puritanism was other-worldly in its outlook and rigoristic in its ethics, it also justified man's attainment of wealth and earthly happiness. The thrift and the energy with which he pursued his 'calling' were evidence of his godliness, and were rewarded by this world's goods as well as by divine favor. Similarly, democracy affirmed the agreement of individual and universal happiness, the individual being so constituted that the enlightened pursuit of his own happiness was at the same time conducive to the happiness of others. Thus both cults provided a sublimation of worldly success. Both gave their blessing to the doctrine of laissez faire—that doctrine of painless piety by which a man may seek his own private gain and at the same time enjoy the comfortable assurance that he is best serving the will of God and the good of mankind at large.

An even more fundamental bond between the practical philosophy of puritanism and that of democracy was their respect for the dignity of man. In both cults the ultimate moral unit was the responsible individual, deserving of reward or punishment. Whether the good was conceived as the satisfaction of natural desires, or the mystical love of God, or the bliss enjoyed by the redeemed in another world, it resided in the individual's fulfillment. That the individual should be saved, whether from ignorance, poverty, and pain, or from the corruption of sin, was the meaning of history. The conception of progress through enlightenment, and the conception of a universe contrived expressly for a segregation of the saved and the damned, testified alike to the individual's high place in the design of the cosmos.

And at the same time that individuals were thus elevated they were equalized. As the appointed objects of God's creative and redeeming purpose—as souls to be saved—the saints were found not among the wealthy or the well-born, but among all classes, and especially among those whom this world despised. The same leveling tendency appeared in the puritan condemnation of luxury, vanity, and arrogance—as, for example, in Calvin's attack upon the "Libertines" of Geneva, and in the rejection by New England of hereditary rank, even when its acceptance would have brought men of substance to the colony.[42] This equalitarianism before God suited well the democratic conception of the equal title of all members of society to be its beneficiaries and the sources of its authority.

Turning to their political creeds, we find in puritanism and democracy a common acceptance of the principle of contract. The democratic state was conceived as a contract among human individuals by which they created a temporal authority and agreed to obey it; the puritan theocracy was a contract among believers by which they agreed to obey God. In both cases the contract was at one and the same time a bond among men and a bond between the aggregate of men and the ruling authority. The contract theory in both of its forms implied that obedience is based upon a quid pro quo. It commended itself to the individual's reason because he, qua individual, could translate it into terms of his own consequent happiness or salvation.

As congregationalists the puritans were inclined against monarchy, and habituated to representative or popular government. Although the minister might, and sometimes did, exercise a tyrannical authority, he did not derive that authority either from God or from St. Peter. He was in theory the choice of his congregation, an eminent individual of their own number, distinguished by his piety and learning rather than by his official status.

The democratic tendencies of congregationalism found fullest expression in the Separatists, whose zeal and impatience moved them to form independent and self-governing communities. "The thought of the Brownists," says Gooch, "was saturated with democratic feeling." [43] The Independents and 'Levellers' of Cromwell's England manifested the same tendencies. John Lilburne, the leader of the latter sect, wrote in 1646:

> God [created men and women] . . . by nature all equal and alike in power, dignity, authority, and majesty, none of them having by nature any authority, dominion, or magisterial power one over or above another; neither have they, or can they exercise any, but merely by institution or donation, that is to say, by mutual agreement or consent, given, derived, or assumed by mutual consent and agreement, for the good benefit and comfort each of other, and not for the mischief, hurt, or damage of any; it being unnatural, irrational . . . wicked, and unjust, for any man or men whatsoever to part with so much of their power as shall enable any of their Parliament-men, commissioners, trustees, deputies . . . or servants, to destroy and undo them therewith. And unnatural, irrational, sinful, wicked, unjust, devilish, and tyrannical, it is for any man whatsoever, spiritual or temporal, clergyman or layman, to appropriate and assume unto himself a power, authority and jurisdiction, to rule, govern or reign over any sort of men in the world without their free consent.[44]

The democratic spirit of Separatism was brought to New England by the Plymouth Pilgrims. The Massachusetts Bay Colony, on the other hand, explicitly repudiated both Separatism and democracy. John Cotton wrote in 1636: "Democracy, I do not conceyve that ever God did ordeyne as a fitt government eyther for church or commonwealth. If the people be governors, who shall be governed?" [45] But the leaven worked nonetheless. The democratic implications of congregationalism were more fully realized in Connecticut than in Massachusetts. Connecticut was at first and for more than a quarter of a century without a charter, and had to improvise its own instruments of government; and the relatively homogeneous character of the settlers made it expedient to broaden the base of political power and to give less control to the elders.[46]

The Fundamental Orders of Connecticut, drafted in response to a sermon delivered by Thomas Hooker before the General Court of

Hartford on May 31, 1638, has been referred to as "the first written constitution of modern democracy." [47] The Biblical injunction, "Take ye wise men, and understanding, and known among your tribes, and I will make them rulers over you," [48] was cited by Hooker with the emphasis on the 'taking' rather than the 'making'; and was interpreted as meaning "that the choice of public magistrates belongs unto the people, by God's own allowance." "They who have power to appoint officers and magistrates," he went on to say, "it is in their power, also, to set the bounds and limitations of the power and place unto which they call them"; because, in short, "the foundation of authority is laid, firstly, in the free consent of the people." [49]

The Reverend Mason L. Weems said, with characteristic eloquence, "Perhaps, God may be about to establish here a mighty empire, for the reception of a happiness unknown on earth, since the days of blissful Eden." [50] The writer was thinking in terms of the goal of democracy, and in terms of that ideology he should have spoken of the State of Nature. His mixture of metaphors may be taken as evidence of the likeness in difference between the puritan and the democratic conceptions of history.[51] The difference was further reduced by the puritan idealization of the primitive church, which had, like the democratic state of nature, been corrupted by the later abuses of tyranny.

In puritanism and the democracy of the Enlightenment there was the same sense of destiny felt by a group set apart to realize the moral purpose of the world; and in both cults that sense of destiny was nostalgic—the homing instinct of exiles from Paradise. In both cults man had fallen from grace: in the one case, through the abuses of institutional authority; in the other, through pride and the temptations of the flesh. In both cults that condition of man in which the circle is completed, and life ends as it began, was a condition of freedom: in the one case, the spontaneous exercise of reason and conscience; in the other, the fearless confidence of creatures in the Author of their being. In both cults man was originally endowed with the faculties requisite for his salvation, and by which he might be trusted to govern himself: he sprang into full realization at the dawn of his being, and required no slow and tortuous process of development. If in this doctrine there was a magnificent disregard of historical fact, both cults were guilty; and both were justified in the same manner and degree as having been blinded by a passion for perfection.

8

The predisposition of puritanism to democracy has been obscured in America by memories of the New England theocracy, with its doctrinal bigotry and its clerical oligarchy. It has been forgotten that Calvin himself through his insistence on the superiority of the spiritual to the temporal power was a political revolutionary, in theory as well as in act. He set the law of nature (or of reason, or of God) above the law of civil magistrates; he proclaimed the doctrines of natural right and contract; and in the name of these principles he defied political tyranny.

Through the habit of identifying Calvinism with its excesses posterity has lost sight of the close and continuous association between Calvinism and the ideas which constitute the basic creed of democracy. Because Roger Williams was persecuted by New England puritans, it is no longer remembered that Williams himself was a Calvinist. He was not a renegade, but a spiritual brother of the great company of liberal Calvinists which included the French Huguenots, William the Silent, the Dutch Arminians, Milton, and Cromwell; he was a cousin of the Cambridge Platonists, and of Calvinistic Anglicans such as Richard Hooker, so greatly esteemed by Locke.

The most significant symbol of this kinship is Locke himself. For if John Locke was the father of modern democracy, he was nonetheless a descendant of Calvin. "Through direct and indirect influences, both orthodox and liberal, Locke became," as a recent writer has expressed it, "a 'carrier' of Calvinism from the Reformation to the revolutions of 1688 and 1776." [52] He came of puritan stock; his early surroundings and his schooling were dominated by puritan influences. His eight years at Oxford fell in its Cromwellian period, and Louis du Moulin, Camden professor of history, whose lectures he attended, was a Dutch Huguenot. Ten later years of Locke's life were spent in France and in Holland in a Calvinistic environment. His sobriety, his philanthropy, his identification of duty with piety, his condemnations of luxury and vice, and his moralizing of social and political relations were all in the puritan tradition.

Thus when the puritan and other Calvinistic clergy of the colonies turned in the eighteenth century to Grotius, Milton, Sidney, Burlamaqui, and Locke, they were citing not only accepted authorities in political philosophy, but men of their own religious creed. It was not surprising that patriotism was preached from the pulpits, and that political agitators should have drawn their inspiration from puritan ministers.

In 1715 the Reverend John Wise, Harvard 1673, Congregational minister at Ipswich, Massachusetts, wrote his famous *Vindication of the Government of New-England Churches.* This was no mere transposition of ecclesiastical to civil forms, but a justification of the internal polity of congregationalism on fundamental grounds—on grounds which had their equally valid applications to political institutions.[53] Wise's argument was fully in the spirit of the Enlightenment, and its revolutionary and democratic political implications were not concealed.

> The first human subject and original of civil power is the people. For as they have a power every man over himself in a natural state, so upon a combination they can and do bequeath this power unto others; and settle it according as their united discretion shall determine. For that this is very plain that when the subject of sovereign power is quite extinct, that power returns to the people again. . . . It seems most agreable with the light of nature, that if there be any of the regular government settled in the church of God it must needs be a democracy. This is a form of government, which the light of nature does highly value, and often directs to, as most agreable to the just and natural prerogatives of human beings. . . .
>
> Also the natural equality of men amongst men must be duly favored; in that government was never established by God or nature, to give one man a prerogative to insult over another; therefore in a civil, as well as in a natural state of being, a just equality is to be indulged so far, as that every man is bound to honor every man, which is agreable both with nature and religion, 1 Pet. 2. 17. *Honor all men.* The end of all good government is to cultivate humanity, and promote the happiness of all, and the good of every man in all his rights, his life, liberty, estate, honor, &c. without injury or abuse done to any.[54]

A religious community accustomed to such ways of thinking needed no new argument, but only the appearance of the appropriate conditions, to support the cause of independence as well as the doctrines by which it was justified. Indeed, Wise's *Vindication* became an important revolutionary tract and earned for its author the title of "the first great American democrat." [55]

The invoking of the theological sanction for political revolution has been thus summarized by Professor Corwin:

> After the Bible, Locke was the principal authority relied on by the preachers to bolster up their political teachings, although Coke, Puffendorf, Sydney, and later on some others were also cited. . . . To the modern reader the difference between the Puritan God of the eighteenth century and Locke's natural law often seems little more than nominal. "The Voice of Nature is the Voice of God," asserts one preacher; "reason and the voice of God are one," is the language of another; "Christ confirms the law of nature" is the teaching of a third. . . . Reason has usurped the place of revelation, and without affront to piety.[56]

The voice of God, like the voice of nature, can be invoked in behalf of revolution: "The man who refuses to assert his right to liberty, property, and life, is guilty of . . . high treason against God." The people have a "sacred and inalienable Charter of the Almighty to . . . alter the Government under which they live." [57]

The Reverend William Jenks of Bath wrote in 1812 of "the zealous, benevolent and learned" Hollis, who had been a benefactor of the Harvard Library both before and after its destruction by fire in 1764:

> This truly *ingenuous* Englishman, in the range and direction of his literary beneficence, effectually refuted the seeming paradox, that a loyal subject of the monarchy in Britain might be an ardent and intelligent friend to the cause of freedom in America. The books he sent were often political, and of a republican stamp. And it remains for the perspicacity of our historians to ascertain what influence his benefactions and correspondence had in kindling that spirit, which emancipated these States from the shackles of colonial subserviency, by forming the "high minded men," who, under Providence, achieved our independence.[58]

It is possible that this writer like others overlooked the fact that the Hollis benefactor was a dynasty rather than an individual. Beginning with Thomas Hollis,* a London merchant who died in 1731, and con-

---

* It was this Hollis who founded two professorships at Harvard, and who, though of Baptist upbringing, attached no religious conditions to their incumbency.

tinuing through his younger brothers Nathaniel and John to Nathaniel's grandson, Thomas of Lincoln's Inn, who died in 1774, this family of Englishmen shipped books to the Harvard Library—some hundreds of books covering a wide range of subjects, and including the political and moral writings of Locke, Milton, Sidney, Harrington, Cudworth, Hutcheson, and Clarke.* Through these and other accessions the Harvard Library became a center of infection and promoted the development of a group of congregational clergymen whose Calvinism was so liberalized that it passed by insensible gradations beyond the line of orthodoxy into Arminianism and unitarianism, and merged with the optimistic and rationalistic temper of the Enlightenment.

This development was not so much a repudiation of Calvinism as the flowering of a certain Calvinistic strain which these clergymen recognized as their religious inheritance. They found a precedent not only in their great European forerunners, such as Milton, Sidney, and the Cambridge Platonists, but in the New England covenant theology. They did not deny revelation, but insisted, as did Locke, Clarke, and Hutcheson, on the essential harmony between revelation and reason, and could attack superstition and 'enthusiasm' in the spirit of the eighteenth century without renouncing the essentials of puritan piety.[59]

Ebenezer Gay, throughout the nearly sixty-nine years (1718-87) of his ministry in Hingham, Massachusetts, sought in every possible way to

---

* A letter from the younger Thomas conveys not only this extraordinary man's zeal for the spread of learning, but the likemindedness which bound the mother country to the colonies: "More books, especially on government, are going for New England. Should those go safe, it is hoped that no principal books on that FIRST subject will be wanting in Harvard College, from the days of Moses to these times. Men of New England, Brethren, use them for yourselves, and for others; and GOD bless you! . . . I confess to bear propensity, affection towards the people of North-America, those of Massachusetts and Boston in particular, believing them to be a good and brave people: long may they continue such! and the spirit of luxury, now consuming us to the very marrow here at home, kept out from them! One likeliest mean to that end will be, to watch well over their youth, by bestowing on them a reasonable manly education; and selecting thereto the wisest, ablest, most accomplished of men that art or wealth can obtain; for nations rise and fall by individuals, not numbers, as I think all history proveth."—A letter written about May, 1766, to the Reverend Jonathan Mayhew in Boston, and another of Oct. 1, 1766, to Edmund Quincy of Boston; both quoted by Francis Blackburne, *Memoirs of Thomas Hollis, Esq.*, 2 vols., London, 1780, Vol. I, pp. 319, 339-40.

break down the opposition between natural and revealed religion, or between reason and faith. He lived to pronounce the funeral sermon on his younger and more brilliant disciple, Jonathan Mayhew, of the West Church in Boston. To Mayhew, as to John Milton, religious piety and the secular struggle for liberty expressed the same fundamental impulse—"true religion, comprising in it the love of liberty, and of One's country." [60]

> Having been initiated, in youth, in the doctrines of civil liberty, as they were taught by such men as Plato, Demosthenes, Cicero and other renowned persons, among the ancients; and such as Sidney and Milton, Locke and Hoadley, among the moderns; I liked them; they seemed rational. Having earlier still learnt from the holy scriptures that wise, brave and vertuous men were always friends to liberty; that God gave the Israelites a king in his anger, because they had not sense and virtue enough to like a free commonwealth . . . and that "where the Spirit of the Lord is, there is liberty"; this made me conclude, that freedom was a great blessing.[61]

In his famous "Discourse Concerning Unlimited Submission and Non-Resistance to the Higher Powers" (1750),[62] occasioned by the anniversary of the execution of King Charles I, Mayhew defended the Puritan Revolution on grounds of reason and natural rights; and before his death in 1766 he had given open evidence, in both letters and sermons, of his firm adherence to that principle of resistance which later, under the leadership of his friends the Adamses, Otis, and Hancock, became the principle of revolt. In the Discourse referred to above, he said:

> We may very safely assert these two things in general, without undermining government: One is, that no civil rulers are to be obeyed when they enjoin things that are inconsistent with the commands of God. All such disobedience is lawful and glorious. . . . Another thing that may be asserted with equal truth and safety is, that no government is to be submitted to at the expense of that which is the sole end of all government—the common good and safety of society.
>
> To say that subjects in general are not proper judges when their governors oppress them and play the tyrant, and when they defend their rights, administer justice impartially, and promote the public welfare, is as great treason as ever man uttered. 'Tis treason, not against one *single* man, but the state—against the whole body politic; 'tis treason against common sense, 'tis treason against God.[63]

The most distinguished of this group was Charles Chauncy, Harvard 1721, and for sixty years the minister of the First Church in Boston. He united a liberalized puritanism with the philosophy of Hutcheson and Locke, and with praise of the light of reason:

> The plain Truth is, an *enlightened Mind,* and not *raised Affections,* ought always to be the Guide of those who call themselves Men; and this, in the Affairs of Religion, as well as other Things: And it will be so, where GOD really works on their Hearts, by his SPIRIT. . . . If we would act up to our Character as Men, or Christians, we must not submit blindfold to the Dictates of others; No, but we should ourselves examine into the Things of GOD and another World; Nor can we be too sollicitous, so far as we are able, to see with our own Eyes, and believe with our own Understandings.

To be sure, Chauncy added in a postscript: "Only in all our Inquiries of this Nature, let the Word of God be our Rule. This only may with Safety be depended on." [64] But "as it [civil order, or government] originates in the reason of things, 'tis, at the same time, essentially founded in the will of God. For the voice of reason is the voice of God." [65] Thus, living in New England at the time of the religious Awakening, of which he was a moderate defender, and at the same time stirred by the fresh breezes of the Enlightenment, Chauncy found it natural, first to prefer dogma to emotion, and then to prefer reason to dogma. He also found it natural and in line with his religious inheritance to become an ardent champion of the patriot cause in the war for independence:

> The Bostonians have always been as much disposed to honor and support constitutional government, as any of the people in England; and it is one of their greatest burdens that they should be brought into such circumstances, as to be even forced into that which is highly disagreeable to them; and if "the good order of Boston" has in any measure, been disturbed, the way to restore peace is to hear our cries, and redress our grievances. . . . Force may for a while keep the people under restraint; but this very restraint may, in time, be the occasion of the out-breaking of their passions with the greater violence; and what the consequence, in that case, will be, God only knows. . . .
>
> Even those who have been distinguished by being called the friends of government, are now fully satisfied, that the plan to be carried into execution, and by forcible measures, is, intire obedience to the demands of despotism, instead of those constitutional laws we are perfectly willing to be governed by. It may reasonably be esteemed an advantage, and a very im-

portant one, to be thus indisputably let into the knowledge of this; as, by knowing that forcing from us our rights and privileges as English subjects, is the grand point in view, we shall naturally be urged on to contrive expedients to prevent, if possible, our being in this way, brought into bondage.[66]

New England congregationalism recognized no barrier between pulpit and politics. James Otis drew inspiration from Mayhew. Samuel Cooper (1725-1783), another of the Harvard liberal group, and a member of the Harvard Corporation, was the intimate friend of John Adams, Benjamin Franklin, and John Hancock and exercised a potent influence on their political thinking.[67] He pleaded the revolutionary cause in his sermons as well as in articles written for the press.

We want not, indeed, a special revelation from Heaven to teach us that men are born equal and free; that no man has a natural claim of dominion over his neighbours nor one nation any such claim upon another; and that as government is only the administration of the affairs of a number of men combined for their own security and happiness, such a society have a right freely to determine by whom and in what manner their own affairs shall be administered. These are the plain dictates of that reason and common sense with which the common parent of men has informed the human bosom. It is, however, a satisfaction to observe such everlasting maxims of equity confirmed, and impressed upon the consciences of men, by the instructions, precepts, and examples given us in the sacred oracles; one internal mark of their divine original, and that they come from him "who hath made of one blood all nations to dwell upon the face of the earth," whose authority sanctifies only those governments that instead of oppressing any part of his family, vindicate the oppressed, and restrain and punish the oppressor.[68]

The political fame of Patrick Henry has obscured the fact that from his eleventh to his twenty-second year he listened to the patriotic sermons of the Reverend Samuel Davies, widely acclaimed as the most eloquent pulpit orator of his day. Davies was a Presbyterian minister of Hanover County, Virginia, and afterward the fourth president of the College of New Jersey (Princeton). He not only founded the first presbytery in Virginia but was "the animating soul of the whole dissenting interest in Virginia and North Carolina," [69] traveling widely, preaching in many pulpits, and vigorously defending the civil rights and liberties of nonconformists against the Anglican authorities. It is said that Patrick Henry adopted this preacher's oratory as his model, but he learned more than eloquence from an orator who taught that the British constitution is "the voluntary compact of sovereign and subject," and who exhorted his hearers "to secure the inestimable blessings of liberty." [70]

9

The political revolution must not be allowed to obscure the continuity of the continental environment. The newly enfranchised citizens of 1776 were still settlers in a newly discovered land. Under the influence of this common experience the bonds between puritanism and democracy were confirmed, and their differences were subordinated.

Since the publication in 1921 of F. J. Turner's *Frontier in American History* the title of that work has been used to embrace three distinct but related facts: contact with nature in the raw, the building of a new society, and the effects of dislocation upon the minds and habits of immigrants. It is clear that these ideas present only a part of the picture. The colonists were never wholly removed from their European environment; and as soon as they had effected a settlement, newcomers and later generations found in that settlement an established American environment. Because Turner, with the zeal of the innovator, presented a one-sided picture, later historians are now, with equal insistence, presenting the other side.* But the peculiarities of the frontier experience, and their profound influence upon the American character in its formative period, remain an indispensable part of the balanced truth.

The original settlers were not savages but small farmers, tradesmen, or gentry imbued with the traditions of contemporary Europe. Nor were they conquerors, acquiring possession of a pre-existing civilization. When they set foot on this continent they felt the impact of primeval nature—suffered its dangers and hardships, responded to its challenge, and exploited its resources. They were vividly aware of this 'wilderness'

* Such as the democratic impulses of the eastern seaboard, the labor movement, the capitalistic system, the plantation system in the South. *Cf.* Charles A. Beard, "The Frontier in American History," *New Republic,* Feb. 1, 1939, pp. 359-62.

in which their lot was cast; and in terms of this encounter they dramatized both their hardships and their providential opportunity.

The experience of the frontier was all-pervasive—spatially, temporally, and culturally. Beginning with the eastern seaboard, the frontier moved to the west and south: to the fall line of the rivers flowing into the Atlantic, to the Alleghenies, the Mississippi and Missouri rivers, the Rocky Mountains, and finally to the southwestern desert. Each of these regions was in succession a theater of life to those who occupied it, and a reserve of opportunity for those living in regions already settled. Each of these regions in turn witnessed successive phases of frontier evolution, from trapping, hunting, and fishing to cattle-raising, farming, mining, the building of railroads and cities, and the development of the arts. Thus every epoch in American history has had its frontier, every region has in turn been that frontier, and every community has its frontier memories.[71]

The profoundest effect of this influence was the emphasis on economic need and opportunity, reflected in the American attitude to nature. As societies grow mature, men's dependence on physical nature is decently veiled. The 'beasts of the field and fowls of the air' testify to the marvel and beneficence of creation. Forests, rivers, and mountains become symbols, and objects of poetic contemplation. The grove is "God's first temple"—"a pillar'd shade, high over-arched, and echoing walks between." The river is the symbol of time, or a "blue rushing of the arrowy Rhone." Mountains are "palaces of nature," "holy altars":

Alps on Alps, in clusters swelling,
Mighty, and pure, and fit to make
The ramparts of a Godhead's dwelling! [72]

But in America the poetry of nature has never eclipsed that other nature from which man has to wrest his title to exist. The most imperative task for settlers on virgin soil is to conquer nature and put it to use. Wild animals are dangerous intruders, or prey to be used for food and clothing; the forest a breeding-place of disease and a source of timber; the river a menace of flood, a convenience of navigation or irrigation, and a source of power; the mountain a formidable barrier and a store of mineral wealth. Thus in America the struggle for existence, beginning with a defense against hunger, hostile aborigines, and the rigors of climate, developed into aggressive exploitation and pursuit of wealth. Nature had first to be disarmed, and then, as man consolidated his gains and improved his instruments, harnessed to the service of multiplied desires.

This same priority of the economic interest lent dignity to manual work. In America, to be sure, it was the businessman rather than the laborer who came to hold the place of highest esteem. But the businessman was only the eminently successful laborer, in whom the impelling motive was shifted from defense to attack—from the satisfaction of need to the accumulation of resources. The businessman was one who worked with other people's hands instead of his own. The fundamental scale of esteem remained the same, the place of eminence being given to him who mastered the forces of nature.

The settler's economic preoccupation agreed with the mind of the puritan, who had been taught that the virtues of thrift and industry, by which he achieved success in his 'calling,' were evidences of piety. His success was felt as something superadded to his own efforts—being deserved and not merely caused. Believing that the merit of economic success lay in the moral qualities by which it was achieved rather than in the appetites to which it ministered, the puritan did not desist from his efforts in order to enjoy their fruits. The businessman was admired, not only as one who was 'self-made' and who 'earned his living,' but as one who died, as he had lived, in harness; for idleness and luxury are, at least in principle, as ungodly in age as in youth. Hence, with this puritan strain is connected that dogged determination with which the American continues indefinitely to exert himself and to postpone his reward.

The idea of 'opportunity,' perhaps the most American of all democratic ideas, derives its peculiar and untranslatable meaning from this context. Opportunity is given, not made; but it has to be seized, and not merely enjoyed; and it is elastic, yielding fruits proportional to effort and zeal. America became the field for the rising man, stimulating him, tempting him, and rewarding him; and the rising man was *any* man who, having the will, could find the way. Thus puritanism and revolutionary democracy, transposed to the frontier, were confirmed and reconciled.

10

The frontier has been a school of individual self-reliance. To appreciate its disciplinary effects it is necessary, in the first place, to recognize that the American Promised Land has never flowed with milk and honey. It has yielded its fruits reluctantly, being resistant, but not insuperable; selective, but not destructive. Humanly, as well as geographically, speaking, it has been temperate rather than either arctic or tropical.

To the cultivated visitor from abroad who compared the American with the European scene, and who lacked both the background of deprivation and the sense of present participation, the life of the American frontier contained little to commend it. Writing in 1842 of the region of St. Louis, Charles Dickens said:

> There was the swamp, the bush, and the perpetual chorus of frogs, the rank, unseemly growth, the unwholesome steaming earth. Here and there, and frequently too, we encountered a solitary broken-down waggon, full of some new settler's goods. It was a pitiful sight to see one of these vehicles deep in the mire; the axletree broken; the wheel lying idly by its side; the man gone miles away, to look for assistance; the woman seated among their wandering household gods with a baby at her breast, a picture of forlorn, dejected patience; the team of oxen crouching down mournfully in the mud, and breathing forth such clouds of vapour from their mouths and nostrils, that all the damp mist and fog around seemed to have come direct from them.[73]

The pioneer was exposed to attack by Indians, and was compelled to fight these enemies with their own weapons and with equal savagery. He was coarsened and even brutalized in the process. He battled with drought, with plagues of insects, and with barren soil; he suffered from disease, undernourishment, cold and heat, and heartbreaking disappointment. Especially tragic was the plight of the old, or of more gentle and sensitive souls, who were not only handicapped by physical disability, but filled with nostalgic longing for the life and friends they had left behind.*

---

* Such as Beret in O. E. Rölvaag's *Giants in the Earth* (Harper, 1927, pp. 32-38, 330-32) and old Mr. Shimerda in Willa Cather's *My Àntonia* (Houghton Mifflin, 1918, pp. 47, 98-99, 102, 115-16).

Those who migrated to the frontier carried few possessions, and lost touch with their places of origin. The cultural arts were not movable, nor could they be communicated from a distance along the slender and precarious threads of connection, by forest and stream, which then existed. Such trappings of civilization as found their way to the frontier —patent medicines, canned goods, or cheap ornaments—revealed by their very incongruity the essentially primitive character of frontier culture.[74]

The bitterness of the frontier experience has left an ineffaceable imprint on the American mind. It helps to explain that "American Malady" of joylessness, to which critics such as Langdon Mitchell have referred. Dickens said that the Americans "are not a humorous people." He observed their "dull and gloomy character"—their "prevailing seriousness and melancholy air of business." We now pride ourselves on our humor, and have, no doubt, acquired some "lightness of heart and gayety"; but the fundamental seriousness and air of business remain. Such qualities are perhaps less the effects of privation than symptoms of a discontent arising from unsatisfied ambition. When men are resigned to their lot they find compensations, and cultivate the art of happiness; harvesting what they can, however meager the crop.[75]

But while the frontier was a school of hardship, it was, broadly speaking, a profitable school. The frontier is not to be confused with the stagnant backwaters of American uplands, where a primitive culture was stabilized and hardship was unredeemed by hopefulness. The life of the frontier was charged with a sense of conquest and adventure. Whether hardship develops character or breeds despair depends on the relative preponderance between the adverse forces of the environment and the moral forces of man. In the long run the American pioneer was on the winning side. That it was a hard victory made it the more exhilarating, and enhanced the victor's sense of power. His social force was not institutional, but the sum of man added to man. Often he faced nature alone in physical remoteness and isolation; dependent on his own resources, he discovered that he possessed them. His experience of self-reliance confirmed the individualism inherent in both democracy and puritanism.

At the same time the ideal of social equality corresponded, as rarely in human history, with the actual state of affairs. When men moved to the frontier they left fixed social hierarchies behind. Stripped of the insignia of rank, they were thenceforth measured by their essential worth, as judged by the new conditions of life. And the sameness of their conditions was reflected in their uniformity of type. They shared a common vocation of labor or enterprise, passing readily from the one to the other through insensible gradations. Inequalities developed, but these were based on evident differences in intelligence or character, and were not great or rigid enough to create fixed cleavages of social status.

11

Political theorists who assumed a State of Nature, and explained institutional authority as a compact dictated by convenience, could cite America, since America provided numerous examples, as Locke said, of "men withdrawing themselves and their obedience from the jurisdiction they were born under . . . and setting up new governments in other places." [76] Pioneers started, socially speaking, with a clean slate. Their life together antedated their social organization. They organized themselves because, being without organization, they saw its need. The notion that social institutions are prior to individuals, being impersonal organisms or the products of immemorial growth, could have no relevance to this practice.

Parties of settlers migrating together across the continent were advised to convert themselves at once from a mere aggregation of chance arrivals into a political and legal entity:

> After a particular route has been selected to make the journey across the plains, and the requisite number have arrived . . . their first business should be to organize themselves into a company and elect a commander. . . . An obligation should then be drawn up and signed by all the members of the association, wherein each one should bind himself to abide in all cases by the orders and decisions of the captain, and to aid him by every means in his power . . . and they should also obligate themselves to aid each other, so as to make the individual interest of each member the common concern of the whole company.[77]

A typical agreement of this sort is described in the *Journal* of Silas Newcombe:

> At a meeting of a Company of Californians on the Banks of the Missouri, May 6th, 1850, the following Preamble and Resolutions were unanimously adopted:
>
> "Whereas we are about to leave the frontier, and travel over Indian Territory, exposed to their treachery and knowing their long and abiding hatred of the whites; also many other privations to meet with. We consider it necessary to form ourselves into a Company for the purpose of protecting each other and our property, during our journey to California.
>
> "*Therefore Resolved,* That there shall be one selected from the Company, suitable and capable to act as Captain or Leader.
>
> "*Resolved,* That we, as men, pledge ourselves to assist each other through all the misfortunes that may befall us on our long and dangerous journey.
>
> "*Resolved,* That the Christian Sabbath shall be observed, except when absolutely necessary to travel.
>
> "*Resolved,* That there shall be a sufficient guard appointed each night regularly, by the Captain.
>
> "*Resolved,* That in case of a member's dying, the Company shall give him a decent burial." [78]

All of the essential ideas of the compact theory are to be found here: the original unorganized multitude, the need of organization felt by each individual, the dedication to a common purpose, the voluntary and reciprocal promise to obey the common authority. This familiar experience, beginning with the Mayflower Compact of 1620 and repeated on various memorable occasions, disposed frontiersmen to a similar interpretation of the foundations of church and state.

Throughout its history American democracy has been distinguished by a ready resort to the method of free association for the meeting of common emergencies. And with this method of voluntary co-operation is associated the appearance of natural leaders. Not only were Daniel Boone, Davy Crockett, John Sevier, James Robertson, George Robertson, William Clarke, Sam Houston, and Andrew Jackson typical products of the frontier environment, but it was characteristic of frontier life that it should have found a use for them. Instead of appealing to established institutions and profiting by their prestige, the American has been traditionally accustomed to improvise his social mechanisms, multiplying them or allowing them to lapse as the situation may require.

The appeal to the aggregate judgment of individuals, rather than to the sanction of historic institutions, explains the powerful influence in American democracy of public opinion and sentiment. Its authority is direct, personal, and intrusive. The readiness of the individual to judge his fellows, the disposition of the mass of like-minded individuals to suspect and penalize every departure from type, and the creation of ad hoc organizations to 'prevent' this or 'promote' that, create the paradox so often remarked by European critics: that American democracy in tracing authority to the individual authorizes him to interfere with his neighbor, and thus tends to the suppression of individuality.

The frontier has been a school of manners, as well as of moral and political thought. The pioneer was a product of European civilization; transplanted to the frontier, he was decivilized rather than uncivilized. There was no fitness between his inheritance and his environment, and he lacked the graces not only of civilization but of a genuinely primitive or a peasant society. There was a disproportion between his human scale of living and the gigantism of forest, mountain, plain, and desert —a disproportion mitigated only by the audacity of his hopes for the future.

Those who, like Charles Dickens, applied a standard of European manners, found in the frontier society of 1842 that same lack of conversation and amenity which has been charged by later critics against the more developed phases of American life. He said of his fellow passengers on an Ohio River steamboat:

> Sitting down with so many fellow-animals to ward off thirst and hunger as a business; to empty, each creature, his Yahoo's trough as quickly as he can, and then slink sullenly away; to have these social sacraments stripped of everything but the mere greedy satisfaction of the natural cravings; goes so against the grain with me, that I seriously believe the recollection of these funeral feasts will be a waking nightmare to me all my life.[79]

A more discriminating critic would have found in the life of the frontier a sociability reflecting the pioneer's peculiar blend of origin and habitat. His reticences indicated the unpracticed tongue, and an inability to cope with novel social situations. If he turned to his plate, it was as much from embarrassment, suspicion, or the lack of conversational resources as from the grossness of his appetite. To inquiries regarding his health or prosperity, he might reply, "Jes' toler'ble. . . . We air makin' out—we air makin' out," * reflecting in his understatement that fear of committing oneself which is characteristic of men in uncertain social situations, or the superstitious dread of making a claim which might tempt the jealousy of fortune. At other times, an overhasty intimacy, contrary to certain canons of good taste, proclaimed his unappeased hunger for human relations and his dependence on the spontaneous co-operation of his fellows. To a frontiersman men were divided into three categories—friends, enemies, and strangers—and he had an attitude appropriate to each. He had no graduated scale of superiority or deference suited to highly differentiated relationships.

Being inexpert in the social art, the frontiersman was relatively helpless in the presence of social forces. He had neither immunity, nor a technique of defense. There is what might be termed a sociability of the unsocialized: a tendency of belief to take on an edge of fanaticism; the ready acceptance of panaceas; the rise of leaders known to the rest of the world as demagogues, but speaking to their followers with an accent of prophetic inspiration; a susceptibility to suggestion on the part of minds undisciplined in criticism, and devoid of certified knowledge. To the effects of inexperience should be added the morbid excesses begotten by loneliness and monotony.

The social characteristics of the frontier mind have appeared not only in the political and economic movements of the agrarian West, but in the multiplication of religious sects, and in periodic waves of revivalism. The experience of the frontier has thus transferred to American democracy certain of the traits of evangelical protestantism—a fervor of collective conviction, a crusading spirit, utopian enthusiasm, and emotional instability.

---

* Expressions attributed to mountaineers of eastern Tennessee by C. E. Craddock.[80]

12

Finally, the experience of the frontier confirmed that idea of destiny which, however differently construed, gave both to the puritan elect and to the founders of American democracy a sense of the special favor of Providence. Harriet Martineau wrote:

> I regard the American people as a great embryo poet, now moody, now wild, but bringing out results of absolute good sense: restless and wayward in action, but with deep peace at his heart; exulting that he has caught the true aspect of things past, and the depth of futurity which lies before him, wherein to create something so magnificent as the world has scarcely begun to dream of. There is the strongest hope of a nation that is capable of being possessed with an idea.[81]

The puritan looked for the proof of his election in his power to endure adversity and to triumph over obstacles. The American patriots of the eighteenth century felt themselves appointed to the historical role of creating permanent institutions which would serve as an instructive and hopeful example to the nations of the world. The conquest of nature and of territory, which, however great the cost, did in fact proceed steadily and triumphantly, served to verify both forms of faith. Sir Charles Elliot, the British diplomatic agent in Texas from 1842 to 1846, marking the westward penetration of the United States, said "they jolt and jar terrifically in their progress, but *on they do get.*" [82]

The territorial expansion of the new republic was so rapid that a man could measure it within the span of his own memory. He could *see* the wilderness brought under cultivation, and remote outposts become thriving cities. The Louisiana Purchase in 1803, the annexation of Texas in 1845, the definitive settlement of the Oregon country boundary in 1846, and the acquisition of California, Arizona, and New Mexico in 1848 were so many giant strides in this onward march.[83] Their occurrence in rapid succession created a sense of perpetual movement and of continental spaciousness.

It is not strange that men reared in the protestant tradition should have found confirmation of their faith in a special providence. The great river courses and varied natural resources seemed designed to link together and enrich the communities for whose advent they were waiting. Referring to the Mississippi, President Jackson wrote to Van Buren in 1829, "The God of the universe had intended this great valley to belong to one nation." [84] Whatever the place of his origin and whatever his racial extraction, the pioneer identified himself with this expansive force. He intermarried with his fellow frontiersmen and founded a new race. The new territories and states which sprang from the westward movement had no colonial past, and were thus wholly American in their memories and their collective sentiment. The pioneers felt a national identity, a national self-consciousness, and a faith in their national future.

The great discrepancy between the pioneer's vision of the future and his present imperfect attainment may account for that mixture of pride and "exquisite sensitiveness" remarked by Mrs. Trollope:

> Other nations have been called thin-skinned, but the citizens of the Union have, apparently, no skins at all; they wince if a breeze blows over them, unless it be tempered with adulation. . . . So deep is the conviction of this singular people that they cannot be seen without being admired, that they will not admit the possibility that any one should honestly and sincerely find aught to disapprove in them, or their country.[85]

It is not strange that the American should have earned and justified a reputation for boastfulness. The frontiersman, like the Homeric warrior and Bedouin Arab, made an art of boasting. He boasted, as it is profoundly natural to boast,[86] as a means of keeping up his courage, and of flooding himself with militant emotion. But he boasted also as a man boasts in the midst of conquest, when he not only feels invincible strength but sees its palpable results in victories already earned. Hence the characteristic American disregard of 'reality,' his contempt for precedent, and his assured conviction that all things are possible when the liberated human faculties are supplemented by abundant opportunity and by the approving will of God.

That this sense of a 'manifest destiny' should have expressed itself in quantitative terms, and that Americans should have boasted of size, of speed, of numbers, and of wealth, was inevitable. Material goods were idealized by their very magnitude. Anything done on a large scale, whatever it might be, acquired a certain dignity from that fact. "The bigness of it all!" exclaims a character in Robert Herrick's *Memoirs of an American Citizen.* "The one sure fact before every son and daughter of woman is the need of daily bread and meat. To feed the people of the earth—that is a man's business." [87]

The growth of America made quantity dramatic. But whether interpreted in puritan or in democratic terms, that quantitative growth was taken as evidence of the essential soundness of American institutions. The role of America was not merely to flourish and expand, but to realize through physical greatness the ideal of civic righteousness. Thus at the time of the annexation of Texas, the boast was not of mere territorial aggrandizement: "The march of the Anglo-Saxon race is onward. They must, in the event, accomplish their destiny—spreading far and wide the great principles of self-government, and who shall say how far they will prosecute the work?" [88]

13

The philosophy of the Declaration of Independence was thus not only familiar to colonial Americans as the common thought of their times, set forth in the books they read, in the speeches and sermons which they heard, and in the tradition which they shared, but *congenial* because of their peculiar experience. However it has seemed to later ages, to Americans of the eighteenth century this philosophy was not doctrinaire. The circumstances of their lives attested the state of nature, if not, as to distantly admiring Europeans, in its idyllic aspect, at any rate in its priority to civil institutions. When the colonies took steps "to dissolve the Political Bands which have connected them with another," they felt that they were renewing the state of nature until such time as they should create new bands among themselves. As Patrick Henry said to the first Continental Congress:

> Government is dissolved. . . . Where are your landmarks, your boundaries of Colonies? We are in a state of nature, sir. . . . The distinctions between Virginians, Pennsylvanians, New Yorkers, and New Englanders, are no more. I am not a Virginian, but an American.[89]

Americans felt themselves to be men of principle dwelling in a wilderness. It seemed to them that their institutions could be suspended without depriving them of their human faculties. They found themselves compelled to make new institutions, with a full consciouness of the benefits to be obtained and the rights to be protected.*

Experience taught Americans that settled society could be dismembered without the destruction of its members, and that an individual could pass out of old societies into new without loss of identity—that society, in short, was an organization rather than an organism. Being palpably successful in their conquest of nature and in their creation of a new state, they felt a confidence in the essential rightness of things. Their religion tended to be disengaged from elaborate ritual, ecclesiasticism, and dogma, and to be identified with gratitude to a purposeful and indulgent God. As self-reliant, co-operative individuals, competent to build their own several futures in an environment which provided room for all, they were predisposed to feel their equality, and to assume a harmony between self-interest and the general good.

---

* "Courts and judges found themselves called upon to make law for the occasion with little else to guide them except the Bible, the precepts of natural law or natural justice, and the community sentiment of what ought to be right and just." [90]

Part Two

APPRAISAL OF PURITANISM

CHAPTER NINE

THE IMPORTANCE OF SALVATION

1

An examination of the reading of the New England and Virginia colonists of the seventeenth century reveals a dominant tone of seriousness. If George Herbert's lines

> *Religion stands on tiptoe in our land*
> *Ready to pass to the American strand*

do not tell the whole story, they sound the keynote of this great migration. Its leaders intended to create a planned and purposeful society, taking account of man's stake both in this world and in the life to come. They did not confine themselves to religious literature such as Arthur Dent's *The Plaine Mans Path-Way to Heauen* or Lewis Bayly's *The Practice of Piety*, but whatever the content, whether science, agriculture, belles-lettres, ancient classics, manners, or general information, the accent was on self-improvement and methodical living. "Instead of idle and frivolous reading matter, the counsellors of our seventeenth century ancestors prescribed good books to 'bob vs continually on the elbowe,' and to 'importune vs to well doing.' " *

A highly saturated puritan life is marked by its preoccupation with religion. When a puritan of the great puritan days wrote his autobiography, he wrote his spiritual autobiography, as containing what was most worth recording. Here, for example, are incidents from "The Life of Dr. Thomas Goodwin," who was president of Magdalene College from 1650 until the Restoration:

* I owe the above citations to Louis B. Wright, "The Purposeful Reading of Our Colonial Ancestors," *Journal of English Literary History,* June 1937, p. 90 and *passim.* This admirable and entertaining article gives an exceptionally rounded picture of the seventeenth-century colonial mind.

I began to have some slighter Workings of the Spirit of God, from the time I was six Years old; I could weep for my Sins, whenever I did set my self to think of them, and had Flashes of Joy upon thoughts of the Things of God. . . .

When I was past twelve Years old towards thirteen, I was admitted into *Christ's College* in *Cambridge*. . . . And that which now, since I came to that College, had quickened and heightened my Devotion, was, that there remain'd still in the College six Fellows that were great Tutors, who professed Religion after the strictest sort, then called Puritans. . . . These Puritan Fellows of that College had several Pupils that were Godly, and I fell into the Observation of them and their Ways. . . .

When I was one day going to be merry with my Companions at *Christ's College*, from which I had removed to *Katherine Hall;* by the way hearing a Bell toll at St. *Edmunds* for a Funeral, one of my Company said there was a Sermon, and pressed me to hear it. I was loth to go in, for I lov'd not preaching, especially not that kind of it which good Men used, and which I thought to be dull stuff . . . they told me it was Dr. *Bambridge,* which made me the more willing to stay, because he was a witty Man. . . . He spake of deferring Repentance, and of the Danger of doing so. Then he said that every Man had his day, it was, *this thy day*, not to morrow, but to day. . . .

So God was pleased on the sudden, and as it were in an instant, to alter the whole Course of his former Dispensation towards me, and said of and to my Soul, Yea live, yea live I say, said God: and as he created the World and the Matter of all things by a Word, so he created and put a new Life and Spirit into my Soul, and so great an Alteration was strange to me. . . . This speaking of God to my Soul, altho it was but a gentle Sound, yet it made a noise over my whole Heart, and filled and possessed all the Faculties of my whole Soul. . . .

I observed of this Work of God on my Soul, that there was nothing of Constraint or Force in it, but I was carried on with the most ready and willing Mind, and what I did was what I chose to do . . . the most eminent Property of my Conversion to God . . . was this, That the Glory of the great God was set up in my Heart, as the Square and Rule of each and every particular Practice, both of Faith and Godliness, that I turned unto. . . . I fixed upon this summary of my whole Life, that I had made Lusts and Pleasures my only end, and done nothing with aims at the Glory of God: and therefore I would there begin my turning to him, and make the Glory of God the measure of all for the time to come.[1]

To an eminent believer such as Thomas Goodwin puritanism was no dogma or external observance, but a certainty founded on experience. Sin and salvation, despair and faith, soul-sickness and cure, human inability and the miracle of divine grace, were facts more incontrovertible than any others that he knew. Of a certain "Mr. *Price* of *Lyn*" Thomas Goodwin said that he was "the greatest Man for experimental Acquaintance with Christ, that ever he met with." [2] Goodwin himself was master of the physiology of the spirit. Human life presented the alternative between a highest good and a lowest evil—a hope of the one and a risk of the other; and this highest good and lowest evil outweighed all the goods and evils of the natural appetites and of worldly achievement. He sensed this awful parting of the ways. Like a man awakened from nightmare he felt himself, to his unspeakable relief, carried to safety from the very brink of the abyss.

To one who does not share his preoccupation the puritan seems to be obsessed with religion. But since the term 'obsession' implies that the matter is not worthy of the attention which it receives, and thus begs the question, it is better to say of the puritan that religion is his profoundest interest, underlying and pervading all his other interests. It found its way, for example, into almost every letter written by Oliver Cromwell, whether to his family, to his friends, or to his collaborators, and into whatever other matters occupied his attention.* This was not a literary affectation, any more than it is an affectation for an arctic explorer to refer to the weather. Jonathan Edwards wrote of a Christian's "practice of religion":

> It may be said, not only to be his business at certain seasons, the business of Sabbath-days, or certain extraordinary times, or the business of a month, or a year, or of seven years, or his business under certain circumstances; but the *business of his life*.[4]

To an unusual degree the puritan *made* religion his business; and when in his correspondence and journals he set down the events of the day, it took the leading place. In another age, when matters of religion are rarely alluded to and the religious vocabulary has fallen into disuse, this habit of discourse is sometimes found distasteful. It is not, however, a question of form or propriety, but of what actually fills the mind and gives the dominant tone to experience and thought.

---

* For Cromwell's characteristic intermixture of affairs, humor, personal affection, and piety, *cf.* his inimitable letter to Richard Mayor, July 17, 1650.[3]

The puritan was distinguished by his preoccupation with good and evil, in a disjunctive and catastrophic sense. But it is quite false to suppose that this preoccupation laid greater emphasis on evil than on good. Puritanism, like all Christianity, extolled a greatest good and at the same time condemned its converse evil. A gospel is a way of salvation; but to be saved implies that there is some condition of misery or privation from which to be saved, as well as a positive state of fulfillment and joy in which salvation consists. There is a danger, and there is an opportunity; and the preaching of the gospel may take the form either of a warning against the one or of an invitation to the other. Which form it shall take in any given situation will depend on the extent to which the need of salvation is consciously felt. A man in acute pain does not need to be persuaded of evil, and will listen eagerly to the glad tidings of good; a man who suffers from a hidden disease, or who, finding his half-life tolerable, does not understand how much more alive he might be, will need first to be alarmed before he is willing to send for the physician. Both forms of evangelism appear throughout the history of Christianity: the gospel of hope, preached to suffering, fear, bereavement, despair, or futility; and the gospel of sin, preached to complacency and shallow optimism.

The reputation of puritanism has suffered from emphasis on the negative rather than the positive aspect of its gospel. Its historians and critics have, as a rule, been worldlings to whom its alarming diagnosis, however true, has been unwelcome. But such an emphasis is false. It is false to the fundamental meaning of religion: a gospel or evangel is *good,* not bad, tidings. It is false to the historical meaning of puritanism, because man's evil condition was a 'fall' which could be understood only in terms of his original eminence—"Adam's felicity in innocency," as a famous Plymouth Pilgrim expressed it.[5] The state of sin was a depravity, a corruption, a degeneration, a banishment, a disinheritance, a forfeiture, the evil of which lay not in its intrinsic painfulness or repugnancy but in the loss of good. The quality of the evil followed from the quality of the good; the degree of the evil was proportional to the greatness of the good.

Since Jonathan Edwards is so often used to document the hell-fire version of puritanism, let us turn to him for further illustration. He did, it is true, depict men as hanging "over the pit of hell" and bade them "haste and escape" for their lives, lest they be consumed.[6] But the full account—fear *and* hope, fear of losing the promise of hope—appears in his description of the revival in Northampton, Massachusetts, in 1735 and 1736:

> Presently upon this, a great and earnest concern about the great things of religion, and the eternal world, became *universal* in all parts of the town, and among persons of all degrees, and all ages. . . . But although people did not ordinarily neglect their worldly business; yet *religion* was with all sorts the great concern, and the *world* was a thing only by the bye. The only thing in their view was to get the kingdom of heaven, and everyone appeared pressing into it. The engagedness of their hearts in this great concern could not *be hid,* it appeared in their very *countenances.* It then was a dreadful thing amongst us to lie out of Christ, in danger every day of dropping into hell; and what persons' minds were intent upon, was to *escape for their lives,* and to *fly from the wrath to come.* . . . Our *young people,* when they met, were wont to spend the time in talking of the *excellency* and dying *love* of JESUS CHRIST, the glory of the way of *salvation,* the wonderful, free, and sovereign grace of God, his glorious work in the *conversion* of a soul, the *truth* and certainty of the great things of God's word, the sweetness of the views of his *perfections,* &c. . . . Those amongst us who had been formerly converted, were greatly enlivened, and renewed with fresh and extraordinary incomes of the spirit of God. . . . Many who before had laboured under *difficulties* about their own state, had now their *doubts* removed by more satisfying experience, and more clear discoveries of God's love.[7]

I would not obscure Edwards's emphasis on the rigors of God's punitive justice. But Edwards himself was aware of the need of preserving a balance between justice and love. And if Edwards's system be taken as a whole, or puritanism be considered in its total meaning, it is clear that the key to the nature of evil can be found only in the nature of good.

2

What, then, was the puritan conception of that 'pearl of great price' which was so good that its loss was the worst of evils? All agree that this pre-eminent good was the love of God. But there are two false interpretations of this good which have first to be set aside—misinterpretations which are customary among unregenerate critics of puritanism, and appeal to the residual unregenerateness of puritans themselves. According to the first, God's love is the one indispensable and all-sufficient means by which a man can satisfy his present natural appetites and worldly ambitions. According to the second, God's love is a spatio-temporal projection and enlargement of natural and worldly goods: heaven is their enjoyment in a celestial region after death; hell is a suffering of their opposites in the 'abyss'; both being endlessly prolonged.

Now while these interpretations were frequently employed as means of adapting higher truths to lower grades of understanding, and while professing Christians have often failed to pass beyond them, there can be no doubt whatever that they are false. The good which was proclaimed in the puritan-Christian gospel was a transformation, and not a mere transposition, of natural and worldly goods; it did not guarantee and extend them, but superseded them. It was a joy, a sweetness, and a glory, sui generis. It may, I think, be justly objected that puritanism through its inordinate desire to emphasize the *super*natural and *other*-worldly dignity of the good, falsely abstracted it from nature and the world. But this objection cannot be entered on the debit side of the account until puritanism is first credited with affirming the idea of a supreme good to which natural and worldly goods were, if not alien, then at any rate subordinate.

This supreme good, or 'salvation,' consisted in a direct and reciprocal relation of man to God—a rebirth of man through love of God into the likeness of God. This was Oliver Cromwell's "sum of all," taken from Scripture and communicated to his son Richard.[8] "What is the chief end of man? Man's chief end is to glorify God, and enjoy Him forever" [9]—so runs the catechism, designed to give the plain Christian answer to precisely the question before us, and designed to summarize the Christian creed and rule of life.* Still more authoritative was Christ's "first and great commandment": "Thou shalt love the Lord thy God

---

* This and all the authoritative catechisms of the day, Roman and protestant, date from the sixteenth and seventeenth centuries, but the catechetical tradition and the substance of its teachings go back to the early centuries of the Christian era.

with all thy heart, and with all thy soul, and with all thy mind." If one looks beyond the record of puritan experience and practice to the systematic thought of puritan philosophy, one finds the same doctrine in Jonathan Edwards. There is an "end for which God created the world," by which all beings compose a perfect harmony. To enjoy this harmony, to contemplate its intellectual coherence, to feel its aesthetic beauty, to participate in its universal agreement of wills, and so to love its Author—this is the supreme good which excels every earthly felicity.[10]

3

So far, then, puritanism is the vivid affirmation, at once emotional, practical, and intellectual, of a supreme good, conceived in terms of man's immediate enjoyment of God. To the specifically theological and metaphysical aspect of salvation we shall return in a later chapter. In the remainder of the present chapter, and in the chapters that follow, we shall be concerned with its moral aspects—its meaning in terms of the puritan's personal and social life, and stripped, so far as possible, of dogmatic technicalities.

Salvation was conceived by the puritan as an effect of faith and grace rather than of works or merit. This may be construed to mean that the goodness of the love of God has to be known, if it is to be known at all, by him who tastes it for himself. Being untranslatable into concepts, it cannot be anticipated or demonstrated by reason. It is as inaccessible to the man without the specific experience as is red to the man who is color-blind. In the one case as in the other it is first necessary to cure a defect of sensibility. Pending such a cure, the felt quality of the good has to be taken on faith, in the sense that its proper evidence is not as yet presented. Its appreciation is conditioned by an act of humility—a submission, and not an assertion, of the mind. To be saved a man must purge himself of arrogance, precisely as does the self-denying student of nature, with, however, this difference: that whereas the student of nature need anticipate experience only by hypothesis, the seeker after God must first *believe* in him. And when God reveals himself there occurs at one and the same time not only an intellectual verification but also, since God is felt as good, an alteration of the will and emotions. This change of heart is the work of 'grace.'

Here in theological guise is the basic moral truth that the supreme goodness of universal love cannot be deduced from, or reduced to, any other terms. As immediate, it cannot be represented in idea, but must be felt; as universal, it cannot be reduced to any narrower love. It will not move a man in terms of any other motivation. It cannot be grafted on self-love, or on familial or national love; it will not live unless it springs from its own independent roots. If these roots have died, then their seed must be replanted. There must be a transformation effected in the soul by a revolutionary experience of good: life being newly oriented, all of its elements shift their positions and assume a new order.

Human inability means that perfected character cannot be achieved by a man who does not yet love God; and the 'irresistibility of grace' means that when that love has become his master motive, his perfection follows as an inevitable consequence. The rejection of 'works' means that a man cannot earn salvation, or attain it by merit, because being a good of a higher order, no accumulation of lesser goods can be considered its equivalent. The highest good is not a payment to man for value received, but is, as judged by any other standard than itself, a complete gratuity.

It is clear, however, that the complete denial of man's participation in his own salvation was impossible. Man was created in the divine image, and the sin of Adam, while corrupting human nature, did not obliterate its essential faculties. Even in the fallen man there were traces of divine kinship, and the very wrath of God testified to human responsibility. It is impossible, on general Christian premises, to deny that man is *capable* of regeneration; and the grace of God could never, therefore, be a complete miracle or a tour de force. Furthermore, the state of faith itself was in some sense a human achievement, which was ardently and methodically sought. It follows that the difference between the optimistic and the pessimistic views of man was a relative and not an absolute difference. Between the 'flamboyant humanism' of the Renaissance, which glorified genius and heroism, and the protestant insistence on original sin and total inability, there were intermediate degrees, such as the "*humanisme dévot*" of the Catholic François de Sales, who found, even in the humblest and most sinful, an "*inclination naturelle à aimer Dieu sur toutes choses.*" [11] If man is originally good, and retains a capacity for goodness while at the same time depending on grace for its recovery and realization, then there is an option of emphasis. Puritanism represents the perennial need of the harsher view of human nature as a corrective of the too indulgent.

4

The most important corollary of the idea of a supreme good is the idea of a hierarchy of value, in which lower evils are outweighed by higher goods, and lower goods by higher evils. This is an indisputable moral principle, by no means peculiar to puritan dogma. It is implicit in the preference of future to present goods, of the durable to the transitory, the universal to the particular, the total to the partial, or the important to the trivial. It is the principle of moral statesmanship, as opposed to mere opportunism. It was summarized as follows by Richard Hooker, perhaps the greatest of the protestant critics of puritanism:

> In which kind axioms or principles more general are such as this, "that the greater good is to be chosen before the less." If therefore it should be demanded what reason there is, why the Will of Man, which doth necessarily shun harm and covet whatsoever is pleasant and sweet, should be commanded to count the pleasures of sin gall, and notwithstanding the bitter accidents wherewith virtuous actions are compassed, yet still to rejoice and delight in them: surely this could never stand with Reason, but that wisdom thus prescribing groundeth her laws upon an infallible rule of comparison; which is, "That small difficulties when exceeding great good is sure to ensue, and on the other side momentary benefits when the hurt which they draw after them is unspeakable, are not at all to be respected." [12]

Puritanism denied none of the implications of this principle, but laid special emphasis on its application to evil. Pain and worldly privation, though evils on the lower level, are as nothing to men who achieve the greater good of salvation. Similarly, there is no profit in natural or worldly gain if a man lose his soul. This plain truth was set forth in allegorical form in Bunyan's *The Pilgrim's Progress.* In the House of the Interpreter Christian meets two little children, Passion, who "seemed to be much discontented," and Patience, who "was very quiet." Christian wants to know the reason for Passion's discontent, and receives the following explanation:

> These two lads are figures: Passion, of the men of this world; and Patience, of the men of that which is to come; for, as here thou seest, Passion will have all now this year, that is to say, in this world; so are the men of this world: they must have all their good things now, they cannot stay till next year, that is, until the next world, for their portion of the good. . . . But as thou sawest that he had quickly lavished all away, and had presently left him nothing but rags; so will it be with all such men at the end of this world. . . . Therefore Passion had not so much reason to laugh at Patience, because he had his good things first, as Patience will have to laugh at Passion, because he had his best things last; for first must give place to last, because last must have his time to come; but last gives place to nothing, for there is not another to succeed. He, therefore, that hath his portion first, must needs have a time to spend it; but he that hath his portion last, must have it lastingly.[13]

5

If life is to be regulated by a hierarchy of value, the sense of evil must be quickened. This does not mean that evil itself is to be increased, but that its existence must be more fully and more vividly realized as the first condition of its being remedied. For evil may be ignored. A man may choose to forget the evil of tomorrow in order to enjoy more fully the pleasure of today. The first condition of prudence is to look these remoter and unwelcome evils in the face. Similarly, a man may through the accident of his station be innocently unaware of the misery that lies all about him in the lives of others. Or, having caught a fleeting glimpse, he may shut his eyes to it because he finds it painful and disturbing. The first condition of social reform is a lively sympathy by which the full volume of human suffering and privation is seen, and held firmly before the mind.

Puritanism is rightly associated with another discovery of evil, the discovery, namely, of the real evil of apparent good. That which leads man to ignore evil of the higher level is not so much its own repellent aspect as the seductiveness of lower good. It is quite true that, having caught a glimpse of hell, a man may for his peace of mind prefer to forget it. But puritanism is not so much concerned with this danger of repression, which implies at least a repugnance to the higher evil. The more insidious danger is that men shall be so satisfied with the lesser goods which they have as to neglect the greater evils to which they are unsuspectingly exposed. The horrors of hell, so laboriously and excruciatingly depicted in Christian painting, sculpture, and literature, and so terrifyingly driven home by all the arts of evangelical eloquence; the legend of satanism, peopling the world with devils, and having through the spiritistic imagination an effect so conducive to superstition and so fatal to science—both have a moral root in the need of alarm.

6

To understand these rhetorical developments, and to appraise them with due regard to their grain of truth as well as their errors of emphasis and exaggeration, it is necessary to examine without prejudice the question of temptation, by which is meant the higher evil implicit in the attractiveness of lower goods. The Devil is the Tempter. It is essential to his role that he should attract. He does not make evil manifest, but disguises it as good. He seduces men from God, that is, from their highest good; but he does so by substantial gifts and promises.

That there is a real evil in apparent good cannot be denied. Under the universally accepted code of prudence, temptation takes the form of the immediate satisfactions of appetite. These absorb the attention, and govern the will and emotions, at the cost of the higher good of total and lasting happiness. The thing most needful for regeneration on this lowest moral level is to regard physical indulgence as evil—as evil, namely, in the higher sense of imprudence. The effect of such an increased tenderness of conscience is to destroy a primitive sense of innocence, and substitute a sense of guilt. This increase of the area of felt evil is not the fault of the puritan, though it is often urged against him. It is dictated by an unfortunate aspect of life which the puritan should not be charged with inventing, but rather praised for recognizing.

To admit so much, and place it to the puritan's credit, does not absolve him from the errors into which, as the extreme exponent of this truth, he is likely to fall. Among these besetting and characteristic errors there are two which, being first noted here, will constantly reappear in the critique of puritanism.

In the first place, the fact that physical pleasures are temptations to imprudence obscures the fact that they are, within limits, good. "And these Lusts," said Thomas Goodwin, "I discern'd to have been acted by me in things that were most lawful, answerably unto that Saying in Scripture, *The very plowing of the Wicked is Sin.*"[14] The point here is that even so good a thing as plowing is lustful when it blinds the wicked to the love of God. But to deny the good of appetites altogether both destroys the good of prudence, which is their restrained and methodical satisfaction, and also contradicts every correlative judgment of evil. If there is no good in the bodily pleasures of this world, there is no evil in the torments of hell. And if there is no good in one's own bodily pleasures, then there is no evil in another man's bodily pains; which fact, if granted, would largely destroy the incentive and the reasonable ground of Christian compassion.

The higher goods themselves are founded on the lower, without which they are abstract and empty. The failure to recognize this truth is responsible for the most notorious of all the failures of Calvinism; namely, its ethics of marriage.[15] Had it not been for the cult of denial and concealment, in which the flame of love is replaced by its cinders and asphyxiating gases, it would not have been necessary for D. H. Lawrence to press the opposite extreme. The cult of primitive appetite, which exalts the subterranean roots of passion, divorces sexual love from every social and cultural value, and evades its moral implications, has acquired an accent of veracity and even of nobility as the champion of outraged nature.[16]

Sexual love is the most powerful of the physical appetites, the most prone to excess, the most unruly and insubordinate. To Calvin it afforded the most signal example of the evil of lower goods: and he conceived it, therefore, as originating with the fall of Adam. Physical passion being essentially sinful, marriage retained only two meanings. In the original state of innocence it meant the begetting of offspring, by which, in accordance with the divine will, the race of men was perpetuated. After the fall it acquired a second meaning; namely, the restriction and regularization of original sin. In other words, physical passion, being identified with lewdness, was excluded from sacred love, and reluctantly conceded as a necessary but indecent evil in profane love. Marriage was thus debased to a biological function plus a mask of hypocrisy. The true meaning of marriage as a sublimation of physical passion, in which the intensity and warmth of natural appetite is retained on the higher level of domestic life, and there enriched with the values of parentage, companionship, and fidelity, is omitted altogether.

The emphasis on the higher evil of lower goods also tends to obscure the higher evil of lower evils, or the imprudence of denial. The frustration of the appetites renders them insistent. Greed is as likely to arise from starvation as from gluttony. Obsession with sexual desire may arise not only from incontinence but from chastity. Poverty, destitution, impotence, sickness, and misery beget recklessness as well as disillusionment. Satan, seeking to lead men into imprudence, should often assume the form of pain, and tempt them to pleasure, not by providing but by withholding it. He should sometimes bring his victims to a mountain where their appetites would be sharpened, not by sight of a promised land, but by a spectacle of privation. The needle of virtue is often more difficult to thread with poverty than with riches. A Satan thoroughly equipped for his task would have both of these techniques at his command, and would know when each might be more effectively used. By the same token a God who wished to recover the love of his creatures would not necessarily inflict misery upon them. In certain situations he would find it more effective to lead them at once into green pastures, where through their sense of goodness they might the more confidently seek to discover more. To allocate the pleasures of appetite to Satan, and the pains of appetite to God, does not do justice to the subtleties of the moral order, even upon the level of prudence. It would be nearer the truth to identify the spirit of excess and one-sidedness with Satan, and to find God in the spirit of moderation.

Puritanism is guilty, then, of exaggerating the moral danger of appetitive satisfactions; of dwelling on their dangerousness so extravagantly as to disparage their good; and of neglecting the dangers which are consequent upon such disparagement. But a fair judgment will make entries on the credit as well as on the debit side of the ledger. Except in moments of millennial expectancy or of monastic asceticism, puritanism has ministered to the appetites. The care of the sick, the feeding of the hungry, the clothing of the naked, have until recently been the exclusive province of the church, whether protestant or Catholic. Through its sanction of marriage it has admitted, however begrudgingly, the demands of physical love. It has urged men to pluck out their eyes only when these give offense. That puritan piety at its best acknowledged the right of natural and worldly satisfactions, and was consistent even with the spirit of indulgence, is attested by Cromwell's attitude to his son's extravagance as revealed in the following letter to his son's wife's father, his "very loving Brother Richard Mayor, Esquire":

> I hear my Son hath exceeded his allowance, and is in debt. . . . I desire to be understood that I grudge him not laudable recreations, nor an honourable carriage of himself in them. . . . Truly I can find in my heart to allow him not only a sufficiency but more, for his good. But if pleasure and self-satisfaction be made the business of a man's life, "and" so much cost laid out upon it, so much time spent in it, as rather answers appetite than the will of God, or is comely before His Saints,—I scruple to feed this humour. . . . I desire your faithfulness . . . to advise him to approve himself to the Lord in his course of life; and to search His statutes for a rule to conscience, and to seek grace from Christ to enable him to walk therein. This hath life in it, and will come to somewhat: what is a poor creature without this! This will not abridge of lawful pleasures; but teach such a use of them as will have the peace of a good conscience going along with it.[17]

7

Having explored the problem of temptation on its lowest, or appetitive, level, let us now follow it to higher levels. A hierarchy of value will embrace not only a highest and a lowest good, but divers intermediate goods; such, for example, as self-interest, familial love, patriotism, or the cultural arts. These would be conceded to be superior to any immediate appetitive satisfaction, but at the same time, relatively to a highest good, they may constitute temptations, and provide a suitable guise for Satan intent on divorcing men from God. Their degree of moral goodness only renders them the more enticing, so that an artful Satan will prefer them to cruder bait. They appeal to conscience and not merely to appetite, and through such appeal they enlist the total person or a community of persons in their support. Here again the facts are not invented, but discovered and proclaimed, by puritanism. They are verified by the universal moral experience.

Self-interest may be a formidable obstacle to public good, a more formidable opponent than self-indulgence. Similarly, familial love is not less tempting for being tender and true. A doting mother or a fond wife may be more violently unneighborly in the cause of her family than in her own behalf. Puritanism did not reject the family affections. The correspondence between Governor John Winthrop and his wife exemplifies the warmth and constancy of marital love as well as the delicacy and literary beauty with which it may be expressed. But the prior claims of religion are never wholly forgotten:

> Deare [*torn*],—I am still detayned from thee, but it is by the Lord, who hath a greater interest in me than thy selfe, when his worke is donne he will restore me to thee againe to o^r^ mutuall comfort: Amen. I thanke thee for thy sweet Lre: my heart was wth thee to have written to thee everye daye, but businesse would not permitt me. I suppose thou hearest much newes from hence: it may be, some grievous to thee: but be not troubled, I assure thee thinges goe well, & they must needs doe so, for God is wth us & thou shalt see a happy issue. I hope to be wth thee to morrowe & a frende or 2: I suppose. So I kisse my sweet wife & rest
>
> Thine
>
> Jo: Winthrop [18]
>
> This 6: daye.

"If any man come to me, and hate not his father, and mother, and wife, and children, and brethren, and sisters, yea and his own life also, he cannot be my disciple." [19] This seemingly harsh injunction can be reconciled with fundamental Christian teachings only if it be taken to mean that lesser loves may even in their very lovingness preoccupy and narrow the affections. Cromwell's letters to his family are pervaded with an almost extravagant ardor, but this must take second place—after the love of God. Thus to his wife he writes: "Truly, if I love you not too well, I think I err not on the other hand much. Thou art dearer to me than any creature; let that suffice." [20]

This same Cromwell has, however, provided a notorious exemplification of the fact that a lesser love when unduly subordinated to a greater love may be transformed into its opposite. Of his nephew Oliver Walton, whose dying regret was that "God had not suffered him to be any more the executioner of His enemies," and whose last request was that the ranks be opened "that he might see the rogues run," Cromwell said that he was a "precious young man, fit for God." After grimly describing the slaughter of the garrison of Tredah, Cromwell concluded: "I wish that all honest hearts may give the glory of this to God alone, to whom indeed the praise of this mercy belongs." [21] Such exultant inhumanity again illustrates the insidious danger inherent in any hierarchy of values. Neither Cromwell nor his nephew was a sadist. To impute their brutality to mere lust of combat or thirst for blood is to miss the moral of the tale altogether. Assume that their leading motive was the love of God. Assume, furthermore, that the God they loved was a loving God. Their hardness of heart would then illustrate the moral error of confusing subordination with negation. A universal humanity may set bounds to a narrower humanity, and at this boundary the humane impulse itself may have to be checked, as the humane surgeon or judge may have to overcome a reluctance to inflict pain. But it is difficult to set bounds to any humane impulse without weakening the humane disposition; and in proportion as that disposition is weakened, room is made for the play of the contrary impulses of rage and hate.

The discipline and ardor of collective enterprise illustrate the same theme. Patriotism is a higher principle than either self-indulgence or calculating self-interest. In pursuit of national expansion, and for the express purpose of creating a pressure of population, Fascist Italy invoked a 'moral sanction,' and this term was not improperly used, since individuals were called upon to sacrifice their private convenience to a communal good. But the result was to create a force for evil surpassing all previous forces, as modern arms and munitions of war employing the latest fruits of science surpass the simpler weapons of a less 'advanced' age. Nationalism destroys higher goods all the more effectively because of its intermediate goodness, and defies God with a good conscience and with enthusiastic unanimity. The completely modernized Satan has learned to tempt with the voice of duty.

But because patriotism may seduce men from the love of mankind at large and must therefore be kept within bounds, it does not follow that it should be denied. The individual who hardens his heart against its appeal is likely to dissociate himself from all collective enterprise, to weaken his disposition of loyalty, and to make room for the baser motives of appetite and self-interest.

8

When puritanism was at its height, however, and stamped its peculiar mentality upon the European mind, nationalism had not yet revealed its devastating possibilities. Its horns and tail were not yet fully visible. Another intermediate good, the enjoyment of beauty, appeared more menacing. Since puritanism is identified in the popular mind with the rejection of aesthetic values and with the decline of art, it will be profitable to examine at length this application of its hierarchical principle.

The common supposition that the Gothic art of the Middle Ages was wantonly destroyed by protestantism is not supported by the facts.[22] Its decline was due in large part to purely artistic causes—to changes of technology, craftsmanship, and taste, in which Catholicism participated unreservedly. The supposition that Catholicism had any peculiar respect for the art of the past is belied by the fact that the remains of ancient Rome were continually plundered to obtain the materials for medieval Christian buildings. Similarly, the old Church of St. Peter was ruthlessly destroyed in 1505 to make way for the new. It was Catholicism rather than protestantism which absorbed the new cultural spirit of the Renaissance, and derived from the humanistic revival a repugnancy to the Gothic tradition.

As to the religious motives which led to a decline of Christian art, these were shared alike by Catholicism and protestantism. There are two fundamental grounds on which religion may criticize art. In the first place, religious art *represents,* and its iconography may therefore be deemed true or false in the light of changing ideas. In the second place, and this immediately concerns our present theme, religious art gives to the object of worship a delightful sensuous embodiment; and may, therefore, deflect worship from its ideal object. The very fact that aesthetic pleasures are higher than physical pleasures renders them the more seductive and the more dangerous to true piety. Satan, in his surpassing guile, and true to his mission of seducing men from the love of God, will assume the form of beautiful images, or of rich vestments, or of stately ecclesiastical architecture, or of sweet incense, or of liturgical music. Those who in all ages, and notably in the present age, confuse piety with what they call 'the beauty of the service,' or with their admiration for artistic monuments, testify to the power of this seduction, especially over more cultivated minds.

This second and deeper motive of iconoclasm has been felt in all periods of Christian history. It has even been contended by Remy de Gourmont that since Christianity proclaims the valuelessness of all sensual values, "there is no Christian art; it is a contradiction in terms." So early and exalted an authority as Origen praised the Jews because they had expelled "all painters and makers of images" and had condemned "an art which attracts the attention of foolish men, and which drags down the eyes of the soul from God to earth." But the Catholic church has, on the whole, subordinated art without negating it. Thomas Aquinas defended the worship of images on the ground of tempering the higher truths of religion to the shorn faculties of humble worshipers. In the fourteenth century Mathias Parisiensis, mindful of the danger of religious art, issued the following warning:

> Unlearned people, following their senses only, are strongly moved by . . . images and by their splendid and artificial appearance. . . . All such folk are prone to idolatry. . . . Let the Church, therefore, be adorned with statues; I oppose not this, nor gainsay in any wise, provided that we be on our guard against the devil's wiles here as in other things.

In November, 1563, the leaders of the Counter-Reformation in the last session of the Council of Trent decreed that:

> If any abuses have crept into these holy and salutary observances, this Holy Synod is vehemently desirous of abolishing such altogether, so that no images of false dogma may be set up, giving occasion of perilous error to simple folk. And if ever it chance that stories and narrations of Holy Scripture are sometimes expressed and figured, as this is expedient for the unlearned multitude, let the people be taught that the Deity is not figured on this account, as though It could be seen with the bodily eyes, or expressed in colours or shapes. . . . Moreover, let all wantonness be avoided, so that images be not painted or adorned with provocative beauty.

Finally, in 1570, the position of the Catholic church was thus stated by Molanus:

> Let us tolerate and permit some things for the sake of the weak. . . . That which the Church tolerates in books, let us also, with her, tolerate in pictures, which the Fathers have justly named the Scriptures of the Simple.[23]

The Catholic view, in short, is indulgent to the immediate values of religious art, and mindful of their educative value as elevating men above a preoccupation with baser appetites. At the same time it recognizes their danger. For the sensuous symbol may be substituted for the spiritual meaning, and the aesthetic pleasures may, owing to their very refinement and elevation, serve as a potent allurement inclining man to stop short of the full knowledge and love of God.

Similarly, protestantism has not, either in theory or in practice, denied art utterly. Even Calvin was "not so scrupulous as to judge that no images should be endured or suffered; but, seeing that the art of painting and carving images cometh from God," he required "that the practice of art should be kept pure and lawful." [24] The strong protestant leanings of Cranach, Dürer, and Holbein are well known. Rembrandt, Hogarth, Gainsborough, and Constable were thoroughgoing protestants of the reformed school. "It is interesting, and perhaps significant," writes Joseph Crouch, "that all the early masters in the English school of landscape painting were born and nurtured in East Anglia. Here Cromwell raised his Ironsides, and here today the strongest flavour of that Puritanism which came to maturity in the seventeenth century still remains." * [25]

The King James version of the Bible was the work of protestant scholars and divines, about evenly divided between the Anglican and the puritan parties. No one would impeach the protestantism or even the puritanism of Spenser, Milton, and Bunyan, and their literary craft and sensitiveness to beauty compare favorably with that of the Catholic or secular critics of puritanism.[27] As to New England puritanism, it is a notable fact that at the close of the seventeenth century Massachusetts ranked second in the British Empire in the volume of its literary publications, and that its schools and colleges fostered the study of the ancient classics.[28]

The costumes and architecture of puritan New England were sober but they were not ugly, and the decline of puritan faith was not accompanied by any notable improvement of taste. A recent student of puritan England and New England has written: "The more I study the Puritans the more I am at a loss to find their 'Puritanism.' " The puritanism which he found was a puritanism which, despite the unfavorable conditions of frontier life, tolerated both music and dancing, and enjoyed them; the puritanism which he had expected to find was a puritanism, invented by its critics, in which these and other arts were totally rejected.[29]

New England puritans emphasized simplicity and decorum. They believed that men should adorn themselves and their lives in a manner appropriate to their social condition and to their spiritual estate as servants of God. They opposed what they judged to be extravagance, luxury, and vanity, but they did not condemn richness or elegance in dress or in domestic furnishings. That they were censorious of the arts is unquestionable. But it is important to understand the difference between prohibition and censorship. Prohibition rejects what it supposes to be unqualifiedly evil; censorship regulates and restricts on what are supposed to be the higher grounds of morals, religion, or social good.[30]

When Charles William Eliot went to Paris as a youth of twenty-nine,

---

* These painters are known as the Norwich School, after that same Norwich in which Robert Browne founded his congregational church in 1580.[26]

and observed the strange worship of the Roman Catholic natives, he recorded the following impression:

> Since I have been in a Catholic country, I have been much struck with the fact (notorious and patent here) that the love of a place, of a form, of an image, of an altar, of its flowers, furniture, decorations or implements, has nothing whatever to do with a moral life, with religion properly so called. . . . Did we not see the altar at the Madeleine, Good Friday night, superbly decorated with the costliest flowers, candles, gold and silver vessels, and gorgeous hangings, and an idolatry at the foot of the altar no better than that of the Feejee Islanders.[31]

Now it is precisely this danger that the puritans emphasized—and exaggerated. It is just to condemn exaggeration, if at the same time pains are taken to admit the validity of that which is exaggerated. The puritans, being purists, and insisting upon the distinctively Christian element in historical Christianity, were quick to detect and denounce the admixture of idolatry which was undoubtedly characteristic of medieval Christian worship. Being peculiarly jealous of the supremacy of religious values, they were peculiarly suspicious of other and rival values. Aware of the blandishments of art, and of man's natural susceptibility to them, the puritans in their zeal and militancy were more disposed to condemn art for its insubordination than to defend its limited rights. And they found a justification in the fact that aestheticism may and does seduce men from piety.

9

The present theme illustrates the tendency of critics, victims of their own wit or eloquence, to take the easy way of ridicule or adulation. The puritan is accused by his enemies of waging a war of extermination upon every value of life other than salvation. "Puritanism," it is said, is "the haunting fear that someone, somewhere, may be happy." [32] This is a modern version of Macaulay's familiar gibe: "The Puritan hated bearbaiting, not because it gave pain to the bear, but because it gave pleasure to the spectators." [33] Mr. Ernest Boyd gives us another variant:

Scandals in politics and commercial dishonesty do not often call forth his [the puritan's] fulminations, for he does not conceive of the people concerned as having a particularly good time. Pleasure is the enemy, not evil, and so the joys of mind and body are under suspicion. . . . All that remains of the traditional stern virtue of Puritanism is a jealousy of everything which offers in this world the consolations advertised as belonging exclusively to the next.[34]

Let me add an even more sweeping indictment, which, despite concessions, holds puritanism responsible for all that the critic considers objectionable in the temper of American life, and illustrates the common fault of identifying the meaning of a gospel with the desiccated and negating phase into which all gospels enter in their decline:

Puritanism, great and powerful influence for good, as it once was, necessary as it once was, has also done limitless harm and continues to do harm to-day. It damages the human soul, renders it hard and gloomy, deprives it of sunshine and happiness;—in short, it takes away from the soul its joy. The Creed, or say the temper which arises from it, wrongs us sadly even to-day. More than to any other single agency we Americans owe it to the Calvinistic philosophy that we have so little of the zest of life; that our social life is so meager. Calvinism has wrought upon us and our forefathers in the Past. It deprived them not only of their music, their ballads, songs and dances, but also of all that almost infinite mass of social activity and opportunity of happiness which goes under the name of Play, and which is vital to the soul of man, lest that soul fall into sorrow; into a barren and sad vacancy, and curse its own being. Man does not live by bread alone; neither does the soul by morals alone. It is not enough to the godlike soul to sing gloomy hymns or to dwell perpetually in the realm of a piety without joy, and frequently without mercy and kindness.[35]

As the enemies of puritanism fail to go to the root of puritanism, and neglect its characteristic truth, so friendly critics fall into an opposite fault of too readily dismissing its defects. Thus Stuart Sherman, apropos of Hawthorne:

If Puritanism means . . . fear of ecclesiastical and social censure, slavish obedience to a rigorous moral code, a self-torturing conscience, harsh judgments of the frailties of one's fellows, morbid asceticism, insensibility and hostility to the beauties of nature and art, Hawthorne was as little of a Puritan as any man that ever lived. But if Puritanism in America means to-day what the lineal and spiritual descendants of the Puritans exemplified at their best in Emerson's New England—emancipation from ecclesiastical and social oppression, escape from the extortion of the senses and the tyranny of things, a consciousness at least partly liberated from the impositions of space and time, freedom for self-dominion, a hopeful and exultant effort to enter into right, and noble, and harmonious relations with the highest impulses of one's fellows, and a vision, a love, a pursuit of the beauty which has its basis in 'the good and true'—if Puritanism means these things, then Hawthorne was a Puritan.[36]

When puritanism is thus identified only with its virtues, or with the fuller truth that has emerged in the light of history and experience, it loses its characteristic physiognomy, and the account becomes a fatuous work of edification like a censored biography subsidized by the deceased's surviving relatives. The meaning of puritanism is not fully grasped until it is seen as justifying both its apologists and its detractors. It contains a fraction of moral truth, and through excessive emphasis on that fraction, possesses characteristic defects of omission and distortion.

10

The puritan was peculiarly alive to the existence and the possibility of evil. He was realistic. He refused to ignore or to sentimentalize the pain, the labor, the misery, the brutality, the perpetual exposure to war and pestilence, the sense of helplessness, and the imminence of death that were the lot of man in the seventeenth century. He was aware of these things, and he did not evade them. It is not surprising that he felt that man suffered from a hereditary curse, and that only heroic measures could save him.

He looked for the remedy not in science and statesmanship but in moral regeneration. His idea was that evil, having first been translated from physical or social into spiritual terms, could then be cured by spiritual methods. The immediate effect of this was to increase the volume of conscious evil. His medicine was homeopathic, evil being treated with evil. Men must be made to feel worse before they could feel better. Over and above the natural evils from which they already suffered they must be made to suffer a 'conviction of sin' from which they had hitherto been free. This sense of depravity was the puritan's bitter medicine. Richard Baxter prescribed it in these terms:

> But carefully examine and inquire, Hast thou been thoroughly convinced of a prevailing depravation through thy whole soul? and a prevailing wickedness through thy whole life? and how vile sin is? and that by the covenant thou hast transgressed, the least sin deserves eternal death? Dost thou consent to the law, that it is true and righteous, and perceive thyself sentenced to this death by it? Hast thou seen the utter insufficiency of every creature, either to be itself thy happiness, or the means of removing this thy misery? Hast thou been convinced that thy happiness is only in God, as the end, and in Christ, as the way to him; and that thou must be brought to God through Christ, or perish eternally? [37]

Here was a cure that was open to men of every station and degree. And it was a cure that was apparently effectual. For while men did not by this cure escape natural evils or attain natural goods, they did through spiritual good find abundant compensation. They could be happy. Puritanism did not, in short, confine itself to the pure science of spiritual medicine: it conducted a free clinic and staked its claims on its practical results.

In proclaiming a supreme good exalted above all natural and worldly goods, puritanism seized upon a truth; and in driving that truth home, puritanism did justice to that truth's practical priority over all other practical truths. In its insistence upon the corollaries of this primary truth—the priority of the supreme good over all intermediate goods, the tendency of intermediate goods through their very goodness to deflect the will from its true orientation, and the possibility of achieving a new will which should flood and regenerate the total life of the individual—puritanism contributed significantly to the history of the human spirit.

11

But while it is proper to use the puritan as the symbol of his characteristic truths, a just criticism will note the distortions arising from his neglect of other truths. While he was alive and responsive to the fact of evil, and thus escaped both complacency and irresponsibility, and while he rightly stressed the higher evil of lower goods, and the cure of lower evils by higher good, he was betrayed into error through the very zeal with which he was addicted to these truths. He tended to be morbidly preoccupied with evil, where a fuller wisdom would have dictated the positive vision of goodness. He did not deny to natural and worldly pleasure, or to health, or to family affection, or to social welfare, or to beauty and the cultural arts, a place in the hierarchy of goods, nor did he exclude them from his life. But in his eagerness to subordinate them he unduly disparaged them.

The inferiority or danger of lower goods is essentially different from intrinsic evil. In what is called his 'prudishness' or 'evil imagination,' and in the harshness of his discipline, the puritan fell into the error of allowing the relative or indirect evil of lower goods to contaminate their innocence. Insisting on the subordination of inferior goods, he neglected the fact that these lower goods will not flourish unless they are given room, and allowed, within broad limits, to be autonomous and spontaneous. Thus art and science and the family affections, if they are perpetually haunted by a censorious consciousness, may for lack of air be killed altogether. The puritan neglected the fact that lower goods will often pave the way to higher; and that the most effective method of dealing with lower evils is not to aggravate them by a sense of guilt, but to meet them on their own ground with the aid of the physical and social arts. He failed to realize that the sense of guilt added to the sense of natural evil may only break a man's heart and complete his feeling of impotent despair. He failed to see that higher goods, divorced from a foundation of sanity and from the satisfactions of the natural man, may themselves be only apparent, consisting in a precarious state of subjective exaltation which will tend to lapse, if indeed it does not beget a reaction to the opposite extreme.

The puritan's harsh insistence on the pre-eminent importance of salvation was suited to the exigencies of reform, or of revolution, or of migration and settlement. It put the moral and spiritual life on a war footing. It was not so good a gospel to live by over long periods of normal relaxation. Like all policies adapted to times of emergency, it curtailed liberty and impoverished the content of life. In the long run, and on the whole, the vision of a supreme good should stimulate and enrich. While giving life direction and order, it should at the same time reach down through all the levels of life, permeate the whole, enliven all of its activities. In short, the first requirement of salvation is that it should save.

CHAPTER TEN

THE MORAL ATHLETE

1

PURITANISM PROCLAIMED a supreme good—and insisted on its supremacy. But the moral hierarchy of value did not coincide with the order of natural inclination. The true way of life was not the line of least resistance, but an unnatural spiritual condition to be achieved by discipline, method, and dogged determination. There was need of what George Herbert Palmer has called "the exercise of . . . subordination." [1] It is this phase of puritanism—its moral rigorism—on which I wish now to focus attention. Indulgently judged, the puritan is the exponent of moral zeal and perfectionism. To less sympathetic judges he is a moral virtuoso; a moral martinet; or a sort of moral Hercules of the worst period, disproportionately developed in his moral muscles.

The puritan's moral rigorism, whether just or excessive, sprang from his dualism. There were several dualities in the puritan system of belief. The elect and the damned formed a complete disjunction: every man belonged to the one group or the other, and no man could belong to both. If one was saved, one was totally saved, and if one was damned, one was totally damned—a duality like that which plays so important a part in modern moral judgments, between those who are in jail and those who are out of jail. The Lutheran doctrine of justification by faith implied, or at any rate generated, a further duality between the occurrence and non-occurrence of a specific religious experience, such as that of conversion or sanctification. The Calvinistic emphasis on the will of God created still another dualism, between acts of obedience and acts of disobedience. When this doctrine was combined with the acceptance of the Bible as a codification of the divine will, there resulted a legalistic distinction between wholly right and wholly wrong, according as the act does or does not conform to the rule. If there is a statute forbidding the riding of a bicycle on the sidewalk, the right and the wrong are divided by the edge of the curb.

All of these ideas tended to present moral differences as white and black divided by a sharp line. But although they fostered a cult of strictness, they did not in themselves define a dynamic antithesis. This second form of moral dualism sprang from a motive more deeply rooted both in the Christian tradition and in the universal moral experience—the inner tension, namely, between will and appetite, or, to use Kant's familiar terms, between duty and inclination. Since the better life did not in principle agree with inclination; since it might, therefore, at any particular time require a departure from inclination; and since inclination was a force—it followed that there was need of a moral counterforce by which inclination could, if necessary, be overcome.

In puritanism, as we have seen, this dynamic antithesis was conceived as a rivalry between the attachments to lower and higher goods. Dr. Thomas Goodwin discovered "that the Spirit not only contradicted and check'd, but made a real natural Opposition, such as Fire do's to Water; so that the Spirit did as truly lust against the Work of the Flesh, as the Flesh against that of the Spirit." [2] On the one hand, there was natural appetite, or worldly ambition, or the love of anything less than the best; on the other hand, there was the love of God, which had to acquire that ascendancy to which it was entitled.

From this root sprang all those conceptions, descriptions, and figures of speech in which the moral life was represented as a battle, a conquest, an overcoming. Man's cure is to be effected by surgery rather than by hygiene or medicine. Something must be destroyed. "He that loveth his life shall lose it: and he that hateth his life in this world shall keep it unto life eternal." The path of virtue is not only steep and rugged, but hard to find and hard to keep: "For narrow is the gate, and straitened the way, that leadeth unto life, and few be they that find it." [3] There is never a moment when it is safe for the Christian warrior to relax his vigilance; there is "a way to Hell," said Bunyan, "even from the Gates of Heaven." [4] Heaven is up and hell is down, in a world in which things naturally gravitate, morally as well as physically. To reach hell it is not necessary to make any effort—it is sufficient to grow faint or lose one's footing.

St. Augustine insisted that Christian women who had been violated by Roman soldiers might nevertheless be said to have preserved their chastity. For wickedness consists, he said, not in the subjection of the body to another's lust, but in the soul's "consent to the desire aroused in its own flesh." [5] Appetite is here represented as possessing an alien or external character, even though it spring up within the individual's consciousness. It is an enemy which has penetrated into the household, but must nonetheless be disowned and repelled. The moral will must keep its attachments uncorrupted and its authority undivided.

This crucial disjunction between one attachment and another, this test of fundamental loyalty, divided men into two groups. Richard Baxter's *Alarm to Unconverted Sinners* was addressed "to all ignorant, carnal, and ungodly, who are Lovers of Pleasure more than God, and seek this World more than the Life everlasting, and live after the Flesh, and not after the Spirit." [6] Against these "enemies of God" were arrayed his servants, and the inner struggle was thus transferred to the physical battlefield, and the lines of moral cleavage were readily identified with those of civil war or class struggle.

The puritan's dualism tended, then, to assume two forms: a sharp linear disjunction, and a dynamic antagonism. Similarly, the puritan's rigorism assumed two forms; namely, purity and effort, strictness and power, precision and forcefulness. In a sermon delivered at Plymouth in 1621 Robert Cushman said of the Virginia colonists that while in England they seemed very "religious, zealous and conscionable," they "have now lost even the sap of grace, and edge to all goodness; and are become mere worldlings." [7] It was expected of the puritan that he should be clearly distinguishable from other men by the perfection of his righteousness and piety, and by his uncompromising allegiance to the supreme good. Let us examine each of these aspects of puritan zeal in turn and at greater length.

2

The puritan's name implies that he was a purist. He had clearly defined standards and he judged himself strictly by them. If his grade was fifty on the scale of a hundred, he did not congratulate himself for rising so high, but condemned himself for falling so short. He recognized that man was by nature sinful, as modern psychology recognizes that man is by nature irrational. Such an acknowledgment of weakness may lead to either of two judgments: one may expect nothing, or one may demand everything. One may say that it is remarkable, considering his corrupt nature, that man is no worse than he is; or one may say, with puritanism, that considering his divine origin and ideal possibilities, it is disgraceful that he is no better. It is this perfectionism which led the puritan to place the generality of mankind so low, and at the same time to exalt the elite of saintliness so high.

The ideal of purity or strictness was, as we have seen, in part an outgrowth of ethical legalism. For the average man in his everyday life the puritan faith translated itself into obedience of God's will as written down plainly in the Bible. Or, if it was not plain, it seemed plain when a certain interpretation of it had become generally accepted. The teachings of the Bible, furthermore, were largely identical with the precepts of the secular conscience. The Bible did not ask impossible things. Some of its teachings, at least, were both plain and within man's power to obey. Within these limits one's righteousness might be absolute: precisely what the rule prescribed, one might perform; precisely what it forbade might be avoided.[8]

Is extreme scrupulousness—adherence to the letter of the precept—an odd and unpleasant vagary of historical puritans and their like, or has it some general ethical validity? There are at least two considerations which support the second alternative.

In the first place, the application of precepts means their crystallization into concrete and largely stereotyped habits. Virtue cannot be practiced until it is converted into specific rules to be complied with literally. It is important, no doubt, that the more general virtue should not be confused with the specific rule, so that the latter may be open to amendment. But when a code is actually operative, the agent is adhering strictly to *some* formula. The cavalier is in this generalized sense not less scrupulous in the details of his courtesy than is the puritan in those of his sabbatarianism.

In the second place, there are virtues that have no virtue save in their strict or literal observance. Such, for example, is the virtue of punctuality. The virtue of this rule lies in its enabling two or more persons to meet in the same place at the same time. It is not observed at all unless it is observed precisely. This is not a case in which one would invoke the spirit rather than the letter of the law. If chronometers were introduced, and hours and minutes reckoned, it would not be felt that the transaction had been degraded. But punctuality is an instance of a large class. All concerted human efforts are engagements, depending on a precise commitment by each party, precisely adhered to. They depend on each party's saying just what he means, on his being understood by the other parties, and on all parties conforming their action to their meaning. If human relations of a more slipshod character are possible, it is because there are 'precisionists' somewhere who have pledged and kept their word.

3

Fundamentally, however, the puritan dualisms were dynamic rather than static, and conduced to a cult of will rather than of scruple. The difference between the saints and the damned was a difference of attitude, a facing of the mind in opposite directions; such as the obedience and disobedience of God's commands, or the acceptance by faith, and the rejection by unbelief, of the offer of the Gospel. There was, in other words, an irreconcilable yes or no. Similarly, the subjective experience of conversion or of sanctification was essentially a profound and abrupt change of heart. There was a crucial choice: one cannot choose both God and Mammon, and he who is for the one is against the other. If one rejects God, it is because one has chosen something other than God—physical pleasure, worldly success, selfish attainment, narrow familial, neighborly, and national goods, or aesthetic gratification.

The puritan's strict rectitude, or scrupulous adherence to the letter of the rule—his static perfectionism—was thus a secondary and not a primary consideration. Insofar as there were specific injunctions to be obeyed, the puritan would manifest his zeal by the perfection of his obedience. But the validity of rules depends on their sanction, and their sanction in this case was a God who called for love, and merited love. Those who loved him would automatically obey him, for love comprises the alignment of the lover's will with the will of his love's object. Hence the Christian who had attained to the perfect love of God enjoyed what was called 'Christian liberty'; that is, being governed centrally by the will of God, he was no longer apprehensive of deviation from the rules in which that will was formulated.

The wholehearted love of God implies the eradication of rival affections. Saving, perhaps, its depicting of the horrors of hell, there is no feature of puritanism that has seemed so absurd to posterity as its sumptuary legislation. In England during the Puritan Revolution, and in New England during the theocracy, the puritan church through the civil authorities prohibited amusements and luxuries that to a later age appear not only innocent but right and reasonable. The inquisitorial eye of the Consistory followed the Genevese citizen "from his cradle to his grave." Even personal adornment was "made an affair of public concernment and welfare."[9] The modern reader dismisses such regulations with amused contempt. But the sumptuary legislation, or so-called blue laws, of the puritan are wholly misunderstood if they are construed as independent judgments of good and evil. They constituted a regimen of abstinence designed to deliver the heart from debasing attachments. They were a social manifestation of what Calvin described as "most diligent efforts to extricate ourselves from these fetters" of the world and the flesh.[10]

The evil of personal adornment, of card-playing, dancing, and similar frivolities, lay not in the deed itself, nor in its immediate consequences, but in the inordinate and disloyal fondness by which it was prompted. Believing that his spiritual progress was a doubtful and hazardous enterprise, beset by many pitfalls, the puritan intended to take no chances. He named as temptations to be resisted and prohibited those practices which in his time and place seemed most conspicuously to represent the contrary of the love of God. He was peculiarly suspicious of the sexual appetite, not only because of its strength, but also because of all the appetites it seems most deeply rooted in the body. At the same time it is of all the appetites the most imaginative, so that it is peculiarly difficult to divide the thought from the deed. The point of puritanism was not to impute the sexual imagination where it did not exist, but to recognize the indivisibility of the imagination from the passion, and to distrust the passion as one of the major rivals of the love of God.

4

The puritan's sharp differences of right and wrong, of election and damnation, of regenerate and unregenerate, of belief and unbelief, reduce, then, to the dynamic opposition between the higher love of God and whatever rival loves may claim or threaten the dominion of the human heart. Piety consisted in fidelity. "I see therefore," said John Winthrop, "I must keepe a better watch over my heart, & keepe my thoughts close to good things, & not suffer a vaine or worldly thought to enter, etc.: least it drawe the heart to delight in it." [11]

In dramatizing the opposition between lower and higher goods, and in insisting that the triumph of the one involves the defeat of the other, the puritans followed the immemorial conscience of man. They affirmed an unwelcome truth about life which all moralists have affirmed, but which does not depend on any authority, pagan or Christian. The puritans because they took it so much to heart have come to symbolize it, but they did not invent it. It expresses the fact that the elements of which a good life is composed offer a certain resistance to the form which goodness imposes on them. The moral life is the making of some harmonious purpose out of impulses each of which is endowed with an independent bias which must be checked if the purpose is to be maintained. The will, representing the purpose, sets a limit to each impulse, and stations a sentinel there with instructions to challenge every trespasser. If the purpose is to be a permanent achievement of character, there must be a judgment that says "No," a power to enforce this judgment, and an impulse which obeys. That the impulse obeys reluctantly is implied in the definition of the situation. The imposed limit blocks the very way which the impulse, if left to itself, is inclined to follow.

In other words, the moral shoe pinches. Let us consider some homely workaday aspect of life. One's general purpose in life requires, let us say, that one shall rise in the morning at six o'clock. This purpose provides for sleep, but sets a limit to it. One is not born, like a wound and set alarm clock, with an impulse to bestir oneself at six o'clock. There are mornings in youth (despite the poetic fiction which associates youth with dawn) in which one is governed by a pure impulse to sleep, *only* to sleep, to sleep *more*, to sleep *on* and *on*. The impulse whispers, "Yet a little sleep, a little slumber, a little folding of the hands to sleep." [12] With this impulse the day's program is in irreconcilable conflict. The program requires that one shall leave that warm, soft bed, dispel that delicious languor, turn from that enticing prospect, and do what of all imaginable things is then and there most repugnant. No method has ever been, nor ever will be, invented by which one can both play one's part in the world and also sleep as much as in one's sleepiest moments one would like to sleep.

Sleep, love, hunger, thirst, have their own primitive, inherent, and independent impulsions, which they never lose. Any moral code whatsoever, even the least and lowliest prudence, must begin by subduing them, and must remain in command. There is the same conflict between the pull of private gain and the requirements of public good, or between a preoccupation with American domestic interests and a duty to mankind at large. Everywhere, on every level, there is an inertia or a momentum of the given interest which for the sake of some larger and more legitimate plan has to be overcome or redirected. This is the plain and unpalatable fact which all experience teaches—the most trite, the most disagreeable, and among the most profound, of all moral truths.

Puritanism is rightly associated with this negative incidence of goodness and piety. That the puritan should have exaggerated an aspect of morality so congenial to his zeal, and so abundantly confirmed by his experience, is not surprising. It is not surprising that in his struggle with human enemies or with the forces of nature he should have supposed that he was 'battling for the Lord.' It was natural that having taken God's side he should assume that God had taken *his*, and that Satan was on the side of his enemies. It is not surprising that the puritan, like other moralists, should have come to associate virtue with disinclination. It was said of John Quincy Adams, as evidence of his taint of puritanism, that

> the fact that . . . action involved an enormous sacrifice would have been to his mind strong evidence that it was a duty; and the temptation to perform a duty, always strong with him, became ungovernable if the duty was exceptionally disagreeable.[13]

Virtue bears the scars of battle, and retains a flavor of tragedy. Its sting lies in its cost. Men remember that reluctance, that giving up or going without, that sheer effort, which gave it birth, and suppose this is the surest mark by which it may be known.

There is a novelty as well as antiquity in this aspect of puritanism, since it is opposed to the recent swing of opinion. It has been superseded by the cult of release. The psychoanalytic attack upon repression and the popular attack upon inhibitions unite in their demand for a freer expression of subordinate desires, which, when too harshly subjugated, assume the form of unconscious 'complexes' and become centers of psychic infection. The cure, we are told, lies in exposing them to light and air.

But the fact that the puritan's dynamic dualism may become an obsession, or serve as a pretext, or be naïvely interpreted and through its dramatization conduce to superstition, or be so one-sided as to exclude its complementary truth, does not furnish ground for its rejection. It is characteristic of the best life, however conceived, that it should be conditioned by self-mastery. It requires a will that is never wholly committed to any subordinate enterprise, or wholly absorbed by any given constituent part of life; a general purpose that is stronger than hunger or thirst or love or ambition or even patriotism. It implies a centralized and unified control which will bring the whole course of a man's actions, feelings, and thoughts into accord with his moral judgment or spiritual faith.

5

Recognizing this need of a centralized control, the puritan proposed to achieve it by extraordinary and systematic effort. This cult of will power, this use of the will for the purpose of strengthening the will, was motivated in the puritan by anxiety. He was tortured by doubt as to the present state and future prospects of his soul. He was forever telling his eternal fortunes, plucking the petals—"He loves me—he loves me not"—the love in question being that divine love which pronounces the word of doom. There can be no doubt of the anxiety. But was it consistent with the basic tenets of puritan theology? Why should the puritan have been anxious about what he imputed to the irrevocable decision of God? Why should he be so much interested in the condition of his will if he was saved by faith and not by works?

These objections are purely academic. He who puts himself in the position of the puritan will not feel any inconsistency. One is either elected to show forth the mercy of God, or damned to manifest his justice. Would one not, on this assumption, like to know which? Has it ever been observed that the candidate for office is indifferent to the returns on election night, even though he realizes that he is now powerless to influence the outcome? It is not surprising, for example, that Cotton Mather should have lived, as he expressed it, "in the very frequent Practice of *Self-Examination*," or that he should have looked anxiously for what he called the "Mark of an *effectually called* Person." On a certain day in his forty-third year he set himself with "a more singular and exquisite Measure of Consideration" than usual to enumerate his favorable symptoms—such as sorrow for sin, the impulse to prayer, complete resignation to the will of God, compassion for his personal enemies—and asked himself "whether the Man that can find these *Marks* upon himself, may not conclude himself *mark'd out*, for the City of God."

Mather's attitude was not wholly one of curiosity. He undoubtedly sought by "Fasting . . . Contritions . . . Humiliations . . . Supplications . . . [and] Abasements" to *create* the symptoms as well as to find them. But considering what the symptoms were, there is nothing astonishing in this. Whether one does or does not possess a certain degree of physical strength may be tested by lifting a weight of a certain magnitude. If one applies the test, one tries to lift the weight. If one believes that ability to lift the weight is evidence of perfect health, and inability evidence of mortal disease, one will exert oneself to lift it in order to convince oneself of that which one prefers to believe. So in this case, since "*Idleness* . . . *Listlessness* . . . Slothfulness . . . Lukewarmness . . . Formality . . . *Pride* . . . Hardness . . . Wantonness" were symptoms of spiritual death,[14] an anxious person such as Cotton Mather would seek to prove his hold on eternal life by manifesting their opposites. His ability to "correspond to the design of God in calling" [15] him would constitute the much desired evidence of his call.

In other words, the puritan was engaged in a trial of strength. The question "Can I?" was experimentally tested by *trying*; and in proportion as he tried, the answer was likely to be affirmative, as he hoped it would be. The effort was doubly motivated: by curiosity as to the answer, and by desire for a particular answer. To this is to be added the further consideration that when the first signs were favorable, confidence rapidly increased because of the doctrine of integral salvation. And this confidence, in turn, generated an access of strength and further increased the desired probability. This is good psychology. Any logical misgivings that remained were easily quieted by the reflection that while God causes all things by his infinite will, he causes many things through man's will; and if what one calls one's own will is in a deeper view of the matter God's, so much the more reason to have confidence in its power.

6

In order to perfect and prove his spiritual strength the puritan engaged in exercises and went into training, much as a youth now sets out to excel in sport. An American schoolboy whom I knew made up his mind to become a high hurdler; not an ordinary everyday high hurdler, but a supreme high hurdler. He placed on his bureau a photograph of

Nurmi, the Finnish long-distance champion. He gazed at this photograph every morning until there came into his face that grim expression which betokens unconquerable and irresistible resolve. This was his prayer. He abstained from candy and tobacco, and ate and drank only what was convertible into those tissues of the body which are employed in high hurdling. This was his fasting. He arranged his vacations, his friendships, his studies, his hours of sleep, his diversions, in the manner that he believed would increase his speed and endurance. Every day he weighed himself and tested himself. Slowly but steadily he clipped fractions of seconds from his record, with a growing assurance that he was one of the elect.

Now let us consider our great puritan champion, Jonathan Edwards. In early life, just after graduating from Yale at the age of seventeen, he went into training to perfect himself in godliness. For several years he recorded in a diary the course of training which he followed. Here are a few selections:

5. *Resolved,* Never to lose one moment of time, but to improve it in the most profitable way I possibly can. . . .

22. *Resolved,* To endeavour to obtain for myself as much happiness in the other world as I possibly can, with all the power, might, vigour, and vehemence, yea violence, I am capable of, or can bring myself to exert, in any way that can be thought of. . . .

38. *Resolved,* Never to utter anything that is sportive, or matter of laughter, on a Lord's day. . . .

Monday, Dec. 24 [1722]. . . . Concluded to observe, at the end of every month, the number of breaches of resolutions, to see whether they increase or diminish, to begin from this day, and to compute from that the weekly account my monthly increase, and out of the whole, my yearly increase, beginning from new-year days. . . .

Saturday evening, Jan. 5 [1723]. . . . This week, have been unhappily low in the weekly account:—and what are the reasons of it? . . . *Resolved,* That I have been negligent in two things:—in not striving enough in duty; and in not forcing myself upon religious thoughts. . . .

Sabbath-day morning, May 12. I have lost that relish of the Scriptures and other good books, which I had five or six months ago. *Resolved,* When I find in myself the least disposition to exercise good nature, that I will then strive most to feel good-naturedly.[16]

It is clear that the young Jonathan Edwards was determined to achieve perfect self-mastery and control through the exercise of his will. He deliberately set his will difficult tasks, as one takes bodily exercise by the use of antagonistic muscles. He made a business of moral virtue, felt his spiritual pulse, took his spiritual weight, and measured his spiritual record.

Another distinguished moral athlete was Cotton Mather. He was even more methodical and businesslike than Jonathan Edwards. He felt that man's moral possibilities were almost limitless, provided one went about it in a systematic way:

> Without abridging yourselves of your occasional thoughts on the question, "What good may I do to-day?" fix a time, now and then, for more deliberate thoughts upon it. Cannot you find time (say, once a-week, and how suitably on the Lord's day) to take this question into consideration:
>
> *What is there that I may do for the service of the glorious Lord, and for the welfare of those for whom I ought to be concerned?*
>
> Having implored the direction of God, "the Father of lights," consider the matter, in the various aspects of it. Consider it, till you have *resolved* on something. Write down your resolutions. Examine what precept and what promise you can find in the word of God to countenance your resolutions. Review these memorials at proper seasons, and see how far you have proceeded in the execution of them. The advantages of these preserved and revised memorials, no rhetoric will be sufficient to commend, no arithmetic to calculate. There are some animals of which we say, "They know not their own strength"; Christians, why should you be like them? [17]

It may be objected that the puritan's emphasis on moral discipline was disproportionate to the matter in hand. The American athlete is felt by many to have overdone athletics. He violates, we say, the amateur code, in the spirit if not in the letter. By his intense effort to surpass records or defeat opponents he makes work out of what should be play. He makes it uncomfortable for those who have neither the time nor the inclination to take the game so seriously. Now many people have precisely the same feeling toward the puritan. He takes his game of morality too seriously. He 'exaggerates' morality, as some colleges are said to exaggerate football. Others who cannot compete with him, because they have only their odd hours to devote to morality, feel that the pace should be slackened. They are advocates of 'morality for all,' 'intramural' morality, morality of a more sportive and spontaneous sort.

But the force of this plea for the amateur spirit in morality is somewhat weakened by the fact that most of those who utter it believe in being professional *somewhere*. They may be professionals in athletics, and although they think that the puritan's perpetual examination of the state of his soul is in bad taste, they have no hesitation in keeping a similar diary of the state of their muscles. Or they may be men of affairs, and want morality tempered to the tired businessman, who, however, is tired because he is so exceedingly businesslike about his business. These critics also think it morbid to balance one's spiritual account, but feel an irresistible urge to balance their bank accounts. And so with the artist, who is perhaps the most contemptuous critic of the puritan. He objects strongly to moral discipline, but devotes himself with infinite patience to the mastery of his own technique.

So it is evident that it is not so much a question of *whether* one shall be strict, as *where* one shall be strict. One will be strict, presumably, about the more important and central things: the athlete about high hurdles, the businessman about profits, the artist about music, painting, or poetry. The difference is over the question of what is important and central, and on this question the puritan held a view which, it must be admitted, is now somewhat outmoded. He held that morality is all-important and all-central.

There is some point in every man's system of ideas at which his sense of humor gives out. If you are a puritan, you may take other things lightly, but morals are no laughing matter. The puritan held, incredible as it may now seem, that morals are more important than athletics, business, or art. He held that to achieve a controlling will by which to conform one's life to what one conceives to be the way of righteousness is the one thing most profoundly needful. Or rather he held that athletics, business, and art should be judged by conscience, and approved only so far as they form parts of that good life—that orderly and integral life, of the person or of society—which must be founded on virtue. Perhaps he was mistaken in his scale of relative values, but at any rate to drive him from this position would require heavier guns than most of his critics carry.

7

Richard Baxter, a divine of the seventeenth century, said of one of the pioneers among puritans:

> My Father never scrupled Common-Prayer or Ceremonies, nor spake against Bishops, nor ever so much as prayed but by a Book or Form, being not ever acquainted then with any that did otherwise: But only for reading Scripture when the rest were Dancing on the Lord's Day, and for praying . . . in his House, and for reproving Drunkards and Swearers, and for talking sometimes a few words of Scripture and the Life to come, he was reviled commonly by the Name of *Puritan, Precisian* and *Hypocrite*.[18]

This "reviling" became a habit and a class prejudice for generations. Said Macaulay:

> To the stern precisian, even the innocent sport of the fancy seemed a crime. To light and festive natures the solemnity of the zealous brethren furnished copious matter of ridicule. From the Reformation to the civil war, almost every writer, gifted with a fine sense of the ludicrous, had taken some opportunity of assailing the straight haired, snuffling, whining saints, who christened their children out of the Book of Nehemiah, who groaned in spirit at the sight of Jack in the Green and who thought it impious to taste plum porridge on Christmas day. At length a time came when the laughers began to look grave in their turn. The rigid, ungainly zealots, after having furnished much good sport during two generations, rose up in arms, conquered, ruled, and, grimly smiling, trod down under their feet the whole crowd of mockers.[19]

What is the real onus of the epithets with which the puritan is so bitterly assailed by his opponents? In the use of these epithets the modern age is but echoing the abuse heaped, derisively or vindictively, upon the Roundhead by the Cavalier during the Puritan Revolution and the Restoration.

No one supposes that Richard Baxter's father, or any other notable puritan, went about trying to persuade people that he was more virtuous than he secretly knew himself to be. There was no notable discrepancy between the inner and the outer life of the puritan. What he professed to others he also confessed to himself. He was not distinguished among men by a lack of candor. Indeed, as George Gissing has suggested, if 'hypocrisy' means cynicism wearing a mask of virtue, then it is quite irrelevant to puritanism.[20] It is pharisaism rather than hypocrisy of which he may more reasonably be accused. Pharisaism does not mean wearing a cloak of righteousness; it means sincerely believing that one is more righteous than one really is. This is a failing that the puritan did, indeed, have difficulty in avoiding. He believed himself to be one of the elect, and that implied a moral eminence which contemporaries or later historians have not always found him to occupy. There seems to be a discrepancy between what he was and what he claimed to be. But so it seemed to him also, and hence the perpetual reproach and haunting doubts which beset him. The puritan believed himself to be called, but since his election implied an unnatural and unusual state of godliness, he could not always feel sure of himself. He alternated between the "very Top of Felicity" and the lowest depths of moral despair. It was a life of mountains and valleys with great and precipitous differences of altitude.

Furthermore, to claim the support of God is to credit God with the victory, and is a form of self-abasement. When Cromwell was most elated by success, humility was always near at hand. The results were too amazing to attribute to himself. There is more of gratitude and trust than of boasting in these words, written after the battle of Preston:

> When we think of our God, what are we! Oh, His mercy to the whole society of saints,—despised, jeered saints! Let them mock on. Would we were all saints! The best of us are, God knows, poor weak saints;—yet saints; if not sheep, yet lambs; and must be fed. We have daily bread, and shall have it, in despite of all enemies. There's enough in our Father's house, and He dispenseth it.[21]

Cotton Mather summed up this oscillation or mixture of attitudes when he signed as follows his "Resolutions as to my Walk with God": "Penned by, *Cotton Mather*; A feeble and worthless, yett (*Lord! by thy Grace!*) desirous to approve himself, a sincere and faithful Servant of Jesus Christ."[22]

The puritan may always be convicted of failure as judged by his own standard; and of over-belief in himself as judged by his own attainment. But who cannot? It is impossible to have standards at all without exposing oneself to precisely such accusations. There is no way of being zealous in right-doing without being 'self-righteous. To have a standard is to set a goal beyond actuality or even possibility; and yet to seek the goal is impossible unless one has moments of belief in one's power to reach it. There is perhaps no one so self-righteous as the man who is fond of calling other people 'hypocrites.' He is excessively ready to assume that he has attained his own ideal of sincerity. When standards are applied in action there will always be some concession to circumstance, some use of means by which the purity of the action is corrupted; so that it will be possible for critics (including oneself) to point out a discrepancy between the deed and the creed. A practical Christian, like Cromwell, must adjust his ideal to the context of affairs and use what weapons are at hand. A man can do his best only by confidently seeking (and perpetually missing) an unattainable perfection.

Why, then, is the puritan's self-righteousness so odious? In the first place, because the critic frankly takes the side of Mammon, and recognizes the puritan as his enemy. His criticism is self-defense or counterattack: "In the mouth of a drunkard he is a puritan who refuseth his cups; in the mouth of a swearer he which feareth an oath; in the mouth of a libertine he who makes any scruple of common sins." [23]

Or consider the complaint of Colonel Hutchinson that the term 'puritan' was an epithet used to discredit every form of decency and piety which took itself seriously:

If any, out of mere morality and civil honesty, discountenanced the abominations of those days, he was a Puritan, however he conformed to their superstitious worship; if any showed favour to any godly honest person, kept them company, relieved them in want, or protected them against violent or unjust oppression, he was a Puritan; if any gentleman in his country maintained the good laws of the land, or stood up for any public interest, for good order or government, he was a Puritan: in short, all that crossed the views of the needy courtiers, the proud encroaching priests, the thievish projectors, the lewd nobility and gentry—whoever was zealous for God's glory or worship, could not endure blasphemous oaths, ribald conversation, profane scoffs, Sabbath-breaking, derision of the word of God, and the like—whoever could endure a sermon, modest habit or conversation, or anything good,—all these were Puritans; and if Puritans, then enemies to the king and his government, seditious, factious hypocrites, ambitious disturbers of the public peace, and finally, the pest of the kingdom.

Such false logic did the children of darkness use to argue with against the hated children of light, whom they branded besides as an illiterate, morose, melancholy, discontented, crazed sort of men, not fit for human conversation; as such they made them not only the sport of the pulpit, which was become but a more solemn sort of stage, but every stage, and every table, and every puppet-play, belched forth profane scoffs upon them, the drunkards made them their songs, and all fiddlers and mimics learned to abuse them, as finding it the most gameful way of fooling.[24]

Macaulay speaks of "the sarcasms which modish vice loves to dart at obsolete virtue." [25] The critic may thus represent not his personal impulses merely, but the general cause of the disparaged values; as at the time of the Restoration, when the pendulum had swung from moral and religious discipline to free indulgence of the physical pleasure, the luxury, the arts, and the human affections and loyalties which had lately been repressed.

But the puritan is also condemned because he is felt to be inopportunely right. A recent writer has illustrated the uncomfortableness of puritanism, as contrasted with Anglicanism:

The difference between the two types of religion is brought out humorously in a pamphlet written in 1566 by an English vicar, Anthony Gilbert. The parson in the dialogue, in speaking against the Puritans, says, "There are very few that can agree to the Genevans' fashion to have nothing in the church but naked walls and a poore fellow in a bare gown, telling a long tale and brawling and chiding with all his hearers. As for my Lord [i.e., his patron] I heard him say that he could never go to any of these Genevan sermons, that he came quiet home, but that there was ever something that pricked his conscience; he always thought that they made their whole sermon against him. But in the reading of Mattins and Evensong at [St.] Paul's, or in my reading of my service in his chapel, he sayeth, he feeleth no such thing, for he is never touched, but goeth merrily to his dinner."

There you have two conceptions of religion which have by no means died out. Some people do not want to have their appetite spoiled by having their conscience pricked. The Puritan did not feel it was quite right to go home from church to his dinner with too undisturbed an appetite, or in too complacent a frame of mind.[26]

Everyone will, if forced, avow his allegiance to some moral code, acknowledge its logical priority over his appetites, and confess his lapses from strict rectitude. But one dislikes to be perpetually reminded of these things. When a puritan is in the neighborhood, one feels the uncomfortable sense of an accusing presence. It is impossible to go on enjoying oneself frivolously in the midst of such gravity. The puritan is the death's-head at the feast. He cannot be lightly ignored, because his admonition is re-echoed and confirmed by one's own conscience. One knows oneself to be vulnerable. Hence one hurls epithets at the puritan, hoping to frighten him away; or, if not, then to divert his attention and put him on the defensive by calling attention to his own shortcomings.

8

Whatever the motives of the critic himself, the puritan's moral athleticism is abundantly open to criticism. It is marked by one-sidedness and distortion—by defects of omission so serious as to amount, in moral judgment and practice, to defects of commission. Its most glaring fault is that which has invariably manifested itself in asceticism, which is only another name for moral athleticism. The ascetic treats the will as though it were in fact a sort of muscle, which could be strengthened by a moral daily dozen. He fails to see that there is no will which is not a will to do this or that. In his effort to isolate the will he divests it of content. He creates a false dualism between his will and his concrete inclinations. He does not see that if his ruthless war upon his impulses were successful, he would have destroyed himself altogether; and that it *cannot* succeed, because he can after all do no more than range one part of himself against another. Instead of achieving peace and harmony, therefore, he aggravates the antagonisms which already divide him, and converts into unnatural monsters the appetites with which he is endowed.

Similarly, the puritan in his zeal to forge a highly tempered and sharp-edged will loses sight of the ulterior purpose which such a formidable weapon is designed to serve. Its purpose is to put the appetites in their place, but this implies that they may justly claim a place. It is as much the task of the moral will to make room for the appetites as to confine them to that room. It is true that their unruliness must be broken, but only in order that they may thrive in peace. This positive provision for concrete goods and satisfactions provides the only moral justification for their subordination, as the claim of God to the obedience of his subjects rests on his provident love.

The puritan in his insistence upon the effective control of his supreme principle harps upon it incessantly, when it should be reserved for crucial decisions. Suspicious of all intermediaries, he neglects their indispensable role. Because the love of God speaks with authority, it does not follow that it must speak all the time. With God and conscience forever looking over his shoulder, a man cannot devote himself to any interest, however innocent, with the absorption which is the condition of its satisfaction. To acknowledge God's authority it is not necessary to run to God with every little problem. It is as though a man should take the Supreme Court as his guide, philosopher, and friend. God and conscience, like the Supreme Court, take no cognizance of the greater part of life. It is their function to determine a general orientation and to define limits. Within these limits subordinate principles—the appetites, prudence, family love, communal loyalties, science, and art—must enjoy autonomy. Without that autonomy they cannot be fruitful of good, and the effect is to create a waste instead of orderly abundance.

The moral will divorced from its natural content, freed from accountability to the human desires which it is designed to serve, proceeds to extravagant lengths. It may lead to a masochistic pleasure of self-denial, or to the hoarding of a personal power which yields no good beyond its own subjective satisfactions. Aldous Huxley has described such a case:

> In a mild and spiritual way Herbert was very fond of his food. So was Martha—darkly and violently fond of it. That was why she had become a vegetarian, why her economies were always at the expense of the stomach—precisely because she liked food so much. She suffered when she deprived herself of some delicious morsel. But there was a sense in which she loved her suffering more than the morsel. Denying herself, she felt her whole being irradiated by a glow of power; suffering, she was strengthened, her will was wound up, her energy enhanced. The dammed-up instincts rose and rose behind the wall of voluntary mortification, deep and heavy with potentialities of force. In the struggle between the instincts Martha's love of power was generally strong enough to overcome her greed; among the hierarchy of pleasures, the joy of exerting the personal conscious will was more intense than the joy of eating even Turkish delight or strawberries and cream.[27]

Excessively developed, and divorced from all positive goods, the moral will takes pride in its own negating, and flaunts it before the world. Deprived of natural delights, it retaliates by affecting to despise them. Instead of conceding the innocence of natural goods until they are proved guilty, it considers them as presumptively guilty, since they have not proceeded from itself. Hence that strange fanaticism, vividly portrayed by Walter Scott, and pilloried with delicate restraint by Richard Hooker:

> There sprang up presently one kind of men, with whose zeal and forwardness the rest being compared were thought to be marvellous cold and dull. These grounding themselves on rules more general; that whatsoever the law of Christ commandeth not, thereof Antichrist is the author: and that whatsoever Antichrist or his adherents did in the world, the true professors of Christ are to undo; found out many things more than others had done, the extirpation whereof was in their conceit as necessary as of any thing before removed. . . . All their exhortations were to set light of the things in this world, to count riches and honours vanity, and in token thereof not only to seek neither, but if men were possessors of both, even to cast away the one and resign the other, that all men might see their unfeigned conversion unto Christ. . . . Where they found men in diet, attire, furniture of house, or any other way, observers of civility and decent order, such they reproved as being carnally and earthly minded. . . . If any man were pleasant, their manner was presently with deep sighs to repeat those words of our Saviour Christ, "Woe be to you which now laugh, for ye shall lament." So great was their delight to be always in trouble, that such as did quietly lead their lives, they judged of all other men to be in most dangerous case.[28]

Fanaticism may assume many different forms, use different symbols, excite different emotions, formulate different ideologies, but whether it be the puritanism of the seventeenth century or the communism and Fascism of the twentieth, its characteristic danger is the same. The measures taken to give a cause ascendancy, to secure allegiance to its supremacy, beget a forgetfulness and reckless disregard of that concrete beneficence which originally commended it, or which at any rate constitutes the only ground on which it possesses a moral justification.

By a curious paradox the rigorism of the puritan evades the most serious difficulties of life. His effort takes the form of a kind of brute strength rather than of skill. The difficulties which he overcomes are forces rather than complexities—forces that can be overcome by a dead heave of the will, and with comparatively little discrimination or understanding. Puritanism *wills* hard rather than thinks hard. Similarly, the puritan's precisionism involves the minimum of intellectual difficulty. The casuistical application of rules, especially of rules that are codified and set down in an authoritative document, is perhaps the simplest form of morality, requiring only a few steps of inference. The rules may go against the grain, and their application may require an overcoming of temptation, it may be difficult to *do* what one ought to do; but to *discover* what one ought to do is comparatively easy.

It is only a small part of morality which can be subserved either by 'main strength' or by the direct application of rules. Abstinence, yes; and punctuality. But temperance, wisdom, loyalty, friendship, happiness, justice, benevolence, liberty, peace—these are goods which require something more than overcoming, and something more than purity or scrupulousness. The supreme moral difficulties are similar to the difficulties of art, requiring judgment rather than exactness or power. Strength of will divorced from the art of its judicious application leads to brutality; and rules divorced from the purpose which justifies and interprets them lead to pedantry.

9

If it is fair to exhibit the puritan's defects, it is also fair to remember, here as elsewhere, those opposite defects which he condemned—to remember them is to feel some sympathy with the puritan's excessive reaction. He regarded his opponents much as the youthful athlete of today regards the libertine. The lack of moral control, whether due to infirmity of will or to violence of emotion, translates itself from age to age into different terms.

The puritan of the seventeenth century had the effect of "bracing character in a period of relaxation." He stood for "the lit lamp" and "the loins girt" against the indulgence and improvidence of his times.[29] That he should have specifically attacked drunkenness, sexual looseness and perversion, the brutality of sport, licentiousness at carnivals and feasts, dancing, card-playing, was in some degree a historical accident. These may or may not remain the most conspicuous symptoms of moral weakness. If not, then others have superseded them. There is always a loose living in some sense, a laxity, a shortsightedness, a recklessness of passion, a narrow preoccupation with the immediate satisfaction, an inordinate fondness for physical pleasures. 'Self-indulgence' is a term of reproach under any code, since it implies an indifference or resistance to that code as such, whatever code it be. Therefore he who takes arms against puritanism must consider that by so doing he gives aid and comfort to the puritan's enemy, who is in some sense also his own.

The puritan's rigorism contains, then, an important element of moral truth, both in that which it champions and in that which it opposes. He may with perfect right be made to serve as the symbol of that which he made peculiarly his own, and for which he sacrificed residual and compensating truths. So to use the puritan does not contradict the sober judgment which discovers his faults. Symbolism is not sober judgment; it is a simplification and subordination of the concrete complexity in order to point a moral. Its one-sidedness is overcome by the use of other symbols. The moral pantheon as a whole corrects the one-sided cults of its component deities: the worship of Zeus and Ares is mitigated by the worship of Athena, Aphrodite, and Apollo.

In his insistence upon the importance of salvation, the puritan symbolizes the choice of a supreme good and its preference over all other goods. Conceived as a moral athlete, the puritan symbolizes the enthronement of such a pre-eminent good—its control of the appetites, its practical ascendancy over intermediate goods, and its scrupulous regulation of conduct. He represents that inflexible adherence to creed which will always appear as fanaticism or obstinacy to more balanced minds—as the faith of the early Christians appeared to their more cultivated pagan contemporaries. He represents the ruthless subordination of every lesser consideration to the one thing needful. The puritan was single-minded—which is, in effect, to be narrow-minded. He stripped for battle by divesting himself of worldly attachments, he economized his spiritual resources by reducing his appetitive liabilities, he tempered his will in the fire of enthusiasm.

Such an ancestor may properly be worshiped in those recurrent periods of individual and social reform when there is an ominous sound as of surf on the rocks. The puritan, said Stuart Sherman,

> comes aboard, like a good pilot; and while we trim our sails, he takes the wheel and lays our course for a fresh voyage. His message when he leaves us is not, "Henceforth be masterless," but, "Bear thou henceforth the sceptre of thine own control through life and the passion of life." If that message still stirs us as with the sound of a trumpet, and frees and prepares us, not for the junketing of a purposeless vagabondage, but for the ardor and discipline and renunciation of a pilgrimage, we are Puritans.[30]

The puritan sailed his ship in the open seas. Despite his cult of moral vigor, he was not a moral introvert. He did not confine himself within his moral gymnasium, but used his strength out of doors, in the world. He pursued his calling, and he participated in the public life of his time and place. In the wars and revolutions precipitated by the Protestant Reformation he assumed the role of statesman and soldier. From this school of discipline came men who were notable for doing what they soberly and conscientiously resolved to do, despite temptations and obstacles—such men as William the Silent, Admiral Coligny, John Knox, Oliver Cromwell, John Milton, and our New England ancestors. The puritans imprinted on English and American institutions a quality of manly courage, self-reliance, and sobriety. We are still drawing upon the reserves of spiritual vigor which they accumulated.

CHAPTER ELEVEN

THE ULTIMATE INDIVIDUAL

1

PURITANISM PROCLAIMED a supreme good, and insisted both on its surpassing goodness and on its effective supremacy. In theory and in practice it accepted the full consequences of this teaching—the subordination of lesser goods, and the need of suppressing insubordination. In the chapters that follow we shall further explore the meaning of this puritan conception of life: first, its individualism; next, its social aspects; and finally, its broader cosmic and theistic setting.

Individualism is the antithesis of two universalisms, abstract and organic. The individual is the concrete particular rather than the abstract nature therein embodied—for example, Socrates rather than man; and the individual is the constituent member rather than the organic whole—for example, Socrates rather than the Athenian society. Puritanism is individualistic in both senses. Neither can be construed absolutely. Men have a common abstract nature, and this will always remain a part of the truth; but there can be no man without men. It is impossible to ignore man's social organization, but it is also impossible to ignore the fact that a social organization is composed of individuals. Similarly, the religious life involves some degree of union between man and God; but without some degree of separateness this union would lose its meaning. If man and God were identical, there might still be a universe, but there could be no religious life, which consists of the dealings of God with men and of men with God. The core of Christian faith and worship lies in a man's finding of God after an estrangement, and his enjoying a God in some degree distinct from himself.

It is a question, then, of relative emphasis as between the terms and the relationship. Which is fundamental and which is derivative—in being, in genesis, in causal explanation, in authority, or in perfection? In this relative sense puritanism is indubitably individualistic. Its stubborn individualism determines its economic and political affinities, and is of the utmost importance in determining its place in the development of modern American institutions. This individualism also distinguishes puritanism from pantheistic and mystical forms of religion, whether Occidental or Oriental.

In puritanism the concrete human individual is known as the 'soul,' and the emphasis which it receives represents puritan individualism in the first sense, the sense, namely, opposed to abstract universalism. But the nature of the soul conditions the relations into which it is qualified to enter, whether with other human souls or with a higher being of the same type, such as a personal God. In discussing the soul, therefore, we shall be laying the ground for a subsequent examination of the puritan's second individualism—his rejection, namely, of organic universalism, whether social or theological.

I shall not attempt any philological precision in the use of terms. The exact meanings of 'soul,' 'spirit,' 'individual,' 'person,' in the different phases of the Christian corpus (Mosaic, prophetic, synoptic, Pauline, Johannine, Hellenistic, patristic, scholastic) and in the different Christian languages (Hebrew, Aramaic, Greek, Latin, English) is a topic of vast complexity on which the scholars are divided, and on which, so far as I am concerned, they must remain divided. The moral and religious life, as the puritan saw and lived it, was composed of unitary and active beings of a certain characteristic sort. It consisted of certain things that happened within these beings, to these beings, among these beings, and by means of these beings. It is a matter of accident or convenience that we should call them 'souls.' The only important question is "What, to the puritan, were they like?"

2

We have, then, first to note that souls were concrete. In proportion as philosophers are, as they tend to be, governed by an intellectual bias, they assign the highest place in the order of being and value to abstract universals. Concrete particulars tend to be disparaged as signifying the minimum of intelligibility, and as the objects of 'mere' sense, affection, or action. Insofar as Christian belief has been interpreted and formulated by such philosophers, as it often has been, abstract deity has been exalted above the persons of the Trinity, an abstract humanity above particular suffering and sinful mortals, a timeless logical order above the creative acts of a temporal will, and the contemplation of abstract truth above the love of particular individuals.[1]

To the naïve Christian believer, however, concrete particulars are not mere negations of intellect, but presentations of experience and primary certainties. The Christian narratives are not allegories or myths in which the higher truths of the intellect are hidden; or symbols substituted for ideas. The ultimate meaning and the popular representation are one and the same. Creation means that God *did* bring man and the natural world into existence—in a distant past looked back upon from the actual present. It is a part of history antecedent to and continuous with the history of Abraham and Moses, of Jesus and the foundation of the Church, and of the Last Judgment. The future life means the *future* life, a more or less remote tomorrow reckoned forward from today. God created the world by the causal efficacy of his will and from the motive of love; will and love being construed in accordance with their plain human meaning. Adam sinned, and transmitted to his descendants a sinfulness which only God's redeeming love can cure. Through that love certain fortunate individuals are saved and restored to the innocence and joy which Adam forfeited.

All of these and like dogmas have, no doubt, their aspect of mysteriousness and their aspect of rationality, the one of which can be allocated to blind faith and the other to reason. But thus to judge them from the standpoint of the intellect, as lying either within or beyond its domain, is to ignore that positive meaning which they have in terms of experience itself: a meaning which is neither blind nor rational, and which commends them to the plain man. He needs no philosopher to tell him the meaning of creative action, of will, of persons, of sin, of repentance, and of love.

Love, as we have seen, is the supreme principle of Christian piety, and also, as we have yet to see, the highest attribute of God. The world as seen with the eye of love is a world of individuals, love being, as Royce pointed out, an "exclusive" passion, which, once it has fastened on its object, is satisfied by no other, even of the same kind.[2] It is directed to the individual on his own account—felt toward the individual for himself. It is a fondness and solicitude evoked by the concrete man, however much or little of the ideal he may embody. Jesus taught that with God not one sparrow is forgotten, and that since men are of more value than many sparrows, they may count, each and every one, on the same untiring and sleepless providence.*

Christian love is directed to the existent particular, in that time and place, and in that kind and blend of qualities, by which it is unique. This is most adequately represented by the attitudes of familial love. In terms of Christian love men are children or brothers, and God is the father, in whom parental love is perfected. The loving parent knows his own children, one by one, with a particular love for each. His children are not mere exemplifications of human attributes, which, once they have served their symbolic purpose, become redundant. The multiplication of children is not a repetitive process, or a series of experiments which, once the essence is grasped, may then be terminated without loss. Each unit adds value, as well as number; and if any individual were lacking, so much value would be lost to the universe. Each individual has a proper, as well as a generic, name; and is precious to the loving parent for being *this one* and no other.

Christianity considered as a body of ideas is an intermingling of Christian experience and tradition with such secular instruments of thought as were available to the Mediterranean world in the early centuries of the Christian era; and these instruments were largely forged by the pagan philosophers. It is impossible to divest any specific Christian doctrine altogether of this pagan ingredient. It is possible, however, to distinguish it, and to note the proportion in which it is mixed with the specifically Christian ingredient. We may then say that puritanism represents here, as elsewhere, an effort to purify Christianity; which, in this case, means to credit the plain statements of Scripture, naïvely and literally construed, and to accept the beliefs most immediately involved in the attitudes and emotions of the average Christian worshiper.

The pagan ingredient in Christian doctrine reflected the intel-

* This is the theme of Francis Thompson's *The Hound of Heaven*.

lectualism and the abstract universalism of Plato and Aristotle. Its adoption as an integral part of Christian thought is represented by the great system of Thomas Aquinas, now recognized as the official Catholic philosophy. Puritan thought, on the other hand, adhered more closely to religious common sense. As it sought to regain the pristine simplicity of worship, so it sought likewise to recover the pristine simplicity of mind; and to accept as authentic that view of God and man which was prior to the influence of Greek philosophy, and which is accessible to the humble believer as well as to the learned doctors. The puritan's religious consciousness was not interpreted and reconstructed by philosophy; it *was* his philosophy. The puritan's world was a dramatic and historical world, in which events were unique in time and place, and in which the principal agents were particular persons, called by proper names and enumerable in a cosmic census. His representations were perceptual and his imagination was pictorial. If he disparaged the senses, this was because of their limited range or their association with the baser appetites, and not because of the concreteness and particularity of their objects.

3

What is this concrete individual, this soul, which the puritan takes as the unit in his moral and religious transactions? What marks it off, and bounds its circumference? It is, of course, a complex being, capable of further analysis; and it is a term capable of entering as a whole into relations with other terms. It is an ultimate unit in the moral and religious realm in the same sense as that in which the molecule composed of atoms of hydrogen and oxygen is the ultimate unit in the realm of water. We must not take it to be a 'substance' of which moral and religious experience is an 'attribute'; or as a receptacle within which this experience is enclosed. We must start with the experience itself, and see what sort of unit it defines.

Now the moral and religious experience is essentially, as we have seen, a diversity of rival attachments, among which some acquire a dominance over others. A series of acts is unified through the sameness of desire which pervades them. Antecedent acts are performed with the expectation that their results will be conducive to other acts which are desired. They are selected as means to an end, and the whole series then assumes the form of a purpose. Two such desires or purposes assume a relationship of antagonism when the acts which they inspire are incompatible; and this antagonism persists until some dominant purpose acquires control, and exercises a censorship upon the rest, supplying a motivating power of its own and permitting other motives to operate only within a limited range. In their antithesis to the environment, whether physical or social, these activities are named by the singular personal pronoun; and the dominant purpose in its antithesis to subordinate desires assumes the name 'I will.' The will, or dominant purpose, in its power to negate or reinforce desires is called 'choice'; and in its power to exercise this control despite the strength of the subordinate desires, the will is said to be 'free.'

It will be noted that the description of the practical and emotional life has involved the use of the term 'expectation,' which is the germ of inference. Sensible sequences beget empirical expectations; identities, revealed by analysis, beget rational expectations. These things happen upon the humblest level of human experience. It is impossible to adopt means to an end without expectations of the future grounded in past experience; it is impossible to obey a rule or to be governed by fear of punishment unless belief is founded on subsumption of the particular under the general. Thus a man cannot hold himself to prudence or strict obedience unless he has an intellectual purpose—the purpose, namely, that his practice shall correspond to the 'facts' of sense or the 'necessities' of logic. And the control exercised by this specific passion constitutes another sort of freedom, a freedom to exercise or suspend the intellect.

These relationships constitute a unit when they bind their terms together in a manner in which these terms are bound to no other terms. Thus the means is bound to the end, when it is *adopted for* the end, in a manner in which the means is bound to no other end, nor the end to any other means. Similarly, the relation of subordination by which a desire is controlled by a dominant purpose does not bind the desire to any other purpose, or the purpose to any other desire. And the evidence which determines an intellectual judgment is bound to that judgment in a manner in which neither is bound to any other term. There is, in short, a set of elements whose reciprocal relations differ from their relations to any elements outside the set, as the relations of atoms within a molecule differ from the relation of these atoms to any other atoms.

In the concrete individual which we call the 'soul,' the internal relations are such as desire, purpose, subordination, will, choice, freedom, self-consciousness, memory, expectation, inference, prudence, and obedience. Its perimeter is the limit of the range of these relationships, the limit beyond which they are superseded by relations of another type, such as time, place, and causality. The exclusiveness of these relationships makes the soul a unit; the character of these relations makes it a moral unit.

The peculiar structure of this integral unit, and its peculiar dignity, are sometimes expressed by calling it a 'person,' or by saying that it is endowed with 'personality.' It is an ultimate unit in the sense that short of this type of inner relationship a unit is not moral; in the sense that, having this inner relationship, a unit is sufficiently endowed to constitute a moral being or person; in the sense that such a unit or person is not composable or decomposable into like units or persons; and in the sense that when two or more such units enter into relationships, such as those of religion, economics, or politics, the moral character of these relationships is derived from the personal character of their terms. The soul as person is the moral microcosm or molecule; and there is no moral macrocosm except in the sense of a system of personal souls.[3]

4

We turn from the internal unity of the soul to its externality—its 'spiritistic' or 'pneumatic' aspect. Insistence upon this aspect of the soul underlies the Christian view of the relations of mind and body.

Professor Etienne Gilson has made it clear that the Christian doctrine of the resurrection of the body was not an accident or a mere atavistic superstition.[4] The concern of Christianity was with the salvation and future destiny of *men,* and it was assumed that men have, or rather are, in some sense, bodies. Modern philosophers speak of the 'problem' of mind and body, arising from their duality: the soul is inextended, the body extended; the soul is known immediately and certainly, the bodily world by dubious inference; the soul is governed by laws of thought, the body by the laws of mechanics. From the standpoint of unsophisticated Christian piety, however, soul and body are one and indivisible. If it is necessary to distinguish the soul from the grossly ponderable body, then it is supplied by the imagination with a second and more ethereal body with which to achieve a freer flight. Body as such is not an enclosing receptacle made of a foreign substance and hampering the soul's intrinsic activities. It is, on the contrary, the vehicle of the soul, through which it engages in intercourse with its natural and social environment.

It is through his body that the individual man has a unique spatio-temporal history. If he has a future beyond the event called 'death,' then that future will be a prolongation of the same history. If *he* is to be resurrected, then he will remember his own past; he will look back upon it from some ulterior temporal position, and *out* upon it from some distant spatial position. If he is to be resurrected and is to live after death, he must carry with him those characteristics which make him a man. This is not a theory which has to await the sanction of speculative philosophy, but merely an extension of the experiences of everyday life. The burden of proof is upon those who would impute to man a cosmic destiny and at the same time deprive him of those familiar characteristics which define his concrete humanity. If it is hard to believe that the body should be resurrected, it is harder to imagine how a completely disembodied man could be a man at all.

It is true that Christianity conceives of body as something to be negated and escaped, but this is in a moral, and not in an ontological, sense, and by no means implies the rejection of corporeality as such. There are certain desires which are intimately associated with the physical organism and its biological inheritance. These give rise to the pleasures of the 'flesh,' and must, as we have seen, be subordinated; or even, when insubordinate, denied altogether. The body as responsive to these temptations is 'infirm.' It is body in this sense which is corruptible, and which returns to dust at death. The body which survives death, or which lives after death, must be incorruptible: "For this corruptible must put on incorruption, and this mortal must put on immortality." There is a "natural" or "terrestrial" body; and there is a "spiritual" or "celestial" body.[5] The pleasures of the natural, terrestrial, or corruptible body cannot be enjoyed in the life to come. There is considerable lightening of the baggage as the soul embarks on its last voyage; though this is offset, no doubt, by the new treasures acquired. But this does not contradict—on the contrary, it accentuates—the fundamental idea that the immortal or resurrected man has some body. And that body, corresponding to his new condition, means precisely what it means upon the higher moral levels of actual human experience, the condition, namely, of recognizability, of identity through change of place and time, and of effective agency.

5

This conception of the individual soul as the concrete human being, moral in its internal structure and at the same time corporeal in its external relations—an inner ascendancy of the love of God over lower passions, having at the same time a local habitation and a name—is confirmed by the puritan conception of the relations between man and God. God has created concrete persons; and it is such that God loves, and seeks to save and perfect. He loves them neither abstractly nor collectively, but each by each with a particular love. "God took me aside," said Thomas Goodwin, "and as it were privately said unto me, do you now turn to me, and I will pardon all your Sins." [6] The elect are individually nominated to Christ:

> The *Father* said unto the Son, *such an elect Soul there is, that I will bring into thy Fold, and thou shalt undertake for that Soul, as a Sufficient and an Eternal Saviour*. Wherefore, I am now, in thy Hands, O my Lord; Thy Father hath putt mee there; and I have putt myself there; O save mee! O heal mee! O work for mee, work in mee, the good Pleasure of thy Goodness.[7]

The particular human individual, whatever his destiny, whether salvation or damnation, is thus through God's interest elevated to a place of exalted dignity in the actual world.

God, in his own nature, is also a soul, a moral entity actuated by unerring and omnipotent love of the good and of the creatures he has fashioned in his image. In his second person, as Christ, God's nature is expressly humanized. In order that God may be man he must live on earth, in a specific time and place, and through an earthly body engage in reciprocal intercourse with a local environment. The humanity of God is represented by Jesus at Gethsemane. Pascal's rendering of this experience in his "*Le mystère de Jésus*"—the blend of loneliness, of patience, of tender compassion, of a faith which holds firm on the verge of despair, and of a suffering borne willingly for the sake of others lonely and suffering like himself—might well be taken as a summary of the essence of the Christian life.

This humanization of God is not a degradation. Never is God so divine, so evocative of love, so clearly entitled to worship and obedience, as in this aspect of triumphant suffering. And his humanity is the same thing as the divinity of man, both consisting in the victory of the moral will over temptation, amidst an environment which is at one and the same time an impediment and a sphere of opportunity. God, in order to be a God of religion, that is, an adorable and saving God, must become a particularized, a struggling, an acting, and a suffering individual. The relation of God to man and of man to God cannot be expressed save as an intercourse between two such souls—save in terms of *moi* and *toi*.[8]

The pneumatic aspect of the Christian soul receives further light from the conception of the Holy Spirit. Waiving the metaphysical difficulties which beset the doctrine of the Trinity, the underlying motive is clear. God is not merely a supreme and providential power, and a moral individual, but also a mobile and palpable force capable of operating locally. When God is considered as working in the individual man and reinforcing his moral will; or as dwelling in the collective life of believers in such wise as to unite them into the body of the church; then he is referred to as the Holy Spirit. The experience of the Holy Spirit is the sense of an access of love, of light, of assurance, and of energy that seems to come from 'without' or 'above.'

6

From the standpoint of critical thought the spiritistic conception of man and God which puritanism shares with Christianity at large is defective in its failure to recognize the sphere of mechanical causation. This defect is widely pervasive in its consequences. Modern physics has established itself by a resolute adherence to the descriptive and quantitative method, and to this method the puritan and Christian preoccupation with the moral and religious experience has proved stubbornly resistant. The Christian consciousness is naïvely anthropomorphic and teleological. It has evaded the serious difficulties arising from the fact that the body of the moral individual is part of a natural world which obeys the laws of physics and chemistry. Through its readiness to accept the causal agency of spirits the Christian mind has short-circuited the patient inquiries of the special sciences, and invoked ad hoc powers whose ways are inscrutable, and whose effects are therefore unpredictable. It has neglected the fact that the human mind is influenced from abroad mainly, if not wholly, by physical stimuli operating upon the bodily senses. It has, in other words, accepted telepathy; which is, to say the least, premature. It has been guilty of the so-called 'pathetic fallacy,' which imputes to the causes of good and evil the friendly or hostile feelings with which they are received.

There is, however, another side of the account. The Christian view of man is not a pure invention, or a mere effect of ignorance. It is, as regards its central core, a record of the moral and religious experience, accentuated and adhered to consistently. This fidelity of doctrine to experience is to be found in the beliefs of common men, rather than in the distinctions and systems with which these beliefs have been rationalized by scholastic philosophers or by theologians. It is a matter of fact, and not of speculation or dogma, that taken in its moral angle the world is a realm of will, of inner struggle, of obedience and disobedience, of despair or of new-found hope and courage. It is a matter of fact that these passages occur within the movable and self-identical spheres of individuals who communicate with one another, and are reciprocally related in space, time, and causality.

Its very unsophistication has saved the Christian consciousness from certain difficulties that have blocked the way of critical thought: the abstraction of the soul from the body, with its resulting impotence and irrelevance to the context of nature; the removal of the soul from time, with the consequent paradox of an agency that has no history; the conception of the soul as a substratum, deprived of its empirical characteristics; the reduction of the individual to an abstract universal or to a larger corporate entity; the hopeless attempt to save the moral and spiritual values of life while destroying or disparaging the sphere of their most unmistakable occurrence. There is, as Professor Gilson has insisted,[9] a Christian philosophy of man and of the moral individual: not merely in the sense that Christianity has imported into the European mind ideas of which secular philosophy has been compelled to take account, but in the sense that the Christian belief itself, as a verified report of experience, must be given a place in the sum of truth.

7

In puritanism, the individual human soul is both the subject and the scene of salvation. Doctrines such as predestination and election suggest that a man's salvation consists in his having his name registered, and that this is effected by a sort of absent treatment of which the fortunate beneficiary is himself unaware. Nothing could be further from the truth as the puritan saw it. A man's being saved meant that something happened to him of which he was fully aware, and in which he participated. He was saved by the grace of God, and he was saved irresistibly—but not unwillingly or unwittingly. Salvation was not a bequest written in God's testament from the beginning of time, opened only at the Last Judgment, and distributed only after the resurrection. The saved entered upon their patrimony here and now. Salvation happened within the life-cycle of the soul and at the very core of its humanity. This general truth I shall now examine under its three aspects: faith, retribution, and regeneration.

Faith is the beginning, albeit the mere threshold or dawning, of a new life. It marks a crucial point, defining a new direction which diverges to ever enlarging distances—the first step on a long journey. It is a human act which initiates the progressive achievement of God's saving grace. This doctrine, together with insistence on the right of private judgment as applied to Scripture, and on the priesthood of believers, forms part of that radically individualistic creed which distinguishes puritan protestantism within the larger stream of Christianity.

The fact that faith is an "evidence of things unseen" must not be allowed to obscure the fact that it is an intellectual act, involving both understanding and inference as well as acceptance. The reading of the Bible and the application of its teachings to life involve a grasp of its meaning and its implications. These acts of the intellect, however restricted, are acts of the same human individual who is their beneficiary: the believer interprets the gospel himself, and accepts it for himself. The minister, instead of being the source or vehicle of magical powers, is the teacher and preacher, who expounds ideas and presents their evidence to other minds. When Cotton Mather in his youth was disturbed by his impediment of speech, he said: "Another thing that much exercised mee was, that I might not bee left without necessary Supplies of *Speech* for my Ministry." [10] That his anxiety was needless, or his prayer, at any rate, answered, is proved by his lifelong volubility. The priesthood of all believers is not a mere rejection of the priestly caste, but an extension to all believers of the priestly vocation of teaching and preaching.

Preaching, with its odor of intrusiveness, differs only in its tone and manner from that more blessed thing called teaching. Teaching and preaching imply both an art of communicating ideas and a capacity to receive them. The idea that these functions should be exercised in some degree by all believers directed attention to free and universal education. The encouragement of intellectual attainment on the part of the ministry requires a similar qualification on the part of their congregations. It is not an accident that Geneva, Scotland, and puritan New England should have played an important role in the history of public education.

The puritan's homiletic volubility and addiction to theological combativeness were conducive to that practice of discussion, that interchange and cross-examination of opinion, which is the life-blood of free institutions. He sowed the seeds of that very tolerance which in his theocracy he sought to suppress. For if you seek to persuade a man, you assume that evidence and not external force is the fit instrument by which to deal with dissenting minds. You assume that each mind has a power and a right to reach its own conclusions, and that the most that another mind can do is to provide the options of intellectual choice. If you wish to persuade, and not merely induce a gesture of outward conformity, then you must wish for others that same receptivity to evidence through which your own conclusions acquire their force of truth. You cannot seek to persuade your neighbor without wishing him to be *open* to persuasion, and if you open his mind, other ideas may find lodgment there. And pending the moment of his persuasion you must accept a contrariety of opinion, and protect it by an appropriate form of liberty.

The right of private judgment implies that the truth is accessible to the isolated individual. The individual who sees or represents the object as it is, possesses all that is necessary to truth—not the whole truth, but the quality of truth. The agreement of other minds is an effect, and not a condition, of truth; minds which direct or yield themselves to the same object will tend to a sameness of judgment or belief. This is the precise reverse of the view that minds governed by the same internal principles, or united as parts of the same over-individual mind, will construct the same object. Puritanism, in common with the whole Christian tradition, was 'realistic' rather than 'idealistic' in its theory of knowledge. Puritan belief was not aware of this issue, being innocent of those subjectivisms, relativisms, and corporate authoritarianisms which, implanted in the European mind in the nineteenth century, have had such tragic consequences in the twentieth. But beneath its specific cosmology and moral code there lay the deeper and more general presupposition of a common objective world and scale of values which reveal themselves to man through his cognitive faculties; or, if not through his natural intellect, then through the added light of revelation.

8

Faith is belief, and belief has, over and above its intellectual character, an aspect of firmness, persistence, and subjective certainty. Burke attributed the "fierce spirit of liberty" in America partly to the religion of the northern provinces, which he said "is a refinement on the principle of resistance; it is the dissidence of dissent; and the protestantism of the protestant religion." [11]

Puritanism was distinguished not only by its spirit of dissent, but by its stubborn adherence to a creed. This attitude was not only different from, but also contrary to, those acts of understanding, inference, and persuasion with which it was associated. The puritan's guilt is, however, mitigated by the unavoidable difficulty which puritanism here shares with all mankind.

The puritan was not a pharmacologist, but a doctor and a patient; he both prescribed and took his medicine. Now to believe, in the practical sense, implies a degree of commitment which the theorist is privileged to avoid; to *live* by an idea requires some degree of fidelity and partisanship. The inevitable effect is to harden acceptance and repel unsettling evidence. In such a situation, which is the universal lot of men who must both think and live and live by what they think, there is a subtle and often insidious contamination of the intellect by passion and will. The will to believe is confused with the light of reason, and the certainty begotten by constancy or by the heat of polemics is mistaken for insight and theoretical demonstration. But if the puritan may be cited as a warning, it is only fair to add that he fell into error through eagerness to make his ideas not only conformable to evidence, but effective in practice.

The puritan is charged with pride of opinion and contentiousness. Individual minds, poorly endowed, scantily furnished, and little disciplined, were turned loose upon the Scriptures, with the assurance that they might there find the ultimate verities for themselves. That text should be divorced from context, and used to support crude individual vagaries; that private opinions should multiply; that their adherents should become their partisans; that dissent should issue in dissension—all this was inevitable. It rightly gave offense to the sweet reasonableness of Richard Hooker:

> Nature worketh in us all a love to our own counsels. The contradiction of others is a fan to inflame that love. Our love set on fire to maintain that which once we have done, sharpeneth the wit to dispute, to argue, and by all means to reason for it. . . .
>
> O merciful God, what man's wit is there able to sound the depth of those dangerous and fearful evils, whereinto our weak and impotent nature is inclinable to sink itself, rather than to shew an acknowledgment of error in that which once we have unadvisedly taken upon us to defend, against the stream as it were of a contrary public resolution! . . .
>
> Think ye are men, deem it not impossible for you to err; sift unpartially your own hearts, whether it be force of reason or vehemency of affection, which hath bred and still doth feed these opinions in you.[12]

Puritan contentiousness was not merely an offense to contemporary taste; it was a seed of inner weakness. It drove puritans themselves to a definition and enforcement of orthodoxy that belied their own principles. It proved their lack of certain indispensable qualities: moderation and flexibility of opinion, regard for the body of collective wisdom and for the authority of competent and learned minds, a modest admission of fallibility.

It is not inconsistent with the right of private judgment that a man should learn from others, or reckon on the possibility that his opponent may be right. This is a matter of temper rather than of principle; and the puritan's temper was often arrogant and combative. Let us admit this, and add to it the charge, no less relevant and just, that to impute the capacity for truth to every man not only elevates the man, but debases the truth. There still remains a large credit to the puritan's account from his doctrine of faith and private judgment: the internality of thought and belief to the individual human soul; the individual as the unique subject of rational assent, and as the object of persuasion; the interrelation within an integral individual of thought and will, so that he may act from his own inner convictions. If these are commonplaces, so much the better; but they need perpetual reaffirmation in a world in which most men are still ready to let others do their thinking for them.

9

Protestantism accentuates the Christian teaching that God's promise of salvation is made to men individually. The individual takes it as a personal matter between himself and God. Said Luther in commenting on the Epistle to the Galatians under the heading "For me":

> For he delivered neither sheepe, oxe, golde nor silver, but even God him selfe entierly and wholy, *for me,* even for *Me* (I say), a miserable and a wretched sinner. Now therefore, in that the sonne of God was thus delivered to death for me, I take comfort and apply this benefite unto my selfe. And this maner of applying is the very true force and power of Faith.[13]

But there is a price which has to be paid, to satisfy the requirements of *justice.* Even God does not evade these requirements, but himself pays the costs, which others have incurred. Among protestants it is the puritan who is the most radical exponent of justice, of both its rigors and its individualism. The topic of justice is of the sort that is confused by oversimplification. The ready-made and current conceptions conceal a complexity of motives. Let us begin with the classic distinction between distributive and retributive justice.

Distributive justice is any principle sanctioned by conscience, or held to be morally valid, by which goods and evils are apportioned among the individual members or classes of society. Thus it may be held that goods and evils should be apportioned equally, or according to capacity, or according to service, or according to need. Retributive justice is a special case of distributive justice, and declares that goods shall be apportioned like to like—good to those who do good, evil to those who do evil. It is the principle of distribution by merit, the maxim that people shall receive, retain, and enjoy what they deserve.

There are at least three interpretations of retributive justice. It may be taken either as an absolute principle, or as a method of control, or as an instrument of education. On the first interpretation it is held to be axiomatic or self-evident that virtue should be rewarded and vice penalized; justice being conceived as a sort of balance of payments and receipts, to be restored whenever it is disturbed. Conceived as a method of control, retribution induces men to do good, and deters them from doing evil. When retribution is conceived as educative, the emphasis is placed upon the alteration of the agent's character or disposition. Criminal justice has to do with negative retribution, or punishment; that is, the apportionment of evil to him who has done evil; there are, therefore, three theories of punishment. It may be conceived as a satisfaction of the demands of abstract justice, as a means of preventing the performance of injurious acts, or as a means of transforming the wrongdoer into a doer of right.

There is another fundamental idea of justice which is not less primitive than distribution and retribution. This is the principle of reparation or compensation. According to a recent observer of the mores of Kenya:

> The ideas of justice of Europe and Africa are not the same and those of the one world are unbearable to the other. To the African there is but one way of counterbalancing the catastrophe of existence, it shall be done by replacement; he does not look for the motive of an action. Whether you lie in wait for your enemy and cut his throat in the dark; or you fell a tree, and a thoughtless stranger passes by and is killed; so far as punishment goes, to the Native mind, it is the same thing. A loss has been brought upon the community and must be made up for, somewhere, by somebody. The native will not give time or thought to the weighing up of guilt or desert: either he fears that this may lead him too far, or he reasons that such things are no concern of his. But he will devote himself, in endless speculations, to the method by which crime or disaster shall be weighed up in sheep and goats.[14]

In compensatory justice attention is given not to the malefactor but to the recipient of injury, and good and evil are apportioned inversely —good to him who has suffered evil, evil to him who has been exceptionally fortunate. When it is stipulated that the compensation allotted to the injured party shall be taken from him who performed the injurious act, the retributive and compensatory ideas are combined.

10

The puritan emphasis on retributive justice and its individualistic implications appears in two doctrines.

In the first place, although a man does not earn salvation, he does earn damnation; though he is not rewarded for his righteousness, he is punished for his sins. But this does not mean that puritanism rejects retribution in its positive application. It means that while men *would* be rewarded by God's favor if they *were* righteous, they are in fact incapable of attaining righteousness unless they already enjoy that favor. What the puritan rejects, in other words, is not the principle of reward for merit, but human capacity for merit. Wherever the puritan influence has been diffused and applied to secular affairs it has supported positive as well as negative retribution; it has encouraged the idea that the righteous have a right to prosper, and that there is a defect in happiness unless it has been earned.

In the second place, although men are not saved for their own righteousness, they are saved through the atoning sacrifice of Christ. This means not that men earn salvation through vicarious righteousness, but that they escape damnation through vicarious punishment. Christ takes upon himself the just deserts of human sin. Hence the strange paradox that the requirements of justice are met by imposing on innocence the penalty that is merited by guilt. Negative retributive justice here violates positive retributive justice. The difficulty can be met only provided the principle of love is allowed to override the principle of justice; and this solution is possible only provided the first and second persons of the Trinity are so identified that in giving his only begotten son as a sacrifice for human sins, God is in reality sacrificing himself.

With the notion of guilt and punitive desert is associated the notion of responsibility. In the puritan philosophy of life, the individual is *held* responsible. This habit of thinking was deeply implanted in the American mind and profoundly affected both English and American institutions. Dicey, speaking of "principles which underlie the whole law of the [British] constitution, and the maintenance of which has gone a great way both to ensure the supremacy of the law of the land and ultimately to curb the arbitrariness of the Crown," continues as follows:

> The first of these . . . is that every wrongdoer is individually responsible for every unlawful or wrongful act in which he takes part, and, what is really the same thing looked at from another point of view, cannot, if the act be unlawful, plead in his defence that he did it under the orders of a master or

superior. . . . This doctrine of individual responsibility is the real foundation of the legal dogma that the orders of the King himself are no justification for the commission of a wrongful or illegal act. The ordinary rule, therefore, that every wrongdoer is individually liable for the wrong he has committed, is the foundation on which rests the great constitutional doctrine of Ministerial responsibility.[15]

Dean Roscoe Pound, in summing up what he believes to be the unfortunate influences of puritanism upon the development of the common law, declares:

> It has given us . . . the notion of punishing the vicious will and the necessary connection between wrongdoing and retribution, which makes it so difficult for our criminal law to deal with anti-social actions and to adjust itself in its application to the exigencies of concrete criminality. . . . The Puritan has always been a consistent and thoroughgoing opponent of equity. It runs counter to all his ideas. For one thing, it helps fools who have made bad bargains, whereas he believes that fools should be allowed and required to act freely and then be held for the consequences of their folly.[16]

No one seriously advocates the total rejection of the principle of retribution. Dean Pound would place a greater emphasis on equity and on social legislation; and in the field of criminal law would give relatively greater attention to the social causes and effects of criminality. But the principle of retribution would still operate in a large area of human conduct, and where operative would still presuppose the responsibility of the individual.

Punishment presupposes that a wrong act which is punished and a penalty which is suffered are events of the same individual history. The second must be attended with a memory and an acknowledgment of the first. The act itself must be attended by an understanding of 'the difference between right and wrong'—which is an intellectual and moral capacity peculiar to the individual mind. Ideally, the guilty man must see and feel that he has done wrong. As in the puritan conviction of sin, there must be an individual sense of culpability and repentance.* The same fixation of responsibility upon the individual is implicit in the conception of positive retribution. There must be acts of will,

* Hence the insistence among the more enlightened puritans, such as Jonathan Edwards, that in order to be guilty sin cannot be merely "imputed." Adam's sinfulness must be revived and re-enacted.[17]

choices, expectations, inferences, memories, identities, which unite into one individual him who sows and him who reaps; and he must feel that the reward is his just due.

The notion of social or corporate responsibility is a figure of speech and a source of confusion. A corporation has its own 'liability,' distinct from that of its individual members; but this means only that under the law debts may be incurred and damages assumed by a collective and impersonal fund. It is correct to say that a corporation is 'soulless,' which means not that it is blameworthy, but that it deserves neither praise nor blame—is neither guilty nor innocent. Culpability and merit must go behind the corporation to the individual officers or members who are responsible for its activities. Society may be considered either as a corporate entity or as a mere aggregation of causes, but in either case it is merely accountable—not responsible. It is not qualified to be the object of a retributive judgment.

The idea of retributive justice, then, is bound up, as the puritans insisted, with the idea of individual responsibility. But what of the idea of retributive justice itself? If this is abandoned, then its individualistic implications go with it. Retribution, taken as an absolute or axiomatic principle, is rightly under suspicion of being a mere rationalization of the primitive impulses of revenge and gratitude. The charge against puritanism on this score will be set forth in another context. But assuming that the puritan is at fault in fostering the idea of the *absolute* rightness and reasonableness of retributive justice, its two other interpretations, as a means of control and as an agency of education, remain unaffected.

When retribution is conceived as a method of control, it has precisely those individualistic implications which the puritan ascribed to it. If punishment is to be employed as a deterrent, or reward as an inducement, it must be imposed upon individuals who are capable of understanding the particular application of a general rule; who, being aware of the consequences of their acts and preferring pleasure to pain, property to impoverishment, liberty to imprisonment, or power to impotence, will choose accordingly; and who, suffering the penalty or enjoying the reward, will ascribe it to their own antecedent acts and recognize their deserts. The use of this method of control assumes that individuals exercising these functions are at the same time effective causes, through whose instrumentality evil may be prevented and good brought to pass.

No modern society has found it possible to abandon the use of retribution as a means of public control. Penological reform has reduced the severity of penalties, but in the hope of making them more sure and effective. Totalitarian states may be censured for their practice of terrorism or for their decoration of synthetic heroes, but such criticism testifies to the misuse, and not the disuse, of retribution as a method of control. And within those areas where retributive control is not exercised by the state, it is practiced by the social conscience and by public opinion. Guilt is penalized by ill repute, and merit rewarded by applause, even more effectively in a totalitarian than in an individualistic society; and a socialistic society which would reduce or abolish the rewards of private profit must proportionally increase the rewards of honor and reputation. The liberal reformer who deprecates coercion must create a social conscience that shall sanction his gospel, and induce its practice by individuals.

Retributive justice may also be conceived as an agency of education. The use of rewards and punishments in altering habits is demonstrated in the training of animals or in the education of children. But it may be argued that its results are only external. The man who refrains from unrighteousness from fear of pain or adopts the righteous course from hope of pleasure has not become in his heart a righteous man, but remains as he was, devoted to his own pleasure and pain. The extent to which the effect of retribution may be internal, and touch a man's deeper dispositions, will depend on the extent to which he imposes it on himself. But it is evident that we have already entered upon another phase of the saint's progress, namely, his spiritual regeneration.

11

When a man's salvation is consummated, he achieves a certain condition of which he is himself aware. Salvation is something that has happened *to* him, and not something that has merely happened *about* him. Call it 'regeneration, 'sanctification,' or what you will, the fruit of the gospel, in fact, the most perfect and precious fruit of creation itself, is to be found within the circumference of the individual soul. It is experienced there; and if it is not experienced there, then it has not occurred. This is the most fundamental and most radical part of puritan individualism.

Like other elements of puritanism, this idea was not invented, but was selected from the general body of Christian teaching for special emphasis both in theory and in practice. It is consistent with other puritan ideas: the sweeping away or drastic simplification of the whole liturgical, sacramental, and ecclesiastical system in order to bring the individual man face to face with God; the equal dignity of all believers; the sharp demarcation between the elect and the damned; the conception of the visible church as a congregation of saints; the rigors of discipline and the practice of self-examination.

There is a direct transition from negative retribution, or culpability, to regeneration. He who acknowledges his guilt has already experienced a change of heart even if he has not yet mended his ways. He who misses God has already found him.* If he accepts his punishment as just, he has shifted his allegiance from the law of the flesh (to use St. Paul's words) to the law of the spirit. When suffering seems meaningless, it induces despair; and when it seems to be unjustly inflicted, it induces resentment and bitterness. But when the victim of punitive suffering acknowledges its justice, then it both expresses and intensifies the sufferer's allegiance to justice. It is attended with a moral exaltation in which its mere painfulness is transcended.

Even more profound is the change which is affected by the experience of being forgiven. This derives its meaning from the sense of a just penalty remitted. The offender must acknowledge that he deserves punishment in order to feel the full force of its remission. The puritan's guilt is more than a mere obliquity; it is an offense against love. The forgiveness of such guilt is evidence of an even deeper love, and induces a correspondingly stronger impulse of gratitude.

Thus salvation, even in its aspect of culpability punished or forgiven,

---

* *"Tu ne me chercherais pas si tu ne me possédais."* [18]

is transformed into an experience of regeneration. The shift from justice to love conceives evil in a form in which it can be cured, and corresponds to the verities of moral experience. An offense forgiven is as though it had never been—the wound which it inflicted is healed. A forgiveness accepted renews and enhances the love which had grown cold in the offender's heart.

The experience of regeneration consists in a sense of power and of certainty, felt by the individual as a relief from frustration and as a resolution of doubt. These experiences can be verified without resort to speculation or dogma. He who is saved knows the goodness of God in the act of loving him; he knows his exceeding goodness, in loving him above all other loves. He derives a new power from the integration of his life—the resolution of inner conflict, the unification and convergence of his total motivation. That of which the 'fall' had deprived him was a capacity to recognize and choose the good. He has now recovered his 'freedom,' in the positive sense of a freedom to love God and to obey him from love, in place of a compulsion to obey him from fear, or to disobey him blindly. Of this surpassing goodness, and of its effect upon himself, he is the direct witness. He is aware of the new orientation of his affections, he tastes its sweetness, and he feels a reinvigoration flowing from his new harmony and single-mindedness.

To the puritan this was by no means the whole of the story. In his sense of assurance he did unquestionably claim, and seem to witness, an intervention from abroad. He seemed to see the hand, as well as the goodness, of God. The presence of this second, and external, factor is evident in prayer. It was characteristic of puritanism that the personal and spontaneous aspect of prayer should have been emphasized. Prayer was the believer's direct resort to God, without intermediaries. It was an exercise in submission and in the direction of the emotions to their supreme object. But it was at the same time a petition that called for an answer.

Unquestionably the average puritan believed that God exerted a transforming influence upon the soul. He found abundant scriptural support for this view in St. Paul; who, while he stressed the moral content of the Spirit, continually spoke of it as from God, as "working on" the soul, and as "delivering" it from the dominion of the flesh. "The fruit of the Spirit is love, joy, peace, longsuffering, gentleness, goodness, faith." [19] Of the fruit, since it ripens within his own breast, the human individual is the most reliable witness. But the puritan was, for better or for worse, committed to a theistic metaphysics. It was presupposed in his sense of security. For the saved soul felt not only purified, exalted, and invigorated, but destined to enjoy that state in perpetuity. His salvation meant that he was not only saved, but safe; and the guarantee of this finality of salvation, expressed in the doctrines of perseverance and irresistibility, could be afforded only by an identity between the forces to which he owed his regeneration and the forces that controlled the future course of the universe.

12

Any critical appraisal of the puritan's idea of personal salvation must therefore distinguish these two components: an immediate experience of inner moral change, and a belief in its divine spiritistic cause. Each has its characteristic difficulties and dangers.

The first is exposed to the danger of excessive emotionality. In St. Paul's exhortation, "be not drunk with wine, wherein is excess; but be filled with the Spirit," it is to be noted that he did not encourage men to be "drunk," even with the Spirit. Emotion imbibed to excess is as fatal as wine to those qualities which the apostle himself enumerated in the same context: "For the fruit of the Spirit is in all goodness and righteousness and truth. . . . See then that ye walk circumspectly, not as fools, but as wise." [20]

It is easy to confuse moral regeneration with emotional intoxication. A sense of elation, in which tensions are relieved and the individual is flooded with fresh streams of energy, may be no more than a phase of manic-depressive psychosis. Emotion may act as an anesthetic, and remove the symptoms of disorder without effecting its cure: taken as a sedative or stimulant, it may make a man a drug addict rather than a saint. The forces of suggestion and contagion may be deliberately created in order to induce a toxic effect. Emotionality, like disease, assumes an acute form when it becomes epidemic, its intensity increasing in proportion to its volume. Divorced from any specific ideational or practical content, liberated from every control, and having acquired a momentum of its own, it may violate every standard of taste, decency, or public order. A specious regeneration, like a fever, will be followed by a chill. Requiring the repetition of exciting stimuli, it will not bear the test of everyday living.

These evils, which mark the history of evangelical revivalism, were known to the puritan and were frequently the occasion of doubts and warnings. They were characteristic of the protestantism of the extreme left, and provided a motive for those puritan persecutions which are usually remembered only as evidences of intolerance. Jonathan Edwards, puritan leader of the Great Awakening, was aware that its emotional manifestations must be strictly judged by standards of piety and right conduct. In his *Treatise Concerning Religious Affections* he took pains to distinguish their mere "fluency and fervour" from the trustworthy signs of their "graciousness." The religious affections, he said, are truly "holy" only when they incline the heart to God, possess a "beautiful symmetry and proportion," and bear fruit in Christian practice.[21] If Edwards's *Faithful Narrative of the Surprising Work of God* is a penetrating analysis of the phenomena of conversion, his longer *Thoughts on the Revival of Religion in New England* is a most thorough appraisal of these phenomena—an appraisal in which the writer, while accepting the whole as a manifestation of the spirit of God, is at great pains to point out its dangerous excesses.

The Reverend Charles Chauncy, who was a contemporary of Jonathan Edwards, but stood apart from the Great Awakening, felt himself to be in the best puritan tradition when he warned his contemporaries that a feeling of regeneration may be purely delusionary unless it is confirmed by conscience, by works, by systematic thought, and by the test of durability.[22] In the spirit of the Enlightenment he distrusted what Bishop Butler called "superstition, and the gloom of enthusiasm."[23]

Puritanism itself, then, realized the need of objective checks, in order to avoid too great a reliance on subjective experience. Although it stressed the individual religious experience, it resisted anarchy, both intellectual and moral. It sought through intellectual sobriety to restrain vagaries of opinion, holding to the idea that thinking minds are brought to agreement by the common truth. It sought through moral sobriety to combat antinomianism, perpetually reaffirming the moral validity which is founded on conscience. And the critic, whether puritan or non-puritan, must at least concede this much to the defendant: that he was a witness of the immediate goodness and transforming power of love; and that here he was face to face with original data of the moral and religious life.

The puritan's theistic explanation of his spiritual regeneration lies less securely within the field of his competence. His difficulty was the difficulty that besets all mysticism, the difficulty, namely, of distinguishing the content of intuition from its interpretation in terms of current beliefs. A mind imbued with the theistic tradition will be almost irresistibly disposed to impute events which are not otherwise explicable to the agency of God. To the puritan this agency was unquestionably at large in the universe, and it was unhesitatingly invoked whenever the effect appeared in kind and in circumstance to be appropriate. The puritan mind was too quick to perceive the hand of God where a modern mind would insist upon a more rigorous and verifiable hypothesis.

Two things remain to be said in extenuation of the defendant's presumptive guilt. In the first place, moral regeneration does occur as a discontinuous change. The moral subject experiences a volte-face—an abrupt change of heart. The new good is not a mere extension of the old good, but a central change of attitude carried to all parts of the periphery. It is a break with habit, and with every prepossession, a change in the scale of values in which every particular value is reappraised. And this does not seem to occur through any effort or discovery which can be imputed to the subject's existing will. He finds himself, sometimes with cataclysmic suddenness, in possession of, or possessed by, a new will. However inadequate his explanation, the puritan is at any rate aware of a phenomenon to be explained.

Secondly, the puritan's belief in an external ground of his regeneration and feeling of security for the future—while it does, no doubt, transcend the limits of his experience, and involve dubious metaphysical hypotheses—may fairly be identified with that hopefulness of belief which is inseparable from moral earnestness. It is difficult to devote oneself to an end, to place it above all ends, and to enlist wholeheartedly in its support, without confidently expecting the co-operation of cosmic agencies. It is proper that this confidence should be considered as faith rather than as rigorous knowledge. But the puritan's assurance of salvation in the sense of objective destiny may be ascribed to the strength of his resolve and the reach of his aspiration rather than to mere superstitious habit or defect of intellect.

In his individualism the puritan testified to moral and spiritual realities of which he was in immediate possession. It was his role to impress on his age and his posterity the prerogatives of the human soul. He knew it as the sphere of those linkages which constitute the life of thought and will, and as both the scene and the witness of salvation. He symbolizes those ideas of individual integrity and responsibility and of personal dignity and destiny to which the American mind has so persistently clung through all its phases of historical change. He is qualified to be their symbol because in him they were carried to excess and allowed to eclipse other truths which have become more evident to a later age.

CHAPTER TWELVE

THE ECONOMIC VIRTUES

1

THAT PURITAN INDIVIDUALISM should have been so completely assimilated to the texture of American life was possible only because of its affinity with laissez-faire capitalism. The puritan tradition has not formed an element apart from the economic life, serving as a check upon its excesses, and an independent standard by which its values were to be assessed; but it has served to strengthen the forces by which the economic life has itself been governed. Instead of providing antagonistic scruples, it has allowed the economic motives free play and given them its blessing.

This is both a fact and a paradox—a paradox because Christianity affirms the vanity of worldly achievement, and because puritanism as a radical form of Christianity might have been expected to utter this affirmation in its harshest and most uncompromising form. How does it happen that puritanism has not only tolerated ambition, the competitive struggle, and the acquisition of wealth, but has invested them with a glow of piety? For puritan Christianity not only permits men to "help themselves," but teaches that "God helps them that help themselves" [1] —when to "help themselves" implies taking and possessing material goods, and when this taking and possessing implies at the same time a taking away and a dispossessing. William Penn was a good puritan when he said of the Reformation, "I am sure 'twas to *enjoy Property* with Conscience that promoted it: Nor is there any better *Definition of Protestancy,* then *protesting against Spoiling* Property *for Conscience."* [2] To solve this paradox is the task of the present chapter.

There is a set of moral attributes or virtues, generally endorsed by the conscience of mankind, that have the effect of promoting the material success of those who possess them. Such acquisitive virtues are, for example, industry, sobriety, frugality, reliability, temperance, and simplicity of living. These are by no means the only, or even the most fruitful, conditions of material success. A man may find it more profitable to be wellborn, or to exercise political power, or to have rich friends, or to be crafty and unscrupulous. But the qualities enumerated and others commonly associated with them play a double role: they both bring profit to their possessor, and at the same time earn moral approbation. They define a common ground which is higher than appetite or malice even though it be lower than justice, love, or the pursuit of beauty and truth.

These virtues were both possessed and admired by puritans because, in the first place, they were the characteristic virtues of their class. As has been pointed out, the protestant religious revolution coincided with contemporary political and economic revolutions; and with the rise of a bourgeoisie which was as resentful of political and of economic privilege as it was of the ecclesiastical hierarchy. Puritanism was a part of the revolt against feudalism. In a feudal system power, wealth, and authority descend from above through a graded hierarchy. The individual who finds himself upon a lower level accepts what is assigned and delegated to him by his superiors, and repays it by loyalty, obedience, and service. The anti-feudal attitude is the refusal to accept inferior status—the resolve to ascend from below. In such an ascent the individual or the class must rely on its own efforts—on its naked capacity and intensity of exertion rather than on the favor of fortune. The yeomen, tradesmen, and artisans from whom the English and American puritans of the seventeenth century were largely recruited were men of this type. They were neither so unfortunate as to be imbued with a sense of helplessness, nor so privileged as to be satisfied with their present status. They possessed just enough to whet their appetites for more and to feel confident of their power to attain it.

To improve one's position in the economic scale through one's own efforts requires a certain technique. This technique is in part specifically economic and amoral. It is necessary to attain some form of skill or to produce some form of commodity for which there is a demand. The development of the technical arts of manufacture, distribution, and finance created economic opportunity. This belongs to the history of the so-called Industrial Revolution, and does not here concern us. The technique of economic self-improvement has also its factor of intelligence, which is likewise amoral. There are qualities of shrewdness, inventiveness, and understanding which enable a man to make the most of his economic opportunity.

But there is also a moral technique—a technique of steadfastness, self-denial, and prudence. This technique is not a sufficient or even necessary condition of gaining wealth, and in any given case it may be less important than intellectual or strictly economic qualifications. Nor does it rank high in the scale of moral value. It has an implication of selfishness, and when it opposes itself to benevolence or to the love of God, it deserves, no doubt, to be accounted as unrighteousness. When we say that 'it pays to be honest' we do not mean that honesty is the only thing that pays, or that there is a market for pure honesty, or that honesty is the decisive factor either in morals or in business. But in honesty two circles overlap, the code of conscience and the code of business success. He who is honest is doubly rewarded, in the market-place, and before the bar of conscience or God. So it is with industriousness, punctuality, thrift, abstemiousness, and other like qualities. These virtues were doubly characteristic of the puritans, as members of an economic class and as members of a religious sect. They were doubly sanctioned: They commended themselves to the puritan as member of a rising class which sought to improve its position by taking shrewd advantage of new economic conditions, and they commended themselves to him as a puritan.

2

In the first place, he found his warrant in the Bible, and especially in the Old Testament, which, while it may be said on the whole to be less lofty than the New, is for that very reason better fitted to serve as a handbook for everyday living. This is notably the case with the Book of Proverbs, which abounds in ready-made, homely precepts, teaching the lessons of worldly wisdom:

Give not sleep to thine eyes, nor slumber to thine eyelids. . . . Go to the ant, thou sluggard; consider her ways, and be wise: Which having no guide, overseer, or ruler, Provideth her meat in the summer, and gathereth her food in the harvest. How long wilt thou sleep, O sluggard? when wilt thou arise out of thy sleep? . . . So shall thy poverty come as one that travelleth, and thy want as an armed man. . . . He becometh poor that dealeth with a slack hand: but the hand of the diligent maketh rich. . . . Wealth gotten by vanity shall be diminished: but he that gathereth by labour shall increase. . . . A good man leaveth an inheritance to his children's children: and the wealth of the sinner is laid up for the just. Much food is in the tillage of the poor: but there is that is destroyed for want of judgment. . . . The rich ruleth over the poor, and the borrower is servant to the lender. . . . He that tilleth his land shall have plenty of bread: but he that followeth after vain persons shall have poverty enough. A faithful man shall abound with blessings: but he that maketh haste to be rich shall not be innocent.

This was not merely a counsel of material self-interest. The same context contains the injunction: "A good name is rather to be chosen than great riches, and loving favour rather than silver and gold." [3] The teaching of worldly prudence is, even in the Book of Proverbs, subordinate to the teaching of divine providence and justice. But the fact remains that the Old Testament, and also the New (as in the parable of the wise and foolish virgins), do affirm and proclaim the fact that diligence, self-control, and foresight conduce to power and riches. And the puritan, given to citing isolated texts, and to the regulation of his life by precepts, found abundant Biblical support for that same code which was proved by his economic experience.*

But the code of economic self-improvement had a more solid support in puritan piety than any mere conformity to the letter of the Scriptures. It was in profound agreement with that subordination of immediate to ulterior goods which is the central motif of the gospel. For worldly prudence is a resistance to the solicitations of immediate pleasure through a sober regard for the morrow: a willingness to postpone satisfaction in order that it may be greater and more durable; a patience begotten by the ordering of values; a dispelling of the illusion of proximity. It re-

---

* Exegesis also played its part, as when in John Cotton's *Spiritual Milk for Boston Babes,* the Eighth Commandment is construed to mean: "To get our goods honestly, to keep them safely, and to spend them thriftily." [4]

quires and rewards that power of self-mastery and that strictness of self-regulation which, as we have seen, the puritan set himself to attain by the cult of the moral will and the discipline of the appetites.

The code of worldly prudence was in harmony with the puritan's self-reliant individualism. It was an application to livelihood and business of the puritan emphasis upon the integrity of the human soul and of its characteristic prerogatives. It was the economic form of the puritan's idea of retributive justice, with its emphasis upon desert and individual responsibility. And it expressed the puritan's temper of personal independence. For though he was willing to admit his dependence on God, he looked to this as a means of emancipation from dependence on men and on nature. Salvation was the only gratuity that he was willing to accept. Wealth which he earned for himself was both a manifestation and a condition of self-reliance. It was a product of his own will and at the same time an instrument of freedom. For he who possesses reserves and resources in his own right may defy the weather of fortune—and he may likewise defy his fellow man, of whatever station. He who controls what a man needs controls the man; he who himself controls what he himself needs is subjected to no control but self-control.

Finally, a laborious life was in accord with the puritan cult of the moral will. It was both a school in which such a will was acquired and a sphere for its exercise. To the puritan, worldly prudence was not an instrument of avarice or self-indulgence, but a quality of character to be esteemed for itself. It was a form of spiritual energy, in which the sheer will triumphs over the natural inclination. It fortifies the soul against temptation, whereas "negligence is the nurse of sin." So the puritan read in that comprehensive encyclopedia of righteousness, Richard Baxter's *Christian Directory: or, a Body of Practical Divinity, and Cases of Conscience* (1673):

Zeal and diligence are the victorious enemies of sin and satan. They bear not with sin: they are to it as a consuming fire is to the thorns and briars. Zeal burneth up lust, and covetousness, and pride, and sensuality. It maketh such work among our sins, as diligent weeders do in your garden; it pulleth up the tares, and burneth them. It stands not dallying with sin, nor tasting or looking on the bait, nor disputing with, and hearkening to the tempter; but casteth away the motion with abhorrence, and abstaineth from the very appearance of evil, and hateth the garment spotted by the flesh, and presently quencheth the sparks of concupiscence: it chargeth home, and so resisteth the devil that he flieth.[5]

3

Worldly prudence is practiced in the world, and its effects are registered there, in terms of worldly success. His esteem for this code of virtue is thus an expression of the puritan's belief that moral forces, instead of operating in a separate realm of their own, govern nature and history. Through his moral will the puritan hoped to control the actual course of events, and to conquer evil not only in himself but through himself in the world at large.

According to this philosophy, if a man is rich, he has himself to thank; if he is destitute, he has himself to blame. The rich man is an object of commendation, and not merely of envy; to be a pauper is not a misfortune, but a disgrace. When an individual possesses the qualities of austerity, reliability, energy, industry, self-control, marital fidelity, frugality, sobriety, thrift, self-reliance, and foresight, the effect is wealth. When, on the other hand, a man is pleasure-loving, untrustworthy, sluggish, idle, dissipated, irregular, extravagant, frivolous, wasteful, dependent, and careless, the effect is poverty. The effect, being traced to its cause, is to be dealt with accordingly.

The first condition of salvation from evil is a hopeful diagnosis which translates the evil symptoms into a form which will yield to treatment. The moral diagnosis of poverty has the effect of bringing it within the range of the puritan's special competence. When poverty is considered as a social disease it is remediable by methods for which the puritan was ill equipped. The more modern diagnosis reflects a new expertness, resulting from the development of science. Given this expertness, it is natural and proper that reform should now seek to cure or prevent poverty by a control of its biological, psychological, economic, legal, and political causes, and by a resort to the new technologies of mass production. Given the lack of this expertness, and a greater familiarity with moral causes, it is equally natural that the puritan should have looked to these for his remedy.

The puritan and the modern views agree, however, in their purpose of reform, and in their rejection of certain alternatives which have played an important part in the history of Christian moralizing—such, for example, as the idea of the caprice and mockery of fortune. Thus Boccaccio, in his *De Casibus,* collected from history a corpus of this wantonness with which fortune reverses itself. Those whom fortune favors today become its victims tomorrow: the higher the eminence, the lower the fall. Lydgate develops this idea in his *Fall of Princes:*

Sodeyn departyng out of felicite
Into miserie and mortal hevynesse,
Vnwar depryvyng of our prosperite,
Chaung off gladnesse into wrechchidnesse.[6]

So far as this idea was assimilated to Christian thought it was used, of course, to point a moral. It drove home the vanity and the essential insecurity of all worldly attainment, and the peculiar vulnerability of the man who has multiplied his hostages to fortune. It taught men to lay up their treasure in heaven, where "neither moth nor rust doth corrupt, and where thieves do not break through nor steal."

But the idea of fortune as an erratic and incalculable force could never be wholly assimilated to Christian doctrine. It contradicted the teaching of divine omnipotence, and of a providential regulation of human affairs. It tended, therefore, to be superseded by a pious quietism—by the idea, namely, that the unequal distribution of worldly fortune is designed by God. That some men should be rich and others poor is in accordance with God's inscrutable will. The pious man will accept his lot; or he will even rejoice in his poverty, as less likely to seduce him from the love of God. However small the degree of his wealth or worldly eminence, a man may yet attain the one thing needful and superlatively important, namely, his reconciliation with his Creator.

To these alternatives, the belief that fortune is essentially capricious and therefore incapable of control, and the attitude of resigned acceptance, puritanism and the modern spirit have presented a common front of opposition. They agree in the conviction that worldly fortune *can* be controlled through a knowledge of its causes, and in their teaching that a man *should* improve his fortunes through the exercise of such control. They differ only in their view of the causes through which this control is to be exercised.

Over and above the direct causal relation of virtue to worldly prosperity, the puritan claimed the inestimable advantage of having God on his side. It was natural to suppose that if God brought his elect aid on the field of battle, he would also look to their service of supply; and that the same power of the spirit and efficacy of prayer which enabled the faithful to prevail in war would enable them to prosper in peace. Poverty was evidence not only of a lack of virtue, but of the absence of God's favor and aid.

Poverty being a sign of spiritual weakness, the puritan cure would be found in reprobation. Poverty is to be condemned rather than pitied or relieved. Its prevention will be sought in the inculcation of that prudence, self-reliance, and piety whose absence is its cause.

Such will be the puritan's method of social reform. It may be asked why, if virtue and piety are ends in themselves, they should be put to use. Why should a man not retreat from the world and devote himself exclusively to moral and spiritual exercises? His virtue and piety being thus attained, why should he not enjoy them in their essence, without reaping those worldly advantages which are fraught with danger to his soul?

The puritan's rejection of the monastic form of piety was based on the truth that active virtue requires a world, a task, a field of operation, in which the will is confronted with obstacles to be overcome and with instrumentalities to be employed. As the soul is no individual soul at all without a body, so virtue is no moral possession of an individual soul unless there be some secular sphere for its enactment. Otherwise it is only a symbol of negation. 'Labor' in its monastic form signifies a mere exercise in humility and renunciation. The real meaning of labor lies in the production of goods, and this meaning can be realized only through engaging in the work of the world in a manner suitable to the economic needs and conditions of the day. Similarly, the real meaning of frugality and thrift lies in their usefulness as a means of acquiring wealth.

The puritan's other-worldliness was not a withdrawal from the world, but a living *in* the world in accordance with other-worldly standards. Instead of abstracting the spiritual part of life and guarding it against contamination, he introduced it into war and politics and even trade, as though to say that a virtue which cannot bear exposure to reality is no virtue at all—no genuine capacity and power of the will. The piety which the puritan cultivated was not an exotic flower requiring an artificial soil and temperature, but a hardy plant acclimated to the outdoor conditions of human nature and human life. To his choice of this bolder course the puritan owes those compromises which have cast doubt on his sincerity, and which have filled the puritan himself with a sense of the ambiguity of his standards. But it is to this choice that he also owes the directness of his influence on human affairs and institutions.

4

Owing to the work of Max Weber and Ernst Troeltsch, attention has been drawn to the connection between the Protestant Reformation, especially in its Calvinistic developments, and the spirit of modern capitalism.[7]

Like many a truth, this important relationship has been confused through the excessive claims of its proponents, and lost to view through the counter-excesses of its critics. If it be contended that modern capitalism was *caused* by the puritan, it is easy to adduce proofs to the contrary. The Florence of the fifteenth century was capitalistic but not puritan; the Boer Republics were puritan but not capitalistic. The Venetians and the Hanseatic League, the Fuggers and the Medici and the Rothschilds, contributed to the development of modern commerce and finance without deriving inspiration from protestantism. Sombart has arrayed an impressive mass of evidence to prove that capitalism grew out of the wealth which popes and temporal rulers accumulated by taxation, and from the need of materials and labor with which to carry out the large-scale enterprises of war and luxury.[8] Even to prove that capitalism as we know it *could* not have developed without the aid of protestant ideas would require an experimental isolation of causes to which history does not lend itself.

It is also clear that puritanism in its beginnings was not capitalistic. The economic ideas of Calvin in Geneva, of John Knox in Scotland, and of the American colonists in New England were, like their political ideas, theocratic and not capitalistic. The society conceived by puritanism in its purity was dedicated to the love and worship of God, and rigorously controlled the worldly and material interests of its members.

Shall we, then, say that the development of economic capitalism and the development of puritan protestantism were unrelated? Both the presumption and the facts are to the contrary. There was so great agreement of ideas between the two developments that any individual or group that participated in the one was thereby predisposed in favor of the other. The two mentalities were and remain congenial. The thesis being thus limited, the evidence is, I think, incontrovertible. In the elaboration of this thesis I shall consider, in turn, the division of labor, the private ownership of property, the freedom and inviolability of contract, the motive of profit, and the accumulation of wealth. I take it that these ideas would be considered central in the creed of modern capitalism. It remains to show that these ideas were confirmed by the moral and religious cult of puritanism.

5

Bringing piety with him into the world, the puritan accepted what he found there as the condition of participation in its affairs. As Aristotle had pointed out, every man has, over and above the common vocation of being a man, some special vocation or sphere of usefulness. This immemorial division of labor, inaugurated, no doubt, when Abel "was a keeper of the sheep" while Cain "was a tiller of the ground," was emphasized by the crafts and guilds of the Middle Ages, and reaffirmed and elaborated by the Industrial Revolution. It was taken over by puritanism as a part of God's providential design. I quote Richard Steele's *The Tradesman's Calling,* published in 1684:

> God doth call every man and woman . . . to serve him in some peculiar employment in this world, both for their own and the common good. . . . The Great Governour of the world hath appointed to every man his proper post and province, and let him be never so active out of his sphere, he will be at a great loss, if he do not keep his own vineyard and mind his own business.[9]

The same lesson of vocational piety was taught in such works as John Flavell's *Navigation Spiritualized: or a New Compass for Seamen* and *Husbandry Spiritualized, or the Heavenly Use of Earthly Things;* and Fawcett's *The Religious Weaver.*

The puritan, whether tradesman, navigator, husbandman, or weaver, will be a better tradesman, navigator, husbandman, or weaver for being a man of God. More will be expected of him, by himself as well as by others, on that account. He will possess every virtue, including those specific virtues of prudence and self-mastery which are effective in the world of affairs. Owing to his power of will he will be exceptionally scrupulous and faithful to his duties. He will have a strong sense of personal responsibility. Being a man of God, he can count upon the aid of God. He will bear God's name before the world, and will be quickened by the esprit de corps of the elect. His piety thus takes the form not of a specifically religious exercise, such as prayer and meditation, or compassion, or ecclesiastical office, or sacramental or liturgical observance, but of an access of motivation, competence, and power in the performance of that task to which he is appointed as his part in the work of the world.[10]

The man who is zealous and faithful in his calling is working both for his own and the common good. His work is a work of co-operation. As Richard Baxter said:

> The public welfare, or the good of many, is to be valued above our own. Every man therefore is bound to do all the good he can to others, especially for the church and commonwealth. And this is not done by idleness, but by labour! As the bees labour to replenish their hive, so man being a sociable creature, must labour for the good of the society which he belongs to, in which his own is contained as a part.[11]

6

As regards private property, the fundamental puritan idea is not that a man has a right to keep what he possesses, but that he has a right to possess what he has earned. There may be a legal right to possess what one has inherited, or received as a gift, but there is no moral right except insofar as legal rights themselves rest upon a moral right of contract—to be considered presently. Still less is there a moral right to the possession of what one has seized by force. To possess what one has earned, on the other hand, is to enjoy what one deserves. It is 'just' that one should possess it. Insofar as property is the product of the individual's exertions, disciplined will, and prudent foresight, it is the expression of his moral personality: it 'belongs,' in the sense of moral fitness, to the same individual whose qualities of character are embodied in it. The righteous indignation with which he resents violation of its possession is very different from a defiant determination to keep what one holds, for it expresses conscience and not merely desire.

To this same idea that a man's earned property is his desert is to be traced the American approval of the 'self-made' man. When wealth is considered as a fund with which he can buy what he wants, and thus enjoy security, comfort, or luxury, it is enviable but not meritorious. The circumstances of its origin are then irrelevant; and if it has cost the possessor nothing—if he has been fortunate enough to inherit or receive it as a gift—so much the better. When, however, wealth is considered as an index of character, then the deeper the depths of poverty from which the possessor has risen, the greater the obstacles over which he has triumphed, the less he has profited by the favor of fortune, the more creditable his wealth. The man of humble origin, surrounded in his youth with every possible disadvantage of lowly station, of ignorance, of material deprivation, or even of ill-health, who has through the pure power of his moral will ascended to the summit of affluence, is the paragon and model of youthful aspiration. His prosperity is accepted without resentment, and applauded by his admiring contemporaries.

The cult of the self-made man is one of the central and most persistent elements of the American conscience. James McCabe wrote in 1871:

> The chief glory of America is, that it is the country in which genius and industry find their speediest and surest reward. Fame and fortune are here open to all who are willing to work for them. Neither class distinctions nor social prejudices, neither differences of birth, religion, nor ideas can prevent the man of true merit from winning the just reward of his labours in this favored land. We are emphatically a nation of self-made men, and it is to the labors of this worthy class that our marvelous national prosperity is due.[12]

The brightest exemplar of his idea is Abraham Lincoln, whose story is used as pointing the moral to American youth:

> Abraham Lincoln was a man sprung from the people, working his way from poverty to fame, from a little log cabin beside a Kentucky stream to the stately White House in Washington. . . . His is a story . . . that you can never know too well; for it tells you how the poorest boy can reach the highest power, through ways more wonderful, and by paths more difficult than were ever trod by hero in wonder story or prince in fairy tale.[13]

Colonel Henry Watterson, citing William Dean Howells's characterization of Mark Twain as "the Lincoln of our literature," goes on to say:

> The genius of Clemens and the genius of Lincoln possess a kinship outside the circumstances of their early lives: the common lack of tools to work with; the privations and hardships to be endured and to overcome; the way ahead through an unblazed and trackless forest; every footstep over a stumbling-block, and each effort saddled with a handicap. But, they got there—both of them—they got there.[14]

The rights which attach to private property, and by which its possession by a given individual is justified, evidently reach beyond the range of his own moral will. There is a right to possess what one has inherited, and to receive an 'unearned' income from capital. Here also there is a sanction which can be found in the puritan's code. His appeal is not to the economic need for capital, or to the social advantages of a 'leisure class.' There may be such justifications, but they are not his. The characteristic puritan justification is found in the contractual theory of law. With this theory we shall be further and more fully concerned in the chapter which follows. But to forestall the charge of its omission it requires mention in the present context.

The puritan mind was deeply impregnated with the idea that society is essentially an agreement, entered into by individuals with their eyes open. The law of contract as affecting property and services is a special application of a principle by which the puritan interprets both state and church. Now if a man enters into a bargain hoping to profit by it, he has no right to withdraw or to complain if he gets the worst of it. This notion is a practical, if not a logical, sequel of moral individualism. The individual is competent to make a contract, and is properly held responsible for its keeping. He understands and takes upon himself whatever consequences it may entail. The individual who makes it, and the individual who profits *or suffers* by it, are the same individual, and the one state is the moral sequel or desert of the other. The application of this principle to the case of unearned property rests on the assumption that the laws of inheritance, or of investment, or of corporations, are agreed on by all individuals, whether they happen in any given case to be beneficiaries or victims. Every individual hopes to be a beneficiary, all cannot; but the consequences are as just in the one case as in the other, since the individual is in both cases equally committed.

7

The fundamental idea of modern capitalism is not the right of the individual to possess and enjoy what he has earned, but the thesis that the exercise of this right redounds to the general good. This justification is necessary if the institution of private property is to be defended against the charge of selfishness. The motive of private gain brings the individual into competitive relations with his fellows: he takes advantage of them, and presses the advantage mercilessly. He buys in the cheapest market and sells in the dearest. In the market he meets his fellow men as competitors for exclusive goods, and his success is at their expense. His brother is his adversary, with whom, if he does not exchange blows, he at any rate matches wits. When there is an increased demand for what he produces or possesses he raises its price, and makes it more difficult to obtain. He profits by his brother's need to buy his brother's labor at the lowest cost, and to keep him in a condition of dependence. He drives the hardest possible bargain, and if the other's bargaining power is weak, so much the better.

Capitalism is not a mere acceptance of this fact—a mere gospel of 'the tooth and the claw'—but a justification of it which enables the selfish competitor to enjoy the sense of an approving conscience. It is pointed out that free competition spurs the individual to efforts which benefit society at large. His private profit depends on his providing at the lowest possible cost goods for which there is a demand, that is, which satisfy wants. The spur of competition impels him to improve by invention the quality, and to lower the cost, of what he has to offer, and thus puts a premium on progress. Even the defeated competitor, who gets the worst of the bargain, shares as a consumer in the general benefit. Competitive success is a test of economic fitness in the exercise of a social function. A highly competitive society will possess a strong bargaining power in competition with other societies. When international trade is 'free,' goods of progressively higher quality and lower cost will be available to consuming humanity at large. Or, if a given society is a closed economy, it will derive from the internal competition of individual with individual a power to defeat and survive its external enemies.

Thus the individual may devote himself to private gain with the comforting assurance that he is a patriot, or a benefactor of mankind. He may *justly* ask to be let alone, and may be allowed to pursue his profitable course without molestation. The popularity of such a creed among successful or ambitious men is not surprising.

A man who accepts the teachings of Jesus will find it hard to reconcile them with the code of such a competitive economy. He will not sell another man what the other wants, still less what the other needs; but will give it to him, though it be the last cloak or loaf of bread. He will leave the business of the world to the non-Christians, or divide himself into two parts, his weekday practicality and his sabbatarian piety. Or, conceding the motive of private profit to be necessary or useful, he will do what he can to mitigate or compensate its harshness. He will make laws against usury, attempt to establish a 'fair price' and a 'minimum wage,' or devote himself to charity, or to exhortations designed to soften the heart of the businessman.

Puritanism, on the other hand, did not apologize for the profit motive in business, or evade it, or weaken it; but integrated it with the motive of piety. This may be considered surprising in view of the fact that puritanism was a radical expression of Christianity. The explanation lies in the fact that its radicalism did not lie in this quarter. It was the Christian conception of God as the omnipotent and just ruler, and not the Christian conception of compassionate love, which puritanism pressed to its extreme logical conclusions. The capitalistic system—profit motive, competition, and all—was simply taken over as God's plan for administering the affairs of this world in the interest of human society as a whole. Thus Richard Baxter says of the rewards of labor:

> It is God's appointed means for the getting of our daily bread: and as it is a more real honour to get our bread ourselves, than to receive it by the gift of our friends or parents, so is it more comfortable to a well-informed mind. We may best believe that we have our food and provisions in mercy, and that they shall be blest to us, when we have them in God's appointed way: who hath said, "If any man will not work, neither should he eat." [15]

Similarly, according to Cotton Mather, the relations of creatures are so organized according to the divine plan that self-interest and the public good are in complete harmony with one another:

> There should be . . . some *Settled Business,* wherein a Christian should for the most part spend the most of his Time; and this, that so he may Glorify God, by doing of *Good* for *others,* and getting of *Good* for *himself.*[16]

And since the fundamental causality that governs all events is the divine will, however selfishly a man may seek profit, he may and should accept it with gratitude and without self-reproach: "In our *Occupation* we spread our *Nets;* but it is God who brings unto our *Nets* all that comes into them." [17]

Finally, the puritan theology accustomed the minds of its adherents to the idea of a privileged body who enjoyed a monopoly of divine forgiveness. A good puritan must endure the thought of being saved, not at the *expense* of his fellow men—for their damnation is not a consequence of his salvation—but *without* his fellow men. He must be willing to be saved knowing that he is one of a favored few, his pity for those who perish being solaced by the thought that they get what they richly deserve. The horrors of hell are vividly depicted to him not in order that he may clear up this abysmal slum and remove its inhabitants to better mansions provided through some enlightened housing plan. Not at all. The purpose is to persuade him to look to his own residential destiny. He has read, no doubt, that there are many mansions in heaven, but the suggestion of the dogma of election is rather that their number is limited, and that he should expect to find one of them reserved exclusively for him.

The effect, if not the intent, is to harden the puritan's heart. That a bourgeoisie should enjoy prosperity while a proletariat remains in penury and dependence, that only the economically fit should triumph or survive, is tolerable to his conscience. Success undisturbed by a large residuum of failure corresponds to the general scheme of things. The competitive system can retain its hard temper and its cutting edge without offense, and its economic rationalization can receive the endorsement of piety.

8

The economist Francis A. Walker wrote: "Capital . . . arises solely from saving. It stands always for self-denial and abstinence. . . . Interest, then, is the reward of abstinence." [18] This sweeping claim is evidently untrue, since there is a point of satiety beyond which the cessation of expenditure costs nothing. If the accumulation of wealth beyond that point is to be moralized, it must be on other ground than asceticism.

An observer from abroad finds it difficult to understand why the American businessman, after he has gained a competence sufficient to satisfy his needs, gratify his tastes, and guarantee his security, does not cease from his efforts but prolongs them to the grave. He continues to go to his 'office,' and to carry the growing burden of his affairs. When he prefers to 'die in harness' or 'with his boots on,' he is commended for his character rather than reproached for his folly. Such behavior is no doubt in large part an effect of habit. The man who has spent his life in labor is ill fitted for leisure, and the man who has devoted his best years to acquisition is not likely to become a spendthrift in his old age. But the deeper motive for the continued accumulation of wealth lies in the persistence of those virtues by which it has been created.

If wealth is esteemed for the qualities which have conditioned it, rather than for the goods which it can purchase, then these qualities are as becoming to old age as to youth and middle age. There is no fixed point at which this ceases to be the case. There is the same merit in increasing one's fortune from $100,000 to $1,000,000 as there is in rising from penury. If industriousness, punctuality, self-control, and thrift are better than idleness and dissipation, then a man will seek as long as possible to possess them and to exhibit them before men. There is no paradox in his accumulating wealth 'beyond the dreams of avarice' or beyond the limits of his wants—for neither avarice nor want is his motive.

The indefinite accumulation of wealth is the economic equivalent of the perseverance of the saints. The elect were not saved by inches, but once and for all; and once saved, always saved. Their actual spiritual fortunes suffered no vicissitudes, though the symptoms might be uncertain and fluctuating. The best evidence of election was to be found in a consistency of virtue prolonged throughout the whole of the life-cycle. As Max Weber said:

> The God of Calvinism demanded of his believers not single good works, but a life of good works combined into a unified system. There was no place for the very human Catholic cycle of sin, repentance, atonement, release, followed by renewed sin. Nor was there any balance of merit for a life as a whole which could be adjusted by temporal punishments or the Churches' means of grace.[19]

By the same token the puritan saint could never rest content with any given level of attainment. If wealth be a proof of godliness, then riches are the cumulative effect of persevering godliness. In Luther the notion of a calling tended to the resigned acceptance of one's lot. It was sufficient to have a place, however humble, in God's plan. With Calvin, on the other hand, a man was called to a perpetual improvement of his situation as evidence of unremitting zeal. To quote Richard Baxter:

> If God shew you a way in which you may lawfully get more than in another way (without wrong to your soul, or to any other), if you refuse this.

and choose the less gainful way, you cross one of the ends of your calling, and you refuse to be God's steward, and to accept his gifts, and use them for him when he requireth it: you may labour to be rich for God, though not for the flesh and sin.[20]

As opposed to Lutheran quietism, Calvinism was congenial to the rising man, whose ambitions knew no limit. Riches already attained created an obligation to labor for more. In reply to the question "Will not riches excuse one from labouring in a calling?" Baxter's answer is:

No: but rather bind them to it the more: for he that hath most wages from God, should do him most work. Though they have no outward want to urge them, they have as great a necessity of obeying God, and doing good to others, as any other men have that are poor.[21]

Of the natural effects of the economic virtues, it is power rather than the pleasures of possession or expenditure that finds a sanction in the puritan consciousness. "The rich ruleth over the poor, and the borrower is servant to the lender"—so runs the proverb. The puritan conscience will sanction power when it is earned and merited, and when it is dedicated to the service of God. This holds of the greater power which is the effect of accumulated wealth. In the exercise of such power the individual realizes himself as a self-sustaining unit freed from all other dependence in order that he may the more effectually serve God—if, happily, in his pride of power, he still remembers God:

Riches may enable us to relieve our needy brethren, and to promote good works for church or state. And thus also they may be loved: so far as we must be thankful for them, so far we may love them; for we must be thankful for nothing but what is good.[22]

9

The puritan cult of the economic virtues represents an advancing worldliness in which Christianity arrived at a reversal of its original profession of faith. The first stage of historical Christianity was the renunciation of this world for the sake of the next. The Christian life was a life apart. Persecuted and rejected by men, Christians engaged in mutual help and prayer while awaiting their translation to that spiritual realm which was their proper sphere. Monasticism developed not as a universal rule of life, to be sure, but as a symbol of the profound divergence between perfected piety and secular affairs.

After the acceptance of the fact that the majority of Christians must spend the greater part of their time in doing the work of the world, and that if they do so they will reap a temporal reward, there still remained at first a lively suspicion of its dangers. The Christian may prosper, but his prosperity is a liability rather than an asset. "*La miséricorde de Dieu est infinie: elle sauvera même un riche.*"[23]

The next stage of advancing worldliness was to esteem prosperity, provided it was purified. Christianity was now brought into the world, but the world must make concessions. A Christian king would temper power, and even justice, with mercy; a Christian knight would temper force with gentleness; a Christian merchant would temper shrewdness with charity, and greed with moderation. Christianity was still in principle alien to the world, but it might dwell in the world and enjoy its rewards, provided it exercised an ameliorating influence.

By an inner dialectic, allied with the temper of the times and the bias of his class, the Christian now advanced to a final stage in which the code and the motives of worldly prosperity were adopted as they stood, and reinforced by moral and religious sanctions. Christianity in this form did not merely dwell at peace with the world through mutual accommodation, but gave the world its blessing. Worldly values were no longer excluded, deprecated, tolerated, or even limited, but reinterpreted and endorsed.

Here the puritan Christian was indeed on treacherous ground. Given moral and religious credentials, worldly values tend to take command. Their moral and religious meaning assumes the form of a 'rationalization' or mere aroma of piety attending a life completely dominated by worldly ends. Prosperity considered as the *criterion* of salvation, and prosperity considered as itself constituting salvation, become in practice indistinguishable. Prosperity, being first commended for its underlying moral qualities or as evidence of divine favor, is now commended in itself; and this commendation is extended indiscriminately, until it embraces luxury and exploitation.

Thus Christian piety, having been transferred to the business of this world, suffered from its own success like a plant withering under the density of its own foliage. The man who had improved himself in the face of adversity could no longer enjoy for himself or for his children the same school of discipline. The Christian conscience was deeply troubled by this apparently inescapable paradox. John Wesley wrote:

> I fear wherever riches have increased, the essence of religion has decreased in the same proportion. Therefore I do not see how it is possible, in the nature of things, for any revival of true religion to continue long. For religion must necessarily produce both industry and frugality, and these cannot but produce riches. But as riches increase, so will pride, anger, and love of the world in all its branches. . . . Is there no way to prevent this—this continual decay of pure religion? [24]

How the New England puritans found themselves condemned to deplore the prosperity which was the fruit of their pious labors has been admirably recounted in Professor Perry Miller's *Declension in a Bible Commonwealth.*[25] The members of this society attributed their success to the special favor of divine providence and to their own faithful observance of God's will. In the early phases of their struggle, when they suffered from dangers and hardships, they looked to God for external goods; but when, after 1660, their prayers had been answered and they had attained security and abundance, the emphasis shifted to a consciousness of guilt. They were evolving from a "Bible Commonwealth" into a modern capitalistic society; and, given their economic circumstances, their own piety had inevitably promoted this evolution. But now that they prospered in outward ways they felt a growing corruption in their hearts. They were becoming proud, self-indulgent, and forgetful of God:

> Through a succession of . . . fast-day and election sermons, in the proclamations, histories and tracts, a standard theme began to emerge, to become the recurrent moral of all these utterances: New England is steadily declining from the high purity of the founders. . . . New Englanders seemed to be deserting the great tradition of their fathers. But they would have deserted it still more had they not labored in their callings with a diligence that was bound to increase their estates and widen the gulf between the industrious and the shiftless, the rich and the poor, between those who made money and those who borrowed it—and paid the interest! [26]

10

Puritanism has allowed itself to become a sanctification of worldly success. It has helped to elevate the system of capitalism to a position of dogmatic authority, and induced men to forget the moral or religious standards by which this, like any other economic system, has in the end to be judged. Prosperity having been justified by piety, piety becomes a mere adjunct of prosperity. In explaining to a delegation from the Methodist Episcopal Church his decision "to put the Philippines on the map of the United States" and keep them there, President McKinley said that he had gone down upon his knees and asked for guidance from Almighty God; whereupon it "came" to him (among other things) that it would be "bad business" to turn the Philippines over to "our commercial rivals in the Orient." [27] Thus success in business having been esteemed as evidence of the hand of God, God is now esteemed as an adviser to business.

The puritan influence has not prevented the development in America of the most advanced and questionable forms of capitalistic enterprise: "Mammon working blindly, almost automatically, yet with a kind of terrible demonic power, and Wall Street the final result of the doctrine of election! Has the whirligig of time ever cast up a stranger or more staggering paradox?" [28] Puritanism cannot be held guiltless of that claim of divine ordination with which the American captain of industry has justified his inordinate privilege:

> "Divine-right Baer," a railroad president of a generation ago, expressed with inadvertent clarity a thought that was in many minds when he said that God had wisely placed the control of the country's wealth in the hands of a few that from the abundance of their profits there might filter down to the many so much of prosperity as would be good for them.[29]

In America puritanism has confirmed the excessive preoccupation with acquisition begotten by the vast potentialities of an incompletely subjugated continent. If that joylessness of which Langdon Mitchell complains [30] is to be ascribed to puritanism, it is not because puritanism is repressive, but because it obliges the individual to be forever improving his economic position. Since there are always others who have exceeded him or who threaten to outstrip him, he is in a state of chronic discontent with his present lot. He regards his superiors with envy, and if he fails, is embittered by disappointment. Since he hopes for something better, he does not endeavor to make the most of what he has. Happiness is perpetually postponed and never realized. There is no cult of leisure. The social mass is too unstable to crystallize into those forms of tradition which express themselves in art and ritual. Puritanism, which is so congenial to the cult of the rising man and the progressive society, must share responsibility for the evils which that cult engenders.

Since religion may properly be expected to correct the defects of secular life, puritanism may properly be reproached for having here only confirmed its harshness and narrow emphasis. It has encouraged men to be forever moving, striving, and making, and has not taught them to live graciously and tenderly in the present. In its emphasis on the instrumental goods of livelihood and wealth, and in its neglect of intrinsic goods such as beauty, contemplation, and social intercourse, it has been no better, as it should have been, than the world in which it lived. If the lust for wealth exists, and is necessary or even beneficent in its indirect effects, it is better to acknowledge this motive candidly than, like Mr. Chadband,* to make gestures of piety while devoting oneself to gain, or prate of the next world when one's real concern is with this.

Even when the modern puritan has subordinated business to ethics, the result is largely vitiated by the inadequacy of the ethics. The puritan's economic moralism has tended to deflect attention from the purpose of economic life, and to represent it as a drama of retribution, or as a school of discipline, rather than as an attempt through science and co-operation to provide an abundant and equitable satisfaction of human needs. Hence the force of Edward Bellamy's satire upon the nineteenth century from the standpoint of a socialist utopia:

> To put the whole matter in the nutshell of a parable, let me compare humanity in the olden time to a rosebush planted in a swamp, watered with black bog-water, breathing miasmatic fogs by day, and chilled with poison dews at night. Innumerable generations of gardeners had done their best to make it bloom, but beyond an occasional half-opened bud with a worm at the heart, their efforts had been unsuccessful. . . . Moreover, urged some

---

* Charles Dickens, *Bleak House*.

eminent moral philosophers, even conceding for the sake of the argument that the bush might possibly do better elsewhere, it was a more valuable discipline for the buds to try to bloom in a bog than it would be under more favorable conditions. The buds that succeeded in opening might, indeed, be very rare and the flowers pale and scentless, but they represented far more moral effort than if they had bloomed spontaneously in a garden.[31]

There is, however, no possible solution to the economic difficulties of mankind that does not embrace the values of effort, ambition, emulation, and self-reliance, and that does not permit the individual within limits to enjoy the fruits of his virtues. For driving home this partial truth, and building it into the habits and dispositions of the modern world, puritanism deserves credit. It is indispensable to any society that men should keep their promises. Otherwise the whole institution of credit, which conditions not only economic life but every species of human co-operation, is dissolved. There is a romantic attractiveness in the cavalier:

Good at a Fight, but better at a Play
Godlike in giving, but—the Devil to Pay![32]

At the same time it is well that the work of the world should be done in a spirit of sobriety. It is well that men should produce, and not merely give or receive. It is well that the individual should count the cost and faithfully discharge his obligations.

There are worse handbooks for the daily living of the average man than the Book of Proverbs or *Poor Richard's Almanac*. However the best society shall be organized, it will be no stronger than the individuals who compose it. Any society, whether capitalist, neo-capitalist, socialist, or Fascist, will depend for its cohesiveness and firmness of texture on the individual's industry, self-discipline, and accountability. The economic virtues, sordid and ignoble though they be when abstracted from the remainder of human life, are essential to its bone and sinew.

CHAPTER THIRTEEN

THE COMMUNITY OF RIGHTEOUSNESS

1

There is a widespread impression that the puritan community in its full theocratic flowering was a sort of Society for the Suppression of Vice, or dictatorship of Anthony Comstock. There is enough truth in this analogy to make it a parody. Puritanism did tend, through the concurrence of a number of motives which will be examined in the present chapter, to assume the form of a community in which piety was enforced both by social ostracism and by legal penalties. At the same time, however, it embraced motives and latent forces which worked in precisely the opposite direction, so that for reasons internal to itself the puritan theocracy was unstable, and paved the way for tolerance and the separation of church and state.

We have first to note that zeal is inherently an expansive force. It is the plain duty of a Christian to disseminate his belief as is set down in the Scriptures: "Go thou and preach the kingdom of God." Puritan authorities reaffirmed this injunction, as when Richard Baxter, having devoted a chapter of his *The Saints' Everlasting Rest* to "The Necessity of Diligently Seeking the Saints' Rest," added another chapter on "The Duty of the People of God to Excite Others to Seek This Rest." In puritanism this function of preaching and excitation was not reserved to the clergy, despite their exalted office and high prestige. The doctrine of the 'priesthood of believers' encouraged every puritan, layman as well as minister, to take it upon himself. The members of a flock which has no appointed shepherd must nose one another into the paddock. It becomes the duty of the nearest at hand to seek out the straggler who has lost his way.

But it would be a mistake to suppose that Baxter's second injunction was merely superadded as something alien to the first. The second is in fact superfluous, for the obedience of the first will, if it be *sufficiently* diligent, entail the obedience of the second. Preaching the kingdom of God is a sort of overflowing of its zealous acceptance. He who has good news and is sure that it is true is irresistibly impelled to communicate it to others, for their edification as well as for their information. He who has found a cure for his ailment does not have to be exhorted to tell others about it—he has to be restrained lest he become a public nuisance. The puritan was nothing if not zealous, and his belief therefore possessed an abundance of this overflowingness. Having discovered a great good, he wished it to prevail, and his joy in its triumph, and in his own contribution to that triumph, was only an expression of his joy in its goodness. Said Cotton Mather:

> I find myself so affected with the Glory of my Lord JESUS CHRIST, that if I can be the Instrument of advancing His Glory in the world, and bringing others to acknowledge it, I am raptured with inexpressible Consolations. . . . I find, that I really reckon my *Opportunities* to serve God and His Interests in the world, the most valuable of all my *Treasures*.[1]

True to his underlying principles, the puritan could not seek credit for his missionary zeal. It was not a form of works by which he might hope to earn salvation. But his "assurance of being already justified, and entitled to eternal life" will so exalt him that he can in good works outstrip any mere "merit-monger." [2] Since the saint's condition of election and regeneration will thus express itself in his emanation of moral and religious truth, the latter may be taken as evidence of the first. A man may therefore be judged by the spiritual condition of those about him who are most susceptible to his influence—his household, for example, and his neighbors—as the strength of a radio-active substance is measured by the rate, intensity, and distance of its spread.

2

This expansive force of evangelical moralism determined the form assumed in puritanism by that natural benevolence which in some degree inhabits every human breast. Familial affection and neighborly solicitude were not created, but were colored, by puritanism. The good which a benevolent man dispenses to others will depend on what he deems good; hence a benevolent puritan will dispense piety. "Our natural affection," said Cotton Mather, "is to be improved into a religious intention. . . . In promoting the good of the neighbourhood, I wish above all, that you will consult their spiritual good. . . . Charity to the *souls* of men is undoubtedly the highest, the noblest and the most important charity." [3]

Cotton Mather was true to this principle, both in precept and in practice. "I will be very inquisitive and solicitous," he said, "about the company chosen by my servants." A faithful servant having been miraculously restored to him after suffering many hardships, this humane puritan wished to show him a signal favor. He did not raise his wages, or relieve him from service, but recorded in his diary: "I sett myself to make him a Servant of the Lord." [4] On another occasion Cotton Mather thought kindly of his brothers and sisters. Whereupon, instead of contriving them some pleasant indulgence, he resolved as follows:

1. To make my Brothers and Sisters, as many as are capable thereof, to take their *Bibles*, when the Scripture is read Morning and Evening before Prayers; and attentively accompany the vocal Reader.
2. To gett my Sisters, as many of them as I can, to spend an *Hour* together every Day. Half of it, in writing and half of it, in furnishing themselves with Knowledge about the Matters of Religion.
3. To sett a better Exemple of Seriousness and Gravity before them.[5]

Parental affection took the same austere form. Speaking of his children, Mather said: "I would frequently admonish them to be sensible of their baptismal engagements to the Lord." [6] No orphan's plight could stir the reader's sympathies as that of poor, be-fathered little Sammy, aged ten, and the devoted object of methodical and improving kindness:

I must think of some exquisite and obliging Wayes, to abate *Sammy's* inordinate Love of Play. His play, wounds his Faculties. I must engage him in some nobler Entertainments. . . . What shall be done, for the raising of *Sammy's* Mind, above the debasing Meannesses of Play! . . . Entertain *Sammy* betimes, with the first Rudiments of Geography and Astronomy, as well as History; and so raise his Mind above the sillier Diversions of Childhood. . . . Heap a great Library on my little *Samuel*. . . . *Sammy* is united with a Society of sober and pious Lads, who meet for Exercises of Religion. I will allow them the Use of my Library, for the Place of their Meeting; and give them Directions, and Entertainments.[7]

Because the puritan's moralism inclined him more to edification than to indulgence, it must not be assumed that he was lacking in benevolence. He *willed the good of others.* His individualism must not be confused with egoism. That piety which he sought to implant in himself and in others had its seat in individual souls, but he was not concerned exclusively with his own soul. Nor must his endorsement of individual prosperity, or his acceptance of a world in which some men are forever excluded from divine favor, be allowed to obscure the fact that for puritanism, as for Christianity generally, the end of God in creation was the happiness of *all* creatures. Whether God's love and justice were in the last analysis consistent is another matter. In any case, whether justice is taken as an independent principle setting bounds to love, or is in the depths of God's inscrutability subordinated to love, there was no place for *self*-love as a principle of piety. Cain was his brother's keeper, and all men were brothers.

The Christian is not allowed, like the priest and the Levite, to pass by on the other side when his fellow man, friend or stranger, falls among thieves. This humanitarian burden the puritan took upon himself. Benjamin Franklin wrote of Cotton Mather's *Essays to Do Good* (in a letter addressed to that same poor Sammy who was the object of so much parental solicitude): "If I have been . . . a useful citizen, the public owes the advantage of it to that book." [8] Of Cotton Mather, again, his editor wrote, "He imposed on himself a rule, never to enter any company, where it was proper for him to speak, without endeavouring to be useful in it." [9] Puritan piety thus embraced a well-wishing interest in all members of the human family. As being both individualistic and benevolent, motivated by a will for the good, not of any abstract or corporate entity but of mankind in their severalty, it was thus readily assimilated to the broad humanitarian purpose of democracy.

3

If fault is to be found with Cotton Mather's relentless benevolence, it cannot be with its humanitarian intent, but rather with its method and its conception of good. Children are as a rule subject to two kinds of parental benevolence, the maternal and the paternal. The mother's benevolence takes the form of giving the child what he needs, and tends to develop into giving him what he wants. It begins as caretaking —feeding, clothing, comforting, and the binding up of wounds—and ends as indulgence, often concealed from the father. It takes as its point of departure the child's actual feelings and desires, and with these the father is less familiar and less concerned. On this the mother and child are tacitly agreed, and they instinctively or from common interest combine against him. The father, whose position is more detached, and who takes the longer view, is not less benevolently disposed, but his benevolence is likely to take the form of giving the child what is 'good for him.' He is willing to forego that instant favor which the mother receives for benefits presently appreciated, hoping that he may be thanked later when the beneficiary is 'old enough to understand.' He is prepared, if needs be, to forgo gratitude altogether, knowing that people are rarely grateful for receiving moral goods instead of immediate satisfactions.

It is, no doubt, a wise provision of nature that the child should be the object of both sorts of benefaction. For each needs to be supplemented by the other. Indulgence may be hurtful, through being too forgetful of remoter goods and of that discipline without which the child grows intolerable to his neighbors and unfit for purposeful living. The fathers of the world can be trusted to press this point. But edifying benevolence has its own pitfalls and seeds of error. Benevolence means willing the good of another, but it can easily become a mere profession of benevolence by which to excuse a willing of one's own good. The good of any given individual is the realization, in the long run, of *that* individual's felt interests—*his* desire, *his* ambition, *his* aspiration, *his* love. The paternal and edifying benefactor is mindful of the long run;

that is his merit. But he is not so quick to discern his beneficiary's will and feelings, and to take these as the clue to his benefaction. Clarence Day wrote:

> I wanted to be a cowboy. I told Father on the way home. He chuckled and said no I didn't. . . . Father briefly explained that their lives, their food, and their sleeping accommodations were outlandish and "slummy." They lived in the wilds, he informed me, and they had practically gone wild themselves. "Put your cap on straight," he added. "I am trying to bring you up to be a civilized man."
>
> I adjusted my cap and walked on, thinking over this future. The more I thought about it, the less I wanted to be a civilized man. After all, I had had a very light lunch, and I was tired and hungry. What with fingernails and improving books and dancing school, and sermons on Sundays, the few chocolate éclairs that a civilized man got to eat were not worth it.[10]

The benefactor who imposes a kindness on other people regardless of their present desires must be very sure of himself. It is as though one were to say: "I know what is good for you better than you know yourself." There is a time when this assurance is unquestionably justified, a time when it is unquestionably presumptuous, and an intermediate phase in which it is of doubtful warrant. If the mother abandons it too soon, the father continues it too long. For the father is nothing if not sure of himself: it is his business to be sure in the field of his vocation, and he brings his sureness with him from the office to the home. 'Paternalism' so named is well named. It would not have done to call it 'parentalism,' still less 'maternalism.'

The philanthropy of Cotton Mather, and of puritanism generally, was philanthropy of this paternal sort. It was a stern kindness, designed to repay the hurts of denial with the greater benefits which will accrue at some remoter time, in this world or the next. It was an inquisitive, because distrustful, kindness, which sought to regulate another's life, rather than to leave that life to the promptings of its own inward impulsions and self-government. It was an arrogant kindness, expressing a conviction so free from doubt as to be untroubled by the protests of the beneficiary.

These are the limitations of the puritan's moralized philanthropy, and may be allowed to qualify our recognition of the fact that it *is* philanthropy: a love of fellow men, extended to all men individually, and a love that is not content with well-wishing, but must express itself, according to its lights, in *doing* good.

4

The puritan's social interest was also actuated by a sense of solidarity —by the belief, namely, that the good of each is bound up with the good of all. His ideas of solidarity consisted in the association of this general idea, which is accepted in all social philosophies, with the puritan's specific idea of the supreme good. It was an application to righteousness and piety of a principle which the modern world would unhesitatingly apply to health, or wealth, or military power. Puritanism affirmed, and endeavored to realize, the ideal of a community of the elect of God. In Nathaniel Morton's *New England's Memorial* the Plymouth Colony was considered as a single body of which the whole must suffer from the defect of any part. "God did once plant a noble vine in New England," which was held to flourish or suffer blight integrally. An earthquake in 1662 suggested to the writer that God had been indulgent, and that the state of New England was not hopeless, since this earthquake was one of the milder kind that serve as "gentle warnings," rather than one of the violent kind that swallow up and destroy. In 1666, "it pleased God to go on in a manifestation of his displeasure against New England," God's displeasure toward the whole community taking the form of striking dead by lightning even its worthy members.[11] It would have contradicted the doctrine of election to say that the salvation of each man depends on the salvation of all men. But *within* the community of the elect the members were conceived as so linked together as to have their spiritual fortunes in common. They were jointly the beneficiaries of God's favor, and that favor was forfeited for all if its terms were violated by any:

> We are knite togeather as a body in a most stricte & sacred bond and covenante of the Lord, of the violation whereof we make great conscience, and

by vertue whereof we doe hould our selves straitly tied to all care of each others good, and of ye whole by every one and so mutually.*

The broad principle of solidarity is divisible for purposes of critical analysis into three distinct but related ideas: the social conditions of piety, its inherently social quality or nature, and the logic of social control.

Among the social conditions of piety the simplest and most evident is contagion. Whatever be the deeper psychological explanation in terms of imitation or suggestion, it is an unquestionable fact that the members of the same social group are in such close physical and mental proximity that good and evil propagate themselves from next to next. The evil condition of one corrupts those about him; no matter how careful a man may be of his own condition, he is exposed and susceptible to evil originating elsewhere. His solicitude for himself will, therefore, include a solicitude for his immediate human environment. This effect of contagion is operative on every level of goods, including religious piety.

Lest the idea of moral and religious contagion be considered as a mere survival of the primitive idea of tribal responsibility—an idea which puritan emphasis on individual culpability and retribution should have superseded—let us consider a modern and presumably enlightened analogy. Health, we say, is a public and not merely a private concern. Given a certain degree of propinquity, the health of one member of the community depends upon the health of all. This undeniable hygienic solidarity depends on the fact that at least some diseases are spread by contagion, so that an individual cannot be saved merely by attention to his own personal diet, rest, exercise, or cleanliness. Nor do the circumstances of life permit him to avoid contact with his fellows. His self-interest, or interest in his family, thus compel him to interest himself in the health of his neighbors. Even if he lives in the better residential district, he must concern himself with conditions in the slums. This hygienic solidarity by which the innocent suffer with

* John Robinson and William Brewster, "Of the coming of diverse godly Men to these Parts and of their Endeavours to establish the Kingdom of God herein, albeit sorely harassed by the Hardships of the Land and by evil Men"; a letter written from Leyden, Holland, Dec. 15, 1617, to Sir Edwin Sandys.

the guilty does not have the effect of relieving the individual of responsibility; on the contrary, it increases his responsibility. Since his own disease may contaminate others, they will hold him responsible; since his own health may be destroyed by the disease of others, he will hold them responsible.

Belief and unbelief, like diseases, are contagious. How far this analogy of physical and creedal hygiene shall be pressed we are not as yet prepared to judge. There are profound differences which divide them and which may well imply totally different methods of control. I would not imply that because thoughts and sentiments are 'dangerous' or 'subversive' they should therefore be suppressed. It may be that the better course is to inoculate the susceptible individual with better ideas and sentiments, or to build up his resistance by the cultivation of his critical faculties. But the fact that ideas and sentiments are spread by contact is undeniable.

This fact is more clearly recognized today than in any historical puritan community. Modern enlightenment has confirmed, and not discredited, the puritan's sense of the dependence of his private creed on the creed prevailing in his immediate neighborhood. Taking his faith to be the one thing essential, more essential than physical health, it is quite intelligible that he should have been concerned with the faith of others. Since he could not avoid all human contacts, he associated with others of like faith, warming himself by their irradiation; and he saw to it that they remained of the same faith lest they become centers of contamination. He felt responsible to others for the state of his piety, since they were exposed to it, in proportion to their propinquity; and he held others responsible for the state of theirs. He regarded an unbeliever as a public enemy from whom all of his neighbors, however scrupulous in their private affairs, would in some degree suffer. It was this argument which, according to Coulton, the Inquisition pressed to its extreme conclusion:

> As Berthold of Regensburg puts it: If I had a sister in a country wherein was only one single heretic, yet I should be afraid for her soul on that one heretic's account.[12]

5

Since unrighteousness was conceived not merely as a private but as a public evil, concerted measures were taken to prevent or to eradicate it, and to create a uniformity of righteousness in the community at large. Thus from contagion we pass to co-operation, as a second social condition of piety. Public health, being a common interest, enlists the support of all, each contributing as best he can, if not by services then by taxation. Special agencies are created, such as hospitals, medical aid, nursing, drainage, water supply, education, housing, and sanitary regulations. These agencies being perpetual, public health thus becomes an institution. Similarly, in a community which is concerned with the health of the soul, and which is aware that here also the health of each depends on the health of all, *spiritual* hygiene tends to become an institution, and a work of general collaboration.

But a broader analogy is afforded by the economic division of labor. The wealth which the individual enjoys, be it great or little, is produced by the community as a whole—by its diversity of skills and services, and by the consolidation of individual efforts. Every man profits by functions, such as production and exchange, to which every man contributes. The full possibilities of the economic life are realized only from the pooled resources of a community. The same is true of civilization and culture in their fuller meaning. The maximum of good is attainable only through the creation of a common fund to which each man contributes his part, but of which, if he have the capacity, he may enjoy the whole, even the contributions of genius.

For the puritan the greatest riches were those of the soul, and the highest culture was moral and religious culture. But the same principle applies. The various gifts of the spirit are distributed among men, so that no man can profit by all of them unless he belongs to a community in which they are all assembled. This spiritual division of labor was set forth in St. Paul's analogy of the body and its members.

> Now concerning spiritual gifts, brethren, I would not have you ignorant. . . . Now there are diversities of gifts, but the same Spirit. And there are differences of administrations, but the same Lord. And there are diversities of

operations, but it is the same God which worketh all in all. But the manifestation of the Spirit is given to every man to profit withal. For to one is given by the Spirit the word of wisdom; to another the word of knowledge by the same Spirit; To another faith by the same Spirit; to another the gifts of healing by the same Spirit; To another the working of miracles; to another prophecy; to another discerning of spirits; to another divers kinds of tongues; to another the interpretation of tongues: But all these worketh that one and the selfsame Spirit, dividing to every man severally as he will. . . . For the body is not one member, but many. . . . And if they were all one member, where were the body? But now they are many members, but one body. And the eye cannot say to the hand, I have no need of thee: or again the head to the feet, I have no need of you. . . . And whether one member suffereth, all the members suffer with it; or one member is honoured, all the members rejoice with it. Now ye are the body of Christ, and severally members thereof.[13]

I do not attempt any exegesis of this famous passage. I am fully aware that the Pauline conception of the church as the body of Christ and vehicle of the spirit lends itself to a corporate view of salvation which is at variance with that emphasis on the individual soul which is so incontestably fundamental, not only in puritanism, but in the Christian teaching and tradition as a whole. I might take refuge in St. Paul's consoling words, "This is a great mystery"; or cite another Pauline text to suggest that even for him the end of the church lay beyond itself, in its providing a means to the regeneration of its members severally: "For through him we both have access by one Spirit unto the Father." [14] In any case, the Pauline metaphor is reconciled with puritan individualism when the body of the church is conceived, not as a higher being which supersedes the souls of men as the final end of creation and redemption, but as a form of union through which each participant may benefit by the special gifts of others in exchange for his own, and through which each may utilize in his own behalf that greater spiritual force which arises from combination. For cooperation is not merely an exchange and a pooling of special gifts; there is also an élan which springs from association in a common enterprise, and which works inwardly upon each of its participants, so as to enhance both the quality and the quantity of his contribution. It is still the participants severally to whom the ultimate benefit accrues. Corporate piety is a means to individual ends.

A man comes to a stream which he cannot cross. He observes others in the same predicament, and it now appears that by combining forces they can build a raft and thus cross together. But it is still the individual man who desires to cross the river, and to whom the successful crossing is a good. Nor does this incident cease to be a history of individuals if in the crossing each man desires not only his own but the safe arrival of all. A joint undertaking, redounding to the advantage of all as well as of each, and motivated at one and the same time by self-interest and by fellow feeling, is still an affair of individuals, because both its driving force and its ultimate satisfactions reside in individual breasts.

6

The solidarity of piety is thus far external, consisting in its social conditions. The individual is confirmed in his own piety, and saved from the contamination of impiety, through dwelling in an environment of piety. He is enabled to promote piety more effectively by co-operation with others who are devoted to the same end. But the full meaning of the solidarity of piety is not grasped until it is understood that piety is intrinsically social in its nature or quality. It is not merely that the piety of the individual cannot be achieved, protected, and advanced, but that it cannot be *possessed* and *enjoyed,* in isolation.

The good life as the puritan-Christian conceived it embraces states and activities which can exist only in the relations of two or more like-minded men. The love of God can exist only in a kingdom of God where certain rules are generally observed. Taken in isolation, the individual can achieve a mastery over his own passions and can contemplate the truth, but he cannot be honest, veracious, peaceful, just, or loving; and these are constituents, not merely conditions, of piety. These forms of piety require not only that there shall be two or more parties, but that both parties shall be actuated by the same piety.

A man may speak the truth to liars, in the sense of outwardly uttering his inward belief, and refraining from deception. But the full virtue of truth lies in a relation of mutual understanding that requires a partnership of veracity. Similarly, the virtue of honesty lies in the security of property, and not in the scrupulous self-impoverishment of a man who practices honesty among thieves. A man may himself refuse to kill, but the value of peace lies not in suicidal nonresistance practiced among assassins, but in the saving of lives, and it takes two to make this sort of peace. Even if virtue is practiced for the sake of example, there must be one who follows as well as one who sets the example. He who turns the other cheek does so not in order to suffer a double injury, but in the hope of softening the heart of the wicked. Justice is not complete until it is recognized both by him who administers and by him who receives. The two 'great commandments' are love of God and love of neighbor, and neither can be obeyed except in a reciprocity of at least two terms—a lover and a loved one. The love of man for God is the filial return of parental love. The love of God for man is, before the fall, and after regeneration, a love which kindles love. The love of man for his neighbor is in its fullness a mutuality, in which each is at one and the same time both subject and object. Thus if truth, honesty, peace, justice, and love are to be perfected, they must reign, and they require a kingdom. He who like the pious puritan seeks these perfections will seek to create a community in which they may be embodied.

There is nothing in the idea of solidarity, even when it thus affirms the intrinsically social quality of the good life, which contradicts the puritan's individualism.* It is still the individual who enjoys and practices the ways of righteousness. Nor does solidarity when so individualistically interpreted imply that any given individual regards his fellows, or association with them, as a mere means to his own private righteousness. His fellow man is not his instrument but his partner. The seat of piety is neither a corporate entity nor the exclusive self. Piety will express itself neither with the impersonal pronoun 'it' nor the first personal singular 'I,' but with the first person plural 'we.' It is not a question of substituting public for private, but of introducing public spirit into the aggregate of private individuals.

A community of piety, such as that of puritanism, is in principle as

* The puritan idea of solidarity did not imply economic communism.[15]

wide as human relations. When the New England Confederation was formed in 1643 the Article of Confederation opened as follows:

> Whereas we all came into these parts of America with one and the same end and aime, namly, to advance the kingdome of our Lord Jesus Christ, and to injoye the liberties of the Gospell in puritie with peace.[16]

The New England puritans found their opportunity of collective life by removal to a distance, where they could escape interference from without. There was need of spiritual solidarity within, but there was no need of extending it to embrace other contemporary societies. Such an extension becomes increasingly imperative when, through the increase of trade and of facilities for transportation and communication, distance is reduced. In a compact world where all societies touch and interpenetrate, each is subject to contagion from the rest, and the maximum achievement of each is found through co-operation with the rest. Unless all parties observe the same principles of justice and peace, their abandonment by one degrades the rest. The full realization of truth, honesty, peace, justice, and love requires that they shall be reciprocated universally, and reign in a kingdom that embraces all nations.

7

The motives which led puritanism, despite its ineradicable individualism, to conceive of a community of the righteous, found their full realization in theocracy.

A pure theocracy would be a society in which religious piety embraced all of the interests, activities, and relationships within the state's jurisdiction, there being no difference between church and state except that the state reserved for itself the exercise of force. While no such condition has been completely realized in human history, it was approximated in New England during the middle of the seventeenth century, when the franchise was limited to church members, the church was supported by public taxation, and the government in which church and state were thus united undertook to prescribe every public manifestation of conscience, belief, and worship.[17]

This theocracy, like the Genevan theocracy of Calvin and the presbyterian theocracy of Scotland, not only dedicated the state to the purposes of religion in principle, but, in its severity and pervasive control, reflected the puritan's characteristic zeal. It undertook to achieve a completely integrated social life founded on identical metaphysical and moral presuppositions; and so to realize the Christian virtues in a fellowship of saints. Although the acceptance of the basic creed was in principle voluntary, it was protected by the civil authorities, and doubt, dissent, unrighteousness, and impiety became misdemeanors, crimes, and treason. So long as society was thoroughly imbued with the traditional beliefs and sentiments of protestant Christianity, such a goal did not leave a greater gap between profession and practice than is characteristic of any society. Indeed, the creed professed and imposed deviated so slightly from habit and common sense as to justify the charge that its rejection was due to a blind and obstinate defiance of the self-evident.

The New England theocracy was in part an effect of geographical isolation. That this theocracy should have occurred a century later than its European forerunners, and that it should have persisted after liberalizing influences had become effective abroad, even in puritan communities, are attributable to this same cause. And this same remoteness, together with the opportunity of building a new society in an unoccupied territory, made it possible to minimize the usual compromises with external and alien influences.

The puritan's habits of thought found nothing abhorrent or even strange in a theocratic polity. The use of the civil power for the enforcement of piety was a general practice of the times.[18] God's government of the world, which was the pattern and prototype of all government, was not only by definition a government by God, but also a regulation of piety by punishments and rewards. While God might forgive, nobody expected him to be tolerant.[19] As for the rigors and the pervasiveness of theocratic rule, the puritan found ample warrant for them in the Bible. The rule of life therein set down, especially in the Old Testament, penetrated into every nook and cranny of life and recognized no line of demarcation between the private affairs of the individual and that social solidarity which was of public concern. God could be offended and the whole community jeopardized by any individual's breach of regulations covering the most minute details of behavior. Above all, the least hint of infidelity to God was construed as giving succor to his enemies, and was punished as treason is punished in time of war. It could mean little to speak of cruelty to minds familiar with the terrible teachings of the Book of Deuteronomy:

> Ye shall walk after the Lord your God, and fear him, and keep his commandments, and obey his voice, and you shall serve him, and cleave unto him. . . . If thy brother, the son of thy mother, or thy son, or thy daughter, or the wife of thy bosom, or thy friend, which *is* as thine own soul, entice thee secretly, saying, Let us go and serve other gods, which thou hast not known, thou, nor thy fathers . . . Thou shalt not consent unto him, nor hearken unto him . . . neither shalt thou conceal him; But thou shalt surely kill him; thine hand shall be first upon him to put him to death, and afterwards the hand of all the people. . . . If thou shalt hear *say* in one of thy cities, which the Lord thy God hath given thee to dwell there, saying, *Certain* men, the children of Belial, are gone out from among you, and have withdrawn the inhabitants of their city, saying, Let us go and serve other gods, which ye have not known; Then shalt thou inquire, and make search, and ask diligently; and, behold, if it be truth, and the thing certain, *that* such abomination is wrought among you; Thou shalt surely smite the inhabitants of that city with the edge of the sword, destroying it utterly, and all that *is* therein, and the cattle thereof, with the edge of the sword.[20]

Willingness to enforce a rule of life is proportional, as we have seen, to the degree of one's assurance that it is good for all concerned, including him on whom it is enforced. One does not hesitate to drag a drowning man from the sea or to carry a half-suffocated victim from a burning building. One does not hesitate to use whatever force may be necessary in order to restrain him who would scuttle the ship or commit arson. These examples illustrate not only the sense of certainty, but also the sense of urgency. Both are illustrated by the state of mind which prevails in time of war, when the enemy is at the gate. It is assumed that self-preservation is good, and that at moments when it is threatened it takes precedence of all other considerations. Under such conditions force is unhesitatingly employed to over-rule objections, and to prevent delay. Liberties are abridged, penalties are increased, and action supplants deliberation.

To understand the New England theocracy, then, it is necessary to remember that to the members of this community salvation was a *certain* good, to be imposed relentlessly on those deluded men who failed to appreciate its worth; while the loss of salvation was an *imminent* peril which required prompt action. It is always possible that a human creed should be raised to a high pitch of subjective certainty and urgency, and should to its adherents justify the sharp repression of dissent, and the saving of dissenters even against their own protest. The modern art of propaganda has learned how such a sense of certainty and urgency can be created and maintained, and a society kept in a perpetual state of alarm.

The puritan theocracy exemplified the truth that a community requires some form of moral cohesiveness which expresses what its members take to be of common and paramount concern. How far the unity of creed shall be enforced depends on the nature and the role of civil authority, and it is the puritan answer to these questions that we shall now examine and appraise.

8

The character of a theocracy will depend, in the first place, upon the content of piety. The puritan theocracy will be a polity in which the members of a community are compelled by the state to live as puritans. But the ground of the compulsion which is exercised—the sanction of political authority—will also be puritan. Thus the character of a puritan theocracy will depend, in the second place, on its own inherent political principles. It is true that reformed or Calvinistic communities which were fortunate enough to find the existing civil authorities sympathetic availed themselves of their support without examining their credentials, otherwise than to impute them in principle to God. But a puritan community which fully expresses the characteristic genius of puritanism will be puritan in the form as well as in the content of polity. It is thus of fundamental importance to see that puritanism had its own justification or logic of social control.

The term 'theocracy' suggests the absolute rule of God, or a polity of passive obedience. From God's will itself there is no appeal. The ultimate value of human life, constituting that salvation which is the goal of Christian endeavor, consists either in the rectitude of conformity to God's commands or in the bliss of unconditional and loving surrender. This constitutes the authoritarian strain in puritan polity, which is ever in the background as a sanction of practice and as a habit of thought.*

But the essence of puritan polity lies in the doctrine of the 'covenant,' in which authority is limited by the terms of an agreement. The 'invisible covenant,' or 'the covenant of grace,' unites the body of the saints in the acceptance of God's offer of salvation. Its 'invisibility' lies in the fact that the identity of the saints is known indubitably only to God. The 'visible covenant' unites in the bond of a common profession, discipline, and worship, persons who are present in the flesh and known to their fellow men. It is evident that the conception of covenant can justify itself both by Scripture and by the Christian tradition. But it is equally evident that it has roots connecting it with the history of secular political theory. The theory of contract, like that of natural law, is so ancient and so pervasive that it has no inventor. It is sufficient for our purposes to note its explicit acceptance by the New England Pilgrims and puritans.

Nathaniel Morton, writing in 1669, thus describes the creation of the Separatist church which migrated to Holland in 1610 and was the forerunner of the community which later migrated to Plymouth:

---

* The authoritarian overtone of puritan piety is illustrated by the catechism contained in John Cotton's *Spiritual Milk for Boston Babes in either England: Drawn out of the Breasts of both Testaments for their souls nourishment, But may be of like use to any Children:* 21

"Quest. *What is the fifth Commandment?*
Answ. HONOUR thy Father and thy Mother. . . .
Quest. *Who are here meant by Father and Mother?*
Answ. All our Superiours, whether in Family, School, Church, and Common-Wealth.
Quest. *What is the honour due unto them?*
Answ. Reverence, Obedience and (when I am able,) Recompence."

> In the year 1602, divers godly Christians of our English nation . . . entered into covenant to walk with God, and one with another, in the enjoyment of the ordinances of God, according to the primitive pattern in the word of God. . . . Being at Cape Cod upon the eleventh day of November, 1620, it was thought meet for their more orderly carrying on of their affairs, and accordingly by mutual consent they entered into a solemn combination. . . . The contents whereof followeth.
>
> We whose names are underwritten . . . having undertaken for the glory of God, and advancement of the Christian faith, and the honour of our King and country, a voyage to plant the first colony in the northern parts of Virginia; do by these presents solemnly and mutually, in the presence of God and one another, covenant and combine ourselves together into a civil body politic, for our better ordering and preservation, and furtherance of the ends aforesaid; and by virtue hereof, do enact, constitute, and frame such just and equal laws, ordinances, acts, constitutions, and officers, from time to time, as shall be thought most meet and convenient for the general good of the colony; unto which we promise all due submission and obedience.[22]

A quarter of a century later, when the New England theocracy was broadened to embrace the larger migrations to Massachusetts Bay and elsewhere, and numbered many churches, the same idea was affirmed in the Cambridge Platform:

> This *Form* is the *Visible Covenant,* agreement, or consent whereby they [the members] give up themselves unto the Lord, to the observing of the ordinances of Christ together in the same society, which is usually called the Church-Covenant; For we see not otherwise how members can have Church-power over one another mutually.[23]

In the year prior to the adoption of the Cambridge Platform in New England, members of Cromwell's army formulated the "Agreement of the People for a firme and present Peace, upon grounds of common-right and freedome." As printed in 1647 this famous document was "proposed by the Agents of the five Regiments of Horse; and since by the generall approbation of the Army, offered to the joynt concurrence of all the free COMMONS of ENGLAND." The extreme equalitarian sentiment of Lilburne and the Levellers combined with congregational ideas of church polity to produce a striking anticipation of the American and French Declarations of the late eighteenth century, embracing: the fundamental law of nature; the institution of the powers of government by voluntary compact among all the people; government subject to the consent of the governed; the reservation of individual liberties, and their protection against the usurpation of government.[24]

According to the doctrine of covenant, an authority is a power which a set of individuals have agreed to obey for the sake of a benefit which they expect to reap and which the authority is pledged to promote. There is a double agreement, one which unites in a common obedience those who obey, and one which unites those who obey with him who commands. He who disobeys is guilty of a double breach of contract: he has broken his pledge to his fellows, and his pledge to the authority.

The contract among the obeying members of such a polity is bilateral, the obligation to obedience by each party being conditional on the obedience of the other parties. The relation between the obeying party and the authority, on the other hand, may be unilateral. There is an important difference between trustful and untrustful obedience. Trustful or 'passive' obedience is based on the assumption that the obeying party is in some degree ignorant of his true interest, and therefore unqualified to impeach the authority. He who obeys leaves to the authority the decision as to whether or not the expected benefit is realized. Such obedience is rationalized by the assumption that the authority is all-wise and all-benevolent, and therefore trustworthy. Once convinced of the authority's qualifications, he who obeys surrenders his judgment utterly.

This relatively authoritarian strain is inherent in the Calvinistic idea of man's relation to God. Man's power to achieve his own good being renounced, he has no course save to throw himself wholly on the divine mercy and wisdom. There is no ground independent of God's will on which he can challenge God's will. God is by definition incapable of being false to his promise. But the logic of covenant is not altered by this fact. In the impossible event of such a breach on God's part, the human believer *would* be released from his obligation. Or the human believer has a right (the exercise of which is unnecessary) to *demand* that God fulfill his promise. The idea of covenant loses its meaning unless it is assumed that man knows its terms, and is in some measure qualified to know whether it is kept. In short, man judges the authority which he obeys, even when that authority is God.

As regards human authorities, civil or ecclesiastical, there is in protestantism no dogma of infallibility, and the implications which are hypothetical in the case of God come into practical force. The believer looks to the clergy or other officers of the church to render that service in exchange for which he voluntarily accepts their authority: namely, the preaching and promotion of what he himself judges to be true piety. They are directly or indirectly of his own choosing, and as he is competent to choose them, so he is competent to reject or disobey them. The civil government is not only a divinely ordained institution, but is expressly designed to carry the law of God into effect in the daily lives of men. It is a religiously created instrument dedicated to a religious purpose. The judgments by which it commends itself, both its authority and its particular acts, are religious judgments. In a puritan community the lay believer is held to be qualified to pronounce such judgments, by virtue of his access to the written Word, confirmed by his personal religious experience.

The spiritual independence of the individual believer was in the seventeenth century offset by credulity and tradition, by the prestige of the clergy, elders, and presbyters, by absolutistic conceptions of God and the civil ruler, and by divers other authoritarian ideas, sentiments, and habits of mind. But the claim of individual judgment was recognized in principle, and in New England, as in Geneva and Scotland, there was for a time an approximation to a theocratic democracy, in which the Christian way of life was imposed by a civil authority which derived its sanction from popular piety. Such a theocracy by consent was possible only so long as there existed a fervent unanimity of belief.

Fervent unanimity on so elaborate a scale as Biblical Christianity, and in a group of highly individualized, educated, and self-reliant men, was a momentary product of the confluence of many forces, and it was impossible that it should long prevail. But such a community embodied a central principle of democracy: namely, the subordination of every social authority to the moral judgment of those whom it controls. "Contrariwise," as was clearly recognized in the struggle of the Cromwellian army with the King—"contrariwise, on the King's part the interest was to discountenance and suppress the power of godliness, or anything of conscience obliging above or against human and outward constitutions."[25] If to set up the godliness and conscience of common men against every human and outward constitution is democracy, then the puritan theocracy was democratic.

9

The fall of the New England theocracy was due to the change of those conditions and the weakening of those forces which were the causes of its origin, and at the same time to the leavening effect of its own inherent individualism. From the middle of the seventeenth century there was a diminishing isolation, and a growing immigration of colonists who were attracted to the colonies for reasons other than piety. The picture of the Calvinistic God and of the divine government of the world faded from the imagination. As the secular interests developed, the Bible became less relevant and adequate as a guide of life. As men felt less certain of the common creed, and as its acceptance seemed less urgent, there was a growing hesitation to impose it by force.

Zeal itself tended to dissent. For, as we have seen, protestantism invited men not only to exercise their own judgment, but also to invoke in its behalf the sanction of divine authority. The puritan spirit and method tended to the multiplication of orthodoxies and of uncompromising and militant sects determined either to secede or to conquer. And as for all of these reasons dissent increased, the enforcement of a single creed became more questionable.

So long as agreement is generally prevalent, its enforcement upon the occasional backslider seems neither brutal nor intrusive; the agencies of enforcement are subject to no excessive strain. But when dissent is chronic and wholesale, the difficulties of its suppression become more evident. Careless lapses from faith can be corrected by intimidation, but a resolute conviction cannot be changed by force; it can only be denied outward expression and driven under the ground. Occasional deviations from the norm of conduct can be occasionally corrected, but to impose on a community a code of conduct at variance with its habits requires a perpetual inquisition. The sporadic dissident can be expelled from the community, but large-scale excommunication is self-destructive.

The formidable growth of apathy and dissension brought the puritan theocracy to a parting of the ways. In such a situation two alternatives present themselves: the revival of flagging zeal and the reconquest of dissent; or a delimitation of the basic political creed to those elements which are indispensable to social cohesiveness, and the creation of spheres of liberty for more specific creeds—in other words, the separation of church and state.

The first of these alternatives is the course of uncompromising zealots such as Captain Edward Johnson, author of *The Wonder-working Providence of Sions Saviour in New England* (1654), who rejoiced in the number of the enemies of God, that he might slay them:

> You are not set up for tollerating times, nor shall any of you be content with this that you are set at liberty, but take up your Armes, and march manfully on till all opposers of Christs Kingly power be abolished: and as for you who are called to sound forth his silver Trumpets, blow lowd and shrill, to this chiefest treble tune; For the Armies of the great Jehovah are at hand. See you not his Enemies stretched out on tiptoe, proudly daring on their thresholds, a certaine signe of their sudden overthrow? be not danted at your small number, for every common Souldier in Christs Campe shall be as David, who slew the great Goliah, and his Davids shall be as the Angels of the Lord, who slew 185000. in the Assyrian Army.[26]

Jonathan Edwards, a century later, was less militant, but his part in the 'Awakening' was not less designed to restore the ascendancy of the strict faith over the minds and institutions of New England. The difficulties of such a theocratic reinvigoration, and the abuses to which it gives rise, are highly instructive, and throw light on contemporary attempts of the same sort.

It is necessary that the remnant of the faithful should lash itself into fury, and then keep itself and the community at large at a high pitch of crusading enthusiasm by perpetual excitation, and by periodically sounding a tocsin of alarm—even imagining or creating dangers where they do not exist—in order to stimulate a mentality of war. It is necessary to suppress dissent with a methodical violence proportional to its extent, so that prosecution becomes persecution. In order to nip opposition in the bud, it is necessary to employ constant vigilance; in other words, a secret police, which creates a pervasive condition of mutual distrust. The party itself must by recurrent 'purges' keep its purity uncorrupted, lest the salt shall lose its savor. And in proportion as this effort is successful, what is the result? The state is not a means of giving effect to a genuine agreement or sober consciousness of community of interest, but an oligarchy in which a ruling class derives a specious appearance of general support from an admixture of hysteria with sullen conformity.

10

While in New England the lesson of theocracy was taught by its failure, in old England that failure was anticipated, and statesmanship discovered and chose the solution which in New England was tardily imposed by a change of circumstance and the infiltration of enlightenment from abroad.

The Cromwellian army was both a fighting force and a convention representing all shades of puritan opinion. A victorious revolutionary party was obliged to create a commonwealth embracing both its own divided members and its vanquished opponents. No situation could be better calculated to bring to light the diverse political motives of puritanism, and the dialectic by which it moved away from theocracy to the separation of church and state and to a 'constitutional settlement' based on democratic processes and the principle of toleration. The so-called Army Debates held during the years 1647-49 at Putney, Whitehall, and elsewhere were recorded by William Clarke, assistant to John Rushworth, secretary of the General and the Council of War; and these Debates, together with appropriate selections from Calvin, Milton, Roger Williams, William Ames, and other leaders of puritan thought have recently been edited with a remarkable Introduction by Professor A. S. P. Woodhouse.[27]

The factions represented in the Cromwellian army ranged from the 'sectaries' (Anabaptists, Levellers, congregational Separatists, and Millenarists such as the 'Fifth Monarchy Men') at the extreme left, through the 'Independents' in the center to the presbyterians and the Erastians on the right. Taken from right to left, this continuum of opinion represented increasing degrees of puritan zeal. The extreme right advocated the authority of the state, even in matters religious; the extreme left advocated the reign of the elect, even in matters political. Next to the left of the Erastians stood those who proposed a state church on the presbyterian model.* Both Millenarists and Separatists identified the church with the community of saints, but while the Millenarists looked forward to the time when this community should absorb and dominate the whole of society, the Separatists were content to withdraw and perfect the Christian life among themselves.

The central or Independent party was composed of men of relatively moderate opinions—strict puritans in their personal convictions and discipline, but adhering to the broad principles of reformed protestantism rather than to any extreme sectarian peculiarity, and feeling a profound sense of civic responsibility. From the left they drew the idea of the priority of religious to secular values, and the basic allegiance of the human soul to the dictates of faith and conscience. From the right they drew the idea of the secular state as the institution dedicated to the maintenance of public order and the conduct of the affairs of the realm at home and abroad. At the same time, taking a statesmanlike view of the situation, they were profoundly impressed by the destructive effects of religious conflict, and the impossibility of imposing on the whole of society any one of the several creeds represented by its members. Hence their policy of religious toleration.

The duty of Christian believers to obey the dictates of their own religious conscience is of the very essence of protestantism. The will of

---

* The equivocal position of the English presbyterians is illustrated by the career of Richard Baxter, whose *Saints' Everlasting Rest* is one of the classic records of the puritan religious experience. He distrusted both the radical left ("I like not the Democratick formes.") [28] and the Anglican-monarchical right, and was in turn distrusted by both; with the result that although he advocated a presbyterian establishment under the King, he was eventually driven into nonconformity.

God as he construes it is to each man the highest sanction of conduct, prescribing not only the rules of his personal life but the form of his collective worship. That the civil ruler should endeavor to control the believer's spiritual affairs is therefore both presumptuous and foolish. It is presumptuous because it sets the judgment of a profane authority above the judgment of spiritual experts. It is foolish because faith and worship cannot be imposed by force. Their essence lies in an attitude which if it is to exist at all must be freely adopted.

Because they desired to begin at once and with all their hearts to live according to the dictates of their own faith and conscience, the Separatists, whether Baptist or congregational, became the pioneers in the movement for religious toleration. The first and in the long run the strongest force for religious tolerance is the desire *to be tolerated* felt by members of a sect zealously devoted to their own peculiar creed, but doomed inescapably to live within a society which they cannot control. Abandoning hope of imposing their creed on their neighbors, they demand a sphere of liberty within which they can profess and practice it themselves. In order to secure this privilege they are willing to concede a like privilege to others, and to abandon the idea of religious uniformity. They see the value of a general rule of tolerance—in its application to themselves. The political sequel to Separatism is the neutral state presiding over a multisectarian society.

A state which exercises this function of protecting each sect from the aggression of its rivals will represent the area common to the diverse religious creeds of its members, an area tending to become smaller and smaller until finally it excludes religion altogether and is confined to a purely political creed. When that limit is reached, the complete separation of church and state is achieved. Thus the state may be the partisan of protestantism in general without identifying itself with any protestant sect; or the partisan of Christianity in general without taking sides as between protestant and Catholic; or the partisan of religion in general, including both Christian and Jew; or the partisan of public peace among believers and unbelievers. The end of this progression is the secular state, within which all diversities in matters religious shall live together and enjoy security. Speaking of the attitude of Parliament at the time of the Puritan Commonwealth in England, a recent historian says: "It had come by painful stages to recall that Elizabeth had sought to give England a broad, tolerant, and flexible religious structure which would permit the free play of enquiry and conscience so long as the civil order was not contravened." [29]

The struggle of Cromwell and his Independents to revive and develop this policy illustrates the transition from the defensive motive of religious liberty to the constructive motive of political principle. To the Scots, who, until decisively defeated at Dunbar and Worcester, would have imposed their presbyterian theocracy on England, Cromwell's army was made up of "perfidious and blasphemous sectaries." To the English presbyterians, this multiplication of fanatical creeds was equally abhorrent. But Cromwell was bound to appease his radical followers while at the same time maintaining an army and erecting a constitution; hence as a ruler of men, responsible for unity of effort and for public peace, he saw the need of dissociating the general bond of political agreement from the peculiarities and fanatical temper of every sect, including his own. Cromwell adhered tenaciously to this policy. The history of his dealings with Quakers, Catholics, Anglicans, Jews, and unitarians illustrates the logic of his position. So long as these sects were themselves aggressively intolerant, they were prosecuted and penalized; so long as they were willing to respect the equal rights of other sects, they were tolerated and protected.[30]

The idea of a neutral state which shall keep the peace among rival religious sects persisted with varying fortunes, and eventually triumphed both in England and in America. Lord Baltimore, who founded the colony of Maryland in 1634, was required by the terms of his charter to establish the Church of England. Being himself a devout Catholic, he was thus compelled to dissociate his role as governor from his personal faith, and to make room for diverse creeds.* The Quakers had in their beginnings been a peculiarly fanatical and unruly sect, and a constant source of difficulty to the authorities. But external coercion in religious matters was flatly opposed to their central conviction of inward

* During the years of the Protectorate and at the time of the Revolution of 1688 the Catholics were themselves persecuted in Maryland and became the exponents of tolerance in self-defense.[31]

spiritual guidance, and when William Penn became the governor of a colony, he saw no necessity for religious uniformity, but only for an orderly society within which religious diversity might be saved from the evils of dissension.[32] He practiced what he had professed some years before in speaking of *England's Present Interest* (1675): "Many inquisitive Men into humane Affairs, have thought, that the Concord of Discords hath not been the infirmest Basis Government can rise or stand upon." [33]

It was for reasons of statecraft that Charles I had advised his son:

> Beware, of Exasperating any Factions, by the Crossness and Asperity of some Mens Passions, Humours, or Private Opinions . . . grounded only upon their Differences in Lesser Matters, which are but the Skirts and Suburbs of Religion, wherein a *Charitable Connivance* and *Christian Toleration* often Dissipates their Strength, whom Rougher Opposition Fortifieth.[34]

Whether or not he remembered his father's advice, Charles II said on the eve of the Restoration: "We do declare a liberty to tender consciences; and that no man shall be disquieted, or called in question, for differences of opinion in matters of religion which do not disturb the peace of the kingdom." [35] This was the dictate of political wisdom to a ruler whose first duty was to keep "the peace of the kingdom." If he did not execute this policy, it was because of those partisans, political and ecclesiastical, who did not feel the same sense of civic responsibility. This lesson of political experience was finally embodied in the Toleration Act of William III in 1689, which omitted Catholics from its provisions only because of the suspicion that they, were they in turn to acquire power, would revert to a policy of religious persecution.

"If there had been in England only one religion," said Voltaire, "its despotism would have been fearful. If there had been two religions, they would have cut each other's throat. But as there are thirty they live peacefully and happily." [36] Religious toleration as thus far described meant a keeping of the peace among existing sects. It represented political wisdom rather than political theory. It was a counsel of expediency designed to terminate the religious wars of the sixteenth and seventeenth centuries. Similarly, the Edict of Nantes in 1598 conceded certain special privileges to the Huguenots in France—privileges which were withdrawn by the Revocation of this Edict in 1685. The Peace of Westphalia in 1648 permitted the princes of the old Empire to choose which of three forms of faith and worship, whether Roman Catholic, Lutheran, or Reformed, they would impose on their subjects. None of these arrangements abridged the right of the political authority to impose religious uniformity within the area of its jurisdiction. From religious toleration in this opportunistic sense is to be distinguished the theory, advocated by philosophers, religious reformers, and statesmen, and later embodied in liberal constitutions, which explicitly distinguishes the private sphere of religion from the public sphere of civility.

11

The historic doctrine of 'the separation of church and state' is not, as this expression unfortunately implies, a merely negative doctrine, but a constructive view of the relations of religion and polity, or of godliness and civility. According to this view the state represents a basic interest which is common to conflicting religious cults, and which arises from the fact that men must live together as men. Whether a man be an Anglican, a presbyterian, a congregationalist, a Catholic, a Jew, or even an atheist, he is a *socius*; and whatever his particular way of salvation, it must be accommodated to the requirements of a social order.

This distinction between a limited and variable sphere of religion and the inclusive and common sphere of polity was not recognized by Calvin. He had declared that the state should concern itself with the regulation of godliness as well as of civility:

> Not one . . . [heathen writer] has treated of the office of magistrates, of legislation, and civil government, without beginning with religion and divine worship. And thus they have all confessed that no government can be happily constituted, unless its first object be the promotion of piety, and that all laws are preposterous which neglect the claims of God, and merely provide for the interests of men. . . . We have already shewn that this duty is particularly enjoined upon them by God; for it is reasonable that they should employ their utmost efforts in asserting and defending the honour of him, whose vicegerents they are, and by whose favour they govern.[37]

The most notable exponent of the opposing doctrine was Roger Williams, in his famous dispute with the Reverend John Cotton.[38] He was at one and the same time a religious thinker and, through his Rhode Island experiment, a man of affairs. Although he came to New England as early as 1631, he frequently revisited old England, and thus fought his battle on both continents.

The essence of Williams's teaching was that religion is, in principle, a private and not a public matter. The state is a ship, whose passengers should be allowed to believe what they like so long as they obey certain rules on which the safety of the ship depends. There is no justification for persecuting Jonah or throwing him overboard so long as he does not annoy his fellow passengers or interfere with navigation. And similarly, the pilot of the ship, like any other expert, is to be judged by the skill with which he exercises his specific social function:

> And hence it is true, that a *Christian Captaine, Christian, Merchant, Physitian, Lawyer, Pilot, Father, Master,* and (so consequently) *Magistrate* &c. is no more a *Captaine, Merchant, Physitian, Lawyer, Pilot, Father, Master, Magistrate,* &c. then a Captaine, Marchant, &c. of any other Conscience or Religion. . . . A *Pagan* or *Antichristian Pilot* may be as skilfull to carry the Ship to its desired Port, as any *Christian Mariner* or *Pilot* in the World, and may performe that worke with as much safety and speed.[39]

As Cromwell fought the presbyterians, so Williams fought Cotton as the exponent of puritan theocracy—as one who "publickly taught, and teacheth . . . that body-killing, soule-killing, and State-killing doctrine of not permitting, but persecuting all other consciences and wayes of worship but his own in the civill State, and so consequently in the whole world, if the power or Empire thereof were in his hand." [40] The state has its own civil and secular business, and its attempt to go beyond its province is self-destructive. The effect is to provoke dissension and to attempt coercion in a sphere of life in which men fear penalties less than the violation of their own scruples. To the state, its subjects are not believers or souls, but citizens, and it is as such that they owe the state their allegiance.

A second document of comparable importance to the polemical writings of Roger Williams is the anonymous pamphlet entitled *The Ancient Bounds, or Liberty of Conscience, Tenderly Stated, Modestly*

Asserted, and Mildly Vindicated, published in 1645. Because, as the title indicates, this tract represented a counsel of moderation, its definitive position on the present question is all the more striking.[41] The author has "reflected much upon the principles and light of nature and the outward good and consisting of societies." With these matters, "the preservation of societies" and "the happiness of societies," the state is concerned. In religion the state does not, it is true, play a purely neutral role. It will spread the light of the Gospel, but it will scrupulously keep "this side of force."[42] In every society, save the peculiar instance of Israel, the king and the magistrate have to do with the immediate interest of man as man, leaving religious matters to the spiritual guidance of conscience and the church:

> That is, differing opinions in religion, being of a secondary and remote consideration to the outward well-being of men, doth not oblige to destroy, or to expose to destruction by mulcts, bonds, or banishment, the persons of men; for whom, and in relation to whose preservation, magistracy was erected. For this is a rule: The law of nature supersedes institutions. Men have a natural being before they come to have a spiritual being; they are men before they are Christians. Now therefore for faultiness in Christianity, you must not destroy the man.[43]

The Quakers, with their emphasis on 'inner light,' could not accept external coercion. Piety and statesmanship alike prompted William Penn to a policy of religious toleration. But like Roger Williams and the author of *The Ancient Bounds,* he went beyond expediency to principle, and recognized a fundamental division between the spheres of religion and politics:

> Nothing is more unreasonable, then to *sacrifice the Liberty* and *Property* of any Man (being his *Natural and Civil Rights*) for *Religion,* where he is not found breaking any Law relating to Natural & Civil Things. *Religion,* under any Modification is no Part of the old *English* Government; *Honeste vivere, alterum non loedere, jus suum cuique tribuere,* are enough to entitle every Native to *English* Priviledges: A Man may be a very good *English* Man, and yet a very indifferent *Church-man.* Nigh 300 Years before *Austine* set his Foot on *English* Ground, had the Inhabitants of this Island a *free* Government. It is Want of distinguishing between *It* and the *Modes* of Religion, which fills every Clamorous Mouth with such Impertinent Cryes as this; *Why do not you submit to the Government?* as if the *English* Civil *Government* came in

with *Luther*, or were to go out with *Calvin*: What Prejudice is it for a *Popish Landlord* to have a *Protestant Tennant*; or a *Presbyterian Tennant* to have a *Protestant Landlord*? Certainly, the *Civil Affairs* of all Governments in the World may be peaceably transacted under the different *Trims of Religion*, where Civil Rights are inviolably observ'd.[44]

After the Restoration, when all disputants were eager to show their loyalty to the civil power, the issue of toleration was again fought out in the famous controversy between Samuel Parker and Andrew Marvell. Parker, of puritan descent but Bishop of Oxford under Charles II, argued that liberty of conscience, defined as "every Private mans own judgment and perswasion of things," was fatal to the public order. Given autonomy in religious matters, it would claim the same authority in civil matters. It was essentially schismatic.* Andrew Marvell, who was of Anglican antecedents, was equally with Parker a supporter of the prerogatives of the crown. But he found the ground of the state's authority, and the guarantee of its stability, to lie in the breadth of its base. The state represents the interests of all of its members, and its task is to secure these interests and enable them to live together rather than to take the part of some against the rest. Its toleration is implied in its peculiar responsibility and trusteeship:

> But they [kings] are the incumbents of whole kingdoms, and the rectorship of the common people, the nobility, and even of the clergy. . . . The care, I say, of all these rests upon them. So that they are fain to condescend to many things for peace-sake, and the quiet of mankind. . . . They do not think fit to require any thing that is impossible, unnecessary, or wanton, of their people.[46]

It would be a serious mistake to suppose that the idea of the secular state implied any derogation of religion. In the ship of state the pilot is the magistrate, and the minister has to obey his orders. But this does not detract from the minister's dignity, any more than it detracts from the dignity of the player that he should submit to the referee, or from the dignity of Jesus that he should submit to Caesar. At the street crossing the traffic policeman is master and everybody must submit, even

* "Every opinion must make a sect, and every sect a faction, and every faction, when it is able, a war, and every war is the cause of God, and the cause of God can never be prosecuted with too much violence." [45]

though he be poet, seer, or saint. So in the doctrine of the separation of church and secular state there is no implication whatsoever as to their relative eminence. The assumption that the kingdom of God is above the kingdoms of this world remains unchallenged.

Thus the argument against theocracy consists fundamentally of the charge of usurpation. Theocracy assigns to the magistrate not only his proper jurisdiction over men's bodies, but what is in effect a blasphemous jurisdiction over men's souls. "Upon his judgement must the people rest," said Roger Williams, "as upon the minde and judgement of Christ." [47] Williams's argument, then, while it denied the hegemony of any religion, affirmed the autonomy of every religion, and even of irreligion. Faith and worship are among those reserved rights which the state does not give or take away, but protects. The state is to abstain from interference, not because religion is trivial or fallacious, but because its supremely important truth can reveal and spread itself among men only through liberty. Errors there will no doubt be, but " 'tis Light alone, even Light from the bright shining Sunne of Righteousnesse, which is able, in the soules and consciences of men to dispell and scatter such fogges and darknesse." [48]

12

Although religious toleration means that the state shall not interfere in matters of faith and worship, it must not be forgotten that there is a condition attached. Religion in order to be tolerated must be tolerable; that is, consistent with the social order; and to be thus tolerable religion must itself be tolerant. A tolerating civil polity and a tolerant religion conspire together.[49] It is for this reason that the development of religious toleration in England and America was conditioned and reinforced by a decline of the inquisitorial and persecuting temper of religious thought.

This development embraced three ideas: the attitude of tolerance as a manifestation of Christian virtue; the doctrine of multiple and progressive revelation; and the emphasis on common essentials rather than sectarian peculiarities. Of the first of these ideas Williams was again a most eloquent exponent. Bigotry and persecution, he maintained, are inconsistent with the true religion.[50] "It is but *Humanity*, it is but *Christianity* to exercise *meeknesse* and *moderation* to all men." [51] William Penn wrote to the same effect:

> And truly it is *high Time,* that Men should give *better Testimony* of their *Christianity*; for *Cruelty* hath *no Share* in *Christ's Religion,* and *Coertion* upon Conscience is utterly inconsistent with the very Nature of his Kingdom: He rebuked that Zeal, which would have *Fire* from Heaven to devour *Dissenters,* though it came from his own Disciples; and forbad them to *pluck up the Tares.*[52]

Williams especially emphasized the inconsistency of intolerance with evangelism. The church may and should require a creed of its own members, but the state should embrace also those from whom the church by exhortation and persuasion recruits its members. These should be regarded as potential believers, suffering only from that ignorance and sin which are the common lot of man, and from which one has oneself been saved only by the grace of God:

> There is a *peradventure* or *it may be*; It *may be* God may give them *Repentance.* That *God* that hath shewen *mercy* to one, may shew *mercy* to another. . . . Hence that *Soule* that is lively and sensible of *mercy* received to it selfe in former *blindnesse,* opposition and enmitie against God, cannot but be patient and gentle toward the *Jewes* . . . the *Turkes* . . . to all the severall sorts of *Antichristians* . . . and to the *Pagans* and *wildest* sorts of the sons of men, who have not yet heard of the *Father,* nor the *Son.* And to all these sorts . . . such a Soule will not onely be patient, but earnestly and constantly pray for all sorts of men, that out of them *Gods* elect may be called to the fellowship of *Christ Jesus.*[53]

The idea of multiple and progressive revelation reflected a decline of intellectual arrogance and a respect for religious truth as exceeding the bounds of any individual mind, or organized group, or historical epoch. It credited every honest conviction and fresh experience, however conflicting it might at the moment appear to be, as contributing some element of knowledge which would be reconciled in the fullness of light. If the way is to be found, men must be allowed to explore for themselves and testify to one another. Truth is delicate and manifold, and must be suffered to grow in its own way. This is the spirit of the declaration issued by Cromwell and Rushworth when they marched into Scotland in 1650:

> Is all religion wrapped up in that or any one form? . . . We say faith, working by love, is the true character of a Christian, and God is our witness, in whomsoever we see anything of Christ to be, these we reckon our duty to love, waiting for a more plentiful effusion of the spirit of God to make all Christians of one heart.[54]

The author of *The Ancient Bounds* sounded the same note:

> I contend not for variety of opinions; I know there is but one truth. But this truth cannot be so easily brought forth without this liberty; and a general restraint, though intended but for errors, yet through the unskilfulness of men, may fall upon the truth. And better many errors of some kind suffered than one useful truth be obstructed or destroyed. . . . This practice of magistracy, to be the dictator of truth, and to moderate with the sword, lays an unhappy caution, and too effectual an obstruction, in the way of truth, which comes not in always at the same end of the town—not always by the learned and eminent in parts or power (John 7. 48: *Have any of the rulers or Pharisees believed on him*?) but even by the people oftentimes.[55]

Even John Robinson in addressing the Pilgrims on the eve of their voyage, and however limited the application he may have had in mind, felt moved to say that "he was very confident the Lord had more truth and light yet to break forth out of his holy Word."[56] But the most impressive advocate of this idea was John Milton. His *Areopagitica*, written in defense of *the Liberty of Unlicensed Printing* has become the classic formulation for English-speaking countries of the doctrine that the truth prevails only when reason is allowed to choose, even at the risk of error.

The swing toward religious toleration within puritanism itself was reinforced by the broad current of liberal religious thought in England. Latitudinarianism bred tolerance, because it stressed the broad principles on which the sects agree, and considered their differences as relatively unimportant. Philosophy bred tolerance because, detaching itself from every positive sect, it generalized the meaning of religion, and recognized the equal legitimacy of its diverse manifestations. The growth of the rational temper promoted by the cult of modern science had the same effect, that of promoting a neutral mind which dissociated itself from religious partisanship. It is to this humanitarian, latitudinarian, philosophical, or scientific temper, already widely diffused in Europe in the seventeenth century, and making itself felt in New England in the eighteenth century, that the rising cult of tolerance owed many of its earliest adherents.

The following views of William Chillingworth, Jeremy Taylor, and Edward Stillingfleet illustrate the tendency to praise that which is universal and to disparage that which is particular in religious belief:

> Why should men be more rigid than God? Why should any error exclude any man from the Church's communion which will not deprive him of eternal salvation? The way to heaven is not narrower now than Christ left it. God does not and man ought not to require any more than this—to believe the scripture to be God's word, to endeavour to find the true sense of it, and to live according to it. . . . Take away this persecuting, burning, cursing, damning for not subscribing to the words of men as the words of God. Take away tyranny. Require of Christians only to believe Christ.

> To make a way to heaven straighter than God made it, to refuse our charity to those who have the same faith because they have not all our opinions, is impious and schismatical.

> What possible reason can be assigned why such things should not be sufficient for communion with a Church which are sufficient for eternal salvation? The unity of the Church is a unity of love and affection, not a bare uniformity of practice and opinion.[57]

The culminating work in this development was the famous *Letter Concerning Toleration* (1689), in which John Locke, of puritan birth and upbringing, latitudinarian and deistic in his own religious philosophy, master mind of the Enlightenment and the chief philosophical source of the Declaration of Independence, links puritanism with democratic liberalism:

> I esteem . . . toleration to be the chief characteristical mark of the true church. . . . The toleration of those that differ from others in matters of religion, is so agreeable to the gospel of Jesus Christ, and to the genuine reason of mankind, that it seems monstrous for men to be so blind, as not to perceive the necessity and advantage of it, in so clear a light.[58]

In brief, the rejection of theocracy and the separation of church and state in the seventeenth and eighteenth centuries marked the triumph of three ideas: the idea of the autonomy of religion as having both the right and the need to live its own life in the faith and worship of its adherents; the idea of the neutral secular state—the protector of all religions, but the partisan of none; the idea that liberality of outlook and temper is not a mere limitation forced upon all religions by the exigencies of civil order, but an excellence intrinsic to religion itself.

13

Those who stress the antithesis of puritanism to democracy rely on the professed rejection of democracy by leaders of puritan thought, the absence of democratic organization and procedure in puritan communities, and divers local and historical accidents. Their conclusions can be admitted, however, without denying the profound democratic implications inherent in the fundamental ideas of puritanism.[59]

The puritan religious society was founded on the thesis that a man's first allegiance was to his faith and moral conviction. To this allegiance he must remain loyal even to the point of defying the civil authority. Calvin, it is true, explicitly rejected pure democracy in favor of "aristocracy or a mixture of aristocracy and democracy"; and he went so far as to advocate a passive submission to "wicked," "rapacious," and "sacrilegious" rulers, provided they "are invested by the will of the Lord with that function, upon which he hath impressed an inviolable majesty." But given the temperamental, practical, and historical motives which inclined Calvin to authoritarianism, his concessions to the political logic of his fundamental principles are all the more striking. The religious judgment of common men remains as a check upon the ruler. Conscience takes precedence of kings and magistrates: "In the obedience which we have shewn to be due to the authority of governors, it is always necessary to make one exception . . . that it do not seduce us from obedience to . . . the Lord"; for "how preposterous it would be for us, with a view to satisfy men, to incur the displeasure of him on whose account we yield obedience to men!"[60]

The full democratic implications of puritanism, however, were developed only among the congregational Separatists, who created their own democratic religious societies and then extended the same principles to human society as a whole. This appears most strikingly in the debates among the several factions represented in Cromwell's army. The Levellers, with their able leader, John Lilburne, were not an excrescence upon the body of puritanism, but only its extreme self-expression. Translating spiritual into political rights, they became, as Gooch has said, "the earliest of British radicals." Their democratic creed was premature and revolutionary, so that they were strongly opposed by the constitutionalists such as Ireton and Cromwell himself, who would not go "too fast." [61] But Lilburne's thought ran the whole gamut of the democratic creed: the sovereignty of the people, against king, parliament, and army alike; government by conscious consent; the unassailable 'native rights' of the individual; wide suffrage and biennial or even annual elections; social reform; the high potentiality of the common man.[62]

Owing to its basic mentality, the army of Cromwell could either take the field against its enemies, or sit as a democratic assembly in which each man spoke his mind, in which the art of disputation was highly developed and in which the method of "free and equal discussion" was employed in order to lead to "truth and consent." As Professor Woodhouse summarizes the matter, puritanism "evolved from its theological consciousness ideas of liberty, of equality, of individualism, of government by consent and agreement, and of a species of privilege which had nothing to do with worldly possessions or existing class distinctions." It was a short and natural step from the view that "in the order of grace all believers are equal" to the view that "in the order of nature all men are equal." To those who thought of the church as "composed of believers all equally privileged," it seemed evident that "the state should be composed of men all equally privileged." The moral law—the law of nature; the covenant of believers—the social compact: thus to reason by analogy from the sphere of religion to the sphere of civil polity was inevitable.[63]

It is not necessary, therefore, that the later historian should build a bridge from puritanism to democracy. The puritans themselves built such a bridge, and many of them crossed it, some decades before John

Locke. Men such as Cromwell, Milton, Williams, and Penn belong alike to the history of protestantism and the history of democracy. The separation of church and state, the diversity of religious creeds freely held and lived within a common civil framework, the spirit of inquiry and discussion, the ideal of voluntary agreement, the appeal from the political authority to the universal human faculties of conscience and reason, the sentiments of equality and humanity—all these were all cherished within the bosom of puritanism against the time when their fuller implications could be realized in appropriate political and legal institutions.

14

The history of puritanism exhibits the interplay of two of its deepest motives: on the one hand, its recognition of the necessity and the ideal of social solidarity; on the other hand, its individualism. Both of these motives are valid, and their conflict in puritanism represents their universal conflict, as regards both the end of a political society and the control which it exerts over its members. A state is an association of men who are bound by a common aspiration; its function is to realize this aspiration; and the legitimacy of the control which it exercises upon its individual members rests upon the assumption that the members, because they share the aspiration, agree to accept the regulation which its fulfillment entails.

If the modern totalitarian state appears to have inverted the order, and to have subordinated morality and piety to the state, this is only because the state itself has assumed the role of a fundamental standard of conduct or object of worship; being justified as the expression of the common ethos, whether national glory, disciplined subordination of part to whole, racial identity, imperial grandeur, or class revolution. Liberal societies which proclaim the divorce of church and state do not escape the fact that this very divorce is founded on a creed, and a creed which is broadly moral or religious in character. Individualism, humanity, liberty, progress, the sacredness of personality, family and property, the cult of service, respect for decorum and decency, constitute a set of common beliefs and sentiments on which the state is founded, and which it is expected to protect, enforce, and develop.

But it is equally true that the good life requires that the individual shall be permitted to follow his own desires and exercise his own judgment. The good life cannot be imputed to society in any abstract or corporate sense, but resides, if it exists at all, in the individual man. It cannot be forced upon a man against his will, because it is not *his* good life unless it coincides with his preference. And while love can be frustrated by external compulsion, it can be elicited only by attraction—by commending an object to its favor.

The same interplay of community and individuality affects also that agreement which conditions and justifies the exercise of political control. Agreement is a sameness of judgments, in which each party endeavors and claims to think truly. But a man cannot be made to think truly; he can only be allowed the opportunity. He may be prevented from acting on the truth as he sees it, but there is no truth save as he or someone like him does see it; that is, affirms it freely in the light of the appropriate evidence. All of these considerations argue against the imposing of any uniform creed upon all members of society, and argue in favor of allowing the individual to act according to his own conscience and his own reason.

The fundamental paradox of a political society lies in the fact that while a solidarity of purpose and of judgment is required if such a society is to be perfected, or even to exist, their enforcement destroys their virtue. Purposes and judgments imposed from without are not genuine purposes and judgments, but only habits or opinions. When they are regimented by force, they are not really shared, but express only the personal or oligarchical wills of those who impose them. They represent the fears, or perhaps the momentary hysteria, of the people, and not their thoughtful conclusions or sober aspirations. Enforcement closes the mind to evidence, both the mind of the enforcer and the mind of the enforced. It arouses combative emotions of oppression and of self-defense. It conduces not to an honest assent of truth-seekers, but to superstition and hypocrisy. Because it violates the fundamental prerogatives of the individual, it tends, by whatever necessity or good intention it may appear to be dictated, to assume the form of 'persecution,' with all the corruption and inhumanity which that term connotes.

The evils of persecution were aggravated rather than mitigated by the puritan doctrine of the priesthood of all believers. It is bad enough to have a common creed imposed upon all by one, or by some detached authority; it is worse to have each man enforce his creed upon his neighbor. Authority then becomes personal and intrusive. The individual is subjected to a constant scrutiny and censoriousness. It is impossible to live either honestly or happily with one's keeper, and if every man may at any time assume this role without official designation or insignia, all social relations are corrupted by concealment and suspicion. Where any neighbor is authorized to represent the Society for the Prevention of Vice, or the orthodoxy of Karl Marx, or the gospel according to Mussolini or Hitler, the liberal feels impelled to institute Melville's "Chinese Society for the Suppression of Meddling with Other People's Business." [64] At the same time that every man suffers from living perpetually among his keepers, he suffers equally from being compelled to play the role of keeper himself. Instead of a becoming modesty and self-distrust, and a respectful regard for the values of his fellow men, he must assume a role of superiority, and harden his heart as well as his mind.

It is this antithesis between the bond of community and the freedom of individuality which liberalism attempts to resolve. It recognizes the fact that every political society must be based on a common creed. But while liberalism is itself a creed, it is a limited creed, which provides for the full concreteness of life through the exercise of diverse liberties.

When a man plants a garden, he dreams of a diverse pattern of flowering. He does not, however, attempt to regulate its growth. He plants seeds, he provides favorable conditions of soil, moisture, sun, and air. He spaces his plants so that in their growth they will not interfere with one another. He may even prune them and train them. But he counts heavily, most heavily, upon the genius of the several plants themselves and upon the principle of growth which is inherent in each. If he did otherwise, if he attempted to substitute mechanism for spontaneity, if he opened the seeds and uprooted the plants, subjecting them to perpetual supervision and manipulation, he would have no garden, but only a dead architectural design.

A man may plan his day to provide for periods of leisure. What is done in these periods is not planned, but is left to the promptings of the moment. Otherwise the spirit and the creative possibilities of leisure would be destroyed. Each is filled with its own activities, and the resulting life is not an abstract schedule, but a fullness of varied satisfactions. Nevertheless the whole may be said to have been designed, and to have been promoted by setting times apart and providing the conditions most conducive to their fruitful use.

Similarly, a liberal polity will define areas within which individuals and groups can grow and flower in accordance with their inherent propensities. It will prevent their mutual interference, it will provide favorable conditions of soil and climate. Its ideal of life is not simple and uniform; on the contrary, it aspires to richness and abundance through the spontaneity of its constituent parts. Regulation will be restrained, lest the tender plants of thought and passion be killed with too much handling, or asphyxiated by too narrow confinement.

CHAPTER FOURTEEN

THE SOVEREIGNTY OF GOD

1

"The spirit of the Puritan sect," said Francis G. Peabody, "was a sense of responsibility to God; its form was the scheme of a state based on the Old Testament." [1] From the theocratic form of the puritan state we turn now to its theocentric spirit.

The metaphysical presuppositions of puritanism fall outside the scope of the present book. To explore the 'evidences' of Christianity, to formulate and criticize the proofs of God, and to examine the tenability of the theistic cosmology which is their sequel, would take us far beyond the limits of relevance. The truths which I have undertaken to salvage are truths which, because they are bound up with no peculiar metaphysical system of the past, are capable of being assimilated to the general stream of modern life: truths which may commend themselves not only to the diverse groups of Christian believers, whether protestant or Catholic, orthodox or latitudinarian, but also to the adherents of secular or naturalistic beliefs which in modern times have sprung from sources outside of Christianity. This does not mean, however, that the fundamental concepts of Christian metaphysics—God, freedom, and the immortality of the soul—can be ignored altogether. For all of these concepts have their practical and social implications, which can be tested by the same ethical norm which has been applied to the puritan conception of salvation—to its rigorism, and to its moral, economic, and political individualism.

The positive gospel of puritanism consisted, as we have seen, in the supremacy of the love of God over all other attachments. The full practical implications of this gospel depend both on God's nature and on God's actuality. As Plato pointed out, and as has been so often reaffirmed, the moral effect of worship depends on the qualities imputed to its object. What flower the love of God, implanted in the breast of man, will yield, depends on the *kind* of God men love—or on what men love God *for*. But the puritan faith was not a mere ordering of values. It was a belief concerning the actual world, to the effect, namely, that a God possessing the attributes of wisdom and goodness is the creative cause and the regulative providence of nature and of history.

It was characteristic of the puritan to address himself directly to God. I do not mean that puritanism rejected intermediaries altogether, but its tendency, like that of protestantism generally, was to reduce the emphasis upon priest, saint, sacrament, liturgy, the Virgin Mary, even the Son of God, and to open a freer access for the common man to the very throne of heaven. Similarly, the puritan tended to neglect secondary causes, and to see the hand of God in every event. He was ever in God's watchful presence; while God, on the other hand, was immediately concerned with the daily vicissitudes of individual men. His name was perpetually on the puritan's lips. "It was God that did draw me by his Providence out of my Father's family. . . . It was God put into my heart to incline to live abroad"; it was God who was responsible for all the major events of his life—such was the testimony of Captain Roger Clap, who landed in Massachusetts Bay in 1630.[2]

One may be a theist in theory—that is, *when the question is raised*—and not raise the question except in occasional moods of inquiry. A theist in this sense will agree that God is the first and fundamental cause; but, having made this affirmation once and for all, he will in the normal routine of life ignore it. The puritan's theism does not differ from such theism in theory, but in experience. His sense of God was not reserved for flights of speculation, but was continual and pervasive. He was pious in season and out, and hence his piety was felt by the more secular-minded to be intrusive. He had no sense of propriety in such matters. If accused of the impropriety of introducing pious phrases into daily discourse, he would have answered that the acknowledgment of God can never be unseasonable.

It is this through-and-through, this daily and hourly, this shameless, admixture of piety with life which has begotten the disparaging epithet of 'cant.' This term suggests that one who perpetually talks, looks, and gesticulates piety cannot possibly mean it. He whose piety is less zealous prides himself on his greater sincerity. He who manifests it perpetually and immoderately is presumed to have substituted the outward sign for the true inwardness.

But the demand for a more reticent piety must not be allowed to obscure the fact that different individuals and groups are capable of different degrees of religiosity without any difference of sincerity. Granted that there is a God, and that God is the original and universal cause, there are different degrees of the capacity to *feel* and *live* as though this were the case. Religious genius has a high degree of this capacity, imparting to religious belief a vividness and a constancy comparable to those of sense perception. Tradition and habit, the circumstances of collective life, familiarity with the Bible and with Christian devotional literature, extended this capacity to the puritan layman, and made it a common capacity; just as in modern times the scientific consciousness is not reserved for a Newton or an Einstein, but is widely diffused, so that the ordinary man may attune his emotions to a world of galaxies and electrons, and practice the most advanced technologies in his daily affairs.

The puritan's sense of God's presence afterward declined, not because men became more sincere, but because men read other books more than the Bible, because they participated in other collective activities more than in religious worship, because the knowledge of secondary causes came to outweigh knowledge of first causes, because physical technology proved more immediately useful than theological technology, and because the things of this world obscured the life to come. God was no longer in the foreground of consciousness, but retreated to the background, where he could be seen only on days of exceptional visibility or by ascending to some high eminence.

2

God was known to the puritan as a ruler who imposed laws on his human subjects, and demanded obedience as the condition of his favor. The relations of God and man were a cosmic projection of the paternalistic state. In both cases there is an authority, a set of laws enacted by the authority, a power to enforce these laws, and an option of obedience or disobedience on the part of a subject. This politico-authoritarian aspect of God is most easily grasped, and affords the best approach to the profounder meanings of the puritan theology. "Since all rectitude of life," said Calvin, "consists in the conformity of all our actions to his will, as their standard, we might consider him as the sole master and director of our conduct . . . he requires of us nothing more than obedience." [3]

Construed most simply, this meant that the Bible is the corpus of the divine law, and that piety begins and ends with the scrupulous obedience to the rules therein formulated. Puritanism, through its zeal, its discipline, and its Biblical literalism, was easily betrayed into a moral legalism rivaling the notorious pedantry of the scribes and pharisees of old.* But legalism is the historical degradation of a higher principle from which no authoritarianism can ever be wholly dissociated. To obey a law is to obey a lawgiver, who is assumed to possess a *claim* upon obedience. Christian legalism was an obedience not of Biblical injunctions in and for themselves, but of the will of God; and imputed to God a *worthiness* to be obeyed. According to puritanism, as to Christianity in general, God's titles to obedience were his attributes: omniscience, omnipotence, and supreme goodness.

In all three cases it is possible to construe the divine attributes as instrumental to natural and worldly goods, and thus to reduce piety to prudence. A man desires victory in battle—God should then be obeyed because he is the wisest counselor, the most potent force, or the most devoted ally. A merely prudential piety may be dismissed as primitive or juvenile provided it be recognized that precisely such primitiveness or juvenility is alive in the world today, and supplies nations, races, classes, and even individuals with their tutelary gods. Primitiveness and juvenility are never eradicated, but are periodically outgrown. Being perpetually recurrent, they may at any time be the latest mode of the religious consciousness. There is today, as always, a tendency to invoke God as the auxiliary of any insistent human purpose, thus reversing the order of the divine government and making man the ruler over God.

* The narrowing effect of this literalistic legalism is one of the chief charges of Richard Hooker.[4]

It is clear, however, that a prudential interpretation of puritan piety would belie its central doctrine. The elect were not merely the more fortunate, who in the pursuit of long life, wealth, power, or victory in battle enjoyed the aid of God, but the regenerate, who had set their hearts on higher things. Worldly success was never more than a symptom of saintliness. Obedience was not a mere shrewdness by which the divine attributes might be turned to existing human uses, but an inclination of the human will to its supreme object.

3

Calvinism not only orients man toward God, but conceives God as absolute and self-sufficient. In the second chapter of the Westminster Confession of Faith we read of God that he

> hath all Life, Glory, Goodness, Blessedness, in, and of himself; and is alone in, and unto himself All-Sufficient, not standing in need of any Creatures which he hath made, not deriving any Glory from them, but only manifesting his own Glory, in, by, unto, and upon them: He . . . hath most Sovereign Dominion over them, to do by them, for them, or upon them, whatsoever himself pleaseth.[5]

Even this extreme expression of God's absolutism is tempered by the recognition of God's attributes, and by the appeal which these make to human faculties. God's pleasure is justified and his glory is admirable. The divine attributes are infinite power, wisdom, and goodness.[6] God being worshiped for his attributes, there are three alternatives of motivation, according to the attribute under which God is conceived. The tendency of the Christian consciousness is to translate power and wisdom into goodness.

First, God as power. It is possible that sheer power should be worshiped—not merely feared, but admired, praised, and obeyed for itself. There is, as modern psychologists have pointed out, a sheer submissiveness in man which inclines him to accept the dictates of a masterful will; and a sheer suggestibility which prompts men to conform their minds, their conduct, and their feelings to any exemplar invested with 'prestige.' There is a masochistic impulse which prompts men to humble themselves before Moloch, and suffer gladly the most brutal arrogance. These motives have played an important part in political and religious history; rulers and priests know well how to invoke them by pomp and ceremony and by the insignia of authority. The God of puritanism was no doubt a majestic and awful being, so depicted by the religious imagination as to inspire abject prostration. There was in puritanism a cult of passive obedience, designed to beget an unquestioning surrender to God's will, *whatever that will might be*—a sheer surrender of creature to Creator.

This aspect of puritanism finds its noblest expression in Jonathan Edwards. The central idea in his theology was the idea of the sovereignty of God. He perpetually affirmed the "absolute and immediate dependence which men have upon God," an "absolute and universal dependence" upon God "for all their good." This dependence was construed not as a promise of good to man, but rather as a glory of God.[7] God's sovereignty was to Edwards not a mere theological idea, accepted for reasons of logical necessity, nor a mere dogma accepted for reasons of Biblical orthodoxy: it was a central fact in Edwards's religious consciousness—an exalting and ecstatic experience. In retrospective account of his religious development he wrote:

> God's absolute sovereignty and justice, with respect to salvation and damnation, is what my mind seems to rest assured of, as much as of any thing that I see with my eyes; at least it is so at times. But I have often, since that first conviction, had quite another kind of sense of God's sovereignty than I had then. I have often since had not only a conviction, but a *delightful* conviction. The doctrine has very often appeared exceedingly pleasant, bright, and sweet. Absolute sovereignty is what I love to ascribe to God. . . . This I know not how to express otherwise, than by a calm, sweet abstraction of soul from all the concerns of this world; and sometimes a kind of vision, or fixed ideas and imaginations, of being alone in the mountains, or some solitary wilderness, far from all mankind, sweetly conversing with Christ, and wrapt and swallowed up in God. The sense I had of divine things, would often of a sudden kindle up, as it were, a sweet burning in my heart, an ardour of soul, that I know not how to express.[8]

In short, to Edwards in his mystical moments the unlimited power of God was a rapturous experience requiring no rationalization in terms of ulterior attributes. This acceptance of God on any terms, this sheer obedience of God for his dazzling omnipotence, is an authentic element in puritan piety, and was always a last reserve when God's ways proved unintelligible to man's reason and conscience.

But Edwards did not let the matter rest there. In his youthful notes on "The Mind" he presented a "universal definition of Excellency" as "*The Consent of Being to Being. . . .* The more the Consent is, and the more extensive, the greater is the Excellency." [9] This definition is designed to satisfy the requirements of ethical theory, and to interpret not only moral judgments, but aesthetic judgments as well. Piety, taken as the alignment of man's will to the will of God, is thus construed as a form of excellency, and God, construed as the harmony, or "cordial" agreement of the parts of Being, is both good and beautiful.[10] Obedience is then not a blind or reluctant acceptance of overpowering might, but the attraction of the will to its supreme object, and the consummate satisfaction afforded to partial being by its affinity to the whole.

Second, God as wisdom. This attribute, too, like that of power, is capable of being worshiped for itself. The intellectual interest has its own ultimate goal, which is complete and flawless knowledge. A God so qualified would be the supreme object of a man who was pure intellect. His God would be the personification of truth, and worship would be the loyalty of thought to this ideal, or the admiring contemplation of its imaginary realization.

But this is not the God of Christianity. It is true that Augustine, the favorite patristic authority among protestants, taught that the light of reason is a divine illumination—"an enlightened, not an enlightening light." [11] But with Augustine there is an ultimate priority of will over intellect—in God, in man, and in the intercourse between the two.[12] Even with Thomas Aquinas, in whom the intellectualistic motive was especially strong, man is not a pure intellect, and requires an object which will satisfy the will and the feelings as well. If Aquinas accepts the Aristotelian definition of man as a 'rational animal,' this is because reason is conceived as a faculty which knows the 'good' and can thus provide a *moral* reason for existence. The omniscience imputed to God is not a mere knowledge of fact, or mere power of explanation and prediction, but a grasp of that good purpose which is the motive of his creation and providential regulation of the world. The creature obeys God as one who both knows the good, and is good.

Obedience of God's infinite wisdom is not a mere confession of ignorance, as though a blind man were to submit himself confidingly to the guidance of one who sees. God's knowledge of the good does exceed that of man, but within its limits the human mind shares and confirms the knowledge of God, and the moral experience and insight of man give meaning to the goodness of God. The inscrutability of God lies not in the values which his perfection embodies, but in their reconciliation with the events of nature and history. There is, as we shall see, a 'problem of evil,' which is never wholly soluble; but unless the meaning of evil fell within the competence of the human mind, there would be no problem.

The analysis of the divine attributes of omnipotence and omniscience thus brings us back to the attribute of goodness. Obedience was not blind, any more than it was prudential. It was not a willingness to trust God's will in total indifference to the terms which it dictated, or a willingness to accept God's wisdom in total ignorance of its content. God's omnipotence was construed as a beneficent force which guaranteed the triumph of the moral will; and his omniscience as a revelation of the good, which confirmed and extended the worshiper's moral judgment. God was obeyed for the sake of that goodness which his power executes, and which his wisdom illuminates.

4

God's goodness, according to the puritan theology, is divisible into the two virtues of justice and love, and the ultimate appraisal of the puritan conception of God turns upon their relative priority.

In the puritan conception of human justice the characteristic emphasis is upon negative retribution, that is, the punishment of evildoing. The same emphasis appears in the puritan conception of justice as an attribute of God. The rigors of criminal justice are not softened in their theological application. The penal code of divine justice is of the greatest imaginable severity—the infinite culpability of sin being punished by the maximum of torture prolonged through infinite time.

Damnation by works does not in the puritan teaching imply justification by works—on the contrary. In the beginning God did not dispense justice to men, but indulgence. When Adam manifested ingratitude, he deserved punishment, and received it—he and his descendants, who inherited his ingratitude. The plan of salvation follows from man's deservingness of punishment. The 'mercy' of God consists in his exercise of the prerogative of pardon, and the greatness of his mercy lies in the magnitude of the punishment remitted. There is more mercy in pardoning a capital crime than a petty misdemeanor. The culprit, while he repents his crime, does not *earn* his pardon. Heaven is not a deserved reward. It is a renewal of the primordial indulgence. The immediate fact to the believer is not this original and normal divine goodness of the Creator, but the extraordinary goodness by which man is saved from his just deserts. Even this goodness, however, has to satisfy the claims of negative retributive justice. Justice is still relentless. The penalty has to be paid, if not by the guilty themselves then by Christ in their behalf—by Christ, whose very innocence enhances the value of his sacrifice.

The puritan sharpens this Christian doctrine, and drives it home. It is not his function to gloss it over, or introduce mitigating and apologetic considerations. Far from that. He glories in it. He takes retributive justice to be an absolute and irreducible principle, and not a mere instrument of re-education or social control. He expresses that strange but undeniable demand, felt in every human breast, that the wrongdoer shall be made to suffer for his wrongdoing, and proportionally to its degree. A crime being committed, there is a discontent that can be appeased only by reprisal. That having been done, at whatever cost to human sympathies, there is a sense of rectification, as though evil were somehow expunged from the record, and an original balance restored. The demand for punitive justice is not a mere feeling of revenge, but may, as for Leibnitz, assume the objectivity of aesthetic judgment:

> There is a kind of justice which aims neither at the amendment of the criminal, nor at furnishing an example to others, nor at the reparation of the injury. This justice is founded in pure fitness, which finds a certain satisfaction in the expiation of a wicked deed. The Socinians and Hobbes objected to this

punitive justice, which is properly vindictive justice, and which God has reserved for himself at many junctures. . . . It is always founded in the fitness of things, and satisfies not only the offended party, but all wise lookers-on, even as beautiful music or a fine piece of architecture satisfies a well-constituted mind. It is thus that the torments of the damned continue, even tho they serve no longer to turn any one away from sin, and that the rewards of the blest continue, even tho they confirm no one in good ways. The damned draw to themselves ever new penalties by their continuing sins, and the blest attract ever fresh joys by their unceasing progress in good. Both facts are founded on the principle of fitness . . . for God has made all things harmonious in perfection. . . .[13]

To consider retributive justice in its deterrent and regenerative aspects is to look beyond the principle of justice to its social effects, whereas the puritan finds justice admirable in and for itself. He deems God worthy of worshipful obedience, as one admires the just judge, not because he protects life and property, but because with close attention to the scales, and undeflected by any humane consideration, he apportions punishment to desert. So conceived, the judge most worthy of esteem would be he who would pass sentence of death upon his own son. Justice is stern, but it is not wanton, because it is merited; hard, but not selfish, because the judge submits himself as well as others to its rule. Retributive penal justice, so conceived, is by the puritan built into the basic structure of the world. The course of universal history is the dramatization of this virtue. It is a tragic theme, no doubt, and to find it good requires that the spectator shall subordinate pity to the logical austerities of moral fitness.

It is because retributive justice was taken to be a good in itself, and not a mere painful necessity, that it was considered as adding to the glory of God, and as an occasion of rejoicing. As Richard Baxter says:

The *principal Author* of hell-torments is God himself. . . . The *place or state of torment* is purposely ordained to glorify the justice of God. . . . As God will then glorify his mercy in a way that is now beyond the comprehension of the saints that must enjoy it; so also will he manifest his justice to be indeed the justice of God. The everlasting flames of hell will not be thought too hot for the rebellious; and, when they have there burned through millions of ages, he will not repent him of the evil which has befallen them. . . . Consider also, that, though God had rather men would accept of Christ and mercy, yet, when they persist in rebellion, *he will take pleasure in their execution.*

> . . . Terrible thing, when none in heaven or earth can help them but God, and he shall rejoice in their calamity! [14]

If justice is the greatest or one of the greatest of goods, if it is good in itself regardless of circumstance and cost, and if justice consists in retribution, then the moral consciousness will applaud it; the soul, whether divine or human, which has rightly ordered its values will be happy that this great good should be.

Negative retributive justice, then, was numbered among the divine perfections. The greatest of the exponents of this theme was again Jonathan Edwards: "Sin entered into the world, as the apostle says, and death by sin. Which certainly leads us to suppose, that this affair was ordered, not merely by the sovereignty of a creator, but by the righteousness of a judge." [15] It is clear that the God whom Edwards deemed worthy of worship was a "righteous judge," and that he admired God *in this role.* The Reverend Joseph Bellamy, a follower of Edwards, was even more explicit:

> To view the vindictive justice of the divine nature, as a beauty in the divine character; is to see, that all heaven ought forever to love and adore the infinitely glorious majesty, for punishing sin according to its desert. . . . And unless it appears to us a beauty in the divine conduct thus to punish sin, we shall be at enmity against his whole plan of government. . . . If vindictive justice is a glorious and amiable perfection, then it was a glorious and amiable thing in God, to bruise HIM, and put HIS soul to grief, who had espoused our cause, and appeared as our representative, although he were his own SON.[16]

5

But is retributive justice the end of creation? It is intrinsically good, but is it also *supremely* good? Is that verdict of goodness which God pronounces upon his creation reserved for the Last Judgment, when the drama reaches its tragic climax? There are within the puritan doctrine itself two reasons for rejecting this interpretation.

If retribution is a manifestation of divine justice, redemption is a manifestation of divine love; so that the purpose of creation must at least be divided between the two. Election is as essential to the glory of God as damnation.* Had justice been the only moral of the tale, it would not have been necessary that sin should be repented, or that God should send his son into the world to bear its penalty vicariously. Mercy is not deducible from justice. The divine pardon is not, like human pardon, an admission of doubt or of extenuating circumstances. The divine pardon is extended to those who are unquestionably and damnably guilty. It is an annulment of justice by a principle that is at least equal and independent.

But if the system is to remain unified and coherent, justice must be subordinated to love. And although this subordination is never completely realized, it lies in the direction in which puritan, like Christian, thought in general, unquestionably moves. God finds his creation "good" on the seventh day, and before Adam has provoked the divine wrath. Creation would, presumably, have remained good had there been no occasion for justice. It is as though the attribute of justice had been reserved for a contingency which *might* never occur. God is in his nature just; that is, disposed to punish sin; but he would have been satisfied had the painful necessity of its exercise not arisen. I use the word 'painful' advisedly. "God had rather men would accept of Christ and mercy." [18] That God does not wish men to sin follows from the very nature of sin, the enormity of which lies in its ingratitude; that is, in its failure to reciprocate love. And the fall is, after all, a *fall.* The normal relation of God to his creatures, in which the essential nature of each is fulfilled, is the relation of mutual love, enjoyed before the sin of Adam in the first paradise, and restored between God and the elect in the second paradise. Sin, with all the train of consequences in which justice is manifested, is a deviation from this norm.

As has been pointed out, the content of the Christian gospel is positive and not negative. The Christian God is the saving God, who promises escape from the rigors of justice. The very darkness of sin and of its just penalty is a background which through contrast makes brighter the promise of eternal life, and demonstrates the full amplitude of divine

---

* This idea of the double glory of God is explicit in Zwingli and Bucer, forerunners of Calvin.[17]

mercy. The world is a world in which no one gets less than he deserves, and some get infinitely more; a world which is at least just, and at most mercifully indulgent.

The puritan conception of divine justice is subordinated not only by these doctrinal considerations, but also by the basic moral insight that mercy is greater in the hierarchy of values. The ten Mosaic commandments, the two 'great' commandments, and the Golden Rule embrace no injunction to punish sin. Their essential teaching is the love of God and neighbor. The injunction to love and to forgive one's enemies forbids resentment, even just resentment. The utterance, "Vengeance is mine, saith the Lord," may, it is true, glorify revenge as a divine attribute; but it is designed to eradicate this hateful attitude from the heart of man.

6

Advancing moral enlightenment has repudiated revengefulness, and has rightly condemned the puritan for harboring its traces. It is sometimes felt that his chief cause of offense is the imputing to God of wrath. But if God loves good, he will, by the same principle, hate evil; and the intensity of the negation will be proportional to the intensity of the affirmation. It is God's prerogative to hate evil, and to hate it purely and unqualifiedly. The wrath of God may be justified as 'righteous indignation.' But if indignation is to be righteous, it must be an indignation felt against unrighteousness in *behalf* of those persons whom it injures; it is an offense to moral insight that God should hate unrighteous persons and wish them harm.

All virtue, as Plato pointed out, must be a manner of doing good, and must express a benevolent intent. It is this idea which is the germ of all modern ideas of penology and criminal justice. Punishment is an inflicting of pain or injury upon persons. Taken in itself, and independently of ulterior considerations, it is the precise opposite of goodness. If it is to be conceived as goodness, it must be construed as an instrument of ulterior beneficence—the greatest beneficence which circumstances permit to society or to the guilty man himself. Therefore if justice is to be a virtue, the damnation of sinners cannot be considered just unless it be a means of preventing sin or of saving the sinner. Otherwise God is guilty of an act of unmitigated cruelty, wholly inconsistent with the assumption of his essential goodness.

It is true that enlightened Calvinists have sometimes thought of punishment as the natural consequence of evildoing. In the reminiscent puritanism of Hawthorne's *Scarlet Letter*, sin punishes itself by its psychological effects:

> Tempted by a dream of happiness, he had yielded himself with deliberate choice, as he had never done before, to what he knew was deadly sin. And the infectious poison of that sin had been thus rapidly diffused throughout his moral system. It had stupefied all blessed impulses, and awakened into vivid life the whole brotherhood of bad ones. Scorn, bitterness, unprovoked malignity, gratuitous desire of ill, ridicule of whatever was good and holy, all awoke to tempt, even while they frightened him.[19]

But this shifts the ground altogether, and has nothing to do with justice. The puritan conception of divine justice, both in its authoritative teaching and in its popular acceptance, rests upon the analogy of government and jurisprudence. Punishment is an artificial evil, deliberately contrived and perpetuated. Hell is not a mental disease or even a fit of remorse, but an institution. Its tortures are invented for their ingenious painfulness. The guilty do not reap hell from the seeds of their wrongdoing; they are condemned and sent there.

Puritanism did not invent revenge. No man who feels a satisfaction when the score is evened, or who when evil has been done feels uneasy until somebody has been made to suffer and then feels at ease, or who rejoices in the punishment of the guilty, can complain of the puritan until he has first purged himself. Nor did puritanism invent hell. It was a central element in all medieval Christianity. The Last Judgment and the 'Doom' of sinners was a favorite theme of medieval sculpture and painting; and the brush and the chisel were even more effective in representing its horrors than the rhetoric of the puritan sermon. "There is no modern religious denomination," says Coulton, "not even the Salvation Army, which emphasizes this subject so frequently and so pitilessly as medieval orthodoxy." * It lay at the basis of the Inquisition, whose tortures were held to be justified by the greater tortures of which they were the foretaste or the prophylactic. And unquestionably puritanism, like medieval Catholicism, finds some excuse in the brutal criminal code of its day.[21]

The fact remains, however, that puritanism through reconsecrating a primitive idea of justice resisted the humanizing influence of the modern age. There is no possible way in which this idea can be reconciled either with moral enlightenment or with the genius of Christianity itself. For the Christian God, while he is a king to be reverenced for his majesty, and a judge to be respected for his justice, is first of all a father to be loved for his tenderness.

7

Love and its priority over other values is the all-pervasive theme of Christian theology, piety, and practice. This needs no proof, and little elucidation. Love is the motive of creation, and the original relation between God and his creatures. The first person of the Trinity is God the Father, and the familial relations, parental, filial, and marital, are continually employed to give concrete meaning to the sublimest truths of religion. While God the Father rather than God the Son is the exponent of justice, he is a Father who has so loved mankind that he has given his only-begotten Son that they may be saved. The office of Christ is created by God. The divinity of Christ implies that Christ's qualities, his love of his Father, his love of little children, his care of the sick and

* G. G. Coulton, *Art and the Reformation*, pp. 306-08. It was the Franciscan friar St. Bernardino of Siena (1380-1444) who wrote: "The damned ought to be tortured for ever by reason of pleasure. . . . Even as continual praise of thanksgiving shall everlastingly resound His [God's] mercy in those that are saved, even so shall wailing and lamentation, sighs and bellowings and cries resound His justice in the damned; therefore, to the ears of the blessed, Hell shall sing to Paradise with ineffable sweetness. Nor would there be in that place a pleasant and completely perfect sweetness of musical song, if this infernal discant from God's justice were lacking to the chant of His mercy." [20]

the poor, his inexhaustible pity and forgiveness, are divine qualities. For the Christian scale of values and standard of life it is more important that God should be Christ than that Christ should be God.

The Christian religious experience, in which the gospel receives its immediate confirmation, is a sense of the restoration of loving rapport between man and God, in which man feels the elevation and purifying effect of loving and at the same time the assurance and the euphoria of being loved. And when the puritan endeavors in his imagination to represent the perfection and the supreme satisfaction of the life eternal. he finds its original or foretaste in the happiness of love.

All of these Christian teachings are retained in puritanism, and constitute the core of its meaning. It was the puritan Richard Baxter who said:

> Lay by all the passionate part of Love and Joy, and it will be hard to have any pleasant thoughts of Heaven. . . . The Scripture, that saith of God, That he is *Life* and *Light,* saith also, That he is *Love,* and *Love* is Complacence, and Complacence is Joy; and to say *God is Infinite, Essential Love* and *Joy,* is a better notion, than . . . to say that *God* and *Angels* and *Spirits,* are but a Thought, or an *Idea.* What is Heaven to us if there be no Love and Joy? [22]

When the puritan Christian used the term 'love,' he meant that tenderness of feeling which expresses itself in giving, providing, ministering, caring, guarding, caressing, or suffering from another's pain and rejoicing in another's joy. Such love is consummated when it is mutual and each loves the other not only for that other's sake but for the other's reciprocal love of oneself. Such love is a sort of harmony, and has some analogy with beauty, but it is significant that Jonathan Edwards, exponent of divine justice, and gifted in the art of philosophical speculation, should have explained harmony by love and not love by harmony:

> As bodies, the objects of our external senses are but the shadows of beings; that harmony, wherein consists sensible excellency and beauty, is but the shadow of excellency. That is, it is pleasant to the mind, because it is a shadow of love. When one thing sweetly harmonizes with another, as the Notes in music, the notes are so conformed, and have such proportion one to another, that they seem to have respect one to another, as if they loved one another. So the beauty of figures and motions is, when one part has such consonant pro-

portion with the rest, as represents a general agreeing and consenting together; which is very much the image of Love, in all the parts of a Society, united by a sweet consent and charity of heart.[23]

The original of that "sweetness" to which Edwards so continually alludes is tasted by the personal affections, and not by the senses or by the contemplative intellect. For Plato, personal love is the shadow of that love of abstract good which is the supreme object of the intellect. Personal love is thus a stage or school of experience beyond which the emancipated mind will ascend to the admiring contemplation of perfection. In its highest forms it is a seeing of the good in one another, or a companionship in its pursuit, where the good in itself lies beyond all persons as an archetypal principle. Human privation does not excite such love, but is tolerated for the sake of the fraction of positive attainment with which it is commingled.

Christian love, on the other hand, is a pitying and helping love of persons elicited by their state of non-fulfillment. It is of the essence of familial love that it should be uncritical, that its dear and familiar personal object should be loved for himself, and not for the qualities of excellence which he embodies. God's love is such a love, evoked by human limitations—more strongly by the sinner than by the saint. And man's love of God has in the Christian revelation, despite its affirmation of God's self-sufficiency, something of this same character. For its evocative object is not the Creator in his full majesty, but the God who in the person of Christ underwent privations and suffered on the cross. He who would grasp the distinctive contribution of Christianity to moral and religious thought must hold firmly to this insight.

Christian love forbids an impersonal God, for only a person can love persons. It forbids a pantheism in which God and man are identical, for personal love implies a duality of persons, each having an independent value as being loved for himself. It suggests, if it does not imply, a God whose task is unfinished, and whom to love is not the mere endorsement of a fait accompli, but the giving of an effectual support. Finally, if the mutual love of God and man is to be something more than a system of mirrors or echoing surfaces, there must be interests at stake other than love itself. The purpose in which God and man are lovingly conjoined is that same moral purpose of fulfilling and reconciling concrete desires and aspirations which gives meaning and authority to social institutions. In short, this exaltation of personal love, sometimes slighted by Christian philosophers but constituting the essence of the common Christian piety, points unmistakably to a pluralistic universe, a limited God, and an immanence of the divine life in the actual affairs of human history.

His inhumane and unenlightened conception of justice being admitted, and his infidelities to his own gospel of love, the puritan is still to be credited with insistence on the moral essence of God. The Lord of puritanism, like the Lord of Elijah, was not in the wind, the earthquake, or the fire, but in the still small voice of conscience. That God is justice and love rather than force and noise is a not untimely truth. Ignazio Silone, describing the demonstrations of Italian nationalism—the tumult, the overwhelming of every scruple and tender sentiment by a wave of hoarse and ferocious patriotism, when every man joins in the clamor, and finds pretexts for marching with the winning side—has said: "The loud speakers proclaiming the outbreak of the war in all the market-places were certainly not the Lord." [24] The present is an age of loud speakers, when the voice of justice and of love is more still and small than ever. All the more reason why, if it be difficult to hear, this voice should be listened for attentively, and acknowledged when it speaks.

8

Puritan piety was not a mere moral insight and preference of the best, but a confident hope that what is best is also first and last. In this linking, through the idea of God, of morals and cosmology, puritanism was true to the genius of religion.

The point may be expressed by saying that while goodness was God's supreme attribute, in the sense of qualifying God to be obeyed, it was not his sole attribute. For God was not only good, but effectually good. He must, therefore, be endowed with the attributes of moral causality, and in an eminent degree. His omniscience was his knowledge of the true good, and of the true means of its realization; his omnipotence was his control of the forces by which the actual world, embracing nature and history, is governed. God was thus a supreme volition, perfectly enlightened and fully implemented.

In this affirmation of the forcefulness of righteousness puritanism assimilated to itself both the teleology of the pagan philosophers and that primitive animism and anthropomorphism which instinctively credits events to the agency of friendly or hostile wills. It vivified and simplified this doctrine through its simple—its all-too-simple—rendering of the course of nature and history in terms of a historical drama of which man was the hero, Satan the villain, and God, in his capacity of playwright and producer, the over-ruling fate. God as Creator was the original cause, and as Providence the regulative cause, by which events were both controlled and explained.

In this triumphant righteousness the pious consciously participated. The elect were not seers of the good merely, who had chosen the better way, but the instruments by which its victory was achieved. They felt the élan of an army going into battle under a Captain of irresistible might and wisdom. They enjoyed so much assurance as to give them courage, but not enough to render them passive. They were not mere passengers in a ship, but oarsmen who themselves supplied a portion of the energy by which it was propelled. They felt their strength renewed and enhanced, not superseded, by the grace of God. They possessed that degree of confidence in which the will is raised to its highest degree of power, in which it can bear hardship, overcome resistance, and endure any finite period of defeat, owing to the conviction that such defeat can only be temporary.

Since sinners as well as saints endure throughout eternity, immortality was not a survival of righteousness qua righteousness, but of souls qua souls. It implied the ascendancy of moral over physical forces. The resurrection of Christ was the symbol of this general principle. But the doctrine had a different meaning for saints and sinners. The sinner would have preferred to forfeit the prerogative of immortality. It was a part of his torment that he could not be annihilated. To the saint, on the other hand, immortality provided the assurance that he in his own person would participate in that future good which lies beyond the term of his natural life, and which is only imperfectly achieved under the conditions of this world. Heaven was that society of souls, bound together by ties of perfect love, which prolongs and purifies those relationships of family, friendly, and neighborly affection which constitute the best of life. This belief encouraged men to give hostages to fortune—to depend on one another's love without fear of bereavement, and to love life without fear of annihilation. The Christian eschatology, in its plain meaning of survival, and of personal and social continuity, was not an accident or a superstition, but an outgrowth of Christian hopefulness combined with the Christian scale of values.

Whatever be the verdict of philosophy on the extension of moral causality to the cosmos at large, puritanism thus becomes a powerful exponent of its operation within the realm of human affairs. It takes its stand on an experience which, within limits, is indubitably authentic. And while it testifies to the efficacy of the will, it at the same time proclaims the inability of the individual to achieve good easily or through his own unaided efforts. The triumph of the Kingdom of God requires intense and patient effort, the collaboration of many wills, and that access of fervor which comes through faith in eventual victory. Cromwell's armies, says Macaulay, "came to regard the day of battle as a day of certain triumph." Cromwell's own account of the battle of Dunbar reveals the perfect union of tactics and fanaticism. He shrewdly observed the "posture" of the enemy, and knew when to attack. But the password of the puritan army was "The Lord of Hosts"; the soldiers felt themselves to be "the chariots and horsemen of Israel," and the enemy "as stubble to their swords." [25]

The story of American puritanism is pervaded by this sense of the conquering might of a righteous God working through human agencies, or of a dedicated mankind reinforced by God. The puritans felt that they had a mission, and that that mission could not fail. Transferred to the "howling desart . . . from fertill Soyle to Wildernesse of Rocks," and beset by savages, they exulted in the "Wonder-working Providence of Sions Saviour":

> And now let the Reader looke one the 102. Psalme, the Prophet Isaia 66. Chapter; take this Sharpe Sword of Christs Word, and all other Scriptures of like nature, and follow on yee valiant of the Lord; And behold the worthies of Christ, as they are boldly leading forth his Troopes into these Westerne

Fields, marke them well Man by Man as they march, terrible as an Army with Banners, croud in all yee that long to see this glorious sight, see, ther's their glorious King Christ one . . . that white Horse, whose hoofes like flint cast not only sparkes, but flames of fire in his pathes.[26]

The American pioneer carried this militant piety with him into the conquest of the western continent. Sherwood Anderson's Jesse Bentley, in his lowly and brutalizing struggle for existence, was sustained by the conviction that he was the instrument of deity:

"I am a new kind of man come into possession of these fields," he declared. "Look upon me, O God, and look Thou also upon my neighbors and all the men who have gone before me here! O God, create in me another Jesse, like that one of old, to rule over men and to be the father of sons who shall be rulers!" Jesse grew excited as he talked aloud and jumping to his feet walked up and down in the room. In fancy he saw himself living in old times and among old peoples. The land that lay stretched out before him became of vast significance, a place peopled by his fancy with a new race of men sprung from himself. It seemed to him that in his day as in those other and older days, kingdoms might be created and new impulses given to the lives of men by the power of God speaking through a chosen servant. He longed to be such a servant. "It is God's work I have come to the land to do," he declared in a loud voice and his short figure straightened and he thought that something like a halo of Godly approval hung over him.[27]

As God's retributive justice requires that the guilty individual shall be himself responsible for his wickedness, and that the will which sins and the will which punishes shall be two wills; as personal love implies independent persons, whose tasks are not finished and who may thus receive aid and succor from one another; so the idea of an army of righteousness and a battling for the Lord implies an opposing unrighteousness not only opposed, but so formidable as to require the united efforts of God and his elect in order to ensure the victory. How these implications of the moral and religious consciousness shall be reconciled with the idea of God's supremacy, how the pluralism of the first shall be reconciled with the monism of the second, constitutes the so-called problem of evil.

9

Of the many attempted solutions of the problem of evil there are two in particular which contribute to the understanding of puritan doctrine. In both cases the significance lies in the attempt rather than in the solution.

The more radical of these attempts proceeds by the reduction of lower evil to higher good. All physical evil being reduced to sin, this in turn is viewed as providing the necessary condition of God's manifestation of justice and mercy. Without sin there would be no guilt to punish or to pardon. Sin is thus a part of the divine purpose, introduced by the Great Dramatist in order to point the moral. Although repudiated by the more authoritative puritan thinkers, this tempting escape from speculative difficulties was congenial to the puritan temper, and found its distinguished exponents. Said Richard Baxter:

> All things must come to their perfection by degrees. The strongest man must first be a child. The greatest scholar must first begin with the alphabet. The tallest oak was once an acorn. This life is our infancy: and would we be perfect in the womb, or born at full stature? If our rest was here, most of God's providences must be useless. Should God lose the glory of his church's miraculous deliverances, and the fall of his enemies, that men may have their happiness here? If we were all happy, innocent, and perfect, what use was there for the glorious work of our sanctification, justification, and future salvation?—If we wanted nothing, we should not depend on God so closely, nor call upon him so earnestly.[28]

It is clear that the writer is here attempting to justify not only the as-yet-unsaved condition of favored mortals, which furnishes the occasion of the glorious work of God's grace, but also the hopeless predicament of those doomed sinners whose role it is to furnish the occasion of his just enmity.

This is the particular application of a general and perennial argument: that which taken in itself is deemed evil, will, if taken in its larger context, assume the character of good—good of a higher order. Thus hardship, pain, privation, and other *natural* evils are seen in the light of their sequel to be the formative elements of *moral* good. Similarly, stoicism subordinates the standard of pleasure to the standard of reason. Judged by the higher standard, pain in itself is 'no evil.' It is pain regarded passionately, as by the man who complains of it, which is evil; whereas pain regarded rationally, as by the man who bears it with fortitude, is good. And so with the Calvinistic analogy. The higher good is not sinlessness, but repentance, the chastened spirit, or the victory over temptation. Sin in itself, then, is not evil; but only sin unrepented, unassimilated, unsubdued. Similarly, as judged by the higher standard of justice it is sin-unpunished and not simple sin which is evil; while sin-punished is good.

That which is most serious from the standpoint of the religious consciousness is the fact that a double standard of good and evil implies a doubling of God. There is the lower God who punishes sin, and who is therefore just; and there is the higher God who creates both the sinner and the punishment as parts of a world in which punitive justice is embodied. The first is the hero of the play, the second is the Author. It is the lower God who is the God of everyday religion; while the second God, the supreme Artist, is reserved for those detached philosophical souls who can rise above moral partisanship to the plane of aesthetic contemplation.

It is not surprising that this doctrine should prove unacceptable, in the long run, even to the austere puritan consciousness. It clearly contradicts both the fundamental premises and the prevailing sentiment of a creed which proclaims the enormity of sin. It is as though a cult devoted to the extinction of fire should transform itself into a cult for the development of a fire department. The devotee would then hope for occasional fires; he might even commit or encourage arson, recognizing that without fire there could be no fire department. His hatred of fire would have been superseded by his pride in the organization and the technique designed to cope with it.

If the argument proves that sin in itself is no evil, it also proves that innocence in itself is no good. But in that case what becomes of the paradise before the fall, and of the paradise to come, both of which consist in the guiltless and unmerited enjoyment of God's love? If the life of Adam before the fall, or of the angels who never fall, or of saints whose regeneration delivers them altogether from the law of retribution, represent types of perfection, then it is impossible to escape the conclusion that an innocent world would have been a better world. The world as it is possesses an inexplicable flaw—inexplicable in terms of almighty goodness.

Even if retribution be accepted as higher than innocence, a world in which the innocent were rewarded would be better than a world in which the guilty were punished. And even if negative retribution be accepted as higher than positive retribution, there still remains an insuperable difficulty, the difficulty, namely, of accounting for the evils which arise upon the higher level of value. The stoic has no way of explaining in a world which is ruled by reason the incontestable fact of unreason. Similarly, in a world which is ruled by justice it is impossible to explain injustice. Evil has changed its form, but the *problem* of evil still remains. Evil-unpunished is just as solid a fact as sin. Even if the injustices of this world are assumed to be made good in the world to come, salvation itself is an unjust discrimination among men who are equally guilty. It is heaven, and not hell, that now becomes inexplicable. And if justice be so great a good as to justify even the sin which it entails, then injustice becomes an evil of corresponding gravity. Even if the standard be again shifted, from moral to aesthetic terms, and the final good of the world be conceived in terms of the tragic 'fitness' of retribution, there still remains an unresolved evil of the same order. For such a dramatic value of divine justice is appreciated only by God himself or by a few of the initiated; and there still remains the unmitigated pain and deprivation suffered by those who play the role of sinners for the sake of a delectation which they do not themselves enjoy.

10

A second attempted solution of the problem of evil abandons the idea that sin is justified by justice, and returns to the view that justice is justified by sin, but imputes sin to man's exercise of freedom. Moral values require the exercise of choice. Piety is not piety unless God be freely loved. But the freedom to love implies the freedom to disobey—

piety cannot be created without the risk of impiety. Desiring in his benevolence to create the highest good—namely, piety—God therefore endows men with a free will, which his creatures then misuse. God does not create, nor does he will, this impiety. It is created by men through the exercise of that faculty with which God endows them. That men will so misuse their freedom is foreknown to God; but this does not deter him, because a tragic moral world is better than a blameless mechanical world in which piety is impossible.

This argument may be interpreted as a form of the first. Sin, the misuse of freedom, is justified as the necessary condition of piety, its right use. But the force of the argument is here weakened by the absence of any clear order of values as between freedom and piety. If freedom is taken to be the higher good, then freely sinning would be as good as freely loving God. If it is piety and not freedom which is accounted the supreme good, then impiety is an evil of the same level, and outweighs the good. There is no assurance, nor even the suggestion, that the pious outnumber or equal the impious. It is as though, taking life as one's ultimate standard, one should seek to justify death by the fact that *some* persons live. But if life be good, then death is equally evil; and it would be more logical to condemn life, on the ground that without life there would be no death.

The introduction of the principle of freedom does not, then, fortify the first argument, but aggravates its weakness. The force of the appeal to freedom lies elsewhere—namely, in the exculpation of God. It provides, or claims to provide, a way of explaining evil in a God-made and God-regulated world while at the same time saving God from its taint. This project would seem to be condemned to failure from the beginning, to be, in short, self-contradictory; and such is, I believe, the case. But it is instructive to examine its futility.

It is argued that God does not create sin, but creates those who create sin. Yes, but God is aware of what he is doing. He does not set going a train of events which later occasion him surprise and dismay. Although he does not create men for the sake of the evil consequences, he knowingly permits these to occur. If sin does not constitute the *motive* of creation, then it is at least a part of its *intention;* and if sin be evil, then the creative will cannot be held blameless.

Seeking to exonerate God, one may argue that sin is intrinsic to the will which commits it, and that blame therefore attaches exclusively to the human sinner, regardless of ulterior causes. It is true that the will of the sinner cannot be effective without the agreement of external circumstance and the employment of physical force. Let it be admitted that the sinner himself, as a chooser of evil, is a product of the past. The puritan, in fact, goes further than the most advanced modern exponent of environment and heredity in his recognition of such concomitant and antecedent causes. But even so, he argues, the human will is the only proper object of blame, because it is the place where the sin resides, and because a judgment of blame can properly address itself only to a responsible will and not to extraneous causes:

> His inability being moral, and lying in willful wickedness, is no more excuse to him, than it is to an adulterer that he cannot love his own wife, or to a malicious person that he cannot but hate his own brother: is he not so much the worse, and deserving of so much the sorer punishment? Sinners shall lay all the blame on their own wills in hell for ever.[29]

But the attempted solution is unsuccessful even though it be assumed that the human will is blameworthy. It is unsuccessful because the sinner's will is not the *only* blameworthy will, and because the judgment of blame properly looks for the ultimate seat of responsibility. If the sinful propensities of later men can be ascribed to the earlier sin of Adam, then Adam is to blame; and if Adam's capacity for sin can be ascribed to God, then this creative will, being ultimately responsible, is ultimately blameworthy.

The heart of the puritan difficulty lies in the fact that the sins of Adam and his descendants flow not from natural causes, but from a will—the will, namely, of the all-creating and all-providential God. In puritan thought and experience this will does not lurk in the background, to be invoked only by speculative philosophy; it is a near and vivid presence. If men are encouraged to leap over secondary causes of good and see the hand of God in their salvation, there is the same reason to see that same hand in the sinful condition which requires salvation. Blame, like praise, seeking a will to hold accountable, and going back of proximate to original causes, then finds itself faced with a profound dilemma. To blame

God is a sacrilege which contradicts not merely the theological dogma of divine perfection, but the attitudes of love and reverence which are the core of piety. To acquit God, on the other hand, is to be unfaithful to the moral consciousness. It requires a splitting of the divine personality as proposed by the Scottish minister who, being questioned by a parishioner concerning God's creation of evil, replied: "You must understand that the Almighty in His public and judicial capacity is obliged to do many things that in a private and personal capacity He would be ashamed to do." [30]

There is, of course, always the possibility of falling back upon the acknowledgment of "mystery." Jonathan Edwards was not a man to qualify either his affirmation of God's causality or his reverence for God's perfection; it was inevitable that these two motives should have met in head-on collision; and it is significant that so resourceful a thinker should have found no way of escape. He was speaking of Adam's sin, to which all subsequent human ills are traceable. How is this initial and catastrophic deviation from righteousness to be explained?

> [It] was by God's *permission*; who could have prevented it, if he had pleased, by *giving* such influences of his Spirit, as would have been absolutely effectual to hinder it; which, it is plain in fact, he did *withhold*: and whatever mystery may be supposed in the affair, yet no Christian will presume to say, it was not in perfect consistence with God's *holiness* and righteousness, notwithstanding Adam had been guilty of no offence before.[31]

It is always possible that faith should exceed the limits of understanding—that is what faith is for. But it is unfortunate, to say the least, that faith should be invoked to escape a contradiction of its own making. For God's all-causality is as much an article of faith as its reconciliation with God's perfection. In this case, furthermore, faith lacks that practical justification which is its chief warrant. It tends to moral confusion and cynicism. Someone has said that "an optimist is a fellow who believes that whatever happens, no matter how bad, is for the best. The pessimist is the fellow to whom it happens." The belief that apparent evil is in some mysterious way 'all for the best' provides too easy an evasion for the relatively fortunate. It reconciles a man to the evil which others suffer; it excuses his failure to remedy it, or even his share in its creation.

And when, on the other hand, this blindly trusting faith is held by the sufferers themselves, it tends to a dulling of their perception and a relaxation of their moral will. It is because faith may thus serve as an 'opiate,' dispensed to allay discontent and thus to induce men to accept their lot rather than improve it, that religion has been considered by many as the enemy of social progress. It allies religion with obscurantism, with reaction, and with moral apathy.

11

The failure of the attempts to 'explain' evil by the requirements of divine justice, or by the exercise of human freedom, leaves evil as an intolerable fact to be eradicated or transmuted into good by the moral will. It cannot be thought away. There remains, then, only the practical alternative of doing away with it by the consolidated effort of mankind under the authority of God. This attitude toward evil—its militant conquest through the exercise of the moral will—was the practical faith of the puritan. Though his methods were not enlightened, his intent and concern were unmistakable.

It has been pointed out that puritanism was fundamentally a gospel, or offer of salvation. It was a signal of alarm, but at the same time an offer of safety. With the puritan's sensitive and realistic acknowledgment of actual human misery and his uncovering of hidden evil there was associated a profound optimism. His central motive was to replace evil with good, or to convert the first into the second. He represents a most resolute refusal to abandon hope, on the part of one who is exceptionally aware of the reasons why one should. To this stubborn hopefulness is to be ascribed the puritan's attempt to convert physical into moral evil. There is a story of a physician who, being unable to cure his patient's actual disease, gave him another disease which he *could* cure. The puritan felt the impossibility of coping with physical evil. He was unfitted for the task both by the state of the times and by his own preoccupations. His competence lay in the field of moral disorder. Consider, for example, the following passage from Cotton Mather's *Diary*, written in 1681:

"About the Middle of this Month, I lost abundance of precious Time, thro' tormenting Pains in my *Teeth* and *Jawes*; which kind of *Pains* have indeed produced mee many a sad Hour, in my short Pilgrimage. In the Pains that were now upon mee, I sett myself, as well as I could for my Pains, to *search and try my Wayes.* I considered, I. Have I not sinned with my *Teeth*? How? By sinful, graceless excessive *Eating.* And by evil Speeches, for there are *Literæ dentales* used in them? II. This is an *old* Malady, from which I have yett been free, for a considerable while. Lett mee ask then; Have not I of late given way to some *old* Iniquity?" [32]

The modern remedy for Cotton Mather's difficulty would be, no doubt, a visit to the dentist. But let us imagine an absence or ignorance of such scientific remedies, together with a strong desire for relief: the effect would be to construe the malady in a form which was remediable. The puritan did not know how to cure the toothache as such, but he did know, or thought he knew, how to deal with sin. This was his special province. Hence he construed the toothache, and similar physical evils, not as diseases but as symptoms. He recognized only one fundamental disorder: namely, moral or spiritual disorder. Evil being so construed, he had a therapy which corresponded to the diagnosis. If the evil was in oneself, the remedy was repentance, faith, and discipline; if it was in others, the remedy was edification, preaching, and punishment; if it was in the community at large, the remedy was moral sanitation and theocratic institutions.

The puritan's method of reform was not enlightened, even in the sphere of moral and religious education. His moral diagnosis of physical evil was, to say the least, of dubious warrant. It served to deflect attention from those actual causes of pain and sickness whose discovery by modern medical science has paved the way to their removal. But the puritan is to be credited with a recognition, however misapplied, of the broad principle that the first and sometimes the last step in the correction of evil is a sound diagnosis. And the puritan's attempt to correct evil, however unsuccessful and misguided, places him squarely on the side of those who believe that the evils of life are remediable.

12

To substitute the practical attitude of doing away with evil for the theoretical attitude of explaining it away is unquestionably to impeach the power of God. It leaves an irreducible opposition of good and evil, and an irreducible manyness of being: a moral dualism and a metaphysical pluralism. If the justice of God is a salutary but painful necessity imposed by the occurrence of sin, then that evil is as external to God as crime is external to the judge who pronounces sentence upon it. The evil which God rectifies is not of his own making—it is non-God; and God is a limited being dealing with an occasion which arises from without. If in order to relieve God of complicity evil is imputed to human freedom, then freedom itself must imply a power on man's part to proceed independently of, even in defiance of, God. If man under God's guidance, and with a confidence begotten by faith in God's power, sets his face against evil and undertakes to destroy it, he implies that evil, even though its defeat be certain, is alien both to himself and to God, causally as well as morally.

These implications, while they may contradict the dogma of omnipotence, do not conflict with religious practice and sentiment. To the pious believer, if not to the systematic theologian, divine justice and atonement are measures by which God meets the deplorable catastrophe of sin—the remedy appropriate to a contingent and regrettable emergency. The puritan is never pantheistic, and mysticism, in any sense that dissolves moral differences and dulls the edge of moral judgment, is profoundly repugnant to his cast of mind. His individualism, his unreserved hatred of sin, his historical and dramatic imagery, his sense of the tragedy of life, shared even by the incarnate God, and his conception of the perfected life in terms of reciprocal love—all these depict a world which is pluralistic in its ultimate metaphysical composition and dualistic in its moral alignment.

Given a God who can be obeyed with the full endorsement of conscience and loved with an undivided heart, the puritan is prepared to wage a long campaign in God's behalf. He knows how to endure and to postpone the victory. He is not accustomed to suppose that the triumph of the Kingdom is an easy triumph. He knows evil and respects its force and subtlety. He is not surprised to find that the enemies of God are numerous and formidable, and is prepared to pay the cost of their eventual overcoming. He would have felt at home in the world of today.

If it be the great merit of Christianity to have humanized God, and to have identified him through the doctrine of the incarnation with the defeat, pain, and privation which beset human life, and with the love that may emerge and triumph over them, it is a fault of puritanism to have compromised God's humanity to man and thereby to have countenanced man's inhumanity to man. Accepting negative retribution as an ultimate principle and failing to see that there is no virtue in justice save as the instrument of love, puritanism gave high sanction to the primitive spirit of revengefulness. Puritanism also exaggerated the deterrent and educative value of punishment. Men cannot be taught to love God by being harshly punished when they fail to do so, especially if it be God himself who inflicts the punishment. The result is to associate God with fear or with the hatefulness of the penalty. The love of God is better implanted in men by representing God's lovableness than by stressing and aggravating the hatefulness of non-loving.

The puritan's exaggerated and unenlightened emphasis on justice being admitted, there yet remains his exaltation of human dignity. Man was the central figure in the great tragic theme of creation, sin, punishment, and salvation. Cotton Mather, as we have seen, was greatly preoccupied with his spiritual fortunes, and was tortured by anxiety. But whether he was damned, or whether, as he hoped and on the whole believed, God had "pull'd [him] out of the *horrible Pitt,*"[33] he was in any case conscious of receiving the personal attention of God. For better or worse, the universe cared about him. The very meaning of history lay in his destiny and in that of others like him. He participated in a great cosmic tragedy, "noble" in Aristotle's sense, since its theme was the painful triumph of justice and of mercy.

The puritan's conception of the sovereignty of God thus saved him, on the one hand from complacency and egotism, and on the other hand from meanness and vulgarity. So long as its essential spirit lives, puritanism will insist on the supremacy of moral values; and, in the hierarchy of moral values, on the supremacy of love qualified only by the necessities of justice. It will insist upon construing the universe in terms of the hard but assured victory of this supreme end over the natural and human enemies by which it is beset. It is a catastrophe that the differences which divide the Christian sects, protestant or Catholic, should ever be allowed to prevent their effectual alliance in this common faith.

Even were the teachings of science to force the abandonment of every Christian dogma, there would still remain this moral mission of mankind as a common ground for all men who take life seriously and who view it in its aspect of universality. The causal efficacy of the moral will is as well attested as any species of causality. There is a moral way of life, which is the way of reflective agreement, all interests being considered, all wills included, and all judgments consulted. This way of life has won its victories—in personal integrity, in family life, in peaceful, orderly, and free communities. It has also suffered its defeats. There are times, such as the present, when the situation appears desperate. But the puritan mind expects defeats, and finds within itself reserves of moral courage with which to continue the battle. The defeats of yesterday and today do not preclude a future turning of the tide. Time is long, and recorded history is short. There is no conclusive reason why patience and effort may not, if necessary, be as long as time.

The content of puritan doctrine has been traced through its phases of evangelism, rigorism, individualism, economy, theocracy, and theism. Through its inheritance of medieval dogma, its Biblical authoritarianism, its fanaticism, its distrust of the natural man, and its exaggerated insistence upon retributive justice, it resisted the advance of ideas endorsed by posterity. But at the same time it contained the seeds of progress within itself. For the puritan was taught to respect conscience and private judgment above any oppressive authority. If he accepted the Bible, he construed its meaning for himself. If he obeyed God, it was because God's worthiness to be obeyed was confirmed by his own conscience and emotional experience.

It was, in short, characteristic of the puritan to give his allegiance to ideas rather than to persons or institutions; or if he obeyed persons and institutions, he did so in terms which he could understand and which commended them to his moral faculties. This is the connecting link between puritanism and democracy. For American democracy was a manifestation of those tendencies whose flowering in the eighteenth century has received the name of the Enlightenment. And the essence of the Enlightenment was the belief that rightful authority lies in a doing of good recognized as such by the individual called upon to obey.

Part Three

APPRAISAL OF DEMOCRACY

CHAPTER FIFTEEN

THE SUPREMACY OF REASON AND CONSCIENCE

1

THE REJECTION OF DEMOCRACY is nowadays regarded as evidence of superior wisdom. Even in those parts of the world where democracy is still professed there are many who privately consider it an exploded myth. Opinion has been veering so swiftly in this direction that while a few years ago the defense of democracy would have been condemned as hackneyed and banal, one who undertakes it now is suspected of seeking notoriety.

There are two condemnations of democracy that clearly beg the question, and need to be disposed of in advance lest they become sources of confusion. People do not beg a question explicitly: but there are those whose argument against democracy is in effect the mere utterance of an inarticulate anti-democratic or pro-democratic prejudice. Such question-begging appears in the judgment which condemns democracy because it is too democratic, and in the judgment which condemns it because it is not democratic enough.

Those who condemn democracy as too democratic are often found in democratic countries, where they have been reared in the democratic tradition. They dislike democracy in proximity, although they were once loud in their praise of it or hot in its pursuit. Such a reversal is not at all unusual, for goals which exert an attractive force at a distance often exert a repulsive force when they are approached more closely. When I was a boy I had a dog whose favorite pastime was chasing cats. Ordinarily this furnished agreeable and harmless exhilaration both to the dog and to the cats. But every once in a while, owing to some unnatural burst of speed or accident of topography, the dog would overtake a cat. Then he suddenly sat down and scratched a flea, or was reminded of some other engagement. Cats were good to chase, but catching them was a very different matter, for which he had neither the appetite nor the technique. He was somewhat disgusted, too, with the cat because it refused to go on escaping. Now it is impossible to pursue an ideal without running the risk, however slight, of overtaking it. There is a strong chance that one will, at any rate, gain on it. And then, as one comes to closer quarters, one is likely to experience a sudden revulsion of feeling. If we look about us, I think we shall find here and there ardent pursuers of democracy who have assumed the posture of that dog—dismayed, annoyed, and embarrassed.

For a long time, feebly and intermittently since the beginning of the Christian era, vigorously and continuously since the beginning of our own national existence, western Europeans have been trying to improve the condition of the masses. It is a great end to pursue, and it has given us a great run. But recently we have been gaining on it; and instead of celebrating the victory, the fastidious withdraw their skirts, anxious housewives deplore the passing of 'the good, old-fashioned servant,' and uneasy employers complain of the increase of wages or the insubordination of the wage-earner. American reformers, beginning with Thomas Jefferson, have eloquently preached the gospel of universal salvation by education. Now that their eloquence has borne fruit, and the youth of the land are thronging to the high schools and colleges, many leaders of education are barricading their doors and posting sentries to keep back the crowd. They are remarking with an air of perfect innocence, as though they had never said anything on the subject before, that, after all, the value of liberal education has been much exaggerated, that the learned professions are overcrowded, and that for most men there is nothing so good as that great public school of *experience* which was opened some time ago by the Creator in the Garden of Eden, and which it costs nothing to operate or attend.

The second kind of question-begging critic objects to democracy because it is not democratic enough. While critics of the first kind profess the theory but shrink from its practice, these complain that it has in fact never been practiced. They beg the question because, although they seem to be advancing arguments against democratic institutions, they are really assuming democracy as their standard of criticism. They are in their hearts its most radical and dogmatic partisans. When such a critic argues that public education does not really emancipate the mind, or that the people do not really rule, or that genuine equality is inconsistent with a capitalistic system, or that the American democracy does not in fact permit those liberties of speech and press which it is pledged to secure, the very bitterness of his lament reveals the depth of his passion for emancipation, popular government, equality, and liberty.

Analogies can be found among the critics of Christianity. There are the pursuing Christians who do not like Christianity at close range, or prefer the profession to the practice. They feel that there is already too much Christianity in the world. Radical Christians, on the other hand, condemn Christendom for being too little Christian, and by this condemnation manifest the rigorous and uncompromising quality of their adherence to Christian standards.

These two sets of critics, then, we may ignore; neither has fairly examined the fundamental question. But today they are being joined by critics of a more thoroughgoing sort, who claim to have considered democracy on its merits and to have rejected it deliberately. They would have us reopen a question that was supposed to have been settled. They would have us reverse the main current of political change during the eighteenth and nineteenth centuries. They would have America, instead of moving forward in the direction of its original impulse and toward its supposed historic destiny, go back and begin over again, modeling its institutions on those very tyrannies which were once denounced.

Those who thus reject democracy advisedly and explicitly may also be divided into two groups: namely, those who reject it for reasons of expediency, and those who reject it for reasons of theory. Critics of the first sort claim that democracy does not 'work.' But such criticism is not fundamental, because whether democracy works or not can be judged only after one has decided what it is for; and to answer that question it is necessary to go back to moral and social first principles. It is the theoretical, and not merely the practical, challenge to democracy with which we shall be concerned in the chapters that follow. A recent writer has said that "the invention of America was far more important than the discovery of America," and adds that "the America which was invented in the eighteenth century on the basis of ideas from the seventeenth century is in jeopardy in the twentieth century." [1] What of these ideas? And how, if at all, can democracy be saved from the theoretical jeopardy in which it is placed by their rejection?

2

"A decent Respect to the Opinions of Mankind" requires that "a People about to dissolve the Political Bands which have connected them with another" should declare "the Causes which impel them to the Separation": [2] whereupon the Declaration of Independence proceeded to recite philosophical reasons, which were supposed to commend themselves to all disinterested minds. It has been objected that American democracy is 'doctrinaire.' If by this is meant founded on principles claiming universal validity, then American democracy is consciously and advisedly doctrinaire. It was instituted in an age which considered itself an age of enlightenment, and it was instituted with the avowed intent of profiting by that enlightenment.

The claim that American institutions were created by the conscious application of sound doctrine was repeatedly affirmed at the beginning of American national history, and is one of the chief grounds of American national pride. In 1777, John Jay, in his "Charge to the Grand Jury of Ulster County," said:

> The Americans are the first people whom Heaven has favoured with an opportunity of deliberating upon, and choosing the forms of government under which they should live. All other constitutions have derived their existence from violence or accidental circumstances, and are therefore probably more distant from their perfection, which, though beyond our reach, may nevertheless be approached under the guidance of reason and experience. [3]

Speaking before the South Carolina ratifying convention in 1788, Charles Pinckney made the same claim:

> To fraud, to force, or accident, all the governments we know have owed their births. To the philosophic mind, how new and awful an instance do the United States at present exhibit in the political world! They exhibit, sir, the first in-

stance of a people, who, being dissatisfied with their government,—unattacked by foreign force, and undisturbed by domestic uneasiness,—coolly and deliberately resort to the virtue and good sense of their country, for a correction of their public errors.[4]

A state founded on "reason and experience," conceived by the "philosophic mind," and realized, as William H. Seward said, under peculiarly "propitious circumstances," will expect to have its superiority conceded by all mankind. America's triumph will lie, not in superior force, but in its successful and exemplary solution of the social and political problems with which every people is confronted. Its success will not be enviously resented but welcomed as "for the benefit of the human race." [5] This pride was voiced with the florid oratory of the American politician by Congressman Ashton C. Shallenberger of Nebraska in 1917:

> To our future jubilee shall come, in the fullness of time when we hold it, not kings and princes as a relic of the imperialism, the barbarism, the despotism of the past; not conquered nations bound to our chariot wheels, as trophies of conquest and all-conquering war, but rather the nations of the earth in peaceful procession, to sit at our feet and learn from a study of America's history the story of man's final emancipation from wrong and oppression and do Columbia reverence as the uncrowned queen of the highest, the freest, and the noblest type of civilization upon the face of the earth. That is the ideal which I hold for my country. That is the mission I would have her bring to mankind.[6]

This sentiment, despite its offense against modesty and good taste, has been shared by many men of other lands. It is freely conceded that this creed makes peculiar demands upon human nature, and may fail ingloriously where these demands cannot be met. Nevertheless it was felt, and is still felt by a large portion of mankind, that, granted the necessary conditions, democracy of the type broadly set forth in the Declaration of Independence is the optimum form of social and political organization.

The defense of democracy as founded on universally valid principles, and as therefore possessing a unique claim to acceptance, stands opposed to all those social philosophies which make their ultimate appeal to the verdict of history. It explicitly rejects historical authoritarianism, historical determinism, historical relativism, and every historical school which would concede the finality of established things merely because they are established. The eighteenth century is fairly charged with a lack of historical knowledge, or with the invention of a mythical history to accord with preconceived ideas. This charge is well grounded and must be placed on the debit side of the account. There was, however, a certain virtue in this defect. Thinkers of the time were not so obsessed with history as to fall into the paradoxes of historicism, according to which, since all actual institutions are historical, all institutions in turn are equally justified. Or rather, none is justified or justifiable.

The social philosophy of the eighteenth century was based on the assumption that a historic institution was not a fatality but a form of life organized for good reasons, and subject to reorganization when and insofar as these reasons were violated. It was assumed that these reasons could be known—not merely affirmed by an act of faith, or formulated after the fact for the sake of putting a fair front on unseemly motives, but proved moral reasons differing, no doubt, from the truths of physics or mathematics in the manner of their proof, but not in their universality or impartiality. It was believed that society might be ruled not by men, or even by positive law, but by principles, of which the personal ruler was merely the agent and the positive law merely the provisional embodiment.

And because it was believed that human institutions rested on principles, and not merely on historical accidents or irrational forces, it was also believed that the best guarantee of the soundness of human institutions lay in the development and dissemination of knowledge. Said Jefferson:

> Enlighten the people generally, and tyranny and oppressions of body and mind will vanish like evil spirits at the dawn of day. Although I do not, with some enthusiasts, believe that the human condition will ever advance to such a state of perfection as that there shall no longer be pain or vice in the world, yet I believe it susceptible of much improvement, and most of all, in matters of government and religion; and that the diffusion of knowledge among the people is to be the instrument by which it is to be effected.[7]

3

The reasons by which democracy or any other specific form of state is justified must be derived from the reasons by which the state itself is justified. If democracy is the best state, it must be because democracy is pre-eminently what the state as such is designed to be. The crucial question is, "Why should there be a state at all?" The state is a power which demands obedience and penalizes disobedience. He who is called upon to pay the costs in taxes, in military service, or in the restraint imposed upon his spontaneous desires—he who because of the state may not do what he likes and must do what he does not like—may properly ask himself why this should be. This does not mean that he asks why he should obey the law, once it is enforced. He asks the more general and fundamental questions: "Why should there be a force which thus constrains me? If there were none, what would induce me to create such a force?" In other words, he wants to know how the authority of the state is to be rationalized.

This question is not universal or necessary. Men find themselves already living under a state when they reach the stage of reflection, and are apt, for various psychological reasons, which are better understood now than in the eighteenth century, to acquiesce. The public authority is invested with pomp and ceremony, and exerts an almost irresistible power of suggestion. There exists a strong and widely diffused sentiment of loyalty, and men are groomed to obedience by social custom. The state in its own interest is prepared with opiates or intoxicants to strengthen the forces of suggestion, loyalty, and custom, and so to maintain a state of either apathetic or passionate acceptance. Neither apathy nor passion asks questions. But when, whether through resentment or curiosity, and despite the forces of inertia and emotional excitement, the critical consciousness persists, and men demand that the state shall justify itself, the attempt to satisfy that demand is the root of political philosophy. Whether this justification is offered in behalf of a state in the making or a state already made does not affect the nature of the question once it is raised and pressed to an answer.

Such an attitude of inquiry is not satisfied by an appeal to custom or to a theory of the 'divine right' of rulers, for that is only to appeal from one accepted belief to another. If God does ordain human governments, then why? If custom prescribes obedience of the ruler, then again why? In an age when religion and ethics were themselves subject to critical re-examination, it did not suffice to rest the state upon the ground of piety. This did not mean that politics was unrelated to religion and ethics, but only that all must be rationalized together, and purged of mystification and arbitrary force.

The political philosophers of the eighteenth century were not skeptics or anarchists. They believed that there *was* a reason for the state beyond its power to impose itself by force or tradition. They looked beyond the state, not in order to reject it, but in order to find the premises from which it could be argued.

The state being a force executed by men called rulers, and placing restrictions upon the activities of other men called subjects, citizens, or members, the crux of the question is the right of the first group to exact obedience of the second. Is it reasonable that some men should command, and others obey? There are two schools of political thought which are divided on this question—*statism* and *moralism*. According to the first school, political rule is self-justifying; according to the second, it is justified by appeal to an ulterior moral standard. American democracy is clearly identified with the second of these schools, but the logic of its position can best be approached by an examination of the first.

4

Statism, or the view that the power of the ruler is self-justifying, is in turn divisible into two doctrines: the doctrine of tyranny, in which the will of the ruler is interpreted as his own private will; and the corporate or organic doctrine, in which the ruler's will is interpreted as the public will.

Although tyranny has many practical exponents, it has few theoretical apologists. But its comparative simplicity commends it as a starting-point for discussion. It is the extremest and least ambiguous political application of the general doctrine of moral solipsism or subjectivity, according to which all judgments of right and wrong or of good and evil are relative to the actual will of him who pronounces them. If I find an end to be in accord with my will, then, and only then, do I judge that end good. That my will should be in conflict with another's will is irrelevant, unless that other will also happens to be an object, or a means to an object, of my own will. This precludes my saying that it would be better if I were to change my will or if my end were also to satisfy other wills. All such impersonal judgments of the form 'it would be better' are meaningless, since 'better' can refer only to my actual preference.

Suppose, for example, that, being Mussolini, I will that all Italians shall have large families. Then large Italian families are good, entirely regardless of the fact that the Italians in question, or some of them, may prefer smaller families. I may hope that they will share my will, as this would help me to execute it; but if they do not, this fact in no way affects the merits of the question. If I adopt measures of violence, I am only doing what is dictated by my moral judgment. If they, on their part, use violence in behalf of their opposing wills, they are equally justified. The outcome, then, is civil war or coercion, each party judging by the standards of its own will and these wills being, unhappily, in conflict. And this is the end of the matter, reason and conscience providing no substitute for force.

Or suppose that, being Mussolini, I will that Italy shall acquire a colonial empire. Then, so far as I am entitled to judge the matter at all, the annexation of Ethiopia is good, the Ethiopians to the contrary notwithstanding. Their opposite will in the matter is evidence to them that my policy is bad—but it constitutes no evidence one way or the other to me; since I, if I am to judge at all, am bound to judge by the evidence of my own will. If war ensues, then each is right and the enemy is wrong; and one right is as right, and one wrong as wrong, as the other.

Recognizing that there is no escape from conflict, and that conflict is aggravated and intensified through the self-justification which each contestant derives from the standard of his own will, one may idealize conflict itself in terms of heroism and victory. After all, one may argue, the great thing in life is to 'live dangerously,' as one does in war—forgetting how little of war is glory, and how much of it is disease, treachery, brutality, degradation, and death; forgetting that war affords by no means the only or the best opportunity of living dangerously. Or one may argue that war brings the survival of the strong—forgetting that the only kind of strength which war in itself selects is warlike strength. But even though belligerent heroism and victory were admirable, such attempted idealizations could have no meaning in this philosophy. For heroism and victory cannot be judged good unless someone wills them, and the judgment of him who wills them can have no possible superiority to the judgment of the pacifist or the defeatist who wills otherwise.

Let us return to a questioning individual who has asked the state to justify itself to *him*. If he happens to be the ruler, or a party member who shares in the ruler's enjoyment of power and plunder, he finds the state to be justified in terms of his own will. If, on the other hand, he is an ordinary citizen who pays the costs while others reap the benefits, the present theory gives him only two alternatives. Either he submits from fear, and finds no justification in a system which can thus intimidate him; or he may suffer a change of will and, in a frenzy of patriotic fervor, enjoy the triumph of the ruler vicariously. But even in this second case he can be offered no reason why his will should be thus altered. As between his former will, representing, let us say, his private interests, his love of liberty, his scruples, or his vocation, and a new will, representing the interest of the ruler, there is no ground of choice other than his own actual preference.

The mark of tyranny is the failure of the ruler to justify himself to the ruled. This failure leads to the second form of statism, in which the ruler's private will is replaced by his public will. There is, according to this organic or corporate form of subjectivism, a collective or general will, a will of the body politic, which by definition embraces the will of the ruled, and of which the ruler is the only authentic and effective expression. Mussolini, for example, does not as 'Duce' speak for himself but for Italy. Officially, he acts and judges by a will which is not the will of a former journalist of Forli, or of Ciano's father-in-law, but the Italian will, the will of all Italians.

There are two crucial questions to be asked about this 'higher' or 'greater' will: What are its claims? Where, if anywhere, is it to be found?

It claims to be the will of all members of the community. But if this is to be anything more than a fiction introduced for the purpose of 'rationalizing' tyranny, it must be construed as a reflective and explicit agreement among those individual members.[8] There is a will of all when and only when the participating individual wills knowingly and deliberately adopt the same end and unite upon its means. But to concede this is fatal to statism, both in theory and in practice. It recognizes a non-political standard by which the ruler's actual power may properly be judged, criticized, and even overthrown, a standard which any thoughtful and well-informed person may comprehend and apply. It invalidates the creation of a general will *by* the state, through the use of propaganda or intimidation, since the power so used would be as yet an illegitimate power. If the state's rightful authority rests upon the reflective and explicit agreement of its members, it can attain and renew that rightful authority only through promoting enlightenment and freedom of choice.

The second question—"Where is the general will to be found?"—leads to a similar conclusion. According to statism, it is to be found in the ruler's public or official will, as distinguished from his private will. But once such a distinction is made, and whatever be the criterion, it is always possible to question the ruler's possession or exercise of power on the ground that it is merely private or personal. His authority is valid only when it is constitutional, or legitimate, or represents the wills of the people at large, or is exercised in the general interest. But who is to judge? If the ruler himself, then *that* exercise of authority is arbitrary; the ruler's authority is invalidly validated. If not, then any man endowed with reason and conscience—any man who is aware of the criterion and informed as to the facts—is entitled to sit in judgment upon the ruler.

Thus statism, if it is to be maintained at all, is forced to adopt in theory that alternative of tyranny which it invariably adopts in practice. The view of Treitschke is at least clear and straightforward. "The State," he says, "is born in a community whenever a group or an individual has achieved sovereignty, by imposing its will upon the whole body"[9] through armed force and coercive regulation. The state so conceived monopolizes both power and right. It explicitly abandons any idea of justifying itself to the "body." Its rulers can justify their exercise of power only to themselves, in terms of their particular will—one will among others, selfishly and effectively imposed.

Tyranny, then, which justifies the ruler's power to himself in terms of his own private will, is the only form of statism that exists in practice or makes sense in theory. So far as its principle is concerned, it matters not whether tyranny is embodied in a single individual, or in a party, or in a bureaucracy. If what goes on behind the closed doors of a modern dictatorship were known, what a disclosure there would be of bargains struck among those of the inner circle, who divide among themselves spoils which they enjoy at the expense of the balance of society! In tyranny, politics is not the art of ruling well, but the art of becoming and remaining the ruler. It is as though the culinary art were conceived not in terms of the production of nutritious and palatable food, but in terms of the rewards of the cook. In tyranny, the ultimate justification of political procedure lies not in benefits conferred, but in benefits received. Benefits conferred are merely concession or cajolery.

Because the principle of tyranny justifies the usurper who covets power as well as the ruler who possesses it, statism resorts to the doctrine of the collective will. If this will were construed literally as a will embracing all wills, then a refractory opponent could disprove its claim by pointing out that his will was not in fact embraced. Hence the fiction which identifies the collective will with the will of the de facto ruler. Faced with the dilemma of acknowledging the principle of force and thus inviting its use by others, or of abdicating in favor of reason and conscience, statism imputes to the functionaries of the state, ex officio, a representativeness which they do not possess of a collective will which does not exist.

The art of tyranny appeases, as well as intimidates, its victims. Its benefits have then to be translated into terms of individual satisfactions, and when so translated they tend to be divisible into two categories: the belligerent satisfactions of the many, and the material perquisites of the few. The article on "Fascismo" in the *Enciclopedia Italiana* contains a statement, attributed to Mussolini, of a fundamental creed which is equally applicable to the other Axis tyrannies, and is explicitly opposed to the individualistic liberalism of democracy, to the class-conflict of Marxist Communism, and to monarchical and ecclesiastical constitutions. The good life is essentially that of a warrior-caste, consisting in physical courage, disciplined obedience, and love of power. The people at large are promised a 'moral' or 'spiritual' good which consists in the subordination of their selfish and material goods to the enduring life of the all-embracing nation-state. The general acceptance of such a code requires that the normal interests of men shall be dissolved in the heat of military ardor; and the rulers of such a state well understand that it is as important for that purpose to have enemies as friends. They invent grievances, nurse resentments, or embark on conquest in order that emotions may be kept at a fighting pitch. But in time of peace such a polity becomes the rule of a privileged party, whose members monopolize the offices, enjoy the plums of patronage, augment their private fortunes, and secure the submission of the rest by fear and deception.

5

Statism is tyranny aggravated by bad metaphysics. It would like to persuade its opponents, but in the end can only silence them. Its apologia does not mitigate its offense, but adds insult to injury—insulting the intelligence of the ruled at the same time that it injures their interests. It practices exploitation and talks edification.

Moralism, on the other hand, bases politics upon non-political foundations. It takes its stand outside the state in ethical principles of right or good, and then appraises the state thereby. In the last analysis it trusts the judgment of all beings who are competent to exercise such appraisal, through their possession of the faculties of reason and conscience.

Moralism implies no disparagement of the state. On the contrary, it alone justifies the state, being enabled to do so because it defines a standard by which to justify. The state has a fitness or a claim to be obeyed which reason and conscience, and not merely fear, will endorse. Moralism concludes that the state is indispensable not only to life, but to virtue and to the good life; and this now means something, because virtue and good have been given a definition which is prior to their political application.

Democracy, in its fundamental modern and American meaning, is the application of moralism to human institutions, and in particular to political institutions. Statism being reduced to tyranny and moralism to democracy, democracy becomes the alternative to tyranny. In short, while Plato opposed one best form of government (aristocracy) to four inferior forms of government (timocracy, oligarchy, democracy, and tyranny); and while Aristotle opposed three good forms of government (monarchy, aristocracy, and polity) to three inferior forms of government (tyranny, oligarchy, and democracy), the view here presented opposes one good form of government, democracy, to one bad form of government, tyranny.*

Moralism reduces to democracy for two reasons. In the first place, moralism holds that the justification of the state lies in the good of its members. However the term 'good' is here interpreted, whether as pleasure, happiness, virtue, well-being, or self-realization, it is applicable to man as such, and not to any privileged individual or class. The only inequality which is implied depends on limitations of capacity, which the good state will endeavor, by education or other agencies, to remove. Moralism is thus democratic in its conception of the social ideal which it is the purpose of the state to promote. In the second place, the knowledge of the good is not associated with any hereditary social or personal qualification, but only with the possession of the universal human faculties of reason and conscience. The proof of good lies in the truth or validity of the judgments which these faculties pronounce, and depends, therefore, upon their free exercise. Every man is therefore a rightful critic of the institutions under which he lives, and may properly

* The force of all such classifications depends, of course, upon the meanings given to the terms. The antitheses of Plato and Aristotle are reducible to the antithesis here presented if one stresses the underlying principles of the Platonic and Aristotelian antitheses. For both of these philosophers, tyranny was the worst form of government; the antithesis between the good and the bad forms of government turned upon the degree in which government was disinterestedly beneficent and enlightened; and in both Plato and Aristotle the attributes of the good ruler, namely, disinterestedness and enlightenment, were parts of that virtue and happiness which it was the purpose of the state to promote among its citizens.

give or withhold his assent. Since the justification of the state lies in its goodness, it is always possible that the private citizen may be right and the state wrong.

In short, the justification of the state lies in its commending itself to the enlightened interest and to the enlightened judgment of those who live under it. These are the basic principles of democracy—its basic social principle and its basic political principle. In the chapters which follow they will be elaborated, and, it is hoped, elucidated.

6

Democracy, then, takes the position that what is defensible politically, including the existence of the state itself, rests upon what is defensible morally; that this ulterior moral defense of the state is in terms of the good of those who live under it and are required to submit to its rule; and that the qualified exponents of this moral defense are these same members, by virtue of their competence to judge what is truly good.

As affirmed by the founders of American democracy, moralism was identified with the doctrine of 'nature'—a doctrine which reflected the excessive lucidity or innocence of an age which was as indisposed to political, as it was to religious, mystification. It is commonly supposed that the doctrine is guilty not only of superficiality but of serious error. The indictment may be divided into two charges: first, that the doctrine of nature confused history and ethics; second, that it was a priori and intuitive rather than empirical and experimental. The doctrine is guilty of both charges, but its guilt is not fatal: its errors may be removed and its essential truth preserved.

Both errors are traceable to the broad philosophical tradition and context of the Age of Enlightenment. This philosophy was, as we have seen, theistic and optimistic. Nature was good because it embodied the creative beneficence of God. It was a harmony of members, each so fitted to the rest that in following its own inner promptings it would infallibly serve not only itself but also every other member. Thus when men spoke of a law more certainly valid than the laws imposed by human governments and courts, they called it a 'law of nature.' When they spoke of rights more purely just than those actually enjoyed by men in the existing state of society, they called them 'natural rights.' When they spoke of a state of human perfection and happiness contrasted with the evil or the mixed condition of the life they knew, they called it the 'state of nature.' But nature was also the earliest chapter in history, because, according to the Book of Genesis, it was created in the beginning; and because whenever the natural is distinguished from the artificial, it is assumed that the former precedes the latter in time. The natural is the most direct and authentic work of God, and at the same time, relatively to man, it is original or primitive.

From this blend of ideas there arose that strange conception of the 'noble savage' or of 'nature's gentleman,' which later anthropology has proved to be entirely fictitious.* The eighteenth century was at one and the same time too theological in its science and too naïvely Miltonian in its theology. Assuming that the world left the hands of the Creator at a definite time in the past, and that it has been leaving them ever since, it follows that the farther one goes back in time, the nearer one comes to God. The primitive state of man, under this inverted conception of nature, was the Golden Age, to which only the poets could do justice. But science has compelled us to say adieu forever to Shelley's "dazzling picture," and to Pope's vegetarian Eden. We have been obliged to substitute the somewhat different image of the Hottentot and the Bushman. As, guided by modern history and prehistory, we work our way back to first beginnings, to the Paleolithic or Neanderthal way of doing things, men seem, in a sense, to be getting more and more natural, but nearer perhaps to "the reign of Chaos and old Night" than to "the reign of God." [11]

It would be a mistake to suppose that the political thinkers of the

---

* "*No man has more contempt than I, of breath;*
But whence hast thou the right to give me death?
Obey'd as Soveraign by thy Subjects be;
But know, that I alone am King of me.
I am as free as Nature first made man,
'Ere the base Laws of Servitude began,
When wild in woods the noble Savage ran." [10]

seventeenth and eighteenth centuries were bent on writing bad history. On the contrary, they were notoriously indifferent to history. Their primary concern was not with the origins of law but with the legitimacy of law. They wanted to say that government is *justified* by the intrinsic human faculties of reason and conscience, that there are prior moral principles from which government is *deduced*, and that there is a happiness of mankind of which government is the *instrument*. They expressed this by saying that reason, conscience, moral principles, and the happiness of mankind *antedated* government. This manner of exposition was in agreement with habits of discourse. It was then, as now, customary in reciting a syllogism to affirm the premises before affirming the conclusion, although the logical 'follows from' has nothing to do with the temporal 'follows after.' The temporal form of presentation also gave a certain dramatic force to the argument. For there will always seem to be a certain presumption in favor of an antecedent state of affairs. Possession is nine-tenths of legitimacy as well as of the law; theft strikes us as a more evident evil than poverty. So the priority of that reason and conscience, which these philosophers praised, to the institutions which they condemned, could be more effectively argued by claiming that mankind had been deprived of an original enlightenment by a subsequent tyranny and obfuscation.

Nevertheless, while the position of moralism is quite independent of history, its statement in terms of history by an age which was ignorant of history has exposed it to legitimate attack by a later age which understands history better.

7

The doctrine of natural rights was also betrayed by its alliance with the a priori and intuitive method in ethics, which can best be understood as a stage in the emancipation of ethics from theism. God was the beneficent Creator of nature, and the traditional ethical code coincided with the rules of his beneficence. There were then two ways in which these rules might be conceived: as the commands of God, or as conducive to the happiness of mankind. Conceived in the first way, they would be obeyed from the motive of piety. Conceived in the second way, they would be obeyed from the motive of benevolence—even with the theological sanction eliminated it would still be rational for an individual to obey them, provided he, like God, accepted the general happiness as his supreme end. This second way was always associated with the first, as love of neighbor was 'like unto' love of God. When, by Hume, Adam Smith, Bentham, and John Stuart Mill, it was freed altogether from dependence on theistic assumptions, it came to be known as utilitarianism. But there is a characteristic cycle of development by which authoritarianism on its way to utilitarianism passes through an intermediate phase of intuitionism. Rules first imposed by the will of a ruler themselves acquire a flavor of imperativeness. Wordsworth's "stern daughter of the voice of God" retains her sternness even after the parental voice has become inaudible. There is a transference of authority from the lawmaker to the law, so that even when the lawmaker is forgotten, the law remains standing, as a self-imposed commandment. Hence during the Enlightenment, while the sentiment of piety persisted, it was redirected from the will of God to the content of what he willed. Moral precepts were regarded with awe and reverence, neither as the will of God nor yet as the rules of human happiness, but as mandatory in their own right.

With this lingering aroma of the rule of God another tendency, no less characteristic of the age, conspired to give to the principles of ethics a character of intuitive self-evidence. The age was, as we know, an age of exaggerated confidence in the emancipated reason. This bred a certain contempt for the past, and for tradition. It led men to trust no judgment but their own, to trust that judgment excessively, and to divorce it from habit and sentiment. Hence Burke's defense of traditionalism:

> Many of our men of speculation, instead of exploding general prejudices, employ their sagacity to discover the latent wisdom which prevails in them. If they find what they seek, and they seldom fail, they think it more wise to continue the prejudice, with the reason involved, than to cast away the coat of prejudice, and to leave nothing but the naked reason; because prejudice, with its reason, has a motive to give action to that reason, and an affection which will give it permanence.[12]

The Age of Reason was persuaded not only that truth was readily attainable by the natural faculties, but that such attainment lay within the competence of the average man. Reason was not only trusted, but was vulgarized. Moral truth was held to be 'plain' and 'self-evident.' The age was, in short, readily disposed to a credulous intuitionism which multiplies unchallenged axioms. Even Alexander Hamilton could say:

> The Sacred Rights of Mankind are not to be rummaged for among old parchments or musty records. They are written, as with a sunbeam, in the whole volume of human nature, by the Hand of the Divinity itself, and can never be erased or obscured by mortal power.[13]

Owing to these two epochal influences, an afterglow of theistic authoritarianism, and a low threshold of certitude, the doctrine of natural law and rights assumed the character of an uncritical acceptance of ready-made maxims, lacking systematic relation to the end of happiness and tinged with unconscious dogmatism. These aspects of the doctrine have exposed it to the scorn of a more rigorous and skeptical age. They have given color to the charge that the a priori dicta of 'nature' were in fact the offspring of practical and emotional rather than of rational motives. The light of reason has seemed too perfectly suited to the exigencies of the revolutions of 1688 and 1776, or to the requirements of economic laissez faire, to have been the product of purely theoretical inquiry.[14]

The doctrine of nature in the form which was prevalent in the seventeenth and eighteenth centuries is thus vulnerable to attack because it was untrue to its own deeper implications. If the commands of God are in fact the rules of human happiness, then they should be intelligible in these terms. It is possible, of course, to take the view that they are thus intelligible only to God—only an infinite mind can know in what human happiness consists, and by what means it can be realized. On this ground Bishop Berkeley advocated "passive obedience"; and Bishop Butler, having some doubt as to the coincidence of duty and interest, invoked the religious premise of "a good and perfect administration of things."[15] But Berkeley and Butler, while they lived in the Age of Enlightenment, were both bishops and preached sermons. It is more in keeping with the genius of that age, at least in its secular manifestations, to insist that the natural reason of man knows more about human happiness and its rules than about God and his commands; and so to take the first as the key to the second rather than the second as the key to the first.

To transform the pietistic and intuitive ethics of the eighteenth century into an experimental utilitarianism frees the theory from its errors without weakening its essential contentions.* For it will still remain true that political institutions and judgments rest upon a moral foundation; that this foundation lies within the scope of man's natural intellectual faculties; and that the supreme principle of goodness, by which the state and all its works are justified, is the happiness of sentient beings.

8

Similar considerations apply to the charge that whereas the political philosophy of the Enlightenment conceived the state as an artificial human construction, in reality it is as original as man himself. Unquestionably the more simple-minded proponents of the doctrine of 'compact,' and most of its proponents in their simple-minded moments, fell into this error. Unquestionably, too, there was at the time in question a general tendency to be simple-minded, and to substitute pseudo-history for logic.

It is false to suppose that the state as a historic institution arose like the Masons, or the Knights Templar, or the C.I.O.—by an act of deliberate organization on the part of men who hitherto had lived under no such rule at all. The historical retrospect, extended even beyond history by modern archaeology and anthropology, reveals no pre-political or uninstitutionalized condition of mankind. Polity seems to be as universal as men, and to have roots in human nature as deep as those of the family. When states do arise, furthermore, they appear to arise in ways that

* Professor Carl Becker, in his *Declaration of Independence* says that the natural rights theory was rejected in the nineteenth century in favor of utilitarianism (*cf.* p. 236). I should prefer to say that its theological presuppositions and its a priori method were subordinated to these principles of benevolence and happiness which it had always embraced.

bear very slight resemblance to the famous social compact. Their origin, if they have an origin, is mysterious, and seems to be due to the enlargement of the family group, or to conquest, or to the assumption by the strong of power over the weak, or to the spontaneous operation of instincts such as gregariousness, imitation, or sympathy. Here again, the Enlightenment was unenlightened in its history and its psychology. It failed to see that institutions are as old as man, or that when they do come into being, they *grow* by the operation of obscure and multiple forces, and only to a comparatively slight degree by conscious volition.

The simple-minded interpretation of the doctrine of compact seemed to be confirmed by the American experience. In America governments were not, like rivers and continents, inheritances from a prehistoric past, fatalities to which man must accommodate himself as best he could. They were human creations, made to meet a need, and made when the need was acutely felt. The American colonists deliberately undertook "to dissolve the bands which have connected them with another," and to replace these with new bands among themselves, in order to escape lawlessness and dissension. This experience was repeated in every frontier community down to the close of the last century. Men whose law and order, like that of Tombstone, Arizona, was the result of having decided to choose their most dangerous desperado as sheriff, in order that he might hang enough other dangerous desperadoes to intimidate the remaining desperadoes, in order that those whose object was to mine silver might be delivered from the perpetual menace of robbery and assassination—such men were not likely to acquire a metaphysical or a mystical view of the state. The authority whose prohibitions and regulations they accepted was an authority of their own making, instituted by agreement among themselves, and obeyed by them because each of them could see the clear advantage of doing so. Tell such men that man is nothing apart from the state, and their experience will refute you. They can remember a time when, unhappily, they had no state. They see the state as the invention and the instrument of individuals, and not individuals as the organs and the members of the state.

Nevertheless the state as a human institution was older than these men. They themselves were products or relics of states; and they had political memories and a political inheritance even during their period of anarchy. The state of nature, taken as the first chapter of universal history, is a fiction; and the compact as an original instituting of all government is a myth. The democratic ideologies of the eighteenth century have exposed themselves to this criticism and have deserved it.

It is now time, however, to remark that the error was gratuitous. The adherents of the doctrine of compact could have accepted the contentions of their critics without conceding anything essential. The point of the doctrine of compact is not a historical statement that once on a time, when there was as yet no state, men met together and resolved to create one, each accepting a limitation of his individual liberty in return for a like renunciation on the part of others, and in order that peace and security might be enjoyed by all; but the moral statement that such a procedure *would have been right and reasonable.* If the state has come into being by some other means, so much the better; for if it had not been found ready-made, it would have been necessary to go to the labor of inventing it.

The institution of the family no doubt arose unconsciously from biological and psychological causes associated with reproduction. This does not contradict the justification of the family as a useful device by which to safeguard the child, care for women during the period of childbearing, educate the young, and protect society against the disintegrating effects of promiscuity. If the family did not exist, it, or something like it, would have to be invented to serve these uses. Similarly, the state is not less useful for being primordial. Blackstone wrote:

> The only true and natural foundations of society are the wants and the fears of individuals. Not that we can believe, with some theoretical writers, that there ever was a time when there was no such thing as society either natural or civil; and that, from the impulse of reason, and through a sense of their wants and weaknesses, individuals met together in a large plain, entered into an original contract, and chose the tallest man present to be their governor. . . . But though society had not its formal beginning from any convention of individuals, actuated by their wants and their fears; yet it is the *sense* of their weakness and imperfection that *keeps* mankind together; that demonstrates the necessity of this union; and that therefore is the solid and natural foundation, as well as the cement of civil society.[16]

In short, the doctrine of compact sets forth the reasons for accepting the state gratefully—for preserving it, and for perfecting it. These reasons of utility appeal to the individual members of the state, in terms of their "wants and fears," and so provide them with a ground of political obligation whenever they demand one. These reasons were emphasized in the eighteenth century because the critical and revolutionary temper was aroused, because authorities were on the defensive, and because it was believed that the faculty of reason, being universal to man, provided the only basis for political agreement and stability.

The opponents of the democratic theory of compact substitute a natural state for a pre-political state of nature. In fact, however, the state is natural in both theories. The real difference lies in the conception of nature. The historical or organic theory stresses elements of irrationality, such as force, gregariousness, the familial ties, habit, and the process of growth. The democratic theory, on the other hand, stresses the reasoning and critical faculties, which are nonetheless natural for being immersed in a context of irrationality. If the democratic theory in its classic form has erred through neglecting factors other than conscience and reason, and for idealizing nature, the opposing view has erred no less in neglecting the importance of reflective thought in the development of institutions, and in neglecting the question of the grounds on which political obedience commends itself to the individual's critical judgment.

Both theories have in some degree committed the same error, that, namely, of identifying what is with what ought to be: democracy because of its conceiving what is in terms of what ought to be; anti-democratic views in conceiving what ought to be in terms of what is. The error is less fundamental in the case of democracy, because in this view the distinction is at least *made*. The theism of the eighteenth century formulated ethical judgments independently, and combined ethics with history through a dogmatic metaphysics; but the critics of democracy have committed the unpardonable fault of confusing the reasons why the state should be with the historical fact that it is.

When natural law and rights are taken as definitions of what ought to be, rather than as descriptions of what is—as moral injunctions rather than as causal explanations—then the perfected society in which they reign is transposed from the beginning to the end. They characterize a state of man to-be-achieved, rather than an original state from which he has lapsed. The characteristics of the state, however, remain the same: a state of harmonious adjustment, regulated by reason and conscience and realizing the maximum of human happiness.

9

It is a first principle of democracy that the state is to be judged on independent moral grounds to which every man has access through his faculties of reason and conscience. The same basic doctrine leads to the democratic principle of tolerance;[17] and gives it a restricted meaning, both as to what is tolerated and as to the act of tolerating.

In the present context that which is tolerated is the exercise of reason and conscience—that is, a judging-for-oneself in matters theoretical and practical—together with the open avowal and persuasive communication of such judging. Action, emotion, or prejudice may be tolerable, but if this is so, it is not to be argued from the supremacy of reason and conscience. In actual practice such lines are difficult to draw, but this does not argue against the difference in principle. It is important to state the principle, in order to make it clear that the right to be tolerated is conditional, imposing certain obligations on him who exercises its privileges. One who asks to be tolerated must be able to prove that he fulfills the terms on which tolerance is defended.

There are also certain implications as regards the *act* of tolerating. To tolerate is to forbear; that is, to allow something to occur when one has the inclination and the power to prevent it. It is commonly said that the test of tolerance is a willingness to tolerate opinions which one finds false or objectionable; and it is customary to quote the statement ascribed to Voltaire—"I disapprove of what you say, but I will defend to the death your right to say it." * It is not tolerance when one is willing that others should think for themselves only provided their conclusions agree with one's own. The declaration that "liberty of conscience is to be

* It now appears that Voltaire made no such statement.[18]

granted to men that fear God" is not tolerance,[19] since it prescribes in advance what shall be thought.* Tolerance must be willing that another should follow the dictates of his reason or conscience *whatever conclusions* he reaches, even though these be deemed erroneous or 'dangerous.' Nor is tolerance the same as skepticism or apathy. It implies having convictions which one desires that others shall hold, and which one is therefore inclined to impose on them.

It is not tolerance to suffer others to think for themselves if one has no power to prevent it. One would not speak of tolerating the winds and the tides. What are the powers which tolerance possesses, but nevertheless withholds? Intimidation, whether this takes the form of legal penalties, private violence, or social disapproval, may be used to prevent the open avowal or communication of judgment; but can it prevent the forming of that judgment? What a man shall conclude from certain premises, how he shall interpret certain data, whether he shall or shall not crystallize his thinking at a certain point and there translate it into acceptance, or pursue reflection further—these are acts of the individual which cannot be controlled directly from without. But they can be controlled indirectly. It is possible to dictate what data and premises shall be accessible. Their communication or publication may be prevented by the intimidation of those who possess them; or they may be falsified, colored, and manufactured by agencies of misinformation. At the same time the mood of thinking may itself be inhibited or dispelled by suggestion; that is, by all the arts, now known as propaganda, by which belief is implanted regardless of evidence.

These are the methods of control which the tolerant man renounces in opposing even what he deems false or in propagating what he deems true. But he does not renounce persuasion. He may proclaim the truth as he sees it, and buttress it with every force of fact and reason that he can command.

---

* *Cf.* the statement attributed to Mr. Fred G. Clark, National Commander of the Crusaders: "Clark said he had no objection to teachers describing conditions in the Soviet Union so long as they made clear that conditions there were bad."—*New Republic,* Apr. 15, 1936.

10

What is the *argument* for tolerance? There is no simple desire to tolerate. Tolerance is not an easy-going good nature, an indifference, or a wish to avoid trouble. It is found in men who have strong convictions, and who nonetheless refrain from imposing them on others. They must, therefore, be deterred by some still deeper conviction or higher scruple. Nor is the claim to be tolerated simply a willful desire to be allowed to do as one *pleases*, in thinking, as in any other matter. It is claimed as a right to be recognized on some more fundamental ground. This deeper conviction, higher scruple, or more fundamental ground is provided by the esteem for truth.

The Enlightenment was marked by its *faith* in truth—by faith not only in its beneficence, but in its power to prevail. Truth is the mind's natural bent, and tolerance is the unfettering of the mind so that it may fly to its appointed goal. When freedom is granted, as Condorcet said, "the truth inevitably succeeds in establishing itself. It is in the very nature of things that error is transitory, and truth, eternal." [20] This was the faith of Milton:

> For who knows not that Truth is strong, next to the Almighty; she needs no policies, nor stratagems, nor licensings to make her victorious; those are the shifts and the defences that error uses against her power; give her but room, and do not bind her when she sleeps, for then she speaks not true, as the old Proteus did, who spoke oracles only when he was caught and bound, but then rather she turns herself into all shapes except her own, and perhaps tunes her voice according to the time.[21]

The intolerant man who backs his opinion by force and refuses to submit it to discussion shows that he doubts the power of his opinion to win acceptance by virtue of its truth; or that he values it more because it is his own than because it is true. This was also the argument of John Locke:

> If his opinion be settled upon a firm foundation, if the arguments that support it and have obtained his assent be clear, good and convincing, why should he be shy to have it tried whether they be proof or not? He whose assent goes beyond this evidence, owes this excess of his adherence only to prejudice; and

does in effect own it, when he refuses to hear what is offered against it, declaring thereby that it is not evidence he seeks, but the quiet enjoyment of the opinion he is fond of, with a forward condemnation of all that may stand in opposition to it, unheard and unexamined.[22]

This disloyalty to truth tends to appear in that field of knowledge which at any given time men deem most important. It betrays itself, for example, in the use of abusive epithets. "An Act concerning Religion," adopted in Maryland in 1649, and said to be the first of its kind on the American continent, contained the following provision:

. . . whatsoever-pson or-psons shall from henceforth vppon any occasion of Offence or otherwise in a reproachful manner or Way declare call or denominate any-pson or-psons whatsoever . . . an heritick, Scismatick, Idolator, puritan, Independant, Prespiterian, popish prest, Jesuite, Jesuited papist, Lutheran, Calvenist, Anabaptist, Brownist, Antinomian, Barrowist, Roundhead, Sepatist, or any other name or terme in a reproachfull manner relating to matter of Religion shall for every such Offense forfeit and loose the some or [of] tenne shillings.[23]

In the seventeenth century religion was important enough for men to quarrel about. Had they been concerned about religious *truth*, however, they would not have abused their religious opponents, but would have sought to learn from them; and would have promoted an atmosphere of discussion, confident that the truth would emerge and prevail on its merits. Their persecuting temper showed that they had become partisans of opinion rather than devotees of truth.

In the present era men quarrel about economic issues, and have developed a vocabulary of economic vituperation including such names as 'communist,' 'Bolshevik,' 'red,' 'radical,' 'brain-truster,' 'reactionary,' 'economic royalist,' and 'Fascist.' Their high charge of 'reproachful' meaning betrays the same disloyalty to truth.

There is a human explanation of this tendency. Truth does not operate in human affairs until it has been converted into belief, and in order that truth shall operate in social affairs there must be agreement. So the emphasis shifts from truth and belief to its propagation, and unbelief or dissent becomes a more serious offense than error. But if the lovers of truth are right, and if economic truth is really as important as mankind now judges it to be, then economics is the field in which men should be peculiarly trustful of truth, most willing to receive it from any source, and most concerned to avoid prejudice.

11

Intolerance not only distrusts truth, but prevents its attainment. It deprives the mind of that free exercise without which it cannot know truly. For knowledge consists in seeing *for oneself*, and in drawing *one's own* conclusions. This was the root of Milton's doctrine of tolerance:

> Well knows he who uses to consider, that our faith and knowledge thrives by exercise, as well as our limbs and complexion. Truth is compared in scripture to a streaming fountain; if her waters flow not in a perpetual progression, they sicken into a muddy pool of conformity and tradition. A man may be a heretic in the truth; and if he believe things only because his pastor says so, or the assembly so determines, without knowing other reason, though his belief be true, yet the very truth he holds becomes his heresy.[24]

A belief or opinion which is imposed from without may happen to be correct, but it is not true knowledge unless it is *evident* to him who holds it. Let us suppose, for example, that a given individual grasps the mathematical proof of the theorem that the sum of the interior angles of a triangle is equal to two right angles; and that he then communicates the conclusion to a second individual who, owing to his confidence in the first, accepts it. It is then the first individual, and not the second, who truly knows. Similarly, it is the physicist and not the engineer who knows the laws of physical nature, because it is he that grasps their experimental evidence. Knowledge is the state of him who draws the conclusion, and not of him who merely borrows and profits by it. If there is to be any knowledge, then some minds at least must be enabled to see why it is so, and not merely believe that it is so.

Knowledge in this strict sense cannot be forced; or if it is forced, it is corrupted through the exclusion and the distortion of the evidence which is its essential constituent, and through the introduction of irrelevant considerations. Wrote Thomas Jefferson:

Almighty God hath created the mind free, and manifested His supreme will that free it shall remain by making it altogether insusceptible of restraint. . . . All attempts to influence it by temporal punishments, or burthens, or by civil incapacitations, tend only to beget habits of hypocrisy and meanness.[25]

Or consider what Locke says of religious faith:

True and saving religion consists in the inward persuasion of the mind, without which nothing can be acceptable to God. And such is the nature of the understanding, that it cannot be compelled to the belief of any thing by outward force. . . . It may indeed be alleged, that the magistrate may make use of arguments, and thereby draw the heterodox into the way of truth, and procure their salvation. I grant it. . . . But it is one thing to persuade, another to command; one thing to press with arguments, another with penalties. . . . For laws are of no force at all without penalties, and penalties in this case are absolutely impertinent; because they are not proper to convince the mind. . . . It is only light and evidence that can work a change in men's opinions; and that light can in no manner proceed from corporal sufferings, or any other outward penalties.[26]

Jefferson was clearly mistaken in saying that external restraints upon the mind could not reach the inner core of conviction, and could only produce a hypocritical pretense of believing. Locke was clearly mistaken in saying that only "light and evidence" could "work a change in men's opinions." Their mistakes arose from an exaggerated estimate of the inherent rationality of the mind. They were, in fact, untrue even to their own view of history; for they believed that the mind of man had in the past been frustrated by tyranny and warped by mystification. Had this not been so, there would have been no need of deliverance. As compared with the present age they were innocently unaware of the extent to which sincere belief and opinion can be indirectly controlled by withholding, falsifying, or coloring the evidence, by exciting the passions, by introducing irrelevant considerations, and by so playing upon the mind that it may seem to draw for itself conclusions which have been artfully implanted.

But they were right in thinking that knowledge of the truth cannot be forced. To know truth requires that an individual shall fit conclusion to evidence, and not to external pressures. Drawing a true conclusion from premises is a transaction between these two elements, the conclusion and the premises, as they lie within one mind. The same is the case in the verification of a hypothesis; the bond of proof is between the entertaining of hypothesis and the observation of fact, and the experimental operation loses its truth-finding virtue when a hypothesis is adopted from fear of its denial, or from the contagion of mass emotion. Tolerance means, then, that the minds of individuals shall be enabled to perform such operations without external interference, to the end that true knowledge may abound and enlighten human affairs.

If men are allowed to think as they choose, that which they choose to think may be false. Freedom of thought implies a risk of error, as freedom of the will implies the risk of sin or wrongdoing. And if men are enabled to think freely, they will in some measure think differently or oppositely. But diversity of judgment is not merely a necessary hazard in the adventure of truth-seeking; it is a positive source of truth, proportionally to the complexity and inexactness of the subject-matter. There is, as Milton pointed out, a fecundity in diversity; the truth has many facets, and the thinking of one man pieces out the thinking of another.

Milton's recognition of this fact is the more remarkable because in the seventeenth and eighteenth centuries men's minds leaped lightly from mathematics and physics to metaphysics, religion, and morals, and exaggerated the ease with which the truth is to be attained. Men mistook custom and familiarity for self-evidence. "And hence it was conceived," wrote Charles Chauncy, "that all the Churches should consider of this Matter, that, if it were a Truth, it should be universally embraced; but if it were an Error or Heresy it might be universally suppressed." [27] How simple this was, as though truth could be distinguished from error by a simple test of litmus paper!

A diminishing sense of certainty in human knowledge has directly contributed to the growth of tolerance.* When there is less certainty of being right, there is less willingness to impose one's views on another, for it is now possible that one may learn something from *him*. Even in the realm of mathematical and physical science there is diversity of opinion, and its effect is to multiply the chances of truth through

* Even in the seventeenth century Pierre Bayle (1647-1706) had contended that *no* knowledge is certain enough to be imposed by force.[28]

profiting by the imagination, the initiative, the special experiences, the idiosyncrasies, and the mutual criticism and cross fertilization of many different individual minds. Where the truth is speculative and devious, the more witnesses the better; the greater reason there is for broadening the base of experience and utilizing the invention and insight of many different individuals. Where, as in the field of the social sciences today, knowledge is deemed both difficult and important, there is a superlative obligation to give room and air to all shades of judgment in order that saving truths may emerge.

12

Although the democratic exponents of tolerance believed that the truth was revealed through diversity, it would be a grave mistake to suppose that they accepted conflict of opinion as the final outcome. The argument proceeds upon the assumption that the truth is one, and that minds will eventually converge upon it in proportion to the extent to which they are enlightened. Free minds fly to the same goal, even though they follow diverse routes. The fact that social institutions must be founded on a sameness of fundamental creed was not ignored. On the contrary, it was stressed; but agreement was sought through objectivity and not through the centralized control of subjective forces.

This difference between uniform indoctrination and evidential agreement is the crux of the matter. When people agree about the simpler mathematical relations or particular matters of observable fact, it is comparatively safe to assume that they have *reason* to agree. When, on the other hand, there is widespread agreement on matters so complex and speculative as religion, metaphysics, or social philosophy, as in the Christian theism of Europe, or the moral code of Western Europe, or the creeds of contemporary communism, Fascism, or democracy, there is ground for the suspicion that non-evidential influences have been at work.

A modern dictatorship has mastered the art of creating a pseudo-unanimity of popular support by enthusiasm, ignorance, and fear. Timid and suggestible minds are dominated by propaganda; bold and clear-thinking minds are intimidated or, if necessary, destroyed. The average man is indoctrinated by censorship, by eloquence, by public ceremony, by myth and symbol, by patriotic education, by music and marching, and by a perpetual play upon the primitive instincts; critical and independent spirits who are insusceptible to these relatively juvenile methods are bribed or threatened. The press, the radio, the billboard, and the loud-speaker provide the mass attack; the mopping-up is done in concentration camps.

That there was likewise a pseudo-unanimity among the adherents of the cult of reason is not to be denied. They hastily assumed that the clearness and certainty of Newton could be duplicated in the metaphysical and moral sciences; and they mistook their own traditional habits of thought for rational self-evidence. But they *intended* that their unanimity should reflect the universality of truth, and were willing through the principle of tolerance to wait for their unanimity until it could be of this sort. In Milton's words:

> They are the troublers, they are the dividers of unity, who neglect and permit not others to unite those dissevered pieces, which are yet wanting to the body of truth. To be still searching what we know not, by what we know, still closing up truth to truth as we find it, (for all her body is homogeneal, and proportional,) this is the golden rule in theology as well as in arithmetic, and makes up the best harmony in a church; not the forced and outward union of cold, and neutral, and inwardly divided minds.[29]

These men understood, furthermore, that merely psychological unanimity was precarious and local. It extends no further and lasts no longer than the social forces which create it. Furthermore, it contains within itself the seeds of dissension. An opposing creed uses the same methods. As between one creed and another there is then no appeal except to force. But the gravest objection of all is that forced unanimity has itself no guarantee of truth, and closes the mind to evidence. These considerations, applied to religion, were thus stated by Locke:

> For, there being but one truth, one way to heaven; what hopes is there that more men would be led into it, if they had no other rule to follow but the religion of the court, and were put under a necessity to quit the light of their own reason, to oppose the dictates of their own consciences, and blindly to

resign up themselves to the will of their governors, and to the religion which either ignorance, ambition, or superstition had chanced to establish in the countries where they were born? In the variety and contradiction of opinions in religion, wherein the princes of the world are as much divided as in their secular interests, the narrow way would be much straitened; one country alone would be in the right, and all the rest of the world put under an obligation of following their princes in the ways that lead to destruction: and that which heightens the absurdity, and very ill suits the notion of a deity, men would owe their eternal happiness or misery to the places of their nativity.[30]

Tolerance is the necessary condition of genuine and lasting agreement. It is also the condition of voluntary obedience: "every man being," as Locke says, "naturally free, and nothing being able to put him into subjection to any earthly power, but only his own consent." [31] If political authority is to be justified, it must itself be authorized by man's intellectual and moral faculties. It must be *truly good* that it should exist. Since its power is so overwhelming, and affects for better or for worse every interest of every man who lives under it, these victims or beneficiaries, as the case may be, are entitled to pass upon its credentials. The stake is too high to justify a blind or even a trusting obedience. It is not reasonable to obey unless one knows for oneself and is oneself persuaded that the authority is beneficial. It is unreasonable to accept authority passively, because authority tends to enjoy itself and to misuse its power for selfish ends. There are reasons which justify authority, and the person who has the best right to appeal to these reasons is the man upon whom that authority is exercised. The reasons which justify authority are not those which justify it to itself, but to those who are asked to obey.

It becomes the duty of political authority, then, to disseminate enlightenment among the ruled. They should be instructed in principles, acquainted with the facts, enabled to draw their own conclusions and discuss their differences, in order that their obedience may be endorsed by their judgment. This is tolerance, practiced and protected by the political authority as the means of perpetually renewing that mandate which alone makes either authority or obedience defensible.

The general meaning of tolerance, so far as it is deducible from the supremacy of reason and conscience, is clear. Taken in this context it means: a faith in the power and virtue of knowledge, and a hospitality to truth, however much it goes against the grain; the promotion of access to data, independence of thought, and freedom of discussion, as being favorable to knowledge; the attainment of underlying agreement through the universality of truth, and not through an artificial unanimity of opinion; the dissemination of knowledge throughout the body of those who live under authority, as a condition of their voluntary assent.

13

Democracy takes its stand on the doctrine that there are moral truths from which the state and its policies derive their justification; that these truths can be discovered by men through the exercise of their generic faculties of reason and conscience, and therefore potentially by all men; and that in order that these faculties may discover basic moral truths and apply them to action, men must be permitted to judge freely in the light of accessible evidence. But a democracy, like any other form of government, requires that men shall obey the same laws; and such obedience rests in turn on common habits and convictions. How is this requirement to be reconciled with tolerance? How is a sameness of public creed to be reconciled with a diversity of private creeds?

Uniformitarianism escapes the problem by imposing a public creed to the exclusion of all private creeds, while separatism multiplies private creeds to the exclusion of any public creed. Uniformitarianism, if it were perfected, would destroy that free exercise of reason and conscience without which a creed loses its claim to truth, and becomes a merely psychological product; or, at best, the private creed of the more powerful. Separatism, if it were perfected, would leave no common ground for the adjustment of conflicting interests or opinions, and would in the long run destroy the private creeds themselves by arraying them against one another. Liberalism is the product of men's riper experience and more lucid intervals. Aware of the tragic futility of either uniformitarianism or separatism, it seeks to solve the problem by simplifying the public creed, and by providing within its framework for the diversity of private creeds.

The doctrine of 'the separation of church and state'—that is, the equal protection of private religious creeds within a common civic creed—is a special application of the general principle of liberalism. It developed historically as a rejection of religious uniformitarianism,[32] in which the public creed consists of a system of religious doctrine certified by an autonomous religious institution. Religion concerns itself originally with matters lying beyond the range of politics—with beliefs concerning a supernatural order. It claims precedence because it deals with man's eternal destiny and true salvation. Uniformitarianism then insists that these higher truths of religion shall be all-pervasive. It refuses to confine religion to any special province, but extends it to the whole of life, including those affairs which are ordinarily assigned to politics. It regards the state as the instrument of the church. It assimilates man's civil affairs, together with every other institution or branch of culture, to godliness or piety.

In opposing religious uniformitarianism liberalism starts with certain human concerns which are confessedly less exalted than religion, but which are more immediate. Whatever their religion, and if, during their terrestrial life, they are to believe and worship at all, the members of any human society must enjoy peace and order among themselves and safety from external enemies. From these mundane necessities, which condition all forms of human achievement, there arises the cult of civility, with its appropriate principles and institutions. It opposes the claims of godliness when, and only when, these conflict with its basic requirements. Civility claims jurisdiction over the preservation of life, personal security, and liberty; public health; the waging of war; and the promotion of social welfare whenever this can best be achieved by a public agency. It resists the use of religious or ecclesiastical control to weaken men's allegiance to the state in matters that fall within the state's province. It regards with suspicion any methods of control within a church which run counter to the political processes of the state, and unfit the members of the church to be good citizens. Whenever a religious body seeks by political means to impose itself on all members of society and in all spheres of life, the liberal state is its enemy; but when the same religious body is subject to persecution or coercion, it looks to the liberal state as its friend and protector.

14

Liberalism is also opposed to *political* uniformitarianism, which finds a classic expression in 'Hobbism.' According to Hobbes, the civil sovereign has absolute authority over all of the life of all of the subjects. It is a sovereign's responsibility to see to it that their belief, as well as their behavior, promotes the purpose of the commonwealth:

> . . . We are to remember, that the Right of Judging what Doctrines are fit for Peace, and to be taught the Subjects, is in all Common-wealths inseparably annexed . . . to the Soveraign Power Civill, whether it be in one Man, or in one Assembly of men. For it is evident to the meanest capacity, that mens actions are derived from the opinions they have of the Good, or Evill, which from those actions redound unto themselves; and consequently, men that are once possessed of an opinion, that their obedience to the Soveraign Power, will bee more hurtfull to them, than their disobedience, will disobey the Laws, and thereby overthrow the Common-wealth, and introduce confusion, and Civill war; for the avoiding whereof, all Civill Government was ordained. And therefore in all Common-wealths of the Heathen, the Soveraigns have had the name of Pastors of the People, because there was no Subject that could lawfully Teach the people, but by their permission and authority.[33]

But with Hobbes the requirements of civility are as yet largely negative. He was a strict political authoritarian, but politics was conceived as a small part of life. The full implications of political uniformitarianism appear in certain contemporary totalitarian dictatorships, in which a comprehensive and all-pervasive creed derived from political sources is propagated by a subservient church. Thus the Union of German Christians, formed in 1934 by National Socialist extremists within the German protestant church, was used to bring the faith of its adherents into conformity with the political regime, to the end that patriotism might be confirmed and intensified by piety. Or the existing church may be suppressed altogether, as proposed by the more radical faction of the Nazi party in Germany. The activities of indoctrination, excitation, and patriotic demonstration are then monopolized by the state itself, through a department of 'propaganda.' Symbols and ritual are invented, myths are created, history is rewritten, the creed is publicly recited, missionaries are sent abroad, and heresy is persecuted at home. Art, music, and even science are forced into a national or racial pattern.

Over and above religious and political uniformitarianism, the economic sphere of human life provides two further possibilities.* Uniformitarian communism derives its fundamental creed from the revolt of the exploited classes against the capitalist. The new state is conceived as the collective power devoted to the production and distribution of material goods. The existing church is suppressed, and superseded by the church of Karl Marx or the worship of the proletarian dictator. The social mores are dominated by the ideas of social revolution, and culture in all its forms is dedicated to the glorification of the worker.

Fascism, on the other hand, represents the extreme claims of capitalism. It uses both church and state to propagate and enforce its capitalistic creed. It idealizes the acquisitive virtues of the rich, and the acceptance of their lot by the laborious and subservient poor. Culture is the privilege of a leisured class, and political power is lodged in the hands of a plutocratic oligarchy.

Whether uniformitarianism begins with religion, politics, or economics, it ends, if it is thorough, by assimilating the others. Religious uniformitarianism arises from the belief that the perfecting of piety requires that it shall pervade all of life, including man's political and economic, as well as his artistic, scientific, educational, and other cultural activities. Political uniformitarianism arises from the belief that devotion to the state should be similarly all-pervasive. It does not ignore economic or cultural activities, but dedicates them to the glory of the state. Communistic uniformitarianism substitutes the hammer and the sickle for the cross, converts the state into a collectivistic economic mechanism, and dedicates every form of culture to the theme of the proletarian revolution. Fascist uniformitarianism accepts wealth as the sign of God's favor, uses the state to protect the hierarchy of privilege, and expects the arts and sciences to serve their patrons. In each case there is a single creed which is so extensive and all-penetrating that it

* Whether these possibilities are exemplified in any actual society I do not here judge. The first is commonly believed to represent a phase in the development of Soviet Russia; the second is imputed to capitalistic countries by the critics of capitalism, and especially by its socialist critics.

leaves no room for any other. It claims a monopoly of belief. This sole and exclusive creed is imposed upon all of its members by the collective force, opinion, and sentiment of the social group.

All forms of uniformitarianism, however opposed to one another, agree in their contemptuous rejection of liberalism. Their instinctive hostility to liberalism is well founded. They know their enemy. For liberalism is opposed in principle to their common principle. Liberalism is equally opposed to any single and all-pervasive creed, whatever its source—whether religious, political, or economic. There must, it is true, be a public creed, even in a liberal society. But that public creed is so framed and limited as to permit of a diversity of private creeds—whether of persons or of groups, and in every sphere of human activity, religious, economic, cultural, and even political.

Liberalism does, it is true, assign a peculiar role to the state. For to the state, and to the state alone, is assigned the function of coercion. But this peculiar right is conditioned by a peculiar obligation. It is bound by its own self-denying ordinance. The liberal state does not exalt itself, but rather humbles itself to the role of a means by which men's private cults may prosper the more abundantly. It reigns, but its reign is a rule of freedom.

It is true that the liberal state does regulate all non-political activities. But to each it dictates no more than its own principle of liberality. Religion within a liberal state must itself be liberal, but only in the sense that each religious cult, being a private cult, must agree to live at peace with its rivals. The economy of a liberal state must be liberal, but only in the sense that it must permit the discussion and experimental trial of rival economies. Art and science within a liberal state are bound only by the maxim of live and let live.

It is true that the liberal state infects all institutions—church, economy, art, and science—with its own liberality. In the long run it is not compatible with any illiberal type of human relationship by which individuals are oppressed or their mouths stopped by any authority, whether domestic, ecclesiastical, economic, scientific, artistic, or educational. But this is not because of any assertion of superiority. On the contrary, it is because the state looks beyond itself, to the private creeds of individuals and non-political groups, for the wisdom by which its own authority is justified and its own policy illuminated; because it respects these creeds and cults as embodying the higher purposes to which its own activities are subordinated; and because these creeds and cults can flourish and abound only under a rule of tolerance.

The essential principle of the democratic state is tolerance—not as a symptom of skepticism or indifference, but as a hopeful intent to foster those faculties of reason, conscience, and imagination by which human life may be variously enriched and progressively perfected. A liberal state is bound to tolerate opposition even to its own creed—its public creed, and not merely the private creeds which lie within its bounds. This last extreme of tolerance creates for liberalism its most subtle and delicate problem, to which it will be necessary to return in connection with the general problem of liberty in a democratic state. But the guiding idea for its solution is to be found, again, in that acknowledgment of the supremacy of reason and conscience which is the theme of the present chapter. The fundamental faith of democracy is the belief that sound institutions are founded on truth; that truth is accessible to all men through the cultivation and exercise of their higher faculties; that truth will in the end unite men rather than divide them; and that to this end men should be permitted freely to think, profess, discuss, and persuade.

CHAPTER SIXTEEN

THE INDIVIDUAL AS THE SEAT OF VALUE

1

It is customary to distinguish social from political democracy, and it is essential in the exposition of American democracy to think of the second as the means to the first. Social democracy is the answer to the question of the purpose for which government exists; political democracy is the answer to the question of the form of government that will best serve that purpose. To use Lincoln's famous expressions, social democracy is government *for* the people, while political democracy is government *of* and *by* the people. The union of social and political democracy means that a government of and by the people is the right and proper means of ensuring a government for the people.

That these two forms of democracy are independent follows from the fact that it is theoretically possible, and even plausible, to combine the purpose of social democracy with a non-democratic form of government. Thus, for example, it may be argued that the best political means of serving the popular good would be a rule of God, since God is by definition omniscient and disinterestedly benevolent. The difficulty, of course, lies in the fact that God rules through men; so that it is necessary first to ascertain the credentials of God's agents, and then trust their fidelity to God's guidance. There is always a question, one of grave importance to the people, as to whether those who claim to rule in God's behalf are really his accredited agents; and whether, being fallible mortals, they are pure in their motives and wise in their translation of God's will into concrete policies. And who are to answer this question if not those whose interests are most concerned?

Or it is conceivable that the best way of promoting the people's good would be to entrust the government to a monarch or a dictator, or to a hereditary class, qualified as men of superior intelligence or honor. This association of political autocracy or aristocracy with social democracy is what is known as 'benevolent paternalism.' Although it encounters the difficulty that no ruler's benevolence can be completely trusted, it is a defensible view; which proves again that there is no necessary connection between social and political democracy.

It is also conceivable, though less plausible, that an aristocratic view of the social purpose of government should be associated with political democracy. If the ultimate good were held to lie in a flowering of mankind, exemplifying the highest possibilities of human nature in a few rare and favored specimens, there would be no logical contradiction in supposing that such a good could best be obtained by vesting political authority in all the people.

American democracy, in other words, is a union of two independent theories: a theory as to the value or good for the sake of which the state exists, and a theory as to the seat of the control which the state exercises. It is thus doubly democratic. Employing Aristotle's famous dictum that "the end of the state is the good life,"[1] American democracy holds that 'the good life' consists in the happiness or well-being of the individuals who compose society; and that the political means to this end is to be found in the sovereignty of these same individuals, who are thus at one and the same time the beneficiaries of organized society and the sources of its power.

2

In the present chapter we are concerned with the basic meaning of 'the good life' according to social democracy. Summarily described, the good life is universal or all-inclusive, and individual, both terms being essential. Plato, who like Aristotle rested his political theory on a conception of social good, spoke of "fashioning the state not with a view to the greatest happiness of any particular class, but of the whole." But Plato, if he was universalistic, as he here professes, was not individualistic; for his "greatest happiness" attached, like the beauty of a statue, to the totality of society and not to its members severally.[2] Or insofar as Plato was individualistic, as in his exaltation of a guardian class whose higher faculties were fully perfected, he was not universalistic; since the warrior and artisan classes were, like the feet of the statue, required to play a baser role. Democracy, being both universalistic and individualistic, finds its good or happiness in individuals, and includes the happiness of *all* individuals.

It will be noted that the individualism which is here in question is a *moral* individualism. Eager to affirm the primacy of the individual in the order of value, the social philosophers of the eighteenth century have said, or seemed to say, that the individual comes first in other ways as well. This view is clearly untenable. It is a biological fact that the minimum human entity is the triad of father, mother, and child; it is a psychological fact that human experience and development are inseparable from familial and tribal relationships; it is an economic fact that human beings are interdependent; it is a political fact that human life is unthinkable without some form of organization and control. The nature of the human individual is penetrated and conditioned in a thousand ways by the society of which he is a member. To recognize these undeniable facts is to reject all of the following individualistic doctrines: the doctrine that in the beginning there were merely individuals, and that society was a subsequent and artificial construction; the doctrine that the individual can live without society; and the doctrine that the individual can satisfy his desires or develop his highest possibilities in isolation.

But granting all this, the fundamental thesis of moral individualism remains unaffected. However great the natural, metaphysical, causal, or historical importance of society, it may still be true that the final values of life begin and end with individuals, and with the states or acts of individuals, such as desire, hope, love, volition, creative imagination, aesthetic or intellectual contemplation. For democracy taken as a standard of human life and a justification of human institutions, individualism is a doctrine concerning the seat or locus of good. The question is, 'Whose good or happiness?' and the answer is, 'The good or happiness of individuals.'

The argument turns upon the nature of goodness, in the most general sense. If 'good' were a simple adjective connoting an unanalyzable quality or character, it would have no essential connection with individuals or with anything else. It would be impossible to know to what it attached except by contemplating objects and seeing that they were in fact good—or indifferent, or bad. As opposed to views of this intuitive type, there stands the view, here taken, that the goodness of anything consists in its relation to feeling, desire, emotion, will, or some similar attitude. It is the assumption of this view which has led European moral philosophy to use the terms 'good' and 'happiness' interchangeably.*

Suppose the predicate 'good' as applied to any object, act, or event to mean that it is aligned with some passional or volitional attitude. Whatever is *favored*, for itself or for its consequences, is then 'good'; and per contra whatever is viewed with disfavor is 'bad.' 'Right,' 'ought,' 'virtuous,' and all other terms of value, whether moral or non-moral, will then be construed as variants of the same fundamental concept. The norms applied to human institutions, such as education, art, industry, law, and government, will be based upon this same polar duality of *for* and *against* which is the central feature of man's conscious motor-affective life.

This much having been assumed, there would then remain the further question as to where such attitudes of favor and disfavor are to be found. The answer of social democracy is that they are found, and found only, in individuals; that is, in one or more of those beings enclosed within a skin, born of woman, subject to natural death after a period approximating threescore and ten years, denominated by a proper name, and numerable in the census.

---

* The argument turns, in the last analysis, upon giving a fixed meaning to a term whose actual use in human discourse is diverse and confused. The acceptable meaning of the term 'good' will be that which brings consistency and clarity into the judgments in which the term is used, and into the experiences to which the judgments are applied. A discussion of this subject is to be found in the Author's *General Theory of Value,* and in controversial articles written in reply to criticisms of that book.[3]

3

All this would be obvious enough were it not for the fact that jurisprudence, sociology, politics, and metaphysics have introduced human beings of another type—corporate entities, or 'concrete universals,' designated by such terms as 'legal person,' 'collective' or 'general' will, 'social mind,' political 'organism,' 'nation,' 'state,' and 'race.' The confusion thus introduced is very different from that produced by conceptions of *infra-* or *supra*-human individuals, such as animals, spirits, devils, angels, or a personal God, where these are considered as entering into external relations with men, and as differing only in the partial or superlative possession of human attributes. The effect of the introduction of such individuals is merely to extend the range of social relations, as happens when new races of men are discovered. The corporate or collective individual, on the other hand, is conceived to be of a higher order, *composed* of individuals of the lower order, and superseding them as regards both being and value. The human individual in the ordinary sense is then degraded to the status of part or member, similar to the status of the cells and organs of the body. Similarly, the interest, will, purpose, or judgment of the whole absorbs those of its members; and the claims of the whole take precedence of the claims of its members.

Needless to say, there is some force in this idea. Corporations may assume certain of the legal functions of 'real' persons; societies do possess an internal solidarity analogous to that of biological organisms, and they may possess a community of interest, will, purpose, memory, opinion, and sentiment in which their members participate, and which divides one society from another. But the fact remains that these mental functions and attributes belong to social entities either fictitiously, as when a corporation is given some of the legal privileges and obligations of a person; or derivatively, that is, by virtue of being possessed by the individual components. Corporate or collective entities as such, and in their own right, do not perceive, feel, remember, will, or judge. Still less do they possess that form of internal unity which constitutes the self-determination and enduring identity of a person. Judged by the norm of a living and thinking human individual, social entities are at best monstrosities. The effect of exalting such an entity above its members is to confer moral authority upon a being which is, to put it mildly, less than a man; or upon some individual man who is prompted by ambition, pride, or illusions of grandeur to present himself as its mouthpiece.[4]

Democratic individualism, in the most fundamental sense, affirms that the 'good life' consists in the enjoyment or successful pursuit by John Doe and Richard Roe of what they themselves consciously desire and will. The error of paternalism lies in conceiving benevolence in terms of the will of the benefactor rather than the will of the beneficiary. The ruler, like the parent, may give in order to satisfy the giver rather than the recipient. The intent of the democratic state is to give people what *they* want instead of what the government wants for them.

It is the besetting vice of non-democratic states to substitute fictitious collective or corporate goods for the real desires of the people. The most flagrant case in modern times is the cult of military glory and territorial expansion associated with imperialism.

> During the jubilee an English beggar on the streets of London was heard to say: "I own Canada, the Australias, colonies in Africa, and the islands of the far Pacific, and here I am, starving for a crust of bread. I am a citizen of the greatest power of the modern world, and all people should bow to my greatness. But yesterday I asked alms of a negro savage, and he repulsed me with disgust." [5]

How many subjects of an imperial state could echo this feeling! Would echo it, were they not misled by the mere glamour of rhetoric and pomp; do echo it in their hearts, where it is suppressed by fear of the ruler or of their neighbors! It is healthy for every man to ask himself: "What do I, and others like me, get out of this state of affairs?" The argument between the income-tax collector and Grandpa Vanderhof, in *You Can't Take It with You*, touched something deeper than farce. The taxpayer wants to know what the Government is "going to do with it," what the Government gives *him*, and is not satisfied to be told that his money will be spent on the Army, the Navy, and the Constitution unless he can translate these into terms of his own personal needs and wants.[6] The American audience feels that Grandpa Vanderhof is asking the right question, and is entitled to an answer. His question cuts through the fog of claptrap, and lays bare the real values of the situation.

The present world-wide tendency to emphasize economic interdependence, and to substitute planning and collaboration for competition, is commonly deplored in the name of individualism. But if we look beyond the means to the end, we discover that in a democratic society the impelling motive of this change is to be found in the demands of individuals, and in their greater awareness of their own interests. If the blessings of free competition have lost something of their appeal, it is because of a belief that these blessings are largely fictitious. It is because more individuals are challenging the existing system and asking, "What do I get out of this?" The movement away from the 'rugged individualism' of the past expresses the growing suspicion on the part of an increasing number of men that others get the individualism while they get only the ruggedness.

In this insistence that the values by which institutions are justified reside in the individuals who live under them, democracy follows the main current of the Christian tradition. The Gospel is a saving of souls—the souls of individual men and women. It stresses the love of persons, as the motive even of creation itself and as the highest form of human activity. Both protestantism and Catholicism, true to this tradition, have sharply condemned the totalitarian exaltation of the corporate state. An authoritative statement of Catholic individualism is to be found in De Wulf. He says:

> The fundamental principle of life in society . . . we may enunciate as follows: "The collectivity exists for the sake of the individual, and not the individual for the collectivity." . . . The group exists for the sake of the members.[7]

The encyclical letters of Pope Pius XI repeatedly protested against the absorption of the individual into the Fascist state:

> There has been an attempt made to strike unto death that which was and that which always will be dearest to our heart as father and as shepherd of souls. . . . Of its very nature the true aim of all social activity should be to help individual members of the social body, but never to destroy or absorb them. . . . Whoever raises the concepts of race, or people, or the state, or the form of government beyond mundane evaluations and makes heathenistic idols of them falsifies the divine order of things.[8]

Even more explicitly individualistic is the Pastoral Letter issued by the Bishops of the Netherlands in 1934:

Undoubtedly the good of the individual and the liberty it requires are subordinate to the common good; but they are not absorbed into it. For after all, the common good can be nothing but the well-ordered good of all, and not something which lies quite outside the good of the individual, such as, for example, mere racial or national expansion, or the power and greatness of the State as such. . . . Undoubtedly the promotion of national well-being, properly understood, is something grand and lofty. It is, therefore, the duty of every citizen to promote it. No one, moreover, is allowed so to pursue his own individual interests that he endangers the harmony of the whole, and therefore the well-being of others. Rather as patriots and social beings we are destined and called to contribute to the prosperity of the whole, the well-being of everyone, in co-operation with our fellow-citizens of every class and rank. But the well-being of the whole is the well-being of *free* personalities, each with his own destiny.[9]

Even totalitarian states of the type whose triumph in the present age has been so hastily celebrated must *appear* to confer benefits upon the individuals who live under their rule. They offer bribes to men of special talent or ambition, and seek to persuade their people of the nutritious value of the stone which they offer in the place of bread. But they so emphasize the consciousness of class, or race, or nationality as to obscure those benefits to the individual which provide the only justification of collective organization. They tend to substitute the collective means for the individual end. They proceed by the method of making people like what it suits the convenience of rulers to give them, rather than by the method of giving to the people what through an emancipated critical consciousness and an awakened sense of power they demand for themselves.*

Friendly critics of democracy, impressed by the apparent success of totalitarianism, and alarmed by the apparent inability of the older liberalism to make head against it, have urged the necessity of emphasizing discipline and participation. Democracy, it is argued, can save itself only by taking a leaf from its rival's book.[10] It is true, as we shall see, that democracy, like any form of human society, must, if it is to survive or prevail, be an object of loyal devotion among its adherents. But if democracy is to be saved, it must be *democracy* that is saved. It will

* *Cf.* the Nazi slogan *Du bist nichts, dein Volk ist alles*—Thou art nothing, thy folk (race, nation) is everything.

not do to say that the members of a democracy must learn to obey and participate, and leave it there. That in which they participate is an organization, and not an organism. Their common goal is not a corporate or collective good, but the good of all—of all individuals. And the root of their adherence will be no idolatrous worship of a fictitious entity, but the personal love and sympathy which bind one individual man to his fellows.

4

The individualistic conception of the good life is embodied in the doctrine of 'natural rights.' A right is, in the first place, an interest or felt desire of an individual or a group of individuals. But a right is, in the second place, a limited sphere within which the individual may act freely upon his interest. It is both permissive and prohibitive. It is doubly limited: limited against the individual himself, as setting bounds to his interest; and limited against other individuals, as affording the first individual security from their interference. It gives to each individual's interest as much scope as is consistent with a like concession to others; and it is assumed that the sphere of the individual's interest should be expanded so far as this condition permits. The logic of this doctrine turns on the principle of moral individualism. For if the ultimate values by which the political system is justified are to be identified with the interests of individuals, then there can be no ultimate ground for denying the interests of one individual save the interests of another.

Rights are 'natural' when they are conceived as morally justified rather than as merely legal. It is true that rights are not effectively guaranteed except by the force of the state; and it is this fact which justifies the creation and exercise of such force. But there is a sense in which rights exist before they are guaranteed. Otherwise there would be nothing for the state to guarantee. Otherwise any right whatsoever which the state enforced would be a right simply because it was enforced. It would, in other words, be impossible to criticize an existing legal system, no matter how oppressive; and it would be meaningless to argue that new legal rights should be created.

The confusion which is created by the attempt to give rights a purely legal meaning is illustrated by the history of the emancipation of women. The proponents of this reform argued that women had rights which were ignored or denied. The opponents replied that women had no such rights (such as rights of suffrage, or of property), since they were not provided for in the existing legal system. But the meaning of this reform, and the ground of its persuasiveness in democratic countries, were perfectly clear. The proponents meant that women had moral rights, which unhappily were not, but ideally would be, embodied in law. They meant that in a society organized as a society should be, women would possess certain legal privileges and guarantees similar to those possessed by men.

The distinction between legal and moral rights is not the same as that between statutory rights, on the one hand, and common-law or constitutional rights, on the other. It is true that common-law rights, being matters of judicial interpretation, are often determined by moral considerations, and that they stand closer than do acts of legislation to the universal interests and relations of individuals. It is true that constitutional law expresses the more fundamental premises of the legal system, and that the decisions in which it is embodied tend to rest in part upon moral reasoning. But when the court makes its decision, it, like the legislature, has made legal what was previously only moral.

The distinction between legal and moral rights, and the justification of the first by the second, avoids two errors. In the first place, it avoids the error of supposing that rights are the arbitrary creations of the state, and have no meaning save in terms of the power which the state exercises. In the second place, it avoids the error of supposing that a legal right, merely because it is legal, possesses a moral claim of which the beneficiary may not rightly be deprived. Any legal right may or may not possess that moral justification which it claims, just as any system of belief may or may not possess the truth which it claims. In the one case, as in the other, there is an appeal beyond the existing institution to the norms of reason and conscience.

The notion of inalienable rights introduces a further consideration. Progress, by which the legal system is modified for the better, is the expansion of the periphery of individual rights. In principle the spheres of interests must be as large as their mutual compatibility will permit. The burden of proof lies on any restriction which would negate interest, and the only proof which is valid is injury to another interest. The art of lawmaking lies in contriving new adjustments by which spheres of compatible interests may be raised to the maximum. But there is also a minimum, short of which the legal system loses its excuse for being. Below this minimum it becomes a systematic oppression, which is worse than anarchy, since the latter at least gives the individual the chance to win something through his own unaided efforts. Thus when 'life, liberty, and the pursuit of happiness,' or 'life, liberty, and property,' are conceived as inalienable rights, it is meant that a state which destroyed these would forfeit all moral claim to obedience.

The first condition of good to the individual is that he should exist. To say that the right of self-preservation cannot be abrogated by any legal system means that legal systems have their warrant only in conferring benefits upon individuals, and that to live is the indispensable condition of any good which the individual can enjoy.

Liberty and property are likewise conditions of any individual good whatsoever. Liberty means that the condition or activity of the individual accords with his own desires: he is where he is, or he is what he is, or he does what he does, or he has what he has, because it pleases him so to be, or to do, or to have. Liberty so defined constitutes good in the generic and basic sense, and to destroy it is to negate all good.

Property signifies the individual's possession of instruments for use, or of objects for consumption. Without such possession or control the individual cannot satisfy his desires. Property as an inalienable right is not to be identified with any particular institution of property, such as the private ownership of capital, or the unlimited accumulation of wealth, or the right of inheritance, or the law of contract. Undoubtedly there is a tendency to assume such identity, but this tendency only proves again the importance of holding fast to the distinction between legal rights and moral rights.

Jefferson's omission of 'property' from the inalienable rights listed in the Declaration of Independence was probably due to his own peculiar distinction between rights such as thought and speech, the exercise of which lie within the individual's own power, and those rights whose enjoyment depends on the security afforded by the collective force of society.[11] Rights of the first sort are reserved in the political compact, whereas rights of the second sort are exchanged for civil rights, or legal guarantees. But the distinction is scarcely tenable. Jefferson himself evidently thought it important that the rights of thought and speech should be written into the Constitution; and the right of property (as Locke recognized) is capable of being exercised in the state of nature. All rights, in short, may be exercised imperfectly and insecurely without the sanction of law, and all may be exchanged for civil rights.

The right to the pursuit of happiness, or the "right to be happy," or the right "of seeking and obtaining happiness," [12] adds nothing new, but rounds out the conception that since society exists for the satisfaction and enjoyment of its members, social institutions which tend otherwise have lost their excuse for being.

Inalienable or minimum rights are, of course, subject to the qualification that limits all rights; namely, that the individual who enjoys them shall not deprive others of them. No individual, says Locke, ought to "take away or impair the life, or what tends to the preservation of the life, the liberty, health, limb, or goods of another . . . unless it be to do justice on an offender." [13] Justice, because of its universal scope, takes precedence of any merely private claim; not because it transcends the rights of individuals, but because it respects the rights of *all* individuals.

In Locke's theory the authority to act as the agent of justice appertains not only to the civil ruler but, in "the state of nature," to all individuals who through their reasons are qualified exponents of the laws of nature. The "offender," who has willfully violated the rights of others, *ought* to be punished, and the question as to who should punish him is a secondary consideration. Punishment is rightly visited upon him who lives "by another rule than that of reason and common equity." He is "dangerous to mankind," and violates that "peace and safety" of mankind for which the law of nature provides. He who punishes does so in order to "preserve mankind in general"; and punishment is justified insofar as it is necessary to deter the mischief-maker, and "by his example, others from doing the like mischief." [14] In other words, the function of punishment is also a moral function, exercised upon individuals for the good of individuals and, in the last analysis, *by* individuals.

The political writers of the Enlightenment were concerned with minimum rather than with maximum rights because they assumed that maximum rights would take care of themselves. They had confidence in the individual's power to profit abundantly by his minimum rights, and to rise in life according to the measure of his capacity and will. It was no part of their doctrine that men should enjoy a bare subsistence or a restricted opportunity. Maximum as well as minimum rights are implied in the basic notion of right itself. Life, liberty, property, and the pursuit of happiness are all variable in degree. Length and abundance of life, soundness of health, range of liberty, amount of property, and degrees of attainment in the pursuit of happiness are all capable of being indefinitely increased. Where shall the limit be set? There is no negative principle except that what organized society does for one man it shall do for all.

Hence the fundamental premises of democratic individualism are consistent with the cult of self-development and perfection; and with such intervention on the part of the state as may bring to individuals a fuller opportunity. These premises are not bound up with any specific legal institution, or with a canon of self-restraint on the part of the state; but only with the principle that the good which the state promotes shall express the actual desires, consciously realized and freely affirmed, of the several individuals of which society is composed.

5

The maximum rights of the individual involve not merely the satisfaction of his desires, but also the realization of his prerogatives. Here is to be found the link between social and political democracy. The good by which government is justified lies in the happiness of the individuals who live under it. But these same individuals are themselves the organs of reason to which human affairs must be submitted. The individual is a finality in the double sense, as being the end and as being the authority; but because reason is a part of human nature, the individual's role as authority is embraced within his role as end. An individual in whom the faculty of reason has been allowed to atrophy or remain undeveloped, or whose faculty of reason is superseded by that of officials acting in the name of the state, is not only an incomplete individual, cut off from the peculiar satisfactions of reason, but a debased individual, in whom the distinctively human part is frustrated. He has not only been cut off, but he has been cut off at the top, where nature designed him to bear his own characteristic human fruit.

Reason here stands for the faculty of judgment both in its theoretical and in its practical exercise. Only the individual can fit the conclusion to the evidence, within the circumference of his own experience and thought. Only the individual can store up the experience of the past and use it for the interpretation of the present and the anticipation of the future. Only the individual can establish an order of preference, and choose from a range of alternatives. Only the individual can by understanding and inference govern his action by a general principle. Only the individual can subordinate means to ends, and create a hierarchy of interests under the regulation of a dominant purpose. These functions of the human individual are the attributes of personality, and elevate the good life to a personal plane.

It is from these attributes of personality that the individual derives his moral responsibility, and this conception of man, common to puritanism and to democracy, is implicit in the English and American system of common law.[15] It is this personal aspect of individualism that is insisted upon by Kant, to which he gives the name of "autonomy," and which is embodied in the maxim "So act as to treat humanity, whether in thine own person or in that of any other, in every case as an end withal, and never as means only."[16]

The moral sentiment which insists that the individual is a moral finality, whose claims are not to be outweighed by any mere counting of heads, is vividly expressed by William James:

> If the hypothesis were offered us of a world in which Messrs. Fourier's and Bellamy's and Morris's utopias should all be outdone, and millions kept permanently happy on the one simple condition that a certain lost soul on the far-off edge of things should lead a life of lonely torture, what except a specifical and independent sort of emotion can it be which would make us imme-

diately feel, even though an impulse arose within us to clutch at the happiness so offered, how hideous a thing would be its enjoyment when deliberately accepted as the fruit of such a bargain? [17]

There are two reasons which justify this sense of the finality of the person. In the first place, his will and his scale of preferences, like his feelings and desires, are not commensurable with those of others. There are no identical units in which the happiness of millions can be reckoned as outweighing the lonely torture of a single lost soul.[18] The finality of the human person means, in short, that the ultimate and irreducible source of value is the feeling, desiring, and willing subject, possessed of his own unique inwardness, his own passionate attitudes and struggles, his peculiar history, memories, and station in the world; all of these elements being ordered and unified from within by the individual subject's own preference and judgment.

But in the second place, the human person derives finality from his faculty of reason. His judgment cannot be outweighed by any numerical calculation, because it is a claim to truth. Since there is no higher court of appeal in matters of truth than the judgment of an individual in the light of evidence, every such judge has to be considered an authority until he is proven wrong. Truth, in practical as well as in theoretical matters, is a question of cogency and not of numbers; and it is always possible that the lonely soul, rather than the millions, should be right.

It is this moral finality of the individual human person, always a part of the American tradition, which in the nineteenth century received so powerful a reinforcement from the influence of transcendentalism. "Everything," said Emerson in his famous address on *The American Scholar*, "that tends to insulate the individual,—to surround him with barriers of natural respect, so that each man shall feel the world is his, and man shall treat with man as a sovereign state with a sovereign state, —tends to true union as well as greatness." [19] Each man is a sovereign because he has a mind of his own, and is as likely as the next man to be the vehicle of truth.

The address on *The American Scholar* was delivered at Harvard in 1837. Three-quarters of a century later, also at Harvard, William James reaffirmed the same obligation of a university to help each individual to see and think with his own mind:

Thoughts are the precious seeds of which our universities should be the botanical gardens. Beware when God lets loose a thinker on the world . . . for all things then have to rearrange themselves. But the thinkers in their youth are almost always very lonely creatures. "Alone the great sun rises and alone spring the great streams." The university most worthy of rational admiration is that one in which your lonely thinker can feel himself least lonely, most positively furthered, and most richly fed.[20]

Walt Whitman reiterated the same teaching of the individual's fidelity to his own vision and his own passion, and saw in it a necessary corrective of the tendency to reduce all men to common terms:

For to democracy, the leveler, the unyielding principle of the average, is surely join'd another principle, equally unyielding, closely tracking the first, indispensable to it. . . . This second principle is individuality, the pride and centripetal isolation of a human being in himself, identity, personalism. Whatever the name, its acceptance and thorough infusion through the organizations of political commonalty now shooting Aurora-like about the world, are of utmost importance, as the world, as the principle itself is needed for every life's sake. It forms, in a sort, or is to form, the compensating balance-wheel of the successful working machine of aggregate America.[21]

The romantic cult of the self-expression of genius is in democracy crossed with the principle of universalism. In democracy it is not a question of giving room and authority to the genius which has already declared itself, and of sacrificing thereto the residual mass of mediocrity, but one of tapping new sources, and discovering genius in obscure and unsuspected quarters. By giving light and air to the hitherto buried masses of mankind, democracy hopes to enrich human culture in the qualitative, and not merely in the quantitative, sense.*

---

* Russian communism has professed this same faith: "We are for the fullest development of the individual capacities of every one of our people; we believe that, when every member of human society, when every human being is able to develop his individuality to its utmost—then out of the activities of millions of individuals who never before had the opportunity to develop themselves, a new rich and beautiful all-human culture will come forth that the earth has not yet seen." [22]

6

The principle of inclusiveness or universalism, which in the democratic creed is the co-equal complement of individualism, has been anticipated; but it now requires examination in its own right.

It will be noted that the Declaration of Independence is explicitly universalistic, as are all bills of rights. They represent benefits to which 'all men' are entitled, and of which 'no man' may be deprived. It is in no sense surprising that democracy should have embraced this principle. The stream of social democracy in Western Europe has been fed by the current of Christianity, with its teaching of neighborly love and its conception of a God who loves his creatures like a father; that is, comprehensively and indiscriminately. Secular European ethics, not only popular creeds but philosophic doctrines both Continental and British, has been almost invariably universalistic. Even Hobbes, who professed himself to be an egoist both in his psychology and in his ethics, constantly slipped into the universalistic way of thinking. Both the "poor, nasty, brutish" condition of men in the state of nature, and the benefits of that peace which is prescribed by the law of nature, accrue to all men alike. When, in the nineteenth century, the ethics of happiness received its full recognition under the name of utilitarianism, this universalistic principle was clearly avowed—not in the ambiguous formula of "the greatest happiness of the greatest number," but in Bentham's dictum that "everybody [is] to count for one, nobody for more than one." [23]

Individualism is not to be confused with egoistic self-interest. As a matter of fact, benevolence is more individualistic than egoism. There is no attitude or sentiment which is so completely individualistic as love, which values its particular human object for itself, and neither as a means nor as a set of abstract attributes. Love for one individual, namely, oneself, can scarcely be said to be more individualistic than the love for many individuals. Universalism is not to be confused with altruism. It does, it is true, imply the love of other individuals, but it does not exclude self-love; and as regards others it includes all, and is not satisfied by a love of one or some.

The idea of universal benevolence is never completely realized in our emotional attitudes. It is clearly impossible that an individual should entertain a feeling of personal regard for each and every member of the aggregate of mankind. Even in the most humane persons the love of mankind depends upon abstraction and generalization; or else means a consistent attitude of benevolence to *whatever* individuals, comparatively few in number, happen to come within the range of feeling. The difficulty appears in the difference between the statistical and the personal forms of benevolence. The reformer is so preoccupied with mankind in the aggregate that he may have little feeling for the concrete individuals with whom he comes in contact; whereas the social worker or the good neighbor is so absorbed by the woes or needs of his acquaintances that he may lose sight of the total situation, and confine himself to local palliatives instead of to social reconstruction. Each of these attitudes may learn from the other. The reformer needs to humanize and personalize his statistics with concrete sympathy; and the social worker or the good neighbor needs to systematize his sympathies by concepts and laws.

Individualism in itself carries no implications as to what individuals shall be reckoned in the sum of good, but merely affirms that good is individual. Egoism, personal favoritism, and class interest give to one or more individuals an exclusive title to good; they are cults of privilege. Universalistic individualism is the unlimited generalization of individualism, confining value to individuals while at the same time extending it to all individuals. Its universalism saves the doctrine from prejudice; its individualism saves it from abstractions and fictions.

The meaning of universalistic individualism is obscured rather than illuminated by putting the question in terms of means and ends. It cannot be said that the individual is the means to a social end, because the social end itself is the happiness of individuals. Nor can it be said that society is the means to an individual end, since society consists of individuals, and has no other meaning save the aggregate and relations of individuals. The end—that is, the happiness of all individuals—is both social and individual; but so are the means, which embrace the services of single individuals, or of groups, or even of the totality. The essential principles are two: that the good is individual in form; and that whenever there is conflict, the good of all individuals takes precedence of the good of one or some.

But this principle is confronted with a serious difficulty. It is impossible, we say, to please everybody; human wills naturally conflict. Nevertheless if the universalistic principle is to be invoked as the justification of institutional authority, then there must be some will of which it can be said that it is, or represents, or voices, the will of all. Democracy excludes two alternatives which have played a leading part in social and political philosophy: the doctrine that there is an individual or class that by divine appointment, or by heredity, or by some other principle of 'legitimacy,' can properly be said, ex officio, to represent the wills of all; and the doctrine that society as a whole, in its organic unity, or in its corporate capacity, can properly be said to embrace the will of all within a higher will of its own. There are no wills but the wills of individuals; no one of these can be substituted for the rest; there is no will of all save the agreement of the wills of all individuals. If there is no such agreement, there is no will of all; and if there is to be a will of all by which the principle of universalism is to take effect, then such a will must be created—by discussion, persuasion, and voluntary assent. How such a will shall be created and what it means as a norm of political action is the central problem of popular self-government.[24]

7

While there is no antithesis between universalism and individualism, there is an antithesis between universalism and egoism. The fact that the two standards may partially coincide in practice is unhappily allowed to obscure the fact that they are independent, and will sooner or later at some crucial point require a choice between alternatives. Neither universalistic individualism nor any other philosophy of life escapes this tragic conflict between the action required by the exclusive good of one or some and the action required by the inclusive good of all. This is the sharp edge of moralism, where duty cuts across inclination.

The crux of the so-called optimism of the Enlightenment, that optimism with which its proponents were so enraptured, and which posterity has condemned as shallow, was the belief that self-interest and benevolence were in pre-established and infallible accord. Although this dogma had its deeper roots in metaphysics and religious faith, it found confirmation in everyday experience, and flattered human wishes. One of the most popular of all eighteenth-century maxims was Franklin's assurance that "God helps them that help themselves." Since men were entirely willing to help themselves anyway, it was comforting to know that they would at the same time enjoy the unearned increment of God's assistance. The inverse of this idea was equally comforting—the teaching that the best way to help God was to help themselves.

It is no wonder that this idea has been eagerly embraced and clung to tenaciously. There is a specific and steady demand in this world for a piety and virtue that shall cost nothing. On the eighteenth-century premise one may seek one's own private pleasure or profit with a glowing conscience, because God promises not only to provide for the rest of mankind but also to make use for that good purpose of one's very self-seeking. All that one has to do is to look out sharply for oneself, and lo! by the constitutional harmony of this best of worlds, one is at the same time the obedient servant of God and the benefactor of mankind.

This is a great improvement on the older gospel. The commandment "Thou shalt love the Lord thy God with all thy heart and thy neighbor as thyself," is amended to read, "Love thyself with all thy heart, and God will love thee and look out for thy neighbor." The revised beatitude is "Blessed are those that possess the earth, for theirs is also the kingdom of heaven." Here is a gospel that is to many Americans the very breath of life. It is so intimately American that it seems almost indelicate to discuss it.

When it is not accepted as a dogma, this doctrine is argued on two grounds: the lower ground of reciprocal prosperity, and the higher ground of the social sentiments. When the lower ground is taken, it is argued that the seller profits by pleasing the customer, or that the producer profits by the consumer's higher standard of living, or that the public profits by the invention and lowered costs which enrich the individual. It is this argument which is used to advocate a world-economy by appeal to the self-interest of a nation or class. This was Bentham's argument, when he said:

> Society is so constituted that, in labouring for our particular good, we labour also for the good of the whole. We cannot augment our own means of enjoyment without augmenting also the means of others. Two nations, like two individuals, grow rich by a mutual commerce; and all exchange is founded upon reciprocal advantages.[25]

Unhappily, the argument is not valid. There will always be a discrepancy between that distribution of prosperity which is dictated by the self-interest of one or some, and that which is dictated by the self-interest of others, and that which is dictated by the interests of all. My prosperity depends to a large extent on the prosperity of others, so that if I seek my own prosperity intelligently I shall to that extent seek to promote the prosperity of others. The prosperity of others depends to some extent on mine, and to that extent I shall, insofar as I achieve prosperity, incidentally benefit others. But only *to that extent*. The extent of others' prosperity which is thus the cause or the effect of mine, and which my self-interest will seek or promote, will never be equal to that which would accrue to them if their prosperity were reckoned in terms of their own interests, or in terms of their interests and mine taken together.

It is sometimes argued that as others learn how to press their own claims forcibly and intelligently, I will find it necessary in my own interest to take full account of them. In proportion, for example, as labor becomes self-conscious and powerful the employer finds that it is to his advantage to make greater concessions to labor—which has what is called a 'nuisance value.' But shall the employer therefore encourage labor to press its claims? There's the rub! What argument is to be used against the employer who seeks by opposing public education and collective bargaining to keep labor in a condition of ignorance and helplessness? It can never be proved that it would be more profitable to *him* that he should encourage other people to force him to share his profits with them. We do not attempt to argue with him on this ground. We ask for a 'square deal.' We say that it is only 'fair' that the claims of others should be considered. We speak of their 'right' to improve their condition, or to alter the balance of power and the distribution of wealth in the direction of *their* interests. And when we put the case in these terms, we no longer argue the general prosperity from the private prosperity of any man or of any class, but from the universalistic or benevolent principle itself as an independent premise.

When we take higher ground, we say that men are socially constituted, so that they identify their self-interest with the interest of others. According to Bentham, men are governed by diverse motives, some of which, such as the motive of sympathy, sometimes prompt men for their own pleasure to perform acts having social utility. When, and insofar as, men are thus disposed, self-interest and universal interest coincide. There is no necessary identity between the two unless it can be shown that the pleasures of sympathy so surpass other pleasures that any enlightened man will prefer them. Bentham himself suggests this when he refers to "that energy, that gayety of heart, that ardour of action, which remuneratory motives alone inspire." [26] This was the ground taken by Benjamin Franklin, following Cotton Mather's dictum: "Pleasure was long since defined, 'The result of some excellent action.' This pleasure is a sort of *holy luxury.* Most pitiable are they who will continue strangers to it." [27]

Unhappily, most men cannot be depended upon, without re-education, to choose this "holy luxury" rather than luxuries less holy, or pleasures less sympathetic. Shelley put the argument on the yet higher ground of self-perfection:

> To me the progress of society consists in nothing more than in bringing out the individual, in giving him a consciousness of his own being, and in quickening him to strengthen and elevate his mind. No man, I affirm, will serve his fellow-beings so effectually, so fervently, as he who is not their slave; as he who, casting off every yoke, subjects himself to the law of duty in his own mind. For this law enjoins a disinterested and generous spirit. Individuality, or moral self-subsistence, is the secret foundation of an all-comprehending love. No man so multiplies his bonds with the community as he who watches most jealously over his own perfection. There is a beautiful harmony between the good of the State and the moral freedom and dignity of the individual.[28]

Of Shelley's individualism there can be no question, but his universalism is either dogmatic or circular. If he means that whoever follows the maxim of self-perfection will by implication serve mankind, he is dogmatic. For in the name of self-perfection, or even of duty and conscience, a man may cultivate social irresponsibility and hardness of heart. If, on the other hand, Shelley stipulates that these inner sanctions shall enjoin "a disinterested and generous spirit," then he has put into them precisely what he wishes to draw out of them. He has proved only that he who seeks to perfect himself in benevolence will, to the extent to which he realizes his end, be benevolent.

Such moralizing is dangerous as well as confusing, for it encourages men to believe that by conscious preoccupation with themselves rather than with the needs, desires, and claims of other persons, they will satisfy the requirements of the principle of universalism. It commits in terms insidious and disarming the fallacy that humanity is an automatic by-product of selfishness.

8

Individualism, affirming the power of each passionate attitude to confer value on its object, and putting trust in the reflective judgment of each particular mind, tends in its social effect to a rich qualitative diversity. Permit a man to be independently governed by his own feeling and judgment and he will never be precisely like any other man. He will possess that irreducible individuality which Emerson proclaimed:

> Is it not the chief disgrace in the world, not to be an unit;—not to be reckoned one character;—not to yield that peculiar fruit which each man was created to bear, but to be reckoned in the gross, in the hundred, or the thousand, of the party, the section, to which we belong; and our opinion predicted geographically, as the north, or the south? Not so, brothers and friends,—please God, ours shall not be so. We will walk on our own feet; we will work with our own hands; we will speak our own minds.[29]

A printed circular distributed in the hotels of San Diego in the year 1918 contained the item "*San Diego*. Population 250,000 (1930)." The significance of this item lay not in the well-known and amiable California weakness for living in the future, but in the extraordinary importance attached to the census. The promoters of San Diego were only too happy "to be reckoned in the gross, in the hundred, or the thousand" —or, better still, the hundred thousand. An individualist would be disposed, when confronted with such a boast, to ask "Two hundred and fifty thousand *what*?"

As judged by mere numbers there is little chance that the cities of men will improve on the ant-hill. The individualist, if he boasts at all, will boast of the *kinds* of humanity that flourish in his community. He will desire that each man shall be the unique product of his own nature and experience, and that in its rich variety the community shall reflect the inexhaustible resources of human nature and of human experience. He will view with dismay those assimilating influences which reduce men to mere numerical units, and will seek by insulation to conserve in each something of that inimitable personal flavor which still distinguishes the isolated rustic or seafaring man.

An individualist will have a keen relish and a strong stomach for the unfamiliar and the unexpected. He will enjoy marriage, friendship, neighborly relations, and casual contacts because of the shock of strangeness which is blended with the sense of congenial sameness. Philosophers, for example, are individualists. They hold from time to time what is known as an 'international congress.' Attending such a congress is not a mere effect of natural gregariousness. Professors who are by nature timid, impecunious, and highly domesticated travel great distances and meet other professors who speak strange languages, think strange thoughts, and feel strange feelings. An international congress of philosophers, in short, is a group of persons who take a great deal of trouble in order to associate with others whom they do not and cannot understand. Their attitude is not one of passive endurance; they rejoice in their mutual unintelligibility.

Although an international congress of philosophers is an exceptional or even a monstrous phenomenon, it has a certain symbolic significance. It is of the essence of an individualistic society that its members should always be in some degree inscrutable to one another, and no one is fit to live in such a society who does not prefer the adventure of novelty to the grooves of habit. The institutions of true democracy will all partake in some measure of this character. Its universities will emancipate rather than indoctrinate, and gladly suffer the clash of temperament, personality, and opinion which results. It was this social quality that William James admired in the student body of Harvard:

> They come from the remotest outskirts of our country, without introductions, without school affiliations; special students, scientific students, graduate students, poor students of the College, who make their living as they go. . . . They hover in the background on days when the crimson color is most in evidence, but they nevertheless are intoxicated and exultant with the nourishment they find here. . . . When they come to Harvard, it is not primarily because she is a club. It is because they have heard of her persistently atomistic constitution, of her tolerance of exceptionality and eccentricity, of her devotion to the principles of individual vocation and choice.[30]

James generalized this norm of individualism, and applied it to all institutions. Speaking of a friend whose colorful idiosyncrasies he greatly admired, he said:

> The memory of Davidson will always strengthen my faith in personal freedom and its spontaneities, and make me less unqualifiedly respectful than ever of "Civilization," with its herding and branding, licensing and degree-giving, authorizing and appointing, and in general regulating and administering by system the lives of human beings. Surely the individual, the person in the singular number, is the more fundamental phenomenon, and the social institution, of whatever grade, is but secondary and ministerial. Many as are the interests which social systems satisfy, always unsatisfied interests remain over, and among them are interests to which system, as such, does violence whenever it lays its hand upon us. The best Commonwealth will always be the one that most cherishes the men who represent the residual interests, the one that leaves the largest scope to their peculiarities.[31]

Individualism is commonly opposed to what is called 'regimentation,' and regimentation is commonly ascribed to the state. Thus Herbert Hoover, who is described as the champion "without equivocation or compromise [of] the doctrine of American Individualism," [32] has in the name of this doctrine attacked the 'New Deal's' policy of increasing the functions of government.

But what is the proper political adjunct to individualism? According to the tradition which former President Hoover so greatly respects, it is the function of the state to intervene between one individual and another, or between an individual and a group, in order to preserve the liberty of individuals. May not the state be precisely the agency which is necessary to implement the resolves which Mr. Hoover himself formulated?

> That . . . we shall *safeguard* to every individual an equality of opportunity to take that position in the community to which his intelligence, character, ability, and ambition entitle him; that we *keep* the social solution free from frozen strata of classes; that we shall *stimulate* effort of each individual to achievement; that through an enlarging sense of responsibility and understanding we shall *assist* him to this attainment.[33]

To prevent regimentation it is necessary to fit the remedy to the causes. The state itself is only one of these causes, and the non-political causes of regimentation may be so potent that in protecting him against them the state becomes the individual's best friend. As a matter of fact, neither of the two causes of regimentation most characteristic of American life is to be identified with the state.

In the first place, the 'free' capitalistic economy has tended to a sameness of habit and outlook, both among entrepreneurs and among workers. It would, I think, be more difficult to distinguish two American businessmen than to distinguish, let us say, their two wives, or two poets, or two professors. If there were any two individuals more difficult to distinguish, it would be two factory workers or two farm laborers. The most extreme examples of sameness afforded by human history are occupational, and appear whenever the conditions of the struggle for existence are so severe as to provide neither mobility nor margin for individual variations—as when the individual, under the pressure of economic necessity, follows the rigid life-cycle of peasant, huntsman, fisherman, or shepherd. Occupations themselves will vary in the degree to which they call for inventiveness and spontaneity. "For two generations," said Parrington (speaking of the late nineteenth century in America), "the Industrial Revolution had been extending over an agrarian people the new sovereignty of the machine, and constraining a free individualism into conformity to a drab industrial pattern."[34] If human life is drably patterned by economic forces, it may be the duty of the state, as the protector of individualism, to 'interfere with business.'

The second notable cause of regimentation is the pressure of unofficial sentiment and opinion. The fear of being thought different is more potent than the fear of being convicted of lawlessness: "Independently of truth or falsehood," said Walter Bagehot, "the spectacle of a different belief from ours is disagreeable to us, in the same way that the spectacle of a different form of dress and manners is disagreeable." [35]

No one who has read Romanoff's *Three Pairs of Silk Stockings,* describing conditions in the early days of Soviet Russia, can question the enslaving effect of inadequate housing conditions which expose the individual directly to the curiosity and censorship of his fellows. A major benefit, perhaps the chief benefit, of improved standards of living is to create an interval between one individual and another. Privacy is the greatest of luxuries, and the chief condition of individualism; and the foe of privacy is not the state—which keeps its distance—but the inquisitive eye and gossiping tongue of the close neighbor. On a higher level, it is the vulgarizing appeal of the tabloid, the radio, or the cinema which sweeps individuals into a common current of sentiment or opinion and extinguishes every individual idiosyncrasy. Here the remedy is to be found in education, which is, again, a function of economic opportunity.

In short, the greatest force for regimentation is a maldistribution of wealth which binds men to the routines of livelihood, reduces life to those animal functions in which men most closely resemble one another, exposes men to the pressures of group opinion and sentiment, and excludes that free play of imagination, thought, and choice which is the most fruitful source of individual differences.

9

Individualism is not to be construed as anti-social, either biologically, psychologically, or morally. The individualist does not deny the fact of society, nor, like the philosophical anarchist or the advocate of solitude, does he disparage it as a regrettable necessity. He considers society as a field of individual activity and development. There is, therefore, no paradox in considering the social traits which are characteristic of the code of individualism, while at the same time freeing this code from certain exaggerations and perversions with which it is commonly associated.

It is no proper part of individualism to be conceited, selfish, consciously eccentric, ill-mannered, snobbish, disloyal, or lawless. While the individualist does not possess these traits either necessarily or ideally, they are defects to which he is peculiarly liable, or of which it is peculiarly natural that he should be suspected.

It is natural, for example, that the individualist should be thought to be conceited. Since it is characteristic of him that he should do his own thinking, and since this will commonly lead him to differ from his neighbor, the neighbor's resentment will naturally express itself in the charge of conceit. The thinking individual will also, from time to time, differ from the general and customary opinion of his time and place. Such procedure is not flattering to the crowd. The man who relies on his own judgment even when he has to stand alone is viewed, like all nonconformists, with suspicion and dislike, and others instinctively seek to take him down and coerce him. He is accused of arrogantly preferring his own single opinion to the collective opinion of the group.

But to accuse the individualist of pride of opinion is to miss the whole point. He does not weigh one opinion against another and prefer the one merely because it is his own. He prefers to all opinion, whether his own or that of others, what he takes to be knowledge. Error and prejudice may result either from subjective bias or from conformity. The individualist seeks to avoid both, and opposes the crowd not from contempt of others, but from love of truth.

A lover of truth is not conceited. Only he who loves it with a love which is strong enough to resist the pressure of vulgar opinion knows how elusive truth is. The last man to be boastful of his intellectual attainment will be the sincere lover of truth. In proportion as he respects the vast stretches of its domain and the stout walls of its fortresses, he will esteem little his own meager and precarious conquests.

Individualism *does* imply self-reliance, but this is a very different thing from arrogance and conceit. The conceited man attaches importance to his attainment, and looks for applause: if others do not give him enough applause, as often happens, he applauds himself. The self-reliant man, on the other hand, trusts his powers—not his past achievements. He seems to others to be arrogant because instead of looking for their good opinion, he submits himself to a higher and more universal standard. He seems proud because he cannot be bought. He may as a matter of fact be a very humble man, humble because he demands so much of himself. It is well to reflect on the fact that so many great men have, like Luther and Kepler, seemed to their fellow men whose opinion they defied to be proud and arrogant, when they were in fact only being humble before their God.

In short, the essence of individualism lies in a man's courageous exercise of his own distinctively human faculties, such as reason, conscience, and taste. The individualist makes up his own mind. If he is to make up his own mind, he must enjoy lucid intervals of thought when he collects himself, when he is neither divided by appetite and passion nor swept by the invading currents of the life about him. He needs a chamber of reflection all his own. It does not follow that he is conceited, but he may seem so to those who find the doors of that chamber occasionally closed against them.

The individualist is not conceited; neither is he, as is so commonly supposed, peculiarly self-interested. The essence of individualism is to think *for* oneself, not *of* oneself. It is no part of being an individualist that one should ignore or neglect the existence of other individuals. The saints and martyrs of the world are not less individualistic than the conquerors. St. Francis of Assisi is as much an individual as Napoleon or Hitler.

The individualist is not consciously eccentric. Willful oddity is a pose and a confession of failure. It argues that a man has to resort to desperate measures in order to attract attention—and that what he desires above all things *is* to attract attention. The individualist does not change his step merely in order to be out of step. A genuinely independent man will go his own gait, regardless of the rhythm of the crowd. A man who is bound to disagree is as readily controlled as if he were bound to agree. The negativist, like the man who refuses to join the chorus, must wait for others to set the key. He is slavishly dependent on the interest which he excites, whether the approval which he arouses by his assent or the flattering attention which he attracts by his dissent. The true individualist will hold to his own independent judgment, even when others agree with him.

Nor is the individualist a boor, distinguished by his bad manners. Joseph Priestley, who was one of the leading exponents of that spirit of emancipation which pervaded Europe and America in the eighteenth century, thought that "a commonwealth" was "unfavourable to *politeness*." "This kind of refinement," he said, "grows more naturally from that spirit of servility which is the effect of despotic government." [36] Now it is true that revolution is likely to distrust any sort of existing practice that depends on the sanction of custom. Revolution demands reasons for what men do, and is likely to be peculiarly suspicious of the amenities of life because their reasons are obscure. A revolutionary age is, furthermore, transitional and self-conscious, and is likely to lack that external grace of life—that ritual of gesture, tone, and idiom—which is an effect of the refinement of an established social order. But it is a mistake to suppose that there is only one kind of politeness, and that this is a by-product of servility. The courtier is not the only kind of gentleman. Even the courtier's code provided for the relation of courtier to fellow courtier, or of royalty to fellow royalty. Courtesy is not essentially a relation of inferior to superior. It does imply deference, but there is a deference which is reciprocal—a deference which asks a like deference in turn, and is free from any hint of obsequiousness.

That there is no necessary connection between individualism and bad manners is attested by the fact that we call bad manners 'vulgar,' when vulgarity is the opposite of individualism. The individualist does not necessarily eat with his knife. Peculiar behavior of this sort is rarely the result of originality of mind, or of sturdy adherence to principle. Most people who eat with their knives do so because they have spent their impressionable years among the knife-eaters. The ripe individualist who lives among fork-eaters will adopt that practice for several reasons. Having discovered that manners are mere conventions, he will take the further step of judging that usually the thing to do with mere conventions is to adopt them. If they are not worth adopting, they are still less worth breaking. In other words, he will save his emancipated reason and his moral scruples for more important things. Or having acquired taste, he will prefer good manners to bad. He will see that individualism has, after all, its social implications, and that below their superficial arbitrariness there is a meaning in good manners, as a mode of life by which two or more individuals so temper their individualism as to live without offense to one another.

Individualism is not exclusive. This is perhaps the commonest of errors—the supposition that individualism expresses merely a desire to hold oneself aloof from other people. There is in individualism a desire to be let alone, but it is associated with a disposition to let other people alone—to respect *their* privacy. Nothing could be a more perfect application of the Golden Rule. One may prefer not to be pounded on the back, or preached to by another man; but one is equally considerate of the other man's back and of *his* reticence. If one reserves something of oneself for one's intimates, or even for oneself alone, one considerately yields the same privilege to others—so that one is living in accord with what is really a social and not a private code.

Individualism, in short, is a mutual affair—a relation of two or more individuals to one another, a compound of self-respect and of deference to others. If individualism consisted in the careless disregard of other people, or their assimilation to one's own private and personal uses, then the greatest individualist would be the cannibal or the spoiled child. If it consisted in a forgetfulness of others, then the monomaniac would lead all the rest. The mark of any individualism that is admirable, or that may serve as a norm of conduct, is the equal acknowledgment of other individuals. It implies something more than an acquiescence in their existence; it is a joy in the association with one's equals, a keen relish for the resistance which they offer and for the differences with which they enrich the group.

The most serious indictment of individualism is the charge that it implies disloyalty, or a lack of collective spirit. As a matter of fact, the precise opposite is the case. In proportion as individualism places less emphasis on rules and regulations, or paternal supervision, it relies to a greater extent upon voluntary fidelity to a social code. There are, in other words, the peculiar responsibilities of individualism, and they are so burdensome that selfish or irresponsible individuals will often prefer the refuge of a benevolent despotism.

Individualism in all of its ennobling and perfecting aspects is the product of organized society. If a man is to become that sovereign entity of which Emerson speaks, he must have his faculties emancipated from urgent biological needs, and enjoy the order, the security, and the opportunity which social institutions alone can provide. Even more evident is it that a man cannot be happy or complete without human relations. He is in a hundred ways dependent on what his fellows can give to him, and on what he can give to them. Men can afford to live apart only after they have learned to live together; they can live for themselves, in a rich and satisfying sense, only when at the same time they live for one another.

Individualism is a fruit of organized society. But there is no guarantee that it will survive or develop even in this soil. It is not the result of inaction or apathy. It is not a mere decomposition of society into its primitive constituents, or an atavistic reversal of the process of historical development. Like the artificial oasis redeemed from the desert, it must be perpetually irrigated. Nature has yielded it reluctantly, and seeks every opportunity to reclaim it. It is the most exquisite and fragile flower of that historic human enterprise which is called civilization.

CHAPTER SEVENTEEN

POPULAR GOVERNMENT

1

"DEMOCRACY," SAYS LEONARD WOOLF, "may be defined as the idea that government should exist for the benefit of free and equal citizens, politically united in a common purpose—the happiness of each and all." [1] Two ideas are here conjoined. There is an idea of the "benefit," for which the state "should exist"; and an idea of the structure of the state, or the proper source and locus of its power. The first of these ideas is social democracy, which defines the purpose of the state as the happiness (or good, or well-being) of "each and all" of those who live under it. The second of these ideas is political democracy, which assigns the power of the state to these same individuals, so that those who live under the state are at one and the same time its beneficiaries and its rulers.

The basic idea of political democracy must not be confused with the procedures by which it is implemented. To define political democracy as the rule of the majority, universal suffrage, or parliamentary government, is to define it in terms of specific mechanisms which should be considered as provisional and experimental. Their failure would not invalidate the basic idea, but only prove the necessity of inventing better methods. The same holds true, a fortiori, of the still more specific mechanisms which distinguish the particular democracies; for example, of England and America. To identify the idea with the mechanism leads to hasty despair if the mechanism fails; or to excessive complacency if it proves in some measure successful. It discourages political inventiveness and encourages external imitation. One of the merits of political democracy is its adaptability to local conditions. But it possesses this merit only when stated in the most general terms. Its essence is not an electoral mechanism, or distribution of executive, legislative, and judicial powers. It may be federal or centralized, direct or representative;

it may even preserve the form of a monarchy. Its essence is its being a government of, by, and for the same people.

A government *for* the people may be a government by God, a ruling caste, an absolute monarch, or even a dictator. Such a government would be paternalistic; that is, benevolent in its purpose but irresponsible in its power. It would have no check save its own benevolence and the wisdom with which this benevolence was carried into effect. Said Edmund Burke:

> Kings, in one sense, are undoubtedly the servants of the people, because their power has no other rational end than that of the general advantage; but it is not true that they are, in the ordinary sense (by our constitution, at least) any thing like servants; the essence of whose situation is to obey the commands of some other, and to be removable at pleasure. But the king of Great Britain obeys no other person; all other persons are individually, and collectively too, under him, and owe to him a legal obedience. The law, which knows neither to flatter nor to insult, calls this high magistrate, not our servant . . . but "*our sovereign Lord the King.*" *. . . As he is not to obey us, but as we are to obey the law in him, our constitution has made no sort of provision towards rendering him, as a servant, in any degree responsible.[2]

Political democracy, on the other hand, regards government as a trusteeship. The ruler is responsible to the beneficiaries, and these reserve an ultimate power to create, change, regulate, and direct the government as their judgment and interest dictate. The beneficiaries, in other words, govern themselves, through agents whose power is limited and provisional. The power to exact obedience is vested in the last analysis in those who pay its cost, and whose good is its only justification.

The same idea may be expressed in terms of 'consent.' What Burke said of kings applies to all rulers: namely, that they are designed to be obeyed, and not to obey. But in a political democracy all obedience is in the last analysis voluntary. Those who are ruled consent to be ruled; that is, they voluntarily create and support a power which may be used against them, believing that it is a good thing in general that particular

---

* Similarly, John Robinson: "I know kings may be said to serve their people, and so to become their servants; but this is only in respect of their love towards them, and care for them; but not in respect of their order, which is a lordship and kingship, by which they reign over their people, as their servants and subjects." [3]

persons and particular acts should be regulated, including their own persons and their own acts.

In proportion as a democracy is complex it is necessary that the rulers or agents of government, whether legislative, executive, or judicial, should be authorized to use their own discretion. It is unthinkable that government should at all times express the desire and the opinion of all the people; unthinkable because all the people never desire and think the same thing; unthinkable because it is impossible that all the people should concern themselves with every act of government. The discretion of the rulers is reconciled with democratic principles by the fact that the rulers are given a mandate which is both limited in time and defined by broad principles of policy. It is to such a system as a whole, involving its disagreements as well as its agreements with their momentary and individual wills, that the people as a whole consent.

All popular political consent is in some measure a consent *in principle.* In elections it is a man who is chosen, or even a type of man, and not his particular acts. Unless he were allowed some discretion, there would be no point in instituting his office. Or it is a general policy which is approved, and not its detailed applications. Legislation, administration, and judicial interpretation translate the general into the particular. Even in cases in which a campaign is fought upon a specific issue, there will always be a difference between the broader formulation upon which the electorate pronounces judgment and the narrower question of the way in which that judgment shall be carried into effect.

A certain amount of confusion, therefore, arises from the use of the expression 'self-government.' If this were taken to mean that any given individual submitted only to his own decision, there would of course be no government at all, but anarchy. There can be self-government only in the sense that there are two selves, the self that exercises the ultimate sovereignty and the self that is called upon for some immediate act of obedience. What the individual citizen in a more general sense approves he is called upon in a more particular sense to obey. And when the moment for obedience arises, there may be not only a duality but a conflict between these two selves. In a speech made in 1932, Senator Borah said that he had been startled to find a large number of armed policemen sitting about in the basement of the Capitol. "But then," he continued, "I reflected that they were there to protect the government from its own people, to protect the government from its hungry people—to protect the government of the people, for the people and by the people, *from* the people." [4]

This is a paradox only in the most superficial sense. One may not only need to be protected against oneself, but one may desire to be protected against oneself. I may say to my friend, "If ever you are trying to rescue me from drowning, and I resist, knock me on the head." Then if my friend has occasion to carry out this mandate, he is obeying my will in a sense more fundamental than that in which he is exercising coercion upon me. It is the appeal from Philip drunk to Philip sober. There is my long-range judgment and my narrower view; there is the judgment which expresses the fundamental needs which I share with the larger group to which I belong, and there is the private greed or impulse of the moment. A government which protects the first against the second is not only expressing my will, but is doing so in precisely that manner for which the function of government is instituted.

These considerations have a direct bearing on government in times of emergency.[5] In such times there is a peculiar need for promptness of action, and for attention to imperative and common needs. A dictatorship which perpetuates itself through intimidation, censorship, hysteria, or ignorance, and a temporary increase of the discretionary powers of government based on preliminary discussion and general consent, are poles asunder. The latter does not signify an abandonment of democracy, but its skillful adaptation to special conditions.

2

An old lady of my acquaintance was standing in an automatic elevator debating with her friends in the hallway outside whether or not to go up to her room. Suddenly the elevator, moved by some invisible agency, started up of its own accord, and the old lady, placidly folding her hands, said, "I've decided." The consent of the governed, as democracy interprets that phrase, is not a forced consent, or a mere passive acceptance of what one is helpless to control. Political democracy does not conceive the citizen as a passenger who remains aboard the ship of state and conforms himself to its itinerary because he has no safe alternatives; but as one who takes passage on a ship which he builds and controls, in order to reach a destination of his own choosing. Consent means, in other words, consent to the existence and exercise of that power which is obeyed.

Without a distinction between forced and voluntary consent the theory of popular government loses all meaning. The power exercised by the rulers of the state is not their individual power, but the overwhelming and coercive power of the collectivity. This will be true however autocratic the form of government. The power wielded by the officers of a disciplined army is the power of the army. The individual soldier is helpless to resist the organized force of which he himself constitutes a part. He is at one and the same time the victim and the member of the firing squads by which disobedience is penalized. He may even be said to choose to obey, since he has the alternative of disobedience and death. Nevertheless the polity of the army is autocratic, because the private soldier does not choose the situation in which he finds himself. He does not choose the state of war, or the strategy of the campaign, or the disciplinary regulations, or the orders of the day. His actual choices are narrowly circumscribed within a system which he does not choose.

Every organized political society is in some degree autocratic. The private individual is in some degree compelled to choose between obedience and the penalties imposed by a system of law which he does not choose, although he himself and others like him supply its powers of enforcement. But a political society is popular or democratic insofar as the private individual chooses the system itself and therefore approves of the commands which he obeys, and of the penalties which his disobedience incurs. He participates in the state not as a mere component of its collective force and by acceptance, through habit or fear, of its decrees, but as maker of polity and policy. Voluntary obedience, in this fundamental sense, is, according to democracy, the leaven in the dough, the gold in the ore, the strain of reason which in human political life is commingled with arbitrary force.

Free consent, in the democratic sense, is not, then, a forced consent;

nor is it a merely tacit or implied consent. Political theorists who would like to borrow the moral force of the principle of consent without accepting its democratic implications pay homage to the principle by inventing a fictitious consent. Richard Hooker, inspirer of Locke, is guilty of this subterfuge:

> Wherefore as any man's deed past is good as long as himself continueth; so the act of a public society of men done five hundred years sithence standeth as theirs who presently are of the same societies, because corporations are immortal; we were then alive in our predecessors, and they in their successors do live still. Laws therefore human, of what kind soever, are available by consent.[6]

In other words, according to this view a man born into a state has already consented to its rule vicariously through the acts of his predecessors. This is the only intelligible meaning, though it is veiled by substituting a corporate society for an aggregation of individuals. But corporations do not consent at all, nor can one individual consent for another without that other's explicit consent. In practice, this idea of fictitious consent annuls the processes of democracy. Since all men are born into a state, their consent has been given in advance to whatever is legally enacted, and any appeal whatsover to their present judgment or interest is superfluous. The theory of fictitious consent implies a blanket endorsement of whatever the duly constituted ruler may choose to impose.

If there is force in Hooker's doctrine, it lies in the fact that the violation of existing law on the part of one man will disappoint the reasonable expectations of another. A political society is a continuing process, and, if existing agreements are changed, this should be done in such wise as to avoid violent dislocations and unfulfilled obligations. But this caveat is itself capable of obtaining and should, on democratic premises, obtain the present and explicit consent of reasonable men.

3

Political democracy is sometimes described as the theory of 'popular sovereignty.' The question of sovereignty, which plays so prominent a part in political theory, is unhappily ambiguous. It may be taken to mean, Where does the power of the state *actually* reside? Or, it may be taken to mean Where does its power *rightfully* reside?

The Austinian view identifies sovereignty with "habitual obedience from the bulk of a given society" to "a determinate human superior, not in the habit of obedience to a like superior." [7] But who are the "determinate superiors"?

It will not do to assume that the final term in the series of actual obedience is the highest *legal* authority. The titular ruler is often suspected of habitually obeying non-political superiors representing a private organization such as the church. The rise of monopolistic and finance capitalism has concentrated economic power in the hands of a few. Former Ambassador James W. Gerard created a sensation some years ago by saying that America was ruled by sixty-four captains of industry, alleging, as have other realistic observers, that big business controls not only little business but politics as well.[8] This is a fundamental thesis of Marxism. We read in the *Communist Manifesto* that

> the class of modern Capitalists, owners of the means of social production and employers of wage-labor . . . has, at last, since the establishment of Modern Industry and of the world-market, conquered for itself, in the modern representative State, exclusive political sway. The executive of the modern State is but a committee for managing the common affairs of the whole bourgeoisie.

Lenin lodged this super-political power not in the whole class of capitalists, but in "a financial oligarchy, spreading a thick network of dependency over all the economic and political institutions of modern capitalist society without exception." [9]

Others, like Professor Harold J. Laski, call attention to the plurality of ultimate political authorities. His well-known article on "The Pluralistic State," [10] admirable as it is, illustrates the confusions which beset this subject. The classic doctrine of "the sovereign state," which the author here criticizes, imputes to the state a unified and an absolute actual power which is at the same time a rightful power. The doctrine may be attacked on two grounds: on the ground of fact, and on the ground of rightfulness. Professor Laski's contention that the state is and ought to be plural is seriously weakened by his lapses into the same logical error of which he convicts his opponents—by the failure, namely, to hold these two questions apart.*

It is often argued that modern democracies are not, as they profess to be, governments by the people. But it is then implied that they *would* be what they profess to be—that is, democracies—if the sovereign power *were* exercised by the people. In other words, political democracy, to its critics as well as to its friends, is an ideal polity and not the description of an existing state of affairs. The problem of which the democratic political philosophy offers a solution is not the problem of where sovereignty resides de facto, or even de jure, in the sense of positive law, but the problem of where it ought to reside, or would reside in a perfected society. This problem cannot be solved by sociology, by history, by comparative politics, or even by constitutional law, but only by ethics, or by whatever branch of inquiry formulates the ultimate principles of good and evil, and of moral obligation. When Thomas Hooker of Connecticut said that "the foundation of authority is laid . . . in the free consent of the people,"[11] he referred to its logical or just foundation. When John Adams said, "As the happiness of the people is the sole end of government, so the consent of the people is the only foundation of it," he added, "in reason, morality, and the natural fitness of things."[12]

Political theorists such as Hooker and Adams, who conceived the democratic theory of sovereignty as a formulation of what ought to be rather than as a description of what is, acknowledged the lamentable fact that what is does not ordinarily coincide with what ought to be. They

---

* It is further weakened by the author's failure to distinguish the permissive and the active functions of the state. The argument for the unity of sovereignty, the need, namely, for a consistent and comprehensive system of human relations guaranteed by the collective force, does not imply that this system may not be functionally decentralized. The unity of the state is implied by the need of some authority which shall define areas of liberty and adjudicate conflicts among interests which may otherwise be autonomous.

were aware that actual political societies are all in some degree deformed—that is, their sovereignty is displaced. They recognized, in short, three problems: the moral problem of what ought to be; the historical or sociological problem of what is; and the practical problem of bringing about the highest possible agreement of what is with what ought to be.

No doubt the early proponents of popular sovereignty were too readily disposed to assume that the people did exercise sovereignty. No doubt the present age is more realistic and better informed on these matters. No doubt the modern state has developed new and formidable methods by which the people can be terrorized or deceived. But the admission of these limitations in the traditional democratic view does not justify the confusion of the problem; nor does it weaken the argument that the people are the rightful sovereigns and should so far as possible be put in actual possession of their title.

Among those, whether democratic or non-democratic, who conceive the problem of sovereignty as the question of the rightful rather than the actual seat of power, there is agreement as to the general form of the argument. It is agreed that the political power should be so placed as to realize the social end for which political institutions exist. For Plato the social end was an organic whole in which the idea of the Good should be embodied; and he allocated the sovereignty to philosophers because philosophers alone possess a true knowledge of the idea of the Good. Modern political philosophers of the Hegelian type conceive that the highest good of man is to participate in the self-realization of the historical society to which they belong. They give to such historical societies, taken as corporate and enduring entities, a claim that is higher than that of any individual. They regard the political structure of such an entity as an authentic expression of its peculiar genius, and allocate sovereignty to those organs of authority which this structure provides. They affirm, in short, that the power ought to reside where it constitutionally resides, but only after they have given the constitution their moral blessing.

Similarly, democratic political philosophy is based upon its individualistic-universalistic social philosophy. Thus John Adams advocated popular government as the form of sovereignty best calculated to secure the "end of government," which is "the happiness of the people." He held, in other words, that a government by the people is of all possible forms of sovereignty the one most likely to be a government for the people.

4

"The sovereign when traced to the source," said James Wilson, "must be found in the man." [13] The argument for political democracy turns on the qualifications of the individuals who live under the state to exercise that control of the state through which it shall realize its social purpose. These qualifications are three: the possession of the faculties of reason and conscience; the possession of interests of which the state is bound to take account; the capacity for human development, in respect both of faculty and of interest, in proportion as the purpose of the state is realized.

The individual's possession of reason and conscience qualifies him for a voice in affairs of state because of the fundamental assumption that the state exists for a good reason. It should be controlled by those who are capable of seeing why in general there should be a state, why this or that state should be preserved or superseded, and why this or that policy should be adopted. But these capabilities are the distinguishing prerogatives of human individuals. The acts of mind by which means are subsumed under ends, and by which moral truths are certified by evidence, occur, when they occur at all, within that entity which is called a person. Through the linking together of power and moral judgment there is the highest likelihood that what is should coincide with what ought to be. There is no alternative save to construe the state as a mere force, and deny that there is any right save might; or to assume that through some miracle or metaphysical predetermination superior force is morally inspired.

There remains the question whether the qualifying capacities of reason and conscience shall be imputed to *all* individuals or persons. Opponents of political democracy limit them, as did Plato, to an intellectual elite.

The answer of democracy is twofold. In the first place, access to truth is a generic attribute of man, possessed in some degree by every individual. The capacity for true knowledge can be denied to no man on personal grounds. There are, to be sure, differences of innate capacity, but these do not coincide with any hereditary or official class. The highest intellectual talents may be hidden in the mass through lack of opportunity for their expression. And every individual, whatever the degree of his talent, has a unique experience through which some truth is accessible to him alone. Furthermore, any individual who frames a judgment has a legitimate claim to knowledge which cannot rightly be rejected until it is heard. There is always the possibility that it *may* be true; and to be rightly rejected it must be tested not by the status of the claimant, but by examination of the evidence which he cites in its support. Every individual is a potential vehicle of truth on any matter to which he directs his cognitive faculties. Democracy seeks a government by enlightenment, and bestows political power on all individuals insofar as they are sources of light; which every individual is, for anything that one can know in advance to the contrary.

In the second place, man is not only possessed of reason by definition, but is educable; that is, capable of having his deficiencies removed. The men of the Enlightenment were disposed to attribute such deficiencies to religious bigotry and political tyranny, and naturally supposed that what society had taken away, society could restore. But it was no part of the democratic creed to ignore individual differences, or to neglect the importance of training. "I know no safe depository of the ultimate powers of . . . society," said Jefferson, "but the people themselves; and if we think them not enlightened enough to exercise their control with a wholesome discretion, the remedy is not to take it from them, but to inform their discretion by education." [14]

Popular education has become a universal democratic institution for several distinct reasons: in order to realize the standard of equality; in order that the citizens to whom political power is granted may exercise that power with the maximum of intelligence; and in order to tap all possible sources of enlightenment. In the present context the emphasis is upon the last of these reasons. Every man is to be considered as a source of that moral truth on which the state depends not only for wise policy, but for its very right to exist. Since the attainment of truth depends on a correct knowledge of the facts, the same reason argues for institutions of public information. The question of the freedom and the honesty of the press and the radio is thus a peculiarly urgent and grave question for a political democracy. The extreme abuse of such agencies, leading to a complete reversal of democratic procedure, is the manufacture *by* the state, through censorship and propaganda, of the very judgments from which it draws its authority.

All governments profess to rest on popular support. But whereas a democratic government will permit, facilitate, and encourage the people to make up their own minds, giving them access to information together with freedom of thought and communication, a dictatorial government will use its powers to propagate and maintain those beliefs which are favorable to the continued exercise of those powers. Democracy is concerned to develop and liberate the faculties of its people, and to provide these faculties with the data suitable to their exercise, submitting itself to such beliefs as may then emerge. Dictatorship, on the other hand, will concern itself with the beliefs themselves, and will so control both faculties and data as to prevent any deviation from those beliefs which it authorizes.*

Popular government assumes the possession by all men of the supreme faculty of reason, and relies on education for the development of that faculty. But popular government also reposes confidence in the judgment of the common man—not only because of his constitutional humanity or his potentiality of development, but because of his very commonness. Rousseau said of Thérèse that she was "limited in understanding," even "stupid," but had an excellent and reliable judgment and good sense, and was "a most excellent adviser in cases of difficulty." Similarly, Jefferson trusted the opinion of farmers, who were "the chosen people of God . . . whose breasts he has made his peculiar deposit for substantial and genuine virtue."[16] The common man is here thought of as less corrupt, less ambitious, and less extravagant. His modest claims

---

* This is the unmistakable tenor of Mussolini's official defense of the electoral law passed by the Italian Chamber of Deputies in March, 1928.[15]

for himself are of the order of magnitude which justice will accord to every man. Through his very simplicity of mind he is the more clearly aware of the basic truths of morals and piety.

This trust in the common man reflects the intuitive and axiomatic emphasis of the ethics of the eighteenth century. It sentimentalizes the common man, in protest against the flagrant defects of the rich and the powerful. It exaggerates the merits of the common man because they are found where least expected. It selects as common a type of character and mentality that is in fact uncommon. It shows an innocent disregard of the intellectual and practical difficulties of social life, as though its problems could be solved by guileless adherence to a few moral maxims.

There remains, however, an undeniable force in the old Aristotelian teaching that the best state is that in which there is a large and powerful middle class. The man who is neither too rich nor too poor, too powerful nor too weak, too ignorant nor too learned, is likely to form those judgments of policy which afford the best promise of general agreement. James Bryce said of the traditional democratic faith in the "common man":

> He is taken to be the man of broad common sense, mixing on equal terms with his neighbours, forming a fair unprejudiced judgment on every question, not viewy or pedantic like the man of learning, nor arrogant, like the man of wealth, but seeing things in a practical, businesslike, and withal kindly, spirit, pursuing happiness in his own way, and willing that every one else should do so.[17]

This description fits the postman, the carpenter, the small shopkeeper, or the farmer. They stand near the center of political gravity. Agreement requires compromise, and the locus of the compromise lies close to the intermediate interest, expectation, and habitual outlook of the average man. Being neither the victim of society nor one of its more privileged beneficiaries, he is the exponent neither of revolution nor of reaction. He represents the kind and degree of attainment which is capable of being brought within the reach of all men. He embodies the basic social virtues of domestic fidelity, industry, honesty, and fair-mindedness, and demonstrates the successful working of these virtues for the general good. He endeavors to improve his position in life, but his ambitions are so moderate that he accepts without difficulty the limitations imposed by the similar ambitions of others. His judgments are so 'reasonable' as to require the minimum of alteration in order to coincide with the requirements of disinterestedness.

5

The first argument for political democracy is that every individual has a capacity for disinterested judgment; the second argument, to which we now turn, is that every individual has interests at stake. The state has an obligation to take account of these interests, and to provide for them so far as is consistent with a similar provision for the interests of other individuals.

Political democracy is founded on the belief, supported by experience, that the best guarantee that any given individual's interests will not be neglected is to give to that individual both the voice and the power with which to obtain a respectful hearing. He, at least, will not forget his interests, and is their most vigilant and untiring advocate. A selfish ruler will neglect them so far as he can safely do so. A well-intentioned ruler, however benevolent in his intent and wise in his statesmanship, will reflect the special interests of his class and the bias of his origin or cast of mind. Paternalism, whether honest or dishonest, is justly suspect. Although it is perpetually commended, and never more frequently than in our own day, as the simplest solution of political difficulties, it is the oldest and most discredited of political forms. Of it Matthew Arnold said:

> If experience has established any one thing in this world it has established this: that it is well for any great class and description of men in society to be able to say for itself what it wants, and not to have other classes, the so-called educated and intelligent classes, acting for it as its proctors, and supposed to understand its wants and to provide for them. They do not really understand its wants, they do not really provide for them. A class of men may often itself not either fully understand its wants, or adequately express them; but it has a nearer interest and a more sure diligence in the matter than any of its proctors, and therefore a better chance of success.[18]

Locke tells us, in effect, that a man is a fool to deliver his interests over to a monarch upon whom he has no check. Better no ruler at all, as in the state of nature; for then his interests would have at least a fighting chance:

> Whereas, in the ordinary state of Nature, he has a liberty to judge of his right, according to the best of his power to maintain it; but whenever his property is invaded by the will and order of his monarch, he has not only no appeal, as those in society ought to have, but, as if he were degraded from the common state of rational creatures, is denied a liberty to judge of, or defend his right, and so is exposed to all the misery and inconveniences that a man can fear from one, who being in the unrestrained state of Nature, is yet corrupted with flattery and armed with power.

It is absurd to allow the ruler to

> retain all the liberty of the state of Nature, increased with power, and made licentious by impunity. This is to think that men are so foolish that they take care to avoid what mischiefs may be done them by polecats or foxes, but are content, nay, think it safety, to be devoured by lions.[19]

Now that the modern dictator has learned to combine the attributes of the polecat and the fox with those of the lion, the folly of submission to tyranny is the more flagrant. And the totalitarian dictator who deceives himself, and believes that he has a special mission to dispense good to subjects who have no defense against him, is not less dangerous than the dictator who craftily conceals his self-seeking under a mask of benevolence.

The validity of this political idea rests upon the doctrine that an individual's good is to be found in his own interests as he feels them, and not in a role assigned to him by the interest of another. The insidious fault of paternalism lies in the fact that even the benevolent ruler finds it extremely difficult to avoid the substitution of his own will for that of his alleged beneficiaries. It is notorious that loving parents are disposed to identify their children's good with what they, the parents, want their children to be. Once it is clearly recognized that to do good to any man means to serve that man's felt interests, it becomes evident that in the last analysis each man knows his own good best. True benevolence will kindle in each individual the liveliest and fullest awareness of his interests, and then provide facilities by which these interests may attain their objects. The best guarantee that benevolence shall assume this form is a political system that will enable each individual to testify to his own interests and at the same time give him the power to insist upon their being taken account of in public policy.

"No man," said Lincoln, "is good enough to govern another man without that other's consent."[20] But misguided or deceitful benevolence is not the worst that is to be feared from the irresponsible ruler. He may not be benevolent at all. He may have achieved power through some principle of succession that is quite indifferent to benevolence. He may have achieved power through ambition and greed, and use his power quite shamelessly to satisfy these motives. Or, granting him at least a modicum of benevolence at the outset, he may not remain benevolent. He may, as Locke says, be "made licentious by impunity." It is a notorious fact that irresponsible power has a degenerating effect. Men are brutalized by their power over animals, parents by their power over children, the keeper by his power over the insane, the jailer by his power over prisoners, the officer by his power over his soldiers, the foreman by his power over the laborer, the employer by his power over the wage-earner. The political dictator is parent, keeper, jailer, officer, foreman, and employer all in one, and his victims are numbered by the thousands or the millions. Even if the titular head of the state be genuinely benevolent in his intent, this inhumanity will develop among his agents. The only means of protecting individuals against it is the possession by those same individuals of a power to protect themselves.

It is this association of interest with power that lies at the basis of the wide extension of the suffrage. All limitations of the suffrage which exclude the interests of a group tend to the neglect of its interests by the government, however benevolent the government's professions or its intentions. Qualification and disqualification for voting should never coincide with interests, but only with attributes, such as age, mental soundness, and literacy, which condition the capacity for conscious choice. Qualifications of sex, property, and even education beyond the simplest rudiments tend to result in the exploitation of the disqualified by a privileged class.

The claim of women to the vote here rests upon their possession of special interests—their own personal interests, and the domestic or social interests which concern them peculiarly. A property qualification will dispose those who exercise political power to use it for the perpetuation of that economic system from which they derive their present differential advantages. As regards an educational qualification, it is simple enough to say that the ignorant should not vote. But who should vote on the question whether the ignorant shall be given an opportunity to become wise? The wise have a strong motive for keeping wisdom to themselves, for in proportion as it is extended, it ceases to yield a special advantage to those who possess it. Proposals to limit education come from those who are already educated, and are jealous of their privileges. They fear the 'disturbing' effect of education upon the unprivileged. The pressure for popular education, on the other hand, comes from those who, not having education, covet and rightly covet for themselves or for their children those social, economic, or cultural goods which are manifestly enjoyed by the educated.

6

The first two arguments for political democracy define a citizen as an individual qualified to exercise disinterested judgment, and possessing interests which he is best qualified to represent—the citizen is the union in one person of the roles of sovereign and beneficiary. The third argument for political democracy assimilates the first to the second. Man is by nature a self-governing finality—through his capacity for moral judgment he enjoys access to that truth which is his highest sanction of conduct. Being so endowed, the exercise of political power, or the function of citizenship, is part of that happiness or self-expression which it is the purpose of his institutions to promote.

In proportion as government provides its people with opportunities for education and self-improvement, they will become not only better qualified to judge public policy for themselves, but increasingly insistent upon doing so. Parents who fulfill their parental obligations will presently bring their children to a condition in which they can no longer be treated as children. The same is true of the state and its members.

Granting the beneficent purpose for which government exists, and granting that it progressively realizes this purpose, it cannot in the long run rest upon any other basis than the deliberate and voluntary consent of the governed, because these, like children, will under favorable conditions grow up and speak for themselves.

Man's full satisfaction will require not only that he shall think for himself, and have what he wants, but that his own thinking shall be regulative of his own wants. A peculiarly effective statement of the present argument was made by Lincoln. The cabins of the poor mountain whites of the South, in the days before the war, were built with their floors on a level with the ground, and the term "mud-sill" came into vogue as a contemptuous name for the servile condition of labor. Slavery was only one of the many forms of this degradation, to which Lincoln, as an exponent of "free labor," was earnestly opposed, both in principle and in feeling:

> By the "mud-sill" theory it is assumed that labor and education are incompatible, and any practical combination of them impossible. According to that theory, a blind horse upon a tread-mill is a perfect illustration of what a laborer should be—all the better for being blind, that he could not kick understandingly. According to that theory, the education of laborers is not only useless but pernicious and dangerous. In fact, it is, in some sort, deemed a misfortune that laborers should have heads at all. Those same heads are regarded as explosive materials, only to be safely kept in damp places, as far as possible from that peculiar sort of fire which ignites them. A Yankee who could invent a strong-handed man without a head would receive the everlasting gratitude of the "mud-sill" advocates.
>
> But free labor says, "No." Free labor argues that as the Author of man makes every individual with one head and one pair of hands, it was probably intended that heads and hands should coöperate as friends, and that that particular head should direct and control that pair of hands. As each man has one mouth to be fed, and one pair of hands to furnish food, it was probably intended that that particular pair of hands should feed that particular mouth —that each head is the natural guardian, director, and protector of the hands and mouth inseparably connected with it; and that being so, every head should be cultivated and improved by whatever will add to its capacity for performing its charge. In one word, free labor insists on universal education.[21]

Lincoln's idea had been anticipated two thousand years before by Plato, in the teeth of his own aristocratic doctrine. There is, said Plato, an analogy between the state and the individual in that each has a ruling part and a subordinate part. As a just state will possess a class of wise rulers supported by a military class and regulating the merchants and artisans, so a just individual will possess a reason, supported by a vigorous will and presiding over the appetites. A man who lacks this ruling faculty, or fails to exercise it—whose ruling part is provided vicariously by his superiors—is so much less a man. He is not only an incomplete man, but he is not a man at all, since he lacks man's defining prerogative. Plato deplored the fact that the mass of mankind, though they may participate in social justice, must lack personal justice, and be, like children, the servants of an elite who do their thinking for them:

> We do not indeed imagine that the servant ought to be governed to his own detriment . . . on the contrary, we believe it to be better for every one to be governed by a wise and divine power, which ought, *if possible,* to be seated in the man's own heart, the only alternative being to impose it from without; in order that we may be all alike, so far as nature permits, and mutual friends, from the fact of being steered by the same pilot. . . . And this . . . is plainly the intention of law—that common friend of all the members of a state—and also of the government of children, which consists in withholding their freedom, until the time when we have formed a constitution in them, as we should in a city, and until, by cultivating the noblest principle of their nature, we have established in their hearts a guardian and a sovereign, the very counterpart of our own;—from which time forward we suffer them to go free.[22]

This "if possible" is the small concession through which Plato's aristocracy is convertible into democracy. A fixed pyramidal structure, in which the fullest development of the individual is limited to a small group of privileged and eminent rulers, cannot be reconciled with the ideal of developing all individuals as far as possible. For possibility here depends on the amplitude of the individual's opportunity—not only his opportunity of education, but also his opportunity of responsibility. Political power, involving as it does in Plato's teaching the application of reason to human affairs, is thus one form of opportunity through which the individual may be brought to the limit of his possibilities. A political democracy creates for its members both the incentive and the conditions which are calculated to evoke his powers, and encourages him to be a complete man possessed not only of appetites and enthusiasm, but of the faculty of rational self-determination. A political democracy will not organize society in advance so as to provide for a class of decapitated men, but will be designed to provide all men with heads and the chance to use them.

If individuals are to be brought to the highest possible level of self-development, the state must provide for the claim to power which will invariably attend that development. What Aristotle says of the warriors —that "it is an impossible thing that those who are able to use or to resist force should be willing to remain always in subjection" [23]—can be generalized. The strong will not tolerate their own exclusion from the function of ruling. If they are not admitted to power by the constitution of the state, there is no alternative but that chosen by dictatorship: namely, their systematic suppression. Their power must either be nipped in the bud by indoctrination and habits of servility, or, if they are allowed to attain a consciousness of power, they must be crushed or intimidated. The right to grow strong, on the other hand, implies the right to the political exercise of that strength.

7

Jefferson, who may be accepted as an authority on American democracy, declared in his First Inaugural that we must "bear in mind the sacred principle that tho' the will of the Majority is in all cases to prevail, that will, to be rightful, must be reasonable: that the Minority possess their equal rights, which equal laws must protect, and to violate would be oppression." [24]

There is no profounder misunderstanding of the meaning of political democracy than to suppose that it means the rule of the majority. Such an interpretation is doubly false: as asserting that the good of a majority is *better* than that of a minority; and as asserting that the judgment of a majority is *truer* than that of a minority. Treitschke was right in saying that a majority as such is only one kind of superior force, and that the exploitation of a minority by a majority is no less brutal than the exploitation of a majority by a minority; and that a higher will, if there be one, must in some sense be a will of the whole.[25] It may be argued that the happiness of a majority is "greater" than the happiness of a minority, the happiness of each counting for one. But this method of reckoning comparative goods makes the assumption that the goods of individuals are either equal or commensurable, whereas each is unique and irreducible. According to democracy, the purpose of the state is not the happiness of a majority of its members, but of all; and only through its devotion to this comprehensive purpose can it be said to take higher ground. That the majority as such is wiser than the minority, merely for numerical reasons, is even more palpably false.

The basic principle of political democracy is not majority, but unanimity. This follows from the principle of universality in all its applications. The faculty of political judgment is a generic property of men and gives to *every* mature and normal individual who is a member of the state a title to participate in the creation of policy. The justification of the state and of its policy is a form of truth, and truth is the same for *all* men. The purpose of the state is to benefit *all* of those who live under it. The contract on which the state is based embraces as its contracting parties *all* of those whom it calls upon to obey, so that obedience is the fulfillment of an obligation which *every* individual has voluntarily assumed, in the light of his interest as he sees it.[26]

The acceptance of the principle of unanimity, taken together with its nonexistence and apparent impossibility, has led political philosophers to desperate measures. These measures are highly instructive. Faced by the evident clash of wills, and the forced submission of dissenters in all actual states, Rousseau invented the "general will," as a metaphysical reality, metaphysics being invoked, as is unhappily so often its role, to give reality to an ideal which is contrary to fact.[27]

A second measure, not less desperate, is to affirm after the manner of Richard Hooker [28] that a unanimous agreement entered into in the past, when the state was instituted, is inherited by posterity. Apart from its historical falsity, this view is essentially non-democratic, since it obliges present individuals to submit involuntarily; that is, for no reason that commends such obedience to them here and now.

A third measure is to affirm that 'silence gives consent.' An individual who has passively acquiesced for a time in the political system in which he was born is said to have committed himself before he knew it; when he becomes consciously critical of political authority it is too late to protest. This idea violates the plain meaning of the term 'consent' as a conscious and rational process.

Democratic philosophers, including Locke, are not guiltless of employing such desperate measures as the above, despite the fact that they are quite gratuitous and are contrary to the genius of the Enlightenment. Locke himself offered an acceptable explanation which permits the assumption that an individual's consent means conscious and willing acceptance on grounds that commend themselves to his present reason.

> For that which acts any community, being only the consent of the individuals of it, and it being one body, must move one way, it is necessary the body should move that way whither the greater force carries it, which is the consent of the majority, or else it is impossible it should act or continue one body, one community, which the consent of every individual that united into it agreed that it should; and so every one is bound by that consent to be concluded by the majority. And therefore we see that in assemblies empowered to act by positive laws where no number is set by that positive law which empowers them, the act of the majority passes for the act of the whole, and of course determines as having, by the law of Nature and reason, the power of the whole.[29]

In other words, the state, if it is to be a state, must act as a whole, and must reach a decision within a finite time, which is greater or less according to the urgency of the question. This all individuals can see as clearly as they can see the purpose of the state. The decision to abide by the vote of the majority provides a way out of what would otherwise be an impasse. Hence it is agreed by all to delegate to the majority obtained by constitutional processes the full powers of the state. Other devices, such as proportional representation, the unanimous vote of the jury, and the two-thirds vote required for overriding an executive veto, are alternative devices suited to the nature of the situation; and their use in democracies is evidence of the fact that the decision of the majority is not an absolute principle but a political instrument.

The principle of unanimity means that all of the people deliberately and for good reason assent to a framework of government under which particular policies may be adopted and enforced without the assent, or even despite the dissent, of some of their number. The fundamental agreement is that there should be a state at all, with power of coercion over its members. This agreement is not a mere inheritance from the past, but is perpetually renewed in each individual's mind when he sees for himself that it is right and reasonable for the common good that there should be a state. Beyond this he assents to the constitution of the particular state under which he lives, with its specific provisions for discretionary power, and with the unpredictable restrictions which it will place upon his momentary will. When his institutions cost him some sacrifice, he is supposed to accept that sacrifice cheerfully, as when a man pays his taxes seeing that there must be some system of taxation and finding that his own share is just. Like Socrates at the time of his execution, he suffers the penalty willingly because his own reason endorses the broad plan of which the penalty is a specific application.

Political democracy employs devices by which the departure from full and immediate unanimity is mitigated. Officials are selected for their expert capacity to anticipate or supplement the rational judgment of their electorate. Power is delegated within certain broad limits of policy, elected officials being called upon to declare their intentions, or parties their platforms, in advance. Power is delegated for limited times, and may be withdrawn if its exercise is disapproved. The party in power is subjected to scrutiny, and an opposition gathers ammunition and becomes a focus of dissent against the day when the people will again express their judgment. He who belongs to a dissenting minority today may cherish a hope of belonging to the triumphant majority of tomorrow. In this respect majorities differ profoundly from fixed classes. They are temporary and revolving, and represent no continuous repression of one social group by another.

It is true that a large part of unanimity takes the form of passive acquiescence. It has been pointed out with reason that only a small portion of the population is continuously interested in politics.[30] But such acquiescence is still consent if it is made with a conscious recognition of its consequences. The non-voter wittingly places power in the hands of the voter, and the latter becomes the agent of the former in the same broad sense in which the official in the exercise of his discretion is the agent of his constituency.

All of these and similar aspects of political procedure in a democracy only serve to emphasize the principle of unanimity as a norm. The ideal polity would be that in which the government always adopted the right measure relatively to the good of the people, and in which the people, knowing this and understanding it, gave it their approval as well as their obedience. Such situations may exist momentarily in limited groups, such, for example, as the family, or a private social organization. They do not and cannot exist in a large and complex modern state. But while the principle of unanimity is grossly inadequate as a description of political facts, and while this inadequacy justifies a realistic school of political science, the principle loses none of its importance as a governing idea and a standard of criticism.

8

Political democracy rests on the principle of unanimity, accompanied, however, by the assumption that this unanimity is a rational unanimity: that is, a unanimity like that of fellow scientists, who reach the same truth because of common access to the evidence on which that truth is based. It is proper to greet with derision President Garfield's eloquent portrayal of the "four millions of Republican firesides" where the destiny of the Republic is decreed by "thoughtful voters, with wives and children about them, with the calm thoughts inspired by love of home and country, with the history of the past, the hopes of the future, and knowledge of the great men who have adorned and blessed our nation in days gone by." [31] Again, however, it is not a question of what actually occurs, but of what, in the maximum degree consistent with human limitations, *should* occur.

Although the forces of unreason have been more clearly recognized in modern times, and their use more methodically cultivated, they are as old as political society itself, and the founders of American democracy were aware of their danger. Fear of the irrational unanimity that may be created by the arts of deceptive propaganda was in men's minds at the time of the adoption of the Federal Constitution. "Power is generally taken from the people," said William Goudy in 1788, "by imposing on their understanding, or by fetters." [32] American critics of extreme democracy, such as Francis Lieber, have used this danger as ground for rejecting the doctrines of the Declaration:

> The true and stanch republican . . . wants no divine right of the people, for he knows very well that it means nothing but despotic power of insinuating leaders. He wants the real rule of the people, that is the institutionally organized country, which distinguishes it from the mere mob. For mob is an unorganic multitude, with a general impulse of action. Woe to the country in which political hypocrisy first calls the people almighty, then teaches that the voice of the people is divine, then pretends to take clamor for the true voice of the people, and lastly gets up the desired clamor. The consequences are fearful and invariably unfitting for liberty.[33]

Lieber's appeal from the people to "the institutionally organized country" pointed to a repudiation of democracy altogether; but his objection to identifying the "true voice of the people" with mere "clamor" may equally well be considered as a warning against the abuses of democracy, and as a clarification of its deeper meaning. For nothing was further from the intent of Locke or of the founding fathers than a justification of clamor, however unanimous. By unanimity they meant an agreement of *minds*, which conducted themselves *as* minds; minds which thought and did not merely feel, and which thought for themselves instead of echoing other minds.

It is clear that democracy, insofar as it is founded on the general premises of the Enlightenment, requires that popular judgment shall be formed freely, thoughtfully, and intelligently—or as freely, thoughtfully, and intelligently as possible. In other words, it is not enough that there should be agreement between the government and public opinion; democracy is concerned with the processes by which opinion is formed. A manufactured public opinion is only a technique by which arbitrary authority becomes self-perpetuating. Popular support is then a mere echo of tyranny. It is achieved by preventing or destroying those very qualities of judgment on which democracy depends: freedom, by intimidation and bribery; thoughtfulness, by hysteria; intelligence, by censorship.

All of these operations were, for example, systematically employed and artfully refined in the creation of the Fascist dictatorship of Italy. Intimidation took the form of unofficial violence perpetrated by 'Black Shirts,' or of transportation to 'the islands' by the public authorities. Igniting hysteria and feeding its flames is an art which has long been known to Italians. This will be understood by anyone who has witnessed a quarrel in Italy—not a fracas speedily culminating in bodily injury, but a prolonged duel in which the weapons are rhetoric and eloquence skillfully designed to lacerate the feelings and to raise the emotional temperature step by step from cold malice to boiling rage, and then from boiling rage to limitless and immeasurable temperatures beyond. This process is called *montatura*—which means arousing men to fury.

Education in Fascist Italy was designed not to inform the mind and set it free in order that it might judge for itself, but to form the mind from early years after the pattern required by the state. It employed censorship as a preventive medicine, and patriotism as a sedative or a stimulant. In a speech which he made in 1921, and in which he was discussing his "conception of the state and of the art of governing the nation," Mussolini used the words: "Accept in the spirit of patriotism, or submit." [34] The younger Fascisti were said to have acquired "a veritable passion for obedience." [35]

The same arts are practiced in Nazi Germany, with differences reflecting the peculiarities of the Germanic mind: greater moral fanaticism, more metaphysics, more credulity, and a more sincere self-deception on the part of the leaders themselves. But the instruments are the same—intimidation, hysteria, censorship, and indoctrination; and they are used to induce a like-mindedness spread over the surface rather than an agreement rooted in individual observation and thought, and reflecting the sameness of fact or logic.

The condemnation of Hitler is sometimes qualified by the observation that, after all, he 'unified' Germany. But there is no virtue in unity as such. A lynching party is unified. There is unity in death, in silence, in the sameness of mind achieved by repression or by intoxication. The only kind of unity that can be said to be a praiseworthy human achievement is a unity that harbors differences and renders them benign. The supreme test of any society is its power to thrive on spontaneity and dissent. A society which achieves unity by force or by hysteria may be excused or pitied, but there is no reason why it should be admired. It is a society in extremis, compelled to resort to desperate measures.

The deliberate use of force and hysteria to create unanimity of popular support is irreconcilable with the fundamental premise of democracy, which puts its trust in enlightenment and the saving power of truth. It does not follow, however, that a democratic political philosophy shall reduce political processes altogether to the conscious ratiocination of independent minds. Reason is the court of last appeal, but it does not follow that this court is, or should be, in continuous session, that every question should be submitted to its judgment, or that its decisions should be subjected to perpetual revision. That human minds are governed by unconscious forces, and grooved by prejudice, is an incontrovertible fact. This fact qualifies the mind's political activities, as it qualifies the mind's religious, economic, or even scientific activities. Men do not live by their critical faculties, but these serve to refresh a more stable body of unreflective belief and sentiment. A political philosophy which denies the irrationality of the human mind is doctrinaire and vulnerable; an enlightened democratic philosophy will recognize irrationality as both inescapable and indispensable.

If the individual's personal life is to be coherent, it must persevere in a certain direction. If its premises are perpetually re-examined, it can possess no internal consistency; if its destination is perpetually altered, it will neither reach nor even approximate a goal. A personal life is a complex system of activities enduring through a period of time, and it can have no unity unless crucial decisions once made are adhered to with tenacity. A mind which is constantly remaking itself is, for practical purposes, no mind at all. What is true of the personal life is true a fortiori of the organized life of the social group, which is both longer in its time-span and wider in its complexity. The individual is committed not only to himself but to others. At any given time the life of society consists mainly of unfinished business and undischarged obligations. Continuity and inertia are therefore as important as reform. Acting in their social or public capacity, individuals must move more slowly than in their strictly private capacity.

Considered in this light, those forces of human nature which make for conservatism appear benign. The force of tradition is not intrinsically rational, but it may be endorsed by reason as giving direction to the stream of history. Custom, though in itself it implies the slumber of the critical faculties, becomes their instrument when it is seen to provide the social structure with a necessary factor of rigidity; just as the individual person may deliberately form habits as the means of firm adherence to a purpose thoughtfully adopted. In both cases inertia is the indispensable adjunct of conscious attention, which, having a narrowly limited radius, requires some guarantee that the areas from which it is withdrawn will remain faithful in its absence. Prejudice, though it is blind to new evidence, is loyal to its own presuppositions, and gives them an experimental demonstration. Even the selfishness of vested interest may be endorsed by benevolence, as providing existing goods with an automatic and unfailing defense against ruthless innovation.

The irrational sources of conservative unanimity may thus be, like the forces of physical nature, appropriated by reason and put to its uses; provided always that certain other irrational forces which make for change are also allowed to operate. The momentary passion of the crowd, the hypnotic spell of the leader, the belligerency of the rebellious individual or faction, the vanity of the innovator—these are all forces which make for change and dissent. None has in itself any evidential validity, but they serve to open closed minds and gain a hearing for new truths; and they give the innovator heart to resist the prevailing view. They serve, in short, to balance the irrational forces of conservatism, and may receive the endorsement of reason when so used.

In short, institutions are neither right nor wrong merely because they are old or new, and the forces of stability and change enjoy no valid claims in and for themselves. The political philosophy which accepts the established system as its major premise is as false as that which proclaims revolution for its own sake. If the old is good, it should be preserved; if the new is better, then it should supersede the old. If there is doubt of the matter, the driver should make haste slowly, using both brake and accelerator, but under the guidance of his steering gear and his map.

9

The basic principle of political democracy is government by consent, and this implies the conscious and reflective agreement of all of those who live under government. There remains the question of what such unanimity means, and how it may be brought to pass.

The agreement which is here in question is a *moral* agreement, which implies not only a sameness of judgments as to what is right and good, but a community of wills in which diverse individuals are governed by the same purpose. Moral agreement has its intellectual and its motor-affective components.

Intellectual agreement in moral matters presents no peculiar difficulties other than those of complexity. Unanimity is theoretically implied in the very nature of judgment itself. Two persons framing judgments about the same matter ought to agree, and will agree in proportion as they are enlightened. A judgment is not fully constituted until its meaning is determined, and its meaning prescribes the evidence which it requires for its support. If two judgments are the same in their meanings, they will appeal to the same evidence, and two judgments conformed to the same evidence will conform to one another. Agreement among scientists is implied in there being any science at all. So long as there is disagreement there is either ambiguity and misunderstanding as to what is meant, or an incorrectness of observation or reasoning, or an incompleteness of evidence—all of which are intellectual limitations removable by advancing enlightenment. This is as true of judgments of right and good as it is of any other judgments.

Agreement is implied in the nature of intellectual judgment, since the intent of intellectual judgment is to conform to the same order of objectivity. This cannot be said of wills. Two individuals *may* will the same object, but there is nothing in the nature of will as such which implies such sameness. It is quite consistent with the nature of wills that they should be in conflict one with another. If one individual judges that peace exists and another judges that war exists, the conflict tends to be removed by appeal to the same facts. But if one individual wills peace and a second wills war, there is nothing in the nature of these two wills themselves that implies a resolution of the conflict. Agreement between a pacific and a bellicose will is not inherent in the nature of either of those wills, but requires the introduction of a new will, or moral will, which embraces and supersedes them both. Such a will is implied in the meaning of 'good' when that term is construed in terms of 'general happiness' or public interest.

Such a moral will is essential not only to the meaning of good but to its practical realization. The moral unanimity underlying political institutions comprises not only a common concept but a common motivation. The members of a political society must not only agree concerning what is good, but must love, desire, and seek the same good. In forming the moral will, individuals at one and the same time demonstrate what good means and become its partisans and the agents of its realization.

The supposition that the moral will is implied in all wills, and that agreement of wills, like agreement of judgments, therefore requires nothing more than enlightenment, is usually based on two fallacious doctrines: the doctrine that all wills are motivated by self-interest; and the doctrine that all genuine self-interest is socially harmonious. In the eighteenth century both of these doctrines were too readily assumed.

Since the time of Bishop Joseph Butler it has been generally recognized, at least among philosophers, that self-interest in the sense of reflexive or centripetal interest—proceeding from and toward the same individual—is a secondary and derived rather than a primitive and universal form of interest. Let it be granted, also, that human nature embraces, either at birth or by early unconscious conditioning, *some* impulses and affectations which require for their satisfaction the good of child or neighbor. There is, even so, no reason whatever to suppose that these springs of action are so distributed among all men, and so nicely balanced against selfish appetites, that each man will find his own maximum happiness in the maximum happiness of every other man. The central fact of the moral situation is the fact that the actual desires of men are in some measure incompatible; and that the enlightened pursuit of these desires, instead of removing this incompatibility, often reveals it more clearly.

The man whom the state is obliged to restrain is not the unenlightened man. On the contrary, the monsters of ambition or avarice are often peculiarly enlightened. Refusing to be blinded by any code or sentiment, they see, only too clearly, that their maximum attainment of power or wealth requires the defeat of a similar ambition or avarice on the part of others. No one would say that Hitler, for example, has been unenlightened in his pursuit of power. He has wittingly deprived others of that which he has coveted for himself; and he has known how to deceive and disarm his competitors, as well as how to overcome them. The path of the enlightened egoist is strewn with slain adversaries and thronged with multitudes whose ignorance or suggestibility has led them to an unsuspecting acquiescence. The collision between egoists is not avoided or mitigated by enlightenment unless they become partners in egoism, which only aggravates their collision with other similar rival partnerships and with the defenseless mass. Such collisions are not mysterious, but the natural effect of the forces at play.

If the enlightened self-interest of one man collides with the enlightened self-interest of another, it follows that one or both will collide with enlightened public interest. It is impossible that two paths which do not coincide with one another should coincide with a third path.

But what, then, can be meant by 'public interest'? One thing only is certain: namely, that it cannot mean the aggregate of all actual interests of all actual individuals. These do not add up to a single interest, taken as they stand. There is no conceivable policy which could effectively promote such an aggregate of interests, because what any policy gave to one it would, sooner or later or in some degree, take away from another. To formulate such a policy would be like arranging a plan which would enable trains starting at the same hour from opposite points on the same track to reach their destinations. Just as in such circumstances no plan is effective which does not re-route the trains or alter their schedules, so no public policy is conceivable which does not alter the course of particular interests. How shall such a transformation be brought about in keeping with the obligation to *all* interests? Here is the crux of the moral problem, and the crux of the political problem for all philosophies which conceive politics in moral terms.

The solution is to be found by looking to the analogy between the person and society. Personal self-interest itself is confronted with the problem of 'doing justice' to all of the individual's more or less conflicting interests. The solution is found in the process of reflection in which all of the individual's interests participate. Although the eventual decision may not satisfy any of the interests—ambition, avarice, hunger, or love—in the sense of giving to it all that it would require for its own maximum satisfaction, it may nevertheless be said to represent them all in the sense that they have all gone into the choosing will which prevails. The interest of this choosing will is a 'personal' interest, as distinguished from a merely appetitive interest; it meets the claims of each so far as is consistent with a like acknowledgment of others; and it constitutes a single interest in the sense that it permits of the framing of an organized procedure by which it can be best promoted.

When we turn to society, we are confronted with the imperfection of the analogy. Unhappily for those who speak of a 'collective' or social will, there is, strictly speaking, no such thing. A system of persons does not possess a will of its own. The solution must be sought in the socializing of personal wills.

The citizen is, as we have seen, both disinterested and interested, both impartial and partial. He is a judge of public good and at the same time the exponent of his own private stake in that good. As disinterested, he uses his faculties of sympathy and imagination to understand the interests of others; and adopting these represented interests together with his own, he then proceeds precisely as in enlightened self-interest. The choosing will which emerges, and which by limitation, rearrangement, and subordination transforms conflict into harmony, is a will in which all interests are taken account of and disarmed. The chooser, thus qualified, is more than a person; he is a statesmanlike or moral person. His reconstituted will expresses the interest of enlightened benevolence.

He may well be suspected of allowing his own private interests to prevail over the represented interests of others. This bias, however, is offset by the similar bias of others. Each individual feels a different perspective in the field of interests, but these perspectives correct one another and are unified in the benevolent will, as the different perspectives of perception are united in thought. This procedure is exemplified when two well-disposed persons attempt to come to a 'fair' arrangement which is 'agreeable' to both. It is exhibited in all of the social arts; in ethics primarily, but likewise in politics and economics. Conflict is removed or mitigated by a division of the goods over whose possession and consumption the dispute arises; by the alternating use of the same good; by compromise; by the elimination or suppression of utterly irreconcilable interests; or by the increase of the total aggregate of goods through co-operative enterprise.

The public interest, then, is the will, not of the collectivity as such, but of each and every individual person when these are in agreement in willing the good of all. The individual has in the course of giving and taking, living and letting live, asserting and conceding, acquired a new will for which he will still employ the first personal pronoun, but which he may now express in the plural, and not merely in the singular number. He may use the word 'we,' not in an editorial or a regal sense, but with confidence that he speaks for others as well as for himself.

This conception of the representative or benevolent will, seated in each person and taking account of all persons, not only provides the moral authority of government and of other social institutions but creates the norm by which such authority is to be judged—the democratic norm, or norm of liberality. Any regime may be condemned if it fails to take account of all interests, or abridges any interest beyond the requirements of social order. The neglect or arbitrary abridgment of interests may take any one of several forms, all of which are exemplified by the so-called totalitarian regimes of the present era. A regime is illiberal or undemocratic insofar as it disregards the interests of other societies, by aggression, conquest, plunder, enslavement; when it exploits any class or group, whether large or small, whether economic, racial, or religious, among its own people; or when it blinds those who live under it to their own personal interests by creating obsessions rather than by inducing reflection.

10

There is a widely prevalent opinion that political democracy, however admirable in theory, has proved a failure in practice. In assessing this opinion it must first be noted that all human institutions leave room for improvement. There is what may be called a constant of failure, arising out of the complexity of the problem, the weaknesses of mankind, and the weight of the obstacles to be overcome. Marriage is a failure, agriculture and industry are failures, religion is a failure, education is a failure. Government, being peculiarly difficult, is perhaps the greatest failure of all. It would be equally true to say of any of these human institutions that it is a remarkable achievement. It all depends upon the level of expectation; and if it be legitimate to remark how badly it is done, it is equally legitimate to wonder that it should be done at all. But from time to time some particular institution becomes the symbol of human shortcoming, and has to bear the brunt of criticism.

In fairness, then, the constant of human failure should be subtracted from the specific bill of indictment brought against democracy. Besides this normal degree of failure, there is also an abnormal degree of failure peculiar to the times. It seems safe to predict that when the curve of human fortunes is charted by the historians of the future, it will show a pronounced dip between 1914 and some year later than 1944. Here again there is a disposition to charge the entire loss to some single institution, such as democracy, on which attention happens at the moment to be focused. But democracy was not responsible for the two World Wars, the Great Depression, international rivalries and quarrels, the maldistribution of raw materials, technological unemployment, the increase of divorce, or the decline of religion. The fact is that with few exceptions everything has worked badly since 1914; and it is just as natural and unreasonable to hold a particular political institution responsible for this as it is to charge every evil against the political party that happens to be in power.

It is to be noted, in the second place, that the charge of failure is brought, not against social democracy, but against political democracy. The proponents of political democracy believe that the desirable social result which the state should promote is an individualistic, free, and, in some sense, equalitarian society. It cannot be this which has failed, for this is the standard by which, in a democratic philosophy, failure is to be judged. To say that it has failed would be like saying that justice, goodness, perfection, happiness, or truth has failed.

The fact is that critics of democracy have not, as a rule, distinguished between democracy as a political means and democracy as a social end.

In the absence of any definite goal which shall serve as a standard of judgment, the charge of failure can only mean that political democracies have failed to preserve themselves, or to promote efficiency in the recognized public services, or to provide that minimum of security and order which conditions *any* form of the good life, including social democracy. Is this charge well founded? Or, if it be conceded that mankind has recently suffered from insecurity and disorder, is this the fault of political democracy?

There is at least that degree of reasonable doubt which is supposed to justify acquittal. Writing in 1929 of the First World War, Professor G. G. Benjamin put the question, "What then do the source materials, the memoirs, and monographs produced since the armistice prove?" The third of the five summary conclusions which he drew was that "the failure of Germany was the failure of absolute power." He then goes on to quote the following from an editorial of the *Manchester Guardian*:

> Speaking at Oxford, the Dean of St. Paul's said that he did not "think we should ever wish for a Mussolini in England, but there is a good deal to be said for that type of government." If we examine the reality that exists beneath all the many dictatorships of modern Europe, there is also much to be said *against* "that type of government." It was Bismarck who once declared that any fool can govern by martial law. All dictatorships govern by martial or semi-martial law. . . . There is not a dictatorship in Europe that does not rule by black-and-tannery. It is a mistake to suppose that a dictatorship brings the able to the top. The exact opposite is true—it eliminates the courageous, the critical, the intelligent. . . .
>
> It is commonly supposed that democracy is a form of mob rule and a dictatorship is the rule of the élite. Again the opposite is true. A dictatorship is organized mob rule through organized lynch law. All great dictators have been great demagogues. The Dean of St. Paul's declares that democracies are ruled by catch-phrases. No premier in any European democracy has so many catch-phrases as Mussolini or Pilsudski and calls forth popular applause so blind and hysterical. It is a mistake to suppose that dictatorships are necessarily unpopular. . . . When they appeal to the emotions of the mob it is nearly always to the bad emotions. . . . Dictatorships thrive only in a war-like atmosphere, and if their foreign policies are peaceful it is only because they are not strong enough to fight.[36]

No one who reads the history of Europe during the years immediately preceding 1914 can fail to be impressed by the political defects of the three great military monarchies: Germany, Russia, Austria. It is to be observed, furthermore, that these three governments were swept away by the war, and that at least three of the nations which emerged victorious—England, France, and the United States—were political democracies. In 1944 it appears that after an even more deadly struggle the democracies are again destined to triumph. Mussolini has already fallen, Hitler and Japanese militarism are facing defeat. Soviet Russia has gathered strength from a growth of liberality and industrial freedom. It is true that democratic France has suffered disaster, but its reviving hopes are oriented toward a better democracy rather than toward dictatorship on the Vichy model. It now seems probable that the new dictatorships, to which many renegades turned for political salvation, will prove in the broader perspective of history to have been ephemeral and morbid symptoms of decay, resulting from the shock of the First World War and from the economic and moral prostration by which it was succeeded.

When the charge of failure is examined more closely, it appears that what is supposed to have failed is not political democracy in general, but only parliamentary government of a specific kind. Political democracy has a good many tricks in its bag. There is, for example, representative government in the old-fashioned sense intended by the framers of the Federal Constitution. There are alternative electoral and party methods, alternative forms of the legislative body, and of its relation to the executive. There is no reason to believe that the political inventiveness of democracy is exhausted. The failures of political democracy, even if they be granted, would suggest not that democracy in general be abandoned, but that in respect of certain specific mechanisms it be varied and improved.

It is true that even in democratic countries there has been a trend toward centralized and authoritarian rule, but in times of stress or calamity political procedures must be temporarily altered. There is nothing new in this. It happens in every country in the event of war, in every community in case of flood or earthquake, in every family in case of accident or illness, in every individual in moments of crisis. There is a temporary stripping for action and a massing of energies where the danger threatens, with sacrifice, abridgment, paralysis elsewhere.

There are, in other words, peculiar modes of organization and control which are required for emergencies. But it would be a grave mistake to define the principles of polity by such requirements. An emergency is by definition something out of the ordinary, requiring extraordinary measures. The use of these measures is to preserve life until the better life can be resumed. When one's leg is broken, one puts it in a plaster cast, but one does not therefore conclude that freely moving limbs are a failure and should be permanently abolished. The ultimate purpose of rigidity is to restore mobility.

Suppose a group of settlers to be trekking west in a covered wagon. Although they have a definite goal, they are compelled, on their way, to meet emergencies. They are overtaken by storms, attacked by Indians, threatened by hunger and drought, impeded by rivers, mountains, heat, and cold. Each crisis has to be met on its own terms. It dictates the weapons which shall be used, and forces the travelers to do things which are not in the direct line of their project. They may be compelled to halt, to make a wide detour, or even to retrace their steps. They may be compelled to burn their supplies for fuel, or slaughter their draft animals for food, or abandon their tools to lighten their baggage. For the moment they are not behaving in a manner that at all suggests the settlement of a new country. But that is their goal, nonetheless; and if they are wise they will cling to their map, their instruments of observation, and the directions for their route, in order that their journey may be resumed when the crisis is over.

What a political society does in time of emergency is not, therefore, a safe indication of its basic principles. It may be necessary, in order to obtain that minimum of security and order which must be had at any price, that the processes of political democracy should be suspended altogether, as a sailing vessel in heavy weather may proceed under power or be towed to port. Such a suspension is a misfortune, a lesser of two evils, a remedy to be discontinued with the return of more favorable weather. Or, as ships may reef their sails, or heave to and ride out the storm, so a political democracy may in times of crisis find the necessary readjustments within its own constitution.

Recent political changes in America are interesting, because they are not revolutionary. Two experiments are being carried on simultaneously.

One is the attempt to modify the capitalistic economy so that it may *save itself* from shipwreck. The other is the attempt to introduce into democracy such flexibility as will enable it to meet the most severe tests without rejecting its own essential principles. As the first is a more constructive economic experiment than communism, so the second is a more constructive experiment than dictatorship. It is a continuing attempt to answer Lincoln's question: "Must a government, of necessity, be too strong for the liberties of its own people, or too weak to maintain its own existence?" [37]

Popular judgment always gives some rope to the government of its choice. It is only a question of how long the rope shall be. A democratic government must be flexible enough to permit of the rope's being lengthened or shortened as the situation changes. Sometimes it is desirable for popular opinion to drive with taut reins, and sometimes with loose. In a crisis it may be well to give the official horse his head. Provided there is no concealment of facts, suppression of opposition, or deliberate confusion of the public mind, this does not imply that the driver has abandoned either his control or his guidance; he is merely adopting the method most likely to bring him to his destination.

The rejection of political democracy as a practical failure implies a willingness to accept some alternative. The alternatives to political democracy have been tried, and it was because they had been tried unsuccessfully that political evolution up to 1914 moved in the direction of democracy. Jefferson remarked in his First Inaugural Address: "Sometimes it is said that man cannot be trusted with the government of himself. Can he, then, be trusted with the government of others? Or have we found angels in the form of kings to govern him? Let history answer this question." [38]

Those whose thoughts turn from democracy to dictatorship forget that dictatorship consists to a large extent of the evils of democracy without its merits. Democracy is charged with corruption. But if by corruption is meant the use of political power for personal profit, then the modern dictatorship in the privileges enjoyed by party members exhibits corruption on the grand scale—corruption monopolized, with no check or corrective. If a critic of democracy were asked to name its most intolerable abuse, he would no doubt name the rule of the demagogue, that "dangerous disease" which Hobbes described as the "Popularity of a potent Subject." [39] But, as Plato pointed out many years ago, the tyrant is essentially the Big Demagogue, who is so artful and unscrupulous in his demagoguery that he drives out all the little demagogues and monopolizes the business of demagoguery for himself.

There is no commoner form of sentimentalism than that with which one colors those forms of government under which one is not obliged to live. Those who preach revolution should saturate their minds with the bloody and brutal details of actual revolutions, and with their debasing effects both upon those who are crushed and upon those who crush them. Similarly, those who preach dictatorship should imagine themselves subjected to peremptory commands in matters with which they are deeply concerned, and on which they feel most competent to judge for themselves. They should imagine themselves compelled to become the tools of men whom they deem ignorant and vicious.

The man who longs for a dictatorship usually dreams that he is the dictator, or at any rate that he is the dictator's best friend and most trusted counselor. He thinks of dictatorship as a means of getting done, promptly and thoroughly, what he believes ought to be done. The fact is that for most people most of the time dictatorship consists not in dictating, but in being dictated *to*; not in getting done what one thinks ought to be done, but in being compelled to submit helplessly to what one thinks ought *not* to be done. It is a great thing, no doubt, to be a dictator, but a dictatorship is that form of government under which there is the least chance of dictating. Power is rigidly restricted to a narrow circle, while the vast majority of persons do not even enjoy the satisfaction of complaint, or the prospect, however distant, of enjoying power in their turn.

It is true that the period between the two World Wars was marked by the spectacular multiplication of dictatorships. But instead of weakening the allegiance of the adherents of democracy, this spectacle should rather confirm their faith by presenting the alternatives in their grim reality. They have been witnesses of the ineffectual invocations and obscene rites of the prophets of Baal.

CHAPTER EIGHTEEN

LIBERTY AND THE LIMITS OF GOVERNMENT[1]

1

SUCH EXPRESSIONS as the 'four freedoms,' the 'civil liberties,' and the 'free world' illustrate the extent to which freedom or liberty has come for contemporary minds to signify the essence of democracy. To clarify this topic it is necessary to begin with the distinction between the metaphysical question of 'freedom of the will' and the narrower political question of 'liberty.' To fix this distinction one cannot, unhappily, rely on the terms 'freedom' and 'liberty,' since they are used interchangeably. Advocates of freedom of the will are often called 'libertarians'; and the advocates of political liberty will often invoke the even richer emotional suggestions of the term 'freedom.' The "sweet land of liberty" is a land in which (perhaps owing to the exigencies of versification) the people exclaim, "Let freedom ring!"

The question of 'freedom of the will' is the metaphysical question concerning the causes of human conduct. In terms of this problem it means nothing to ask whether men should or should not be free. It means nothing to ask whether bodies should or should not be governed by the force of gravitation; the only possible difference of opinion is between those who affirm and those who deny that this force actually operates. Similarly, as respects the determination of human conduct there is a difference of opinion as to whether the will is or is not 'free.' It is a question of the unchangeable constitution of man, which sets the limits and prescribes the conditions to which polity and policy must conform.

The meaning of 'freedom' in this metaphysical and pre-political sense is best set forth in terms of a series of antitheses. The first of these is the antithesis between determinism and indeterminism. Given an act of will, the question arises whether it has a cause beyond itself by which its occurrence is inevitable and predictable. The antithesis arises because of the rivalry of the scientific desire to find an explanation of every event, so that it may be anticipated or brought to pass, and the moral desire to fix ultimate responsibility upon the agent, so that he may be praised or blamed. In this antithesis freedom means *indeterminism*: that is, strictly construed, the absence of causality. Indeterminists, ancient and modern, who have adhered to this idea have seen that it means the same thing as chance; or, if not chance, then pure and immediate spontaneity. The defect of the idea, over and above its frustration of the scientific impulse, lies in the fact that it does not even satisfy the moral motive from which it springs. For responsibility implies a man behind the act of will—a continuing person who can be held responsible, and is susceptible to punitive, educational, or other causal influences.

The question of the freedom of the will is sometimes held to turn not on the presence or absence of determination, but on the *kind* of determination. The alleged universality of mechanical causation implies that while human acts appear to be governed by interest, and to be capable, therefore, of being controlled by the excitation of feeling, they are in fact governed wholly by the physico-chemical forces which operate in the body, and in particular by its neuro-muscular mechanisms and their external stimuli. The partisan of freedom here holds that men do in fact act because of conscious motives; that, in other words, what men do results from what they desire to do.

Among moralists, however, it has been customary to define the issue upon a higher level of mental development. Desire is conceived as a form of natural causation, and freedom enters on the scene only when desire is negated or controlled by the faculties of reason and will. A man is said to lack freedom owing to the very power of the appetites which 'enslave' him. Appetitive determination, to use Kant's expressions, is a species of "heteronomy" as opposed to that "autonomy" under which a man does not what he merely likes, but what he judges to be right, for reasons that commend themselves to his intellectual faculties.

There remains one further doctrine of the will's freedom. The second and third doctrines affirm the claims of higher phases of biological evolution against lower—of interest against mechanism, of will against appetite. The fourth doctrine rests upon the antithesis between the human will and some still higher or more comprehensive will. This is the issue of freedom which arises from extreme claims for the sovereignty of God, or from the modern vogue of historical determinism and metaphysical monism.

With the question at issue between determinism and indeterminism, democracy is not concerned. Consideration being limited to the three remaining antitheses, democracy presupposes the determination of conduct by conscious interest as against the exclusive efficacy of physico-chemical causes; by reflective choice, as against the exclusive efficacy of appetite; and by human individuals, as against the exclusive efficacy of more exalted beings. Democracy presupposses that within some area, however small, men act as they desire or choose, and so act in their individual capacity. One can then expect to influence human history by implanting or exciting an individual's interests, and by communicating to his intellectual faculties facts, ideas, inferences, and evidence.

The idea of 'liberty,' in the political sense of the term, turns upon certain further considerations. The idea of freedom of the will imputes to man certain capacities. The idea of political liberty, on the other hand, stresses the fact that this capacity exists in different degrees, that it may be more or less developed, and that circumstances will more or less facilitate or impede it. In the second place, the idea of political liberty raises the question of value. The libertarian here contends that it is good to be free, and to be more free rather than less free. Thirdly, the idea of liberty derives its meaning from the social context. The social, as well as the physical, environment sets limits to freedom; and social organization provides a method of control by which these limits can be contracted or expanded. Libertarianism is the maxim that society should be so organized as to enable individuals to enjoy in a high degree their capacity to act as they desire or choose. Applied to nations, it is the maxim that international relations should be so arranged as to promote this capacity both in nations and in their individual members.

2

Every freedom or liberty has its negative and its positive sides. There is a liberty 'from,' and there is a liberty 'to' and 'for.' Negative liberty signifies the absence of interference, human or otherwise; positive liberty signifies the control by an interested individual of the means by which his interests may be effective.

One does not speak of liberty at all unless there is a disposition to perform an act. Given such a disposition, negative liberty is relative to some obstacle external to that disposition. The most rudimentary obstacle is the restraint of bodily movements by superior force, as when the child is held in the grasp of an adult, or when some barrier, such as prison bars, is interposed. With such an obstacle in mind, negative liberty means merely its absence, and the promotion of liberty means merely its removal.

In the more highly developed human relationships, the obstacle takes the form of penalty. What the individual desires to do is not rendered impossible by the application of superior physical force, but is associated with a more strongly repugnant sequel. A motorist, for example, is not at liberty to park his car within ten feet of a fire plug. This does not mean that the forbidden area is fenced off, or that the traffic policeman exerts upon the car from without a force greater than that of its engine, but that if the motorist parks his car in the forbidden area, he will be fined or imprisoned. Physically speaking, he is at liberty to park there if he likes, but if he does he is deprived of the liberty to retain possession of ten dollars or to sleep at home; and these other liberties he prizes above the first.

It has been affirmed that in England every man has a right to say what he thinks, and that the state has a right to punish him. Insofar, however, as thought is penalized, the negative liberty to speak as one likes is destroyed. There is no forcible gagging, but the individual is presented with the alternative of either remaining silent or suffering some more intolerable frustration. 'Your money or your life' destroys for most men the liberty to keep their money, though they have not yet been forcibly deprived of it. While the code of criminal law appeals to certain universal and standard fears, it is important to note that all fears have the same restrictive effect. The fear of offending the sentiment of the community is often stronger than fear of the legal penalty, as when a man would rather pay a fine than suffer public disgrace.

Negative liberties are associated with human experiences of interference, struggle, and overcoming or escape. Their meaning is made up of the familiar and menacing infringements—such as the barriers of mountain, river, or sea interposed by the natural environment, the retaliation of human rivals, the dominance of the strong, and the penalties imposed by church or state or public opinion.

Restraints upon liberty imply a felt interest. In an age of religious zeal negative liberty will mean liberty from an oppressive church; when men aspire to the management of their own affairs, they will covet liberty from a tyrannical state; when they desire to rise from a low level in the economic scale, negative liberty will mean escape from the controls of an industrial hierarchy; when they already enjoy economic wealth and power, negative liberty will mean the non-interference of government. To writers, liberty means relief from censorship; to drinkers, repeal of prohibition; to pacifists, the absence of compulsory military service; to agitators and doctrinal minorities, unrestricted speech and assembly.

The idea of negative liberty will vary not only with the interest, but also with its intensity. The idea of negative liberty plays a small role in the lives of apathetic men, and will take a high place in the codes of men whose desires and ambitions are strong, and who feel the obstacle with a proportional intensity—as the heat generated by impact upon a resisting body is proportional to the projectile's velocity and mass. This is why the demand for liberty is peculiarly strong in a nation, class, or individual which is already conscious of its power, and whose interests have gathered momentum.

But liberty 'from' is not liberty unless there is at the same time a liberty 'to' or 'for,' unless there is capacity as well as a mere absence of external restraints. A man is not at liberty to walk unless he has sound limbs, or to travel unless he has the fare; it signifies little that no barrier prevents, or no authority forbids. Liberty from prison bars is not enjoyed except by an individual who is capable of moving his body; the absence of censorship, persecution, or tyranny is not liberty except to those who possess the resources for artistic creation, for worship, or for self-government.

The extreme case and the crucial test is provided by liberty of thought. The Stoics proclaimed the doctrine that no man can be deprived of this liberty by external force: his negative liberty of thought is unassailable. As Spinoza expressed it, a man is "the master of his own thoughts." [2] He may be cast into prison or even put to death, but neither this nor any other form of external restraint can prevent his thinking what he likes or behaving virtuously; that is, taking the rational attitude toward his misfortunes. But the Stoics neglected the fact that this liberty, indestructible in its negative aspect, is no liberty at all without the capacity to think, and that it is therefore nullified by mental disease, habit, indoctrination, hysteria, or lack of education. The art of oppression has in modern times learned how to penetrate into the Stoic's stronghold.

The neglect of the positive half of the meaning of liberty leads to the idea that the state promotes liberty only by removing obstacles, including itself. Or it leads to the idea that the mere absence of obstacles somehow implies the presence of capacity; as when the advocate of 'free enterprise,' meaning the non-interference of government, takes this to mean that the individual is "free to move about as he likes economically, socially and politically." [3] But the individual's freedom "to move about as he likes" can be nonexistent owing to his impotence—owing to his disease, malnutrition, ignorance, arrested development, or non-possession of the instrumentalities by which his interests are executed. The absence of liberty may well express itself in the words: "My poverty and not my will consents." If liberty depends on capacities and resources, then the state may promote liberty by supplying them; or, through its failure to provide them, it may nullify liberty by default.

The same holds true of national liberty. A nation does not become free merely by the absence of aggression from without. Unless a nation has resources by which it can achieve its ends and satisfy the needs and aspirations of its people, its freedom is imperfect. For this reason the distinction sometimes made between political self-determination and economic resources or social welfare, as though these were unrelated, is a false abstraction. They are the complementary parts of freedom.

It not infrequently happens that the achievement of negative liberty, sustained during a period of struggle by resentment and combativeness, is thereafter left without content. Obstacles having been removed and interference successfully overcome, there is no liberty to be 'enjoyed,' for lack of a constructive program of positive liberty. One of the weaknesses of traditional liberalism is its identification with a mere resistance to oppression. The future of liberalism turns on the possibility of converting the removal of obstacles into a positive passion, and on the utilization in its behalf of advancing science and technology.

Liberty, then, to be real must be effective. A man enjoys liberty in proportion as he has interests, and in proportion as these interests are both unimpeded from without and implemented from within. No one can be said to be an advocate of liberty, nor can any state or policy be said to promote it, unless liberty is thus roundly conceived.

3

According to Lord Acton, "liberty is not a means to a higher political end. It is itself the highest political end. . . . A generous spirit prefers that his country should be poor, and weak, and of no account, but free, rather than powerful, prosperous and enslaved." [4] The view that liberty ranks high, if not highest, in the order of goods is widely held among diverse schools of political thought. It is a fundamental contention of democracy. In the political thought of the seventeenth and eighteenth centuries this eulogy of liberty was characteristically formulated in terms of 'nature.' Liberty was a 'natural right,' prescribed by the 'laws of nature' and enjoyed in the 'state of nature.'

The moral justification and appraisal of liberty begins with the recognition of its generic meaning. There is a liberty common to all liberties, and which springs directly from the nature of interest itself. Every desire or will desires or wills its means as well as its end, seeks to overcome obstacles, and resents interference. Every interest feels an interest not only in its object but also in its ability to attain that object. Liberty in this generic sense manifests itself on every plane of interest, from the most selfish or elemental appetite to the most humane or spiritual aspiration.

Now it is a part of the democratic theory that this generic liberty, whatever the level on which it manifests itself, possesses a valid claim—a claim, namely, to be *considered.* It may not be disregarded or overruled except on the ground of its interference with other liberties. This is quite different from saying that every liberty is a right. It becomes a right only when its claim is limited to provide for the like claims of other liberties; that is, to meet the requirements of a system of liberties. But the principle which governs such a system is the principle of live and let live. Generic liberty is the stuff that rights are made of.

A liberty takes moral ground, not when it merely asserts itself as it stands, but when it appeals to the standard of universal liberty—as when it claims to be harmless or helpful to other liberties, or protests against their excess. Thus a liberty evokes moral sympathy when it appears to be wantonly attacked or carelessly ignored. It is characteristic of democratic sentiment to sympathize with the underdog, however canine his attributes. So long as the underdog is the victim of superior might he plays the role of innocence; and being the exponent of an interest which is being wrongly negated, his protest serves to correct the wrong. Even when the victim takes the same selfish ground as the oppressor, his cause is for the moment the cause of righteousness. Here lies the explanation of the fact that oppressed and courageous minorities, or small nations fighting for independence, are admired exponents of liberty so long as the odds are against them; whereas when, without any change of motive, they in turn become top dogs, they are condemned.

It is characteristic of democratic sentiment to sympathize even with truculent assertions of liberty, where these are directed against oppression. David Crockett expressed such sympathy with the nullification party in South Carolina in 1834:

> "Well," ses I, "them there people down there fought desperate in the old war. They whipped Captain Cornwallis, and scared Sir Harry Clinton out and out; and I reckon then no more nor now they don't like nobody to wrong them out of their rights." [5]

The spirit of liberty which Crockett symbolizes is a man's insistence upon his interests against those who would override them, and his willingness, if needs be, to resort to force before submitting to oppression.

In comparing modern with ancient democracy, Bluntschli said: "Among the ancients men started from the State and sought to secure the liberty of all by dividing political rule equally among all. Now they start from individual liberty, and strive to give away as little of it as they can to the State, to obey as little as possible." [6] In other words, in modern democracy of the American type, the presumption is in favor of the existing interest, whatever and whosesoever it is. The moral burden of proof is on its opponents. To thwart an interest is to do evil, and if such thwarting is to be justified, it must be in the name of a more liberal provision for interests all around. Government is not thought of as having a right on its own account, with concessions made so far as necessary or expedient to protesting interests. On the contrary, government, since it imposes laws and penalties, and thus forbids certain interested individuals to do what they would like to do, is itself reluctantly accepted only because it is necessary or expedient in the interest of all interests.

The same sentiment appears in the democratic attitude toward national liberty. A nation fighting for its liberty against aggressors appears not in the role of sheer self-assertion, but as the exponent of the claim to have its claims respected. Its liberty is right because the aggressor, in his ruthlessness, is wrong. At the same time it is recognized that the oppressed nation forfeits its right at the moment when it becomes aggressive, and may rightly be overruled by an international sanction which speaks in the name of all nations.

The claim of a liberty to be innocent and beneficent is illustrated by what may be called 'cultural liberty,' by which I mean the unhampered, uncontrolled, and implemented activities of science and art. Truth serves all interests, and its use by one interest does not prevent its being freely used by others. Insofar as science, governed by the love of truth, is successful, it results in a fund of truth freely available to all. Similarly, beauty is a sharable good. The enjoyment of painting, sculpture, poetry, and music by one individual does not deprive others of their enjoyment. Scientists and artists are, of course, human beings, and their activities involve the use of physical instrumentalities; and the physical access to these instrumentalities, or to the works in which truth or beauty is embodied, is subject to incompatibilities. But the fact remains that intellectual and artistic liberties in themselves are innocent and reciprocally enhancing. They unite men across the boundaries of personal, class, or national divisions, and are commonly invoked to mitigate the divisive effect of those 'practical' interests which take from one what they give to another.

The scientific interest is pure in proportion as it is motivated by the desire for truth; the artistic interest is pure in proportion as it is motivated by aesthetic enjoyment, whether appreciative or creative. Insofar as the scientific or artistic interest is controlled or compromised by motives of wealth, fear, ambition, or propaganda, it is prevented from yielding its peculiar fruits, those fruits, namely, which possess the quality of universality. Tyrants of the older type were commonly 'patrons' of science and art; that is, they protected the scientist or the artist, supplied him with the requisite leisure and resources, and left him largely to his own scientific and artistic devices. They thus contributed to the creation of a universal culture and to the sum of moral goods. Modern dictatorships, on the other hand, are politico-cultural. In depriving culture of its purity they not only stifle its growth, but rob it of all claims to a unique place in the scale of liberties. It becomes a mere instrument of national interest, and may become a tool of oppression.

4

Liberty is morally justified when its exercise is consistent with, or conducive to, the exercise of other liberties; or when it resists encroachment by other liberties which fail to take account of it, and make room for it. A liberty may satisfy this criterion regardless of its motives, and even, as in the case of self-defense, when it is opposed to other liberties. Its moral quality is then external or circumstantial. There remain for special consideration those liberties which are governed by a *regard* for other liberties, and which may be said to possess their moral quality internally. Their right is intrinsic rather than merely extrinsic.

Thus a personal will or rational self-interest has a superior moral claim to that of an appetite or impulse, because it takes account of appetites and impulses and provides for them in some comprehensive plan of life. It is this which Bishop Butler had in mind when he said that man is qualified for liberty because "he hath the rule of right within . . . Liberty, in the very nature of it, absolutely requires, and even supposes, that people be able to govern themselves in those respects in which they are free." [7] The personal will has a special claim to liberty, because it embraces and reconciles the liberties of its constituent interests. Their conflicts are resolved, their vehemence moderated, and their recalcitrancy overruled. This claim of personal liberty is forfeited insofar as some of these constituent liberties are forgotten, and others are inordinately intensified by the heat of passion, by the power of suggestion, or by the routine of habit.

It is a part of the purpose of the democratic state that individuals should be allowed and encouraged to exercise the prerogatives of personality, and that they should be protected against those influences which proceed spontaneously from individual to individual, or which may be fomented by the state itself, and which disintegrate personality, enslaving the individual to one of his own appetites and creating a uniform mass of sentiment, opinion, and action instead of a group of autonomous persons governed each by his own judgment.

While personal liberty is intrinsically right insofar as it provides for the person's own interests, it may be, and often is, extrinsically wrong in its relations to the liberty of other persons. A higher intrinsic right is enjoyed by a will which speaks for the liberties of all persons within society. 'Love of liberty' is subject to this criterion. The love of one's own liberty may, as we have seen, create a needful corrective of oppression, but it is morally incomplete. Patrick Henry's "Give me liberty, or give me death!" is thus ambiguous. If he meant that he preferred death to the loss of his private liberty, he did not rise above a level of passionate self-interest. But if he meant that he preferred death to the destruction of a social system under which all individuals enjoyed their just rights, then his sentiment was 'noble,' and the liberty he set above life was possessed of intrinsic moral value on the higher social plane. The utterance remains ambiguous because, while the speaker may have been moved primarily by his own impatience of restraint, he was associated with others similarly moved, and so participated in an effort to achieve a distributed liberty. If, however, his sentiment possessed the form of socialized morality, it would have found a fitter expression in the words "Give *us* liberty, or give *me* death."

The extent to which a man may be considered a lover of liberty in this moralized sense is then to be measured in terms of his passion for the liberty of others. Burke said that the slaveholders of the South were more attached to liberty than the Northerners. "Freedom is to them not only an enjoyment, but a kind of rank and privilege." [8] The liberty of which Burke here speaks is at best a liberty against its abuses by others. It has no intrinsic moral quality. Indeed, those very qualities of pride, courage, and violence which impelled the Southerner to resist interference and to insist on having his way, hardened his heart against those whom he in turn enslaved. His intractability was precisely opposed to that spirit of concession which is required for moral liberty. The inherent moral value of liberty lies in giving and not in 'taking' liberties; and in its maximum degree it consists not in a reluctant consent but in magnanimity.

Santayana speaks of "English liberty." It is, he says, "in harmony with the nature of things"; and consists in a spirit of adaptability, compromise, and co-operation.[9] This liberty is in harmony with the nature of things in the sense that it represents the fundamental fact of social life; namely, the interaction of personal interests and the practical necessity of their being accommodated one to another. The spirit of this "English liberty" is intrinsically moral insofar as it is infused with a desire for diverse and distributed liberties. It implies that the Englishman is not only disposed to insist upon his private liberty, but at the same time adaptable to libertarian institutions, and disposed to enjoy a general environment and reciprocity of liberty.

Precisely the same principles apply to the relations of nation to nation. The national will, or the will of its government, may claim a moral right in proportion as it is the exponent of the personal liberties of its people; but even then it is subject to a further restriction. The similar claims of other national liberties are entitled to consideration. The love of liberty is as yet morally incomplete until it has assumed the form of a love of all national liberties, or devotion to a world-wide order of liberties. Only an interest in all liberties can be said to possess a claim to absolute liberty.

5

Liberty in general means the absence of external obstacles which prevent, and the presence of resources and capacities which promote, the power of any individual to realize his desires or execute his will. Such a power exists in greater or less degree in the constitution of man and in his relation to his environment. When we praise liberty, advocate a high rather than a low degree of it, and organize society accordingly, we introduce moral standards, such as the extent to which any liberty is consistent with, and favorable to, the exercise of other liberties. In the appraisal of specific liberties it is of prime importance to recognize that any standard by which liberties are justified at the same time defines their abuse. If a liberty is right insofar as it satisfies certain requirements, then it is wrong insofar as it violates those requirements.

A convenient classification of liberties—whether positive or negative, whether deriving their right from their internal motive or only from their external effects—is provided by their different relations to government. There are liberties *under* government, *against* government, and *for* government; or legal liberties, civil liberties, and political liberties. We begin with legal liberties, or liberties under government.

The widely diffused idea that liberty is created by the state is both false and confusing. It is entirely conceivable that an isolated individual, possessed of suitable faculties and bodily mechanisms and a favorable physical environment, or an individual living in an unorganized society of individuals whose interests were happily compatible with his own, should possess and enjoy full and praiseworthy liberty.

This reservation being made, it is then in order to affirm that no high degree of liberty is possible without security under the sanction of government. A state of nature would be, and is in times of lawless violence, "nasty, poor and brutish"; because, as Hobbes has shown, men in that state are so preoccupied with fear that they have little time or energy to devote to the positive pursuit of their interests.

The most serious hindrance to a man's interest is the rival interest of his neighbor. Suffering or fearing this hindrance, he must postpone his interest until the hindrance is removed. This is why war becomes every man's first business. It is clear that the only permanent remedy lies in the systematic delimitation of interests. There is a greater liberty to be enjoyed through the acceptance of such delimitation than through the unrestrained assertion of a claim of limitlessness.

If this is reasonable, then it is evident to all men in proportion as they are endowed with reason; and they will proceed accordingly to restrain liberty for the sake of liberty. This is Locke's point—that limited liberty is "natural," that is, reasonable, the state being left out of account. But although men are by definition endowed with reason and disposed to regulate their affairs thereby, it is unhappily the case that this faculty is so unevenly distributed, and may in some men be so deficient, that a man cannot safely count upon the rational self-restraint of his neighbor. The individual is then confronted with this alternative: either he must be prepared himself to impose forcible restraint upon his errant neighbor, or he must join in establishing and supporting a public power which shall by penalties induce all individuals to behave as though they were reasonable.

Liberties defined and enforced by law clearly demonstrate their limited character. They are set forth in general terms as rights, but are then interpreted by judicial decisions which protect the community from their abuse. The exercise of its police power permits the state to interfere against liberties in behalf of the other liberties which they transgress. No individual has a right to life, liberty, or property when this jeopardizes the life, liberty, or property of other individuals. There is no liberty so fundamental or so axiomatic that its exercise may not be denied as a 'nuisance'—a continuing offense against the health, decency, or tranquillity of the community as a whole.[10]

Government, deriving its overwhelming force from the combined forces of individuals, intervenes between man and man. It confines the behavior of each, so that others may enjoy security within their similar boundaries. While the state neither creates nor justifies liberty, it does create security; and it is upon security that the fuller and more constructive liberties of civilization depend.

Its failure to recognize that the only effective liberty is legal liberty, and that this is the product of government, has exposed the democratic doctrine of the eighteenth century to the scorn of such critics as the author of that strange pro-slavery treatise called *Sociology for the South, or The Failure of Free Society:*

> The only free people in the world are the Digger Indians of the valley of the Great Salt Lake and the Australians of New Holland. They know nothing of government, of society, of castes, classes, or of subordination of rank; each man digs for worms and climbs for birds' eggs on his own hook: they are perfectly free, famished and degraded.[11]

The antithesis of 'liberty' and 'license' is misleading because it seems to deny that liberty is, like license, doing as one wills. The antithesis is valid if license means the unlimited doing as one wills. The fact is that there is more rather than less of doing as one wills if it is confined within fixed boundaries, and it is the state which, by prescribing and generalizing these boundaries, raises the power of the individual will to the higher levels which are enjoyed in advanced societies. Liberty under law is a fuller freedom than the nominally unlimited, but in fact narrowly restricted, freedom of lawlessness. The equal application of this principle to the relations of societies to one another—the greater freedom enjoyed by nations within an international system of security—is evident.

It is moral, rather than legal, liberty that speaks the last word. The restrictions which government imposes are in the last analysis morally justified only by the interests or wills for which government makes room. It is always possible for any given system of legal liberties to fall short of that maximum of room which it is morally bound to make. It is this maximum which constitutes the norm for the criticism or the improvement of the existing legal system. Those who under that system enjoy a more spacious liberty than their fellows are inclined to invest legal liberties with a moral validity, and to claim a 'right' to their present advantages. The effect of this confusion is to disarm the underprivileged victims by the hypnotic spell of moral rhetoric. Or they may feel a resentment against all government and conclude that anarchy is to be preferred to law. To avoid this confusion and its unfortunate consequences it is necessary, while conceding the practical necessity and desirability of legal liberty, to remember that it is no more than the instrument of those just liberties which are sanctioned by reason and conscience.

6

While legal liberty is universally acclaimed (by all save avowed philosophical anarchists), it is customary to conceive it as a form of negative liberty, and to affirm that the duty of the state is limited to the protection of the private individual or group against the interference of other individuals or groups. This was not Locke's idea.

> But for as much as we are not by ourselves sufficient to furnish ourselves with competent store of things needful for such a life as our Nature doth desire, a life fit for the dignity of man, therefore to supply these defects and imperfections which are in us, as living singly and solely by ourselves, we are naturally induced to seek communion and fellowship with others; this was the cause of men uniting themselves at first in politic societies.[12]

The doctrine that legal liberty is essentially negative rests upon two lapses of thought. In the first place, it is forgotten that liberty can be lost by privation as well as by interference, and that if liberty is to be promoted, the state must therefore give and not merely protect. In the second place, it is forgotten that individualistic ends can be promoted by collectivist means.

The use of collectivist means for individualistic ends is at the worst only an indirect threat to liberty, arising from the fact that means once created tend to become ends. It is in principle the precise opposite of a polity in which individualism is employed for a collectivist end. The flagrant case of this latter polity is, of course, totalitarianism. But such a collectivist polity may disguise itself, as when the rights of private business are invoked in support of a capitalistic *system* without regard to the condition of the human individuals who live under that system. Whatever name it may adopt, no society is libertarian which does not yield positive results in terms of individual happiness and development justly distributed among all concerned. There is some ground for the charge that totalitarian polities have, even in the name of the corporate whole, sometimes done more for the employment, the health, the recreation, and even the self-respect of private individuals than have democratic polities which profess the creed of individual liberty.

Lord Acton, a distinguished proponent of liberty against government, said:

> By liberty I mean the assurance that every man shall be protected in doing what he believes his duty against the influence of authorities and majorities, custom and opinion. . . . In ancient times the State absorbed authorities not its own and intruded on the domain of personal freedom. In the Middle Ages it possessed too little authority and suffered others to intrude. Modern states fall habitually into both excesses.[13]

Of which excess the writer would convict the contemporary democratic state it is difficult to judge. He would perhaps have ranked monopolistic capitalism high among those "other" intrusive influences against which the state must give the individual protection. He would also, perhaps, have seen that a man's "doing what he believes his duty" cannot be assured by merely "protecting" him.

If it be the duty of government to promote the liberty of every man within its jurisdiction, this duty must be construed to embrace positive and not merely negative liberty. If a man is to do what he desires, wills, or believes to be his duty, he must possess the means, and not merely the permission. The most persistent and oppressive enemies of liberty are not external hindrances, whether physical or human, but poverty and ignorance. It is a major fault of prosperous and enlightened men that they forget this fact.

There is a significant phrase in the report of a committee appointed by the British Labor party to formulate a program of reconstruction after the First World War—the phrase "effective personal freedom." This means freedom that can actually be used to advantage. If you cast a man into stormy waters far from land and tell him that there is nothing to prevent his swimming to shore, there is clearly something lacking in his liberty. For first he has got to keep his head above water. Even if by great and prolonged exertions he can do that, there is little chance of his living to achieve more. The man who demands "effective personal freedom" wants to be put on shore to start with. Similarly, if you dismiss your son from your door without food, money, or education and tell him that the whole wide world is now open to him, you have not given him "effective personal freedom." He may be ignorant of the possibilities which the whole wide world affords, or impotent to realize those which he sees. Circumstances may compel him to accept your terms, hard and dictatorial though they may be. Freedom in such a sense is a threat and not a promise.

Similarly, if you rear a man in a low social station, in the midst of poverty and ignorance, with the necessity of livelihood forced upon him from an early age, and then tell him that he is free to become President of the United States, he is to be forgiven if he does not appear enthusiastic and grateful. He knows that there is a tyranny of deprivation and circumstance more fatal than that of rivals or rulers; that the worst of all tyrannies is the tyranny of existing things—of that established system which has sprung from human action, but for which no human individual now feels responsible. Liberty demands that institutions shall annul this tyranny of circumstance, and perpetually reconstruct the existing system so that the amplitude of choice shall be somewhere nearly commensurate with interest and potential capacity. There is no more bitter fraud than that of giving the name of liberty to mere neglect. If government is under obligation to promote liberty, and if liberty is a positive and not merely a negative thing, then the state is under obligation to promote the capacity and the power of its members. What it does in the way of education, public information, health, housing, increased wages, reduced hours of labor, or the redistribution of wealth is as much a service of liberty as its protection of men against interference from one another or from itself.

The degree of the positive rather than of the merely negative liberty of its members is the measure of the state's achievement. The most favorable symptom of political health is the happy preoccupation of men with non-political interests. The true limiting principle of the state is not definable by the amount and the range of its power, but by the subordination of that power to ends beyond itself. The dignity of the state is not unduly exalted by the multitude of its services, provided they are recognized as services and evoke gratitude rather than worship.

7

The topic of 'civil liberty' is one of the most prominent and, unhappily, one of the most confused of contemporary issues. The expression has at least five distinct meanings which are rarely distinguished. It is sometimes used to mean legal liberty, in the sense discussed above. It is sometimes used to mean political liberty, in the sense to be discussed below. It is sometimes used, without definition, to refer to the specific liberties enumerated in bills of rights, or in the Fourteenth Amendment of the Federal Constitution: the liberties of speech, press, assembly, and religion; the rights of life, liberty, and property or happiness; the rights of petition, habeas corpus, 'due process' of law, trial by jury, and the inviolability of the home or person; and other rights embraced under the formula of 'common-law rights.' It is sometimes used, again without definition, to refer to a narrower group of the liberties listed above; namely, those liberties which have to do most directly with allowing individuals and groups to give effective public utterance to their own opinions. Finally, civil liberty is sometimes taken to mean the 'constitutional' liberties which limit the powers of the executive and legislative branches of the government, or of the government 'in power.' The expression will here be employed in the fifth of these senses.

The virtue of determining the *principle* of civil liberty rather than merely enumerating its specific instances lies in the fact that such a principle will serve as a standard by which the specific civil liberties can be explained and limited. Unless they are to be regarded as 'sacred,' the civil liberties have a reason, and are rights only insofar as they satisfy that reason. The principle of civil liberty rests upon the assumption that government in general has a function which sets bounds to its proper exercise, or defines the line between the use and the abuse of its powers. This principle has meaning only in a political philosophy, such as democracy, in which it is affirmed that government, instead of being an end in itself, is under obligation to benefit the individuals who live under it. The civil rights thus embrace those goods by the destruction or prevention of which government loses its excuse for existence and forfeits its title to obedience.

The debates between federalists and anti-federalists at the time of the adoption of the Federal Constitution reveal amidst many differences of opinion the common ground of civil rights. There was a difference of opinion as to whether the civil rights needed to be embodied in the constitution of a government founded on popular sovereignty, subject to the check of periodic elections, and invested with delegated powers. But there was no difference on the fundamental doctrine that any government in power must respect certain fundamental liberties, such as those embodied in the common law, the Declaration of Independence, and the bills of rights of the several state constitutions; because otherwise it would defeat its own end, and violate the compact from which it derived its authority. "A bill of rights . . . ought to set forth the purposes for which the compact is made." A government which violated the liberties set forth in the bills of rights would be "guilty of a breach of trust." [14] Jefferson, writing to James Madison about the proposed Constitution, and after commending certain features of it, went on to say:

> I will now add what I do not like. First the omission of a bill of rights providing clearly, & without the aid of sophisms, for freedom of religion, freedom of the press, protection against standing armies, restriction against monopolies, the eternal & unremitting force of the habeas corpus laws, and trials, by jury in all matters of fact triable by the laws of the land & not by the law of nations. . . . Let me add that a bill of rights is what the people are entitled to against every government on earth, general or particular, & what no just government should refuse, or rest on inferences.[15]

"What the people are entitled to against every government on earth" has been, as Jefferson desired, explicitly embodied in the Constitution. The effect is to embrace within the law itself the individualistic premises of the democratic political philosophy. Civil liberty thus becomes a form of legal liberty; with the result that there are two systems of law: the constitutional law, which embodies the minimum liberties which government is pledged to respect; and the statutory and administrative law by which the government uses its powers, thus limited, to raise the liberties of individuals to a maximum.

The principle of civil liberty implies a tendency of government to defeat its legitimate end, and to become an abuse rather than a utility. The state serves its purpose by the use of force: in order to secure liberty it must possess and use a power to negate liberty. Government can be considered, therefore, as a threat to liberty, and many a battle for liberty has been fought, and rightly fought, against it. This suspicion or fear of government is deeply rooted in the American tradition.[16]

8

There are three ways in which government may become the enemy of liberty: by disloyalty, by excess, and by inefficiency.

By disloyalty of government is meant any deviation from its public function due to the private self-interest of the ruler.

> "Let us not flatter ourselves," said the writer of "The Letter of Agrippa," "that we shall always have good men to govern us. If we endeavor to be like other nations we shall have more bad men than good ones to exercise extensive powers. That circumstance alone will corrupt them. While they fancy themselves the viceregents of God, they will resemble him only in power, but will always depart from his wisdom and goodness." [17]

This is the chronic evil and the chronic suspicion associated with the name of tyranny; and democracy enjoys no immunity from them. Whereas a monarch may assume the burdens of office reluctantly, as a hereditary and inescapable obligation, a democratic ruler is a candidate. He 'runs for office,' and it is safe to assume that he desires to rule, and enjoys the role when he is successful. The democratic ruler is likely to be ambitious, if not avaricious. He may seek and enjoy office because it will give him power, wealth, or the opportunity of dispensing favors to his friends. An organized party represents a solidarity of self-interest, and its discipline is largely dependent on the spoils of victory. It seeks not only to attain but to hold office. No inconsiderable portion of its activity is devoted to the task of winning the next campaign. To shut one's eyes to these facts is to be ignorant of the actual political processes in a democracy and to forget that here as well as elsewhere disinterestedness is comparatively rare, and commonly reinforced, when it exists at all, by self-interest.

This fact in itself does not imply tyranny. A man need not be a reluctant ruler in order to be a good ruler. It is a fortunate thing that private ambition and self-seeking coincide with society's need of leadership and a masterful will. Tyranny begins only when these two courses of conduct, that dictated by self-interest and that dictated by the general good, diverge. But all authority, whatever its function or ulterior purpose, tends to become a vested interest; lust for the power and the emoluments of office tends to grow in proportion to their range and duration. The ruler will possess from the outset a bias of temperament, of local or class interest, of dynastic pride, or of partisan solidarity, and this bias will be strengthened by the circumstances of office. He is isolated by his exalted role from the experience of the average man, and is surrounded by flatterers whose interest it is to increase that isolation in order to augment their influence. He will easily persuade himself that he is indispensable, or has a mission to mankind; and he will possess an unusual degree of humility and objectivity if he does not in some degree mistake his own interest for the public good, and his private judgment for the inspired voice of truth.

The popularity of government does not suffice to save it from tyranny, but may create new forms of tyranny. Popular government lends itself to tyranny of the majority over dissenting minorities, and of the masses over the classes. It lends itself, furthermore, to the tyranny of the demagogue, who conceals his self-interest by flattering the people, and appeals to their baser instincts against their reflective judgment—that "stale contrivance, to get the people into a passion, in order to make them sacrifice their liberty." [18]

The corrective of tyranny in these popular forms does not lie in relating government more immediately to the existing will of those who live under it, but in the scrupulous protection of civil liberties, and in a system of education that shall emancipate the critical faculties and develop a resistance to irrational appeal.

9

There is a threat to liberty not only in disloyal government, but also in excessive government—not only in tyranny, but also in paternalism. A popular government is peculiarly liable to this abuse. It tends to be trusted by those who live under it, since it speaks in their name; and it tends to be invoked by them as a benefactor, since they have created it, and given it the power which it exercises. Popular government tends, furthermore, and for the same reasons, to be used by an individual or a group who have obtained the support of the majority to enforce their opinions upon all.

From this likelihood that government will tend to encroach unduly upon the domain of private activity, and deprive men of more liberty than it bestows, there springs a specific libertarian motive, expressed in the maxim that a government should govern *as little as possible,* or in Hobbes's declaration that the greatest liberty of the subject depends on "the silence of the law." [19] But the minimum of government would be no government at all, and Hobbes would be the first to admit that the total silence of the law would place the individual at the mercy of his fellow men.

The maxim that government should be reduced to a minimum derives its present meaning to most Americans from its application to 'business.' But the French physiocrats, among whom the doctrine of laissez faire first arose, and Adam Smith, to whose famous *Wealth of Nations* this doctrine owed its vogue in English-speaking countries, were impregnated with the deistic optimism of the eighteenth century, and disposed to believe that what the state did not regulate would be automatically and beneficently regulated by 'nature.' As Adam Smith expressed it, the individual in promoting his own private affairs is "led by an invisible hand to promote an end which was no part of his intention." * [20]

Contemporary apologists of laissez faire are still influenced by this theology. They are disposed to assume that an economy of competitive private enterprise is 'natural,' and that because it is natural it is right and reasonable. The ancient dogma serves in a more critical age as a 'rationalization' of the status quo.

Men are disposed to regard a legal system which is customary, and which confers palpable benefits on themselves, as somehow rooted in the constitution of the universe. They ignore or belittle the extent to which it is founded upon the laws of property and contract. The beginning of sound thinking on this matter is to see that the economic system known as laissez-faire capitalism is not an effect of 'the silence of the law.' Men who are merely let alone to do as they please do not compete with one another; they plunder one another. 'Free competition' depends no more on letting men do as they please than on preventing them from doing as they please, and forcing them to do as they do not please. In fact, no man is quicker to invoke the interference of the government in his own behalf than the exponent of laissez faire.

The degree of governmental restraint which private liberty requires will vary from time to time, and from place to place. Corporations, being admitted as legal competitors, in turn beget trusts, holding-companies, and cartels. But these economic monsters constitute a new and formidable threat to economic liberty. The small businessman asks to be protected against them, and if such protection is to be effective, the state must exercise a force proportional to that of the new oppressor.

As large-scale corporate business may render its business rivals helpless to compete, and thus by the success of its competing nullify the benefits of the competitive system itself, so owners of capital may exclude from competition the mass of workers, dependent on a daily wage

---

* T. E. Cliffe Leslie says of the school of Adam Smith: "We shall see that the original foundation is in fact no other than that theory of Nature which, descending through Roman jural philosophy from the speculations of Greece, taught that there is a simple code of Nature which human institutions have disturbed, though its principles are distinctly visible through them, and a beneficial and harmonious natural order of things which appears wherever Nature is left to itself." [21]

and having a narrow margin of subsistence. The wage-earner is at the mercy of his employer until he can pool his resources and consolidate his forces. He is less cheered by the hope of gaining more than oppressed by the dread of losing the little he has. "For there is nothing," says R. H. Tawney, "which frightens thin sheep like the fear of being thinner." [22] If the state has any business at all to interfere between man and man, it has a duty to interfere in such a situation—always provided that the net result of its interference is to substitute liberty for oppression.

The state must not only protect private individuals and groups from the oppression of other private individuals and groups, but it must also protect its own liberty. Corporate industry, which is so insistent that the government shall keep its hands off business, is not always scrupulous as to the use of its own hands. The concentration of wealth confers on its owners or executives a disproportionate power to influence government, through the control of instruments of publicity, the lobby, contributions to party funds, and the inducements or threats which it can offer to candidates for office. Insofar as this is the case, the state becomes the instrument of a privileged class, and loses that justification which it derives from the just representation of all interests.

In the light of these considerations the issue of government 'interference' becomes the question of how much the government shall interfere, and whether it shall interfere in old ways or in new.

10

The state may, in the third place, be a menace to liberty through its inefficiency; that is, through the unsuitability of its mechanisms and agencies to the uses which they are asked to serve. The uses to which an instrument can profitably be put depends upon the nature of the instrument: there are limits to what it *can* do, even at best.

Thus the state employs instruments of enforcement, but if enforcement is to be effective, it must command a wide support from public opinion and sentiment. It is unwise, therefore, to attempt the enforcement of regulations such as 'prohibition' which represent only a majority, or a majority which is likely to be temporary. Where convictions are deep-seated, the effect of an attempt to control them from without may have the effect of enlisting the combative emotions in their behalf. Against the force of the state they become more obstinate and firmly rooted.

Enforcement depends upon clear evidence of innocence or guilt, and such evidence is usually inconclusive if it relates to thought, intention, or other states of mind which are known best by the defendant himself. The attempt to obtain evidence in such matters leads to the creation of agencies of espionage and censorship which, even if effective for their immediate purpose, readily lend themselves to abuse. They tempt the government in power to stifle opposition; and once created, and the people habituated to their use, they are ready at hand for those who would abolish democratic powers altogether. Such agencies of enforcement, in short, are *dangerous* instruments, which should therefore be created and used with restraint.

The agencies which will effectively regulate opinion, sentiment, or artistic creation are coarse instruments, unsuited to a delicate operation. If a hammer and a saw were the only tools of surgery, it would be difficult to remove the diseased portions of the body without injuring the adjoining parts. The result might be to kill the patient rather than to cure him. Similarly, the mechanisms of public enforcement are ill suited to distinguish between art and lubricity, or between science and dogma, or between persuasion and propaganda, or between education and indoctrination. Unless, therefore, government is to do 'more harm than good,' it may be prudent to leave the regulation of these matters to the control which private organizations such as the church and the family exert over their own members, or to the control of taste and conscience.

As the functions of the state are multiplied, so is its personnel. In developing a large class of permanent officials the state creates, as is suggested by the disparaging suggestions of the term 'bureaucracy,' a governing caste having its own habits and bias, and tending to lose touch with the generality of mankind. There is, therefore, a presumption against the increase of governmental activities, lest human affairs be controlled by the derived and vested interest of officials rather than by the primary interests from which government rightly springs and whose fulfillment is the proper measure of its success.

Every instrument may be dulled or broken by overuse. A state which is asked to do too much may do nothing well. Its functions may increase more rapidly than its competence. It is prudent, therefore, to limit the functions of the state out of regard for the human limitations of its rulers.

The inefficiency of the state may consist not in the imperfection of its own instruments, but in its failure to profit by other instruments. It is self-evident that the state should derive the utmost public benefit from the motive of private self-interest. It is false to assume that the general interest of society and the private interest of each of its several members coincide in principle. Nevertheless there is a large area within which they do coincide, and here the motive of private self-interest may be stronger and more reliable than the disinterestedness of government, and its use more economical.

In a competitive economy of the traditional American type the rewards of private wealth, the speculative possibility of attaining the command of great wealth, and the zest of rivalry induce initiative, effort, organizing capacity, and progress. It is commonly believed that the businessman who enjoys the opportunity of rising in life and of enjoying the fruits of his own success will be more efficient in any given field of activity than the same man in the same field when he has become a public official. Insofar as this is true, the state serves its purpose better by keeping its hands off than by assuming control—doubly better, in that the yield of public benefit is greater at the same time that liberty is less restrained. This argument is traditional in America. Thus James Fenimore Cooper wrote in 1828:

> The secret of all enterprise and energy exists in the principle of individuality. Wealth does not more infallibly beget wealth, than the right to the exercise of our faculties begets the desire to use them. The slave is everywhere indolent, vicious, and abject; the freeman active, moral and bold. It would seem that is the best and safest and, consequently, the wisest government, which is content rather to protect than direct the national prosperity, since the latter system never fails to impede the efforts of that individuality which makes men industrious and enterprising.[23]

Communism is one of the oldest of social philosophies. In America both the idea and the practice were familiar in early colonial New England; and contemporary observers were quick to complain that such a system robbed men of incentive and self-reliance, and made the industrious the caretakers of the idle.

There is no doubt of the fact that effort and invention can under favorable conditions be induced by the desire for the general good, or by the desire to excel in well-doing. The history of religion, art, science, war, and even politics abounds in instances of men who have strained their capacities to the utmost with no thought of personal profit, but only from motives intrinsic to the activity itself. How far even the American businessman is motivated by avarice and personal ambition, and how far by creative or social impulses, is itself obscure. It cannot be said with finality that in a more socialized state in which the temptations of private wealth and power were removed, public officials might not display an equal zeal; and in any case, as in Soviet Russia today, there would remain spheres of liberty in which self-interest, emulation, and individual self-expression would continue to operate. The extent to which the increase of control and regulation by the state would profit or injure society through a change of motivation is not certain. But it is clear that a thrifty state will use and not destroy the motive of private self-interest where this clearly coincides with the public good.

The 'American system' has not only stimulated zeal and initiative, but has also developed a capacity for private organization and collective action. It has been characteristic of American life to develop 'natural leaders,' and generate esprit de corps. This was the impression, for example, made upon observers by the American troops upon their arrival in Europe in 1917:

> The New England saw-mill units have caused a furore of enthusiasm. They came with absolute Yankee completeness of organization—with duplicate parts of all their machinery, tents, cooks, pots, and pans, and everything ship-shape. The only question they asked was: "Say, where the hell are them trees you want sawed up?" That's the way to do a job! Yankee stock is made high here by such things as that.[24]

This was boastful, but it was not sheer boastfulness. It manifested a spirit of readiness, confidence, and goodwill which a mere disciplined obedience cannot create. It is an effect of the self-reliance begotten by experience, and of the self-confidence begotten by opportunity. It would be a wanton dissipation of energy to destroy this social spontaneity. A state which finds men disposed of their own accord to effective collective action will, so long as the results are generally beneficent, gratefully employ this disposition, and scrupulously refrain from destroying the habits and the incentives from which it springs.

Civil liberty sets limits to the government in power, and its rationale lies in the fact that the government in power tends, unless so restrained, to tyranny, paternalism, and inefficiency. If so, then civil liberties are not immutable and self-evident truths, but are subject to revision by the application of the criterion of social good. Judged by this criterion, old civil liberties may be abolished, and new civil liberties added by procedures which the fundamental law provides for its own change. It is unavoidable that there should be an intermediate zone within which the right decision is difficult and doubtful. There is only one fundamental principle in this matter, which is that the total system of law should take as its end, and so far as possible promote, the reciprocal liberties of all individuals concerned.

11

Among the moral, legal, and civil liberties there are certain liberties which are justified not merely as a protection of one private interest against others, or of private interest against government, but as indispensable to the functioning of government. Any liberty when so justified becomes a 'political' liberty.

The distinction between liberties which are merely moral, legal, or civil liberties and those which are also political liberties is often obscure. It is the line between the individual as the beneficiary of the state and the individual as source of its authority. There is no doubt, however, regarding the liberties which enable the individual to form judgments for himself and to communicate his judgments to his fellow men. Among these liberties are the liberties of speech, of press, of assembly, and of religion, when these are conceived as essential to the processes of political democracy. So-called academic freedom, or the liberties of research and of teaching, though they may be guaranteed by educational institutions and only indirectly chartered by the state, are applications of the same principle; so are liberties of radio or cinema, or any other form of communication which advancing technology may devise.

The meaning of these liberties depends on the assumption that a distinction can be made between judgment and practice. The liberty to judge that property should be held in common does not imply a liberty to practice communism; the liberty to hold the theory of free trade does not imply the liberty to bring goods across the frontier without paying a duty. Given any act whatsoever, there is a distinction between its acceptance in idea and its performance. A similar distinction holds also between persuasive communication and incitement to action. The line is hard to draw. Nevertheless the liberty to convert others to a judgment which if acted upon would be lawless does not imply the liberty to induce the performance of lawless action.

The liberties of judgment and persuasive communication have a place in every domain of liberty, and their examination provides an occasion for reviewing the principles discussed above before turning to that principle of political liberty with which we are here primarily concerned.

As negative liberties they underlie the maxim of tolerance, which is the withholding of interference with thought and utterance, and the removal of obstacles which stand in their way. As positive liberties they create the need of education. The principle by which liberty, negative and positive, is morally justified is the principle of inclusiveness. On this ground an individual ought to be allowed to think as he pleases, write what he pleases, talk as he pleases, foment and organize what he pleases, provided in so doing he does not interfere unduly with the liberties of others. This reservation does not abridge the inner liberty of thinking for oneself, since this activity is by nature non-interfering. Communication, on the other hand, involves social relations and external facilities, and may have to be restrained in 'fairness' to all. Private religious faith, for example, needs no restraint; but liberty of worship, meaning the open and collective profession of a religious creed, together with such forms of ritual and discipline as that creed prescribes, must be compatible with a like liberty on the part of similar groups. If it is so compatible, then the cult in question, whether enlightened or superstitious, has a right to live as it will. Thus religious liberty was justified by Locke as being both just and innocent. The church is "a spontaneous society," a "private" and not a public individual: "And therefore peace, equity, and friendship, are always mutually to be observed by particular churches, in the same manner as by private persons, without any pretence of superiority or jurisdiction over one another." [25]

The liberty of science derives justification from the fact that the scientific interest is an inclusive or creative rather than an exclusive or acquisitive interest. Art, as well as science, is in its essential nature humane, and unites its devotees through a common objectivity, or through innocent and mutually enhancing satisfactions. In a democracy science pursued for truth, and art pursued for beauty, are among the common ends of life, and in giving them liberty the state directly serves its purpose of promoting harmonious happiness.

Liberties of thought and communication have an additional claim, since they embrace the principle of inclusiveness within themselves. Religion possesses such a claim insofar as it is inwardly motivated by the love of innocence and justice, and insofar as the church seeks to promote the spiritual interests of its members or of mankind. The individual's self-regulation, in which his component interests are integrated by a personal end and judged by himself in relation to that end, is an application of the principle of inclusiveness within the circumference of the individual's own interests. The libertarian interest itself, the interest in liberty conceived as an institution the benefits of which are extended to all, is similarly self-justifying. This liberty of moral judgment in its personal, social, or international applications, rightfully exercised because it embraces the principle of rightness within itself, is what is meant by liberty of conscience.

All of the liberties of judgment and persuasive communication may be conceived as moral liberties, external or internal. Insofar as they are guaranteed, they are legal liberties, and insofar as their definition is constitutional rather than legislative or administrative, they are civil liberties. And finally, they assume the specific form of political liberties when they are conceived not as benefits which the state owes and guarantees to its members, but as conditions of the state's own existence.

A democratic polity is pledged to the principles of *enlightenment* and *consent,* and the liberties of judgment and persuasive communication are corollaries of these principles. In a state otherwise conceived, as founded on dogma or power, political liberty has no place.

First, democracy puts its trust in the achievement and dissemination of enlightenment. Both the existence of the democratic state and its specific policies rest in theory upon true judgments concerning what is and what ought to be. But knowledge can be achieved only by minds which are freed from coercion in order that they may be faithful to evidence. Said Bagehot:

> Arguments always tell for truth as such, and against error as such: if you let the human mind alone, it has a preference for good argument over bad; it oftener takes truth than not. But if you do not let it alone, you give truth no advantage at all; you substitute a game of force where all doctrines are equal, for a game of logic where the truer have the better chance.[26]

Knowledge is a potential achievement of every inquiring mind. The maximum advance of true knowledge thus depends on giving to every mind a commission to explore the facts and exercise its reasoning capacities. The essential political liberty is thus liberty of thought and inquiry. Religion, when considered in this context, has a liberty in the domain of moral or metaphysical knowledge. Justice Holmes said that according to "the theory of our Constitution," the test of truth is experimental, and "the ultimate good desired is better reached by free trade in ideas." [27] The liberties of speech, press, assembly, and teaching are conducive to the production of knowledge through criticism, confirmation, and discussion; at the same time they provide for the distribution and general availability of existing knowledge.

Every liberty is limited by its justifying principle. Those who claim liberty of judgment and persuasion for the sake of enlightenment submit themselves to that standard. The liberty of blind affirmation, or of impassioned utterance, or of artfully propagating error, or of silencing opponents, or of personal polemics, cannot be justified as conducive to the achievement and spread of that enlightenment to which the democratic state is pledged. Such liberties may be claimed, and perhaps rightly claimed, on other grounds; but every thinker, speaker, writer, or teacher who claims his liberty on the ground of political enlightenment is thereby bound to intellectual disinterestedness and good faith.

Second, the liberties of judgment and communication are essential to the constitution of the democratic state as conditions not only of enlightenment, but also of that consent from which government derives its just authority. The fundamental principle of political democracy is not the agreement of the people with the government, but the agreement of the government with the people. If this is to occur, there must be an antecedent and independent agreement among the people themselves. The people do not choose collectively, but only as individuals. There must be choice by individuals, communicated to other individuals, and resulting in an identity of choice in an aggregate of individuals.

Here again the justifying principle imposes limits on liberty. If liberty is to be claimed on the ground of consent, then its exercise must conduce to consent. This argues that the government must refrain from dictating the decision from which it derives its mandate. It must not only avoid interference, but must positively assist the people to choose for themselves. But consent also implies a genuine decision; that is, an act of deliberate choice from the widest possible range of alternatives. He who claims the liberty of judgment and communication on the ground of consent is bound by the nature of consent. He cannot, on this ground, claim a right to use communication as a method of intimidation, or of inflaming blind passion, or of reducing alternatives to one through the dissociating effect of suggestion.

12

Political liberty may be exercised in relation to the government in power, or in relation to the political constitution taken as embracing the principle of political liberty itself. The first of these uses of political liberty is its partisan use, and the second its revolutionary use.

It is evident that if the existing government is to rest on enlightenment and consent, its policies must have been, and must continue to be, debatable pro and con. The recognized device by which consent is obtained is through the party system, in which a single party or a block of parties exercises the power of government for a limited time, after election by secret ballot. It is an essential feature of this procedure that the election should be preceded by a popular discussion of issues and candidates, and the government elected is supposed to conform its policies to the judgment which has prevailed. Liberty to form this judgment, and to support it by public speech, assembly, press, radio, and organization is an essential part of such procedure.

Consent is periodically renewed or withdrawn by the same processes as those by which it is originally given. The party in power, at the same time that it frames statutes and performs administrative acts in accordance with the popular mandate from which it derives its authority, will also respect the political liberties of its opponents, which may be used for its own defeat. Each party when in power thus serves both itself and its opponents, or both its own partisan end and that general end of popular government to which it is pledged in common with its opponents—precisely as in sport each contestant is governed by two interests, the interest in victory and the interest in the sport itself. Every party will have two loyalties, one to itself and one to the broad purpose of the system at large. Every good Republican or good Democrat will at the same time be a good American, and will respect this quality in his opponent, despite the bitterness of partisan rivalry.

The crucial difference between a political democracy and all other forms of government is to be found here. A democratic government is pledged to maintain a general procedure which implies the possibility or even the likelihood of its own overthrow, and will thus use its power against, as well as for, itself; an undemocratic government will use its power in whatever manner is conducive to its own perpetuation. An absolute polity is like a game that has no rules, but only such opportunistic procedures as may ensure victory. There is no threat to political democracy in a shift of emphasis from private to public regulation, or from state to federal control, or from the legislative to the executive branches of government. The diagnosticians who are watching these changes have applied their stethoscopes to the wrong spot, and may arouse a needless alarm while permitting the real disease to develop unobserved. The enlightened guardian of democracy will scrutinize the government's attitude to its opponents and to public opinion. Does it use its power to intimidate and corrupt? Does it outlaw opposition and stifle criticism? Does it drug the public mind? Or does it rely for its possession of office on the merits of its policies as these are freely judged by a well-informed and free electorate? If not, then, and then only, is political democracy in jeopardy.

A résumé of the arguments for a partisan use of political liberty will serve at the same time to define its limits. Its abuses are the opposites of its proper uses.

If the liberty here in question is justified as a means of determining the policy or the official personnel of government, it may not be used lawlessly or to advocate lawlessness. The limit of the liberty is to be found in its purpose, which is to institute a government by enlightenment and consent. It is a part of that purpose that the government so instituted should be in fact a government obeyed even by dissenting individuals and minorities until changed by the same processes as those by which it was instituted.

It follows that the opposition's attack upon official or candidate should not be so bitter as to discredit the authority of the office, or the attack upon the policy so bitter as to discredit the authority of the law. There is a zone of controversy in which this line is hard to draw, and even when it can be drawn it may be inexpedient that the government itself should intervene. Here as elsewhere it is necessary to take account of the limits of government, owing to its tendencies to disloyalty, excess, or inefficiency. But these reservations do not weaken the principle that the partisan use of political liberties, if they are to secure the purpose by which they are justified, should be restrained within the bounds of law-abidingness and respect for authority.

If partisan political liberties are defended as moral liberties, they are limited by the principle of inclusiveness. To exercise these liberties in such wise as to infringe the similar liberties of other individuals or groups defeats their purpose to create an order or a system of liberties which can live at peace with one another. As there is no justifiable liberty of property or person which does not concede a like liberty to others, so there is no justifiable partisan liberty of thought, speech, press, or assembly which does not tolerate as well as exercise such liberties.

Advancing to the standard of enlightenment, it is evident that partisan opposition which assumes the form of personal invective, excitation of primitive emotion, appeal to acquired prejudice, suggestion, contagion, hypnosis, or intimidation is excluded and not justified. These are forces which make for darkness rather than light. The fertility of discussion is inversely proportional to the arousal of crude combative instincts. Epithets used as weapons do not clarify issues or enrich understanding. With the radio, and to a considerable extent the press, persuasive communication is unilateral, and inflammatory utterance is not even neutralized by resistance or counter-attack. A wide public is then defenseless against the potent influence of rhetoric, which may be used with mendacious intent, and which in any case will obscure the facts and short-circuit the reasoning faculties.

Finally, if the principle of consent is to be invoked, weight must be given to its negative as well as its positive implications. The exercise of partisan liberties must be propitious to the emergence of acts of choice. In reaching a decision the people act as exponents of interests as well as vehicles of truth. It is proper, then, that they should be made vividly aware of their interests, and that to this end their emotions should be stirred. But if the people are to be made 'alive' to their interests, the representation of their remoter interests is as important as the presentation of their immediate interests. In short, consent requires reflection, and whatever negates reflection can derive no support from the principle of consent.

The excitement of passion tends to prevent and not to promote that independent and considered choice from which the government in power derives its mandate. This is especially true when the passions are intensified by the power of suggestion; when personality, which is the agent of choice, is disintegrated and dissolved in a welter of hysteria. If it were to be conceded that a mass uniformity produced by artfully manipulated psychological forces was what is meant by 'the consent of the governed,' the battle for political democracy would already have been lost.

13

Whatever the difficulties in practice, partisan liberty involves no fundamental difficulty of theory, because it is clearly embraced within a democratic framework. But what if an anti-democratic faction arises within a democracy, claiming the partisan liberties but pledged, in the event of securing power, to destroy them? An anti-democratic cult may be safely tolerated when its adherents are in the minority, or during the phase of their rise to power. In this phase they are often the most redoubtable champions of so-called tolerance. But they are not on that account tolerant. They are defensively tolerant in order that they may become offensively intolerant. Meanwhile the tolerance which they enjoy is embodied not in themselves but in the democratic regime which, having the power to suppress them, nevertheless gives them freedom to profess and promote their opinions. What, if any, right do they have to be tolerated?

In earlier days this issue was associated with religion. It still arises in connection with Catholic minorities in protestant countries, assuming that they desire to profit by tolerance but do not themselves possess it either as a virtue or as a conviction. Their ecclesiastical polity, dogma, discipline, and habits are largely authoritarian. The principles which they profess and apply among themselves would, in the event that the population became predominantly Catholic, be extended to the whole of society. Or so it is alleged.

It was for this reason that notable exponents of toleration, such as Milton and Locke, excluded the 'Papists' for having the intent of exalting an authoritarian church above the state.[28] During the controversy which stirred America at the time of the candidacy of Alfred E. Smith for the presidency this issue again became prominent. Some apologists of Roman Catholicism candidly admitted that tolerance was a policy of expediency, to be superseded, whenever it might prove possible, by the policy of creating a fully Catholic community through the alliance of church and state.[29] The same issue has been forced to the front by the rise of communism and Fascism, and constitutes the central paradox of political democracies. It is argued that the democracies harbor and nourish their own enemies, and thus foster the seeds of their own destruction.

Up to a certain point the question of the revolutionary use of political liberty is parallel to the question of its partisan use. A political constitution may permit thought, speech, press, and assembly even when those are directed against itself. It may grant the legal privileges of partisanship not only to political parties in the ordinary sense, but to a 'revolutionary' party; that is, a party which, if it should succeed in securing power, would abolish altogether the party system, or the electoral system, or the parliamentary system. Such a liberty can be justified so long as theory is distinguishable from practice. The violation of the law guaranteeing civil liberties would be intolerable, as would the incitement of such violation; but room can be made for the theoretical advocacy of a new system of law within which, if adopted, these liberties would no longer be legal. The difficulty of distinguishing between revolutionary philosophy and revolutionary action is great but not insuperable. It requires that careful examination of concrete cases and circumstances for which the courts exist.

The fact that it is by faith and doctrine disposed to trust the inherent beneficence of liberty, and to fear its suppression more than its abuse, exposes political democracy to the grave danger of condoning illegality. A state which permits the free discussion pro and con of its own constitution has permitted the forging of a dangerous weapon, and must protect itself the more vigilantly against the misuse of that weapon. And it is a misuse of political liberties if in their name men foment revolution, or so act as to encourage and propagate a spirit of violence. This holds without exception. One form of lawbreaking is as lawless as another, whether the lawbreaker be governed by the ignoble passion of the thief or the assassin or by the philosophical, political, or religious creed of the revolutionary. The revolutionary may be nobler than the 'criminal,' but he is no less lawless; and it is his lawlessness rather than his nobility which determines the duty of the state.

Assuming the political liberties to be guarded by the distinction between theory and practice, discussion and violence, or organized opinion and conspiracy, their revolutionary use is justified by the same principles that are applicable to their partisan use, and is subject to the same limitations.

The most powerful argument for the revolutionary use of political liberties lies in the principle of consent. It is essential to a democratic polity that not only its specific policies but its fundamental creed, its premises spoken and unspoken, should be freely affirmed by those who live under it. The sort of agreement which democracy contemplates is that agreement, founded on objective evidence, which can meet the test of criticism. It is impossible to appeal to reason *for* democracy without admitting evidence *against* democracy. It is impossible that the mind should know without freedom to draw its own conclusions, and if it be given this freedom, its conclusions cannot be predicted in advance. The possibility of truth is conditioned by the hazard of error.

The principle of consent is, here again, restrictive in its implications. The revolutionary use of political liberty is clearly indefensible as a means of securing consent when it is deliberately used to confuse the choosing mind, or by excluding evidence to narrow the range of alternatives. Revolutionary propaganda is dubiously defensible as a means of securing consent when, however sincere the conviction of truth, it generates more heat than light, mingling argument with emotion or with the coercive threat of group opinion and sentiment. It is then defensible, if defensible at all, only on *other grounds.* If it is so exercised as to be consistent with other liberties, it may be argued on the general ground of the right of a person to do what he desires or wills so long as he is innocent and just. It may be defended on the ground that it cannot be prevented; because the attempt to prevent it will only give it the added strength of martyrdom. Or it may be defended on the ground that the agencies which could prevent it would do more harm than good.

So far, the partisan and revolutionary uses of political liberty are similar. We now reach the point at which they diverge. Partisan liberty is an instrument of democracy—a means of realizing the end of free government. He who practices partisan liberty wills the perpetuation of free institutions; the success of his partisanship in no degree endangers them. He who practices revolutionary liberty, on the other hand, wills the destruction of free institutions; insofar as he succeeds, they will cease to exist.

Here the libertarian political system appears to be facing an impasse. Its fundamental principle does not permit it either to prevent or to permit revolutionary liberty. In the one case it violates its principle in act, and in the other case it violates its principle in effect. Whatever it does, its means appears to contradict its end. This apparent contradiction rests, however, on confusion arising from a failure to make a clear statement of the means and the end.

The difficulty is not peculiar to liberty, and it will be illuminating to consider certain familiar analogues. The promoting of health or the healing of the body sometimes requires surgery, or the injuring of the body. If this is carelessly stated, the means contradicts the end; if it is clearly stated, there is no contradiction. If the end were to avoid any cutting of bodily tissues, no matter what the cost, then surgery would contradict the end. But if the end is the future health of the body, then a present act of bodily injury is not its contradictory but may even be its necessary implication. Similarly, the end of a pleasant life on the whole may and often does require the present inflicting of pain, and the general security of person and property may require particular seizures of person or of property, in the form of punishment.

The clearest analogy is afforded by the pursuit of peace. Peace is a system of relations between man and man or between nation and nation in which, when created, the use of violence is excluded; and the pursuit of peace so conceived may, and often does, require the present use of violence. In that case, there is no contradiction. If, however, the devotee of nonresistance regards the use of violence as a 'sin,' if, that is, the end is to avoid the use of violence, then there is a contradiction. The devotee of nonresistance may take other grounds. He may believe that if he uses violence, God will punish mankind by raising up enemies against him, so that his refraining from violence under any circumstances will be the right means to peace. But he is then bound to abandon this means if it fails to work, or if for any reason he doubts his theological premises. Or he may believe that nonresistance will disarm his opponents, and spread peace by example. But then he is bound to consult human experience to discover whether this effect does or does not usually occur, and if so, under what circumstances; and he must be prepared to abandon his nonresistance if he finds it to be an ineffectual instrument. He must not, in other words, be governed by an unalterable scruple.

Following those analogues, if the libertarian end be the creation of a stable political system in which the political liberties of all are raised to a maximum, then this end may sometimes be best served by a particular denial of political liberty. When that is the case, there is no contradiction; there is, on the contrary, an obligation. There is a contradiction only provided the end is conceived as the conceding of liberty no matter what happens. If the absolute libertarian argues that God will look out for the libertarian polity provided men will refrain from suppressing particular liberties, then the argument stands or falls with this pious conviction. If he argues that the government will best promote the right use of political liberties by leaving men to their own consciences, then he is bound to abandon this method if it fails.

In other words, there is a scrupulous libertarianism and there is a purposive libertarianism, as in the parallel case of peace. The first takes the non-suppression of liberty as an absolute, the second takes the libertarian political system as its goal. It can never be consistent with a scrupulous political libertarianism to deny liberty of judgment or persuasive communication, so that such a libertarian is bound by the logic of his own principle to allow libertarian institutions to perish when by a denial of liberty he might save them. A purposive libertarian, on the other hand, is not only permitted but obliged by the logic of his principle to employ the denial of liberty when this is the most effective means to his libertarian end.

It is easy to confuse these two libertarianisms, because up to a certain point they may agree in practice. Any denial of liberty must be reckoned a danger to the libertarian end and be used with caution and reluctance. It is difficult to prohibit liberties, even to a revolutionary party, or in times of crisis, without weakening devotion to libertarian institutions. The means tends to compromise the end, and to corrupt the purity of the will. The agencies created for the effective repression of political liberties in particular cases are tempted to extend their application, and to be used by the enemies of liberty to suppress all liberties, and in the net effect do more harm than good. Although designed to protect libertarian institutions against their revolutionary enemies, they may fall into the hands of these enemies and be turned against the friends of liberty.

On the other hand, there is reason to fear that the transition from libertarian to non-libertarian institutions would be irreversible. Recent developments in the techniques of force and propaganda have made it more difficult than ever before in the world's history to overthrow an authoritarian regime once it is in power. A democracy already in power should not lightly surrender its command of the instruments of control.

These and many other like considerations make the decision difficult in any concrete case. But the first step, and a long step, toward solving difficult problems is a clear definition of the standard of judgment, and the determination of what considerations are legitimate. The democratic political standard is the attainment, the perfection, and the preservation of a system in which government is implemented by enlightenment and based on the consent of the governed, and in which liberties of thought and persuasive communication are cherished so far, and only so far, as they conduce to this end.

CHAPTER NINETEEN

EQUALITY AND FRATERNITY[1]

1

THE DECLARATION that men are born not only free but "equal" has been the butt of an extraordinary amount of labored and irrelevant wit, such as this of Calhoun's: "Taking the proposition literally, there is not a word of truth in it. It begins with, 'all men are born,' which is utterly untrue. Men are not born. Infants are born. They grow to be men." John Adams and others have from time to time made the profound and, as they have seemed to think, annihilating discovery that no two objects are "perfectly alike."[2] Even contemporary writers occasionally indulge in these hollow polemical victories. But it is a safe maxim never to impute to doctrines which have played a great role in history meanings which must have been palpably absurd to their own contemporaries. The eighteenth-century exponents of equality knew as well as Calhoun and Adams or more modern critics that men are endowed by nature with unequal capacity, as they are endowed with unequal stature, strength, fingerprints, or cephalic indices. The equality of which they spoke drew its meaning, not from a mere disregard of facts, but from a group of ideas which had their roots in Greek and Hebrew antiquity and their proof in the moral, political, and religious philosophy of the age.

The equalitarian doctrine can be summarily expounded. It was not an assertion that the several individual members of the human race are *as a matter of fact in all respects* alike; but that they *are and ought to be* alike in *certain* respects; and that these likenesses have a great deal to do with the aims of organized society.

In the first place, all men are equally men—which means not that they possess human attributes in the same degree, but that they possess the same attributes in some degree. All members of an audience, whether they sit in boxes or in the pit, possess the same type of skeleton, the same organs, and the same physiological functions. Whether a man is born in a hovel or in a palace, the reproductive process is the same; whether a man works in a private office on Wall Street or in a coal mine in Pennsylvania, he draws his energy from the combustion of food, and gives off carbon dioxide. But the generic sameness of men is not confined to these baser anatomical and physiological levels; they possess the same psychological traits, from the simpler reflexes of coughing and sneezing to the so-called higher processes of memory and thought. All men experience pleasure and pain, hunger and thirst, fear and anger, love and hate, joy and despair. All men recollect their past, anticipate their future, and perceive their present. All men exercise in some degree the activities of generalization and inference. This fact may be summarily expressed either in naturalistic or in religious terms. All men belong to the same species in the hierarchy of evolution; or all men are created in the same image of God.

What is true of the constitution of man is true also of his life-cycle, and his fundamental relationships to his fellow men and to his physical environment. All men are born, grow old, and die. They traverse the same ardors of youth, the same sobrieties of middle age, and the same scleroses of senescence. All men inhabit the same planet, are exposed to its alternations of season and weather, and are dependent on its resources. All men have parents, and most men have brothers and sisters and children. All men have neighbors, with whom they must establish terms of reasonable accord. All men suffer from the necessity, or enjoy the opportunity, of living with their fellows. They all have one life to live, face the same inevitable death, and hear the same crack of doom.

Owing to many causes, men are disposed to forget or ignore these indisputable facts. Generic sameness tends to be eclipsed by differences of individual and class. Equalitarianism exhorts us to reverse this tendency: to be reverently disposed toward the commonplace, and to be astonished by what is taken for granted. Chesterton says:

> Ordinary things are more valuable than extraordinary things; nay, they are more extraordinary. Man is something more awful than men; something more strange. The sense of the miracle of humanity itself should be always more vivid to us than any marvels of power, intellect, art or civilization. The mere

man on two legs, as such, should be felt as something more heartbreaking than any music and more startling than any caricature. Death is more tragic even than death by starvation.[3]

According to the way of thinking characteristic of the eighteenth century, the notable differences between man and man, such as that between king and subject, noble and commoner, priest and layman, or rich and poor, are products of organized society. This idea led to the habit of abstracting from organized society, and from the differences which it has created. Men were imaginatively divested of institutional accretions—their trappings, powers, and privileges; and when thus denuded and reduced to the ranks they looked strangely alike. The doctrine that equality is 'natural' was a way of saying that the more palpable and invidious inequalities are artificial.

That which is artificial can be unmade, and the purpose of social change was thus conceived as the restoration of a primitive equality. But, as was the case with the conception of 'nature' in all its applications, this retrospective manner of speaking concealed the essence of the matter. Fundamentally, nature signified what men *could* be and *ought* to be, rather than what they *had* been. When man's past came to be better known, the state of nature was transferred from the past to the future, and conceived as an attainable and valid ideal rather than as a historical beginning.

Men's equality of endowment came thus to be conceived in terms of a sameness of potentiality rather than of attainment, and faith in human nature assumed the form of a belief in his educability. This faith was still extravagant, but the locus of its extravagance was shifted. It became an excessively optimistic view, not of what men are or have been, but of what they are capable of becoming when the frustrations and malformations due to human institutions are corrected. Given the air and the sun and the moisture which they require, all individuals of the species are capable, it was believed, of the same flowering. The error now lay in underestimating the inborn differences which predetermine the limits of growth.

The biological emphasis on inherited traits and the psychological emphasis on inherited aptitude and intelligence belong to a later age from that in which American democracy was born, and their acceptance modifies one of its premises. But democracy accepts innate limitations reluctantly. It gives to every man the benefit of the doubt, and the doubt is so far justified as to make the gift significant. The rival claims of heredity and environment are still disputed, and no final adjudication of them is yet in sight.

Anti-democratic social philosophies justify inequalitarian institutions, as Aristotle once justified slavery. It is claimed that the inequalities of power and privilege in organized society are a mere projection of the native and ineradicable inequalities of its members. Men get what they are fit for, and what they are fit for will in the long run determine their happiness. This theory affords a suspiciously convenient justification for those who are most favored by the existing system, as did the puritan theory that power and privilege are the just earnings of virtue. Reformers are accused of making humble people discontented with a lot which corresponds to their inborn capacity and provides the only kind of happiness of which they are capable.

The democratic social philosophy, on the other hand, emphasizes the degree to which mental and moral traits are an effect of the social environment, and proposes that this environment shall be made as auspicious as possible. The extreme hereditarian position is, in the present state of the question, as dogmatic as the doctrine of equal potentiality. Even the commonly accepted opinion of the relative superiority of races is a product of pride and vested interest rather than of science. The least that can be said for the equalitarian view is that it is the more generous and fruitful of two dogmatisms between which science allows an option.[4]

Insofar as native differences of capacity are admitted, there is a tendency in democracy to conceive them as differences of vocation rather than of merit or dignity. And if the idea of generic equality tends to be superseded by the idea of equal opportunity, which affirms only that each man shall be enabled to raise his attainment to the limit of his capacity, this is still accompanied by the belief that such capacity is high. Democracy retains, if only as a regulative principle of social organization, an elixir of hopefulness. For what men attain is, in part, an effect of their belief in themselves and of the confident expectation of others.

Generic equality, then, is the idea that beneath the clothes they wear, and the status or occupation which organized society has bestowed upon them, all men are men, with the same faculties, the same needs and aspirations, the same destiny, and similar potentialities of development. Granting that the reservations are more evident to ourselves than to our fathers, this is still true. No one will deny it, once the question is raised in this form.

Why is this unquestionable fact so neglected that it has to be proclaimed? The founders of democracy were right not only in affirming the fact, but in their explanation of its neglect. The generic sameness of men is overlaid with surface differences. Men wear clothes and insignia, and they wear them on the outside of their persons where they are most in evidence. Every man has a station in life into which he is born, or to which he attains. This station is in part a matter of space and time. A man's spatio-temporal location distributes other men along radii of proximity; his neighbors are near, and others are distant. Those who are near can be seen easily, while those at a distance require the straining of the eye or an unnatural exercise of the faculty of imagination. But his station is also functional, consisting in the role he plays in the drama of life, and determining the relations in which he stands to his fellow actors.

These differences of station are not only more palpable but more interesting. Attention is fastened, not upon the common physiognomy of man, but upon those differences of feature, emphasis, and expression which distinguish the individual face with which one may claim acquaintance. And the functional differences that divide men are of commanding importance, in the sense of practical urgency. One's transactions are not with mankind, but with distinct individuals, or limited groups of individuals. Having an aching tooth, it is more important to consider a dentist as such than to reflect that he is a man, like oneself. The worker's struggle for existence forces upon his attention the difference between those who own capital and those who, like himself, depend upon the wages which the capitalist dispenses.

Man's generic sameness tending thus to be ignored, what is the means of heightening it and investing it with feeling? It might be supposed that modern science in its application to man would have provided such a means. Biology, anthropology, and psychology concern themselves with structures, functions, and laws common to all men. But the scientist, while he is interested in man, is not in his scientific capacity interested in men. Nor is it sufficient merely to acquire perspective. It is true that distance tends to render individual differences unnoticeable. To the European, all Chinese or even Orientals tend to 'look alike.' From an astronomical distance all men, as earth-dwellers, present an aspect of sameness that subordinates the uniqueness of genius and the significance of historic events. But it is also true that distance extinguishes interest in individuals. If human suffering occurs at a sufficient distance, it produces apathy; the suffering or the death of a few thousand, more or less, signifies little.

Neither science nor distance will create equalitarianism, which is an interest in individual men, combined with a recognition of their sameness. It is an appreciation of their common value. It is not a perception or a judgment, but a sentiment.

2

Equalitarianism as an article of the democratic creed is not an equation, but an attitude of love and admiration evoked by all men irrespective of their differences. Its mainspring is compassionate love, felt by one member of the genus for another. This humane feeling, or humanity as it is more simply called, is evoked in one human individual by the presence or the image of another human individual as such. It is rooted in the deep and universal human capacity of fellow feeling or love of kind.

It is said that Greek and Turkish peasants once lived peaceably in Asia Minor as neighbors, before they were divided by religious and national antagonisms. Their feelings toward one another were dictated by their generic human sameness, the common struggle for existence against the physical environment, and the vicissitudes of their common lot and cycle of life. To each, the other was a man rather than a Greek or a Turk, a Christian or a Mohammedan. Similarly, a man may meet his employer, his dentist, or even his ruler on this common ground of birth, marriage, sickness, or death. Catastrophes and emergencies heighten this effect. A man in danger must be rescued, whoever and whatever he is. In case of shipwreck, as Chesterton has said, we do not cry out "Bad citizen overboard!" [5]

The generic love of men is an attribute, perhaps the distinctive attribute, of the Christian God. His promiscuous love of man is not an effect of science. He is neither biologist, psychologist, anthropologist, sociologist, nor statistician. The universality of his interest in mankind is not an effect of distance; God, at any rate the Christian God, is not a spectator viewing human life from so remote a station that all men look as alike as do ants to the eye of man. His is an intimate and fond love by a Father for his children, the very hairs of whose heads are numbered.

The Christian God is conceived after the analogy of the familial relationships because these relationships typify an interest that is personal, comprehensive, and undiscriminating. It is quite true that the family as a structure assigns stations to its several members, and gives rise to differentiated feelings in which each is conceived qua parent, child, brother, or husband. But such is the intimacy of daily contact that the common, elemental vicissitudes of each are matters of vivid concern to the rest. The life of the family centers in birth, marriage, and death, in health and sickness, in the cycle of age, in livelihood and vocation, and in the fluctuations of success and failure, pleasure and pain, or happiness and despair. It is this intimacy that causes the tensions, the frictions, and the galling preoccupations of family life, but it also makes the family a school of humanity. It is in the family that each can be most certainly assured of the solicitude of others, no matter what may be his place in the world, and his level of talent or attainment; it is in the family that each is most likely to acquire that interest in concrete individuals which takes them as they are and loves them for what they are.

Sympathy has its narrowing as well as its expanding effect. It is likely to be associated with some limiting principle. The family, while it creates sympathy among its members, is likely to harden its heart against those who fall outside the circle. The same is true of other sympathetic intimacies, such as those of friendship, neighborhood, or class. They tend not only to excite sympathy but to focus and confine it. The sympathy of God is not thus restricted, because his family embraces all mankind. If the sympathy of men, excited by their closer intimacies, is to possess that unlimited extension which characterizes the sentiment of humanity, it needs to be freed from every sense of exclusive solidarity. The faculty which renders this possible is the faculty of imagination.

A group of thirty people once gathered to listen to an Aeolian organ recital at the home of a winter resident of Santa Barbara—a beautiful Spanish house, a richly furnished music room with a large solid plate-glass window looking over the Pacific, the isle of Santa Cruz on the western horizon. Altar pieces, copes, tapestries, rugs, statuettes, and furniture had been gathered from all quarters of the globe. The whole was based on the appreciation of $50,000 worth of common stock acquired twenty-five years before by the father of the present owner. The members of the audience were living similarly on the income from inherited investments. Their thoughts and feelings were pure and refined. They were enjoying leisure, and enjoying it on a high plane. Among themselves there was a bond of reciprocal intimacy, which manifested itself in kindly feelings and deeds.

But their very community of feeling and of interest shut them off from the rest of mankind. Their chief bond with society at large, their umbilical cord, was the dividend check. They were protected by laws of inheritance and property which they took as a matter of course, without any lively awareness of the incidence of these laws on others who occupied less-favored positions. Beyond their wealth there lay a background of toil and deprivation. The daily lives, the hurts and frustrations, the hard and narrowing routine, the numbing fatigue, the familial anxieties, the defeats and disappointments, of those from whose labors they profited were ignored. These favored of fortune cherished no malice toward their fellow men, and salved their consciences with the vague assurance that the system which benefited them so eminently was at the same time generally beneficent. But they did not realize the human life that lay beyond the narrow circle of their class. It did not excite them, disturb them, or govern their conduct.

The only corrective of such self-absorption, other than the shock of protest and class conflict, is a kindling of imaginative sympathy; and through this faculty an extension to remoter and less congenial men of that sense of common kind and common lot which is vividly felt toward familiar associates.

The equalitarian effect of sympathy is heightened by compassion, felt most intensely toward the unfortunate. Compassion is excited by the aspect which life presents at the lower end of the scale of happiness. It regards life concretely as an aggregate of suffering, struggling, hoping men and women, with the result that it tends to the comparative neglect of institutions, laws, and general principles. It is essentially remedial rather than progressive, and applies itself to raising the minimum rather than the maximum. It would halt the vanguard of civilization in order that those who are dropping by the way or lagging in the rear may be brought abreast of the marching column. It is less interested in the perfection of the few, who demonstrate the heights to which human nature can attain under the most favorable conditions; it is more interested in providing the unfortunate with the staple goods of health, food, and protection.

3

Equalitarianism derives its primary interest in generic mankind from the sentiment of fellow feeling. It derives its element of admiration from an emphasis on human prerogatives. Men are intrinsically admirable because of their possession of reason and conscience—the faculties for truth and moral goodness. Since these are generic faculties, the individual man derives dignity from their possession. Different men, it is true, possess them in different degrees; they may, therefore, either be disparaged for what they lack or respected for what they possess or are deemed capable of developing. Equalitarianism chooses the second of these alternatives.*

---

* Equalitarianism in this sense has been raised to a metaphysical level among certain philosophers who conceive of reality as a society of equal and eternal persons. Charles Renouvier in France, and Thomas Davidson, G. H. Howison, and Josiah Royce in America, were exponents of this idea, variously known as Personalism or Pluralistic Idealism.[6]

All men, furthermore, participate vicariously in the dignity of their most eminent fellows. As the family may enjoy just pride in the attainment of any one of their number, so the lowliest men may say of the greatest human genius, "He is one of us." The whole race of men is dignified by distinguished human achievement, as demonstrating the heights to which human nature at its best can rise. Said Melville:

> Men may seem detestable as joint stock-companies and nations; knaves, fools, and murderers there may be; men may have mean and meagre faces; but man, in the ideal, is so noble and so sparkling, such a grand and glowing creature, that over any ignominious blemish in him all his fellows should run to throw their costliest robes. That immaculate manliness we feel within ourselves, so far within us, that it remains intact though all the outer character seem gone; bleeds with keenest anguish at the undraped spectacle of a valor-ruined man. Nor can piety itself, at such a shameful sight, completely stifle her upbraidings against the permitting stars. But this august dignity I treat of, is not the dignity of kings and robes, but that abounding dignity which has no robed investiture. Thou shalt see it shining in the arm that wields a pick or drives a spike; that democratic dignity which, on all hands, radiates without end from God; Himself! The great God absolute! The centre and circumference of all democracy! His omnipresence, our divine equality!
>
> If, then, to meanest mariners, and renegades and castaways, I shall hereafter ascribe high qualities, though dark; weave around them tragic graces; if even the most mournful, perchance the most abased, among them all, shall at times lift himself to the exalted mounts; if I shall touch that workman's arm with some ethereal light; if I shall spread a rainbow over his disastrous set of sun; then against all mortal critics bear me out in it, thou just Spirit of Equality, which hast spread one royal mantle of humanity over all my kind! Bear me out in it, thou great democratic God! who didst not refuse to the swart convict, Bunyan, the pale, poetic pearl; Thou who didst clothe with doubly hammered leaves of finest gold, the stumped and paupered arm of old Cervantes; Thou who didst pick up Andrew Jackson from the pebbles; who didst hurl him upon a war-horse; who didst thunder him higher than a throne! Thou who, in all Thy mighty, earthly marchings, ever cullest Thy selectest champions from the kingly commons; bear me out in it, O God! [7]

The equal dignity of mankind thus rests not only on vicarious pride in the eminent achievement of genius, but also on the fact that the most admirable qualities are found widely distributed through all ranks of the social scale. When John Ball sought to encourage the humble folk who participated in Wat Tyler's rebellion in 1381, he said:

When Adam delv'd and Eve span,
Where was then the gentleman? [8]

He did not mean that prior to the social hierarchy introduced by organized society there were no gentlemen, but that gentility depended on characters of heart and mind to which such artificial distinctions were quite irrelevant. There is a false gentility which is recognized in the world, and there is true gentility which is independent of worldly status.

In Charles Kingsley's *Alton Locke*, Mr. Saunders McKaye proposed to strip mankind of their clothes, and then proclaim them brothers "on the one broad fundamental principle o' want o' breeks." [9] This is to suggest that men resemble one another at the base rather than at the top of the scale of values; that their common ground is low ground. It is agreed that when men are stripped of the vestments of organized society, they look alike; but it is further implied that in their common nakedness they have lost what gives them decency. According to the equalitarian creed, on the other hand, the stripping away of the trappings of rank uncovers the *real* claims which men have to love and respect. If men are deprived of the powers given them by organized society, as when they are cast upon a desert island, or disorganized by some great natural catastrophe, their relations are often reversed, leadership being assumed by him who possesses the intrinsic qualifications of intelligence and courage, rather than merely titular or imputed qualifications.[10] The plain man is often superior to his 'superiors.'

The Stoics attributed to all men the capacity to enthrone reason above passion, and to accept with cheerful acquiescence the parts assigned to them in the harmonious order of the universe. Virtue in this highest sense was equally within the competence of the slave and the emperor. Christianity taught that the highest qualities of man are the simple and humble qualities of love, industry, and long-suffering, which are most widely distributed, and which are corrupted by worldly ambition and pride. It was the rich man or the potentate who had the greatest difficulty in entering the kingdom of Heaven; it was the child that exemplified the highest virtues.

When Burns sang "a man's a man for a' that," he did not mean merely that a man of lowly station possesses the generic human attributes; but that he is 'king of men,' distinguished by his eminent possession of innocence, honesty, kindliness, frugality, and industry:

To you I sing, in simple Scottish lays,
The lowly train in life's sequester'd scene;
The native feelings strong, the guileless ways; . . .

Compar'd with this, how poor Religion's pride,
In all the pomp of method, and of art;
When men display to congregations wide
Devotion's ev'ry grace, except the heart,
The Power, incens'd, the pageant will desert,
The pompous strain, the sacerdotal stole;
But haply, in some cottage far apart,
May hear, well-pleas'd, the language of the soul,
And in His Book of Life the inmates poor enroll. . . .

Princes and lords are but the breath of kings,
"An honest man's the noblest work of God";
And certes, in fair Virtue's heavenly road,
The cottage leaves the palace far behind.[11]

A more modern version of the same idea is set forth in the following passage from William James. That which "makes life significant" is to be found widely on every social level:

Wishing for heroism and the spectacle of human nature on the rack, I had never noticed the great fields of heroism lying round about me, I had failed to see it present and alive. I could only think of it as dead and embalmed, labelled and costumed, as it is in the pages of romance. And yet there it was before me in the daily lives of the laboring classes. Not in clanging fights and desperate marches only is heroism to be looked for, but on every railway bridge and fire-proof building that is going up to-day. On freight-trains, on the decks of vessels, in cattle-yards and mines, on lumber-rafts, among the firemen and the policemen, the demand for courage is incessant; and the supply never fails. There, every day of the year somewhere, is human nature *in extremis* for you. And wherever a scythe, an axe, a pick, or a shovel is wielded, you have it sweating and aching and with its powers of patient endurance racked to the utmost under the length of hours of the strain.

As I awoke to all this unidealized heroic life around me, the scales seemed to fall from my eyes; and a wave of sympathy greater than anything I had ever before felt with the common life of common men began to fill my soul. . . . *There are compensations*: and no outward changes of condition in life can keep the nightingale of its eternal meaning from singing in all sorts of different men's hearts. . . . If the poor and the rich could look at each other in this way . . . how gentle would grow their disputes! What tolerance and good humor, what willingness to live and let live, would come into the world! [12]

4

The doctrine of equality means, then, that the differences which loom largest in organized society are superficial and accidental differences, which should not be allowed to obscure the generic characteristics of men, or the essential spiritual values which appear on every level of the social hierarchy. It is also a part of the equalitarian creed to affirm that the differences which society creates imply no absolute and irrevocable claims either to the exercise of power over men or to the enjoyment of special favors. When we are thinking of the purposes for which organized society exists, and the seat of its just control, we must disregard these differences, and go back to the original claims which a man possesses simply because he is a man.

It is equality in this sense of moral and political rights that was in the mind of Locke when he held men to be equal in the state of nature; [13] and in the minds of the founders of modern democracy when they said that men were created or born equal.

The following paragraphs from a speech delivered by Charles Sumner in 1849 have the merit of distinguishing this meaning of equality from the equalitarian man of straw which critics have so easily and so irrelevantly destroyed:

> Obviously, men are not born equal in physical strength or in mental capacity, in beauty of form or health of body. Diversity or inequality in these respects is the law of creation. From this difference springs divine harmony. But this inequality is in no particular inconsistent with complete civil and political equality. . . .
>
> "All men are *created* equal," says the Declaration of Independence. "All men are *born* free and equal," says the Massachusetts Bill of Rights. These are not vain words. . . . Here is the Great Charter of every human being draw-

ing vital breath upon this soil, whatever may be his condition, and whoever may be his parents. He may be poor, weak, humble, or black,—he may be of Caucasian, Jewish, Indian, or Ethiopian race,—he may be of French, German, English, or Irish extraction; but before the Constitution of Massachusetts all these distinctions disappear. . . . He is one of the children of the State, which, like an impartial parent, regards all its offspring with an equal care. To some it may justly allot higher duties, according to higher capacities; but it welcomes all to its equal hospitable board.[14]

There are two senses of equality which concern the foundations of polity: an equality of right to control it, and an equality of right to participate in its benefits.

Locke wrote that in the state of nature no man has authority above another. To Locke this was not a negation of authority, an equality of mere willfulness, but the possession by all men of "perfect freedom to order their actions, and dispose of their possessions and persons as they think fit, within the bounds of the law of Nature."[15] In the state of nature all men are possessed of the faculty for apprehending the fundamental principles of right living and the capacity to apply these principles to their conduct. Since this faculty possesses the supreme title to authority, no man possesses authority over any other man. The authority of man over man is not original or intrinsic, but created and delegated. Authority is unequal only in a secondary or derived sense, which obtains its warrant from that primary sense in which all men are equal. This is the meaning of Jefferson's assertion that "the general spread of the light of science has already laid open to every view the palpable truth, that the mass of mankind has not been born with saddles on their backs, nor a favored few booted and spurred, ready to ride them legitimately, by the grace of God."[16]

Equality of right to govern, resting on the universal possession of the ruling faculties of reason and conscience, is emphasized by those exponents of democracy who, like Locke, are primarily concerned with the grounds of political authority. But there is another right which rests upon the universal possession of interests which the state is bound to serve. This is the right, enjoyed equally by all men, to participate in the benefits of government.

The most fundamental question that can be asked about polity is the question, "Whom is it for?" This question is prior to the question, "Who shall govern?" For it is evident that they who should govern are those who are most likely to serve those for whom the polity exists. The democratic answer is that that polity exists for all those who live within it. It is justified by the benefits which it confers upon those who suffer its restrictions and penalties. The qualification which entitles them to its benefits is their possession of those desires, needs, and feelings which generate good in the basic and inalienable sense. This qualification is possessed by individuals, only by individuals, and by all individuals. The individuals of which organized society is composed are equal in their possession of this qualification and in the claim upon government which this qualification implies. They do not possess the same interests, or the same intensity or number of interests, but their interests possess the same finality. None may legitimately—that is, rightly—be overlooked, dismissed, or subordinated.

This principle of equality of rightful claim has been left largely to religion and ethics. It has been proclaimed by Christian humanitarianism, and in later days by utilitarianism. It constitutes the true meaning of that Golden Rule which is a part of the code of paganism as well as of Christianity. This rule prescribes that men shall give the same weight to the inner lives of others that they give to their own. We expect other men to consider *our* desires and feelings: why, then, should we not consider theirs, which are of the same kind and have the same title? This is Richard Hooker's meaning when he speaks of all men as "equals in nature"; or of the relation of equality between ourselves and those that are as ourselves.[17]

Every man attaches value primarily to the objects of his own felt interests; he has to be exhorted to attach value to the objects of his neighbor's interests, which he does not directly feel and can realize only through sympathy and imagination. The Golden Rule is a correction of that distortion which is due to the bright, warm inwardness of self as contrasted with the pale, cold outwardness of others. As Royce said:

> If he is real like thee, then is his life as bright a light, as warm a fire, to him, as thine to thee; his will is as full of struggling desires, of hard problems, of fateful decisions; his pains are as hateful, his joys as dear. Take whatever thou

knowest of desire and of striving, of burning love and of fierce hatred, realize as fully as thou canst what that means, and then with clear certainty add: *Such as that is for me, so is it for him, nothing less.*[18]

If the will, the pains and joys, the desire and striving, the love and hatred, of others is as authentic as one's own, then they have the same power to invest their objects with value; and they have the same claim upon any institution, such as the state, which is justified by its beneficence. This equal claim of all men to the state's beneficence has special force in its application to education, as thus set forth by Theodore Parker:

> The State, in theory, is not for the few, not even for the majority, but for all; classes are not recognized, and therefore not protected in any privilege. . . . A man is born to all the rights of mankind; all are born to them, so all are equal. Therefore, what the State pays for, not only comes at the cost of all, but must be for the use and benefit of all. . . . The aim must be, not to make priests and gentlemen of a few, a privileged class, but to make men of all; that is to give a normal and healthy development of their intellectual, moral, affectional and religious faculties, to furnish and instruct them with the most important elementary knowledge, to extend this development and furnishing of the faculties as far as possible. . . .
>
> In a democracy there are two reasons why this theory and practice prevail. One is a political reason. It is for the advantage of the State. . . . The other is a philosophical reason. It is for the advantage of the individual himself, irrespective of the State. The man is a man, an integer, and the State is for him; as well as a fraction of the State, and he for it. He has a man's rights; and, however inferior in might to any other man, born of parentage how humble soever, to no wealth at all, with a body never so feeble, he is yet a man, and so equal in rights to any other man.[19]

5

The expression 'equality before the law' may be taken to mean those equalities of right—the right to govern and the right to benefit by government—on which the whole system of law reposes. But it has a more restricted meaning, which is a corollary of the meaning of law itself, whatever may be its ulterior premises. It is this more restricted meaning that appears in the Fourteenth Amendment to the Constitution, in the phrase "equal protection of the laws." A law is a general rule, impersonal in its formulation. It applies to, and will so far as effective be imposed upon, all persons who fit the meaning of its terms, no matter *who* they may be.

It is customary to say that the law must not be 'discriminatory.' What does this mean? If it means that the law shall promote the public rather than any private interest of person or class, then we are brought back to the equal right of all men to benefit by the law. But granted that the law is in the public interest, or that in its ultimate effects it benefits all alike, it does discriminate. It discriminates between those to whom it does and those to whom it does not apply. Even the prohibitions of the criminal law apply only to those who are in their right minds. The laws governing the suffrage discriminate between those who are citizens, literate, and twenty-one years of age and those who lack these qualifications. The tariff laws distinguish between importers of one commodity and importers of another. The laws governing the Federal income tax discriminate against those whose net income is above a certain minimum. The laws governing military service and jury duty are discriminatory as between men and women, adults and minors. Laws are not only thus discriminatory in their application, but also in their penalties against those who disobey them. The mere word 'discriminatory,' then, is not illuminating.

What is meant is that the law defines generalized modes of conduct, and applies to persons only in respect of such conduct. If the law imposes a penalty on the crime of forgery, then this penalty shall be inflicted on any individual found guilty of that crime as defined in the law. It is inflicted on Joe Doe qua forger, not because he is John Doe, and not because he is rich or poor, of high or low social station. If the law imposes a certain rate of taxation on all net incomes over $1200, then the tax shall be paid by John Doe qua qualified tax-payer, whether he be friend or enemy of the tax-gatherer, and whatever his religion or creed. The law is no respecter of persons, or of conditions and circumstances beyond those specified or implied in the law.

It may be said that this follows from the meaning of law itself, and that the expression 'equality before the law' affirms no more than that there shall be law and that it shall be impartially—that is, strictly—enforced. To admit this, and at the same time to deny that this form of equality is peculiar to democracy, does not disparage the principle. Democracy here simply incorporates a principle common to all polities in which government is by law rather than by ad hoc executive decrees or bills of attainder. It limits the ruler by its requirements of generalization and consistency. To the governed it gives security, as regards both themselves and their fellows. However harsh the terms of the law, the individual can adapt himself to its provisions, and within these provisions order his own life in an orderly social environment.[20]

As regards the creed of democracy, however, the fundamental principle is not legal, but moral, equality—not equality before the law, but the equalitarian constitution of the law itself in embodying the equal authority and the equal claims of those who live under the law.

6

Although it is not true, as is sometimes affirmed, that modern democracy is the offspring of laissez-faire capitalism, the idea of free and open competition occupies a central place in its creed, under the formula of 'equal opportunity.' This idea found peculiarly favorable soil in a country such as America in which abundant natural resources were combined with a spirit of individual resourcefulness, so that opportunity did not mean chance, but the promise of attainment through the application of an energetic will to a plastic environment.

The idea of opportunity has the peculiar merit of reconciling equality with inequality. Inequalities of native capacity and inequalities of attainment are both admitted; and the intention is that inequalities of attainment shall represent genuine inequalities; that is, natural and moral inequalities. Men should not be artificially handicapped or artificially helped by the stations into which they are born. They should toe the same mark at the start of the race, in order that each contestant may at the finish take the place that he *can* take and *deserves* to take. Equality of this sort means, says R. H. Tawney,

> not absence of violent contrasts of income and condition, but equal opportunities of becoming unequal. . . . The inequalities of the old régime had been intolerable because they had been arbitrary, the result not of differences of personal capacity, but of social and political favouritism. The inequalities of industrial society were to be esteemed, for they were the expression of individual achievement or failure to achieve. They were twice blessed. They deserved moral approval, for they corresponded to merit. They were economically beneficial, for they offered a system of prizes and penalties. So it was possible to hate the inequalities most characteristic of the eighteenth century and to applaud those most characteristic of the nineteenth. The distinction between them was that the former had their origin in social institutions, the latter in personal character.[21]

Equality of opportunity not only distributes the prizes of life according to talent and effort, but provides an incentive to the development of talent and the increase of effort. It calls into play the powerful motives of ambition and emulation. Men desire to overtake or surpass their fellows in the race. Every activity of life—art, science, and public service, as well as money-getting, politics, and 'society'—matches one man against others, and distributes the competitors in a scale of comparative failure and success.

The motive of emulation prompts a man to exceed the attainment of others, and it also makes him resent another's victory when it is not earned. Emulation thus begets the demand for fair play, or a 'square deal.' The race must be to the swift, not to those who from the start find themselves already at or near the goal through no efforts of their own, or to those who are assisted from the side lines. The man who wins despite initial disadvantages, the 'self-made man,' is doubly honored; but such initial disadvantages are nonetheless regarded as contrary to the code of sportsmanship. All competitors should be given an even start; that is to say, opportunity should be equalized.

The benefits of equal opportunity are evident and familiar. It spurs a man to 'make the most of himself.' It reconciles men to inevitable inequalities; for they do not resent the prizes won by others if they feel that they are fairly won, or if they may hope to win them themselves at some later day—they or their children. It enriches the collective life by bringing to light talents which would otherwise go unused. It permits the native differences of men, their grades of excellence and various talents, to germinate and flower over a wide field. And since success, especially in the economic field, depends upon the support of the general public, the contestants bid against one another for the public favor by the zeal and the quality of their public service.

From the motive of emulation which prompts a man to rise in life and equal or exceed his fellows it is important to distinguish the motive of envy which prompts a man to hold others down. Envy is doubly vicious. It is negative and it is destructive. The true motive of emulation prompts men to exert themselves, and to resent only that which prevents their earning their deserts. Envy, on the other hand, prompts men to retard those who excel them, or to visit upon others those very disabilities which emulation seeks to remove. And envy is malicious. It derives satisfaction from defeat and failure. Whereas emulation seeks equality by clearing the course and speeding up the race, envy seeks equality by slackening the pace and impeding the leaders. Emulation devotes itself to a cult of merit, and aims to exalt the record of attainment by removing every artificial hindrance; but the envious man would rather win unfairly in a slow race than be surpassed by his fellows in a swift.

It is envy, and not emulation, which tends to vulgarity. Insofar as this motive is widespread and powerful, men avoid eminence from fear of incurring popular disfavor. They cultivate a sham colloquialism of speech, or roughness of manners; they hide their knowledge, wealth, or power behind an affectation of inferiority. But dissimulation and dishonesty are not the worst of vulgarity. It discourages every sort of high attainment, and robs society of the services of the expert and the leader. And it flatters the inferiority of the inferior, removing the incentive to excel, and teaching him to be proud of that failure which should fill him with discontent. It renders a people, as Mrs. Trollope said it had rendered Americans, incapable of graduating a scale by which to measure themselves; [22] or it tends to depress standards to the level of the lowest attainment, as was unconsciously suggested by an admirer of Calvin Coolidge who is supposed to have said of his hero that "his success should be an inspiration to the youth of the land, since it proves that anybody could be President."

It is envy rather than equal opportunity that is the root of what Plato described as "the forgiving spirit of democracy":

. . . the "don't care" about trifles, and the disregard which she shows of all the fine principles which we were solemnly affirming at the foundation of the city—as when we said that, except in the case of some rare natures, never will there be a good man who in his early youth has not made things of beauty a delight and a study—how grandly does she trample our words under her feet, never giving a thought to the pursuits which make a statesman, and promoting to honour any one who professes to be the people's friend.[23]

There is only one way in which equality of attainment can be brought about; namely, by reducing life to the lowest terms. It would be possible to arrange that all men should run a hundred yards in twenty seconds, but not that all men should run a hundred yards in ten seconds. It is possible to level down, but not to level up. It is said that a mutinous Russian sailor, being asked why he had wished to kill his officers, replied: "Otherwise we shall never be on the same level. They must die to make us level."[24]

The envious nature which would hold life down to the level of the incompetent or hold it back to the pace of the sluggard can have no justification on any grounds whatever. It is a sort of social suicide, which cuts off every head that thrusts itself above the surface. The ideal of social democracy implies a spirit that is more rare and more difficult. It implies a magnanimity of soul which will acknowledge genuine superiority wherever it appears, and prefer a pyramid of excellence to a plane of mediocrity. A true social democracy will recognize the unalterable inequalities of endowment, and the inevitable inequalities of attainment. It will encourage eminent attainment, as enriching the common life, and as embodying higher degrees of that perfection to which all aspire.

The stability of any society must in the long run depend on its members' belief that they have been allowed to prove themselves. The desire for special privilege may be denied, but to deprive a man of his deserts makes that man, in heart if not in deed, the enemy of that society, and a focus of discontent. When, on the other hand, men are convinced that higher attainments are theirs provided they show the requisite capacity and make the necessary effort, they become friends of those attainments.

Men who enjoy the opportunity, however dubious and remote, to enrich themselves tolerate the acquisition and enjoyment of wealth. But this applies to other values as well. Science, art, and education will be viewed with hostility by those who feel themselves arbitrarily excluded, cherished by those who feel that these spheres of life are open to all qualified aspirants, including, perchance, themselves or their children.

7

The maxim of equal opportunity owes its place in the American creed not only to the alleged personal and social benefits of competition, but also to the assumption that, since all men are endowed with the same faculties of reason and conscience, and since natural resources are abundant, the effect of equal opportunity will be to raise all men to *approximately* the same high level of attainment. The fact is that equality of opportunity is at best a secondary principle, subordinate to the principle of the maximum possible benefit to all individuals. There is no ethical axiom to the effect that individuals are entitled only to what they have earned or achieved for themselves. As between the maxims 'Each man should be rewarded in proportion to his service' and 'To each according to his needs,' the ethics of universalistic individualism is clearly on the side of the latter. Ethically speaking, there is no limit to the benefit which the state should confer on its members save its power to confer such benefits.

The competitive system in its ordinary economic sense has its own peculiar limitations. Even though it be admitted that economic goods are promoted by the system of laissez faire, it does not follow that this system is equally favorable to the so-called creative goods of art and science, "where to divide is not to take away." [25] To covet excellence in art and science does not imply that one shall outstrip or deprive others, but that one shall judge oneself by some standard of perfection.[26] It may well be that the state can best promote goods of this sort by furnishing qualified individuals with the requisite means, education, and leisure, thus relieving them from the pressure and the preoccupations of competitive struggle. Whatever in this sphere of life it can do is what it ought to do, without respect to any prejudice in favor of independent livelihood.

But the secondary character of equal opportunity is best demonstrated by stressing the fact that any free competitive struggle predetermines the attributes of the successful contestant. Its freedom is relative to the rules, the rules define the form of the achievement, and the form of the achievement favors those who possess the corresponding form of capacity. All orderly competitions encourage something. Competition for wealth puts a premium upon the qualities of acquisitiveness. This may or may not be desirable; in any case, it is important to recognize its negative as well as its positive implications. Insofar as society as a whole is cast into the form of the traditional laissez-faire capitalism, it sanctions greed and guile as well as industry and invention.*

It is important, furthermore, that if the race is to be 'fair,' the contestants should be at all times free from handicaps other than the ineradicable handicaps of native aptitude. But since the economic struggle is a continuing struggle of families and groups, the individual in some measure inherits the gains or losses of his antecedents; and he finds himself not at the start of a race where all are abreast, but at some later stage where the contestants are already spread in a column of advancement.

Public education is an attempt to remove this handicap of birth. It does so only to a limited degree. It may provide the individual of the younger generation with free 'tuition,' or even give him 'room and board,' but it cannot discount the effects of the domestic environment. It cannot free the son of poor parents from the pressure of livelihood, or the lack of 'spending money,' or the social ignominy of caste. So long as there are marked differences which surround the individual during his early years and create advantages and disadvantages of 'background,' it cannot be said that the contestants in the economic struggle are equal. The individual also finds himself competing, not with other individuals, but with durable and centrally controlled aggregations of corporate wealth.

* Robert Herrick's *The Memoirs of an American Citizen* bears eloquent testimony to the disillusioning and brutalizing effect of opportunity when this is conceived only in terms of the opportunity to rise in the economic scale.[27]

It is this which is fundamentally accountable for the socialistic strain in modern social thought. Professor Tawney says:

> In the absence of measures which prevent the exploitation of groups in a weak economic position by those in a strong, and make the external conditions of health and civilization a common possession, the phrase equality of opportunity is obviously a jest, to be described as amusing or heartless according to taste. It is the impertinent courtesy of an invitation offered to unwelcome guests, in the certainty that circumstances will prevent them from accepting it.[28]

At any stage of the contest, furthermore, the individual finds himself permanently favored or handicapped by his gains or losses up to that time. He runs only one race. Suppose him to be a man whose powers mature late, or who is the victim of accidental misfortune, or whose aptitudes lie elsewhere than in the economic struggle for existence. He enters the race at an early age, and being outdistanced, can never from henceforth compete on equal terms with his fellows.

Much has been said of the value of struggle as a school of character. But this school is commonly judged by those who succeed in graduating —little is heard of those who fail. The experience of adversity is benign to those who triumph over adversity. To those who fail, especially if they believe that their failure has been due to no fault of their own, adversity is often a cause of bitterness and moral dissolution. As the struggle for existence becomes more desperate, the number of moral casualties increases and the number of victors declines.

It never has been and never will be possible for a democratic state to avoid bestowing gratuities on its people with a view to promoting the equality of their competitive positions. It owes to all individuals as much of further positive good as it can dispense. It owes this in the sense that this is the reason for its being. In setting the terms of competition it assumes responsibility for the effect of those terms on the individuals who compete. It is obliged to make the terms of the race fair in substance and not merely in name; but it is no less obliged to consider the effect of the race upon the contestants, both upon those who win and upon those who lose. It has a duty, furthermore, toward the creation and distribution of those goods which flourish best under non-competitive conditions. These considerations amply justify measures which democratic states have in fact undertaken: to provide facilities for individual development, to correct the abuses of competition, to foster the arts and sciences, to protect the standard of living, to succor the ill, the poor, or the unemployed, and to redistribute wealth.

Gross inequalities of wealth tend, furthermore, to destroy that spirit of fraternity and of mutual respect which we have yet to consider, and which constitutes the spirit and flavor of a democratic society. "Where conditions are such," as Professor Tawney says, "that two-thirds of the wealth is owned by one per cent. of the population, the ownership of property is more properly regarded as the badge of a class than as the attribute of a society." [29] Democracy defeats its own purpose if it merely substitutes for a hierarchy of birth, or of ecclesiastical or political privilege, a hierarchy based on the advantages and the disadvantages of accumulated wealth, or the degree of economic opportunity which its members enjoy. Said James Fitzjames Stephen:

> Equality, like liberty, appears to me to be a big name for a small thing . . . Upon the whole, I think that what little can be truly said of equality is that as a fact human beings are not equal; that in their dealings with each other they ought to recognize real inequalities where they exist as much as substantial equality where it exists. That they are equally prone to exaggerate real distinctions, which is vanity, and to deny their existence, which is envy.[30]

But this is not "a small thing." The writer of these words commits the opposite and more serious error of making little of much—of making nothing of what is in a sense everything. For from these mixed equalities and inequalities and from the attitude taken toward them is compounded the very essence of social life.

8

It is impossible that men should be in all respects equal. It would be regrettable if it were possible. If there are to be individuals at all, men must exceed one another in those qualities which distinguish them. Even were men equal in wealth, there would still be aptitudes and forms of achievement which would define orders of rank. But it does not follow that inferiority in this or that respect need constitute a social stigma, attaching to the person as a whole.

Granted that men are equal in some respects and unequal in others, it is always possible to view one's fellows under the one or the other of these aspects. There is, in short, an *option* of social attitudes, which finds its most authentic expression in the democratic code of manners. Inequalities of capacity and attainment are intersected by planes of equality, and standing on these planes a man may look upon his fellows with a level glance, according to others the same respect which he demands for himself. Men are equal as men, each having both interests which deserve recognition and those ruling faculties of reason and conscience which are the ultimate sanction of political authority. There is a dignity of manhood which each man may acknowledge in every other man. There is the comradeship that springs from the common lot, the common hazards, and the common hopes of life. There is at the core of every life some self-justifying warmth of interest, some spark of heroism, or at least some pathos of failure. This is what is meant when men are declared to be equal under God. Whether men be officers or privates, they are fellow soldiers in the army of mankind, and must in some ultimate sense suffer common hardships, and go down to a common defeat or exult in a common victory, as destiny may decree.

From these basic equalities democracy proposes to form the essential human relationship. It harps on these equalities, makes much of them, focuses attention on them. In a democracy a man *treats* his fellow as an equal, despite their inequality; and this means that his attitude, his manner, his tone of address, are based on the fact that his fellow is in some respect as good as or better than himself rather than on the fact that his fellow has a smaller income, or a smaller IQ, or less distinguished parents, or an inferior office. There are both sorts of facts, and it is always possible to choose one or the other as the social bond.

This equalitarian emphasis generates the tonic flavor that distinguishes the air of American life. It justifies and gives a deeper meaning even to the vulgarities of American humor. A man is not allowed to disown his common manhood, however uncommon be his talents or his achievement. If he assumes a posture of aloofness and self-importance, there is always someone near at hand who will know infallibly how to break the spell. There seems to prevail in America the opinion that a dignity that will not keep is not worth keeping; and that homage should be sparingly dispensed. If a man pays too much homage to himself, other people are disposed to withhold it. This was apparently not the case at General Headquarters in Kreuznach, if one is to judge by the *Story* of General Ludendorff:

> The Field-Marshal and I, as well as other officers, lived in a villa which had once formed the home of the Emperor William I. . . . Our office was in the Oranienhof. The distance to it was short, and my regular walks to and fro afforded an opportunity to many kindly disposed people who wished to please me by their greetings and at times by gifts of flowers. Otherwise I led a secluded existence, because—I know men.[31]

Consciousness of merit such as this does not flourish in the American climate. Theodore Roosevelt, hero though he was, and endeared to the American people by many a bluff familiarity and amiable weakness, was never forgiven his modest admission that he had led a victorious charge at San Juan Hill. We tolerate the insignia of superiority only when there is no danger of their being taken too seriously. The comedian may wear a silk hat with impunity; and the political orator may use long words, provided it appears probable that he does not know what they mean. In these cases there is no doubt of the common clay of which the man is molded. But genuine superiority may not parade itself, lest it imply arrogance in the possessor and require subservience on the part of others.

It is in America, in all social classes and in all periods of its national history, that the art of 'taking down,' of abasing conceit, has reached its most delicate refinements. Thus the local celebrity of Angel's, a mining town in the Sierras, inquired of a friend who had recently visited the outer world: "Any political news from below, Bill?" And Bill replied: "Not much. The President o' the United States hezn't bin hisself sens you refoosed that seat in the Cabinet. The ginral feelin' in perlitical circles is one o' regret." [32] There is no country in the world in which flamboyant eloquence has soared to such unsteadying altitudes, nor any in which its bubble has been so neatly pricked—as by Mark Twain's friend from Arkansas City who interrupted his interlocutor to remark:

"Wait—you are getting that too strong; cut it down, cut it down—you get a leetle too much costumery onto your statements: always dress a fact in tights, never in an ulster." [33]

This is the comedy or the parody of the American spirit of fraternity. But in its essential meaning fraternity does not imply easy familiarity. Democratic manners are not the same as bad manners, nor are they inconsistent with reserve. It has been said of the relations between privates and officers in the American army that "the American soldier does not like the French familiarity nor the English patronizing ways, and intercourse should be in keeping with the customs of the service." [34] The spirit of fraternity is entirely consistent with differences of position, and with the absence of intimacy which such differences produce. There may be any amount of distance, provided it is not a distance of altitude. The desire for privacy, or the preference of selective to promiscuous intimacy, implies no claim of superiority, and is usually reciprocated.

President Charles W. Eliot of Harvard was an impressive and somewhat aloof man, presenting a striking contrast to his younger contemporary, Theodore Roosevelt, who 'mixed' readily and heartily with all comers. And yet one would hesitate to say that he was a less-authentic embodiment of the spirit of fraternity. He did not appear to *feel* superior, nor did he inspire a feeling of inferiority in others—however inferior, in fact, they usually were. He wrote a little book about his neighbor at Mount Desert Island, *John Gilley, Maine Farmer and Fisherman.* When the author spoke of this man's industry and frugality, of his skill and courage, of his "honorable career" and "sterling character," one felt that this was praise without reserve—that for Eliot, John Gilley was in all essential respects a complete man for whom he had unqualified respect:

Now in estimating the aggregate well-being and happiness of a community or a nation, it is obviously the condition of the obscure millions, who are sure to be absolutely forgotten, that it is most important to see and weigh aright. . . . This is the life of one of the forgotten millions. It contains no material for distinction, fame, or long remembrance; but it does contain the material and present the scene for a normal human development through mingled joy and sorrow, labor and rest, adversity and success, and through the tender loves of childhood, maturity, and age. We cannot but believe that it is just for countless quiet, simple lives like this that God made and upholds this earth.[35]

9

The basic ideas of democracy have a double application: to oneself and to others. It is important for democracy that individuals should demand liberty and tolerance for themselves, if only to offset the excessive self-assertion by others. But the fuller meaning and the higher moral attainment appear only in the will to tolerate, and in the according of liberty to others. The same distinction applies to equality.

It is essential to democracy that a man should demand equality, and resent the arrogance or the condescension of others. No high-spirited man can tolerate contempt. This is a different thing from the dislike of superiority. It is dislike of conscious superiority, or of the airs of superiority; because, in the first place, these aggravate accidental advantages, and ignore merit; because, in the second place, they imply an attitude of disparagement toward oneself, and induce a posture of self-defense.

Humiliation begets implacable hatred. In the French Revolution monsters of cruelty, such as Marat and Carrier, were seeking balm for the incurable wounds inflicted upon their self-esteem when they were despised subordinates in the establishments of great nobles. Even Mme Roland, as Le Bon says, "was never able to forget that, when she and her mother were invited to the house of a great lady under the *ancien régime*, they had been sent to dine in the servants' quarters." The same author points out that it was not those who had the most solid grievances who led the Revolution, but the bourgeoisie, who despite their wealth or professional success were contemptuously snubbed by the aristocracy. In a measure, then, Napoleon was justified when he said, "Vanity made the Revolution; liberty was only the pretext."[36]

But this explanation ignores the deeper aspect of the matter. Vanity is accidental and temperamental. The mainspring of revolt is not vanity, but the self-confidence and the self-respect which must inevitably accompany attainment. A democracy of opportunity must be at the same time a democracy of personal esteem. In a society which enables the majority of its members to taste success, or to dream of it, the sentiments of pride, honor, and dignity will be widely disseminated, and can no longer be regarded as the exclusive prerogatives of a caste. This fact is as pertinent today as ever. If a fashionable class, an employer class, a 'respectable' class, a 'highbrow' class, or a white race feel themselves to be superior, that feeling will infallibly be scented, and will arouse a resentful and rebellious spirit among those who have become conscious of their own worth. There is no escape from this dilemma. Either the masses of mankind must be broken in spirit, and convinced by subjection of the utter helplessness of their lot, or, if they are once allowed to travel on the highroad to success, their pride must be respected. A man cannot be given opportunity without the acknowledgment of his dignity.

The spirit of fraternity is fully expressed, however, not in the claiming of equality but in the granting of it to others. Lincoln put his finger on this with his usual infallibility:

> When we were the political slaves of King George, and wanted to be free, we called the maxim that "all men are created equal" a self-evident truth; but now when we have grown fat, and have lost all dread of being slaves ourselves, we have become so greedy to be masters that we call the same maxim "a self-evident lie." [37]

The acid test of the sentiment of equality is the dislike, not of the other's superiority, but of his inferiority. An equalitarian spirit which stops short of this justifies the parodies by the enemies of democracy: "Every man is as good as every other man, and a little better," or "When everybody is somebody, nobody will be anybody." The full spirit of fraternity acknowledges the just pride of others, and gives in advance that which the other's self-respect demands. It is the only possible relation between two self-respecting persons. It does not imply intimacy or friendship, for these must depend upon the accidents of propinquity and temperament; but it implies courtesy, fair-mindedness, and the admission of one's own limitations. It must underlie the closer relations of family, neighborhood, or vocation; but it must be extended to the broader and less personal relations of fellow citizenship and fellow humanity. It is the essential spirit of that finer companionship which even kings have coveted; but in a diffused and rarefied form it is the atmosphere which is vital to a democratic community.

It would be fatuous to shut our eyes to the fact that social democracy will have to be paid for. The only root which will bear this flower is generosity. Are we prepared to pay by surrendering personal advantages that we now enjoy? Most of those who read these words would lose materially by a more equal distribution of opportunity and attainment. If we enjoy more than the average good fortune, are we willing that it should be curtailed until such time as those who enjoy only the minimum shall be abreast of us? Are we willing to give up some of our own dear and familiar satisfactions? Or are we democratic only insofar as it costs us nothing? If so, we are not ready for a democratic future.

The whole of democracy will be less indulgent to us than the half of it we have already accepted. Without some previous self-discipline we shall many of us greet its dawn with a wry face. But insofar as we have learned to live more austerely, and to find our happiness in those things which are not diminished by being widely shared, we may in the time to come have the heart to be cheerful despite the realization of the ideal to which we profess our devotion.

The realization of democracy must depend finally not on the self-assertion of the unprivileged and the forced, or even willing, concessions of the privileged, but on their common preference of a higher form of life. There must be not merely a claim and a yielding of rights, but a relish for that reciprocity in which a man associates with his fellows on terms of equality. Democracy bids us search out in each man that generic humanity, that inner passion or obscure heroism, which can ennoble him in our eyes. The democratic faith is the belief that such an ennobling quality can always be found by one of sensitive imagination and tender sympathy. The highest reason for seeking it is because mutual respect between man and man is the relationship in which both makes the best of each, and expresses each at his best.

Treat another as inferior and you place him in a dilemma. He must either suffer humiliation or show resentment. You either break his will or antagonize it. Feel superior, and you do something equally injurious to yourself: you acquire a narrowing insensibility and a stagnant complacency. Arrogance and contempt are sterile, both in him who gives and in him who receives; in self-abasement life is shriveled and degraded. The most enlivening and fertilizing of social relationships is hopeful confidence and esteem, felt stoutheartedly by each man for himself and generously by each man toward his fellows.

CHAPTER TWENTY

THE UNIVERSAL HUMANITY

1

AT THE TIME when President Wilson conceived the League of Nations and exhorted the people of Europe to give their adherence to it, this was felt to be the sort of thing that might appropriately be expected of America. Later, these same Europeans were somewhat resentful that we should have abandoned the League of Nations, and that some among us should have appeared even to derive satisfaction from its failure. It was not merely that we seemed to have been untrue to our word, but that we seemed to have been untrue to ourselves. Similarly, no European debtor nation would have expected another European nation having legal claims to cancel them. In asking such large-mindedness of us, they paid us a high compliment, which I fear we did not wholly appreciate. But they were taking that view of us which we by our professions had encouraged them to take. He who thinks well of himself and takes no pains to conceal the fact can scarcely complain if others take him at his word, and form their expectations accordingly.

During the greater part of our national history we have taken high ground, and pledged ourselves to principles. Sometimes boastfully and rhetorically, sometimes humbly and sincerely, we have affirmed ideals and have proclaimed them to the world. These ideals have been humane and universal. They have defined for us a certain role in history. There are certain things which are in keeping with that role, and other things which are out of character with it. If we mean to be what, historically, we have claimed to be, then it is fitting and logical that in all enterprises for promoting peace and international co-operation we should belong to the party of faith and action rather than to the party of skepticism and inertia.

There have been three ideas of the role of America in the world at large: expansion, isolation, and example. The settlement of the West, and the vast territorial acquisitions from the Treaty of Paris in 1783 to the acquisition of California and New Mexico in 1848, represented the idea of expansion. The occupation of land and the acquisition of natural resources were animated by the spirit of discovery and conquest. Americans looked covetously beyond their existing boundaries to Canada, Central and South America, the West Indies, and the islands of the Pacific, as well as to the unexplored regions of the Arctic and the Antarctic, and resolved to exclude their European rivals and attain a hegemony over the whole of that portion of the earth's surface lying between the Atlantic and the Far East. This movement of aggrandizement culminated in the annexation of Alaska, Hawaii, Puerto Rico, and the Philippine Islands, and in the use of armed force to support the economic penetration of Central and South America. America took its place among the 'imperial' powers.

This idea of expansion was from the beginning accompanied by the idea of isolation. America was settled by men who for one reason or another were discontented with their European place of origin. Most of those who came to America did so in order to get away from something —from poverty, from military service, or from political and religious oppression. Their love of America was mingled with a hatred of Europe, and this negative feeling was often stronger than the positive tie of common race or nationality. It has sometimes been difficult, for example, to say whether the Irish-American was more deeply imbued with the love of Ireland or the hatred of England. Similarly, German-Americans have been anti-French, and Franco-Americans anti-German; American Jews, formerly anti-Russian and anti-Polish, are now anti-German; American Greeks and Armenians were once anti-Turkish; German, Italian, and Russian refugees are anti-Nazi, anti-Fascist, and anti-communist. Every European state, and every European institution, political, ecclesiastical, or cultural, has been sooner or later hated by some group of Americans.

The summary effect of this was to implant in the American mind a general antipathy to Europe, aggravated throughout a great part of our history by the colonial's sense of inferiority to the mother country. To this was added the sense of geographical remoteness and material self-sufficiency. America was safe from invasion, and could live its own life free from interference. It was abundantly provided with natural resources and needed no help from outside its boundaries, save such as came through peaceful trade. All that was necessary in order that America might fulfill its destiny was that Europe should avoid trespassing on America's natural sphere of influence. The Monroe Doctrine thus represented both the positive idea of expansion and the negative idea of aloofness. It was this negative idea that culminated after the First World War in the refusal to enter into political commitments with European powers, even in the interest of trade and peace. It was this idea which prompted Americans to despair of Europe, to liquidate its foreign interests, and to resolve not to participate in any future war, no matter how it might appear to involve the American pocket or the American conscience.

Both of these ideas—the positive idea of expansion, and the negative idea of isolation—were qualified by a third idea, that of example. All three ideas—expansion, isolation, and example—were fused in the idea of destiny, the sense of its predestined greatness of a nation set apart from the rest of mankind in order the better to serve mankind. Having extended and stabilized its boundaries and detached itself from the conflicts and vicissitudes which troubled the rest of the world, America could achieve a perfected society which would not only benefit its own members, but give light and comfort to less fortunate societies. Superstitions incurably prevalent elsewhere might here be dispelled; hopes elsewhere frustrated might here be realized.

America's exemplary mission was closely associated with the doctrine of the 'state of nature,' and with the sentimental cult of nature, both in vogue in Europe in the eighteenth century. How these blended with the experience of the frontiersman to create a sense of virginal purity and fresh promise is abundantly set forth in Crèvecœur's *Letters from an American Farmer,* describing the American experiences of this naturalized Frenchman in the 1760's and 1770's, and first published in 1782. The writer discourses on the "misguided religion, tyranny, and absurd laws" which "depress and afflict mankind" throughout the rest of the earth. "Here," he says, "we have in some measure regained the ancient dignity of our species." Simplicity, mutual affection, freedom, tolerance, the fecundity of nature, the joys of labor, the spur of ambition, and the rewards of possession distinguish this "most perfect society now existing in the world," where all men "are become men" and "rank as citizens."[1]

America as a land where the human race can escape the corruption of old civilizations, make a new start, and prove the full possibilities of human life under optimum conditions is the theme of George Berkeley's famous "Westward the course of empire takes its way," written when American independence still lay in the future:

In happy climes, the seat of Innocence,
Where Nature guides and Virtue rules,
Where men shall not impose, for truth and sense,
The pedantry of courts and schools:

There shall be sung another golden age,
The rise of empire and of arts,
The good and great inspiring epic rage,
The wisest heads and noblest hearts.[2]

If at the time of the First World War France was peculiarly disposed to idealize us, to judge us by our professions rather than by our practice, and to look to us for an unnatural magnanimity, it was for the best of historical reasons. The American and French democracies had sprung from the same epoch, exchanged adolescent pledges of friendship, and shared their youthful enthusiasms. The yet unborn nation of the western hemisphere and the declining monarchy of the Bourbons had looked to the same philosophy, the one for its creation, the other for its regeneration.

This role of America as the visible realization of the dream of Europe found for the imagination of France a dramatic representation in the meetings between Franklin and Voltaire in Paris in 1778. Voltaire was then eighty-four years of age, in the last year of his life, while Franklin, though twelve years younger and in the full vigor of manhood, was scarcely less venerable in character and appearance. Voltaire's biographer, Condorcet, describes the occasion when Franklin presented his young nephew to Voltaire, who blessed him with the words "God and Liberty"; and the scene at the meeting of the Academy of Sciences at which the public insisted that these two philosophers embrace, afterward acclaiming the incident as the embrace of Solon and Sophocles.[3] America as embodied in Franklin signified the liberty of man under the Providence of God. Philosophy, to employ Franklin's own words, was that which "let light into the nature of things." [4] America, to its own admiring consciousness and that of Europe, was the child of light, uncorrupted by fanaticism, dogmatism, and superstition–infallibly destined to happiness by its practice of wisdom and virtue.

The real burden of Washington's Farewell Address was not a counsel of irresponsibility and self-interest, but one of alliance with mankind as a *whole* rather than with any particular nation or group of nations. "It will be worthy of a free, enlightened, and at no distant period, a great nation, to give to mankind the magnanimous and too novel example of a People always guided by an exalted justice and benevolence." [5]

This idea was a persistent theme in the public utterances of American statesmen. Henry Clay referred to "this last and glorious light which is leading all mankind, who are gazing upon it, in the hope and anxious expectation that the liberty which prevails here will sooner or later be advanced throughout the whole of the civilized world." [6] From more recent times a single example will suffice. When in 1917 President Wilson addressed the soldiers of the new National Army, he referred not to what these soldiers might by their arms achieve, but rather to what they, and through them America, symbolized:

> You are undertaking a great duty. The heart of the whole country is with you. . . . For this great war draws us all together, makes us all comrades and brothers, as all true Americans felt themselves to be when we first made good our national independence. The eyes of all the world will be upon you, because you are in some special sense the soldiers of freedom.[7]

Even in the era of despair which followed the First World War, the same idea was advanced to justify the survival of America. America must avoid being involved in the debasing and destructive consequences of war. America, like Noah, might alone be saved from the universal catastrophe, but, like Noah, it would repeople the earth. Though the rest of the world lapse into barbarism or destroy itself, America must remain to carry the torch of civilization. In order that this might be, America must be strong; hence the justification of its territorial and economic expansion, and of its 'defensive' armaments. Americanism must remain pure and undefiled: the American 'standard of living' must be protected, and the American ideology preserved against contamination. Hence the justification of aloofness. If it was too late to make the whole world safe for democracy, then democracy must be withdrawn into that part of the world which remained safe. This was taken by Americans to be more than a policy of self-preservation. For what was to be preserved was not merely America, but democracy; and democracy was conceived not as a merely American interest, but as the ideal form of life. Hence in preserving its own existence and quality America was serving that very world which it seemed to be abandoning.

So long as there was room for expansion on the North American continent and within broad and flexible frontiers to which Americans could with some show of justice claim a right, the idea of expansion was compatible with the ideas of isolation and example. With the Spanish-American War, however, it became apparent that when expansion became imperialistic it not only destroyed isolation through drawing America into the conflicts of rival empires, but invalidated America's claim to exemplary virtue. Thus William Graham Sumner, writing in 1898, said that imperialism meant the abandonment of "all American standards," and putting "shame and scorn on all that our ancestors tried to build up here." [8]

It should be clear, then, that from its beginning America has claimed, and has often been accorded, a mission to mankind. If its mission has been attended with misgivings, it has been because of doubts as to how it should be realized, and because of a conflict between America's destiny of material greatness and its moral creed.

The twentieth century has witnessed a progressive and profound alteration, both in thought and in deed, of the American role in the world at large. If its expansion has not ceased, it has at any rate been reinterpreted. The Monroe Doctrine has been superseded by the Good Neighbor Policy. The idea of unilateral destiny has been superseded by the ideas of reciprocity and mutual obligation. Two world wars within twenty-five years have proved the impossibility of isolation. Never has there been a more conscious and determined attempt to practice isolation than in the years following the first of these wars; and never has America's participation in world affairs been so complete and so irretrievable as in the second. The idea of isolation has now become permanently obsolete through crucial and far-reaching technological changes in the spheres of communication and industry. Safety is no longer assured by distance, or profit by domestic enterprise. The world is moving toward the condition in which both peace and prosperity are indivisible, and America participates in that change. The idea of example is doubly discredited. Having less consciousness of merit, as regards both the validity and the application of these principles, Americans no longer regard themselves as worthy of imitation. Being brought into multiple and inescapable relations with other peoples, they realize that in these relations they must practice, and not merely exhibit, democracy.

2

America's participation in the life of mankind at large is a return to its original character and a resumption of its original premises. It is rooted in the nation's initial cosmopolitanism—its baptismal dedication to universal values. It has been reproached, often by its own critics, for its lack of a national culture. Whether this be reckoned a merit or a fault, it has at any rate enabled America to escape the blight of tribalism, conscious or unconscious. However nationalistic it may have been in its politics, it has never confused the norms of truth, beauty, and goodness with the peculiarities of a historical race or with the fiction of racial purity.

The geographical remoteness of the United States, instead of generating an insular culture, has incited its people to nourish themselves upon all cultures. The mixed origin of its population has brought diverse cultures to its shores. Its comparative safety in times of trouble has made it a place of refuge for independent spirits who cared more for what they believed than for their place of residence.

Americans have been charged by European observers with a lack of the philosophical spirit, as by Lowes Dickinson after his three months' tour of America in 1901:

> The most intelligent people in the world, they severely limit their intelligence to the adaptation of means to ends. About the ends themselves they never permit themselves to speculate; and for this reason, though they calculate, they never think, though they invent, they never discover, and though they talk, they never converse. For thought implies speculation; discovery, reflection; conversation, leisure; and all alike imply a disinterestedness which has no place in the American system.[9]

I am not blind to those of our national traits which have given to this critic's comment its superficial plausibility. It is true that it has not been characteristic of America to breed a leisured class, and to cultivate that dispassionate contemplation which distinguishes the older cultures of Europe and Asia. It is true, furthermore, that as a people we have been peculiarly preoccupied with livelihood and the accumulation of wealth. Men do not commonly carry philosophy into the market-place, and Americans spend much of their time in the market-place.

But while this is a fact, it is not in itself profoundly significant. Philosophy appears not so much in what people do as in the reasons which they give themselves for doing it. It is a fact that Americans are bent upon business, but it is more significant that they should conceive business in a certain way—as evidence of individual self-reliance, as opportunity of self-improvement, or as a conquest of nature and regulation of human affairs in the interest of human progress. These reasons are in turn based upon assumptions concerning human nature, the rights of the individual, the function of institutions, and the place of man in history and the universe. This philosophy is perhaps not the philosophy of Lowes Dickinson. It is an optimistic philosophy of the type that justifies both the fact and the hope of material progress. But whatever the validity of the American philosophy, there can be no doubt of the fact that it is philosophy.

To reproach America for a lack of philosophy shows an astonishing lack of historical understanding. Puritanism may have its faults, but it can scarcely be reproached for a lack of philosophy. It would perhaps be fair to say that no community of men has ever existed with a livelier sense of man's cosmic role, or with a more conscious and elaborate adjustment of daily life to the structure of the universe, than those prolific and hardy settlers of New England. It is peculiarly characteristic of American history that this little corner of the land was settled by men with ideas. The passengers of the *Mayflower* no doubt brought furniture for their houses, but they also brought furniture for their minds, and there are more authentic survivals of the latter than of the former. Persecuted people not only have ideas, but they are acutely conscious and peculiarly tenacious of them. Their governing purpose is not to accommodate their ideas to the environment, but to find or create an environment which is suited to their ideas. America has been peopled by men who asked not merely to live, but to live in a certain way which their reason and conscience approved.

Passing from the colonial to the revolutionary period, we find that from its first moments of self-consciousness the national aspiration of America expressed itself in the name and in the vocabulary of philosophy. Its institutions were framed to fit a philosophical creed. America sprang from a political revolution, and a political revolution is essentially philosophical, since it appeals from practice to theory, and from what is to what ought to be. The initial fault of America was perhaps an excess of philosophy. The Declaration of Independence was a philosophical tract, and is commonly reproached for being so. Its doctrines have remained the familiar and common creed of Americans up to the present day.

The philosophical quality of the American tradition disposes Americans to a constructive and hopeful attitude toward international relations. Simply to be philosophical-minded, regardless of the specific content of the philosophy affirmed, implies a universality of outlook. It implies that local and national problems shall be considered as special cases of general problems that beset all men in their dealings with one another and with their common environment. Insofar as the political life of any nation is consciously philosophical it will be accompanied by the sense of a common task, in which each nation is both concerned with its own affairs and at the same time contributing to the advancement of political enlightenment in the world at large.

Every political philosophy envisages some pattern and norm of internationality, even if it be no more than a struggle among self-asserting and self-aggrandizing units. If this struggle is conceived in terms of a Darwinian struggle for existence, it implies the survival of the fit and the strong. If it is conceived in terms of historical relativism, it implies that each nation shall develop the institutions best fitted to its own genius. If it is conceived in terms of a historical dialectic, it implies the emergence of more adequate truths out of warring abstractions. In each case there is a standard, whether of power, of self-expression, or of concreteness, which is applicable to all nations; and each nation so far as consciously animated by such a philosophy will feel a sense of participation in the history of mankind.

But when the authors of the Declaration of Independence acknowledged "a decent respect to the opinions of mankind," they meant something more simple and explicit than this. They meant that reason and conscience were faculties common to all men, and that these faculties yielded universal truths that were directly applicable to institutions and policies. All men by virtue of the possession of these faculties constituted a court of appeal competent to pronounce judgment upon any society. Such judgments would not be a mere self-assertion of the particular critic or group, but the enunciation and application of common principles. The several nations of men would then be rivals, not in the sense of enmity, but in the sense of emulation, seeking to surpass one another in their fidelity to these principles, and in the translation of them into concrete procedures and policies. The victory of one would thus be a victory for all.

The philosophy of democracy is thus a manifestation of the cosmopolitanism of the age which gave it birth. By cosmopolitanism is meant a man's allegiance to universal culture rather than to the particular social group to which he belongs. If, as in the eighteenth century, a general is primarily a master of the military art, and is relatively indifferent to the nation which he serves, he is a cosmopolitan. If, as in the eighteenth century, a man's code of manners is dictated by common principles of gentility rather than by the local customs of his country, he is a cosmopolitan. A scientist, a painter, a sculptor, or a poet who is loyal to the standards of his vocation, and comparatively indifferent to the peculiarities of his domestic environment, is a cosmopolitan. A Europe such as that of the eighteenth century which enjoys the fruits of human genius, regardless of the nationality of a Locke, a Newton, a Walpole, a Hume, a Voltaire, a Rousseau, a Franklin, or a Jefferson, is infused with a cosmopolitan spirit.[10]

In the democratic philosophy this same cosmopolitanism is transferred to politics—to that field of human activity which is the last and the best-fortified refuge of localism. But the political cosmopolitanism of the democratic cult is not reserved for the members of an elite of experts; it is all-pervasive. For every man, whatever his more particular vocation, has a concern with politics. The exponent of political democracy will, in the cosmopolitan spirit of the eighteenth century, feel a kinship with all democratically minded men, however divided by their non-political creeds, their origin, their station in life, or their race, habitat, and nationality. A man's allegiance to his 'country' will be felt as a manifestation of his deeper allegiance to the political dictates of reason and conscience. Enlightenment will first free him from the effects of propinquity, habit, and established authority, and constitute him a free individual; it will then unite him with other emancipated individuals in a voluntary solidarity of rational and moral agreement.

3

Cosmopolitanism tends to weaken local attachments, but does not in itself imply a union of entire persons. It has the narrowness of a purely cultural bond. Its relations are wide, but they are thin. If democracy is committed to an all-comprehensive concord of human interests, this is because, over and above its cosmopolitanism, democracy endorses the sentiment of humanity, and extends it to all mankind as members of one family. The following allegory is quoted from that essentially American philosopher Benjamin Franklin, in a letter addressed in 1782 to his friend and fellow philosopher Joseph Priestley:

> In what light we are viewed by superior beings, may be gathered from a piece of late West India news, which possibly has not yet reached you. A young angel of distinction being sent down to this world on some business, for the first time, had an old courier-spirit assigned to him as a guide. They arrived

over the seas of Martinico, in the middle of the long day of obstinate fight between the fleets of Rodney and De Grasse. When, through the clouds of smoke, he saw the fire of the guns, the decks covered with mangled limbs and bodies dead or dying; the ships sinking, burning, or blown into the air; and the quantity of pain, misery, and destruction the crews yet alive were thus with so much eagerness dealing round to one another, he turned angrily to his guide and said: "You blundering blockhead, you are ignorant of your business; you undertook to conduct me to the earth, and you have brought me into hell!" "No, sir," says the guide, "I have made no mistake; it is really the earth, and these are men. Devils never treat one another in this cruel manner; they have more sense, and more of what men (vainly) call humanity." [11]

What are the attitudes embodied in this allegory? In the first place, we are invited to contemplate the state of mankind by the light in which it is viewed by superior beings. Instead of being blinded by passion and deceived by prejudice, we are to rise in imagination to heights from which the history of man is spread before us like a map. We then see that men in general, including ourselves, have been seized by a sort of madness. Having won a precarious footing in nature and a faint hope of heaven, instead of consolidating their gains and improving their opportunity they are furiously engaged in destroying one another. Clinging to the edge of an abyss out of which they have laboriously climbed, and with the summit emerging from the clouds above, instead of extending a helping hand they are rapping one another's knuckles and dragging one another down.

The irony of the picture depends on the underlying assumption. If it were assumed that the object was to climb upon another's prostrate form, or to obtain exercise, or to live dangerously, or to register the tragic emotions, or to test endurance, or to be chastened by suffering, then the effect upon the spectator would be very different. Instead of saying, "How shocking! How absurd!" he would say, "How admirably does history express the meaning of life!" But it is assumed that the object of the enterprise is to bring all members of the human family along together as far as possible toward the summit. This assumption is what "men call humanity"—their mutual solicitude and responsibility, extended universally. Their inhumanity, so astonishing to the visiting angel, is their failure to recognize the stranger as a brother, and their forgetfulness of the common task and original partnership.

This is the Christian element in the allegory, unrecognized even by Plato, the most humane of the ancients:

> I affirm that all the members of the Greek race are brethren and kinsmen to one another, but aliens and foreigners to the barbarian world. . . . Therefore when Greeks and barbarians fight together, we shall describe them as natural enemies, warring against one another; and to this kind of hostility we shall give the name of *war*; but when Greeks are on this sort of footing with Greeks, we shall say that they are natural friends, but that in the case supposed Greece is in a morbid state of civil conflict; and to this kind of hostility we shall give the name of *sedition*.[12]

Greeks did not always treat one another like brethren and kinsmen, but Plato urged them to, pointing out the likeness and the common interests which bound them together against the outer barbarians who were their natural enemies. The Stoics, the Hebrew prophets, and the founders of Christianity urged men to go further and to recognize all fellow men as natural friends; thus implying the total abolition of war, since there are no longer any barbarians to be treated as natural enemies. Such hostility as remained would then be considered as domestic, morbid, and remediable.

The sentiment of humanity is open to the charge of being a mere pious phrase. It is true that extension of human acquaintance does not, as has sometimes been supposed, automatically promote the sentiment of humanity. The present painful predicament of mankind, in which nations and social classes are extraordinarily inflamed by hatred and suspicion, has arisen at a time when men are brought as never before into one another's presence. The greater the exposure to human contacts, the more room for hatred and suspicion, as well as for sympathy and love. It is evident that the cult of humanity involves not merely a multiplication and an intimacy of human relations, but at the same time a development and a strengthening of the kindly emotions.

Is it possible that these emotions should be extended to all mankind? And are these emotions not falsified by the impossible attempt to extend them? This is the opinion expressed in James Fitzjames Stephen's vigorous and honest-minded critique of democratic catchwords:

> I cannot but think that many persons must share the feeling of disgust with which I for one have often read and listened to expressions of general philan-

thropy. Such love is frequently an insulting intrusion. . . . It would be pedantic to attempt anything like a definition of love, but it may be said to include two elements at least—first, pleasure in the kind of friendly intercourse, whatever it may be, which is appropriate to the position of the persons who love each other; and next, a mutual wish for each other's happiness. If two people are so constituted that such intercourse between them as is possible is not agreeable to either party, or if their views of what constitutes happiness are conflicting, I do not see how they can love each other. . . . Love for Humanity, devotion to the All or Universum, and the like are thus little, if anything, more than a fanatical attachment to some favourite theory about the means by which an indefinite number of unknown persons (whose existence it pleases the theorist's fancy to assume) may be brought into a state which the theorist calls happiness.[13]

It is evidently impossible to love individually persons whom one does not know individually. It is possible, however, to look with pity and solicitude upon the spectacle of aggregate mankind—the vast procession of suffering, hoping, striving men and women. And it is possible that a sentiment should be directed to a class of objects: most, if not all, sentiments are so directed. One can, for example, hate snakes in general, even though one's acquaintance with particular snakes be very slight. But this means that one possesses a permanent disposition such that *any individual* snake excites antipathy. It is in this sense, presumably, that Stephen himself hated sentimentalists. By the same token it is possible to love men in general—in the sense, namely, of being so disposed that the presence or image of any man, whoever he be so long as he is recognizable as a man, will excite love.

Remoteness and difference do unquestionably reduce the intensity of love. There is a difference between my blood-brother and my fellow townsman. If I call the fellow townsman my brother, I do not mean that he is to me all that a blood-brother can be, and that the bond of the family counts for nothing. I mean only that something of the quality of brotherhood, a flavor of *brotherliness,* may still attend the more distant relationship. Similarly, the love of a stranger cannot be the same love as that felt for a neighbor. But it is possible to transfer to the first relation something of the quality of the second, and to act and feel in a neighborly way to him who is not literally and in the full sense of the term my neighbor.

Humanity does not mean the reduction of the more saturated to the more diluted form of fellow feeling, when the former is possible. In the character of Mrs. Jellyby, Dickens represented what he called the "telescopic philanthropy" of one who left her own house in squalor while concerning herself with the natives of distant Africa:

> She has devoted herself to an extensive variety of public subjects, at various times, and is at present . . . devoted to the subject of Africa; with a view to the general cultivation of the coffee berry—*and* the natives—and the happy settlement, on the banks of the African rivers, of our superabundant home population. . . . The room, which was strewn with papers and nearly filled by a great writing-table covered with similar litter, was, I must say, not only very untidy, but very dirty. We were obliged to take notice of that with our sense of sight, even while, with our sense of hearing, we followed the poor child who had tumbled downstairs . . . Mrs. Jellyby preserved the evenness of her disposition. She told us a great deal that was interesting about Borrioboola-Gha and the natives; and received so many letters that Richard, who sat by her, saw four envelopes in the gravy at once. . . . During the whole evening, Mr. Jellyby sat in a corner with his head against the wall, as if he were subject to low spirits.[14]

Carlyle, having in mind, perhaps, the household of his neighbor Leigh Hunt, remarked that "though the *world* is already blooming (or is one day to do it) in everlasting 'happiness of the greatest number,' these people's own *houses* (I always find) are little Hells of improvidence, discord, unreason."[15]

'Charity begins at home,' not only because it is more effective at close quarters, or because there is a peculiar and prior responsibility for family and neighbors, but because the original meaning of humanity is to be found in the tenderness, the consideration, the delicacy of feeling, the respect, and the loyal helpfulness that are sometimes attained in the more intimate relationships. The sentiment of humanity widens and dilutes these attitudes while preserving something of their essential quality. It avoids whatever is opposed to these attitudes, and it invites their fuller development. It says to any human stranger: "Owing to circumstance, you are not my friend. But did circumstances permit, you might be. I shall regard you in that light, as a possible friend. At least I shall refuse to treat you as an enemy. I shall constantly remember that we are both of the same great human family. As such we can understand one another and be of help to one another. In the fundamental concerns of life we strive for the same goal, share the same defeats, rejoice in the same victories, and undergo similar hardships."

Whether, as Stephen suggests, love is intrusive and impertinent depends on its quality and not on its diffusion. A love which is untimely and insensitive, or a love which imposes on its object a 'good' which is only a projection of the lover's ego, is not love in any admirable sense, whether it be directed to wife, child, brother, friend, neighbor, or mankind at large. For love on every level, and in every degree, consists essentially in the desire that the object of love shall be happy in his own terms. It offers and gives, but it does not demand; and is as dependent on delicacy and restraint as it is on warmth of heart.

4

Modern democracy is pledged to the creation of a just and humane international order by virtue of its major moral premise: namely, its universalistic individualism.

The locus of good and evil is the individual, possessed of desires and feelings, and capable therefore of happiness or unhappiness. The locus of moral good and evil, of right and wrong and duty, is the human (or superhuman) individual, possessed not only of desires and feelings, but of reason and conscience, and capable therefore of regulating his conduct by a regard for the general good.

The meaning of 'individual' is in both cases universal—not one individual, or some individuals, but all individuals. An individual's happiness is good, whoever he is; an individual, whoever he is, has a duty toward all individuals, whoever they are. As regards the fundamental obligation to regulate action by the maximum happiness of all whom the action affects, all distinctions between man and man are irrelevant. Put one man on one side of a line and a second man on the other side, and each is morally bound to take account of the other, regardless of the character of the line—whether it be sex, wealth, education, race, or nation. The line may be erected into a barrier—but this, while it may make the obligation less evident or less easy to fulfill, in no way diminishes its moral force. Selfishness is easy to explain, but impossible to justify.

The universalistic-individualistic ethics provides the justification of the national state, but also defines and transcends its limits. The nation-state is concerned with the general happiness of a particular social group bound by many ties other than a common government, but the fundamental duty of men is to all men, whatever the social group. No man obtains immunity from it by acquiring the status of a political ruler or a citizen. An individual may possess just *political* claims only upon the government or fellow members of the particular state to which he belongs, but he possesses *moral* claims upon the consideration of all men. A man's legal obligation is limited to such regard for his fellow men as is imposed by courts, whereas his moral obligation is conditioned only by the existence of sentient mortals within the range of his action. Morality being conceived unqualifiedly in terms of the relations of human individuals as such, its duties are inescapable, and extend automatically, by their very meaning, to mankind at large.

The same ethics which justifies the state, and governs its dealings with its own members, applies to the state in its dealings with individuals and aggregates of individuals beyond its own borders, including other states. It is a notorious fact that the state acts selfishly in its conduct of diplomacy or war, save so far as it may be restrained by considerations of prudence. If this be justified on the ground that public officials act as agents of the people, and are bound to serve only those who employ them, then the responsibility rests upon the people. If the head of the state claims authority in his own right, then he must be prepared to accept the blame. The disregard of human interests that lie outside the state is wrong, and responsibility for the wrong rests somewhere.

The only escape from this conclusion is to suppose that selfishness changes its moral quality when it changes its diameter: the selfishness of the individual who considers only himself is wrong; the selfishness of members of a nation who consider only themselves is right; the selfishness of a family or a class is somewhere between the two. But a partial unselfishness does not annul the residual selfishness. It tends rather to increase it, as when family, class, or national loyalties harden men's hearts and intensify their antipathies beyond the privileged circle. They are fired by what the Italian statesman Salandra once termed a "sacred egoism,"[16] which requires individual self-sacrifice, and derives from this fact a consciousness of merit. But it is still egoism.

"Sacred egoism" is commonly associated with the view that the nation-state is not an organization composed of a limited number of individuals, but a being of a higher order whose will is the ground of all moral obligation. It creates the obligations of its individual members, but is itself under no obligations, whether to members or to non-members. Adopt an ethics of universalistic individualism, however, and this moral immunity becomes meaningless. There are only 'public' individuals acting in the name of the state, or private individuals from whom these have derived a delegated power. Outside the state there are other individuals, public or private, having the same moral claims. There is no individual, public or private, who escapes obligation to all other individuals.

Since egoism means a disregard of actual interests lying beyond some focal region, egoism can never in the nature of the case be "sacred." Even when, as in collective egoism, it transcends the interests of any one of its component individuals, it is, as regards the interests which it disregards, necessarily blameworthy. "Sacred egoism" is a monstrous fantasy, a bastard offspring of morality and immorality. Democracy unmasks its ambiguous ancestry, discloses its immoral strain, and applies the judgment which it merits. It will, for example, judge national aggression as a crime of the same quality as rape. It will not be misled by the fact that in order to perform aggression successfully individuals must sacrifice their private interests to what they consider a national good; any more than it will excuse the murderer on the ground that the prosecution of his crime requires a certain measure of courage, forethought, and self-control.

The fact that nations commit crimes with a good conscience does not mitigate the crime, but testifies to the incomplete development of conscience. Johnson's remark that "Patriotism is the last refuge of the scoundrel," takes on an even more sinister meaning than that which is commonly understood. In patriotism the scoundrel may acquire immunity not only from the judgment of others but from his own scruples. The state has played a leading role in the history of human wickedness.

To admire the state, however great the emphasis on its internal aspect of justice, tends to the condoning of its accustomed unscrupulousness and violence. Even in the discharge of its obligations to protect its people against the lawbreaker or the invader, the state employs force, and to worship it as an end in itself tends to exalt might above right. It would be better on the whole to regard it as a regrettable necessity, like the soldier, the policeman, or the public executioner. Statism is the worst of all superstitions, because it singles out for worship that agency which is compelled, owing to practical exigencies, to practice what the perfecting of life would eliminate.

It is commonly supposed that the moral defect of national selfishness lies in ignorance and that it can be corrected by enlightenment. It may be true to say that 'enlightened self-interest' is the utmost that can, at any given moment in human history, be expected of nations; or that even enlightened self-interest would be an improvement upon past international practice. But to say that conduct intelligently calculated to satisfy the desires and ambitions of one nation *exclusively* must coincide with conduct intelligently calculated to satisfy the desires and ambitions of all nations *inclusively* is evidently false. It may be that the term 'enlightened' is intended to imply unselfishness; those who employ the expression 'enlightened self-interest' rarely undertake to define it.

Consideration for others can be reduced to enlightened self-interest up to a certain point. A nation's wealth and power depend up to a certain point on the goodwill of other nations, and therefore a nation governed by enlightened selfishness will seek to earn the goodwill of other nations by conferring benefits on them. A nation's own wealth is promoted by the wealth of its customers, and its power by the power of its dependents or allies—up to a certain point, but not beyond that point. These selfish gains may, after a certain point, be attainable only at the *expense* of other nations, and require a hardening of the international heart.

It is true that in proportion as men or nations are moved by sympathy or prefer universal to merely private goods, their very self-interest will impel them to unselfish conduct. But unhappily, not all men and nations are so constituted. Grinding the poor or exploiting the weak will profit the sordid and the ambitious men so long as they remain sordid and ambitious. They lose something, to be sure, but they do not feel the loss, nor can it be measured in terms of their selfish gain and power. They cannot be made to recognize their loss until they develop social interests of another sort and experience the peculiar satisfactions of living among friends and equals.

Self-interest may, in other words, have a broad base or a narrow base. It may take the long view or the short view, the total view or the partial view. It may express the desires, the needs, and the aspirations of all, or of something less than all—the momentary appetite of the single individual, the class, or the nation. The all-inclusive interest—that is, the moral or just interest—cannot be proved to a man in terms of any narrower interest which he may happen to feel and choose to call his own. He may be so inclined, and is often so inclined, that he has less to gain by giving-and-taking than by merely taking. To create an international order we must implant, arouse, spread, and enlist a sentiment of all-inclusive justice and humanity. We must learn to say 'we' rather than 'I'; and in saying 'we' to mean not any single nation, or any limited group of nations, but all nations and all mankind united.

Democracy implies internationality, then, by the expansion of its basic moral principles to the total aggregate of mankind. Christianity is international because a soul is a soul to be saved, regardless of nationality. Democracy is international because the moral claims of one man's happiness and the obligations of another man's will are not canceled by political frontiers. The same principle of inclusiveness which gives the national group a moral priority over its members gives to the total aggregate of the members of all nations a priority over the members of one of its constituent nations. In other words, democracy is impelled by its own universalistic-individualistic logic to seek the creation of an orderly and co-operative society in which the happiness of all is the duty of each.

5

All political philosophers save egoists, relativists, and adherents of the historical-organic school, have regarded the creation of a world polity as implicit in the fundamental moral premises of any polity. Immanuel Kant is the most illuminating and relevant of these prophets, because his views were formulated at the close of the eighteenth century and embodied the same ideas as those which constituted the foundation of modern democracy. In 1784, a year after American Independence was recognized in the Treaty of Paris, he published an essay entitled "The Natural Principle of the Political Order, Considered in Connection with the Idea of a Universal Cosmo-political History"; and his more famous "Eternal Peace" * appeared in 1795, just after the recognition of the French Republic by the Treaty of Basel. In these contemporary developments Kant saw not only the realization of the moral idea of the state, but the promise of a moral world order through a federation of republics.

Kant's individualism, his universalism, and his insistence that all personal embodiments of humanity are to be taken as ends in themselves, have international as well as national political implications:

> What avails it to labor at the arrangement of a commonwealth as a civil constitution regulated by law among individual men? The same unsociableness which forced men to it becomes again the cause of each commonwealth's assuming the attitude of uncontrolled freedom in its external relations, that is, as one State in relation to other States; and consequently any one State must expect from any other the same sort of evils as oppressed individual men and compelled them to enter into a civil union regulated by law. Nature has accordingly again used the unsociableness of men, and even of great societies and political bodies, her creatures of this kind, as a means to work out through their mutual antagonism a condition of rest and security. . . .
>
> And, at last, after many devastations, overthrows and even complete internal exhaustion of their powers, the nations are driven forward to the goal which reason might easily have impressed upon them, even without so much sad experience. This is none other than the advance out of the lawless state of savages and the entering into a federation of nations. . . .
>
> However visionary this idea may appear to be . . . it is nevertheless the inevitable issue of the necessity in which men involve one another. For this necessity must compel the nations to the very resolution—however hard it may appear—to which the savage in his uncivilized state was so unwillingly compelled when he had to surrender his brutal liberty and seek rest and security in a constitution regulated by law.[18]

---

* "These words," said Kant, "were once put by a Dutch innkeeper on his signboard as a satirical inscription over the representation of a church yard." [17]

Polity for Kant was rooted in what he called "the unsocial sociability of man." [19] Human interests conflict, and must be reconciled. Men need security, and can obtain it only by delegating authority to a government which, invested with the collective force of the community, can guarantee the predictable and orderly conduct of its component individuals or groups. By organization men not only can avoid the destructive consequences of violent conflict, but can combine their efforts and secure by division of labor a greater fund of goods than is possible by the separate action of the parts. If the advantages of peace, security, and co-operation argue for the national state, they argue with equal force for a more inclusive polity that shall eliminate national violence and insecurity, and obtain the benefits of a world-wide co-operation.

The civil polity has come into being by a more or less unconscious biological and historical process, and requires only to be better fitted to its use. In the case of the world-polity nature has been less bountiful, and it is necessary to create it almost de novo. But in the democratic theory this difference is not fundamental. In considering the justification of the civil polity, one concludes that if there had been none, it *would have been* reasonable to create it; in considering the justification of the world polity, one concludes that since there is none, it *is* reasonable to create it. The world-polity is, owing to its magnitude, complexity, and diversity, exceedingly difficult to create; it may even be doubtful whether it can be created. Nevertheless it is right and reasonable that it should be created, if possible, or so far as possible. It is a morally valid goal of aspiration and effort.

The democratic, or contractual, theory begins with actual persons, and argues for the creation of political institutions. The reasoning proceeds from the parts that are to the whole that ought to be—and ought to be for the sake of the parts. The opposite, or historical-organic, theory begins with the actual political entity and argues for the obedience of its members. Reasoning here proceeds from the whole that is to the parts that ought to be—and ought to be for the sake of the whole. There is no constructive solution of the present conflict between existing civil polities save by the democratic or contractual theory. If there were an actual world-polity, then one could argue, in accordance with the organic theory, that its member-polities should obey it. But it does not exist, and there can, on this theory, be no obligation to create it; for that would be to argue from the members to the organism, or from the parts to the whole.

The democratic argument for a world-polity can be formulated in terms of the state of nature, whether that state of nature be conceived in the pessimistic terms of Hobbes or in the optimistic terms of Locke. According to Hobbes, life in the state of nature is "solitary, poor, nasty, brutish, and short," and the laws of nature oblige men to escape it by *seeking* peace, and by transferring their right of independent action to a power that can *keep* the peace. According to Locke, the state of nature is already in some degree a rule of peace, since reason dictates peace, and since all men are endowed with reason; but an organized polity is nevertheless desirable for reasons of convenience. The present international state of nature resembles the revolting spectacle depicted by Hobbes rather than the more idyllic picture drawn by Locke. Both, however, imply a world-wide order of mankind in accordance with the laws of nature. For Hobbes, this order would require an irrevocable surrender of sovereignty to a world Leviathan, and would depend on the wholesome fear inspired in its naturally egoistic member states; for Locke, the sovereignty of the world polity would represent, and be answerable to, the judgment of reasonable and moral men.

There are several widespread misunderstandings that cloud the question of world-polity. In the first place, it is assumed that sovereignty is absolute—all or nothing—and that the creation of an international polity therefore implies the complete surrender of sovereignty by the component nations, and its unlimited exercise by a super-state. Kant did not propose a super-state, but a "federation of free states," created expressly for the purpose of putting "an end to all wars forever." Such a federation would not exercise coercive powers over its members, but would consist of an agreement which each member state imposed on itself. Such an agreement, Kant hoped, would be effective if the federated states were republics, in which the people who paid the costs of war would be in control.[20] Although Kant's proposal reflected the over-optimism of his day, it did at least suggest that the possibilities of federation had not been exhausted. It suggested, furthermore, that an international organization might at the outset limit itself to the prevention of armed aggression, and leave broader powers of legislation to the future. It was an enlightened attempt to reconcile the imperative necessity of abolishing war with the autonomy and the cultural identity of free nations.

In the second place, it is often assumed that in entering an international system the constituent nations would surrender their 'rights' of sovereignty. The precise opposite is true. The individual acquires rights when he is brought within a system of rights in which the rights of each are limited by their universality. So long as they are considered as having no obligations to one another, individuals have no rights, but only varying degrees of power. And only when a civil system of individual rights is translated into law and generally observed can these rights be secured. The same holds of nations. An international system which defines the freedom of each nation, and at the same time prescribes its limits, is the only way by which the freedom of nations can become a moral right; and only when the conduct of nations toward one another is actually regulated by such a system can such rightful freedom be confidently enjoyed.

Finally, the idea of an international polity must not be allowed to obscure the individualistic premises on which the whole democratic way of thinking is founded. The first obligation of any polity is to its people. International polity extends this obligation so as to embrace all people. Political authority and political rights attach intrinsically only to persons, by virtue of their attributes of reason and conscience, and their capacity for happiness. The nation-state, like the corporation, may be described as a 'juridical person'—in the sense of a legal fiction or procedural convenience. But it is not a real or a moral person, and such rights and obligations as it has must eventually be translated into the rights and the obligations of its individual members.

It follows that the moral justification of an international polity lies in the greater freedom and happiness which it brings to the people who live under the several national governments. How highly centralized it shall be is a question of method, and not of principle—precisely analogous to the question of the degree of centralized control within the nation-state. The extreme exponents of a 'super-state' would have the international authority related directly to the universal people—represent them and serve them. The exponents of the opposite view, taking account of the immense volume and complexity of human life, and of its diversities of speech, locality, custom, and attachment, would derive the international authority from the several peoples, and distribute its benefits to them only indirectly through their national governments.

Between these two views there are many intermediate possibilities, some one of which is more likely than either extreme to afford the wisest solution. But amid all the doubts and difficulties that beset the constitution of the optimum world order, one idea must be held clearly and tenaciously in mind—that governments have no rightful authority save such as they derive from their people, nor any rightful gains save such as they pass on to their people. The right of self-determination is a right of people to possess their government, and not a right of government to possess its people. There is no moral justification of an international system which delivers people from external tyranny and exploitation only to subject them to tyranny and exploitation from within.

6

"I would it were as sure," said St. Augustine, "that there were no war to be falsely called god, as it is plain that Mars is no god." [21] This might be said to represent the view of enlightened democracy in the present age. The two world wars have robbed war of much of its glamour, and through intensifying and spreading its destructive effects have revealed Mars as the monster he is rather than as the god which in shining armor he sometimes appears to be.

The following account of British naval maneuvers appeared in a London daily paper in 1932: "Divisions are mustered. The band plays 'Voices of the Guns,' and standing beneath the 15-inch muzzles, we sing in the bright sunlight 'Hark, My Soul, it is the Lord'—a strangely moving proceeding. The next moment we are down to brass tacks." [22] "Getting down to brass tacks" here signifies a procedure which is the precise opposite of that love of fellow man which is proclaimed to the soul by the voice of "the Lord." This same contradiction between the piety which is sometimes invoked to sanction war and the actualities of war is driven home by the biting satire of Mark Twain's "War Prayer":

O Lord our Father, our young patriots, idols of our hearts, go forth to battle —be Thou near them! With them—in spirit—we also go forth from the sweet peace of our beloved firesides to smite the foe. O Lord our God, help us to tear their soldiers to bloody shreds with our shells; help us to cover their smiling fields with the pale forms of their patriot dead; help us to drown the thunder of the guns with the shrieks of their wounded, writhing in pain; help us to lay waste their humble homes with a hurricane of fire; help us to wring the hearts of their unoffending widows with unavailing grief; help us to turn them out roofless with their little children to wander unfriended the wastes of their desolated land in rags and hunger and thirst, sports of the sun flames of summer and the icy winds of winter, broken in spirit, worn with travail, imploring Thee for the refuge of the grave and denied it—for our sakes who adore Thee, Lord, blast their hopes, blight their lives, protract their bitter pilgrimage, make heavy their steps, water their way with their tears, stain the white snow with the blood of their wounded feet! We ask it, in the spirit of love, of Him Who is the Source of Love, and Who is the ever-faithful refuge and friend of all that are sore beset and seek His aid with humble and contrite hearts. Amen.[23]

On the premises of democracy, as well as of Christianity, war has always been essentially evil, inasmuch as it substitutes hate for love, cruelty for gentleness, selfishness for benevolence, and force for persuasion. A Treitschke who justifies war by appeal to its "virile features," or to the "grandeur of history," and who declares that "the laws of human thought and of human nature forbid any alternative, neither is one to be wished for," [24] must argue from premises which constitute a complete inversion of the democratic order of values. There is no fundamental justification of war unless one accepts as intrinsically and supremely good either the sheer power of survival, however ugly and debasing the terms of the struggle and however ignoble the attributes of the victor; or the subjective quality of heroism, regardless of the cost to its victims; or the fictitious will of a hypostasized state, whatever its relation to the happiness of its component individuals. The Axis dictatorships in which the cult of war has been revived have appropriately adopted and propagated some or all of these ideologies, with the result that as never before in history the cleavage between the opponents of war and its partisans coincides explicitly with the cleavage between the democratic and the anti-democratic philosophies of life.

As the art of war has developed, its inherent brutality has more unmistakably emerged. Ruthless attacks upon civilian populations, cold and calculating cruelty by officers who are themselves in no personal danger, mental shock more hideous than the effects of physical wounds, wholesale devastation and economic ruin—all serve to reveal the real intent of war, which is to employ whatever degree or form of violence may break resistance. Military codes of honor and chivalry have all but disappeared. While overt warfare destroys men's bodies and property, propaganda and espionage corrupt their minds. War is no longer confined to the professional soldier or the military caste, but engages every element of society, so that its evils are all-pervasive. At the same time that the evils of war have become more evident and more shameless, its probability of occurrence has increased; so that the whole world is preoccupied with fear, poisoned with suspicion, and disturbed by a sense of insecurity. War has thus become, as never before in the world's history, an imminence of catastrophe; while peace has become not only an ideal good, but an absolute and paramount necessity.

The cause of international peace lies in the direction of democratic aspiration, and defines the duty of all who accept democratic premises, whether this duty be undertaken with hopeful resolve and grim determination or abandoned in despair.

Although the recent experience of mankind has accentuated the evil of war and the necessity of peace, the moral issue has been obscured by identifying pacifism with the cult of nonresistance. Peace is a durable state of affairs involving two or more social groups in which conflicts of interest are adjusted without resort to physical violence. If a pacifist is one who pursues peace, he should adopt the most effective means to this end, even though it be the use of violence. The refusal by any individual or group to take up arms may or may not conduce to peace; he whose refusal is governed by a personal scruple or a religious taboo may in fact be the enemy of peace.* If he adheres unqualifiedly to the maxim 'Do

---

* An examination of approximately 1000 of 3000 "conscientious objectors" in the United States Army at the time of the First World War disclosed the fact that 90 per cent gave religious reasons, while 75 per cent were of the "religious-literalist" type (such as Mennonites) to whom war was forbidden by a categorical Biblical injunction.[25]

not use violence,' he must be prepared to add, 'whatever the consequence'—even though it should be the perpetuation of war. It is unfortunate, to say the least, that this moral attitude should have acquired the name of 'pacifism.'

It is sometimes assumed that the way to bring about an ideal state of affairs is to behave as though that state of affairs already existed—so that the way to bring about the state of affairs called peace would be to behave peacefully. The error of this assumption is evident. To achieve a leisurely form of life it may be necessary to work; to achieve a libertarian social system it may be necessary to impose restraint; to achieve security of life and property it may be necessary to take life or seize property. Similarly, to achieve an international organization in which war is eliminated may require the making of war. A 'war to end war' is not a paradox.

Whether the non-use of violence in any given situation would or would not conduce to a state of peace is a matter of experience and not of principle. Since peace is a form of reciprocity, the effectiveness of nonresistance is primarily a psychological question. What, in the light of experience, is the probable effect of the first party's non-use of violence upon the second party? Will it disarm him, or will it tempt him to the use of force through the prospect of gaining an easy success? Will it increase or diminish the number and the militant temper of the warmakers? It is evident that no general answer is possible—the effect will depend on the characters of the two individuals or groups, on the nature of their relationships, on habit and tradition, and on countless other circumstances. Suffice it to say that nonresistance will under *some* conditions be the surest road to war, and that the will to use violence will sometimes be the surest road to peace. This being the case, it behooves every pacifist first to ask himself whether he is or is not a lover of that organized and durable state of affairs called peace, and is prepared to adopt whatever means is, in the light of experience and all available facts, most likely to conduce to that end.

A second source of confusion is the failure to distinguish between two sorts of peace: a peace of justice, and a peace of intimidation and servility. Democracy is dedicated to the end of peace because, in the first place, of adherence to the code of humanity. But democracy is equally pledged to liberty and equality. Its standard is not satisfied by a condition of non-violence, no matter how durable or deeply implanted, provided this condition is obtained at the cost of certain fundamental human rights. Public order is for democracy not an end in itself, but a means by which individuals may satisfy their interests and exercise their prerogatives without interference; it is quite conceivable, therefore, that the resort to violence, or the threat of violence, in the defense of rights may bring a closer approximation to the democratic good than would a mere condition of physical safety and disarmament.

The maxim of 'peace at any price' implies that the warmakers may always be bought off. It is true that men commonly wage war in order to impose their wills upon opposing wills, and it is then possible to remove the cause of war by voluntary withdrawal of the opposing will. Intimidation is a method by which sheer force may triumph without violence. But even submission and servility afford no guarantee of peace—unless it be the peace of death. But men sometimes make war because they enjoy making war, or because they prize the warrior's qualities, or because they desire to exterminate rivals or inferiors. Submission does not then disarm the murderer, but merely makes his work easier. He would as soon cut the throats of sheep as wrestle with lions.

It is customary in this context to cite the aphorism, "The blood of the martyrs is the seed of the Church." Waiving the fact that martyrs may be made by forceful resistance as well as by passive submission, it is to be noted that Tertullian had in mind the historic Church, and affirmed the efficacy of heroic example upon the imagination and the conscience of posterity. If the blood of the martyrs is to germinate, it must be sown in favorable soil, and cultivated by the racial memory. Martyrdom does not touch the hearts of ruthless men. The blood of unknown martyrs bears no fruit. And if martyrdom is justified by its historical effects, then, by the same token, so is the use of violence—when, and if, violence will be more effective.

It is sometimes said that values cannot be either preserved or destroyed by violence. This is true, however, only on the assumption that all values are supernatural. If a man passively submits to martyrdom, his recompense in heaven is not destroyed; and the essence of his virtue may be said to remain unaffected in an eternal world of Platonic ideas. But as an embodiment of righteousness he ceases to exist, and as an agent of righteousness he ceases to exert power, his place being taken by a victor who is the embodiment and the agent of unrighteousness.

The moral virtues are embodied in the dispositions and the convictions of living men, and perpetuated in organized institutions. But all historical forms of collective life are vulnerable to physical forces. It is possible by violence to destroy a just or humane society, either by destroying the just and humane men who compose it, or by extinguishing the sentiments of justice and humanity through control of the external influences by which men's minds are molded. He who refuses from personal scruples to resist such uses of violence becomes himself a passive instrument of that very reign of violence which he professes to abhor.

Democracy is pledged to promote, by persuasion if possible, by force if needs be, an extension of its domestic peacemaking institutions to the interrelations of peoples and states. It has been said that the first European to grasp and to advocate this idea of a concord of all mankind was Alexander the Great. He seems in this respect to have advanced beyond the teachings of his Greek masters, who adhered to the distinction between Greeks and barbarians, and beyond the example of his imperialistic predecessors, who practiced the enslavement of conquered peoples.[26] Whatever be the degree of Alexander's adherence to this idea, or his claim to be its author, it has haunted the European mind since Alexander's day. Whatever may be thought of its consistency with Macedonian, Roman, or modern imperialism, there can be no doubt of its place in the program of democracy.

There is, according to democratic principles, no justification of authority save agreement. What 'we' agree upon has authority over each of 'us.' Otherwise an authority exercised by either over the other is unjustifiable. There is in democracy no limiting condition which prescribes that 'we' shall both belong to the same race or state. It is unjustifiable that Germans or Japanese should subjugate Poles or Chinese because Germans or Japanese desire territory, natural resources, or imperial glory; or even for the 'good' of Poles and Chinese, regardless of what

Poles or Chinese actually desire. The moral solution of conflict is not obtained by superior force, but only when both parties, viewing the matter roundly, each alive to its own interests, but recognizing the rights of the other, agree upon a plan which promises the maximum fulfillment of the demands of both.

It is clear that for democracy the way to peace is by treating the causes of war rather than its symptoms. There is only one persistent cause of war: namely, conflict of interest, real or fancied. "The same reason that makes us wrangle with a neighbour," said Montaigne, "causes a war betwixt princes." [27] The actual desires of men, whether taken as individuals or as groups, are incompatible. This difficulty is met within a social group by the social conscience, by the economic processes of production and distribution, by law, and by government. But the very agencies which achieve a moral solution within the group aggravate the difficulty as between one group and another: because, in the first place, the conflicting rivals are more powerful; because, in the second place, the public agencies of the state, and the emotions of nationalism, create fictitious interests. The moral way of meeting this predicament, on the premises of democracy, is twofold: to establish a world-wide conscience and a world-wide economic, legal, and political system which shall achieve for the several nation-states what each nation-state accomplishes for its individual members; and, by the internal liberalization of each nation-state, to dispel the fictitious interests of officialism, statism, and nationalism.

On democratic premises the purpose and norm of international polity is world-wide agreement based, not on fear, ignorance, despair, or hysteria, but on benevolence and enlightenment. It is a part of the democratic political philosophy to recognize that there will always be an element of irreconcilable dissent which will require coercion. The penalties imposed by the state are justified by the absence or the weakness of the will to agree, or by defects of benevolence and enlightenment. In these cases fear must be substituted for reason, and coercion for voluntary assent.

The international counterpart of this coercive force is the international armed force. How such an armed force shall be composed, and whether it shall be attached to a central international authority or to alliances of nations bound by treaty, are questions of expediency. In any case it is intended that such a force shall represent the whole; that it shall be so overwhelming and so inexorable as to act as a deterrent; and that the normal conduct of mankind shall be governed not by fear and coercion but by enlightenment and goodwill translated into public opinion and habit.

7

The term 'international' has acquired a bad name in some quarters, because the 'internationalist' is supposed to be a man who is attached to no nation, or equally attached to all—which comes to the same thing. He is viewed with suspicion as alien, uprooted, and unpatriotic. But to construe internationalism as opposed to nationalism is as absurd as though one were to construe that inter-individualism is opposed to individualism. The opposite is true. It is through organized society that individuals are multiplied and protected; and similarly, it is only through an international order that a multitude of nations can exist safely and freely upon the same planet. Isolation being no longer possible, nations, if they are to live at all, must contrive to live in relations with one another—that is to say, internationally.

While international, like national, polity implies agreement, democracy implies that agreement shall provide for the maximum degree of liberty and autonomy among the members. Just as in national polity the presumption is in favor of the individual's being left to the control of his own will, so in international polity the presumption is in favor of self-determination. Just as the liberty and the self-development of individuals imply the exercise and use of their own ruling faculties—each pair of hands, to use Lincoln's expression, being regulated by that head with which it is conjoined by nature—so the liberty and the self-development of a nation imply the creation and the use of its own institutions of control. The same principles which argue against the paternalistic state argue against an imperial or a world-wide paternalism.

As the democratic state is a harmony of diverse and largely autonomous individuals, so a democratic internationalism will be a harmony of diverse and more largely autonomous nations, each following its own genius, developing its own culture, discharging its obligations to its people in its own way, and obeying its own judgment, limited only by the necessities of peace and the benefits of co-operation. The lesser propinquity and intimacy between nations permits of a looser bond and a larger measure of liberty than is possible among members of the same nation. The virtue of unity will lie in its preservation and promotion of manyness; the whole will be measured by its contribution to the parts. The purpose will be to benefit the constituents by organization rather than to absorb and identify them by organism.

Just as a state will encourage such distance between man and man as shall enable each to obey his own will unmolested by interference, dwelling in amity but dwelling apart, so an international polity modeled on the same pattern will enable and encourage each nation to manifest its own unique characteristics. It will be a meadow rather than a forest, each tree being exposed to the sun on all sides. The whole will consist of a broad framework of non-conflicting spheres within which the parts may live their own lives. The purpose of community in the one case, as in the other, is not that all may become one, but that each may be itself, profiting by its relations to the rest. Community will consist negatively of non-interference, and positively of a fund of economic and cultural resources which can be adopted and utilized by the members, each according to its own lights.

As the democratic individual will rejoice in individual otherness, so a truly democratic nation will not only let alien nations alone in return for being let alone itself, but will enjoy its intercourse with them because of, and not despite, their alien character. "Other nations of different habits," says Whitehead, "are not enemies: they are godsends." [28]

The tolerance by one individual of others, even the desire that others shall be different, does not contradict the individual's essential confidence in himself. The wholesome conviction that he is right and that others are wrong may properly support him in his private chamber of self-consciousness. An afterglow of these moments of moral recuperation may properly attend him out in the world, and save him from weakness and obsequiousness. But there is a difference between this inner conviction and those airs of superiority and arrogance which offend the self-respect of his neighbors. Similarly, a nation may believe itself right, and prefer itself, while at the same time according others the same privilege. It is entirely possible to be a patriot without offense to other patriotisms. The first condition of this is the absence of ostentation and pretension to infallibility. International comity, like good manners in personal relationships, consists in believing that one is right while at the same time acknowledging that one may be wrong, and conceding that the other is at any rate entitled to a hearing. It is this marriage of pride and modesty, of self-confidence and deference, that marks the highest form of human intercourse, whether between a man and his neighbors, or between the United States and Latin America, or between America and Europe, or between Occident and Orient.

Tolerance is a more important condition of international peace than acquaintance, or even intimacy. It was once naïvely supposed that the modern development of communication would inaugurate an era of mutual understanding. With newspapers, radios, moving pictures, and opportunities for travel, all the nations of the world would know one another better, and this better knowledge would lead to sympathy and love. But every occasion of understanding also creates possibilities of misunderstanding. Indeed the only situation in which people can completely avoid misunderstanding is the situation in which they have never even heard of one another.

Increase of travel has multiplied the menace of the eyewitness—the man who speaks with authority because he has 'been there.' The traveler's judgment is distorted by accidental impressions which he trusts because they are immediate and personal. What could be more pathetic and childlike than the following protest contained in a letter to the *Times* of London:

> I have travelled often on the Continent. both before and since the War, and I hope and believe that my work makes me to some extent an observer of things. Perhaps, therefore, my impressions of the German people may merit equal space and equal prominence with that accorded by *The Times* to the recent letter of Dr. Compton-Rickett. In that letter he described the German

people as suffering from 'mass hysteria' and 'fear,' with other concomitant evils. To this I would make reply that the experience of weeks of sojourn in the Rhineland compels me, in the interests of truth, to record my contrary impressions. . . . I cannot imagine a people more happily united in a spirit of peaceful comradeship. The care of the poor children in the towns and the arrangements for their holidays in the country are so widespread and successful that other nations might well follow in this respect. Their kindness to animals is a revelation to me, and I have seen no ill-fed or ill-looking beast anywhere.

My lasting impressions will be of good-looking, well-conditioned horses at work—quiet cattle in wagons—endless window-boxes of geraniums in towns and villages and all along the terraced restaurants in the Rhine and Mosel, and, finally, of the kindly, good-humoured welcome given to an English traveller indebted to many Germans speaking English so well that he seldom needs to attempt their own language himself.[29]

It would have been better if this traveler had remained at home, and read his own newspapers. He would at least have escaped the error of supposing that a window box of geraniums which you see yourself is more significant than a concentration camp which is proved by the testimony of others.

Or the traveler may find his worst suspicions confirmed. He discovers that foreign countries are inhabited by foreigners, who are unintelligible, unreliable, and queer. The impression that the traveler makes upon the native is even worse. The typical traveler is a self-indulgent and insolent plutocrat. He is curious and intrusive, and his patronizing ways are endured only because of the money which may be made out of him. To exploit him is the natural method of reprisal. If there is anything more unpleasant than the impression which travelers make upon the countries which they visit, it is the impression which they make upon one another. Each returns home more sure than ever that he and his own kind are the salt of the earth.

The multiplication of human contacts by the modern arts of communication multiplies the effects of otherness. If the peace of the world were to be postponed until complete understanding was attained, the world would have to wait longer than it can afford to wait. Nor is such an understanding possible without the reduction of all national minds to their common denominator, or the dominion of one over the rest. Indeed, it may be said that the deepest understanding is possessed by those who acknowledge its impossibility—feel vaguely beyond the horizon of clear vision, refuse to measure the incommensurable by their pocket yardsticks, and after living, and not merely traveling, among an alien people can still say, as D. H. Lawrence said of Mexicans, that their "way of consciousness" is not our way of consciousness.[30]

A residuum of unintelligibility is essential to the flavor of all human relations, international as well as domestic and neighborly. Peace and fullness of life alike depend not on complete understanding, but on the enjoyment of the strange, the impenetrable, and the unpredictable. A democratic organization of international relations would encourage each nation to be its own peculiar self while at the same time respecting other nations and relishing the shock of difference.

As in the case of the state, so also in the case of mankind at large the ultimate obligation is to the system of tolerance itself. If the purpose of democracy transcends the boundaries of the state and contemplates a world-wide state of affairs in which national liberties, like personal liberties, are secured and raised to the maximum, then democracy is pledged to employ the means to this end. If a nation asks to be tolerated in order to destroy such an order, or to make it forever impossible, such a nation has no claim upon the tolerance of other nations.

Any state which professes to serve the cause of a world-order so constituted by custom, sentiment, policy, and international law as to enable each state to live in security, and in the perfection of its own distinctive culture, is bound to employ the means by which, to the best of its knowledge, that end will be realized. It will not judge the question of isolationism or participation in world affairs, of embargo or commerce, of friendliness or hostility—or even of peace or war—in the light of an absolute imperative or prohibition, but as a question of cause and effect. There may be reason to believe that the preservation or creation of a liberal world-order will be best served by a nation's abstinence, in order to keep its own institutions intact. There may be reason to believe that such an end can best be served by example and persuasion. But if, after reckoning the costs and hazards, it appears that diplomatic, economic, or even military intervention will be a more effective means, then the nation will decide accordingly.

8

If democracy is to survive and prevail in the world at large, it must be a fighting faith—at least in the metaphorical sense, and at worst in the literal sense. Faith is an essential ingredient of the democratic tradition. Adherents of democracy must "encline to hope rather than fear, and gladly banish squint suspicion." [31]

The heart of democratic enterprise is a faith in human nature, which emphasizes man's generic and eminent faculties of reason and conscience, and credits them with high potentialities through education and social reorganization. Democracy inherits from Christianity that untiring evangelism which admits no ultimate failure, no unforgivable sin, no incurable sickness. Democracy has faith in the future of mankind, which may or may not be linked with a faith in its beginnings. Democracy has faith in the power of the human will, counting on the broad truth that a being endowed with will becomes thereby in some measure the author of his own destiny. This is what is meant, and must be meant, by will—a force by which ideas are translated into achievements and by which hopes are realized. Applying this fundamental but often neglected truism, democracy resolves to be the maker and the master of its own institutions. At the same time, democracy has appropriated the Occidental and modern faith in the control of nature through the applications of science—a faith which has been confirmed, renewed, and extended in every decade in man's recent history.

In America these articles of faith have been reinforced by a native buoyancy of temper which is an effect of rich natural resources, of climate, and of racial composition. The sum of it all is that workaday optimism which philosophers call 'meliorism'; that progressivism and indomitable spirit of reform which, like all hope, is naïve, but which, unlike mere idle wishing or pious aspiration, is willing to make the effort and pay the cost.

Democracy, then, is optimistic, in a sense which is sharply opposed to Sorel's revolutionary syndicalism and to Hegelian absolutism, both of which have insisted upon the ineradicable presence in the world of suffering and of conflict. A recent writer on Sorel says:

"Democratic" ideology . . . stands for "Liberal" doctrine, the pacific, rationalist, and hedonist temper of social democracy; and is inseparably bound up with the conception of man's natural goodness, his perfectibility, and the necessary progress of the species. Against all this, Sorel stands for "classical pessimism," which is to mean, not the mere disillusionment of the shallow optimist, but the belief that man's nature has in it a radical evil, and can only come to good by heroism and the sublime, in short, by war.[32]

Bernard Bosanquet, a characteristic exponent of the Hegelian form of pessimism, declared his sympathy with Sorel's view, and referred to the liberal creed of progress as "a profoundly contrasted view of life and the world," which holds that "pain and badness are somehow a mistake in the world, and a mistake *prima facie* of our own making, something not meant to be, so to speak. Undo our mistake and all will be well." [33]

The active optimism of democracy which believes "pain and badness" to be remediable is opposed not only to pessimism, but to a static optimism which affirms the actual goodness of the whole despite the evil of the part, or the actual goodness of reality despite the evil of appearance. Democratic optimism rests neither on metaphysical conviction nor on sublimation. It is a militant optimism which, having a realistic respect for the enemy, nevertheless believes in the possibility of victory with that degree of confidence which raises effort and invention to the maximum.

America has been guilty of complacency and shallowness because of a rapidity and ease of partial success. The man or the society that has risen fast is likely to believe that the summit has been reached. A false optimism of this type was bred by the material prosperity of the nineteenth century. The spirit of this optimism, with its characteristic flamboyancy of rhetoric, appears in the following paragraphs taken from a report of the president of the New York Mercantile Library Association in 1853:

Here, the penniless youth just stepping upon the world's arena, may supply the deficiencies of education, and lay broad and deep the foundations of a practical knowledge, and prepare himself for future usefulness and honor. . . . Here, if he will but avail himself of the advantages subject to his command, the clerk of to-day, when he shall have become the merchant of to-morrow, may adorn and dignify that class of men, who have left their footprints upon the burning sands of the equator and the frozen snows of the polar zone. For the merchant is the man of *this* age. He has contributed more essentially than any other class to break down the barrier of feudal institutions, to change the spirit of a more chivalric era from the love of military glory, conquest, and renown, to the love of peace and peaceful institutions.

Under the influence of the mighty spirit of this mercantile era, all the energies of the human mind and all the principles of progression have been called into action. The arts have been carried to a greater degree of usefulness and perfection. . . . The treasures of the land and the treasures of the seas have been scattered among the nations. For his use and his mostly, the lightning has been wrested from heaven and placed upon the wires, and is scarce rapid enough to communicate men's ideas to each other, and convey from mart to mart, the changes in value and the revolutions of trade. Mingled with the roar of the surges that lash the shores of the Pacific, is heard the hum of cities built in a day, the engine of the steamship, and the hammers of the artisan; whilst from Oregon to Australia, new States and new Governments attest his daring enterprise and mighty genius.[34]

This mood of self-congratulation has passed, along with its style of utterance. So long as large numbers even of Americans—who are in respect of material goods the most fortunate people in history—suffer from poverty, insecurity, and frustration, the task of social democracy is scarcely begun. When mankind labors under the perpetual menace of war, when jealousy and hate divide both nations and classes, when that laboriously woven fabric which we call civilization hangs on the issue of an angry word or an irresponsible impulse, the time calls for repentance and alarm, and not for eulogy.

American democracy staked its success on the spread of enlightenment. It was not designed to be a rule of the masses, or of a higher corporate being, or of a superior elite, but an agreement of citizens conducting their joint affairs with wisdom and goodwill. This hopeful aspiration finds itself frustrated by its own partial success. The people have been raised to a level of bare literacy which exposes them to new techniques of mass appeal. Minds are debauched rather than informed, and unscrupulous propaganda has outrun education. The events of recent years have given new force to the Miltonic conception of humanity's ordeal:

And Man there placed, with purpose to assay
If him by force he can destroy, or, worse,
By some false guile pervert.[35]

Not only does the western world fall short of its own standards, but these standards themselves are rightly questioned. There is a humility begotten by social disorder and by war, but there is also a humility begotten by preoccupation with material goods and technological advance. An era of moral confusion and even of despair has followed hard upon man's greatest triumphs over the forces of nature. The contact between the West and the East, and a more philosophical contemplation of life as a whole, arouse misgivings concerning the direction of progress as well as its degree.

It was once customary in America to condemn China by the standard of "the strenuous life." Theodore Roosevelt, the great exponent of that gospel, warned us that "we cannot, if we would, play the part of China, and be content to rot by inches in ignoble ease within our borders"; and he went on to predict that "we should find, beyond the shadow of question, what China has already found, that in this world the nation that has trained itself to a career of unwarlike and isolated ease is bound, in the end, to go down before other nations which have not lost the manly and adventurous qualities." [36]

Despite the apparent fulfillment of this prediction, it is impossible to read any sympathetic account of the older Chinese civilization without feeling that despite its military and industrial weakness it possessed something of the quality of final perfection. The constant factors in the human cycle—birth and death, sex and marriage, youth and senescence, health and sickness, agriculture and trade, and the rhythm of the seasons—were poetized by symbols and ritual, and invested with an immediate sense of aesthetic or moral value that raised them above the level of harsh necessity or calculating expediency. Human experience was ennobled by delicacy of perception and instructive wisdom. Life had been set long enough to permit its acquiring form. Organization had reached the stage in which its reciprocity of benefits was associated with a sense of participation.

To see life so consummated, as also in antiquity and the Middle Ages, is to feel that the modern European world, though building on a broader base, is still in the phase of scaffolding and steam shovels. These doubts are well founded, and justify humility. It is well that democracy should share them, and be deeply imbued with a sense of failure and difficulty.

But this very experience at the same time discloses the end more clearly, and enhances its appeal.

In the image of a goal to be attained conjoined with a sober sense of its remoteness, in a fixing of the will upon a goal that seems worth the effort which it costs—here is to be found the cure for the so-called restlessness of the present age. For the uneasiness of youth is due not to original depravity, but to the lack of a great cause; and what young men and young women really need is neither indulgence nor repression, but a moral tonic. They miss that ardor, that keen interest in great issues, which is natural to those who are buckling on their armor. 'Flaming youth' suffers from asphyxiation rather than from combustion—from inflammation rather than from flame.

Democratic faith is not sheer faith. It rests its case on enlightenment of mind and agreement of will, and there are reasons why in the long run both of these should prevail. Enlightenment reflects the facts and the nature of things, which will outlive the vagaries and dogmatisms of opinion. The ideal of agreement is reinforced by the bitter lesson of conflict and the sobering fear of catastrophe. It is the one ideal which has its appeal to every man, to every class, to every nation, and to every epoch.

9

Democracy is not in itself a religion, if religion be taken to embrace a set of beliefs regarding God and the human soul. Or if, in the broader sense of zealous devotion to a moral cause, democracy be termed religious, then it is still consistent with a rich variety of religions in the narrower and fuller sense. The attempt, in the name of 'Positivism' or 'Humanism,' to reduce religion to democracy is an abortion and an infidelity. Because democracy is the friend of science is no reason for its being the enemy of faith and metaphysics; because democracy centers its attention on man is no reason for its equating man with the universe. Democracy cannot ally itself with such negations or subjectivisms without sinning against its own spirit. At the same time, however, democracy exercises a characteristic influence upon all social institutions; and if democracy comes to prevail in the world, it will in the future as it has in the past make a difference to religion, however that term be construed.

In the first place, being fundamentally humane, democracy will encourage those religions, such as Christianity, which elevate love to the supreme place in the hierarchy of values; and within Christianity itself, it will encourage an emphasis upon God's compassion rather than upon his justice or his power. Thus democracy will favor an interpretation of divine love in terms of personal and familial love, or neighborly kindness; of divine goodness in terms of human happiness; of evil in terms of that misery or pain with which mankind is unhappily familiar; and of salvation in terms of that redeeming value of faith and of love which is proved by human experience.

In the second place, democracy, claiming a general validity for its premises and envisaging the totality of mankind, will support universal religions. It will be unfavorable to all religions which emphasize the interest of a class or a nation, and which tend thereby to intensify rather than to reconcile the antagonisms that divide mankind. Among universal religions it will reject those teachings which make salvation a matter of accident or privilege, and support those teachings in which salvation is offered, with some degree of hopeful promise, to all men.

Thirdly, democracy will encourage an emphasis on temporal goods, being concerned with the happiness of mankind here and now—or if not now, then in some finite future. No religion has wholly neglected the mundane values, nor does democracy reject values that are not of this world. But democracy will insist that the good of man must *at least* embrace his immediate needs and present desires. It will refuse to accept a faith which abandons men to poverty, sickness, failure, or frustration during their terrestrial lives, even if that be no more than a part, and the less important part, of their total lives. A religion which teaches men to resign themselves to their lot, however lowly or dependent, will find itself uncomfortable in a democratic society, and will be accused of conspiring with privilege and reaction. This does not mean that religion should abandon the office of consolation, or its emphasis on the spiritual values of hardship and struggle, but only that this counsel should strengthen and not deaden the forces of progress.

Democracy does not deny immortality, but refuses to ignore, through preoccupation with immortality, man's more evident and indisputable mortality. Democracy will not deny the need of salvation, but will insist that this good, however great it be and of whatever paramount concern, shall supplement and not supersede the improvement of man's condition in this world. Democracy directs man's eyes not down, or back, to the original constitution of the universe, or up to an overarching vault of eternity, but forward in time to man's perpetual betterment.

Democracy does not, however, presume to embrace the entire lives of its members. It conceives of human society and of the terrestrial phase of life as a corridor through which all men pass, whatever their origin, their destiny, or their ulterior concerns. It demands that this life of men together, both in its co-existence and in its historical progression, shall be governed by its own laws, and directed to the achievement of its own proper ends. The goods which democracy itself creates are minimum rather than maximum goods, and goods for all men rather than for their more eminent representatives. It does not negate other-worldly goods, but asks only that these shall be added to worldly goods. Democracy gives men liberty; but it does not prescribe what men shall do with their liberty, provided they do not use it to destroy liberty. It organizes men in order that their unorganized spontaneities, their personal development, and their soaring aspirations may the more abound.

Modern democracy sprang from the Age of the Enlightenment, and will be opposed by its tradition, its genius, and its explicit teachings to any dogmatic or authoritarian restraints upon freedom of thought. It will be opposed to obscurantism, and suspicious of any religious emotions that becloud or debase the reason. It will tend to the rejection of miracles and special providence, or any doctrine out of keeping with the habits of mind inculcated by science. It will subject dogmas to critical scrutiny and encourage their perpetual revision in form if not in substance. It will advocate public education, and attempt to raise the general average of knowledge. It will *trust* enlightenment and not fear it, and will therefore lend no aid or comfort to any religious cult that rests upon ignorance, exploits it, or seeks to persuade men that it does not matter. Democracy does not reject either faith or authority, but only their priority to knowledge. On democratic premises faith may supplement knowledge, but must not replace it; authority may serve as a carriage for infants, or a crutch for the lame, but may not supersede the intellectual self-determination of the man who can walk alone, or impede the acquisition of that power.

Finally, democracy's code of tolerance forbids its interfering with any religion, provided that religion is similarly disposed to abstain from interference with rival cults, whether religious or secular. Democracy developed at the close of an age of religious wars, and knew their destructive effects. It recognizes religion as a general human propensity having diverse expressions. It does not demand a reduction of religions to a least common denominator—a procedure which might well result in the destruction of religion altogether. For to any concrete religion its exclusive loyalties, its solidarities of feeling, its peculiarities of faith and dogma, its characteristic symbols and forms of worship, are the very breath of life. Democracy, the friend of individualism and of nationality, is also the friend of religious uniqueness. It permits and protects each religion in the development of its own genius.

But there is a condition attaching to this tolerance. A religion which profits by this liberality must itself be liberal in its social philosophy. Its intensity of conviction may never take the form of the denial of a similar right to its rivals. It must be content to serve mankind not by imposing, but by offering, itself, enriching the range of possibilities submitted to the choice of free men.

CONCLUSION

1

Puritanism and democracy, under these or other names, form a substantial part of the heritage of Americans. The chief source of spiritual nourishment for any nation must be its own past, perpetually rediscovered and renewed. A nation which negates its tradition loses its historic identity and wantonly destroys its chief source of spiritual vitality; a nation which merely reaffirms its tradition grows stagnant and corrupt. But it is not necessary to choose between revolution and reaction. There is a third way—the way, namely, of discriminating and forward-looking fidelity.

Puritanism springs from the very core of the personal conscience—the sense of duty, the sense of responsibility, the sense of guilt, and the repentant longing for forgiveness. No man, if he grows to maturity, escapes these experiences. Every man, sooner or later, feels himself rightly exiled from paradise and looks for a return. Puritanism is the elaboration of this theme, and the inculcation of its stern implications: some things are better than other things, and the discovery of the best is of paramount importance; the order of better and worse does not coincide with the natural order of strength among human motives, and if a man is to cleave to the best he must therefore overcome the second-best, until its subordination shall have become his second nature; the best prescribes rules of action, to be scrupulously observed; judged by the standard of the best, human life is a record of tragic and ignominious failure, and the recognition of this failure is the condition of its redemption; to live well requires the forging of a will which is stronger than any natural appetite; the reorganization of the natural individual under the authority of his moral faculties constitutes personality, which is the essence of man as distinguished from his fellow animals; society, in proportion as it is human, is an association of persons in which mutual respect is mingled with solicitude and a sense of common responsibility; there is hope of salvation both for the person and for mankind, and indomitable perseverance in the moral struggle alone gives cosmic dignity to the human race.

He who would reject these ideas must be prepared to accept in some degree one or more of their opposites: a frivolous disregard of moral questions, together with aimlessness and inconstancy; a confusion or a promiscuity of values; a blurring of moral distinctions, and a lack of principle; a shallow optimism or a complacent self-satisfaction, bred by the ignorance or the condoning of evil; self-indulgence, infirmity of will, corruptibility, lack of self-discipline; a reckless irresponsibility and indifference to the true well-being of one's neighbors; a cynical admission of failure, and acquiescence in the meaninglessness of life.

But there are certain ingredients in which the puritan mixture is deficient, or which it omits altogether. For lack of these things even the good ingredients lose their flavor, and the dish is bitter to the taste. The puritan saw a limited truth, and what he saw was distorted because of what he failed to see. This distorted puritanism consists of a narrow preoccupation with morality, to the exclusion of the graciousness and the beauty of life; a pharisaical emphasis on the letter of the rule at the expense of its spirit; evil imagination, prudishness, and canting humility; a hard repression of all spontaneities and natural impulses, resulting in the masking of real motives by virtuous and edifying pretension; a morbid habit of introspection; censoriousness; hardness, intolerance, and an aversion to joy, especially the joy of other people; obsequious submission to a cruel and despotic God, and through preoccupation with the moral law a neglect of those aspects which nature and the universe present to the senses, the affections, and the reason.

Democracy, like puritanism, has its perennial spring in the moral consciousness. It expresses man's spontaneous interests and sociability as setting limits to discipline and as constituting its only ultimate justification. It insists that man's natural faculties shall be freely developed, in order that they may serve as the guide and the sanction of life. It conceives the values of life in terms of the desires and the felt satisfactions of concrete individuals, and concedes to these individuals the right to be both the exponents and the guarantors of their own interests. The purpose of institutions is to be found in the material and the spiritual profit of individuals as judged by these individuals themselves; and the beneficence of institutions is therefore measured by the degree of freedom which is provided within their framework. Democracy expresses the social consciousness in the most naïve sense, as an awareness of the plurality and the otherness of individuals; and in the most humane sense, as feeling of kind, compassion for the unfortunate, and appreciation of those higher relationships which are founded on modesty, respect, and mutually enhancing differences. Man derives dignity from his inalienable capacity for joy and suffering, from his capacity for self-determination, and from his tragic but faithful and age-long effort to live and to live better through intelligence and co-operation.

He who rejects democracy chooses its alternatives: atavism and obscurantism; the absorption of the individual into the mass, his assimilation to a pattern, or the exchange of his genuine interests for a fictitious corporate good; slavishness, intimidation, or blind obedience of the many under the authority of institutions diverted from their proper use, or subject to irresponsible power of the few; the surrender by all save a privileged class of the opportunities of personal choice; a society of rank, with arrogance toward those lower in the scale and obsequiousness toward those above; the hardening of the heart and the disowning of fellow men beyond some boundary of self, class, nation, or race; desertion of the cause of human progress, and the acceptance of its defeat.

Historic democracy has suffered ill repute owing to its exaggerations and defects. Through its failure to recognize the forces of unreason it has misconstrued human nature and has underestimated the power of its enemies. It has failed to probe the depths of human interdependence and solidarity, and has confused public good with self-interest. It has seemed to forget that a government must govern, and that government implies obedience. It has confused liberty with anarchy. Through its anxiety to emphasize the equal dignity and rights of men, it has neglected their inequalities of native endowment and of achievement. Like that democracy which the ancients held in disesteem, it has been an exponent of vulgarity rather than of eminence. Through neglect of the economic sphere of life, it has allowed its name to be used as a cloak for greed and exploitation. In both the political and the economic fields it has been too easily satisfied with the nominal rather than the real, and so has exposed itself to the charge of sentimentalism. Intoxicated by its early successes, it was too ready to assume that its triumph was written in the stars, and that progress and universal peace were guaranteed merely because they were reasonable and good. Hence democracy was unprepared to meet the shock of disillusionment, and is now as inclined to the excesses of despair as once it was to the excesses of hope.

2

Puritanism and democracy are in a measure coincident and allied, and where this is the case, they are subject to the same errors. Thus they are both individualistic—in their conception of the good, and in their conception of human faculties. They both affirm the same Occidental, Christian code of justice, compassion, and personal dignity. But they both exaggerate the self-sufficiency of the individual. Both underestimate the intricacies of human relations—as between individuals, classes, or nations. They have as yet found no cure for either domestic exploitation or external war, and their failure has been due not only to ignorance but to infidelity. They suffer both from senility and from corruption.

But if puritanism and democracy reinforce one another's truths and aggravate one another's errors, they also serve to correct and complement one another's limitations. Puritanism is the exponent of the harsh necessities of the moral life. Morality is essentially the imposing of a form of personal integrity and of social justice upon the natural life of man. But morality has no justification except in terms of that very natural life to which it does violence. Personal integrity is justified by the fuller play which it gives to spontaneity, and social justice by the room which it gives to personal self-expression. Puritanism sees that life must be curtailed, to which democracy adds 'in order that it may abound.' As puritanism stresses the sinfulness of Adam after the fall, so democracy stresses his innocence before. Puritanism supplies the pessimistic realization of man's present predicament, democracy the optimistic affirmation of his hopes and possibilities.

The priority of puritanism over democracy means that the ordering of life is the first condition of its humanity, and that life is not in order as it comes. Nature must be considered as plastic to the moral will. But if morality exercises the functions of shaping and control, it is nature which provides the goods of life, without which the rule of morality is barren. Human life receives its content of intrinsic worth from the interests which it embraces and from the satisfactions and the joys which their fulfillment yields. The good life is life organized to the end that its constituent parts may flourish, grow, and bear their natural fruits.

It follows from these mixed judgments concerning puritanism and democracy that there are reasons both for their reaffirmation and for their rejection. Their mixture of truth and falsity, of adequacy and inadequacy, of inclusion and omission, of insufficiency and exaggeration, creates an option: to cleave to them for their merits, or to repudiate them for their faults. It is important for the national health that the critical faculties should be applied to past impurities. But, as Whitehead has said, "if men cannot live on bread alone, still less can they do so on disinfectants." [1] In the particular case before us, then, it is proposed that we, as Americans, take puritanism and democracy as symbols of piety, reaffirming that which we find true; looking for their constituents of truth in order that we may reaffirm them; reaffirming them in order thereby to maintain our moral identity and the stream of the national life.

3

There are meanings of patriotism which do not imply those qualities of the patrioteer, the professional patriot, or the 'hundred per cent American' which have given to the word its present flavor of disparagement. There is, for example, that gratitude which is felt most consciously by foreign-born Americans, or by the first generation of their descendants, who have not yet come to take America for granted. Ralph Henry Lasser, a young Jewish boy who left Harvard in his freshman year and was killed in action in France in the First World War at the age of nineteen, wrote quite unaffectedly to his mother: "We must all give everything we have, even that which is nearest and dearest. . . . We have received from our dear country everything, and now we are called upon to render service in return. I want to serve my country." [2]

Or patriotism may mean the devotion of a people to its creed. Patriotism in this sense implies neither boastfulness, nor aggression, nor reaction. A creed is a standard of perfection, and its adoption implies a willingness to be judged by its requirements. It leads to humility rather than to a sense of superiority; since there is always a gap between present attainment and the perfection which the standard defines, it becomes a goal of effort demanding innovation and change.

Beyond this point there lies the difference between one creed and another, often dividing men into fanatical and conflicting groups—conflicting because their exclusive claims are incompatible. Each cult erects itself on a narrow base, and then attempts to annex every other cult to its own narrowness. This is the principle of solipsism applied to the will. Its corrective is that moral disinterestedness, or rather all-interestedness, which seeks to make the maximum allowance for a plurality of wills, whether of individuals or of cults. Organized society is then devoted not to the intensification of one passion to the exclusion of others, but to the inclusion of diversity, excluding only hatred and aggrandizement.

But the ideal of inclusiveness or liberality is itself a creed. It is impossible for an individual to *be* a liberal without preferring liberalism above all other doctrines. To adhere to the creed of inclusiveness and at the same time acknowledge its opposite as equally valid is self-contradictory in theory, and self-destructive in practice. Inclusiveness has nothing to do with skepticism or relativism. To be a liberal does not mean believing in nothing; it means believing in liberalism.

A democratic state, like any other state, takes its fundamental presuppositions to be true. Its adherents believe such propositions as the following to be true: that moral and spiritual truth is a progressive revelation, attended with doubt; that men disagree, and cannot be forced into conformity without destroying their capacity to be vehicles of truth; that coercion of the mind is conducive to hypocrisy; that the good is hospitable, inclusive, varied, and individual; that even this very creed itself shall, as becomes its truth, be freely accepted—that is, propagated by persuasion rather than by fear or habit, and accepted in the presence of all available evidence to the contrary. A democratic state stands on these principles, and enforces them. To the adherents of other creeds it will offer hospitality but not abdication. The illiberal who accepts this hospitality in the spirit in which it is offered becomes thereby a liberal. The illiberal who accepts this hospitality in order to dispossess his host has to be treated as an exponent of error to be corrected, or of misconduct to be prevented. How far hospitality shall be carried at the risk of dispossession is a question of method and not of principle.

Antoine de Saint-Exupéry, in his *Wind, Sand and Stars,* attacks the creeds of his day as being "carnivorous idols" which "divide men into rightists and leftists, hunchbacks and straight-backs, fascists and democrats." But he fails, apparently, to see that the tolerant humane ideal which he himself proclaims—"a goal towards which all mankind is striving"—is no less an ideal than the "carnivorous idols" which he condemns.[3]

The trouble with the world is not the strength of the conflict of creeds, but the weakness the creed of non-conflict. To refuse to regard peacemaking as a creed, and to deprive it of the forces by which creeds prevail, can result in nothing but its extinction, leaving the field to perpetual conflict or that so-called peace which consists in the bleak tyranny of the last survivor.

If the morality of inclusiveness is itself an ideal, then its adherents cannot afford to leave unused the active measures by which ideals are implanted and realized. They will, it is true, place a special reliance on persuasion, because they believe that their creed is essentially reasonable. But a reasonable creed needs to be propagated as much as does a cult of unreason. Even natural science, where proofs are intellectually unassailable, needs the support of the passion for truth, and this passion, like any other passion, must be excited if it is to prevail. A social creed, furthermore, cannot bear fruit until it is supported by a widely diffused sentiment. It must command the support not only of private but of collective passion.

If a creed is to live and prevail, it must appeal to youth. If it be novelty that appeals to youth, then illiberalism enjoys no advantage on this score. Its detractors speak of liberalism as an outworn creed, and even its adherents style themselves 'old-fashioned.' But it is, in fact, newer than its rivals. All of the elements of which anti-liberalism is composed are as old as Adam, or at least as old as Cain. Because they are revived in the twentieth century, or shamelessly professed, or use new instruments, there is no moral novelty in ambition, hate, superstition, hysteria, selfishness, conquest, tyranny. In the history of human societies tribal solidarity, military dictatorship, doctrinal uniformity, the exploitation of ignorance by cynical augurs, and even the holding of property in common, are primitive and antique. The newest, most daring adventure of history is the attempt to organize mankind in such wise as to achieve the fullest possible liberty, the highest possible development of human nature, and the widest possible distribution of liberty and personal development among all human individuals and groups.

The fatal confusion which paralyzes the man of goodwill is the confusion between ends and scruples. A scruple is a rule of action, usually negative. Morality is construed by its scrupulous adherents in terms of a set of prohibitions, such as "Thou shalt not use violence," "Thou shalt not excite emotion," "Thou shalt not deprive any man of liberty." Morality as a going concern may perish while the moral purists both wring their hands and wash them. Morality as an end is an all-inclusive and stable organization of human life. But if this end is to be realized, or if such stages of it as are already realized are to be safeguarded, account must be taken of conditions of its existence, physical, biological, psychological, and historical. Scrupulosity is as impotent as celibacy to bring about its reign on earth.

4

The ideal of a puritan democracy, or moral liberalism, has a long way to go, and it must pay as it goes—which implies that it must both go and pay. It cannot expect to win adherents either by pious phrases or by promises indefinitely postponed. It must begin at once to be what it hopes to be. Unfortunate and dissatisfied men cannot be expected to wait indefinitely. The appeal of revolution lies in its speed. The good it aims to achieve, and the evil which it seeks to remove, are often the same as those of its conservative opponents; the difference is that it proposes to do something about it now. If revolution is to be averted, it is necessary that progress shall be palpable. The rate of change must be rapid enough to create a sense of movement within the life-span of a generation.

Revolution is the taking prematurely of what is too tardily given. But it tends to destroy the gains already made. It is customary to speak of a breakdown of civilization as a return to the life of the brute, but this is unjust to the brute. In every subhuman form of animal there is a sort of perfection which is the free gift of nature; man must earn what perfection he has, and when he is deprived of it, he is something below the level of natural goodness. Man is not equipped with fur, and when, as in civil war, he is stripped of civilization, he presents an aspect of indecent nakedness. A degraded man is not an animal—

A monster then, a dream,
A discord. Dragons of the prime,
That tare each other in their slime
Were mellow music match'd with him.[4]

The very faculties which exalt man to the highest place in the order of living creatures, in their corruption debase him to the nethermost depths.[5] Man, like Lucifer, falls from High Heaven so far that a special region has to be created to receive him. Only man is capable of cold malice, of perpetual fear, of universal suspicion, or of the mental distortions of secret conspiracy. These are qualities which abound when, as in revolution, man reverses the process of moral development.

The future of mankind would be black indeed if it were necessary to choose between reaction and revolution, between the cult of stagnation and the cult of destruction. Romain Rolland prefers "that great misery which swoops down and slays or forges anew" to "the misery of ever recurring ill-fortune, that small misery which trickles down drop by drop from the first day to the last." [6] There is a moral idealism which refuses to choose between these two miseries. It seeks to remove the monotonous miseries of reaction without subjecting mankind to the cataclysmic miseries of revolution, which may, unhappily, swoop down and slay without forging anew.

Parrington has been cited as saying of Sinclair Lewis's *Babbitt* that it marked "the final passing in America of the civilization that came from the fruitful loins of the eighteenth century." [7] This view has been widely held by American critics of America. Nonetheless it is to that same eighteenth century that we find ourselves turning again today for our fundamental premises.

The fault of the eighteenth century lay not in its idea of perfection, but in its belief that perfection was natural. The nineteenth century brought a sobering pessimism. Its studies of history, biology, anthropology, and psychology disclosed the darker side of man, both his irrational depths and the primitive phases of his evolution. It remained for the twentieth century to make a cult of atavism, or to glorify the state of nature in the grim and realistic sense. Cynics and satirists uncover the raw materials and forces of human life, and hurl epithets of hypocrisy and sentimentality against the culture which has covered them. They make a cult of this uncovering, as though there were some virtue in returning from modern plumbing to surface drainage. They reaffirm the doctrine of human depravity, but without a standard or a gospel of redemption; they accept the unredeemed man, and glory in him.

The good life of man consists of an organization of the original forces and materials of the natural life by the distinctive human faculties. The conflicts of passion are resolved through the governing and regulative function of the moral will; the darkness of passion is illuminated by knowledge; the brutality of the strong is checked by justice; the vegetative and animal functions are by taste, imagination, and symbolism transmuted into friendship, romantic love, festival, and art. It is this patiently woven fabric, embroidered with beauty, gentleness, honesty, truth, freedom, mutual respect, reverence, and the whole catalogue of virtues and amenities—it is this, and not merely life and property, which is torn to shreds in eras of revolutionary violence. It is this fabric, called civilization, which constitutes the good life of man, and which men of moral earnestness will guard and perfect by rational and concerted effort.

The revolutionary should read history with an eye for the destructive and debasing effects of violence. The reactionary should read history and his own heart with an eye to the inertia of human selfishness. Possession is said to be nine-tenths of the law; it appears to the possessors to be the whole of righteousness. Possessors who are unwilling to give, and who confuse the ideal state with the status quo, become, indirectly, the causes of violence. They build a dam across the stream until the accumulated pressure of the current overflows its banks, breaks through, and sweeps away all landmarks in a devastating flood.

Reactionaries often display a remarkable flexibility in the application of their ancient maxims. They may profess adherence to the sacred principles of property and yet boast of predatory ancestors. They may affirm that the laborer is entitled to the fruits of his labor, and only to the fruits of his labor, and yet enjoy inherited wealth or bonuses with an easy conscience. They may resent the interference of the government in business—except in behalf of their special interests. They may profess a broad humanitarianism and yet be more susceptible than their radical opponents to race prejudice. They object in principle to class conflict, but have no objection to class superiority. Revolution is destructive; reaction is obstructive. Revolution is a hatred of existing limitations and restraints; reaction is a morbid fear of losing what one has. The one is reckless, the other timid; both are blind. The revolutionary forgets what it is that he is trying to create, the reactionary what he is trying to keep. The one reaches out to grasp what he has not, the other hugs his possessions; both are greedy. Both rationalize their greed, but both are in fact unfaithful to their professed ends.

In America both reactionaries and revolutionists may swear allegiance to the Constitution. The revolutionist forgets that the Constitution is a frame and a system of checks and balances, and is indignantly surprised when the frame sets limits or the forces of government actually check and balance. The reactionary forgets the libertarian content of the Constitution, and is indignant when people claim and exercise their liberties. Both revolution and reaction dramatize and oversimplify the processes of history—see ghosts, impute malice, create devils to satisfy their fears, see a conspirator in every bush, divide mankind into friends and enemies, tend to become fanatics and monomaniacs.

Gradualism is the only mode of reform which is consistent with democratic political institutions. Democratic procedure implies fluctuations of public opinion. The party in power must tolerate opposition and be prepared after a brief period to surrender its power to its opponents.

Changes and alternations of policy must be considered normal. But if changes of policy are too abrupt, one of two things will happen: either the party in power will seek to perpetuate its rule in the name of social stability; or every change of government will be revolution—social life will suffer from chronic disorder, and long-range constructive activity will be paralyzed by a sense of insecurity.

Gradualism, or a change for the better which is slow enough to conserve the gains of the past while rapid enough to create a hopeful sense of forward movement, is unquestionably the counsel of wisdom. Such counsel has little power to excite the primitive emotions. It must depend for its support on the agreement of sober judgments rather than on the fusion of passions. Its strength is the strength of good sense, enlightenment, and truth. In short, while it is essential to a democratic polity that the pendulum should swing, and it is necessary that the arc should be short, this does not mean that there will be no linear progression, but that this progression shall consist of a series of oscillations in which the forward exceeds the backward component. In the long run the change may be indefinitely great, but each segment will have been doubly traversed, and the ground gained will have been consolidated through habit, expertness, organization, opinion, and sentiment.

5

At the dawn of the present century it was generally felt that the cause of Christian democracy, supported by irresistible cosmic and historical forces, could with confidence claim the future as its own. Wars, revolutions, and economic crises sweeping across the world have converted that confidence into skepticism, or even into vindictive apostasy. Some men speak of the end of civilization and, having cause to expect the worst, feel a certain unholy glee in the confirmation of their despair.

One thing is certain—the passing through this valley will be an indelible chapter in human experience. Men will never again be as innocently hopeful as they were at the close of the nineteenth century. They will never again expect Utopia to be the instant and spontaneous effect of a cult of reason, or of the advancement of the physical sciences, or of the adoption of constitutions. They are unlikely again to put their trust in a providential entity called Progress. If they continue to put their trust in God, it will be a God who expects his creatures to suffer, whether for their sins or from prolonged and laborious effort.

Granting that the reinstatement of illusions is impossible, it remains to find a sober hopefulness founded on knowledge and springing from the very bitterness of experience. A man must endeavor, says Tawney, "without being a simpleton, to avoid being a fatalist." [8] One looks not for crumbs of comfort, but for grounds which justify effort.

There is some hopefulness to be extracted from history. There are many chapters in human history which have seemed to contemporaries to be the last, but which to posterity have appeared as phases of transition. There is no present evil of human suffering, brutality, and degradation which cannot be duplicated, in kind if not in degree, in the records of the past. We thought that we had left these things behind, and it appears that we have not; but man has survived them, and can probably survive them again. Americans have been disloyal to their own creed, and have in this sinned repeatedly, but they have recovered their faith.

History alters the measure of time. Periods that seem long in the living appear short in retrospect. In history thirty years is a brief time. There was once a Thirty Years' War—and a Hundred Years' War. The noxious weeds that have sprung up during the last three decades have as yet shallow roots; there has been as yet no proof of their power to survive. The lessons of history teach patience and the folly of final judgments precipitately arrived at. They prove, to borrow Emerson's words, that a popgun is sometimes mistaken for the crack of doom.

But history is strewn with the bones of dead empires, and even entire civilizations have been known to die. Hope must find some more positive ground. Such a ground is to be found in the revulsion of feeling created by the very excesses of contemporary evil. It is as though totalitarianism had been created in order to exhibit evil in its most repulsive aspect. It has by opposition illustrated and confirmed the moral judgments of Western Christendom and the political judgments of modern democracy. Its brutalities, hysterias, and tyrannies have quickened the love of gentleness, of reason, and of liberty.

If hope is to be justified, however, there must be some evidence that the good has in it some power of survival, and not a mere capacity to excite nostalgic longing. There must be a congruence between Christian-puritan democracy and the conditions of existence. There is, I believe, such a congruence.

Democracy is founded on truth. It is the one form of human society which is not only unafraid of truth, but looks to truth as its ally. But truth, in the original and only defensible sense of that term, reflects the nature of things, and is adapted to the permanent environment of human life. Societies may for a time insult and neglect the truth, but only because they live on the accumulated truths of the past. Men may be indoctrinated with superstition, but they do not stay indoctrinated, because the facts are more persistent than propaganda. Even societies founded on superstition require leaders who are themselves emancipated; and in the long run either the emancipation of the leaders will spread to the masses, or the leaders will themselves be corrupted and rendered impotent by the very doctrine which they use to control the masses.

Christian morality is qualified to survive because its design agrees with the design of human nature, if it be granted that conscience and reason are human faculties which even in their dethronement are never destroyed but remain as deep potentialities which define the direction of human effort. And Christian morality is qualified to survive because love and agreement, which unite men, are stronger than hate and fear, which divide them. There is a human-racial instinct of self-preservation which is asserting itself at this very moment, and which impels men and nations, however selfish and defiant, to come to terms with their neighbors; since, if men and nations are to live at all, they must live at peace, and since they can live at peace only when their social instincts are cultivated and when their institutions are founded on reciprocal respect and aid.

The true ground of hope for Christian democracy lies, then, in its correspondence with the nature of things through enlightenment, and in its correspondence with human nature through its provision for human faculties and human solidarity. This should suffice to give to every man of goodwill enough heart to persist in the effort to translate his creed into actuality. "And thus," as Cromwell said, "to be a seeker is to be of the best sect next to a finder." [9]

America is fortunate in its economic, racial, and climatic diversity, and enjoys a unique opportunity of preserving national unity without cultural impoverishment. Americanism in this sense of tolerant inclusiveness does not consist in a common coating of vulgarity; still less does it consist in a sameness of primitive appetites and emotions stirred up from the bottom levels of human nature. It consists in a common creed of diversity, adopted by each individual and group because of liberty enjoyed, and because of the fructifying intercourse of multiple liberties. These motives will prompt an American to identify himself with the world-wide and age-long adventure of mankind. The only bounds set to personal or national aspiration will be those which are prescribed by peace, and which will serve, not as restrictive barriers, but rather as channels of mutual enrichment. Nations, like men, will no longer live in walled castles from which they make occasional armed forays, but in the valleys and plains where without loss of domestic privacy they enjoy together the fruits of the earth and the achievements of human genius.

REFERENCES

NOTES TO PREFACE

1 *Main Currents in American Thought,* 3 vols., Harcourt, Brace, 1927-30, Vol. III, p. 326.

CHAPTER ONE

1 From an interview given to E. S. Van Zile and published in the *Washington Post,* Feb. 29, 1920, pp. 3, 18.

2 Daniel K. Whitaker in the *Southern Quarterly Review* (of which he was editor), Vol. I (April, 1842), p. 496; quoted by F. L. Mott, *A History of American Magazines,* Harvard University Press, 1930, Vol. 1, p. 724.

3 *Thirty-second Annual Report of the Board of Direction of the Mercantile Library Association in the City of New York,* January 1853, pp. 23-24.

4 "The New American Poetry," in J. C. Bowman, ed., *Contemporary American Criticism,* Holt, 1926, p. 295.

5 *Civilization in the United States: An Inquiry by Thirty Americans,* ed. by Harold E. Stearns, Harcourt, Brace, 1922, pp. vi, vii. *Cf.* also the sequel, *America Now,* Scribner, 1938.

6 From *Upstream* by Ludwig Lewisohn, published by Liveright Publishing Corporation, 1922, pp. 235-236.

7 *The Beginnings of Critical Realism in America, 1860-1920* (Vol. III of *Main Currents in American Thought*), p. 235.

8 *Ibid.,* p. 369.

9 *Cf. The Autobiography of Lincoln Steffens,* 2 vols., Harcourt, Brace, 1931, Vol. II, pp. 865 ff.

10 *More Contemporary Americans,* University of Chicago Press, 1927, p. 5.

11 *Op. cit.,* Lippincott, 1902, p. 9.

12 For other contributions to what Owen Wister called "the unfreezing of George Washington," *cf.* his *Seven Ages of Washington,* Macmillan, 1907; and Henry Cabot Lodge, *George Washington,* 2 vols., Houghton Mifflin, 1909 (American Statesmen), Vol. I, Introd.

[13] *Cf.* Sydney George Fisher, "The Legendary and Myth-making Process in Histories of the American Revolution," *Proceedings of the American Philosophical Society*, Vol. LI (1912), pp. 53-75, especially pp. 57-59.

[14] *Cf.* A. M. Schlesinger, *New Viewpoints in American History*, Macmillan, 1922, Chap. VII and Bibliographical Note, pp. 181-83.

[15] *Cf.* Bessie L. Pierce, *Public Opinion and the Teaching of History in the United States*, Knopf, 1926, Chap. VII.

[16] *Op. cit.*, Holt, 1921, p. 268.

[17] Percy H. Boynton, *Op. cit.*, p. 6.

[18] Arthur M. Schlesinger, "A Critical Period in American Religion, 1875-1900," *Proceedings of the Massachusetts Historical Society*, Vol. LXIV (June 1932), pp. 523-47.

CHAPTER TWO

[1] *The Vanity of Dogmatizing*, reproduced from the edition of 1661, Columbia University Press, 1931, pp. 122-23, 129.

[2] *Our Social Heritage*, Yale University Press, 1921, pp. 16-17.

[3] "The Farewell Address," from *The Writings of George Washington*, ed. by W. C. Ford, 14 vols., 1889-93, Vol. XIII, pp. 287-88, courtesy of G. P. Putnam's Sons.

[4] *The Memoirs of Prince von Bülow*, translated by F. A. Voigt, 4 vols., Little, Brown, 1931-32, Vol. I, p. 650.

CHAPTER THREE

[1] *The Vanity of Dogmatizing*, pp. 128-29.

[2] *Pilgrim's Way*, Houghton Mifflin, 1940, p. 282.

[3] *The Heavenly City of the Eighteenth Century Philosophers*, Yale University Press, 1932, p. 44.

[4] *The Will to Believe*, Longmans, Green, 1897, p. 205.

[5] *Op. cit.*, p. 3.

[6] *Life of George Washington, with Curious Anecdotes*, Philadelphia, 1832, title page.

[7] "Hyperion," Bk I, l. 51.

[8] (*Enthüllung ohne Entseelung.*) I owe this phrase to my friend Professor Robert Ulich.

[9] "Stelligeri," and "American Literature," *Stelligeri and Other Essays Concerning America*, Scribner, 1893, pp. 11, 94-95.

[10] "History," *Essays, First Series,* rev. ed., Houghton Mifflin, 1888 (Riverside edition of *Emerson's Complete Works*), p. 42.

[11] *The Letters of William James,* ed. by Henry James, 2 vols., Atlantic Monthly Press, 1920, Vol. II, p. 40.

[12] "Young America," *Seven Arts,* December, 1916, pp. 146-47.

CHAPTER FOUR

[1] *The Works of Thomas Goodwin,* 5 vols., London, 1681-1704, Vol. V, p. vi.

[2] Henri Bremond, *Histoire littéraire du sentiment religieux en France,* 11 vols., Paris, 1916; Vol. I, *L'Humanisme dévot,* p. 13; translated by the Author. A Catholic puritanism appeared also in the seventeenth century among the French Oratorians and Jansenists.

[3] From "The Act of Supremacy," *Select Statutes and . . . Documents . . . of Elizabeth and James I,* ed. by Sir G. W. Prothero, Clarendon Press: Oxford, 1894, p. 6. By permission of the publishers. *Cf.* also *Ibid.*, pp. 1-20.

[4] "Convocation of 1563: Puritan Demands," *Ibid.*, p. 191.

[5] Thomas Fuller, *The Church-History of Britain; from the Birth of Jesus Christ, Untill the Year M.DC.XLVIII.* London, 1656, Bk. IX, Sec. I, p. 66.

[6] "Camden, Annales, p. 132; s.a. 1568" (*invidioso Puritanorum nomine*), Prothero, *Op. cit.*, p. 195; "Extracts from the First Admonition" [to Parliament, composed by Cartwright, Sampson and others], 1572, *Ibid.*, p. 198; "Queen's Proclamation against Nonconformists," 1573, *Ibid.*, p. 208; "The Queen's Speech in Parliament," 1585, *Ibid.*, pp. 221-22.

[7] *Ibid.*, p. 283.

[8] Formulated at the Westminster Assembly of 1643.

[9] Sir C. G. Robertson, ed., *Select Statutes, Cases and Documents to Illustrate English Constitutional History, 1660-1832,* London, 1904, p. 15, courtesy of G. P. Putnam's Sons.

[10] *Ibid.*, p. 14.

[11] *Cf.* "The Toleration Act, 1689," *Ibid.*, pp. 70-75. This Act inaugurated 'toleration' in the sense, not of equal privileges, but of immunity from the earlier penalties, such as fines, imprisonment and death. For an account of this limited settlement and of the legal disabilities which were *not* subsequently suspended, *cf.* Henry W. Clark, *History of English Nonconformity,* 2 vols., London, 1911-13, Vol. II, pp. 114-28, especially pp. 125-26.

[12] William Bradford, *History of Plymouth Plantation,* 2 vols., Massachusetts Historical Society, 1912, Vol. I, p. 22.

[13] Curtis P. Nettels, *The Roots of American Civilization,* Crofts, 1938, pp. 74-75; *cf.* also N. M. Crouse, "Causes of the Great Migration, 1630-1640," *New England Quarterly,* Vol. V (January 1932).

[14] John Winthrop, *History of New England,* 2 vols., Boston, 1853, Vol. II, p. 37.

[15] *Cf.* Perry Miller, *Orthodoxy in Massachusetts,* Harvard University Press, 1933, Chaps. IV, VI.

[16] S. M. Crothers, *The Dame School of Experience and Other Essays,* Houghton Mifflin, 1920, p. 184.

[17] *Cf.* Perry Miller, *Op. cit.,* pp. 164 ff.

[18] *Thoughts on the Revival of Religion in New England.* First published in 1740, this work went through many editions under slightly varying titles, *Some Thoughts Concerning the Present Revival of Religion in New England* being that under which it appears in the edition used in this book, *The Works of Jonathan Edwards, A.M. with an Essay on his Genius and Writings by Sereno E. Dwight,* rev. and corrected by Edward Hickman, 10th ed., 2 vols., London, 1865, Vol. I, pp. 365-430. All later quotation is from this edition.

[19] *Seasonable Thoughts on the State of Religion in New-England,* Boston, 1743, pp. 309, 314, 397-98.

[20] *Cf.* Arthur M. Schlesinger, *New Viewpoints in American History,* pp. 5-6.

[21] *Cf.* Elmer T. Clark, *The Small Sects in America,* The Cokesbury Press, 1937.

[22] J. B. Thayer, *A Western Journey with Mr. Emerson,* Little, Brown, 1884, p. 39.

[23] *Cf.* W. W. Sweet, *The Story of Religions in America,* Harper, 1930, Chap. III; also J. S. M. Anderson, *History of the Church of England in the Colonies and Foreign Dependencies of the British Empire,* 3 vols., London, 1845-56, Vol. II, pp. 515-29, 686 ff.

[24] S. H. Sutherland, *Population Distribution in Colonial America,* Columbia University Press, 1936, p. xii.

[25] Including not only communicants but members of their families, casual church attendants, and persons coming under the influence of the church. The estimates here given have been furnished to me by Professor George S. Coleman, author of an unpublished doctor's dissertation (Harvard, 1933) on "The Religious Background of the Federal Constitution."

[26] No figures on the Huguenots are available.

[27] The number of *communicants* in the Methodist church in 1776 was 4,921; in 1784 it was 14,988; and in 1800 it had reached the figure of 64,894. These figures are from Daniel Dorchester, *Christianity in the United States,* Hunt & Eaton, 1895, pp. 42, 284.

[28] Within this category belong not only 'infidels,' who were few in number and secret in their profession, but Freemasons and adherents of the many gradations of liberalism (deism, unitarianism, etc.) who reflected the rationalizing influence of the Enlightenment.

CHAPTER FIVE

[1] *Reason in Religion*, Scribner, 1905, pp. 92-96.

[2] *Cf.* James Owen Hannay, *The Spirit and Origin of Christian Monasticism*, London, 1903, Chap. I.

[3] *Op. cit.*, London, Vol. I, pp. 3, 8.

[4] John Calvin, *Institutes of the Christian Religion*, translated by John Allen, 3 vols., Philadelphia, 1813, Vol. II, p. 19 (Bk. III, Chap. II, § VII).

[5] Preface to the *Magnificat*, quoted by W. T. Whitley, "Sects (Christian)," in *Encyclopaedia of Religion and Ethics*, ed. by James Hastings, Vol. XI, p. 322.

[6] I John 2: 20, 27. *Cf.* Heb. 8: 10: "I will put my laws into their mind, and write them in their hearts."

[7] *Cf.* Calvin, *Op. cit.*, Vol. II, pp. 311-12 (Bk. III, Chap. XIX, §§ 4-5).

[8] For the proposed compromises between Augustinian determinism and "Pelagian" or "Semi-Pelagian" libertarianism, *cf.* Adolf Harnack, *History of Dogma*, 7 vols., London, 1896-99, Vol. V, pp. 168 ff.

[9] *Cf.* W. K. Jordan, *The Development of Religious Toleration in England*, 4 vols., Harvard University Press, 1932-40, Vol. III (*1640-1660*), pp. 452-53.

[10] *Cf.* Georgia Harkness, *John Calvin, the Man and His Ethics*, Holt, 1931.

[11] Perry Miller, "The Marrow of Puritan Divinity," *Loc. cit.*, pp. 293-94.

[12] *The Gospel-Covenant; or The Covenant of Grace Opened*, London, 1651, p. 322.

[13] *Ibid.*, pp. 382-83.

[14] II Cor. 6: 16, 17.

[15] *Cf.* W. K. Jordan, *Op. cit.*, Vol. I: *From the Beginning of the English Reformation to the Death of Queen Elizabeth*, pp. 270-71, 297-99.

[16] *Annals of the Reformation and Establishment of Religion, and Various Occurrences in the Church of England, during Queen Elizabeth's Happy Reign*, 4th ed., 4 vols., Oxford, 1824, Vol. I, pp. 2, 271; quoted by W. K. Jordan, *Op. cit.*, Vol. I, p. 296.

[17] *A Declaration of Faith*, issued in 1611 by Thomas Helwys and his fellow Baptists, p. 12; and John Smyth, *A Confession of Faith*, 1612, p. 84; both reprinted in part in Walter H. Burgess, *John Smith, the Se-Baptist; Thomas Helwys and the First Baptist Church in England with Fresh Light upon the Pilgrim Fathers' Church*, James Clarke & Co., 1911, pp. 215, 255. See also the small volume, probably written by Leonard Busher and issued in 1614 by Helwys's congregation under the title *Religious Peace, or a Plea for Liberty of Conscience*; as well as *Persecution for Religion Judg'd and Condemn'd: in a Discourse, between an Antichristian and a Christian*, printed in Holland in 1615, and probably written by Helwys's successor, John Murton, or one of his associates; both reprinted in *Tracts on Liberty of Conscience and Persecution, 1614-1661*, ed. by E. B. Underhill, London, 1846, pp. 1-181.

[18] *The Journal with Other Writings of John Woolman*, with Introd. by Vida D. Scudder, Dutton (Everyman's Library), p. 65.

[19] *Cf.* G. P. Gooch, *Political Thought in England from Bacon to Halifax,* Holt, 1914 (Home University Library), pp. 152-57.

[20] *Cf.* Godfrey Davies, "Arminian versus Puritan in England, ca. 1620-1640," *Huntington Library Bulletin* No. 5, 1934, pp. 157 ff.

[21] *Cf. A Careful and Strict Enquiry into the Prevailing Notions of that Freedom of Will, Which Is Supposed to Be Essential to Moral Agency, Virtue and Vice, Reward and Punishment, Praise and Blame,* first published in 1754, usually and hereinafter referred to under the title *On the Freedom of the Will, Works,* Vol. I, pp. 1-93.

[22] *Cf. Two Dissertations: I. Concerning the End for Which God Created the World. II. The Nature of True Virtue,* first published posthumously in 1765, and included under the same titles in *Ibid.,* Vol. I, pp. 94-142.

[23] *Cf.* "The Great Christian Doctrine of Original Sin Defended" (1758), *Ibid.,* Vol. I, pp. 143-233.

[24] "Remarks on Important Theological Controversies," Chap. III: "Concerning the Divine Decrees in General, and Election in Particular," *Ibid.,* Vol. II, p. 527.

[25] *Loc. cit.*

[26] *Works,* Vol. II, p. 528.

[27] *Cf.* W. W. Fenn, *The Christian Way of Life . . .* Essex Hall Lecture, 1924.

[28] *Cf.* Calvin, *Op. cit.,* Vol. III (Bk. IV, Chap. III, § 15).

[29] I Cor. 5: 7-13.

[30] Robert Browne, *A True and Short Declaration, Both of the gathering and Ioyning Together of Certaine persons* (undated but written probably not long after Browne's departure for Scotland at the end of 1583). There is a London ed. of 1882, p. 6; quoted in Henry Martyn Dexter, *Congregationalism . . . as Seen in Its Literature,* Harper, 1880, p. 67. See also Browne's *A Booke which Sheweth the life and manners of all true Christians,* Middleburgh, 1582. For a discussion of the complex interrelations between Browne, organized Separatism, the Dutch Anabaptists (both in Holland and in England), and the early English Baptists, *cf.* W. K. Jordan, *Op. cit.,* Vol. I, pp. 261-99.

[31] *A Book which Sheweth . . .* 1582, Chap. 3; quoted by W. K. Jordan, *Op. cit.,* Vol. I, p. 269.

[32] Robert Browne, *A True and Short Declaration . . .* quoted by H. M. Dexter, *Op. cit.,* p. 68.

[33] *The Works of John Robinson,* ed. by Robert Ashton, 3 vols., Boston, 1851, Vol. II, p. 132.

[34] *Cf. Ibid.,* Vol. II, p. 7.

[35] As quoted by H. M. Dexter, *Op. cit.,* p. 394.

[36] *Works,* Vol. II, p. 259.

[37] *Cf. Ibid.,* Vol. III, p. 418, *A Just and Necessary Apology of Certain Christians . . .* first published in Latin in 1619, in English in 1625; and Perry Miller, *Orthodoxy in Massachusetts,* pp. 63-64, 82.

[38] *Conscience,* translated out of the Latine, London, 1643, p. 140. *Cf.* also Perry Miller, *Op. cit.,* pp. 160-63.

[39] *Cf. Ibid.,* p. 100.

[40] Perry Miller, "The Half-way Covenant," *New England Quarterly,* Vol. VI (1933), p. 678.

[41] *Cf.* A. S. P. Woodhouse, ed., *Puritanism and Liberty*, London, 1938, pp. 15-17.

[42] John Brown, *The English Puritans*, 1910, p. 54, courtesy of G. P. Putnam's Sons.

[43] *Cf.* John Dall, article on "Presbyterianism," *Encyclopaedia of Religion and Ethics*, Vol. X, p. 247.

[44] "Of Power Ecclesiasticall," *Leviathan*, Chap. XLII.

[45] This view was named for Thomas Erastus (1524-83), but its most authentic exponents were Grotius, Althusius, and Zwingli. *Cf.* Hugo Grotius, *De Imperio Summarum Potestatum circa Sacra*, The Hague, 1614.

[46] This policy was anticipated in 1579 in the northern provinces in the Union of Utrecht, drawn up by John of Nassau, William's brother; *cf. Cambridge Modern History*, 12 vols., Macmillan, 1903-12, Vol. III, p. 251.

[47] Edition of 1659, p. 221; quoted by H. W. Schneider, *The Puritan Mind*, Holt, 1930, p. 16.

[48] *Op. cit.*, Vol. III, pp. 517-18 (Bk. IV, Chap. XX, §§ II-III).

[49] "Charter of Rhode Island and Providence Plantations," *Select Charters . . . of American History*, 1606-1675, ed. by William MacDonald, Macmillan, 1904, p. 128.

CHAPTER SIX

[1] John Jones, M.D., *Of the Naturall Beginning of All Growing and Liuing Things*, London, 1574, p. 33.

[2] From *Modern Democracies*, 2 vols., 1924, Vol. I, p. 4. By permission of The Macmillan Company, publishers.

[3] *The Works of John Adams*, ed. by C. F. Adams, 10 vols., Little, Brown, 1850-56, Vol. X, p. 172.

[4] Letter to Lord Kames, January 3, 1760, from *The Works of Benjamin Franklin*, ed. by John Bigelow, 12 vols., 1904, Vol. III, p. 248, courtesy of G. P. Putnam's Sons. For similar predictions of George Berkeley and Richard Wells, *cf.* Moses Coit Tyler, *Literary History of the American Revolution*, 2 vols., Putnam, 1897, Vol. I, pp. 275-76.

[5] Letter to James Warren, March 25, 1771, *Warren-Adams Letters*, Massachusetts Historical Society Collections, 1917, Vol. I, p. 9, quoted by R. V. Harlow, *Samuel Adams, Promoter of the American Revolution: A Study in Psychology and Politics*, Holt, 1923, pp. 171-72.

[6] Carl Becker, *The Declaration of Independence: A Study in the History of Political Ideas*, Harcourt, Brace (now Alfred A. Knopf), 1922, Chap. III. By permission of the author.

[7] *Cf.* C. H. McIlwain, *The American Revolution: A Constitutional Interpretation*, Macmillan, 1923.

[8] *History of English Thought in the Eighteenth Century*, 2 vols., London, 1902, Vol. II, p. 131.

[9] Carl Becker, *Op. cit.*, p. 3.

[10] The Declaration of Independence as it reads in the parchment copy, as quoted by Carl Becker, *Op. cit.*, pp. 185-86.

[11] Letter of May 8, 1825, to Henry Lee, from *The Writings of Thomas Jefferson*, ed. by P. L. Ford, 10 vols., 1892-99, Vol. X, p. 343, courtesy of G. P. Putnam's Sons.

[12] Gilbert Chinard, *Thomas Jefferson, the Apostle of Americanism*, Little, Brown, 1929, p. 87.

[13] *Select Charters . . . of American History, 1606-1775*, pp. 56-57.

[14] Notes on the debates in the First Continental Congress as summarized later in his Autobiography, John Adams, *Op. cit.*, Vol. II, p. 374.

[15] *Cf.* Benjamin F. Wright, Jr., *American Interpretations of Natural Law*, Harvard University Press, 1931, Chaps. II-IV.

[16] *Works*, 10 vols., London, 1812, Vol. V, p. 209.

[17] *Op. cit.*, pp. 277-79.

[18] "The Substance of American Democracy," in Max Ascoli and Fritz Lehmann, *Political and Economic Democracy*, Norton, 1937, pp. 323-24.

[19] Philip Davidson, *Propaganda and the American Revolution, 1763-1783*, University of North Carolina Press, 1941, p. 410.

[20] Edward S. Corwin, "The 'Higher Law' Background of American Constitutional Law," *Harvard Law Review*, Vol. XLII (1929), p. 403. By permission of the publisher and the author.

[21] Quoted by Henry Adams in his *History of the United States of America during the First Administration of Thomas Jefferson*, 2 vols., Scribner, 1909, Vol. I, p. 78. *Cf.* Chap. I, *passim*.

[22] *Cf.* C. Edward Merriam, *A History of American Political Theories*, Macmillan, 1920, pp. 126, 131. For Burke, *cf.* John MacCunn, *The Political Philosophy of Burke*, London, 1913.

[23] "The Senate," *The Federalist*, Paper LXIII, Colonial Press, p. 348. (Whether this Paper was written by Madison or Hamilton is a subject of controversy.) *Cf.* also E. M. Burns, *James Madison, Philosopher of the Constitution*, Rutgers University Press, 1938, Chap. III and p. 154. That men judge government from the standpoint of their interests, and that among these their economic interests will take a leading place, cannot be doubted. It follows that in protecting property against the consolidated power of the impecunious masses the Constitution of 1788 would appeal to the propertied classes. Political conservatism coincides with the desire for stability, fulfillment of contractual obligations, and the protection of minority rights on the part of men who enjoy a comparatively advantageous position in the existing distribution of wealth. *Cf.* Charles A. Beard's famous *An Economic Interpretation of the Constitution of the United States*, Macmillan, 1913, Chap. VI.

[24] *Cf.* Jeremy Bentham, *A Fragment on Government*, Oxford University Press, 1891, Chap. I, *passim*, especially the Introduction by F. C. Montague, p. 84. *Cf.* also Bentham's *An Introduction to the Principles of Morals and Legislation*, Oxford, 1876, Chap. II, § XIV, note.

[25] *Cf.* J. B. McMaster, *The Acquisition of Political Social and Industrial Rights of Man in America*, Imperial Press, Cleveland, Ohio, 1903.

[26] James Thomson, *Coriolanus*, 1749, Act. III, Scene iii, p. 34.

[27] Letters of Apr. 24, 1816, and Nov. 13, 1787, *Op. cit.*, Vol. X, pp. 23-24; Vol. IV, p. 467.

[28] Bills of rights had already been incorporated in the constitutions of Virginia, Massachusetts, Maryland, North Carolina, New Hampshire, Pennsylvania and Vermont; and in the French *Déclaration des droits de l'homme* (1789). *Cf.* George Jellinek, *La Déclaration des droits de l'homme, et du citoyen,* translated by G. Fardis, Paris, 1902, p. 18, and Chaps. III-V.

[29] "On Alleged Defects in the Constitution," *The Federalist,* Paper LXXXIV, Colonial Press, p. 475; quoted by C. Edward Merriam, *Op. cit.*, pp. 117-18.

[30] Albert M. Kales, " 'Due Process,' the Inarticulate Major Premise and the Adamson Act," *Yale Law Journal,* Vol. XXVI (May 1917), pp. 526, 548.

[31] *Cf.* Zechariah Chafee, Jr., "Freedom of Speech in War Time," in his *Freedom of Speech,* Harcourt, Brace, 1920, p. 34.

[32] Thomas Jefferson, "Notes on Virginia," quoted by Henry Adams, *Op. cit.*, Vol. I, p. 147.

[33] J. S. Bassett, *The Life of Andrew Jackson,* 2 vols., 1911, Vol. II, pp. 423-24. By permission of The Macmillan Company, publishers. The "guest" quoted was James Hamilton, Jr., in a letter of Mar. 5, 1829, to Martin Van Buren.

[34] *Ibid.*, Vol. II, pp. 426-27.

[35] *Cf.* Arthur M. Schlesinger, *New Viewpoints in American History,* pp. 86-88, 204-05. I am much indebted to this book for its admirable survey of the subject of the present chapter.

[36] James Russell Lowell, *My Study Windows,* 22d ed., Houghton Mifflin, 1886, pp. 193-94; *cf.* also John R. Commons and associates, *History of Labour in the United States,* 2 vols., Macmillan, 1918, Vol. I, Pts. II-III; Frederick J. Turner, *The Frontier in American History,* p. 327; Ralph Waldo Emerson, "New England Reformers," *Essays: Second Series,* Houghton Mifflin, 1884 (Riverside edition), pp. 239-42.

[37] *Cf.* Emerson D. Fite, *History of the United States,* 2d ed., Holt, 1923, p. 287.

[38] *The Flowering of New England,* Dutton, 1936.

[39] Ralph Waldo Emerson, "Nature," *Nature, Addresses, and Lectures,* Houghton Mifflin, 1884 (Riverside edition), pp. 78-79; "New England Reformers," *Essays: Second Series,* p. 269.

[40] *Cf.* C. Edward Merriam, *Op. cit.*, pp. 207-16.

[41] *Cf. Ibid.*, pp. 216-48.

[42] Abraham Lincoln, *Complete Works,* ed. by John G. Nicolay and John Hay, 2 vols., Century (now D. Appleton-Century Company), 1894, Vol. I, pp. 690-91.

[43] "Speech of the Dred Scott Decision, Springfield, Illinois, June 26, 1857," *Ibid.*, Vol. I, p. 232.

[44] Quoted without reference by C. Edward Merriam, *Op. cit.*, p. 224. *Cf.* Lincoln's "Speech at Peoria, Illinois, in Reply to Senator Douglas. October 16, 1854"; "Letter to George Robertson, Springfield, Illinois, August 15, 1855"; "Second Inaugural, *Op. cit.*, Vol. I, pp. 195, 215-16.

[45] James Russell Lowell, "Lincoln," *Op. cit.*, p. 176.

[46] Article VI; *cf.* also Article III, Section 2; Article V; Amendment X; and C. E. Merriam, *Op. cit.*, pp. 258, 286.

[47] *Cf. Ibid.*, pp. 263-64, 266-67, 286.

[48] *Cf. Ibid.*, pp. 312-14. Its most eminent representatives in America, after Calhoun, were Theodore Dwight Woolsey (1809-1889) and John W. Burgess (1844-1931).

CHAPTER SEVEN

[1] *Writings*, Vol. X, p. 256.

[2] B. Fay, *L'Esprit révolutionnaire en France et aux Etats-Unis à la fin du XVIIIe siècle*, Paris, 1925, pp. 16-17.

[3] From *The Rise of Modern Religious Ideas*, 1922, pp. 11-12. By permission of The Macmillan Company, publishers.

[4] From A. N. Whitehead, *Science and the Modern World*, 1925, p. 65. By permission of The Macmillan Company, publishers.

[5] "The Epistle to the Reader," from *An Essay Concerning Human Understanding*, ed. by A. C. Fraser, 2 vols., Clarendon Press, Oxford, 1894, Vol. I, p. 14. This is the edition cited throughout. By permission of the publishers.

[6] "De Principiis Cogitandi," (Thomas) *Gray's Poetical Works, English and Latin*, Eton, 1847, p. 107.

[7] *Cf.* E. A. Burtt, *The Metaphysical Foundations of Modern Physical Science*, Harcourt, Brace, 1925, pp. 280 ff.

[8] Colin Maclaurin, *An Account of Sir Isaac Newton's Philosophical Discoveries*, 3d ed., London, 1775, pp. 3-4, quoted by Carl Becker, *The Declaration of Independence*, pp. 49-51. *Cf.* also *Ibid.*, pp. 40-51.

[9] Quoted by Henry Fairfield Osborn, *From the Greeks to Darwin*, Macmillan, 1894, p. 141.

[10] H. R. Fox Bourne, *The Life of John Locke*, 2 vols., Harper, 1876, Vol. II, p. 514; Vol. I, p. 306.

[11] *Op. cit.*, Vol. XI, p. 384.

[12] C. H. Van Tyne, "Influence of the Clergy . . . on the American Revolution," *American Historical Review*, Vol. XIX (1913-14), pp. 54-55.

[13] Max Farrand, ed., *Records of the Federal Convention of 1787*, 4 vols., Yale University Press, 1911-37, Vol. I, pp. 451-52, n.15.

[14] *An Address to the Pastors and People of these United States on the Chaplaincy of the General Government*, Washington, D.C., 1857, pp. 3-4.

[15] *An Essay Concerning Human Understanding*, Bk. IV, Chap. XIX, § 4. *Cf.* also "The Reasonableness of Christianity," *Works*, Vol. VII, p. 147; A. C. McGiffert, *Protestant Thought before Kant*, pp. 201, 203.

[16] Matthew Tindal, *Christianity as Old as the Creation*, London, 1732, p. 343.

[17] "Religious Thought in England," *Essays by the Late Mark Pattison*, collected and arranged by Henry Nettleship, 2 vols., Clarendon Press, Oxford, 1889, Vol. II, pp. 47-48; by permission of the publishers.

[18] *The Theory of Moral Sentiments*, 11th ed., London, 1812, p. 565.

[19] Samuel Clarke, *A Discourse Concerning the Being and Attributes of God,* etc., London, 1719, Pt. II, pp. 47-48, 86-87.

[20] "An Inquiry Concerning Virtue," reprinted in L. A. Selby-Bigge, *British Moralists,* 2 vols., Oxford, 1897, Vol. I, pp. 12, 37, 65.

[21] *Cf. An Essay Concerning Human Understanding,* Vol. I, Introd., § 5, and the Epistle to the Reader.

[22] *Ibid.,* Vol. II, pp. 304, 327.

[23] *Ibid.,* Vol. II, pp. 156, 208. *Cf. Ibid.,* Vol. II, p. 347.

[24] *Ibid.,* Vol. II, p. 208.

[25] *Ibid.,* Vol. I, p. 67.

[26] *Ibid.,* Vol. I, pp. 303, 474-76.

[27] *Ibid.,* Vol. I, p. 68.

[28] *Ibid.,* Vol. I, p. 70.

[29] "The Reasonableness of Christianity," *Works,* Vol. VII, pp. 144, 147.

[30] *An Essay Concerning Human Understanding,* Vol. I, p. 475.

[31] Jefferson's letter of May 30, 1790, to T. M. Randolph, *Writings,* Vol. V, p. 173. *Cf.* also p. 181. F. W. Hirst refers to Jefferson as "a disciple of Adam Smith."—*Life and Letters of Thomas Jefferson,* Macmillan, 1926, p. 256. For Franklin's personal acquaintance with Smith, *cf.* Carl Van Doren, *Benjamin Franklin,* Viking Press, 1938, p. 281.

[32] *The Theory of Moral Sentiments,* pp. 325, 308ff.

[33] The best examination of this question is to be found in Glenn R. Morrow, *The Ethical and Economic Theories of Adam Smith,* Longmans, Green, 1923.

[34] *The Theory of Moral Sentiments,* p. 315; *An Inquiry into the Nature and Cause of the Wealth of Nations,* 2 vols., Dutton, 1931 (Everyman's Library), Vol. I, p. 13. (Hereafter referred to as *The Wealth of Nations.*)

[35] *Cf. The Theory of Moral Sentiments,* pp. 312-16.

[36] *Cf. Ibid.,* pp. 327-30.

[37] *The Wealth of Nations,* Vol. I, p. 400. The same expression occurs in *The Theory of Moral Sentiments,* p. 318.

[38] *The Wealth of Nations,* Vol. II, p. 168.

[39] Edward S. Corwin, "The 'Higher Law' Background of American Constitutional Law," *Loc. cit.,* Vol. XLII (1929), pp. 380-81.

[40] 2 vols., Dutton, 1925 (Everyman's Library), Vol. I, p. 150.

[41] *Ibid.,* Vol. I, pp. 155, 162.

[42] *Ibid.,* Vol. I, p. 182.

[43] *Cf.* A. O. Lovejoy and George Boas, *Primitivism and Related Ideas in Antiquity,* Johns Hopkins Press, 1935, Appendix, "Some Meanings of 'Nature.'"

[44] Richard Hooker, *Op. cit.,* Vol. I, pp. 190, 193.

[45] *Ibid.,* Vol. I, pp. 154-55. This list is not necessarily complete. There is also a "law of nations," etc. (*Cf. Ibid.,* Vol. I, pp. 199, 224.) The important point is that there is one *fundamental* (eternal) law, divisible into diverse parts which differ in their regions of application, or in their "manner of binding." (*Cf. Ibid.,* Vol. I, p. 197.) Thus Thomas Aquinas said that natural law is the participation of rational creatures in the eternal law. (*Summa Theologica,* Prima secundae, qu. 91, art. 2.)

[46] *Op. cit.,* Vol. I, pp. 203-04, 210.

[47] *Ibid.,* Vol. I, pp. 199, 205, 199, 161.

[48] *Ibid.*, Vol. I, p. 180.

[49] *Ibid.*, Vol. I, pp. 188-89.

[50] H. R. Fox Bourne, *Op. cit.*, Vol. II, p. 557.

[51] For Locke's view of will, *cf. An Essay Concerning Human Understanding*, Vol. I, pp. 344, 348, 360.

[52] *Leviathan*, reprinted from the edition of 1651, Oxford, 1909, pp. 121-22.

[53] "An Essay Concerning the True Original, Extent and End of Civil Government" (more generally known, and hereafter cited, as "The Second Treatise of Civil Government"), *Two Treatises of Civil Government*, Dutton, 1924 (Everyman's Library), pp. 119-20.

[54] *Ibid.*, pp. 186, 185.

[55] *Op. cit.*, p. 97.

[56] "A Third Letter for Toleration," *Works*, Vol. VI, p. 225.

[57] Alexander Pope, *Essay on Man*, Third Epistle, ll. 147-50.

[58] *The Letters of Percy Bysshe Shelley*, ed. by Roger Ingpen, 2 vols., Pitman, 1909, Vol. I, p. 170.

[59] Edward S. Corwin, *op. cit.*, p. 383.

[60] *Op. cit.*, p. 99.

[61] *The Second Treatise of Civil Government*, pp. 125, 126, 118.

[62] Edward S. Corwin, *op. cit.*, p. 393.

[63] *Op. cit.*, p. 180.

[64] *Works*, Vol. VI, p. 10.

[65] *The Second Treatise of Civil Government*, p. 129.

[66] *Ibid.*, pp. 130-32, 141.

[67] *Works*, Vol. VI, p. 216. *Cf.* Sir Frederick Pollock, "Locke's Theory of the State," *Proceedings of the British Academy*, 1903-04, pp. 237-49.

[68] *Cf.* Léon Duguit, *Jean-Jacques Rousseau, Kant et Hegel*, Paris, 1918.

[69] *The Second Treatise of Civil Government*, p. 233.

[70] *Ibid.*, p. 179.

[71] *Ibid.*, pp. 120, 180. For Locke's statement of the origin of government, see pp. 158-60.

[72] *Cf. Leviathan*, Chap. XVII.

[73] Richard Hooker, *Op. cit.*, Vol. I, p. 228; quoted by Locke, *Op. cit.*, p. 161.

[74] W. E. Curtis, *The True Thomas Jefferson*, Lippincott, 1901, p. 18.

[75] H. D. Foster, "International Calvinism through Locke and the Revolution of 1688," *American Historical Review*, Vol. XXXII (April 1927), p. 492.

[76] *Op. cit.*, Vol. I, pp. 185, 201.

CHAPTER EIGHT

[1] *Cf.* above, page 126.

[2] *The Works of Theodore Roosevelt,* 25 vols., Scribner, 1906-10 (Elkhorn Edition), Vol. VI, p. 270.

[3] "The Age of Reason," *The Writings of Thomas Paine,* Modern Library, 1922, p. 214.

[4] "Dialogue Concerning Virtue and Pleasure," and "A Second Dialogue between Philocles and Horatio Concerning Virtue and Pleasure," from *The Works of Benjamin Franklin,* edited by John Bigelow, Vol. I, pp. 387, 393-95.

[5] *Cf.* Douglas Campbell, *The Puritan in Holland, England, and America,* 2 vols., Harper, 1892, Vol. I, pp. 233-35; Vol. II, pp. 465-67.

[6] Charles McLean Andrews, "Conservative Factors in Early Colonial History," *Authority and the Individual,* Harvard University Press, 1937 (Harvard Tercentenary Publication) pp. 164-65, 169.

[7] "Speech in the Case of Harry Croswell," from *The Works of Alexander Hamilton,* ed. by H. C. Lodge, 12 vols., 1904 (Federal Edition), Vol. VIII, p. 421, courtesy of G. P. Putnam's Sons.

[8] Letter to H. Niles of Jan. 14, 1818, *Works,* Vol. X, p. 275.

[9] "Common Law," *Encyclopedia of the Social Sciences,* 15 vols., 1930-35, Vol. IV, p. 55. For the characteristically individualistic emphasis of American legal thought, *cf.* also G. Jellinek, *La Déclaration des droits de l'homme et du citoyen,* pp. 48 ff.

[10] *Op. cit.,* ed. by Thomas M. Cooley, 2 vols., Callaghan, Chicago, 1872, Vol. I, pp. 38-41. To Blackstone ethics and natural law were synonymous; *cf. Ibid.,* Vol. I, p. 39; *cf.* also Cooley's Introduction to this edition, Vol. I, pp. x-xi; and B. F. Wright, Jr., *American Interpretations of Natural Law,* pp. 10-11. For the wide vogue enjoyed by the *Commentaries* in the colonies prior to the Revolution, *cf.* Julian S. Waterman, "Thomas Jefferson and Blackstone's Commentaries," *Illinois Law Review,* Vol. XXVIII (1932-33), pp. 629-59. "By 1776 nearly twenty-five hundred copies were in use here, one thousand five hundred of which were the American edition of 1772; a sale which Burke said . . . rivaled that in England."—*Loc. cit.,* p. 630.

[11] *Cf.* H. D. Hazeltine, "William Blackstone," *Encyclopedia of the Social Sciences,* Vol. II, pp. 580-81; B. F. Wright, Jr., *Op. cit.,* pp. 64-70; Edward S. Corwin, "The 'Higher Law' Background of American Constitutional Law," *Loc. cit.,* pp. 398-99; James Otis, *A Vindication of the House of Representatives of the Province of Massachusetts Bay,* Boston, 1762, and *The Rights of the British Colonies Asserted and Proved,* Boston, 1764.

[12] "Sir Edward Coke," *Encyclopaedia Britannica,* 14th ed., Vol. V, p. 981.

[13] Letter to James Madison, February 17, 1826, *Writings,* Vol. X, p. 367. "Coke Littleton" was Coke's commentary on Littleton's *Tenures.*

[14] *Cf.* "Civil Liberty" (section on the United States written by Morris L. Ernst), *Encyclopaedia Britannica,* 14th ed., Vol. V, pp. 742-43.

[15] "Bonham's Case" and "Calvin's Case," *The Reports of Sir Edward Coke,* ed. by J. H. Thomas and J. F. Fraser, 6 vols., London, 1826, Vol. IV, pp. 21, 375; quoted by Edward S. Corwin, *Op. cit.,* pp. 368-69.

[16] *Op. cit.,* p. 394.

[17] *Op. cit.,* London, 5th ed., 1721, pp. 22-27. The notes are from Coke's *Second Part of the Institutes of the Laws of England,* 4th ed., London, 1671. Care's book was originally published in 1682.

[18] *Cf.* C. H. McIlwain, *The American Revolution: A Constitutional Interpretation,* p. 19.

[19] William MacDonald, *Select Charters and Other Documents Illustrative of American History, 1606-1775,* p. 73. *Cf.* the Charter of Maryland (above, page 126); and the Fundamental Orders of Connecticut (below, page 138); also William Penn, Concessions and Agreements of West New Jersey, 1676-77, and Frame of Government of Pennsylvania, 1682, as well as The Resolutions of the Stamp Act Congress, 1765, reprinted in MacDonald, *Op. cit.,* pp. 174-83, 192-99, 313-15.

[20] Attributed to Hubert Languet or to Duplessis-Mornay.

[21] *Op. cit.,* 2 vols., Philadelphia, 1805, Vol. II, pp. 92-93. Sidney's citation is from Tertullian.

[22] By Ray Forrest Harvey, *Jean Jacques Burlamaqui,* University of North Carolina Press, 1937.

[23] *Op. cit.,* translated by Thomas Nugent, 2 vols. 2d ed., London, 1763, Vol. I, Chap. II, p. 51.

[24] Ray Forrest Harvey, *Op. cit.,* p. 121.

[25] *Cf.* below, p. 448.

[26] *Cf.* above, p. 156.

[27] "Considerations on the Nature and Extent of the Legislative Authority of the British Parliament," *The Works of the Honourable James Wilson,* 3 vols., Philadelphia, 1804, Vol. III, pp. 205-06.

[28] Carl Becker, *The Declaration of Independence,* p. 108.

[29] George Mason, "Original Draft of the Declaration of Rights" (Virginia), Appendix X in K. M. Rowland, *The Life of George Mason,* 2 vols., 1892, Vol. I, p. 434, courtesy of G. P. Putnam's Sons.

[30] Rom. 2:14-15.

[31] *Cf.* J. Neville Figgis, "Political Thought in the Sixteenth Century," *Cambridge Modern History,* Vol. III, esp. pp. 764-65.

[32] *Cf.* A. L. Cross, *The Anglican Episcopate and the American Colonies,* Longmans, Green, 1902, esp. pp. 233-35.

[33] R. A. Guild, *Chaplain Smith and the Baptists,* American Baptist Publication Society, 1885, p. 161, n. 1.

[34] C. H. Van Tyne, "Influence of the Clergy . . . on the American Revolution," *Loc. cit.,* p. 47.

[35] E. S. Corwin, *Op. cit.,* p. 397; *cf.* Isaac Backus, *History of New England,* Providence, R. I., 1871, pp. 197-98.

[36] The presbyterian clergy were disposed by their Scottish "philosophy of common sense," as well as by their Calvinism, to the acceptance of the principles of the Enlightenment. While it is true that this philosophy was not widespread in America until after the arrival of John Witherspoon at Princeton in 1768, Lord Kames

and Hutcheson were already known a decade or more before that time. Jefferson's interest in Lord Kames and his acceptance of Dugald Stewart's ethical teaching afford evidence of the fact that Scottish realism and the philosophy of the Enlightenment were readily assimilated to one another.

[37] Lorenzo Sabine, *The American Loyalists, or Biographical Sketches of Adherents to the British Crown in the War of the Revolution,* Boston, 1847, pp. 30-31.

[38] *Cf.* H. W. Schneider, *The Puritan Mind,* pp. 241 ff.

[39] Abridgment by Benjamin Fawcett, New York, 1758, p. 84. This work first appeared in 1649.

[40] *Cf.* Van Wyck Brooks, *The Flowering of New England,* pp. 59-60; S. E. Morison, *The Founding of Harvard College,* Harvard University Press, 1935, pp. 157 ff.

[41] Jefferson's report of the Commission on Education appointed in 1818 by the Governor of Virginia, quoted by James C. Carter, *The University of Virginia: Jefferson Its Father, and His Political Philosophy,* University of Virginia, 1898, pp. 10-11.

[42] *Cf.* S. E. Morison, *Builders of the Bay Colony,* Houghton Mifflin, 1930, pp. 83-84.

[43] G. P. Gooch, *Political Thought in England from Bacon to Halifax,* p. 142.

[44] John Lilburne, *The Free-man's Freedom Vindicated,* 1646, as quoted in A. S. P. Woodhouse, *Puritanism and Liberty,* p. 317.

[45] Letter to Lord Say and Sele, quoted by William Jenks, in the *New England Historical and Genealogical Register,* Vol. X (January 1856), p. 12. Henry Ainsworth had said the same thing as early as 1608 in his *Counterpoyson; cf.* the edition of 1642, London, p. 103.

[46] *Cf.* Perry Miller, "Thomas Hooker and the Democracy of Early Connecticut," *New England Quarterly,* Vol. IV (October 1931), pp. 663-712; and G. L. Walker, *Thomas Hooker: Preacher, Founder, Democrat,* Dodd, Mead, 1891, Chap. VI.

[47] G. P. Gooch, *Op. cit.,* p. 142.

[48] Deut. 1:13.

[49] "Abstracts of Two Sermons by Rev. Thomas Hooker," in the years 1638, 1639, *Collections of the Connecticut Historical Society,* 1860, Vol. I, p. 20. The full text of this sermon has not been preserved. It is probable that it was never written out, and only the shorthand notes taken at the time by Henry Wolcott, Jr., have survived. *Cf.* also the similar action in the New Haven colony in 1639.

[50] *A History of the Life and Death, Virtues and Exploits of General George Washington,* p. 75.

[51] *Cf.* Milton's identification of the fall with the transition from the state of nature to civil polity in his "Tenure of Kings and Magistrates" (1699), in *The Prose Works of John Milton,* 2 vols., Philadelphia, 1847, Vol. I, pp. 377-78.

[52] H. D. Foster, "International Calvinism through Locke and the Revolution of 1688," *Loc. cit.,* p. 485 and *passim.* This article contains an admirable summary of the Calvinistic anticipations of the central doctrines of eighteenth-century democracy.

[53] John Wise drew largely upon Samuel Pufendorf, who, although the son of a Lutheran pastor, was notable for his individualism and challenge of political authority. *Cf.* his *De jure naturae et gentium,* first published in 1672.

[54] *A Vindication of the Government of New-England Churches,* Boston, 1772, pp. 28, 39-40.

[55] Moses Coit Tyler, *A History of American Literature during the Colonial Time,* 2d ed., 2 vols., Putnam, 1897, Vol. II, p. 115; *cf.* also A. M. Baldwin, *The New England Clergy and the American Revolution,* Duke University Press, 1928, p. 9, n. 10; p. 30, n. 24.

[56] Edward S. Corwin, *Op. cit.,* p. 396.

[57] Quoted by C. H. Van Tyne, *Op. cit.,* pp. 57-58. The first quotation is from *American Archives,* 4th series, Vol. I, p. 335; the source of the second is not given. For an excellent account of the subject, *cf.* also A. M. Baldwin, *Op. cit.*

[58] *An Eulogy, Illustrative of the Life, and Commemorative of the Beneficence of the Late Hon. James Bowdoin, Esquire,* Boston, 1812, p. 21.

[59] *Cf.* H. W. Schneider, *Op. cit.,* Chap. VI. This author's description of the movement as an *undermining* of Calvinistic piety fails, it seems to me, to do justice to the broader currents of historical Calvinism. Even Cotton Mather, in his *Christian Philosopher: a Collection of the Best Discoveries in Nature with Religious Improvements,* had already in 1721 praised the beauties and harmonies of nature as testifying to the beneficence of God. Hutcheson was a Scotch presbyterian, Clarke an Anglican clergyman with liberal and rationalistic tendencies similar to those of Locke.

[60] *Christian Sobriety,* Boston, 1763, p. ix.

[61] "The Snare Broken, a Thanksgiving-Discourse" preached at the West Church, May 23, 1766, "occasioned by the Repeal of the Stamp Act," *Sermons,* Boston, 1766, p. 35.

[62] Reprinted by J. W. Thornton, who admiringly described it as "the morning gun of the Revolution," in *The Pulpit of the American Revolution,* Boston, 1860, pp. 41-104. *Cf.* especially pp. 43, 86-87, 93-95.

[63] *Ibid.,* pp. 86-87.

[64] *Seasonable Thoughts on the State of Religion in New-England,* pp. 326-27, 424. *Cf.* also his later work on *The Benevolence of the Deity,* Boston, 1784. Chauncy was famous for his controversy with Jonathan Edwards, whose *Treatise Concerning Religious Affections* (1746) was a reply to *Seasonable Thoughts,* which in turn had been written against Edwards's *Thoughts Concerning the Present Revival of Religion in New England* (1742).

[65] *Civil Magistrates Must Be Just, Ruling in the Fear of God: A Sermon Preached May 27, 1747, Being the Anniversary for the Election,* Boston, 1747, p. 9.

[66] *A Letter to a Friend,* by T. W., A Bostonian (Charles Chauncy), Boston, 1774.

[67] *Cf.* William B. Sprague, *Annals of the American Pulpit,* 7 vols., New York City, 1857, Vol. I, pp. 441-44.

[68] *Sermon . . .* Oct. 25, 1780, Boston, 1780, pp. 14-15.

[69] V. L. Collins, *Princeton,* Oxford University Press, 1914, p. 59.

[70] Samuel Davies, "Religion and Patriotism," *Sermons,* 3 vols., Philadelphia, 1864, Vol. III, pp. 80, 102.

[71] *Cf.* Frederick Jackson Turner, *The Frontier in American History, passim;* also F. L. Paxson, *History of the American Frontier, 1763-1893,* Houghton Mifflin, 1924.

[72] W. C. Bryant, *A Forest Hymn;* Milton, *Paradise Lost,* Book IX, l. 1106; Matthew Arnold, *The Future;* Byron, *Childe Harold,* Canto iii, stanza 71; *Ibid.,* stanza 72; Thomas Hood, *Ode to Rae Wilson;* Thomas Moore, *Rhymes on the Road* (Extract 1, l. 26).

[73] *American Notes and Pictures from Italy,* Dutton, 1907 (Everyman's Library), pp. 181-82.

[74] *Cf.* "Mrs. Skaggs's Husbands," *The Writings of Bret Harte,* 19 vols., Houghton Mifflin, 1896-1903; Vol. II, p. 92; also Introd., *Ibid.,* p. xxi and *passim.*

[75] *Cf.* Langdon Mitchell, *Understanding America,* Doran, 1927, pp. 78-109; also Dickens, *Op. cit.,* p. 246.

[76] *Second Treatise of Civil Government,* p. 175.

[77] R. B. Marcy, *The Prairie Traveller,* Harper, 1859, pp. 6-7.

[78] Quoted in *The Oregon Trail,* W.P.A. American Guide Series, Washington, D. C., 1939, pp. 40-41.

[79] *Op. cit.,* p. 168.

[80] *The Prophet of the Great Smoky Mountains,* Houghton Mifflin, 1885, p. 44.

[81] Written in 1834, quoted by F. J. Turner, *Op. cit.,* p. 214.

[82] Quoted by E. D. Adams, *The Power of Ideals in American History,* Yale University Press, 1923, p. 81; *cf.* Chapter III, *passim.*

[83] *Cf.* A. B. Hart, *National Ideals Historically Traced,* Harper, 1907 (Vol. 26 of *The American Nation: A History,* ed. by A. B. Hart), map opposite p. 18; *cf.* also Emerson D. Fite, *History of the United States,* map of "Territorial Growth of the United States," opposite p. 308.

[84] Quoted by John Spencer Bassett, *The Life of Andrew Jackson,* Vol. II, p. 674.

[85] F. M. Trollope, *Domestic Manners of the Americans,* London, 1832, pp. 282-84; *cf. Ibid.,* p. 325.

[86] *Cf.* Mark Twain, *Life on the Mississippi,* Chap. III; also Dickens, *Op. cit.,* pp. 149-50.

[87] *Op. cit.,* Macmillan, 1905, p. 60. *Cf.* also V. L. Parrington, *Main Currents in American Thought,* Vol. II, p. 350.

[88] Quoted from the *Washington Union,* the administration paper, by E. D. Adams, *Op. cit.,* p. 85.

[89] *The Works of John Adams,* Vol. II, pp. 366-67.

[90] C. G. Haines, *The Revival of Natural Law Concepts,* Harvard University Press, 1930, p. 52.

CHAPTER NINE

[1] *Works,* Vol. V, pp. v, vi-vii, ix-xi, xiii-xv.

[2] *Ibid.,* p. xv.

[3] *Oliver Cromwell's Letters and Speeches,* ed. by Thomas Carlyle, New York, 1846, p. 364.

[4] "A Treatise Concerning Religious Affections," *Works,* Vol. I, p. 314.

[5] From Robert Cushman's "Discourse" of Dec. 9, 1621, *Chronicles of the Pilgrim Fathers,* Dutton, 1910 (Everyman's Library), p. 235.

[6] "Sinners in the Hands of an Angry God," *Op. cit.,* Vol. II, pp. 10, 12.

[7] "A Faithful Narrative of the Surprising Work of God in the Conversion of Many Hundred Souls in Northampton" (written in 1736), *Ibid.*, Vol. I, p. 348.

[8] *Cf.* II Pet. 1:4; Phil. 3:8-10. Cited by Oliver Cromwell in a letter to his son, Apr. 2, 1650, *Op. cit.*, p. 354.

[9] From the Shorter Westminster Catechism.

[10] "A Dissertation Concerning the End for Which God Created the World," *Op. cit.*, Vol. I, p. 95, and *passim.*

[11] Henri Bremond, *Histoire littéraire du sentiment religieux en France,* Vol. I, p. 117.

[12] *Of the Laws of Ecclesiastical Polity,* Vol. I, pp. 177-78.

[13] Dutton (Everyman's Library), 1932, pp. 34-35.

[14] *Op. cit.*, Vol. V, p. viii.

[15] *Cf.* Georgia Harkness, *John Calvin, the Man and His Ethics,* Chap. VII.

[16] *Cf.* D. H. Lawrence, "Pornography and Obscenity," *Phoenix,* 1936.

[17] Letter of July 28, 1651, *Op. cit.*, pp. 448-49.

[18] Robert C. Winthrop, *The Life and Letters of John Winthrop,* 2 vols., Ticknor & Fields, 1864-67, Vol. II, p. 179. See also *Ibid.*, Vol. I, pp. 380 ff.

[19] Luke 14:26.

[20] Letter of Sept. 4, 1650, *Op. cit.*, p. 391. *Cf.* also his letters to his daughters of Oct. 25, 1646, and Aug. 13, 1649, pp. 161-62, 289.

[21] *Ibid.*, pp. 123, 296.

[22] For a thorough and convincing examination of this question, together with a bibliography, *cf.* G. G. Coulton, *Art and the Reformation,* Knopf, 1928.

[23] *Ibid.*, pp. 323, 372, 377-78, 381, 386, 387.

[24] *Institutes of the Christian Religion,* Bk. I, Chap. XI, Sec. 12; quoted by G. G. Coulton, *Op. cit.*, pp. 407-08.

[25] *Puritanism and Art,* London, 1910, p. 337.

[26] *Cf.* above, Chapter V, Section 10.

[27] *Cf.* Edward Dowden, *Puritan and Anglican,* 3d ed., London, 1910, pp. 12-34 and *passim;* also P. T. Forsyth, *Christ on Parnassus,* London, 1912, pp. 280 ff.

[28] *Cf.* S. E. Morison, *The Puritan Pronaos,* New York University Press, 1936.

[29] Percy A. Scholes, *The Puritans and Music in England and New England,* Oxford University Press, 1934, p. 90 and *passim. Cf.* also V. F. Calverton, *The Liberation of American Literature,* Scribner, 1932, Chap. II.

[30] *Cf.* Alice Morse Earle, *Home Life in Colonial Days,* Macmillan, 1898, and *Two Centuries of Costume in America,* Macmillan, 1903. *Cf.* also R. G. Usher, *The Pilgrims and Their History,* Macmillan, 1918, Chap. XVII. For the relation of sumptuary regulations to the *class* legislation of the times, *cf.* A. M. Low, *The American People,* 2 vols., Houghton Mifflin, 1909-11, Vol. I, Chap. XII.

[31] Henry James, *Charles W. Eliot,* 2 vols., Houghton Mifflin, 1930; Vol. I, pp. 125-26.

[32] Definition of puritanism by H. L. Mencken and George Jean Nathan in "Clinical Notes," *American Mercury,* January 1925, p. 59.

[33] *The History of England from the Accession of James II,* 3 vols., Dutton (Everyman's Library), Vol. I, p. 129.

[34] *Portraits: Real and Imaginary,* Doran (now Doubleday, Doran and Company), 1924, p. 109.

[35] Langdon Mitchell, *Understanding America*, pp. 110-11.

[36] *Americans*, Scribner, 1923, pp. 136-37.

[37] *The Saints' Everlasting Rest*, abridged by Benjamin Fawcett, introductory essay by Thomas Erskine dated 1824, pp. 94-95.

CHAPTER TEN

[1] G. P. Adams and W. P. Montague, eds., *Contemporary American Philosophy*, 2 vols., Macmillan, 1930, Vol. I, p. 18.

[2] "The Life of Dr. Thomas Goodwin," *Works*, Vol. V., p. xiii.

[3] John 12:25; Matt. 7:14.

[4] Quoted by R. H. Tawney, *Religion and the Rise of Capitalism*, Harcourt, Brace, 1926, p. 201.

[5] *The City of God, The Works of St. Augustin*, Christian Literature Society, Buffalo, 1886 (*Select Library of the Nicene and Post-Nicene Fathers*), p. 17.

[6] London, 1780, p. iii.

[7] From Robert Cushman's "Discourse" of Dec. 9, 1621, in *Chronicles of the Pilgrim Fathers*, p. 235.

[8] For puritan legalism and casuistry, *cf.* Edward Dowden, *Puritan and Anglican*, pp. 19-20.

[9] *Cf.* Mark Pattison, *Essays*, Vol. II, p. 25.

[10] *Institutes of the Christian Religion*, Vol. II, p. 184. (Bk. III, Chap. IX, §2.)

[11] Quoted in E. D. Hanscom, ed., *The Heart of the Puritan*, Macmillan, 1917, p. 252.

[12] Prov. 6:10.

[13] Quoted from J. T. Morse, *John Quincy Adams*, Houghton Mifflin, 1882, pp. 175-76, by J. H. Allen, *Christian History in Its Three Great Periods: Third Period, Modern Phases*, Roberts Brothers, Boston, 1891, p. 89.

[14] *Diary of Cotton Mather*, 2 vols., Massachusetts Historical Society Collections, Seventh Series, Vols. VII-VIII, 1911-12, Vol. VII, pp. 511, 510, 22, 15, 11, 28.

[15] John Calvin, *Op. cit.*, Vol. II, p. 155 (Bk. III, Chap. VI, § 2).

[16] *Works*, Vol. I, pp. lxii-lxiii, lxvi, lxix.

[17] Cotton Mather, *Essays to Do Good*, new ed., Dover, Eng., 1826, pp. 39-40.

[18] *Mr. Richard Baxter's Narrative of the Most Memorable Passages of His Life and Times*, London, 1696, p. 3.

[19] *The History of England from the Accession of James II*, Vol. I, pp. 307-08.

[20] *Cf. The Private Papers of Henry Ryecroft*, Modern Library, 1918, pp. 230-39.

[21] Letter of Sept. 2, 1648, to Lord Wharton, *Letters and Speeches*, pp. 226-27.

[22] *Diary, Loc. cit.*, Vol. VII, p. 5.

[23] Quoted from an undesignated source by John Brown, *The English Puritans*, p. 3.

[24] *Memoirs of the Life of Colonel Hutchinson . . . by His Widow Lucy*, ed. by C. H. Firth, 2 vols., London, 1885, Vol. I, pp. 114-15.

[25] *Op. cit.*, Vol. I, p. 143.

[26] Oscar Maurer, *A Puritan Church and Its Relation to Community, State, and Nation,* Yale University Press, 1938, pp. 193-94.

[27] "The Claxtons," *Brief Candles,* Harper, 1929, p. 131.

[28] *Of the Laws of Ecclesiastical Polity,* Vol. I, pp. 133-34.

[29] Edward Dowden, *Op. cit.*, pp. 15-16.

[30] *The Genius of America,* Scribner, 1923, p. 75.

CHAPTER ELEVEN

[1] For an excellent account of the rivalry between the intellectualistic, universalistic tendency, represented in medieval Christianity by Thomas Aquinas, and the voluntaristic, individualistic tendency, represented by Duns Scotus, *cf.* Josiah Royce, *The Conception of God,* Macmillan, 1897, pp. 217-71.

[2] *Cf. Ibid.*, pp. 258-65.

[3] For a discussion of the Christian conception of personality, as distinguishing the *human* individual, *cf.* Etienne Gilson, *L'Esprit de la philosophie médiévale,* Première série, Paris, 1932, Chap. X.

[4] *Ibid.*, Chap. IX.

[5] I Cor. 15:53, 40.

[6] *Works,* Vol. V, p. xi.

[7] *Diary of Cotton Mather, Loc. cit.*, Vol. VII, pp. 1-2.

[8] *Cf.* Blaise Pascal, *Pensées,* ed. by Léon Brunschvicg, 3 vols., Paris, 1921; Vol. II, pp. 434 ff; Matt. 26:36-45. I owe this citation of Pascal as evidence of *"la pérennité et l'éminente valeur de l'individu comme tel,"* to Professor Etienne Gilson, *Op. cit.*, p. 176.

[9] *Ibid.*, Chap. I.

[10] *Op. cit.*, Vol. VII, p. 2.

[11] "Speech on Moving His Resolutions for Conciliation with the Colonies, March 22, 1775," *The Works of the Right Honourable Edmund Burke,* 7 vols., Boston, 1826-27; Vol. II, pp. 28, 30.

[12] *Of the Laws of Ecclesiastical Polity,* Vol. I, pp. 89-90, 143.

[13] *A Commentarie of M. Doctor Martin Luther upon the Epistle of S. Paule to the Galathians, out of Latine faithfully translated into English for the unlearned,* London, 1580, Chap. II, Verse 20.

[14] From *Out of Africa,* by Karen Blixon-Finecke, New York, Random House, 1937, p. 280.

[15] From A. V. Dicey, *Introduction to the Study of the Law of the Constitution,* 3d ed., 1889, pp. 197-98. By permission of The Macmillan Company, publishers.

[16] *The Spirit of the Common Law,* Marshall Jones, Boston, 1921, pp. 44-45, 53.

[17] *Cf.* Edwards's *The Great Christian Doctrine of Original Sin Defended.*

[18] Blaise Pascal, *Op. cit.*, Vol. II, p. 441.

[19] Rom., Chaps. 6, 7, 8; Gal. 5:22.

[20] Eph. 5:18, 15.

[21] *Cf.* especially Pt. II, Sec. III, and Pt. III, Sec. X.

[22] *Seasonable Thoughts on the State of Religion,* etc., pp. 7-8, and *passim.*

[23] Joseph Butler, *Sermons, Charges, Fragments & Correspondence,* ed. by J. H. Bernard, Macmillan, 1900, p. 262.

CHAPTER TWELVE

[1] One of the maxims prefixed to Benjamin Franklin's *Poor Richard's Almanack,* 1733.

[2] *England's Present Interest Discover'd,* London, 1675, p. 32. There was at least one other printing of this work in 1675 which varies only in spelling and punctuation from that here cited.

[3] Prov., 6:4, 6-7, 11; 10:4, 13:11, 22, 23; 22:7; 28:19-20; 22:1.

[4] *Op. cit.,* Cambridge, 1656, p. 5.

[5] *Op. cit.,* 2 vols., London, 1825; Vol. II, pp. 607, 606.

[6] Quoted by W. Farnham, *The Medieval Heritage of Elizabethan Tragedy,* University of California Press, 1936, p. 86.

[7] *Cf.* Max Weber, *Gesammelte Aufsätze zur Religionssoziologie,* 3 vols., Tübingen, 1922, especially that part of Vol. I which was translated into English in 1930 by Talcott Parsons under the title of *The Protestant Ethic and the Spirit of Capitalism,* London, 1930; Ernst Troeltsch, *Die Soziallehren der christlichen Kirchen und Gruppen,* Tübingen, 1912 (*The Social Teaching of the Christian Churches,* translated by Olive Wyon, Macmillan, 1931), and *Die Bedeutung des Protestantismus für die Entstehung der modernen Welt,* Berlin, 1911 (*Protestantism and Progress,* translated by W. Montgomery, Putnam, 1912). This theory is ably presented from the Catholic point of view in George O'Brien, *An Essay on the Economic Effects of the Reformation,* London, 1923, Chap. II. This writer holds the Protestant Reformation responsible for *both* capitalism and socialism, the second being a reaction against the individualistic excesses of the first.

[8] *Cf.* Werner Sombart, *Krieg und Kapitalismus,* München, 1913; *Luxus und Kapitalismus,* München, 1913; *Der moderne Kapitalismus,* 3d ed., 2 vols. in 1, München, 1919. For a moderate criticism of Weber and Troeltsch, *cf.* R. H. Tawney, *Religion and the Rise of Capitalism,* pp. 316-17 and *passim.*

[9] For these titles, as well as the quotation above, *cf.* R. H. Tawney, *Op. cit.,* pp. 240, 321.

[10] *Cf.* A. C. McGiffert, *Protestant Thought before Kant,* pp. 38-40; Adolph Harnack, *History of Dogma,* Vol. VII, pp. 195 ff.

[11] *Op. cit.,* Vol. II, p. 580.

[12] James D. McCabe, Jr., *Great Fortunes, and How They Were Made; or the Struggles and Triumphs of our Self-Made Men,* Maclean, New York, 1871, p. 5.

[13] Elbridge S. Brooks, *The True Story of Abraham Lincoln, the American, Told for Boys and Girls*, Lothrop, 1896, pp. 223, 239.

[14] From speech by Colonel Henry Watterson delivered at the *Public Meeting under the Auspices of the American Academy and the National Institute of Arts and Letters, Held at Carnegie Hall, New York, November 30, 1910, in Memory of Samuel Langhorne Clemens (Mark Twain)*, American Academy of Arts and Letters, 1922, pp. 101-02. The Howells quotation is from *My Mark Twain,* Harper, 1910, p. 101.

[15] *Op. cit.*, Vol. II, p. 582.

[16] *Two Brief Discourses*, Boston, 1701, p. 38.

[17] Cotton Mather, *Sober Sentiments*, 1722, p. 25; quoted by A. Whitney Griswold, "Three Puritans on Prosperity," *New England Quarterly*, Vol. VII (1934), p. 481.

[18] *Political Economy*, Holt, 1888, pp. 66, 220; quoted by V. L. Parrington, *The Beginnings of Critical Realism in America, 1860-1920*, p. 112.

[19] *The Protestant Ethic and the Spirit of Capitalism*, p. 117.

[20] *Op. cit.*, Vol. II, pp. 585-86.

[21] *Ibid.*, Vol. II, p. 579.

[22] *Ibid.*, Vol. II, p. 70.

[23] Quoted from Anatole France, *Le Puits de Sainte Claire*, 7th ed., Paris, 1895, by R. H. Tawney, *Op. cit.*, p. 1.

[24] Robert Southey, *The Life of Wesley,* 2d American ed., 2 vols., Harper, 1847, Vol. II, p. 308.

[25] Reprinted from the *Proceedings of the American Antiquarian Society* (April 1941), 1942.

[26] *Ibid.*, pp. 17, 35.

[27] General James F. Rusling, "Interview with President McKinley," *Christian Advocate*, Vol. LXXVIII (Jan. 22, 1903), p. 137; quoted by Charles S. Olcott, *The Life of William McKinley*, 2 vols., Houghton Mifflin, 1916; Vol. II, pp. 109-11.

[28] Kemper Fullerton, "Calvinism and Capitalism," *Harvard Theological Review,* July, 1928, p. 194.

[29] "Mammon in the Vestry," editorial in *Christian Century*, March 25, 1942, p. 374.

[30] *Cf.* above, Chapter IX, p. 240.

[31] *Looking Backward, 2000-1887*, Houghton Mifflin, 1889, pp. 404-06.

[32] Thomas Moore, *Memoirs of the Life of the Right Honourable Richard Brinsley Sheridan*, Philadelphia, 1825, p. 596. It is not clear from the text whether Moore was the author of this couplet or whether he quoted it from an undesignated source.

CHAPTER THIRTEEN

[1] *Diary, Loc. cit.*, Vol. VII, pp. 515-16.

[2] *Essays to Do Good*, p. 38.

[3] *Ibid.*, pp. 60, 64, 114.

[4] *Ibid.*, p. 59; *Diary*, Vol. VII, p. 203.

[5] *Diary*, Vol. VII, pp. 23-24.

[6] *Essays to Do Good*, p. 48.

[7] *Diary*, Vol. VIII, pp. 357, 459, 473, 476, 499. Cromwell's love of wife and children also assumed an edifying, though less studied, form. *Cf.* the letter to his wife of Apr. 12, 1651, *Oliver Cromwell's Letters and Speeches*, p. 437.

[8] Letter to Samuel Mather, May 12, 1784, *Works*, Vol. X, p. 321.

[9] "The Editor's Preface," *Essays to Do Good*, p. 4.

[10] Reprinted from *Life with Father*, 1935, pp. 12-13, by permission and special arrangement with Alfred A. Knopf, Inc.

[11] *Chronicles of the Pilgrim Fathers*, pp. 193, 207, 223.

[12] G. G. Coulton, *Art and the Reformation*, p. 313.

[13] I Cor. 12:1, 4-11, 14, 19-21, 26-27.

[14] Eph. 5:32; 2:18.

[15] How the Plymouth colony passed from a collectivist to a private system of land tenure, both being defended on fundamental religious grounds, may be learned from a reading of "Cushman's Discourse of the State of the Colony, and the Need of Public Spirit in the Colonists," *Chronicles of the Pilgrim Fathers;* and Bradford's *History of Plymouth Plantation,* Vol. I, pp. 301-03.

[16] Bradford, *Op. cit.*, Vol. II, pp. 354-55.

[17] The identification of citizenship with church membership was in force from 1631 to 1664; the church was supported by taxation from 1638 to 1655. For a brief description of this polity, *cf.* H. L. Osgood, "The Political Ideas of the Puritans," *Political Science Quarterly*, Vol. VI (1891), p. 22; Perry Miller, *Orthodoxy in Massachusetts*, Chaps. VI-VII.

[18] *Cf.* C. Edward Merriam, *A History of American Political Theories*, pp. 6, 9-11, 14.

[19] For the analogy between the Calvinistic conception of God and political absolutism, *cf.* the Boston Platform of 1680, Chap. II, p. 2, in Cotton Mather, *Magnalia Christi Americana,* 2 vols., Hartford, Conn., 1853-55, Vol. II, p. 184.

[20] 13:4, 6, 8-9, 12-15. *Cf.* C. E. Merriam, *Op. cit.*, pp. 3-4.

[21] *Op. cit.*, Cambridge, Mass., 1656, p. 4.

[22] "New England's Memorial," *Chronicles of the Pilgrim Fathers*, pp. 7, 23.

[23] *The Cambridge Platform of Church Discipline* (adopted in 1648), Boston, 1653; Chap. IV, par. 3; quoted by H. W. Schneider, *The Puritan Mind*, p. 19, n. 6. For the development of this idea in William Ames, Robert Parker, John Cotton and Thomas Hooker, *cf. Ibid.*, p. 18.

[24] A. S. P. Woodhouse, *Puritanism and Liberty*, Introd., pp. 70-71 and *passim*. For the original version and later modification (1649) of this Agreement, *cf. Ibid.*, pp. 342-67, 443-45.

[25] "The Remonstrance of Fairfax and the Council of Officers," Nov. 16, 1648, *Ibid.*, p. 459.

[26] *Op. cit.*, ed. by J. F. Jameson (Original Narrative Series of Early American History), Barnes & Noble, Inc., 1910, p. 30.

[27] *Op. cit.*

[28] *A Holy Commonwealth*, London, 1659, Pref., pages not numbered; quoted by G. P. Gooch, *Political Thought in England from Bacon to Halifax*, p. 139.

[29] W. K. Jordan, *The Development of Religious Toleration in England*, Vol. III (*From the Convention of the Long Parliament to the Restoration, 1640-1660*), p. 74, Harvard University Press.

[30] For an admirable account of these developments, *cf. Ibid.*, Vol. III, pp. 170-218.

[31] *Cf.* M. P. Andrews, *History of Maryland*, Doubleday, Doran, 1929, Chaps. I-IV, for a full discussion of Maryland's early religious history.

[32] *Cf.* William Penn, *The Great Case of Liberty of Conscience*, London, 1670; *England's Present Interest Discover'd*, London, 1675; *Address to Protestants*, London, 1679; *Good Advice to the Church of England, Roman Catholic and Protestant Dissenter*, London, 1687.

[33] *England's Present Interest Discover'd*, London, 1675, p. 39.

[34] Quoted by William Penn, *Ibid.*, pp. 49-50.

[35] Declaration of Breda, 1660.

[36] *Lettres sur les Anglois*, Amsterdam, 1736, p. 42; quoted by J. S. Schapiro, *Condorcet and the Rise of Liberalism*, Harcourt, Brace, 1934, p. 51.

[37] *Institutes of the Christian Religion*, Vol. III, p. 525 (Bk. IV, Chap. XX, § 9).

[38] *Cf.* Williams, *The Bloudy Tenent of Persecution*, London, 1644; Cotton, *The Controversie Concerning Liberty of Conscience in Matters of Religion*, London, 1646; Cotton, *The Bloudy Tenent Washed and Made White in the Bloud of the Lamb*, London, 1647; Williams, *The Bloody Tenent Yet More Bloody*, London, 1652.

[39] Roger Williams, "The Bloudy Tenent of Persecution," *Publications of the Narragansett Club*, First Series, 6 vols., Providence, 1866-74; Vol. III, pp. 398-99. (I owe this, and many of the citations that follow, to the admirable summary in W. K. Jordan, *Op. cit.*, Vol. III, pp. 472-506.)

[40] Williams, "Mr. Cottons Letter Lately Printed, Examined and Answered" (1644), *Loc. cit.*, Vol. I, p. 328.

[41] *Cf.* A. S. P. Woodhouse, *Op. cit.*, p. 35.

[42] From the abridged reprint in *Ibid.*, pp. 251-52.

[43] *Ibid.*, p. 257.

[44] *England's Present Interest Discover'd*, 1675, pp. 31-32.

[45] *A Discourse of Ecclesiastical Politie . . .* , London, 1670, pp. 6, 16.

[46] *The Rehearsal Transposed, The Complete Works . . . of Andrew Marvell*, ed. by A. B. Grosart, 4 vols., London, 1873, Vol. III, pp. 171-72.

[47] "The Bloudy Tenent of Persecution," *Loc. cit.*, Vol. III, p. 309.

[48] *Ibid.*, Vol. III, pp. 80-81.

[49] *Cf.* W. K. Jordan, *Op. cit.*, Vol. III, pp. 499-500.

[50] *Cf. Op. cit.*, Vol. III, p. 496.

[51] "The Bloody Tenent Yet More Bloody," *Loc. cit.*, Vol. IV, p. 28.

[52] *England's Present Interest Discover'd*, 1675, pp. 56-57.

[53] "The Bloudy Tenent of Persecution," *Loc. cit.*, Vol. III, pp. 92-93.

[54] Declaration of the army of England upon their march into Scotland (July 20, 1650); quoted by W. K. Jordan, *Op. cit.*, Vol. III, p. 134.

[55] A. S. P. Woodhouse, *Op. cit.*, pp. 247, 255.

[56] Quoted in a "Memoir of Rev. John Robinson" by Robert Ashton, *The Works of John Robinson*, Vol. I, p. xliv.

[57] Chillingworth, *The Religion of Protestants*, in *Works*, 3 vols., London, 1820; Taylor, *The Liberty of Prophesying*, in Vol. V of *The Whole Works* of Jeremy Taylor,

10 vols., London, 1850-54; Stillingfleet, *Irenicum*, London, 1662; as quoted by G. P. Gooch, *Op. cit.*, pp. 206-07, 210-11. *Cf.* also John Hales, *Concerning Schism and Schismatics*, in *Several Tracts*, London, 1636; Ralph Cudworth, *Sermon before the House of Commons*, Cambridge, England, 1647; Henry More, *Divine Dialogues*, 2 vols., London, 1668.

58 *Works*, Vol. VI, pp. 5, 9.

59 The most effective exposition of the democratic implications of puritanism is to be found in A. S. P. Woodhouse, *Op. cit.* In the following writers the emphasis is rather on the non-democratic elements of puritanism: Charles McLean Andrews, "Conservative Factors in Early Colonial History," *Authority and the Individual*, pp. 154-69; Perry Miller, *Orthodoxy in Massachusetts*, pp. 206 ff., and Chap. VII, *passim;* Mark Pattison, "Calvin at Geneva," *Essays*, 1889, Vol. II, pp. 1-41; A. F. Scott Pearson, *Thomas Cartwright and Elizabethan Puritanism*, Cambridge, England, 1925, pp. 337 ff., 406 ff. It is, of course, not to be denied that puritan leaders such as John Cotton explicitly repudiated what was in their time known as democracy. *Cf.* also above, Chapter VIII, Sec. 7.

60 *Institutes of the Christian Religion*, Vol. III, pp. 524, 549, 548, 551 (Bk. IV, Chap. XX, §§ 8, 29, 32).

61 G. P. Gooch, *Op. cit.*, pp. 81, 91.

62 *Cf.* above, Chapter V, p. 107 ff. See also "Agreements of the People," in Woodhouse, *op. cit.*, pp. 342-67, especially pp. 352, 363, 367, 357, 366. The Levellers had their own left-wing communistic group, led by Gerard Winstanley, who found that "Jesus Christ is the head Leveller." Quoted by G. P. Gooch, *Op. cit.*, p. 129.

63 Woodhouse, *Op. cit.*, Introd., pp. 64, 69, 75, 76, 86. *Cf.* also "The Solemn Engagement of the Army," of June 5, 1647, *Ibid.*, pp. 401-03. The same William Ames whose theology so profoundly influenced the New England ministry wrote in 1639 a work on *Conscience*, in which he identified natural law with the moral law implanted in every man, discernible by reason or 'natural light,' and defining the principles of civil welfare. Henry Parker and John Goodwin rationalized the resistance to the throne on similar grounds.

64 *Moby Dick*, Dutton, 1907 (Everyman's Library), p. 394.

CHAPTER FOURTEEN

1 Sermon reported in the *Daily Crimson*, Cambridge, Mass., Nov. 8, 1886, p. 1.

2 Quoted by H. W. Schneider, *The Puritan Mind*, p. 33.

3 *Institutes of the Christian Religion*, Vol. III, pp. 194-95 (Bk. IV, Chap. X, § 7).

4 *Cf.* his *Of the Laws of Ecclesiastical Polity*, Bk. II.

5 *The Confession of Faith, Together with the Larger and Shorter Catechisms, Composed by the Reverend Assembly of Divines Sitting at Westminster, Presented to Both Houses of Parliament*, 5th ed., London, 1717, p. 25.

6 *Cf.* Article I ("Of God") of the Confession of Augsburg (1540).

[7] "God Glorified in Man's Dependence," a public lecture in Boston, July 8, 1731, *Works,* Vol. II, p. 3.

[8] From what his biographer, S. E. Dwight, called Edwards's "Personal Narrative," written when Edwards was forty years old, *Ibid.,* Vol. I, p. lv.

[9] Appendix IV: "Remarks in Mental Philosophy—The Mind," *Ibid.,* Vol. I, p. cclxxi.

[10] *Cf.* "The Nature of True Virtue," *Ibid.,* Vol. I, p. 128.

[11] Tractate XIV of "Lectures or Tractates on the Gospel According to St. John," *Works,* Vol. VII, p. 94.

[12] *Cf.* H. Wheeler Robinson, "Soul (Christian)," *Encyclopaedia of Religion and Ethics,* Vol. XI, p. 735.

[13] Quoted by William James, *Pragmatism,* Longmans, Green, 1907, pp. 26-27; translated from "Essais de Théodicée." See *Œuvres de Leibniz,* ed. by M. A. Jacques, 2 vols., Paris, 1842-45, Vol. II, pp. 109-10.

[14] *The Saints' Everlasting Rest,* pp. 138, 139, 140, 141.

[15] "The Great Christian Doctrine of Original Sin Defended," *op. cit.,* Vol. I, p. 173.

[16] *An Essay on the Nature and Glory of the Gospel of Jesus Christ,* London, 1784, pp. 91-92, 210.

[17] *Cf.* A. C. McGiffert, *Protestant Thought before Kant,* p. 83.

[18] Richard Baxter, *Op. cit.,* p. 141.

[19] *Op. cit.,* Dutton, 1919 (Everyman's Library), p. 268.

[20] Quoted, *Ibid.,* pp. 311-12. *Cf.* also Thomas Aquinas, *Summa Theologica,* Third Part (Supplement), qu. XCVII, "Of the Punishment of the Damned."

[21] *Cf.* J. H. Allen, *Christian History in Its Three Great Periods: Third Period, Modern Phases,* pp. 54 ff.

[22] "Epistle to the Reader," *Poetical Fragments,* London, 1681, pp. 4-5.

[23] Appendix IV: "Remarks in Mental Philosophy—The Mind," *Op. cit.,* Vol. I, p. cclxxi.

[24] *Bread and Wine,* Harper, 1937, p. 243.

[25] T. B. Macaulay, *The History of England from the Accession of James II,* Vol. I, p. 99. *Oliver Cromwell's Letters and Speeches,* pp. 386-87.

[26] Edward Johnson, *The Wonder-working Providence of Sions Saviour in New-England,* pp. 22, 47, 49. *Cf.* also Edward Dowden, *Puritan and Anglican,* p. 27.

[27] From *Winesburg, Ohio,* by Sherwood Anderson. Copyright, 1919, by B. W. Huebsch, pp. 64-65. By permission of The Viking Press, Inc., New York.

[28] *Op. cit.,* p. 101. *Cf.* also Jonathan Edwards, *Miscellaneous Observations Concerning the Divine Decrees, Op. cit.,* Vol. II, pp. 516-17, 545.

[29] Richard Baxter, *Op. cit.,* p. 100.

[30] G. A. Gordon, *My Education and Religion,* Houghton Mifflin, 1925, p. 269.

[31] "The Great Christian Doctrine of Original Sin Defended," *op. cit.,* Vol. I, p. 221.

[32] *Loc. cit.,* Vol. VII, p. 24.

[33] *Ibid.,* p. 19.

CHAPTER FIFTEEN

[1] D. Elton Trueblood, "The Invention of America," *Friend*, Oct. 17, 1940, p. 131.

[2] Preamble to the Declaration of Independence.

[3] From *The Correspondence and Public Papers of John Jay*, ed. by H. P. Johnston, 4 vols., 1890-93, Vol. I, p. 161, courtesy of G. P. Putnam's Sons.

[4] *The Debates in the Several State Conventions on the Adoption of the Federal Constitution*, ed. by Jonathan Elliot, 5 vols., Washington, D.C., 1836-45, Vol. IV, p. 331.

[5] Speech on "Patriotism"; *Works*, ed. by George E. Baker, 5 vols., New York City, 1853-84, Vol. III, p. 201.

[6] *Congressional Record*, Vol. LIV, Pt. 4, p. 3445.

[7] *Writings*, Vol. X, p. 25. *Cf.* also *Ibid.*, Vol. IV, pp. 268-69.

[8] For a fuller examination of the notion of "social mind," *cf.* the Author's *General Theory of Value*, Longmans, Green, 1926, pp. 431-59 and ff.

[9] From *Politics*, by Heinrich von Treitschke, translated by B. Dugdale and T. de Bille, 2 vols., 1916, Vol. I, p. 26. By permission of The Macmillan Company, publishers. *Cf.* also pp. 31, 63.

[10] John Dryden, *The Conquest of Granada*, first produced, and "with great Applause," in 1670, Pt. I, Act I, scene i; *Dramatic Works*, ed. by Montague Summers, 6 vols., London, 1931-32, Vol. III, p. 34.

[11] "Paradise Lost," Bk. I, l. 543.

[12] "Reflections on the Revolution in France," *Works*, Vol. III, p. 107.

[13] "The Farmer Refuted," *Works*, Vol. I, p. 113.

[14] *Cf.* Francis Wayland, *Elements of Political Economy*, Sheldon, 1938. The intuitive acceptance of natural law is here blended, in its economic application, with the "common sense" of the Scottish school.

[15] George Berkeley, sermon on "Passive Obedience," from *Berkeley's Complete Works*, ed. by A. C. Fraser, 4 vols., 1901, Vol. IV, p. 102, Clarendon Press, Oxford; by permission of the publishers; Joseph Butler, Sermon III, *Works*, Vol. I, p. 57.

[16] Sir William Blackstone, *Commentaries on the Laws of England*, Vol. I, pp. 46-47.

[17] For a consideration of the specific question of religious toleration, *cf.* above, Chapter XIII. For the relation of tolerance to 'civil liberty,' *cf.* below, Chapter XVIII.

[18] *Cf.* Bartlett's *Familiar Quotations*, 11th ed., Little, Brown, 1937, p. 1053, note. Also Stevenson's *Home Book of Quotations*, 4th ed., p. 2276, where the fallacy is fully set forth.

[19] *Cf.* H. L. Osgood, "The Political Ideas of the Puritans," *Loc. cit.*, pp. 20, 208.

[20] *Correspondance générale*, Vol. I, p. 333, quoted by J. Salwyn Schapiro, *Condorcet and the Rise of Liberalism*, p. 139.

[21] From *Areopagitica*, by John Milton, ed. by W. Haller, 1927 (Modern Readers' Series), p. 60. By permission of The Macmillan Company, publishers.

[22] "On the Conduct of the Understanding," *The Philosophical Works,* London, 1854, Vol. I, pp. 50-51.

[23] *Archives of Maryland: Proceedings and Acts of the General Assembly of Maryland,* ed. by William Hand Browne, Maryland Historical Society, 1883, Vol. I, p. 245.

[24] *Op. cit.*, pp. 44-45.

[25] "A Bill for Establishing Religious Freedom" (which with a few slight changes became The Statute of Virginia for Religious Freedom), *Op. cit.,* Vol. II, pp. 237-38. For an impressive statement of Jefferson's general plea for tolerance, *cf.* "Notes on Virginia," *Ibid.*, Vol. III, pp. 263-65.

[26] "A Letter Concerning Toleration," *Works,* 1812, Vol. VI, pp. 11-12.

[27] Quoted from p. 3 of a "Manuscript Copy of the Proceedings of the Synod, in 1637" by Charles Chauncy, *Seasonable Thoughts on the State of Religion in New England,* p. vi, note.

[28] *Cf.* his *Philosophical Commentary on the Text "Compel them to come in"* (Luke 14:23), translated from the French, London, 1708.

[29] *Op. cit.*, pp. 44-45.

[30] "A Letter Concerning Toleration," *Op. cit.,* Vol. VI, pp. 12-13.

[31] *Two Treatises of Civil Government,* p. 177.

[32] *Cf.* above, Chapter XIII.

[33] *Leviathan,* p. 421.

CHAPTER SIXTEEN

[1] *The Works of Aristotle Translated into English,* rev. ed. by W. D. Ross, 11 vols., Oxford, 1908-31; Vol. X: *Politica,* translated by Benjamin Jowett, Bk. III, Chap. 9, Secs. 1280^b–1281^a.

[2] *The Republic,* translated by Benjamin Jowett, Oxford, 1881, p. 156 (Bk. IV, 420^b, Bk. V, 466^a).

[3] *Cf. Journal of Philosophy,* Vol. XXVIII (1931), pp. 449, 477, 519.

[4] *Cf.* the Author's *General Theory of Value,* Chap. XV, "Is Society a Person?" *Cf.* especially pp. 455-57.

[5] Source unknown; quoted by Congressman D. J. Lewis, *Congressional Record,* Feb. 17, 1917, Vol. LIV, Pt. IV, p. 3504.

[6] Moss Hart and George S. Kaufman, *Op. cit.,* Farrar and Rinehart, 1937, pp. 39-45.

[7] Maurice de Wulf, *Mediaeval Philosophy Illustrated from the System of Thomas Aquinas,* Harvard University Press, 1922, pp. 117-18.

[8] "Concerning Catholic Action," *New York Times,* July 4, 1931; *After Forty Years, Encyclical Letter on Labor,* May 24, 1931, Barry Vail Corporation, p. 34; *Mit Brennender Sorge,* Mar. 14, 1937, quoted by Lillian Browne-Olf, *Pius XI, Apostle of Peace,* 1938, p. 217, and reprinted here by permission of The Macmillan Company, publishers.

[9] Quoted by John Eppstein, "The Totalitarian State," *Church and State,* London, 1936, pp. 230-31.

[10] *Cf.*, for example, W. E. Hocking, *The Lasting Elements of Individualism,* Yale University Press, 1937, Chap. IV.

[11] *Cf.* Gilbert Chinard, *Thomas Jefferson, The Apostle of Americanism,* pp. 80-85.

[12] C. E. Merriam, *A History of American Political Theories,* pp. 49, 53. *Cf.* above, Chapter VIII, pp. 184-87.

[13] *Two Treatises of Civil Government,* p. 120.

[14] *Ibid.*, pp. 120-21.

[15] *Cf.* Roscoe Pound, *The Spirit of the Common Law,* Chaps. II and IV, especially pp. 42-44, 89-90.

[16] Immanuel Kant, "Metaphysic of Morals," translated by T. K. Abbott and included in his *Kant's Critique of Practical Reason and Other Works on the Theory of Ethics,* London, 1889, p. 47.

[17] *The Will to Believe,* p. 188.

[18] *Cf.* the Author's *General Theory of Value,* Chap. XXI, especially pp. 257-60.

[19] *Nature, Addresses and Lectures,* pp. 112-13.

[20] *Memories and Studies,* Longmans, Green, 1912, p. 354.

[21] "Democratic Vistas," from *The Complete Writings of Walt Whitman,* 10 vols., 1902; Vol. II, pp. 94, 95; courtesy of G. P. Putnam's Sons.

[22] From a speech by D. O. Bogomoloff before the Pan-Pacific Association in Shanghai, Nov. 22, 1935, excerpts printed in the *China Weekly Review,* Shanghai, Nov. 30, 1935, p. 456.

[23] Quoted by John Stuart Mill, *Utilitarianism,* Dutton, 1925 (Everyman's Library), p. 58.

[24] *Cf.* below, Chapter XVII, Secs. 6-8.

[25] Jeremy Bentham, *The Theory of Legislation,* ed. by C. K. Ogden, Harcourt, Brace, 1931, p. 53.

[26] *Loc. cit.; cf. An Introduction to the Principles of Morals and Legislation,* Oxford, 1876, Chap. X, §§ 3-4.

[27] *Essays to Do Good,* p. 117.

[28] *Letters,* Vol. I, pp. 354-55.

[29] *Op. cit.*, p. 114.

[30] *Op. cit.*, pp. 352-53.

[31] *Ibid.*, pp. 102-03.

[32] W. F. Dexter, *Herbert Hoover and American Individualism,* Macmillan, 1932, p. 3.

[33] Herbert Hoover, *American Individualism,* Doubleday, Page, 1923, p. 9. Italics added; in the book the whole passage is in italics.

[34] "The Development of Realism," in Norman Foerster, ed., *The Reinterpretation of American Literature,* Harcourt, Brace, 1928, p. 139.

[35] "The Metaphysical Basis of Toleration," *The Works of Walter Bagehot,* ed. by Forrest Morgan, 5 vols., Traveler's Insurance Company, Hartford, 1889, Vol. II, p. 341.

[36] *Lectures on History and General Policy,* 2 vols., Philadelphia, 1803; Lecture XLI, Vol. II, p. 79.

CHAPTER SEVENTEEN

[1] *After the Deluge,* 2 vols., Harcourt, Brace, 1931, Vol. I, p. 335.

[2] "Reflections on the Revolution in France," *Works,* Vol. III, pp. 46-47.

[3] "Answer" to Francis Johnson's Animadversion on a passage in Mr. Robinson's reply to Richard Bernard, Robinson, *Works,* Vol. III, p. 482.

[4] Reported in the *New York Times,* Dec. 25, 1932.

[5] Adaptability to crises is a feature of all government, and not a peculiarity of modern times. *Cf.* W. Y. Elliott, *The Pragmatic Revolt in Politics,* Macmillan, 1928, p. 348.

[6] *Of the Laws of Ecclesiastical Polity,* Vol. I, pp. 194-95 (Bk. I, Sec. X, Subsection 8).

[7] *Cf.* A. D. Lindsay, "Sovereignty," *Proceedings of the Aristotelian Society,* New Series, Vol. XXIV (1923-24), pp. 235-54.

[8] *Cf.* James Gerard's list in "Our Sixty-Four 'Rulers,'" *Literary Digest,* Sept. 6, 1930, p. 7; *cf.* also Walter Lippmann, *A Preface to Politics,* Kennerley, 1914, pp. 17-22.

[9] Karl Marx and Friedrich Engels, *Manifesto of the Communist Party,* authorized English translation, ed. and annotated by Friedrich Engels, tr. by J. T. Kozlowski, The Marxian Educational Society, Detroit, 1919 (reprinted from the edition of 1888), pp. 12, 15. Lenin, *Imperialism: The Latest Stage in the Development of Capitalism,* The Marxian Educational Society, Detroit, 1924, p. 126.

[10] Reprinted in his *The Foundations of Sovereignty and Other Essays,* Harcourt, Brace, 1921, pp. 232-50.

[11] "Abstracts of Two Sermons," *Loc. cit.,* Vol. I, p. 20.

[12] "A Proclamation by the Great and General Court of the Colony of Massachusetts Bay," formally adopted by the Council and the House of Representatives of Massachusetts in 1775, *Works,* Vol. I, p. 193.

[13] *Chisholm v. Georgia* (1793) 2 Dall. 419, 458. Quoted by J. S. Waterman in "Thomas Jefferson and Blackstone's Commentaries," *Loc. cit.*

[14] Letter to W. C. Jarvis, Sept. 28, 1820, *Writings,* Vol. X, p. 161.

[15] *Cf.* "Why Italy Rejects Democratic Rule," and "Official Text of the New Italian Electoral Law," *Current History,* May, 1928, pp. 180 ff., 202 ff.

[16] *Cf.* Rousseau, *Confessions,* 2 vols., Dutton, 1931 (Everyman's Library), Vol. I, p. 304; "Notes on Virginia," Jefferson, *Op. cit.,* Vol. III, p. 268.

[17] *Modern Democracies,* The Macmillan Co., 1924, Vol. I, p. 149. For Aristotle's famous doctrine that the best state is the rule of the "mean," or the middle class, *cf. The Politics of Aristotle* (Bk. IV, Sec. 11), translated by Benjamin Jowett, 2 vols., Oxford, 1885, Vol. I, p. 12.

[18] "The Future of Liberalism," *Mixed Essays, Irish Essays and Others,* Macmillan, 1883, p. 383.

[19] *Two Treatises of Civil Government,* pp. 161-63 (Chap. VII, §§ 91, 93).

[20] "Reply to Senator Douglas at Peoria, Illinois: The Origin of the Wilmot Proviso, Oct. 16, 1854." *Complete Works,* Vol. I, p. 195.

[21] *Op. cit.,* Vol. I, p. 582.

[22] *The Republic,* translated by J. L. Davies and D. J. Vaughan, Burt, 1891, marginal pp. 590-91 (Bk. IX). Italics mine.

[23] *The Politics of Aristotle,* Vol. I, p. 222 (Bk. VII, Sec. 1329a).

[24] Mar. 4, 1801, Jefferson, *Op. cit.,* Vol. VIII, p. 2.

[25] *Politics,* Vol. II, pp. 277-78.

[26] *Cf.* Locke, *Second Treatise of Civil Government, Two Treatises,* pp. 164-65, Chap. VIII, § 95.

[27] *Cf.* "The Social Contract," *The Social Contract and Discourses,* Dutton, 1920 (Everyman's Library), pp. 86-87.

[28] *Cf.* below, Chapter XVIII, Sec. 1.

[29] *Op. cit.,* p. 165.

[30] *Cf.* W. B. Munro, *The Government of the United States,* new ed., Macmillan, 1925, pp. 367, 371.

[31] Quoted by Graham Wallas, *Human Nature in Politics,* Houghton Mifflin, 1909, p. 111.

[32] Speech before the North Carolina ratifying convention, quoted by Jonathan Elliot, ed., *Debates . . . on the Federal Constitution,* Vol. IV, p. 10.

[33] *On Civil Liberty and Self-Government,* 2 vols., Lippincott, 1853, Vol. II, p. 118.

[34] Quoted by W. Y. Elliott, *Op. cit.,* p. 341.

[35] H. W. Schneider, *The Making of the Fascist State,* Oxford University Press, 1928, p. 249.

[36] "Recent Documents and Literature on the Outbreak of the World War," *Historical Outlook,* May, 1929, p. 216; quoted from the *Manchester Guardian,* Feb. 8, 1929.

[37] "Message to Congress in Special Session, July 4, 1861," *Op. cit.,* Vol. II, p. 58.

[38] Standardized spelling and punctuation have been substituted for the abbreviations in the original text, which appears in *Op. cit.,* P. L. Ford, ed., Vol. VIII, p. 3.

[39] *Leviathan,* 1909, p. 256.

CHAPTER EIGHTEEN

[1] Some paragraphs of this chapter have been reprinted from the Author's "Liberty in a Democratic State," in Ruth Nanda Anshen, ed., *Freedom: Its Meaning,* Harcourt, Brace, 1940, pp. 265-77.

[2] *Theologico-Political Treatise,* in *Chief Works,* 2 vols., London, 1883-84 (Bohn's Library), Vol. I, p. 258.

[3] Quoted from a lecture by Nicholas Murray Butler, in the *New York Times,* Sept. 6, 1943.

[4] From *The History of Freedom and Other Essays,* 1909, pp. 22-23. By permission of The Macmillan Company, publishers.

[5] *Life of Col. David Crockett,* Philadelphia, 1859, pp. 212-13.

[6] Johann Caspar Bluntschli, *The Theory of the State,* translated by D. C. Ritchie, P. E. Matheson, and R. Lodge, 2d ed. from German 6th ed., 1892, p. 458; Clarendon Press. By permission of the publishers.

[7] *Works,* Vol. I, pp. 53, 241.

[8] *Works,* Vol. II, p. 31.

[9] *Character and Opinion in the United States,* Scribner, 1920, pp. 227-30.

[10] *Cf.* Zechariah Chafee, Jr., and S. P. Simpson, eds., *Cases on Equity,* pub. by the editors, Cambridge, Mass., 1934, Vol. I, pp. 215-17.

[11] George Fitz-Hugh, *Op. cit.,* Richmond, 1854, p. 170; cited by C. E. Merriam, *A History of American Political Theories,* p. 244. By permission of The Macmillan Company, publishers.

[12] *Second Treatise of Civil Government,* p. 124 (Chap. II, § 15).

[13] *Op. cit.,* pp. 3-4.

[14] P. L. Ford, ed., *Essays on the Constitution of the United States,* Historical Printing Club, Brooklyn, N. Y., 1892, pp. 117, 28. For the discussion of the question of including a bill of rights in the Federal Constitution, *cf., Ibid., passim;* also W. M. Meigs, *The Growth of the Constitution in the Federal Convention of 1787,* Lippincott, 1900, pp. 314-15.

[15] *Writings,* Vol. IV, pp. 476-77.

[16] *Cf.* C. E. Merriam, *Op. cit.,* pp. 76 ff.

[17] P. L. Ford, ed., *Op. cit.,* p. 114.

[18] *Idem.*

[19] *Leviathan,* London, 1894 (Morley's Universal Library), p. 104.

[20] *Wealth of Nations,* ed. by J. R. M'Culloch, Edinburgh, 1846, p. 199 (Bk. IV, Chap. II). *Cf.* James Bonar, *Philosophy and Political Economy,* London, 1922, Chaps. VII-VIII; and T. E. Cliffe Leslie, "The Political Economy of Adam Smith," *Essays in Political and Moral Philosophy,* Dublin, 1879.

[21] *Op. cit.,* p. 151.

[22] *Equality,* Harcourt, Brace, 1929, p. 195.

[23] *Notions of the American,* 2 vols., Philadelphia, 1828, Vol. I, pp. 19-20; quoted by Jesse Lee Bennett, *The Essential American Tradition,* Doran (now Doubleday, Doran and Company), 1925, p. 119.

[24] Burton J. Hendrick, *The Life and Letters of Walter H. Page,* 2 vols., Houghton Mifflin, 1922, Vol. II, p. 291.

[25] "A Letter Concerning Toleration," *Works,* Vol. VI, p. 18.

[26] *Works,* Vol. II, p. 343.

[27] *The Dissenting Opinions of Mr. Justice Holmes,* Vanguard Press, 1929, p. 50.

[28] John Milton, "Areopagitica," in *Areopagitica and Other Prose Writings,* p. 61; Locke, "A Letter Concerning Toleration," *Works,* Vol. VI, pp. 46-47.

[29] *Cf.* C. C. Marshall, "The Issue Is Joined," and Hillaire Belloc, "The Catholic Position," *Atlantic Monthly,* March 1930, pp. 404-21. In the same year this interpretation of Catholic polity found confirmation in the incident of Malta, when the Catholic authorities praised the action of the Maltese Bishops who in a Pastoral Letter exercised their disciplinary authority to compel the faithful to vote against the party of Governor Strickland. (*Cf.* Isaac Foot, letter on "The Right of Electoral Freedom," *Times,* London, July 2, 1930.)

CHAPTER NINETEEN

[1] Some paragraphs of this chapter have been reprinted from the Author's "What Do We Mean by Democracy?" *International Journal of Ethics,* July 1918.

[2] Quoted by C. E. Merriam, *A History of American Political Theories,* p. 230 ff. By permission of The Macmillan Company, publishers. *Cf.* also pp. 229-30.

[3] *Orthodoxy,* 1927, Dodd, Mead, pp. 82-83.

[4] For a convenient summary of the literature on this subject, *cf.* V. F. Calverton, "A Defense of Democracy," *Current History,* Vol. 28 (1928), p. 83. A classic instance of the extreme environmental position is afforded by Helvetius. "The inequality observable among men," he said, "depends on the government under which they lie; on the greater or less happiness of the age in which they are born; on the education; on their desire of improvement, and on the importance of the ideas that are the subject of their contemplations."—*Essays on the Mind,* London, 1810, p. 361. *Cf.* also *A Treatise on Man, His Intellectual Faculties and His Education,* translated by William Hooper, 2 vols., London, 1777, Vol. I, Sec. II, Chap. I, pp. 90 ff. The view of Helvetius is associated with an empirical psychology and theory of knowledge, according to which all knowledge is received from abroad through sensation and attention, and stored by memory.

[5] *George Bernard Shaw,* Lane, 1909, pp. 214-15.

[6] *Cf.* the Author's *The Thought and Character of William James,* 2 vols., Little, Brown, 1935, Vol. I.

[7] *Moby Dick,* pp. 113-14.

[8] David Hume, *The History of England,* 1865, 4 vols., Albany, N. Y., Vol. II, p. 5, n. 1.

[9] *Op. cit.,* new ed., London, 1876, Chap. XXII, p. 233, quoted by J. M. E. McTaggart, *Some Dogmas of Religion,* London, 1930, p. 35.

[10] *Cf.* Sir James Matthew Barrie, *The Admirable Crichton,* London, 1923.

[11] "The Cotter's Saturday Night," and "Is There for Honest Poverty?" *The Complete Poetical Works of Robert Burns,* Houghton Mifflin, 1897 (Cambridge Edition), pp. 28, 30, 31, 294.

[12] *Talks to Teachers,* Holt, 1899, pp. 274-75, 301.

[13] *Cf.* the *Second Treatise of Civil Government,* pp. 118-20 (Chap. II, §§ 4-7).

[14] "Equality Before the Law: Unconstitutionality of Separate Colored Schools in Massachusetts; Argument before the Supreme Court of Massachusetts," *Works,* 15 vols., Lee & Shepard, 1875-83; Vol. II, pp. 341-42.

[15] *Op. cit.,* pp. 118-19 (Chap. II, § 4).

[16] Letter to Roger C. Weightman, June 24, 1826, *Writings,* Vol. X, pp. 391-92.

[17] *Of the Laws of Ecclesiastical Polity,* Vol. I, p. 180.

[18] Josiah Royce, *The Religious Aspect of Philosophy,* Houghton Mifflin, 1887, p. 158; *cf.* also, William James, "On a Certain Blindness in Human Beings," *Op. cit.*

[19] *The Collected Works of Theodore Parker,* 14 vols., London, 1863-76; Vol. VII, pp. 187-88.

[20] *Cf.* C. H. McIlwain, "Government by Law," *Foreign Affairs*, January 1936, pp. 185-98.

[21] *Equality*, pp. 122-23.

[22] F. M. Trollope, *Domestic Manners of the Americans*, p. 264.

[23] *The Republic of Plato*, Jowett translation, p. 256.

[24] *New York Tribune*, Apr. 4, 1918.

[25] R. H. Tawney, *Op. cit.*, p. 272.

[26] *Cf.* John Stuart Mill, *Principles of Political Economy*, Longmans, Green, 1904, p. 453 (Bk. IV, Chap. VI, § 2).

[27] *Cf.* pp. 50-58, 93-95.

[28] *Op. cit.*, p. 135.

[29] *Ibid.*, p. 69.

[30] *Liberty, Equality, Fraternity*, Holt, 1873, pp. 253, 254, 255.

[31] *Ludendorff's Own Story*, 2 vols., Harper, 1919; Vol. II, p. 77.

[32] Bret Harte, "Mrs. Skaggs's Husbands," *Writings*, 1900 Standard Library Edition, Houghton Mifflin & Co., Vol. II, p. 85.

[33] *Life on the Mississippi, Mark Twain's Works*, 37 vols., Harper, 1929, pp. 294-95.

[34] Maj. F. R. McCoy, *Principles of Military Training*, Collier, 1917, p. 143.

[35] *Op. cit.*, Beacon Press, 1899, pp. 3-4, 71-72.

[36] Gustave Le Bon, *The Psychology of Revolution*, translated by B. Miall, Putnam, 1913, p. 83.

[37] From a letter of Aug. 15, 1855, to the Hon. Geo. Robertson, *Complete Works*, Vol. I, pp. 215-16.

CHAPTER TWENTY

[1] J. Hector St. John de Crèvecœur, *Letters from an American Farmer*, Dutton (Everyman's Library), pp. 12, 41, 42, 211.

[2] "Verses on the Prospect of Planting Arts and Learning in America," written in 1726, *Works*, Vol. VI (*Miscellaneous Works*), p. 365.

Franklin's opinion "that the *foundations of the future grandeur and stability of the British empire lie in America*" was a claim of future power rather than of exemplary virtue. (Letter of January 3, 1760, to Henry Home, Lord Kames, *Works*, Vol. III, p. 248.) The same is true of Richard Wells's prediction in 1774 of the transfer to America of the British throne: "Should the Georges in regular succession wear the British diadem to a number ranking with the Louises of France, many a goodly prince of that royal line will have mingled his ashes with American dust."—"A Few Political Reflections Submitted to the Consideration of the British Colonies, by a Citizen of Philadelphia," quoted in M. C. Tyler, *The Literary History of the American Revolution*, Vol. I, pp. 275-76.

[3] *Cf.* Condorcet, *Vie de Voltaire*, Bibliothèque Nationale, Paris, 1895, pp. 140-41.

[4] *Cf.* Franklin's plan for "The American Philosophical Society," *Op. cit.*, Vol. II, p. 70.

[5] "Farewell Address to the People of the United States," *Writings*, Vol. XIII, p. 311, courtesy of G. P. Putnam's Sons.

[6] Speech of Feb. 5 and 6, 1850, on the Compromise Resolutions, *Works of Henry Clay*, ed. by Calvin Colton, 7 vols., Henry Clay Publishing Company, New York, 1897, Vol. III, p. 345.

[7] "The President's Message to the National Army" (dated Sept. 3, 1917), *The Messages and Papers of Woodrow Wilson*, ed. by Albert Shaw, 2 vols., The Review of Reviews Corporation, 1924, Vol. I, p. 426.

[8] "The Conquest of the United States by Spain," *War and Other Essays*, ed. by A. G. Keller, Yale University Press, 1913, p. 334.

[9] *A Modern Symposium*, Doubleday, Doran, 1930, pp. 99-100, 102.

[10] *Cf.* R. B. Mowat, *The Age of Reason: The Continent of Europe in the Eighteenth Century*, Houghton Mifflin, 1934, pp. 30-34. As embodiments of the spirit of cosmopolitanism, the author mentions particularly Gibbon, Rousseau, Voltaire, Benjamin Thompson (Count Rumford), Franklin, Sir John Acton, and Goethe.

[11] Letter of June 7, 1782, *Op. cit.*, Vol. IX, pp. 215-16.

[12] *The Republic*, translated by Davies and Vaughan, p. 182 (Bk. V).

[13] *Liberty, Equality, Fraternity*, pp. 256-257, 283.

[14] *Bleak House*, pp. 32, 35, 38-39.

[15] Quoted by Emery Neff, *Carlyle*, Norton, 1932, p. 162.

[16] Quoted in Sir Pennell Rodd's Foreword to Antonio Salandra, *Italy and the Great War*, translated by Z. K. Pyne, London, 1932, p. 11.

[17] *Eternal Peace and Other International Essays*, translated by W. Hastie, World Peace Foundation, 1914, p. 68.

[18] *Ibid.*, pp. 14-15.

[19] *Ibid.*, p. 9.

[20] *Ibid.*, pp. 82-86, 98.

[21] *The City of God*, translated by John Healey, 2 vols., Edinburgh, 1909, Vol. I, p. 211 (Bk. VII, Chap. XIV).

[22] Quoted in the *New Statesman and Nation*, July 23, 1932.

[23] *Europe and Elsewhere*, Harper, 1923, pp. 397-98.

[24] *Politics*, Vol. I, pp. 21, 65.

[25] *Cf.* Mark A. May, "The Psychological Examination of Conscientious Objectors," *American Journal of Psychology*, Vol. XXXI (1920), pp. 152-65.

[26] *Cf.* W. W. Tarn, "Alexander the Great and the Unity of Mankind," *Proceedings of the British Academy*, Vol. XIX (1933).

[27] "Apology for Raimond Sebond" (Montaigne's *Essays*, Bk. II, Chap. XII), *The Works of Michel de Montaigne*, translated by C. Cotton, 4 vols., Hurd & Houghton, 1866, Vol. II, p. 167.

[28] *Science and the Modern World*, p. 290.

[29] July 24, 1934.

[30] *Mornings in Mexico*, London, 1927, p. 105.

[31] John Milton, "Comus," ll. 412-13.

[32] Georges Sorel, *Reflections on Violence*, translated by T. E. Hulme, Huebsch, 1914; quoted by Bernard Bosanquet, *Social and International Ideals*, 1917, p. 183. By permission of The Macmillan Company, publishers.

[33] *Op. cit.*, p. 179; Bosanquet goes on to say: "To the present writer the true

thing in M. Sorel's speculations is his insistence on the necessity of suffering and conflict."—p. 188.

[34] *Thirty-second Annual Report of the Board of Direction of the Mercantile Library Association in the City of New York,* January 1853, pp. 31-32.

[35] John Milton, "Paradise Lost," Bk. III, l. 90.

[36] "The Strenuous Life," *Works,* Vol. XIII, p. 322.

CONCLUSION

[1] A. N. Whitehead, *Science and the Modern World,* pp. 83-84. By permission of The Macmillan Company, publishers.

[2] M. A. DeWolfe Howe, *Memoirs of the Harvard Dead,* 5 vols., Harvard University Press, 1920-24; Vol. III, p. 256.

[3] Reynal and Hitchcock, 1939, pp. 288-95.

[4] Tennyson's *In Memoriam,* LVI.

[5] *Corruptio optimae pessima* (Thomas Aquinas, *Summa Theologica,* Prim. Sec., i, 5).

[6] *Jean Christophe: Youth,* translated by Gilbert Cannan, Holt, 1915, p. 325.

[7] *Cf.* above, Chapter I, Sec. 5.

[8] *Equality,* p. 268.

[9] In a letter to his daughter Bridget Ireton, of Oct. 25, 1646, *Letters and Speeches,* p. 162.

INDEX